Research Methods in Criminal Justice and Criminology

Sara Miller McCune founded SAGE Publishing in 1965 to support the dissemination of usable knowledge and educate a global community. SAGE publishes more than 1000 journals and over 800 new books each year, spanning a wide range of subject areas. Our growing selection of library products includes archives, data, case studies and video. SAGE remains majority owned by our founder and after her lifetime will become owned by a charitable trust that secures the company's continued independence.

Los Angeles | London | New Delhi | Singapore | Washington DC | Melbourne

Research Methods in Criminal Justice and Criminology

Callie Marie Rennison
University of Colorado Denver

Timothy C. Hart
Griffith University

Los Angeles | London | New Delhi
Singapore | Washington DC | Melbourne

FOR INFORMATION:

SAGE Publications, Inc.
2455 Teller Road
Thousand Oaks, California 91320
E-mail: order@sagepub.com

SAGE Publications Ltd.
1 Oliver's Yard
55 City Road
London EC1Y 1SP
United Kingdom

SAGE Publications India Pvt. Ltd.
B 1/I 1 Mohan Cooperative Industrial Area
Mathura Road, New Delhi 110 044
India

SAGE Publications Asia-Pacific Pte. Ltd.
3 Church Street
#10–04 Samsung Hub
Singapore 049483

Acquisitions Editor: Jessica Miller
Content Development Editor: Laura Kirkhuff
Editorial Assistant: Rebecca Lee
Marketing Manager: Jillian Ragusa
Production Editor: Veronica Stapleton Hooper
Copy Editor: Sheree Van Vreede
Typesetter: C&M Digitals (P) Ltd.
Proofreader: Wendy Jo Dymond
Indexer: Jeanne R. Busemeyer
Cover Designer: Anupama Krishnan

Printed in the United States of America

Library of Congress Cataloging-in-Publication Data

Names: Rennison, Callie Marie, author. | Hart, Timothy C., author.

Title: Research methods in criminal justice and criminology / Callie M. Rennison, University of Colorado, Denver, Timothy C. Hart, Griffith University.

Description: First Edition. | Thousand Oaks : SAGE Publications, [2018] | Includes bibliographical references and index.

Identifiers: LCCN 2017042992 | ISBN 9781506347813 (pbk. : alk. paper)

Subjects: LCSH: Criminal justice, Administration of—Research—Methodology. | Criminology—Research—Methodology.

Classification: LCC HV7419.5 .R46 2018 | DDC 364.072/1—dc23
LC record available at https://lccn.loc.gov/2017042992

This book is printed on acid-free paper.

SUSTAINABLE FORESTRY INITIATIVE
Certified Chain of Custody
Promoting Sustainable Forestry
www.sfiprogram.org
SFI-01268
SFI label applies to text stock

18 19 20 21 22 10 9 8 7 6 5 4 3 2

Brief Contents

Preface   xvii

Acknowledgments   xxiii

About the Authors   xxv

PART 1   GETTING STARTED   1

Chapter 1   Why Study Research Methods?   2

PART 2   SETTING THE STAGE OF YOUR RESEARCH   29

Chapter 2   Identifying a Topic, a Purpose, and a
Research Question   30

Chapter 3   Conducting a Literature Review   62

PART 3   DESIGNING YOUR RESEARCH   99

Chapter 4   Concepts, Conceptualizations,
Operationalizations, Measurements, Variables, and Data   100

Chapter 5   Sampling   136

PART 4   COLLECTING YOUR DATA   173

Chapter 6   Research Using Qualitative Data   174

Chapter 7   Survey Research   208

Chapter 8   Experimental Research   243

Chapter 9   Research Using Secondary Data   276

Chapter 10   GIS and Crime Mapping   312

Chapter 11   Evaluation Research   345

PART 5   ANALYSIS, FINDINGS, AND WHERE TO GO FROM THERE   377

Chapter 12   Analysis and Findings   378

Chapter 13   Making Your Research Relevant   420

Chapter 14   Research Methods as a Career   449

Appendix   A-1

Glossary   G-1

References   R-1

Index   I-1

Detailed Contents

Preface   xvii

Acknowledgments   xxiii

About the Authors   xxv

PART 1 GETTING STARTED   1

Chapter 1 Why Study Research Methods?   2

Learning Objectives   2

Introduction   2

Why Are Research
    Methods Important?   3
    Knowledge and Ways of Knowing   3
        Information From Everyday Life   4
        College Student Victimization   4
        *Violent Crime in the
            United States*   6
    Other Sources of Knowledge   9

Typical Stages of Research   10
    Developing a Research Question   10
    ▶ **Research in Action:** Postrelease
        Behavior: Does Supermax
        Confinement Work?   11
    Conducting a Literature Review   12
    Designing the Research   13
    Collecting Data   13
    Selecting an Analytic Approach   13
    Generating Findings, Conclusions,
        and Policy Implications   14

⚖ Essential Role of Ethics in Research   14
    Unethical Research Examples   14
        *Nazi Research on
            Concentration Camp Prisoners*   14
        Tuskegee Syphilis Experiment   15
        Milgram's Obedience to Authority   15
        Stanford Prison Experiment   17
    Foundational Ethical Research
        Principles and Requirements   18
    Role of Institutional Review
        Boards (IRBs)   20

Researcher Case Studies
    and a Road Map   21
    Featured Researchers   21
        Rachel Boba Santos, PhD   21
        Rod Brunson, PhD   22
        Carlos Cuevas, PhD   22
        Mary Dodge, PhD   23
        Chris Melde, PhD   24
        Heather Zaykowski, PhD   24
    Road Map to the Book   24

Chapter Wrap-Up   25
    ▶ **Applied Assignments**   26
    Key Words and Concepts   27
    Key Points   27
    Review Questions   27
    Critical Thinking Questions   28

PART 2 SETTING THE STAGE FOR YOUR RESEARCH   29

Chapter 2 Identifying a Topic, a Purpose, and a Research Question   30

Learning Objectives   30

Introduction   30
    Wheel of Science   30

Why Identify a Topic, a Purpose,
    and a Research Question?   32

How to Identify a Research Topic   32
    Published Research   32
    Data   34
    Theory   35
    Requests for Proposals (RFPs)   36
    Personal Experiences   36
        Reading   37
    ▶ **Research in Action:** Mental Illness and
        Revictimization: A Comparison of
        Black and White Men   38
        Viewing   39
        Listening   39

Working on Research Projects
    With Professors   39
    Internet   40

How to Identify the Purpose/
Goal of Research   40
    Exploratory Research   40
    Descriptive Research   41
    Explanatory Research   41
    Evaluation Research   41

Gathering More Information
    and Refining the Topic   43

How to Construct the Research
Question   43
    Why Have a Research Question?   44
    Evaluating the Research Question
        to Avoid Common Pitfalls   44
    Research Questions From
        Our Case Studies   46

⚠ Common Pitfalls When
Developing Topics, Purposes,
and Research Questions   47

⚖ Ethical Considerations When
Developing Your Topic, Purpose,
and Research Question   48
    The Contemporary Role of IRB   49
    Vulnerable Populations   50
        Pregnant Women, Human
            Fetuses, and Neonates   51
        Prisoners   51
        Children   52
        Potentially Vulnerable Populations 53
        Exempt, Expedited, or Full Panel
            Review at the IRB   54
    Training in Protecting Human Subjects   54

IRB Expert—Sharon Devine,
    JD, PhD   55

Chapter Wrap-Up   56
    ▶ Applied Assignments   58
    Key Words and Concepts   59
    Key Points   59
    Review Questions   60
    Critical Thinking Questions   60

Chapter 3   Conducting a
Literature Review   62
    Learning Objectives   62

Introduction   62

Why Conduct a Literature Review?   63

A Road Map: How to Conduct a
    Literature Review   63

About Sources   64
    What Are the Best Sources?   64
        Empirical Peer-Reviewed
            Journal Articles   65
        Theoretical Journal Articles   66
        Literature Review Journal Articles 66
        Government Research and
            Reports and Policy Briefs   66
    Avoiding Predatory Publishers and
        Predatory Journals   67
    Inappropriate Sources   68
    ▶ Research in Action: Police Impersonation
        in the United States   69

Finding Primary or Original Sources   70
    Develop Search Terms   70
    Search Using Boolean Operators
        and Filters   71
    Identify Initial Primary Sources   73
    Read Abstracts to Narrow the List
        of Sources   74
        The Anatomy of an Empirical
            Research Article   74

Writing the Literature Review   78
    Summarize Each Original Source   78
        Someone Has Already Focused
            on My Topic!   81
    Create a Summary Table   81
    Preparing for the First Rough Draft   83
        Organizational Approaches   83
        A Writing Strategy: MEAL   85
    Write the First Draft   87
    Edit, Proof, and Polish   87

⚠ Common Pitfalls of Literature
Reviews   87
    Not Allowing Enough Time   87
    Failing to Focus on Themes   88
    Lack of Organization and Structure   88
    Quoting Problems   88
    Miscellaneous Common Errors   88
    Failure to Justify the Need for the
        Proposed Research   89

⚖ Ethics and the Literature Review   89
    Plagiarism   89
    Accurate Portrayal of
        Existing Research   90

Literature Review Expert—Sean
McCandless, PhD   91

Chapter Wrap-Up   92
▶ Applied Assignments   95
Key Words and Concepts   95
Key Points   96
Review Questions   96
Critical Thinking Questions   97

PART 3   DESIGNING YOUR RESEARCH   99

Chapter 4   Concepts, Conceptualizations, Operationalizations, Measurements, Variables, and Data   100
Learning Objectives   100

Introduction   100
Two Primary Types of Data:
Quantitative and Qualitative   100

Why Focus on Concepts,
Conceptualizations,
Operationalizations,
Measurements, Variables,
and Data?   102

What Are Concepts?   103
Examples of Concepts   103

What Is Conceptualization?   105
Example: Conceptualizing
College Student   106

What Is Operationalization?   107
▶ Research in Action: Victim Impact
Statements, Victim Worth, and
Juror Decision Making   108

What Are Variables?   109
Revisiting Research Questions
With a Focus on Variation   109
Type of Variables: Dependent,
Independent, and Control Variables   111
Dependent Variables   111
Independent Variables   112
Control Variables   113
Memorizing IVs, DVs, or
CVs—It Doesn't Work   115

What Are Measures?   115

Example: Measuring College Student   115
How Many Measures?   117

What Are Data?   118
Attributes   118
Mutual Exclusiveness and
Exhaustiveness   120
Levels of Measurement   121
Collect Data at the Highest
Level of Measurement Possible   123
Discrete and Continuous Variables   123
The Role of Validity   123
Face Validity   123
Content Validity   124
Criterion Validity   124
The Role of Reliability   124
Reliability and Validity—Don't
Necessarily Exist Together   125

Overview of the Road From
Concepts to Variables   125

🛆 Common Pitfalls in Concepts,
Conceptualizations, Operationalizations,
Measurements, Variables, and Data in
Research Design   126

⚖ Ethics Associated With
Concepts, Conceptualizations,
Operationalizations, Measurements,
Variables, and Data   127

Concepts, Conceptualizations,
Operationalizations, Measurements,
Variables, and Data Expert—
Brenidy Rice   128

Chapter Wrap-Up   130
▶ Applied Assignments   131
Key Words and Concepts   133
Key Points   133
Review Questions   134
Critical Thinking Questions   134

Chapter 5   Sampling   136
Learning Objectives   136

Introduction   136

Why Is Sampling Important?   136

What Is Sampling?   138

Populations and Samples   139

Census or a Sample?   139
Census Advantages and Disadvantages   140
Sample Advantages and Disadvantages   140

Sampling Error	141
Bias	142
Unit of Analysis	143
Individual	143
▶ **Research in Action:** Low Self-Control and Desire for Control: Motivations for Offending?	144
Groups or Organizations	145
Geographic Regions	145
Social Artifacts and Interactions	145
Unit of Analysis Versus Unit of Observation	146
Ecological Fallacy	146
Individualist Fallacy	147
Choosing a Sampling Approach	147
Probability Sampling	148
Simple Random Sampling	149
Systematic Sampling	150
Stratified Sampling	151
Cluster Sampling	151
Multistage Sampling	153
Nonprobability Sampling	154
Convenience, Accidental, Availability, or Haphazard Sampling	154
Quota Sampling	155
Purposive or Judgmental Sampling	156
Snowball Sampling	157
How Large Should My Sample Be?	157
Purpose of the Research	157
Type of Research	162
Nature of the Population	163
Resources Available	163
⚠ **Common Pitfalls Related to Sampling**	**163**
Ecological and Individualist Fallacies	164
Generalizing Findings That Are Not Generalizable	164
⚖ **Ethics Associated With Sampling**	**164**
Sampling Expert—Sam Gallaher, PhD	**165**
Chapter Wrap-Up	166
▶ **Applied Assignments**	167
Key Words and Concepts	171
Key Points	171
Review Questions	171
Critical Thinking Questions	172

PART 4 COLLECTING YOUR DATA — 173

Chapter 6 Research Using Qualitative Data	**174**
Learning Objectives	174
Introduction	174
Why Conduct Research Using Qualitative Data?	175
What Is Research Using Qualitative Data?	178
Stages of Research Using Qualitative Data	179
Benefits and Limitations of Research Using Qualitative Data	180
Considerations: Research Using Qualitative Data	181
Inductive Reasoning	182
Sampling Considerations	182
Sample Size	183
Approaches Used to Gather Qualitative Data	184
Interviews	187
Individual Interviewing	188
Focus Groups	189
Observation and Fieldwork	190
▶ **Research in Action:** Public Health Problem or Moral Failing? That Might Depend on the Offender	191
Complete Participant	192
Participant as Observer	192
Observer as Participant	193
Complete Observer	193
Documents	193
Content Analysis	194
Recording Qualitative Data	195
Organizing and Analyzing Qualitative Data	196
Examples of Qualitatively Derived Themes: Brunson and Weitzer's (2009) Research	198
Computer-Assisted Qualitative Data Analysis (CAQDAS)	199
Advantages and Disadvantages of CAQDAS	199
⚠ **Common Pitfalls in Research Using Qualitative Data**	**200**
Loss of Objectivity—Going Native	200

⚖ Ethics Associated With Research Using Qualitative Data 200

Qualitative Data Research Expert—Carol Peeples 201

Chapter Wrap-Up 202
▶ Applied Assignments 204
Key Words and Concepts 205
Key Points 205
Review Questions 206
Critical Thinking Questions 207

Chapter 7   Survey Research 208
Learning Objectives 208

Introduction 208

Why Conduct Survey Research? 209

What Are Surveys? 209

General Steps in Survey Research 210

Surveys Across Research Purposes 211
Surveys and Exploratory Research 211
Surveys and Descriptive Research 211
Surveys and Explanatory Research 212
Surveys and Evaluation Research 213

How Are Surveys Distributed? 214
Mail/Written Surveys (Postal Surveys) 214
Advantages 214
Disadvantages 215
Online and Mobile Surveys 216
Advantages 217
Disadvantages 218
Telephone Surveys 218
Advantages 220
Disadvantages 220
Face-to-Face (In-Person) Interviews 221
Advantages 221
Disadvantages 221

Designing Your Own Survey 222
Survey Questions 222
Design and Layout 227
▶ Research in Action: Understanding Confidence in the Police 228
Pretesting of Survey Instruments 229

Survey Administration 230
Notification Letters 230
Fielding the Survey 231

Follow-Up to Nonresponders 231
Survey Processing and Data Entry 231

Easy-to-Use Survey Software 232
SurveyMonkey 233
Qualtrics 233
LimeSurvey 235

⚠ Common Pitfalls in Survey Research 236

⚖ Ethical Considerations in Survey Research 236

Surveying Expert—Bridget Kelly, MA 237

Chapter Wrap-Up 238
▶ Applied Assignments 240
Key Words and Concepts 240
Key Points 241
Review Questions 241
Critical Thinking Questions 242

Chapter 8   Experimental Research 243
Learning Objectives 243

Introduction 243

Why Conduct Experimental Research? 244
What Is Causation? 244
Association Is Not Causation 245

What Is Experimental Research? 248

True Experiments 248
Experimental and Control Group 249
Random Assignment 250
Matching in True Experiments 250
Researcher Manipulation of Treatment 252
True Experimental Designs 252
Two-Group Posttest-Only Design 253
Two-Group Pretest–Treatment–Posttest Design 254
Solomon Four Group Design 255

Validity 256
Internal Validity Threats 257
Experimental Mortality 257
History 257
Instrumentation 258
Maturation 258
Selection Bias 259
Statistical Regression 259
Testing 259

External Validity Threats 260
    Interaction of Selection Biases
        and Experimental Variables 260
    Interaction of Experimental
        Arrangements and
        Experimental Variables 260
   ▶ **Research in Action:** Acupuncture and
   Drug Treatment: An Experiment
   of Effectiveness 261
    Interaction of Testing and
        Experimental Variables 262
    Reactivity Threats 262

Reliability 262

Beyond True Experiments 263

Pre-Experimental Research 263
   One-Shot Case Design 264
   One-Group Pretest–Posttest Design 264
   Static-Group Comparisons 265

Quasi-Experimental Research 265
   Nonequivalent Groups Design 265
   Before-and-After Design 266

Natural Experiments 266

⚠ **Common Pitfalls in Experimental
Research** 267

⚖ **Ethics and Experimental Research** 268

**Experimental Research
   Expert—Chris Keating, PhD** 269

Chapter Wrap-Up 270
   ▶ **Applied Assignments** 272
   Key Words and Concepts 273
   Key Points 274
   Review Questions 274
   Critical Thinking Questions 274

**Chapter 9 Research Using
Secondary Data** 276
   Learning Objectives 276

Introduction 276

Why Conduct Research Using
   Secondary Data? 277

What Are Secondary Data? 278

Frequently Used Secondary
   Data 280

ICPSR 280
Federal Statistical System (FedStats) 283
U.S. Department of Justice 284
   Federal Bureau of
        Investigation (FBI) 284
   ▶ **Research in Action:** Do Offenders
   "Forage" for Targets to Victimize? 287
        Bureau of Justice Statistics (BJS) 288
U.S. Department of Commerce 290
   Census Bureau 290
Geospatial Data 291
Center for Disease Control and
   Prevention 293
State Statistical Agencies 294
Local Statistical Agencies 295

Disadvantages of Using
   Secondary Data 296

Reporting Findings From
   Secondary Data Analysis 298

⚠ **Common Pitfalls in Secondary
Data Analysis** 300

⚖ **Ethics Associated With
Secondary Data Analysis** 301

**Secondary Data Expert—
   Jenna Truman, PhD** 302

Chapter Wrap-Up 305
   ▶ **Applied Assignments** 308
   Key Words and Concepts 309
   Key Points 309
   Review Questions 310
   Critical Thinking Questions 310

**Chapter 10 GIS and Crime
Mapping** 312
   Learning Objectives 312

Introduction 312

Why Conduct Research Using GIS
   and Crime Mapping Techniques? 313

What Is GIS? 314
   Data 315
   Technology 317
   Application 319
   People 319

What Is Crime Mapping
   and Analysis? 320
   Administrative Crime Analysis 320

Tactical Crime Analysis 321
Strategic Crime Analysis 322

Crime Analysis in Academic
Research 323
Crime Hot Spot Mapping 324
Predictive Policing 325
Risk Terrain Modeling 327
Aoristic Analysis 329
Repeat Victimization and Near Repeats 332
▶ Research in Action: Using Risk
Terrain Modeling to Predict
Child Maltreatment 334
Geographic Profiling 335

Reporting Findings From GIS
and Crime Mapping Studies 335

🔺 Common Pitfalls in GIS and
Crime Mapping Analysis 336
Geocoding 337
Modifiable Areal Unit Problem (MAUP) 337

⚖ Ethical Considerations in GIS
and Crime Mapping Research 338

GIS and Crime Mapping Expert—
Henri Buccine-Schraeder, MA 339

Chapter Wrap-Up 340
▶ Applied Assignments 341
Key Words and Concepts 342
Key Points 342
Review Questions 343
Critical Thinking Questions 343

Chapter 11   Evaluation Research 345
Learning Objectives 345

Introduction 345

Why Use Evaluation Research? 346

What Is Evaluation Research? 347
Guiding Principles of
Evaluation Research 348
Seven Steps of Evaluation Research 348
The Policy Process and Evaluation
Research 350

Types of Evaluation Research 351
Formative Evaluation 351
Needs Assessment 352
Process Evaluation 353
Summative Evaluation 355
Outcome Evaluation 355
Impact Evaluation 356

Distinctive Purposes of Evaluation
and Basic Research 356
Knowledge for Decision Making 356
Origination of Research Questions 358
Comparative and Judgmental Nature 359
Working With Stakeholders 359
Challenging Environment 359
Findings and Dissemination 360

Characteristics of Effective
Evaluations 360
Utility 361
Feasibility 361
Propriety 362
Accuracy 362
▶ Research in Action: Evaluating
Faculty Teaching 363

🔺 Common Pitfalls in Evaluation
Research 364
Evaluations as an Afterthought 365
Political Context 365
Trust 366
Overselling Your Skills as an Evaluator 366

⚖ Ethics Associated With Evaluation
Research 366
Failure to Be Nimble 367
Confidentiality 367
Politics 368
Losing Objectivity and Failure to
Pull the Plug 368

Evaluation Research Expert—
Michael Shively, PhD 368
Chapter Wrap-Up 370
▶ Applied Assignments 372
Key Words and Concepts 372
Key Points 373
Review Questions 374
Critical Thinking Questions 374

PART 5   ANALYSIS,
FINDINGS, AND WHERE
TO GO FROM THERE 377

Chapter 12   Analysis and
Findings 378
Learning Objectives 378

Introduction 378

Why Analysis? 379

How Should Data Be Analyzed? 379

Analysis of Quantitative Data 380
  Describing Your Data 380
    Distributions 381
  Measures of Central Tendency 381
    Mean 381
    Median 382
    Mode 383
  Measures of Dispersion 384
    Range 384
    Interquartile Range 384
    Variance 385
    Standard Deviation 385
  Beyond Descriptives 387
    Associations 387
    Differences 390

Qualitative Data Analysis 390

Data Analysis Software 392
  Software Applications Used in
    Quantitative Research 392
    Excel 392
    SPSS 393
    Other Commercial Packages 395
  Software Applications Used in
    Qualitative Research 395
    QDA Miner 396
▶ **Research in Action:** Reducing Bullying
  in Schools 397
    NVivo 398
    ATLAS.ti 398
    HyperRESEARCH 399

Alternative Analytic Approaches 400
  Conjunctive Analysis of Case
    Configurations (CACC) 400
    SPSS 401
    STATA 402
    SAS 402
    R 402
  Geostatistical Approaches 403
    Introduction to Spatial Statistics 403
  Spatial Description 403
    Mean Center 403
    Standard Distance 404
    Convex Hull 404
    Spatial Dependency and
      Autocorrelation 404
    Spatial Interpolation
      and Regression 405

Reporting Findings From
  Your Research 406
  Tables 407
  Figures 408

⚠ **Common Pitfalls in Data Analysis
and Developing Findings** 409

⚖ **Ethics Associated With Analyzing
Your Data and Developing Your
Findings** 411

**Analysis and Findings Expert—
  Sue Burton** 412
  Chapter Wrap-Up 413
  ▶ **Applied Assignments** 416
  Key Words and Concepts 416
  Key Points 417
  Review Questions 417
  Critical Thinking Questions 418

**Chapter 13 Making Your
Research Relevant** 420
  Learning Objectives 420

Introduction 420

Why Conduct Policy-Relevant
  Research? 421

What Is Policy-Relevant Research? 422

What Is Policy? 422

Who Are Policy Makers? 424

The Policy Process 425
  Problem Identification/Agenda Setting 426
  Policy Formulation 427
  Policy Adoption 427
  Policy Implementation 428
  Policy Evaluation 428

Challenges of Getting Research
  to Policy Makers 428
  Relationship and Communication
    Barriers 429
  Nonaccessible Presentation of Research 430
  Competing Sources of Influence 431
    Media 431
    Fear 431
    Advocacy and Interest Groups 432
    Ideology 433
    Budget Constraints 433

▶ **Research in Action:** Type of Attorney
and Bail Decisions 434

Maximizing Chances of Producing
Policy-Relevant Research 435
Plan to Be Policy Relevant From
the Start 435
Relationship 435
Translating Your Research 436

Ⓐ **Common Pitfalls in Producing
Policy-Relevant Research** 436
Producing Research That Is
Not Policy Relevant 436
Failing to Recognize How Your
Research Is Relevant 437
Failure to Know Relevant Policy Makers 437
Going Beyond Your Data and Findings 438

⚖ **Ethics and Conducting Policy
Relevant Research** 438

Policy Expert—Katie TePas 439
Chapter Wrap-Up 440
▶ Making a Policy Brief 441
▶ **Applied Assignments** 446
Key Words and Concepts 446
Key Points 447
Review Questions 447
Critical Thinking Questions 448

**Chapter 14   Research Methods
as a Career** 449
Learning Objectives 449

Introduction 449

Why Research Methods as
a Career? 449

Where Do I Get Started? 450

Career Search Documents 452
Cover Letters 452
▶ What Makes a Great Résumé? 453
Résumés 454
▶ **Research in Action:** Unexpected Career
Choices for Criminal Justice
Graduates 457

Sample Résumé 458
Letters of Recommendation 458

Public- Versus Private-Sector Jobs 461
Working in the Public Sector 461
USAJOBS 461
Applying to State and Local Positions 463
Working in the Private Sector 464

Where to Look for a Career 466
Online Job Searches 467
Social Media 468
Facebook 468
LinkedIn 469
Twitter 470
▶ Top Twitter Job Search Hashtags 471
Internships 471
▶ Tips on Turning an Internship
Into a Full-time Job 471

Interviewing Well 471
Before the Interview 471
Preparing Questions by (and for)
the Interviewer 472
During the Interview 472
Asking the Right Questions 473
Your Professional Portfolio 473
After the Interview 474
Professional Interviewing Tips 474

Ⓐ **Pitfalls and Career Searches** 475

⚖ **Ethics and Career Searches** 475

**Research Methods as a Career
Expert—Nora Scanlon, MA** 476
Chapter Wrap-Up 479
▶ **Applied Assignments** 480
Key Words and Concepts 480
Key Points 481
Review Questions 481
Critical Thinking Questions 481

Appendix A-1
Glossary G-1
References R-1
Index I-1

Preface

Our Approach

The most widely used research methods texts tend to use an approach that convinces students that research methods are irrelevant to their lives and future careers (unless they are going into academia), and the course they are sitting in is one through which they must suffer and complete to graduate. Current texts tend to introduce research as an abstract set of concepts that are used according to a rigid set of rules that leave students questioning the relevance of the material for them. These books fail to ignite imagination, motivate, and engage students. They fail to share the creative and exciting process of generating knowledge—a process that students can engage in. Existing texts are too often like a recipe that results in dry, crumbly, flavorless cookies. In reality, all cookie recipes should result in irresistible, tasty, buttery, and delicious cookies! Our text shows students how they can create equally amazing research.

We also believe that current textbooks miss the opportunity to illustrate to students the very real importance of understanding research methods. This is true for all students, including those seeking a wide range of careers. Research methods matter for those whose careers will generate research, those whose jobs may be affected by research findings, and those who will be consuming research to create policy. Simply, current texts focus too much on the nuts and bolts of "how" and fail to bring to life the exciting and vivid "why" of research methods.

After years of teaching research methods, we have developed interactive, informative, and intellectually stimulating ways to engage and excite students about research methods. We have homed in on ways that demonstrate the challenges, creativity, enjoyment, and overall value of conducting research on relevant and current criminal justice topics. One way we do this is by illustrating and providing a narrative focused repeatedly on the "why" of research, which is a theme carried throughout the text. We emphasize strategies for students to generate exciting questions, ways to go about gathering data to address their questions, challenges inherent in conducting studies that will answer those questions, and how to deal with research when things inevitably go wrong. We emphasize to students how their research can influence policy (in positive and negative ways) and how they absolutely can conduct research that can address important issues.

We find that our approach resonates with the learning styles of today's students who flourish in team environments, value applied research, and want to understand how these research methods skills will enable them to make a positive difference in society. With this text, students will leave class excited about what they have learned. In many cases, their motivation and passion fuel them to continue with additional methodological and statistical courses as well as to consider career paths that use these valuable skills.

In short, this text provides an appealing and competitive alternative to the existing texts by using a narrative approach to first introduce students to exciting research and then get them engaged with the topic. They can learn how researchers from a variety of backgrounds tackled real-life issues associated with research. Students hear about successes and failures. They also see the connection between current issues in the news and research (in terms of both being critical consumers of existing work as well as engaging in that research themselves in their future careers). By using this book, students are able to see themselves in the role of a researcher and the relevance of research for them.

Coverage

The text provides broad, comprehensive, and contemporary material about research methods, especially as they pertain to criminology and the criminal justice system. This includes introductory materials as well as practical strategies for how to develop a research question, write a literature review, identify the framework for designing a research study, gather data (via a variety of strategies, including survey research, qualitative data, and the use of secondary data), and present findings. In addition, we go beyond traditional approaches and include a chapter on making research relevant, and how to use these skills to begin a career. A way we diverge from existing texts is that the topic of ethics is not confined to a single chapter. We feel strongly that in the context of studying criminology and the criminal justice system, ethics are extremely important and should be a discussion that begins in Chapter 1 and ends only when the book ends.

Relevance

Perhaps the greatest limitation of current research methods texts is their failure to convey the relevance of research methods, especially for students whose career paths may not be clearly associated with research presented in a more academic-centered format. As noted, extant books are heavy on the "how" element of research methods while almost neglecting the "why" element. Presented as many texts currently do, students see research methods as limited to publishing scholarly articles rather than as a process of posing questions and systematically answering them to create a body of knowledge that can be disseminated to a variety of audiences. Recognizing they are answering an important and relevant question helps students to understand why the research endeavor is important. Furthermore, it illustrates why the approaches used in methods are important. This helps students understand the need to be knowledgeable consumers of research. A wide variety of careers are affected by research directly (as analysts or policy makers) or indirectly (via policy initiatives that influence those working in the criminal justice system as well as related fields). A text that identifies the variety of ways research can be used and that enforces the need to discern quality research from problematic studies will engage a range of students. This approach makes clearer the "why" of research methods.

Voice

Our text is not akin to an encyclopedia full of information. Rather, our text is speaking directly to the students about research and how it is conducted. By talking directly to students, we can show them why parts and approaches associated with research methods matter. By talking directly to them, we can tell them that they too can do this. We can encourage them to try and show them many examples of people just like them that are using these skills every day. We tell students directly that this material can be used to put themselves in a fulfilling career and life. Research methods skills are not magic. They are something that all students can master. Our text and our directly speaking to students are designed to show them this.

Distinctive Characteristics of This Text

Case Studies

One way our text engages students is by telling the story of the research process as it unfolds. This is done by following six researchers who describe actual research they have conducted. The text reveals elements of each piece of research slowly as the student moves throughout the chapters. This approach demonstrates how the material in the chapters is interconnected as a system versus being discrete unrelated elements. We find in the classroom that the slow revelation of research case studies holds students' attention and facilitates learning more readily. The information we share about each of these six pieces of research is based on hours of interviews that cover the full research process from the initial steps of identifying a research question to the completion of the research project and how it has influenced policy, society, or both. The research covered in these case studies covers issues of interest to students such as the relationship between gang members, violence and fear, police interaction with young males in the St. Louis area, Latino adolescent victimization, high-intensity policing strategies, help seeking behavior among violent crime victims, and policewomen posing as prostitutes. We recognize that contemporary students are public-service minded, and applied research resonates with them. We show them how six researchers feel the same, and how they can join the ranks of researchers making a difference.

Equal Treatment of Qualitative and Quantitative Data

Most research methods books are simply books focused on gathering quantitative data with a chapter devoted to qualitative data. Our book differs. We discuss the elements of research such as sampling, research questions, ethics, and pitfalls for both quantitative and qualitative data throughout. We do devote a specific chapter to qualitative research and data gathering—just like we do to gathering other approaches. But make no mistake, qualitative research and data are not an afterthought in our text.

Careers

A theme in this text is that research methods skills can lead to a variety of rewarding careers. To highlight this, we have included career sections highlighting an expert using these skills in each chapter. Not only do these sections show clearly how these skills are used in a variety of rewarding ways (that pay good salaries), they show that those in these careers lead interesting and fun lives. The goal of this feature is for these professionals to demonstrate why research methods are vital to the work they do, as well as to describe exactly how they use these skills. To this end, the book will educate students on the myriad of careers these skills can help them obtain. Plus, we devote the final chapter in the text to finding a career with these skills. This includes material on how to effectively find work and conduct interviews with those working in these types of jobs. This approach will better allow students to visualize themselves in these careers.

Ethics

As mentioned, a repeating theme in each chapter is the vital importance of ethics. One limitation with current texts is that ethics as a topic is treated in a single chapter. It is then rarely spoken of again. Ethics should not only be a consideration at the beginning of research, but they should also be a consideration every single day from the beginning to the end of a project. Typically, ethics as a topic in existing texts is focused on the classic examples including the Stanford Prison Experiment, Laud Humphreys, and Milgram. These examples are important and are included in our text; nevertheless, we greatly expand on these discussions throughout our text. We also include specific examples from our six case studies and research in the media to emphasize the important role of ethics and ethical behavior in research. By making ethics a thread woven throughout the text, its ubiquitous importance is better shown throughout the process of research versus as a consideration that occurs only at the beginning of the endeavor. Those engaged in work in the criminal justice and criminology fields need to have a deep and appreciative understanding of ethics.

Failure and Pitfalls

Failures, errors, or unanticipated bumps in the road are a normal part of research that is not discussed in existing texts. In contrast, our text repeatedly discusses what can go (and has gone) wrong to show that glitches are normal and that researchers must be nimble and ready to adjust plans if needed. By understanding the many ways errors in methods can lead to failure, students can better understand why some methods are preferable to others. For example, incidents when a researcher fails to word a survey question carefully and ends up with useless data will be included. Certain failures can be prevented, but others cannot. The best laid research plans sometimes just do not work out. We find it is important to demonstrate to students that errors, changes in plans, and sometime failures can happen and are not necessarily the end of the research project.

Research in Action Boxes

Each chapter includes a "Research in Action" box. These features have several purposes. First, they emphasize the ability of research to influence policy (in positive and negative ways) and convey to students that they too can conduct or consume research that addresses important issues. Too often, there is a failure to link research with the "real world" and real policy. These features help to avoid that pitfall. Second, our research in action boxes offer another opportunity to help students understand that they will find themselves in positions to create, review, or be affected by policy. It is imperative then for them to understand the connection between research and policy. Third, these boxes allow a discussion as to why research has too often failed to inform policy. Examples of existing research will be used to illustrate this. These boxes keep the policy discussion alive throughout the text and serve to lead students to Chapter 13, which focuses on making our research relevant.

Digital Resources

edge.sagepub.com/rennisonrm

SAGE edge offers a robust online environment featuring an impressive array of tools and resources for review, study, and further exploration, keeping both instructors and students on the cutting edge of teaching and learning. SAGE edge content is open access and available on demand. Learning and teaching has never been easier!

SAGE edge for Students provides a personalized approach to help students accomplish their coursework goals in an easy-to-use learning environment.

- Mobile-friendly **eFlashcards** strengthen understanding of key terms and concepts.

- Mobile-friendly practice **quizzes** allow for independent assessment by students of their mastery of course material.

- Carefully selected chapter-by-chapter **video links** and **multimedia content** to enhance classroom-based explorations of key topics.

- EXCLUSIVE! Access is provided to full-text **SAGE journal articles** that have been carefully selected

SAGE edge for Instructors, supports teaching by making it easy to integrate quality content and create a rich learning environment for students.

- **Test banks** provide a diverse range of pre-written options as well as the opportunity to edit any question and/or insert personalized questions to effectively assess students' progress and understanding.

- Editable, chapter-specific **PowerPoint® slides** offer complete flexibility for creating a multimedia presentation for the course.

- **Lecture notes** summarize key concepts by chapter to ease preparation for lectures and class discussions.

- **Sample course syllabi** for semester and quarter courses provide suggested models for structuring one's course.

- Chapter-specific **discussion questions** to help launch engaging classroom interaction while reinforcing important content.

- EXCLUSIVE! Access to full-text SAGE journal articles that have been carefully selected to support and expand on the concepts presented in each chapter to encourage students to think critically.

- Carefully selected chapter-by-chapter **video links** and **multimedia content** to enhance classroom-based explorations of key topics.

End-of-Chapter Features

In addition to the features discussed, the text includes several "End of the Chapter Features." These include:

- **Key Points.** Students are provided with summary statements that emphasize major concepts discussed in each chapter. These summary statements and key points will provide the student with a review of the most important things to grasp after reading the chapter.

- **Key Terms.** Terms and concepts that the student may not be familiar with are highlighted and introduced in each chapter. They are listed in this section, and their corresponding definitions may be found in the glossary at the end of the book.

- **Review Questions.** Review questions designed to assist the student in reviewing the most important material in each chapter are included. This material helps students identify whether they fully understand important topics covered in the chapter.

- **Critical Thinking Questions.** These questions are offered to spur independent thought about topics and can be used by the professor/instructor to promote class discussion. These questions are designed to show students that many (most?) issues are not black and white but far more complex in nature and outcome.

For Whom Is the Book Suited?

The primary market for this book is undergraduates and beginner masters students in criminology and criminal justice. The audience also might include related social science undergraduate and graduate programs such as sociology, public affairs/policy, and political science. In addition, the text could be used in high school courses designed to prepare students for the university experience.

Acknowledgments

Thank You

Writing a text requires a lot of work and time. As an author, I know that very well. I also know that writing a text is not possible without the efforts and sacrifices of many others who contribute their time, comments, and critiques. Those contributions lead to a text that is greatly enhanced. A genuine thanks go to the researchers featured throughout the text: Drs. Rod Brunson, Carlos Cuevas, Mary Dodge, Chris Melde, Rachel Boba Santos, and Heather Zaykowski. I've been lucky enough to be their colleagues and can speak firsthand of their dedication, rigor, and passion to make our world a better place through research. Each freely offered a lot of time over the course of a year in interviews where they shared their thoughts and experiences. I greatly appreciated our discussions as they offered opportunities to take time to reflect on my own research. I hope the readers of our book can see their dedication, as well as that each is a fun and interesting person.

Sincere thanks go to the experts highlighted in each chapter: Sharon Devine, Sean McCandless, Brenidy Rice, Sam Gallaher, Carol Peeples, Bridget Kelly, Chris Keating, Jenna Truman, Henri Buccine-Schraeder, Michael Shively, Sue Burton, Katie TePas, and Nora Scanlon. Each of these individuals freely shared his or her thoughts and passion about how they use research methods in a variety of roles. Our intention is to show students how research methods skills are useful and can lead to careers that make a difference. We think each of our experts demonstrated this well.

Other colleagues not explicitly identified in the text were instrumental in completing this text. Clearly, Tim Hart PhD, my co-author, is greatly deserving of many thanks. After almost 20 years of working together, I still think he is a great collaborator, as well as a terrific person in general. I'm happy he's my colleague and so thrilled to have embarked on the journey of writing this text with him. It simply could not have been completed without him.

Heartfelt thanks also go to Kathryn DuBois, PhD, who listened to my brainstorming (often involving talking to myself), and provided ideas and critical feedback on my work. Thanks go also to Lucy Dwight, PhD, who read some of the earliest chapters and provided feedback although she had a very full plate at the time. In addition, my TA Jessica Rosenthal provided fresh eyes to many of the chapters during the writing process. Although it was a valuable experience for her as a student, it was equally valuable to me to get her feedback.

Last, but definitely not least, thanks go to my family, in particular my husband, Dave Vaughan. Even though he may not fully understand what compels someone to write a text, he supported me nonetheless. He always was there with the best margaritas available at the end of long days. I also offer great love and thanks to others in my family, especially Dayle B. Rennison, who sat by me as I wrote much of this text. His calming presence made a huge difference to me during the entire process.

This text would simply not have happened without the support of Sage Publications. Thanks to Jerry Westby who worked with us at the beginning stages. In addition, deep thanks go to Jessica Miller who took the helm after Jerry retired to manage the text flawlessly. Other amazing Sage team members were also key including Laura Kirkhuff, Jennifer Rubio, Rebecca Lee, Jillian Oelson, Veronica Stapleton Hooper, and Sheree Van Vreede.

Unseen by readers of the text are the many reviewers lined up by Sage who offered excellent and meaningful critiques of the text. I am deeply appreciative of the important feedback each reviewer provided that positively influenced this text.

Callie Marie Rennison

Publisher's Acknowledgments

SAGE wishes to acknowledge the valuable contributions of the following reviewers:

Eileen M. Ahlin, Penn State Harrisburg

Christine Arazan, Northern Arizona University

Megan Bears Augustyn, The University of Texas at San Antonio

Kevin M. Beaver, Florida State University

Ashley G. Blackburn, University of Houston—Downtown

Sriram Chintakrindi, CSU Stanislaus

Douglas Devaney, PhD, MA, MSCJ

Tina L. Freiburger, University of Wisconsin-Milwaukee

Brooke Gialopsos, Mount St. Joseph University

William K. Marek, PhD, CSU-East Bay, Central Michigan University

Fawn T. Ngo, University of South Florida Sarasota-Manatee

Peter T. Paluch, SUNY Delhi

Jamie A. Snyder, University of West Florida

Rebecca Stone, Suffolk University

Lindsey Vigesaa, PhD, St. Cloud State University

Jennifer Wareham, PhD, Wayne State University

Jessica J. Warner, Miami University Regionals

Qiang Xu, Indiana University South Bend

About the Authors

Callie Marie Rennison is a professor in the School of Public Affairs (SPA) and the former associate dean of faculty affairs in SPA. Currently, she serves as the director of equity and is Title IX coordinator for the University of Colorado Denver and Anschutz Medical Campuses. Callie earned her PhD in 1997 in political science from the University of Houston, University Park, where she also received a BS in psychology, MA in sociology, and MA in political science. In 2016, she was awarded the Bonnie S. Fisher Victimology Career Award from the Division of Victimology, American Society of Criminology. She has also served on a National Academies Committee examining domestic sex trafficking of minors in the United States and was a senior researcher at the Department of Justice's Bureau of Justice Statistics. Her areas of research include the nature, extent, and consequences of violent victimization with an emphasis on research methodology, quantitative analysis, measurement, and crime data. Her research examines violence against several groups including women, African Americans, American Indians, Hispanics, and those in rural locales. In addition, much of her research focuses on victim interaction with the criminal justice system and college student victimization. Callie's research has appeared in many venues including journals such as the *Journal of Quantitative Criminology, Justice Quarterly, Violence and Victims, and Violence Against Women*. She has authored multiple books including two editions of the *Introduction to Criminal Justice: Systems, Diversity and Change* (with Dr. Mary Dodge; Sage Publications). Along with Dr. Carlos Cuevas, Callie published the *Wiley Handbook on the Psychology of Violence*. Dr. Rennison has taught a variety of undergraduate and graduate courses including Research Methods, Statistics, Murder in America, Crime and the Media, and Introduction to Criminal Justice.

Timothy C. Hart is a senior lecturer in the School of Criminology and Criminal Justice at Griffith University. Tim earned his PhD in criminology and criminal justice from the University of South Florida. In 1997, he was awarded a Presidential Management Fellowship with the Bureau of Justice Statistics at the US Department of Justice. He has also served as a program analyst for the Drug Enforcement Administration (DEA) and as a research analyst for the Hillsborough County (Florida) Sheriff's Office. Tim is also the former Statistical Analysis Centre (SAC) director for the state of Nevada. His areas of interest include survey research, applied statistics, geographic information systems (GIS), and victimization. His scholarship appears in various academic journals, including the *Journal of Quantitative Criminology*, the *Journal of Research in Crime and Delinquency, Criminal Justice and Behavior,* and the *British Journal of Criminology*. He has also been awarded numerous research grants, including studies funded by the Queensland Police Service, Australian Institute of Criminology, the National Institute of Justice, and the Bureau of Justice Statistics.

Getting Started

Welcome to research methods! Before getting into the meat of the material, it is important to make clear why research methods are important, what research methods are, and the role of ethics in conducting research. Whether you recognize it or not, you use research findings every day, so understanding what goes into that research so you use it well is imperative. We want you to learn how to conduct research well for the same reasons. This begins by making clear why research methods are important, not only for the purposes of the class but also in your everyday life. Once you learn why, you will better grasp the material presented in the rest of the text. If you do not understand why research methods matter, then the learning the rest of this material is going to be more difficult (and less fun) than it should be. So let's get started with a basic question: What are research methods?

CHAPTER 1

Why Study Research Methods?

Learning Objectives

After finishing this chapter, you should be able to:

1.1 Define knowledge, social science, research, and research methods.

1.2 Summarize why understanding research methods is important.

1.3 Evaluate and describe each of the major steps taken to conduct research, as well as the importance of each step.

1.4 Develop research questions that would describe, associate, and predict variables. Compare the different types of research questions.

1.5 Assess what makes ethics an important consideration during research by summarizing examples from the classic cases of unethical research.

1.6 Describe the impetus and purpose of the Nuremberg Code and the Belmont Report. Evaluate the guidelines and requirements of ethical research according to these foundational documents.

Knowledge: In this context, it is defined as information believed to be true and reliable. Knowledge can come from a variety of sources both scientific and nonscientific. This text is focused on assessing and creating scientific knowledge.

Science: Challenging and much debated definition that is defined here as a branch of knowledge derived from observable and falsifiable information, data, or evidence gathered in a systematic fashion.

Research: According to the Common Rule refers to a systematic investigation or examination that will contribute to generalizable knowledge.

Social science research: Area of science focused on society and human relationships in society. Criminal justice, criminology, and sociology are a few disciplines within the social sciences.

Introduction

You are enrolled in a class on research methods (probably because you are required to) and you likely have no idea what research methods are. Don't worry, you are not alone. We will get into it more deeply, but for now know that research methods help you become a better consumer and creator of information and knowledge. In addition, understanding and using research methods can help you get a job and be successful in a career.

To understand what research methods are about, it is useful to place them into a larger context of knowledge. What is **knowledge**? There is no universally agreed definition of knowledge, but for the purposes of this text, knowledge is defined as information believed to be true and reliable. Knowledge can be gained in many ways, one of which is via science. **Science** (another challenging and much debated definition) is a branch of knowledge that uses **research** to develop that knowledge. Research is conducted in many fields, and in this text, we focus specifically on **social science research**. Social science research is focused on society and human relationships in society. Criminal justice, criminology, and sociology are some disciplines within the social sciences.

Research in criminal justice and criminology is guided by the goal of answering a specific research question. Once you have a research question, you would then systematically gather observable, and falsifiable, evidence or **data** that are used to answer this research question. Answering this research question requires a specific method—a set of procedures, frameworks, processes, or steps. **Research methods** outline the systematic processes, frameworks, steps, or procedures a person uses to conduct social science research. It is useful, therefore, to view research methods as a how-to guide or as a basic recipe for conducting research.

Research methods identify the systematic steps used by scholars to gather data, analyze it, and reach findings and a conclusion used to answer a research question. Just like there are many recipes for making enchiladas, margaritas, or pies, there are many research methodologies that can be used when conducting scientific research in criminology and criminal justice. Research methods offer the tools needed to solve the puzzle of how to best conduct the research of interest given many acceptable options. Learning about the suitable options available in research methods, the logic behind each, and the advantages and disadvantages of each is the purpose of this book.

With an understanding of *what* research methods are, you can get the most out of the material offered in this book. Understanding that research methods are simply the process used to conduct social science research places the material that follows in that larger context. In doing this, research methods should make greater sense. Not only that, with an understanding of what research methods are, you might find that you enjoy the material in this course. Even better, you will learn that you can apply this material to parts of your everyday life as you become not only an intelligent and critical *creator* of knowledge but also an intelligent and critical *consumer* of knowledge. Importantly, these skills are easy to translate in the "real world" to find a job and build a career.

This chapter begins your journey into research methods by first introducing why methods are important. We then move to a brief description about the typical stages of research including developing a research question, gathering data, and selecting an analytic approach. The chapter then turns to an important discussion of the role of **ethics** in life and in research. From this point, we discuss principles of ethical research. We conclude the chapter by introducing you to six researchers and a piece of research each conducted. We will discuss their research throughout the text to provide real-world examples of how they conducted their research from the beginning to the end.

Data: Information that takes a variety of forms, such as words, observations, measurements, descriptions, and numbers. The individual pieces of information or evidence gathered, analyzed, and used to answer the research question. Data can be numeric and non-numeric in nature.

Research methods: Methods, processes, or steps used to conduct social science research.

Ethics: Norms for behavior that distinguish between what is and is not acceptable. Ethics are not necessarily what our feelings or laws direct us to do but what the common norms of moral behavior in society dictate.

Why Are Research Methods Important?

In addition to understanding what research methods are, it is equally important to understand *why* research methods are important. More bluntly, why should you use your valuable time learning about research methods? The answer is that understanding research methods influences what you know by offering you a systematic way to assess and gain knowledge. Understanding research methods provides you with practical skills that allows you to produce, and to consume, findings, facts and information with the assurance that it was arrived at systematically. These skills are not only useful in college but also in private businesses, nonprofits, government agencies, and other places you can get a job.

Knowledge and Ways of Knowing

How do you know what you know? Throughout your life, you have been exposed to knowledge in a variety of forms such as information available on the Internet, research findings, documentaries, writings, opinions, and your own observations and experiences. You have taken some of that knowledge, and it has become a part of what *you* know. Some of the information you were exposed to was scientifically generated, and some of it was not. Available knowledge based on well-executed scientific processes (i.e., systematic gathering of observable and falsifiable data that are carefully analyzed to reach a conclusion) comes from sources such as legitimate peer-reviewed research journals, academic books, and information from substantive experts (to name a few). Available knowledge generated in nonscientific ways includes information you have been told by people you trust, things you have personally observed, intuition, or information gleaned from social and mass media (to name a few). Thinking about all the types of available information you have been exposed to, what has guided you to accept or reject any piece of information? How did you assess that information before accepting or rejecting it? Is what you know based on knowledge that was carefully assessed and created? Or was it accepted for other reasons?

One approach to deciding whether to accept knowledge is to carefully assess or evaluate it. A means of assessing it is to examine the methods used to generate that knowledge. When exposed to knowledge, you might ask, "What evidence was used to generate this knowledge?" "How was this evidence gathered?" and "Do the conclusions and findings follow from the evidence presented?" By using this approach, you can make an informed choice about that knowledge and then offer evidence to support your choice to accept it or reject it. Learning research methods provides you with the tools needed to ask and answer these questions and, in turn, to assess and create meaningful knowledge.

Another commonly used (and not recommended) approach in accepting knowledge is to assess it based on characteristics unrelated to the actual knowledge. This type of noncritical assessment means that knowledge was accepted without considering *how* the knowledge was created. Perhaps the decision to accept the knowledge was based on where it was obtained (e.g., local news or blogs), from whom it came (e.g., celebrity, priest, person wearing a white coat, family member, or guy in a bar), or just a general gut feeling about that information (e.g., instinct, it just sounds good, or it agrees with what I already believe). Obtaining knowledge in this way is fast and easy, but this approach can come at the price of accepting erroneous and, at times, dangerous knowledge.

The focus of this book is to understand how to create and assess knowledge that is scientifically sound using social science research methods. Some examples of the usefulness of thinking critically about research methods follow.

Information From Everyday Life

Each day we are bombarded with a lot of new information—some of it seemingly contradictory—and yet most people are confident they "know" about these topics. For example, most people, especially those who watch local nightly news, "know" that crime is at an all-time high and out of control. How did they reach that conclusion? What evidence do they have to support that conclusion? (Crime is not at an all time high. Rather, crime rates continue to be relatively low.) It is the responsibility of a savvy consumer never to merely accept what you are told, read, or observe but instead to critically assess the evidence and steps used to reach that conclusion. The next sections offer actual examples in the popular media that have gained a lot of traction. When reading about them, ask whether you believe this information or not, and why that is.

College Student Victimization

Krebs, Lindquist, Warner, Fisher, and Martin (2007) published conclusions from their research titled "The Campus Sexual Assault (CSA) Study." The goal of this investigation was to estimate how much sexual assault was experienced by university students to develop targeted intervention strategies. This research sat in relative obscurity from the public until recently. In fact, findings from the CSA research are the source for what is perhaps the most widely cited contemporary statistic regarding sexual violence against college women: the "1 in 5" statistic. Headlines and other modes of popular media frequently report that 1 in 5 women are raped on campus (or some similarly stated variant). In fact, you may have seen this type of information posted around your campus. What is your assessment about the 1 in 5 statistic? Do you find it to be accurate? Why? Why not?

The appropriate way to assess this and any information is to access the original research and learn about the research methodology used to conduct the research. By doing so, you might be surprised to learn that Krebs and his collaborators never concluded that 1 in 5 college women were raped on campus or anywhere. Reading their clearly articulated methodology, you would learn about the actual research, rather than relying on poor and incomplete descriptions of it found in the media and elsewhere. You would learn that this research was based on a **sample** or a subset of 18- to 25-year-old college students attending two large public universities in the United States. Students who were eligible to participate in the research had to be enrolled at least ¾ time. Data from the survey were gathered from 5,466 women and 1,375 men. An examination of the methodology would make clear the particular **definitions** and **measurement** used to estimate rape and sexual assault perpetrated against those college students in any location. You would also see that **behaviorally specific questions** were used to identify who had been victimized. These questions are more graphic in nature and leave little doubt in the mind of the respondent about what rape and sexual assault means in this specific research.

One of the many conclusions from the Krebs and colleagues research was that 19% of female college seniors had experienced an attempted or completed rape or sexual assault (which includes forced kissing or unwanted groping of sexual body parts) since entering college. Furthermore, you would learn by examining the research methodology that in contrast to the name of the study, only one question was asked about whether the event happened on campus. The 19% statistic represents rapes and sexual assaults perpetrated against these college women in any location. Another very important piece of information available in the published research study is that these findings apply only to the two universities that participated in the study, and that findings do not reflect any other university or any other student outside of those two universities. This research has been so frequently misstated that Krebs and Linquist (2014) wrote a second piece titled "Setting the Record Straight on '1 in 5,'" where they stressed that

> [f]irst and foremost, the 1-in-5 statistic is *not* a nationally representative estimate of the prevalence of sexual assault, and we have never presented it as being representative of anything other than the population of senior undergraduate women at the two universities where data were collected—two large public universities, one in the South and one in the Midwest. (para. 3)

How does understanding a bit about the research methodology of the CSA study alter your view of the "1 in 5" statistic? How might you view newer headlines with similar claims? Hopefully this example encourages you to find the original research *and* consult the methodology before making an assessment. With the information you'll learn in this text, you will be a savvier consumer of material and hold informed views on topics that are based on scientific research.

About eight years after Krebs and his collaborators finished their work on the CSA, the *New York Times* (Perez-Pena, 2015) ran a headline proclaiming that "1 in 4 Women Experience Sexual Assault on Campus." What is your assessment about this headline? Is it your experience that 25% of the women you know were sexually assaulted on campus? Do you believe it to be accurate? Why? Why not? How might you investigate this claim to ascertain whether you find it credible?

To assess this information, you should examine the specific research methods from the Association of American Universities (AAU) study by Cantor and colleagues that led to that conclusion (Cantor et al., 2015). If you accessed the original research by Cantor and his colleagues, you would learn more. A lot more. In the case of the *New York Times* headline, you would learn that this study came from a nonrepresentative sample or subset of students attending 27 institutes of higher learning (IHEs) in the United States. You would learn that males and females enrolled at these IHEs who were at least 18 years of age or older were surveyed. In total, about 150,000 students participated. Furthermore, you would learn about the particular definitions and measurement used in this study, specifically that they are not the same as those used in the Krebs et al.'s (2007) research. In addition, contrary to the headline, there were no estimates or statistics provided regarding how many students, or women,

Sample: Subset of a population of interest from which information or data is gathered. Samples are often composed of people, but they can also be other things including geographic areas (e.g., cities or organizations) or documents (e.g., newspaper reports).

Definition: Clarifying the precise meaning of a particular concept when used in research. For example, in one piece of research, injury may be defined as physical harms perpetrated to another person against his or her will. In some other piece of research, injury may be defined as physical, emotional, psychological, and financial harms perpetrated against another person against his or her will.

Measurement: Process of quantifying a concept. Measurement can be conducted in a variety of ways such as through survey questions (e.g., on a scale from 1 to 10, how happy are you today? How many cigarettes have you smoked this week? and What is your current GPA?), counting behaviors during observation, taking blood pressure measurements, or recording one's age.

Behaviorally specific question: In research, a question that tends to be more graphic in nature, which leaves little doubt in the mind of the respondent about the type of information the research is after.

were sexually assaulted *on campus* in Cantor and colleagues' research. There is no question in the survey asking where a victimization took place. There is one question in the survey asking about *perceptions* of risk of sexual assault on versus off campus (students perceived no difference in risk: 5.0% on campus and 5.3% off campus).

Perhaps the most important information about this study available in the methodology is that the researchers state that the estimates of sexual victimization differ greatly across campuses, and that the findings from this research are not generalizable to any other university in the nation. The findings from this research cannot and do not tell anyone about risk of sexual assault against women on (or off) campus for any place other than the 27 IHEs included in this research. In fact, Cantor and his colleagues stated this clearly on page v:

> The wide variation across IHEs puts in stark perspective prior discussions of single-IHE rates as representing a "standard" against which to compare results. For example, many news stories are focused on figures like "1 in 5" in reporting victimization. As the researchers who generated this number have repeatedly said, the 1 in 5 number is for a few IHEs and is not representative of anything outside of this frame. The wide variation of rates across IHEs in the present study emphasizes the significance of this caveat.

The descriptions of Krebs and colleagues' CSA research and Cantor and colleagues' AAU research show that each of these studies used different samples, definitions, measurements, and other means to gather the data. Neither used a sample that allows them to generalize the findings to other universities or university students. Still, now that you are aware of the research methods used in both studies, you can see that findings from both are frequently misreported as providing estimates of sexual violence on campus. Given what you know now about the methodologies used in these two studies, what is your assessment about the "1 in 4" and the "1 in 5" statistics that are so widely reported? Are people being unnecessarily frightened about college campuses given this widely reported information? Or are they using these misreported findings to feel safe in situations when it is not warranted? The material in this text offers information that will make clearer the importance of research methodology for consuming knowledge (or rejecting it), proposing and conducting studies, and creating knowledge.

Violent Crime in the United States

Let's consider another example. Every year, the Department of Justice (DOJ) releases annual crime statistics for the United States. One set of crime rates is disseminated by the DOJ's Federal Bureau of Investigation (FBI). A second set of crime statistics is disseminated by the DOJ's Bureau of Justice Statistics (BJS). In 2014, the FBI estimated that the national violent crime rate was 3.66 offenses per 1,000 people (FBI, 2014).[1] In contrast, for the same year, BJS estimated that the national violent crime rate was 20.1 violent victimizations per 1,000 people (Truman & Langton, 2015). Note that the BJS estimate is six to seven times greater than the FBI estimate. There was also a lack of agreement between the two sources regarding violent crime rates over time: BJS found that the violent crime rate was stable from 2013 to 2014, whereas the FBI found that violent crime had declined over that same period.

Generally, FBI and BJS crime estimates are released and reported in the media at about the same time, leading to a series of predictable questions and comments such as "statistics lie," "government researchers are biased, idiots, or lying," "an idiot must have made

---

[1]FBI estimates are provided in a "per 100,000" rate. This has been adjusted to make the comparison with the National Crime Victimization Survey (NCVS) rates equivalent.

those numbers up because crime is bad where I live," and "my cousin was robbed so these numbers are not right." What are your thoughts about comments such as these? Do you agree with any of them? How can you account for the fact that BJS violent crime estimates are so much greater than the FBI crime rates? How might you explain that BJS finds that violent crime was stable over the year, yet the FBI concluded it was declining?

The FBI considers arson a violent crime, but the NCVS does not. How might this affect violent crime rates published by each organization?

Hopefully, this chapter prompts you to recognize that research differences in the research methodology used by each federal agency to generate these crime rates account for these differences in estimates. This is exactly the case. BJS violent crime estimates are based on data from the National Crime Victimization Survey (NCVS) on nonfatal violent criminal victimization. This survey defines violent crime as including rape, sexual assault, robbery, aggravated assault, and simple assault. It does not include murder because NCVS data are gathered directly from the victims of violence (victims of murder cannot be interviewed). The NCVS gathers data from a sample of people (not every person in the United States is interviewed), and the published NCVS violent crime rate tells us how many *violent victimizations* (not how many victims or how many incidents or offenses) occurred per 1,000 people age 12 or older.[2] That the NCVS crime rate focuses on victimizations (and not on victims or incidents) is an important piece of methodological information in understanding these figures because there can be multiple victims in each incident, and each victim could experience multiple victimizations in each incident or offense.

The FBI produces violent crime estimates using a completely different approach or methodology. First, FBI crime data are gathered from police agencies who submit crime information to the FBI on a voluntary basis. This means if a victim of a crime does not report the incident to the police, or if the police do not record an incident, or report crime data to the FBI, it will not be reflected in the FBI numbers or estimates. The FBI defines violent crime as including murder, rape, robbery, aggravated assault, and arson. Note that sexual assault along with simple assault (the most common form of violence in the United States according to the NCVS) are not included in FBI violent crime estimates. Also, as noted, murder, the least common form of violence in the United States according to the FBI, is included in FBI violent crime estimates. Moreover, the FBI includes arson, which is not recorded in the NCVS. FBI crime estimates describe crime committed against all people in the United States, regardless of their age (the NCVS focuses only on victims age 12 or older), regardless of where they live (recall that the NCVS focuses only on persons in a housing unit—no people living in institutional housing or the homeless are included), and includes commercial crimes (the NCVS does not count crimes against a business). Also, FBI crime rates refer to offenses, and offenses are counted differently depending on the specific violent crime considered. According to the FBI, when considering assault and rape, an offense is equal to the number of victims. For robbery, an offense equals the number of incidents. This means that a single robbery counted by the FBI could include numerous victims. These are only some of the differences in the methodologies used to generate violent crime estimates by the NCVS and the FBI. See Table 1.1 for some UCR and NCVS methodological differences.

The NCVS and FBI estimates are based on different approaches, definitions, measurements, and ways to count violent crime. Now with a better understanding of differences in methodologies

---

[2]The NCVS data do allow for the calculation of incident and prevalence rates; nevertheless, most BJS reports are focused on victimizations.

Table 1.1 Differences in Construction of Violent Crime Rates—FBI's UCR and BJS's NCVS

	Uniform Crime Reports—FBI	National Crime Victimization Survey—BJS
Purpose	The UCR Program's primary objective is to provide a set of criminal justice statistics for law enforcement administration, operation, and management.	The NCVS was implemented to provide previously unavailable information about crime (including crime not reported to police), victims, and offenders.
Source of Data	Administrative data. The FBI compiles data from monthly law enforcement reports or individual crime incident records transmitted directly to the FBI or to centralized agencies that then report to the FBI. Includes only crimes that were reported to the police and estimates data when it is either incomplete or not submitted.	Data directly from crime victims. On an ongoing basis, BJS interviews a nationally representative sample of approximately 169,000 people age 12 or older living in U.S. households. Households remain in the sample for 3.5 years. New households and persons rotate into the sample monthly.
Exclusions	Excludes crimes reported to the police against any person of any age occurring in any location that can be used in FBI crime rates. Does not include crime not reported to the police.	Excludes persons younger than age 12 and institutionalized persons not living in a housing unit (e.g., military barracks, prisons, homeless). Violence against a person that occurred outside the United States is not included.
Differences in Violent Crimes Covered for Annual Estimates Released (both data collection systems gather other additional information)	Murder, rape, robbery, aggravated assault, and arson. The UCR includes, but the NCVS excludes, homicide, arson, commercial crimes, and crimes against children younger than age 12.	Rape, sexual assault, robbery, aggravated assault, and simple assault. The NCVS includes, but the UCR excludes, sexual assault (completed, attempted, and threatened), attempted robberies, verbal threats of rape, simple assaults, and crimes not reported to law enforcement.
Differences in Violent Crime Definitions	Although names of crimes may be the same, definitions differ. For example, until January 1, 2013, rape in the FBI's UCR did not include male victims. Consult the methodology of each for more details.	Although names of crimes may be the same, definitions differ. For example, until 2013, rape in the FBI's UCR did not include male victims. Consult the methodology of each for more details.
Counting Differences	The basic counting unit for the UCR is the offense. For some crimes, such as assault and rape, the frequency of offenses is equal to the number of victims. For other crimes, such as burglary or robbery, the number of offenses equals the number of incidents.	The basic counting unit of the NCVS is the victimization. A victimization is a specific criminal act that affects a single victim. A victim may experience multiple victimizations in an incident.
Rates Reported	The UCR reports violent crime rates using "per 100,000 people in the United States."	The NCVS reports violent crime rates using "per 1,000 people age 12 or older in the United States."

Adapted from http://www.bjs.gov/index.cfm?ty=pbdetail&iid=5112; and Rand, Michael R. and Callie Marie Rennison. (2002). True crime stories? Accounting for differences in our national crime indicators. *Chance, 15*(1), 47–51.

used by BJS and the FBI, do you have a more informed understanding about the extent of violent crime in the United States? Can you now articulate some reasons why the NCVS suggests stability in crime rates over the year, whereas the FBI measures a decline? Can you offer evidence for why you know this? Can you better understand why NCVS estimates might be higher than FBI estimates? Can you see why stating that statistics and researchers are biased or that "statistics lie" is not only intellectually lazy but also incorrect? Given all of these differences, is it at all surprising to you that the two pieces of research reach different conclusions? It should not be.

Other Sources of Knowledge

Chances are that each of us has knowledge we hold dear that is not based on a scientific approach. In fact, having only knowledge from scientific inquiry would make day-to-day living impossible. Imagine requiring scientific evidence to determine how to best cook, eat, bathe, drive, read, study, interact with others, converse, or any number of other daily activities. This section identifies common sources of nonscientific knowledge and notes some limitations of these sources.

- **Tradition, customs, and norms**. Tradition, customs, and norms are used to pass on knowledge or beliefs from person to person over time. This knowledge is thought to be true and valuable because people have always believed them to be true and valuable. Examples include how strangers are to be greeted, treatment of the U.S. flag, manners used while eating, and what is viewed as appropriate food sources (e.g., no horse or dog for dinner [or breakfast either]). A limitation of this type of knowledge is that it is subjective, nonresearch based, and not concluded from systematically collected data. Also, this information is often not falsifiable or reproducible. The knowledge is simply accepted as fact.

- **Personal experience**. Personal experience is a powerful source of nonscientific and nonresearch-based knowledge. This knowledge is believed to be valuable and true because you have personally experienced it. For example, you may have the personal experience that babies in restaurants are loud and messy (based on seeing one or two loud and messy babies; you probably didn't notice the clean and quiet babies, although they were there too). Or you may hold particular stereotypes of others based on a few personal experiences. This may be your experience; your experience is subjective, however, and does not necessarily accurately reflect the larger truth. This knowledge also suffers from not being concluded from systematically collected data. It is not falsifiable, and it is not reproducible.

Some find babies to be poor restaurant patrons based on personal experience. Does this meant that all babies are unruly at restaurants, or might that knowledge be based on personal experience only?

- **Authoritative sources**. Knowledge also can include information taken from authoritative sources including parents, clergy, news sources, bloggers, social media, professors, or others. For some, if a source is trusted, the information they share is trusted. Examples can include knowledge such as that prayer is useful, the president is a jerk, crime is out of control, and research methods are useful. Although knowledge gathered in these ways can be valuable (and even be based on scientific research), you should research that information to assess its value because it too can be imperfect or incorrect.

Tradition, customs, and norms: knowledge or beliefs passed on from person to person over time. This knowledge is thought to be true and valuable because people have always believed it to be true and valuable.

Personal experience: Knowledge accepted based on one's own observations and experiences.

Authoritative sources: Knowledge based on information accepted from people or sources that are trusted such as parents, clergy, news sources, bloggers, social media, or professors.

Intuition: Knowledge developed based on a feeling or gut instinct.

Research question: Question that guides research designed to generate knowledge. This question guides the research endeavor.

- **Intuition**. Knowledge based on intuition is believed and valued because you have a feeling, sense, or gut instinct it is "good" information. Examples include initial perceptions about others or feelings about particular places or situations. Imagine meeting an individual at a party where your intuition immediately suggests he or she is a shyster and not to be trusted. This is your intuition talking, and what it is saying may or may not be true. It is also the case that this information is not research based or scientific (even if you have been correct in other initial assessments). Like the other categories described here, this knowledge is not falsifiable, not reproducible, and not scientifically based.

Typical Stages of Research

Subsequent chapters provide greater detail about the foundational elements and stages important for conducting scientific research. For now, this section briefly outlines these major steps and things used in research, including developing a research question, conducting a literature review, selecting appropriate research methods (such as samples and ways of gathering data such as surveys and observations), selecting analytic techniques, and developing and disseminating findings and conclusions.

Developing a Research Question

Research begins with, and is guided by, a **research question.** The research question when answered increases our understanding and knowledge about a topic. Research is never guided by a statement of fact. As basic as this distinction between question and statement seems, students new to research methodology frequently offer a statement rather than a question when asked to pose possible research questions. Every step that is taken to accomplish research is informed by that research question. There is an endless number of possible research questions. Some examples include

- What is the effect of gang membership on self-reported violent victimization among adolescents?

- Is violence against college students more likely to occur on or off campus?

- What are the differences between the perceptions and experiences of Black and White youth with police officers?

- How do female police officers serving as prostitution decoys view this work?

- Will an offender-focused, high-intensity policing strategy in a hot spot lead to a reduction in crime?

- What role does reporting violence to the police play on a victim's likelihood to access victim services?

- What are the rates of dating violence by Latino victim gender?

Do you have a research question in mind that you would like to explore? If not, you are not alone. Many students are anxious and feel that they cannot possibly think of a research question. Happily, all students can pose research questions once they recognize that they can be developed in many ways, including listening to others speak, reading a text and research literature, learning about theories, reading and watching the media, going to professional meetings,

From 1970 to the early 2000s, the incarceration rates in the United States exploded, as did the amount of research focused on incarceration. That research overwhelmingly shows that incarceration does not effectively reduce a person's odds of recidivating compared with other approaches that include probation or shorter prison sentences. What has not received much attention, however, is how the type of incarceration affects recidivism and other postrelease behaviors. Specifically, it is unclear how supermax confinement influences odds of recidivism and other postrelease behaviors. Supermax facilities are costly to operate, and confinement typically involves confinement to a cell for 23 hours a day with few or no opportunities for socialization with staff or other inmates. Butler, Steiner, Makarious, and Travis (2017) found two studies that examined the influence of supermax confinement on recidivism. Neither study found that supermax confinement had an effect on offenders' odds of recidivism. To build on that research, the current examination by Butler et al. compares recidivism rates of offenders exposed to supermax confinement in Ohio with those derived from a matched sample of offenders not exposed to supermax confinement. In addition, this research considers both short- (1 year) and long-term (7 years) effects of exposure to supermax confinement. Finally, Butler et al. consider the influence of supermax confinement on other postrelease behaviors such as employment and treatment completion.

To address these research purposes, the researchers used a randomly selected sample of 1,569 men taken from a list of all men released under postrelease supervision in Ohio from about 2003 to 2005. Data about each offender were collected from several official sources such as case files, and offenders were followed for a full year after release. Measures of whether each offender was reincarcerated for any reason or reincarcerated for a new crime within 7 years of his release were also obtained and used in the analysis. The analysis consisted of finding a similar sample of incarcerated men who differed from the supermax sample only in terms of having not spent time in a supermax facility. By comparing their outcomes with the supermax sample, the researchers can now point to the effects of supermax exposure.

Findings from Butler et al. show that exposure to supermax confinement had no effect on recidivism in the short term. Similar to the findings from the analysis of recidivism in the short term, the odds of recidivism over the long term were nonsignificant. Thus, supermax confinement did not affect offenders' odds of recidivism over the long term either. When considering other postrelease behaviors, findings show that exposure to supermax confinement does not affect other postrelease outcomes for offenders released under postrelease supervision. In sum, supermax exposure leads to equivalent outcomes when compared with offenders not exposed to supermax.

The policy implications of this work by Butler et al. point to the costs versus the benefits of supermax. The cost of operating a supermax facility is far greater than the cost of operating a typical maximum security prison. If outcomes are equivalent, this suggests the need to consider the feasibility of running expensive supermax operations. It appears cheaper and equally effective alternatives exist.

Butler, H. D., Steiner, B., Makarious, M. D., & Travis, L. F. (2017). Assessing the effects of exposure to supermax confinement on offender postrelease behaviors. *The Prison Journal, 97*(3), 275–295.

Literature review: Review, summary, and synthesis of extant knowledge on a topic. Literature review sections in journal articles review, present, organize, and synthesize existing understanding on a topic at the time the research was conducted. They are used to place the published research into context and to demonstrate how it adds to our understanding of a topic.

and so on. Sometimes it takes practice to see that one's innate curiosity or a desire to develop information can lead to research questions. Imagine you are in class listening to a police officer identifying the ways you can distinguish a police impersonator from a legitimate police officer. This officer discusses subtle characteristics in an officer's uniform or personal appearance (e.g., facial hair) that can be used to identify an impersonator. The officer's presentation gets you wondering more broadly about police impersonators, which leads to several questions:

- What is the gender, race, and age of most police impersonators?
- What types of victims do most police impersonators target?
- What are the main motivations of police impersonators?
- Are police impersonators more likely than other types of criminals to brandish or use a weapon? To injure the victim?

These are all interesting questions, and all are suitable research questions.

Imagine now that you taking a university-required training about college student sexual violence. You find that the material in the training is focused on sexual violence against female students only. This raises several questions in your mind:

- Are college women victims of nonsexual violence such as robbery? If so, to what extent?
- What is the extent to which male college students are sexually and nonsexually victimized?
- Does violence against college students differ from violence against noncollege students in terms of rates and characteristics?
- Are bystanders more likely to be present during a college versus a noncollege student victimization? Is this the same for male versus female college students?

These are all suitable research questions. With the skills learned in this book, each of these research questions can be answered by you. Once a research question (or questions) has been identified, the next step is to learn what is already known about that topic. That is accomplished via a literature review.

Conducting a Literature Review

A research question is the foundation of proposed research. Once you have identified a research question (or questions), the next step is to conduct a review of scientific literature on that research topic. A **literature review** serves many purposes. It

- summarizes and synthesizes existing understanding on the topic of interest,
- identifies limitations and gaps in existing research,
- offers justification for the proposed study, and
- places the new study in context of the existing literature.

Although you may develop a creative and fascinating research question, it might be that others have already addressed it. That is okay! Reading about existing studies focused on the same question will assist in refining your research question. Understanding details about the methodology used in prior research offers the opportunity to identify possible improvements on that methodology in your project. Perhaps the existing studies are very old. This means a new look at this old question using newer or improved data can increase our understanding of the topic. Or perhaps the older study used very basic analytic approaches because computer power was not available at the time that research was conducted. It may be that the research question can be reexamined with more powerful analytic approaches and technology available today. This means the new study can provide an enhanced understanding of the issue.

Designing the Research

Designing the research study is the next major step in conducting research. Designing the research is where you identify the precise steps that will be used to answer the research question. Some of those steps may be identifying concepts of interest, making them measurable (operationalization), measuring those concepts, and selecting a sample. It is imperative that the precise steps taken to conduct research be thoroughly considered and documented. Documentation of your methodology is needed for consumers of your work to critically assess it, and so future researchers who want to replicate your study can do so exactly.

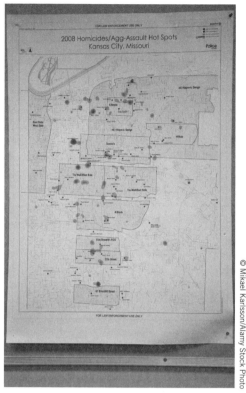

Crime mapping is the source of much criminology and criminal justice knowledge. How do you think it added to our understanding about where crime occurs?

Collecting Data

Once the research methodology has been identified, the next step is to gather the data or information that will be analyzed to answer the research question. Researchers gather data that are most effective, efficient, and affordable to answer the research question. Data may be gathered in any number of ways, including survey research, in-person interviews, focus groups, observations, experiments, quasi-experiments, document analysis, and so on. At the conclusion of data gathering, a researcher has the data needed to answer his or her research question. The next step is to analyze those data.

Selecting an Analytic Approach

To answer the research question posed, a researcher takes the systematically gathered data and analyzes it. How the data are analyzed depends on the nature of the research question and the data gathered. If a researcher wishes to explore or describe a topic using numeric data, he or she might use percentages or rates. If a researcher is working with non-numeric data in the form of text, interviews, or observations, he or she might use an approach that identifies themes, concepts, or core meanings. If a researchers wishes to identify associations among variables, then correlations might be an appropriate approach. If the researcher is interested in investigating causal relationships using numeric data, a statistical technique such as regression might be the most suitable approach. Many considerations including whether the data sought are numeric or non-numeric in nature go into selecting the appropriate analytic technique, but all ultimately are selected based on the best way to answer the research question.

Generating Findings, Conclusions, and Policy Implications

Answering the research question to create knowledge is the goal of the research. Nevertheless, answering the question is not enough. You as a researcher must also make sense of the findings. This can be accomplished by placing the findings in the context of the existing literature (again, the literature review is useful during this step). Do your findings support what was found in other literature? Do findings in the current research deviate from the findings in the literature? What are possible reasons for this support of, or deviation from, existing literature? How might this new knowledge be used to affect policy and improve everyday life? This step requires thinking about the research and what it means in the larger context of the issue.

Essential Role of Ethics in Research

In everyday life, and especially in the fields of criminal justice and criminology, ethical behavior is imperative. This includes the practice of criminal justice and criminology research. Attention to ethics must occur *throughout* the research process, not only in the planning stages. Ethics are norms for behavior that distinguish what is and is not acceptable. Ethics are not necessarily what feelings or laws direct us to do but what the common norms of moral behavior in society dictate. The next section offers information on some classic unethical studies conducted in the name of research. Understanding them places into context why ethical considerations must be constant and why oversight in research is imperative.

Unethical Research Examples

You might believe that an intentional and constant attention to ethics is unnecessary because researchers would not act unethically. If you believe this, you are incorrect (and there is a lot of evidence demonstrating that). It is shocking the sheer number and nature of unethical research that has been undertaken, all in the name of science. Even more surprising is that many researchers engaged in these studies did not view their research as unethical while it was ongoing. Clearly, humans require additional oversight than that provided by self-reflection alone.

Nazi Research on Concentration Camp Prisoners

During World War II, German doctors conducted research experiments on prisoners held in concentration camps. These grisly experiments included altitude experiments in which prisoners were put in low-pressure chambers to determine the effects of altitude on the body, as well as experiments in which prisoners were submerged in freezing water to test the effects of, and effective treatment for, hypothermia. Other concentration camp prisoners were exposed to diseases such as tuberculosis, typhoid fever, yellow fever, and hepatitis allowing doctors to conduct experiments on possible vaccines. Some prisoners were subjected to bone-grafting experiments, others were shot to learn about blood clotting, and still others were exposed to mustard gas that provided data used to identify possible antidotes to poisons. Millions of concentration camp prisoners were subjected to forced sterilization experiments as German doctors tried to discern inexpensive and efficient ways to sterilize those deemed inferior. It hardly needs to be stated, but this type of research is absolutely unethical, yet it was conducted by many researchers, in the name of science, and *it continued for years.*

Tuskegee Syphilis Experiment

If you are thinking that researchers in the United States would not engage in such savage, unethical research, think again. Consider the U.S. Public Health Service's Tuskegee Syphilis Experiment, which took place in Macon County, Alabama. The purpose of this study was to identify the natural course of syphilis in Black men. Syphilis is a severe disease that leads to damage to body parts including the brain, heart, eyes, liver, bones, joints, and nerves. It can also lead to paralysis, blindness, mental illness, and death. Six hundred impoverished Black men volunteered for the study, but they were not told they had just volunteered for research on syphilis. Rather, they were told they would be treated for "bad blood." Bad blood was understood to mean an assortment of medical issues including anemia and fatigue. In return for volunteering for this study, the men were offered free medical examinations, transportation to and from the clinic, meals while at the clinic, treatment for minor problems, and burial stipends paid to their families after their death. These were highly valuable incentives for such impoverished individuals.

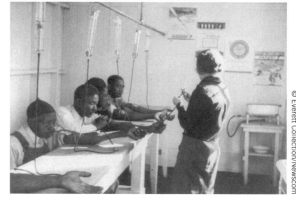

© Everett Collection/Newscom

The Tuskegee Syphilis Experiment is an example of highly unethical research that cost many unsuspecting Black men their health and their lives. What benefit was gained from conducting this research?

At the beginning of the experiment, 399 of the 600 participants were known to be infected with syphilis (the remaining 201 were considered the comparison group). None of the infected men were told they had syphilis, however. When the Tuskegee Syphilis Experiment began in 1932, there was no cure for syphilis. In an astoundingly unethical turn of events, when penicillin was identified as a cure to treat syphilis in 1947, penicillin was withheld from the infected participants in the study. In fact, efforts were made to obstruct study participants from receiving penicillin anywhere so as not to jeopardize the study. In contrast, although these men were denied available treatment for syphilis, the study's sponsor was establishing "Rapid Treatment Centers" to treat syphilis in the general population.

This ghastly experiment was finally halted in 1972, more than 20 years after the discovery of penicillin. Many had called for the study's termination earlier given its unethical nature, but those demands were ignored. Only when a whistle-blower, Peter Buxtun, leaked information regarding the experiment to journalists was the research halted. At the time the experiment was stopped, only 74 of the original 399 infected men were still living. Twenty eight had died from syphilis, 100 had died from related complications, and 40 spouses and 19 children had been infected. In 1997, President Bill Clinton formally apologized for this government-sponsored study. In attendance at this formal presidential apology were five of the eight surviving experimental research subjects.

Milgram's Obedience to Authority

Unethical research in the United States has not been confined to federal government sponsors either. Consider the infamous work of Stanley Milgram (1963). The purpose of his 1961 research was to identify the willingness of people to obey authority figures even when that requested behavior conflicts with a person's conscience. The impetus for the study was the death of millions of people killed in gas chambers in concentration camps during the Holocaust. Milgram (1975, p. 1) noted that "[t]hese inhumane policies may have originated in the mind of a single person, but they could only have been carried out on a massive scale if a very large number of people obeyed orders." To conduct the study, Milgram advertised for volunteers to participate in an experiment about learning. Forty male volunteers were selected to participate. The experiment began as two men showed up as volunteers. The first order of business was to determine who would be the teacher and who would be the learner in the research on "learning." These roles were determined by drawing slips of paper out of

In one iteration of the Milgram experiments, the teacher and learner sat next to one another. In this case, the learner had to place his own hand on the shock plate. When he refused to do so at 150 volts, the teacher was ordered to physically force the learner's hand on the shock plate. Thirty percent of teachers forced the learner's hand onto the plate all the way up to the maximum 450 volts. Would you have done so? Why or why not?

a hat. Both men drew a slip of paper, and each announced his role. Both slips of paper in the hat had "teacher" written on them. In reality, one volunteer was a confederate working with the research team. Although the confederate drew a slip that stated "teacher," he stated he was the learner. The true volunteer would serve as the teacher, and his behavior was the focus on the actual experiment.

After identifying roles, the teacher watched the fake learner get strapped into a chair where the learning would take place. The teacher was then seated in front of a board with 30 switches, each of which would deliver a shock to the learner. Shock intensities began at 15 volts and increased at 15-volt increments to a maximum of 450 volts across the 30 switches. In addition to identifying the voltage of each switch, each switch was labeled using a phrase such as "Slight shock" to "Danger: Severe Shock." At that time, the teacher was administered a small shock to demonstrate what the learner would feel in the beginning. In reality, the learners were not shocked during the experiment.

After the subjects were situated, the teacher was instructed to read a series of word pairs. The learner was required to recall one of these word pairs. If the learner failed to identify the correct word, the teacher was required to announce the voltage level he was administering and then administer the shock (although a shock was not administered). With each incorrect answer, the level of shock was increased. As the severity of shocks increased, the learner increased his vocalization of distress from pleas, cries, begs, and moans, ultimately culminating with silence. If the teacher hesitated or refused to administer the required shock, the researcher (wearing a white laboratory coat) urged the teacher to continue using four demands delivered in sequence (Milgram, 1963, p. 374):

1. Please continue, or please go on.

2. The experiment requires that you continue.

3. It is absolutely essential that you continue.

4. You have no other choice, you must go on.

If the teacher asked the researcher about his own liability for harm to the learner, the researcher stated, "Although the shocks may be painful, there is no permanent tissue damage, so please go on." If the teacher told the researcher that the learner did not want to continue, the researcher responded, "Whether the learner likes it or not, you must go on until he has learned all the word pairs correctly. So please go on." If at any time during the experiment the teacher refused to continue after hearing four demands from the researcher, the experiment was halted. Milgram found that the earliest a teacher stopped the experiment was at 300 volts (five teachers). Sadly, 26 teachers (65% of the teachers) administered the maximum 450-volt severe shock even when they were visibly shaken while doing so. Milgram offered two important conclusions from this research. First, the strength of obedient tendencies demonstrated by teachers in the experiment was unexpectedly and surprisingly high. The second conclusion was that although the experiment generated extraordinary tension in the teachers, it was not enough for them to disengage from the experiment.

Many erroneously believe Milgram conducted this famous experiment only once. In fact, he conducted 19 experiments in which characteristics of the experiment varied. Variations in the subsequent experiments included the physical location of the experiment, the physical closeness of the learner to the teacher, the ability of teacher to see the learner, the gender of the learner, whether the teacher had to physically place the learner's hand on a shock plate to receive the shock, and so on. All iterations of the experiment concluded the same: A large percentage of people obeyed authority even when it was stressful and conflicted with their personal beliefs.

Milgram's work prompted others to conduct similar experiments, including some that did not involve human subjects. Thinking that perhaps teachers in Milgram's research did not really believe the learner was being shocked, Sheridan and King (1972) designed an experiment in which a "cute, fluffy, puppy" was shocked. In this research named "Shock the Puppy," undergraduate psychology students volunteered to act as teacher to the puppy. The students were told that the puppy was learning to stand to the left or the right of his cage depending on whether he saw a steady or a flickering light. When the puppy failed to respond correctly to the light stimulus, the student was directed to shock the dog. For each incorrect action by the dog, the level of the shock was increased by 15 volts. When shocked, the puppy initially barked, then jumped, and finally howled in pain. This demonstrable show of pain deterred few students from administering the painful shocks. Although the 13 female and 13 male student volunteers were visibly upset during the experiment, each continued administering and increasing the shock level when instructed by an authority figure. In fact, all 13 of the women and 7 of the men shocked the puppy using the maximum 450 voltage.

Most believe they would not administer shocks and suffering to humans, but Milgram's results suggest differently. How about administering painful voltage to a puppy? Would you do this? What sort of information would make doing this worthwhile in your opinion? Why?

Stanford Prison Experiment

In part, in response to Milgram's work, Haney, Banks, and Zimbardo (1973) designed the Stanford Prison Experiment, which investigated identification conformity and the role of social situations on behavior. An additional purpose of this work, sponsored by the U.S. Office of Naval Research, was to better understand conflict between military guards and prisoners. After placing an advertisement for college student volunteers in 1971, 24 males judged to be psychologically stable and healthy were selected to participate. The study was designed to last for two weeks and took place on the Stanford University campus in a basement make-shift prison complete with a solitary confinement cell. Volunteers acting as guards were instructed not to physically harm or withhold sustenance from the prisoners. Still, guards were reminded that they had all the power while the prisoners had none. Guards were issued mirrored sunglasses, khaki uniforms, and wood batons.

Those volunteers serving as prisoners were not told when the experiment would begin. They left the university and resumed their normal lives. To their surprise (and humiliation), they were unexpectedly taken into custody in front of friends and loved ones in public places. Prisoners were placed in a police car and taken to the "jail" where they were fingerprinted, strip-searched, deloused, photographed (mug shots), issued poorly fitted smocks and stocking caps, and had a chain placed around their right ankle. Each prisoner was then given a new prisoner number and not referred to by name again.

Almost immediately, guards and prisoners internalized their roles. Prisoners responded in a variety of ways. Some began resisting guard demands, whereas some passively accepted the psychological abuse heaped on them. Some acted insane. Five prisoners exited the experiment before its conclusion as a result of the trauma they experienced. Guards exhibited dehumanizing authoritarian behaviors and attitudes and forced prisoners to engage in degrading tasks, subjecting prisoners to psychological torture. Findings indicated that one third of the guards exhibited sadistic tendencies; guards even began controlling prisoner access to the toilet.

Even Zimbardo, the principal investigator of the study, failed to recognize the unethical nature of this experiment until it was pointed out to him by a graduate student. Only then did

Courtesy of Philip G. Zimbardo, Inc.

Guards actively humiliating several Stanford prisoners in sadistic and authoritarian means. Do you believe you would have been a sadistic guard? Zimbardo concluded anyone in that position would. Do you agree? Why or why not?

he see the escalating brutality of the situation, as well as his own contribution it. Zimbardo recognized that he had begun acting as the executive leader of the prison, rather than as an objective researcher conducting an experiment. It was then, six days after beginning the experiment, that it was ended. Zimbardo concluded that a brutal environment leads to brutal behavior.

Foundational Ethical Research Principles and Requirements

These few examples of unethical research point to the need for research oversight to prevent abuses of human subjects. Two historical and important documents provided the initial moral framework that continues to guide researchers today. After the research atrocities perpetrated in Nazi Germany, the Nuremberg Code (Ivy, 1948) outlining ethical principles to guide research, was created in 1947. It identifies ten points of guidance:

1. Required is the voluntary, well-informed, understanding consent of the human subject in a full legal capacity.

2. The experiment should be aimed at positive results for society that cannot be procured in some other way.

3. It should be based on previous knowledge (like an expectation derived from animal experiments) that justifies the experiment.

4. The experiment should be set up in a way that avoids unnecessary physical and mental suffering and injuries.

5. It should not be conducted when there is any reason to believe that it implies a risk of death or disabling injury.

6. The risks of the experiment should be in proportion to (that is, not exceed) the expected humanitarian benefits.

7. Preparations and facilities must be provided that adequately protect the subjects against the experiment's risks.

8. The staff members who conduct or take part in the experiment must be fully trained and scientifically qualified.

9. The human subjects must be free to immediately quit the experiment at any point when they feel physically or mentally unable to go on.

10. Likewise, the medical staff must stop the experiment at any point when they observe that continuation would be dangerous.

A limitation of the Nuremberg Code (Office of History, National Institutes of Health, n.d.) is that it offered no mechanism for compliance or enforcement. The code relied on the researchers themselves to govern themselves, which as the past shows is not effective:

> The duty and responsibility for ascertaining the quality of the consent rests upon each individual who initiates, directs or engages in the experiment. It is a personal duty and responsibility which may not be delegated to another with impunity. (item 1)

Sadly, the Nuremberg Code did not end unethical research. Note that the Tuskegee Syphilis Experiment described earlier began before the Nuremberg Code was established, yet that experiment continued for almost 30 years after the introducing the Code. Given the Nazi experiments, the Tuskegee Syphilis Experiment, and many more examples of unethical research than this book can cover, the National Research Act of 1974 was passed by Congress. This law created the National Commission for the Protection of Human Subjects of Biomedical and Behavioral Research (referred to as The Commission), which was charged with developing human subject research guidelines. A document from the 1974 Commission was the *Belmont Report: Ethical Principles and Guidelines for the Protection of Human Subjects and Research* (National Commission for the Protection of Human Subjects of Biomedical and Behavioral Research, 1979), which was published in the U.S. Federal Register in 1979. The Belmont Report identifies three core ethical principles and three requirements that all researchers must adhere to when conducting research on human subjects (unfortunately, the cute, fluffy puppies were not protected by the Belmont Report, which focuses on humans).[3] The following are three fundamental *principles* outlined in the Belmont Report:

1. **Respect for persons.** Individuals should be treated as autonomous agents, and that autonomy must be acknowledged. Persons with diminished autonomy are entitled to protection, and protection is required of those with diminished autonomy.

2. **Beneficence.** Researchers are obligated to do no harm, to maximize possible benefits, and to minimize possible harms to all participants in a study. Study participants include respondents, researchers, and bystanders.

3. **Justice.** Research subjects must be treated reasonably and fairly. Selection of participants should not be conducted in which some due to their easy availability, their compromised position, or their manipulability are taken advantage of, or shoulder the bulk of the costs of the research. Selection of subjects in research should be related directly to the problem being studied. Costs and benefits of the research should be shouldered fairly.

The following three *requirements* for human subjects research are indicated by the principles of respect for persons, beneficence, and justice in the Belmont Report:

1. **Informed consent.** Participants in research can choose what shall or shall not be done to them. To provide informed consent, **voluntary participation** requires that participants choose to engage in the study after having been given sufficient **information** about the study. In addition, information about the research must be provided in a way that is **comprehensible** to the participant.

2. **Assessment of risk and benefits.** It is required that all parties engaged in research examine whether the benefits outweigh the risks. It is the researcher's responsibility to properly design a study, and to ensure the selection of subjects is fair and just. It is a review committee's responsibility to identify if risks, if any, to the participants are justified. Participants must assess whether they will or will not participate.

3. **Selection of subjects.** This requirement calls for the fair selection of, and fair distribution of, outcomes associated with the selection of research subjects for research conducted.

---

[3]Some documents now available do focus on ethics when it comes to animal research. One such example was written by Bernard Rollin and can be found at http://animalresearch.thehastingscenter.org/report/the-moral-status-of-invasive-animal-research/#footnote-1, and at http://www.apa.org/monitor/jan03/animals.aspx.

Respect for persons: First principle of ethical research outlined in the Belmont Report. It states that individuals should be treated as autonomous agents and that autonomy must be acknowledged. Persons with diminished autonomy are entitled to protection, and protection is required of those with diminished autonomy.

Beneficence: Second principle of ethical research outlined in the Belmont Report. It states that researchers are obligated to do no harm, to maximize possible benefits, and to minimize possible harms to all participants in a study.

Justice: Third principle of ethical research outlined in the Belmont Report. This principle indicates that research subjects must be treated reasonably, justly, and fairly.

Informed consent: First requirement of ethical research stated in the Belmont Report. Informed consent indicates participants can choose what shall or shall not be done to them.

Voluntary participation: Required in ethical research. A participant's engagement in a study must be grounded in having received comprehensible information about the study.

Information: Required by the Belmont Report for ethical research. Those considering participating in research must be provided information about the study they are considering.

Comprehensible:
Requirement from the
Belmont Report of the
information given possible
study participants.
That the information
be comprehensible is
required before the
participant can offer
informed consent.

**Assessment of risk
and benefits:** Second
requirement of ethical
research stated in the
Belmont Report. It is
required that all parties
engaged in research
examine whether the
benefits of the study
outweigh the risks.

Selection of subjects: Third
requirement in the Belmont
Report that requires that
subjects in research should
be fairly selected and that
the benefits and risks of
the research should be
fairly distributed.

**Institutional review
boards (IRBs):** Committee
convened and tasked with
reviewing, approving, and
monitoring health and
social science research
involving humans in the
United States. With few
exceptions, all research
that is supported in any
fashion by the U.S. federal
government requires IRB
oversight; other funding
sources may also require
IRB approval for human
subjects research.

Today, **institutional review board (IRB)** committees frequently serve as the review committees identified in the second requirement for human subjects research.

Role of Institutional Review Boards (IRBs)

IRBs that review behavioral human subjects research today resulted from two primary sources. First, in 1966. the U.S. Public Health Service (USPHS) issued a memorandum requiring all proposed research using Public Health Service grant funds be reviewed by a board of institutional associates:

> No new, renewal, or continuation research or research training grant in support of clinical research and investigation involving human beings shall be awarded by the Public Health Service unless the grantee has indicated in the application the manner in which the grantee institution will provide prior review of the judgement of the principal investigator or program director by a committee of his institutional associates. This review should assure an independent determination: (1) of the rights and welfare of the individual or individuals involved, (2) of the appropriateness of the methods used to secure informed consent, and (3) of the risks and potential medical benefits of the investigation. A description of the committee associates who will provide the review shall be included in the application. (p. 351)

Great improvements in terms of research oversight stemmed from this memorandum as independent reviewers were required and enforcement was tied to funding.

The second cornerstone document leading to IRB committees was that the ideas in the 1966 USPHS memorandum were expanded to include a broader group of federal agencies and departments with the work of the National Research Act of 1974. This law prompted the establishment of IRB committees to review almost all federally funded behavioral human subject research at the local level (generally in universities). IRBs are tasked with reviewing, approving, and monitoring health and social science research involving humans in the United States. With few exceptions, all research that is supported by the U.S. federal government requires IRB oversight. Exceptions include research in which the only involvement of human subjects include research (National Research Act of 1974, 2009)

- conducted on normal educational practices in established or traditional educational settings.

- involving cognitive, diagnostic, aptitude, or achievement educational tests (exceptions to this exemption are provided in the original source).

- involving the collection or investigation of existing data, documents, records, pathological specimens, or diagnostic specimens, if these sources are publicly available, or if the information does not contain means to identify the subjects.

- including demonstration projects that are conducted by or subject to the approval of department or agency heads, which are designed to study, evaluate, or examine public benefit or service programs, or the procedures used in these programs.

- including taste and food quality evaluation and consumer acceptance.

For the full text of the exceptions, see http://www.hhs.gov/ohrp/regulations-and-policy/regulations/45-cfr-46/index.html

IRB committees are required to ensure that the requirements and obligations outlined in the Belmont Report are followed and that the rights of humans participating in research are honored. Nevertheless, IRB committees are not without controversy, especially when social science research is considered. Finding a frustrated social scientist who has tangled with an IRB committee is not very difficult. These frustrations often stem from the burdens placed on social science researchers trying to satisfy IRB regulations that grew out of medical and health research. Furthermore, frustration stems from changing requirements based on changes in the committee membership. Attempts to ameliorate this friction are ongoing. Although IRB committees can be challenging to work with at times, review of research procedures and an independent body to ensure human subject treatment is ethical have proven necessary given past research shenanigans. As Dr. Carlos Cuevas of Northeastern University, one of our featured researchers who will be introduced in more detail later in this chapter, noted, "IRB is like the IRS, no one likes them; but they are very much needed."

Researcher Case Studies and a Road Map

One limitation of existing research methods books is that they often present research as static, dry, boring, and a linear process where a researcher completes step one, then step two, then step three, without every circling back to improve or refine parts of the process. In addition, too often, research methods books do not demonstrate how much fun research is! They do not share the anticipation of what the results show or when the results show something completely unexpected. This is fun! It is unfortunate that the fun is often neglected because research is an investigation, an exploration, and the answer that the researcher ultimately uncovers can come as a great surprise. It is similar to opening a wrapped gift while excitedly anticipating what is inside.

To illustrate the dynamic and fun nature of research and research methods, several engaging researchers will be sharing stories about their own research experiences in this text. These accomplished researchers have studied a range of criminal justice and criminology topics, gathering a variety of types of data, using a variety of research methodologies. Throughout the remainder of the book, they share, often in their own words, stories about successes and hurdles they have encountered as they have attempted to answer important and interesting research questions. This information was gathered in a series of personal interviews conducted via videoconference, many of which were recorded.

The next section introduces each researcher we follow throughout the research process in the text. This section also introduces one piece of research each researcher published in an academic journal. We will discuss the process each engaged in throughout the text to illustrate research methods in action. Table 1.2 follows and offers the full citation for each researcher's work. For additional information about each researcher, consult the corresponding academic webpages that are available in the "Web Resources" section at the end of this chapter.

Featured Researchers

Rachel Boba Santos, PhD

Rachel Boba Santos, PhD, is a professor in the Criminal Justice Department at Radford University. Her research interests include conducting practice-based research, which is implementing and evaluating evidence-based practices in the

"real world" of criminal justice. In particular, her research seeks to improve crime prevention and crime reduction efforts by police in areas such as crime analysis, problem solving, accountability, as well as leadership and organizational change. Her research has used a variety of methods, including experimental research and program evaluation. In addition, she has recently completed the fourth edition of her book, *Crime Analysis With Crime Mapping* (2016), the only sole-authored textbook for crime analysis.

Santos was first exposed to research when she was an undergraduate in college. She was enrolled in a research methods class where she designed her own survey. Her professor asked her what her future plans were and encouraged her to pursue a PhD. As she progressed through her education, she recognized that she has a talent for identifying and conducting pragmatic and relevant research that mattered to police agencies and the community they serve. Throughout the text, we learn more about Santos's research and the very practical application of it. Her work offers a useful blend of experimental and evaluation research that can be quickly translated to the field to assist police officers on the street. The particular piece of research we focus on is an examination of the influence of offender-focused, high-intensity police intervention to identify whether this approach reduces property crime in known hot spots in a suburban environment. This article was conducted with her colleague Roberto Santos, PhD (Santos & Santos, 2016). Although we are focusing on Rachel Santos in this text, it is important to recognize Richard Santos's collaborative role in this work.

Rod Brunson, PhD

Rod Brunson, PhD, is a professor and dean at the Rutgers University School of Criminal Justice. His research examines youth experiences in neighborhood contexts, with a specific focus on the interactions of race, class, and gender, and their relationship to criminal justice practices. He has authored or co-authored more than 50 articles, book chapters, and essays using a variety of research methods, including gathering and analysis of qualitative data and evaluation research.

Courtsey of Rod Brunson

Brunson was first exposed to research when he was in graduate school and got invited to participate on a professor's research project. In this capacity, he went into a juvenile detention center and spoke to juveniles involved with gangs. Brunson was surprised and intrigued by the willingness of people to share intimate details of their lives. The purpose of that project was gangs, but Brunson learned so much about the living conditions that these young people faced every day that it made him more curious. From this experience, a researcher emerged. Since then, Brunson has studied myriad topics in the field (and behind the computer) that demonstrate the practical benefits of his work.

To learn more about Brunson's research, we consider a piece of research he was once told by a senior faculty member had no relevance: police relations with urban disadvantaged males. It turns out that critic was wrong and that understanding how disadvantaged male adolescents view and interact with police is timely and relevant. In particular, Brunson examines whether there are differences between those experiences and perceptions between Black and White youth living in similarly disadvantaged urban neighborhoods. Like others, Brunson collaborated on this research. His collaborator was Ronald Weitzer, PhD, a sociologist at George Washington University (Brunson & Weitzer, 2009). Although Weitzer's contribution is important (in this piece and in his body of research more generally), we focus on Brunson throughout this text.

Carlos Cuevas, PhD

Carlos Cuevas, PhD, is an associate professor in the Criminology and Criminal Justice Department at Northeastern University. His research interests are in the area of victimization and trauma, sexual violence and sexual offending, family violence, and psychological assessment. He focuses on victimization among Latino women, youth, and under-studied populations, and how it relates to psychological distress and service utilization, as well as the role cultural factors play on victimization. In addition, he is studying the impact of psychological factors on the revictimization of children and how it helps explain the connection between victimization and delinquency. He uses a variety of methodologies to conduct his research, including secondary data analysis and original data collection.

Courtesy of Carlos Cuevas

Cuevas never intended to be a researcher but instead started his program in clinical psychology to become a clinician. From very early on in his graduate program, Cuevas recognized that he was good at research, and he found himself admiring the creative research conducted by his mentor. He graduated and began doing the opposite of what he originally intended. Today he spends about 90% of his time conducting research and publishing, and the remainder working as a clinician. We will learn more about the research Cuevas conducts by considering his research using data from a large national survey focused on adolescent Latino victimization. Surprisingly, research on victimization of Latinos in this nation has lagged, although the work of Cuevas and several others is changing that. In the research we'll consider throughout the text, Cuevas and his colleagues examined the rates of victimization, and the risk factors and cultural influences on dating violence experienced by Latino teens. Collaboration among researchers is common. This research is no exception as Cuevas worked with an excellent team, including Chiara Sabina, PhD, and Heather M. Cotignola-Pickens (Sabina, Cuevas, & Cotignola-Pickens, 2016). Sabina is an associate professor of social sciences at Penn State Harrisburg and the lead author on this featured research. The third author, Heather Cotignola-Pickens, was a student at the time this research was conducted. Heather is beginning her doctoral studies at Loyola University Maryland in clinical psychology.

Mary Dodge, PhD

Mary Dodge, PhD, is a professor in the School of Public Affairs at the University of Colorado Denver. Her research focuses on women in the criminal justice system, white-collar crime, policing, prostitution, and courts. Most of her work focuses on qualitative data to gain a deep understanding of the topics she examines. Dodge uses a variety of approaches, including gathering original data and evaluation research.

Courtesy of Mary Dodge

She was first exposed to research as an undergraduate when she began working as an assistant to a professor where she gathered data in a geriatric unit in a hospital. As a doctoral student, Dodge recognized how interesting research was when researching a project involving a university, alleged illegal acts by doctors, cover-ups, and whistle-blowers. Anyone who thinks research cannot be fun should give a good look at the research Dodge has conducted. For our purposes, we focus on research she conducted with two of her former students: Donna Starr-Gimeno and Thomas Williams (Dodge, Starr-Gimeno, & Williams, 2005). Donna Starr-Gimeno is a member of the Denver Police Department, and Thomas Williams is a member of the Aurora (Colorado) Police Department. This particular piece of research explores the perspectives of female police officers who serve as decoys in prostitution stings. Her work offers insight into how these women feel about themselves and others involved in the stings. Prior to this research, researchers had only speculated about how women view this type of work. In general, that speculation viewed these roles as further evidence of the subjection and degradation of women in law enforcement.

Chris Melde, PhD

Chris Melde, PhD, is the associate director of the School of Criminal Justice, director of graduate studies, and an associate professor at Michigan State University. His primary research interests include juvenile justice, street gangs, youth violence, adolescent development, individual and community reactions to crime and victimization risk, and program evaluation. His research uses methodologies including survey research, original data collection, evaluation research, experimental research, and secondary data analysis.

Melde was first exposed to research when he was a sophomore in college. With the encouragement he received from a professor, he pursued a PhD. It was not until late in his PhD course work that he got excited about criminal justice research—about asking his own interesting questions and finding a way to answer them. He realized too that he was good at it. Initially, he did not think being a student could be a profession, but in reality, researchers are perpetual students. That part of research—the opportunity to continually learn and solve puzzles—motivates much of Melde's work. We will learn more about Melde's research by focusing a piece of research that examines an apparent contradiction in the literature: Gang members talk about how being in the gang protects them from victimization, but at the same time, research shows that being a gang member is associated with greater experiences of being violently victimized. With his collaborators, Melde's research offered insight into this apparent inconsistency. Melde's collaborators include two close colleagues: Finn-Aage Esbensen, PhD, and Terrance J. Taylor, PhD (Melde, Taylor, & Esbensen, 2009). Both are on faculty in the Department of Criminology and Criminal Justice at the University of Missouri–St. Louis.

Heather Zaykowski, PhD

Heather Zaykowski, PhD, is an associate professor in the Department of Sociology at the University of Massachusetts Boston. Her research interests include victimization, youth violence, the intersection of victimization and offending, police–community relationships, and help-seeking among victims. Her research uses both qualitative and quantitative data, as well as a variety of approaches, including analysis of secondary data, evaluation research, and collection of original data.

Although Zaykowski was always interested in learning new things, she did not fully understand what research was or that she could do it as a job until the end of her undergraduate education. She had a senior thesis project that required the collection of original data. In completing this work, she realized how much she appreciated the opportunity to move beyond a research methods/statistics class to try to answer a question of her own. The ability to address her own curiosity by conducting research is a consistent thread in Zaykowski's work. We see this when we review her research addressing the puzzling question about what it takes for victims of violence to access and use victim services (Zaykowski, 2014). Zaykowski's work examines the factors associated with accessing victim services for male and female victims (most research only considers female victims), including characteristics such as whether the violence was reported to the police and victim demographics. Unlike our other case studies, this research was conducted by Zaykowski alone, without collaboration.

Road Map to the Book

This text is presented in six parts. Part I, the current chapter, offered information on what is meant by research methods and why research methods are important. It showed that

Table 1.2 Researchers and Their Research	
Rod Brunson	Brunson, R. & Weitzer, R. (2009). Police relations with Black and White youths in different urban neighborhoods. *Urban Affairs Review, 44*(6), 858–885.
Carlos Cuevas	Sabina, C., Cuevas, C. A., & Cotignola-Pickens, H. M. (2016). Longitudinal dating violence victimization among Latino teens: Rates, risk factors, and cultural influences. *Journal of Adolescence, 47,* 5–15.
Mary Dodge	Dodge, M., Starr-Gimeno, D., & Williams, T. (2005). Puttin' on the sting: Women police officers' perspectives on reverse prostitution assignments. *The International Journal of Police Science & Management, 7*(2), 71–85.
Chris Melde	Melde, C., Taylor, T., & Esbensen, F. (2009). "I got your back": An examination of the protective function of gang membership in adolescence. *Criminology, 47*(2) 565–594.
Rachel Santos	Santos, R. B., & Santos, R. G. (2016). Offender-focused police intervention in residential burglary and theft from vehicle hot spots: A partially blocked randomized control trial. *Journal of Experimental Criminology, 12,* 373–402.
Heather Zaykowski	Zaykowski, H. (2014). Mobilizing victim services: the role of reporting to the police. *Journal of Traumatic Stress, 27*(3), 365–369.

understanding methods offers information needed to be a better consumer, producer, and proposer of knowledge. Being an informed consumer, proposer, and producer of research and knowledge is a vitally important skill regardless of the path in life you or anyone takes. Plus it provides a new path in that you can become a researcher yourself. Part II presents information on the beginning stages of conducting research. This includes developing a research topic or research question and conducting a literature review. In addition, it demonstrates that preparing for research is not a linear process, but each part informs the other. It requires constant looping back to refine your approach. Part III of the book moves into the introduction and description of important foundational elements used in designing, proposing, and conducting a study. This includes concepts, conceptualizations, operationalizations, variables, measurements, and samplings. Part IV focuses on the ways a researcher can collect different types of data that will be used to answer the research question. It covers approaches used to gather qualitative data, the use of secondary data, experimental research, crime mapping, and several others. Part V focuses on basic analytic approaches you can use to generate findings to answer a research question. In addition, this section discusses approaches to make your research broadly relevant especially in terms of policy. In this chapter, we offer the policy implications of our highlighted articles. Part VI, the final part of the book, synthesizes all of the information presented in the text to demonstrate how these skills can be used practically in careers in criminal justice and criminology (and beyond). In addition, this section presents valuable information about things you can do to turn these skills into a rewarding and influential career. This includes discussing where to search for jobs, documents needed in these searches, interviewing skills, and other important basics.

Chapter Wrap-Up

This chapter presents foundational material regarding what research methods are and why they are important. Research methods were placed in the larger context of knowledge and social science research. This chapter offered a first glimpse at the steps used in conducting research, and how this knowledge can be used to assess existing information and create new knowledge. A brief introduction to the steps in research was provided, including generating a research question; engaging in a literature review; identifying data, samples, definitions, analytic techniques; and finally, making and disseminating conclusions. An important topic introduced and emphasized was ethics in research. Classic research examples in which ethics were absent were discussed as well as contemporary guiding principles and requirements of conducting ethical research to avoid problems from the past. Finally, this chapter introduced you to several prominent criminology and criminal justice researchers who will share stories about their own research throughout the text. Better understanding what each did and why they did it, when conducting their own research, will illustrate the reality of research that includes both successes as well as hurdles, and problems to be solved. Decisions, hurdles, and roadblocks are a normal part of research, and understanding how they were dealt with in reality by a variety of researchers will make you a stronger researcher. Next, we move to Part II of the book that provides insight into the foundational steps of conducting research. We first focus our attention on developing a research question, and then we turn to conducting a literature review.

Applied Assignments

1. Homework Applied Assignment: Unethical Research

Students should find an example of unethical research. The example does not have to be from the social sciences and can include research from the military, medicine, or elsewhere. Do not use an article that has been widely discussed, including those discussed in this chapter, such as Zimbardo, Milgrim, or the Tuskegee Syphilis Experiment. In your thought paper, present the following: a summary of the research—purpose, methodology, and findings. Describe specifically why you believe the work is unethical. Which principles of ethical research were violated? Discuss whether the research question may have been researched in another more ethical way? Do you believe that what was learned outweighs the ethical problems with this research? Turn in a summary of the unethical research along with your discussion of it as your thought paper. Be prepared to discuss what you found in class.

2. Group Work in Class Applied Assignment: Unethical Research

As a group, discuss one of the pieces of unethical research described in this chapter. As a group, be able to offer a synopsis of this research, including a summary of the

research—purpose, methodology, and findings. Describe specifically why you believe the work is unethical, if you do. If you do not believe it was unethical, be able to defend your position using information from this chapter (e.g., principles of ethical research). Discuss whether the research question may have been researched in another more ethical way. How might it have been done more ethically? Do you believe that what was learned outweighs the ethical problems with this research? How is what we learned from this research relevant today?

3. Internet Applied Assignment: Using These Skills to Get a Career

Do a search of the many career positions available for those with research methods skills in the criminology, or criminal justice fields. Some helpful search terms include "analyst" or "research" or "data." Also look to some specific agency websites such as Rand, Abt, Weststat, and RTI (Research Triangle Institute). Be sure to consider looking at businesses that hire those with methods skills. Search for roles using these skills in the local and federal government. Write a paper that focuses on the many jobs that one can get using these skills. Reflect on how mastering these skills will be useful in the "real world." Identify those skills you want to especially focus on to make yourself marketable.

KEY WORDS AND CONCEPTS

Assessment of risk and benefits 19
Authoritative sources 9
Behaviorally specific questions 5
Beneficence 19
Comprehensible 19
Data 2
Definition 5
Ethics 19
Information 19

Informed consent 19
Institutional review board (IRB) 20
Intuition 10
Justice 19
Knowledge 2
Literature review 12
Measurement 5
Personal experience 9
Research 2

Research methods 2
Research question 10
Respect for persons 19
Sample 5
Science 2
Selection of subjects 19
Social science research 2
Tradition, customs, and norms 9
Voluntary participation 19

KEY POINTS

- Research methods identify the process and approaches available when conducting research.

- Research methods are important because they offer information on the options available when conducting research that ensures quality creation of knowledge as well as a critical means for assessing existing knowledge.

- In different research studies, there may be differences in definitions, measurements, and samples used (as well as in other methodological elements) that explain the differences in findings. Just because two studies result in different findings does not mean one or both are bad studies.

- There is no universally agreed-upon definition for many concepts studied in criminology and criminal justice.

- One gains knowledge from scientific and nonscientific sources. Nonscientific sources are easy to use, but they come with the limitation that they may be incorrect.

- Research is guided by a research question. The purpose of the research is to answer the research question and enhance knowledge on the topic.

- Literature reviews summarize and synthesize existing understanding about a topic.

- Designing research means planning the precise steps used to answer the research question.

- Every step of research must involve ethical considerations.

- The Belmont Report provides three fundamental principles of ethical research, including respect for persons, beneficence, and justice. The requirements of these principles include informed consent stemming from comprehensible information used to volunteer for the study, assessment of risks and benefits by all involved, fairness in selecting subjects, and ensuring risks and benefits are justly distributed among subjects in the research.

- IRB committees are charged with reviewing, approving, and monitoring health and social science research conducted involving humans in the United States (with few exceptions).

REVIEW QUESTIONS

1. What do we mean by "research methods"?

2. Why is understanding research methods an important skill?

3. Why is developing a research question valuable?

4. What can a literature review offer in regard to research methods?

5. Why is scientific knowledge especially useful?

6. What is offered by understanding the research methods used in a particular piece of research?

7. Concepts used across pieces of research may be defined and measured differently. Why is that important to understand when assessing and designing research?

8. What was the impetus for the Nuremberg Code and the Belmont Report?

9. What was the importance of the Nuremberg Code and the Belmont Report?

10. Why are IRB committees important, and what caused them to come into existence?

CRITICAL THINKING QUESTIONS

1. The FBI and NCVS use different crimes in their definitions of violence. Which do you feel is better (if either), and why? Would you add any crimes that are missing from either? Which crimes? How would you measure them?

2. The FBI and NCVS count crimes differently. Do you believe counting victimizations, victims, or offense/incidents is more appropriate? Why? How would changing NCVS estimates from victimizations to victims change crime statistics?

3. Defenders of the Tuskegee Syphilis Experiment argue that by preventing participants from accessing penicillin, much was learned about syphilis. Do you believe that the benefits gained from this research outweighed the costs to those men and their families? Why or why not? Is there another way this same information could have been accessed?

4. Many argue that IRB committees should be disbanded when it comes to social science. What are the advantages and disadvantages of disbanding IRB committees? Would you be in favor of this? Do you believe social science researchers would be able to police themselves? Why or why not?

5. In *Damned Lies and Statistics* (2012), Joel Best notes that no research is perfect but some is less perfect than others. Given this introduction to research methods, what are some ways some research can be made closer to perfect in your opinion?

Setting the Stage
for Your Research

The first chapter in the text addressed the important questions of why research methods are important, what research methods are, and the role of ethics in research. The first chapter is intended to make clear why the material in the rest of the book is important. Research matters, and how you conduct research matters. If you do not understand why research methods matter, then the learning the rest of this material is going to be more difficult (and less fun) than it should be.

In this second section of the text, we begin by describing tasks you need to accomplish to properly design your research. In this section, we cover two important topics—topics that are often neglected in methods texts. First, we provide information on how to select a research topic and develop a suitable research question. For many new researchers, this can be an intimidating task. We think, however, that given the material presented here, you will find choosing a topic you care about, and using it to develop a research question, to be manageable (Chapter 2). The next major task covered in this foundation section is the literature review (Chapter 3). This topic is also generally never discussed in a methods text to the detriment of students. The literature review is frequently dreaded by students, but we strongly believe that terror stems from the fact that few students are taught how to write a literature review. The literature review material presented here offers step-by-step directions on what literature you should search for, how to search for it, and how to craft that information into an excellent literature review. We find with the clear directions provided that student anxiety about literature reviews is greatly reduced and that writing them may even be enjoyable. With these foundational steps completed, you as researcher can move onto designing your research, which is the topic of the third section of this text.

Identifying a Topic, a Purpose, and a Research Question

Learning Objectives

After finishing this chapter, you should be able to:

2.1 Describe why a research topic is necessary, and identify several sources for developing a research topic.

2.2 Compare and contrast the four primary purposes of research.

2.3 Identify the purpose of a research question, and demonstrate your ability to evaluate a research question.

2.4 Evaluate the importance of the Federal Policy for Protection of Human Subjects, its subparts, and the role of the Common Rule.

2.5 Summarize a "vulnerable population," and identify the ways in which a group may be vulnerable.

2.6 Define "human subjects" and "research" according to the Common Rule.

Introduction

In building on the information presented in Chapter 1, this chapter addresses initial steps in conducting research: identifying a research topic and developing it into a research question. All research is guided by interest in a topic. For example, perhaps you, like Heather Zaykowski, one of our featured researchers introduced in Chapter 1, are interested in what makes a victim of violence more or less likely to access victim services (Zaykowski, 2014). Or perhaps your interest lies in wondering about differences in young Black and White males perceptions and experiences regarding contact with the police. Research begins with an interest in a topic like this. Although having a topic of interest is the key, research is based on a narrower focus—a question that you as a researcher want to answer—a research question. You as a researcher conduct research to answer that research question. How then does a researcher decide on a topic of interest? And how does a researcher form a research question about that topic? Where do hypotheses fit into this? Before moving onto the remainder of this chapter, it is informative to take a look at the wheel of science.

Wheel of Science

Science is a recursive process, meaning it is never ending and works as a continuous loop. Knowledge created from scientific discovery leads to new ideas, these ideas lead to new testable questions, and these questions can be answered by more empirically based research. Nearly 50 years ago, Walter Wallace created a visual depiction of this scientific process, which has become known as Wallace's **wheel of science** (Figure 2.1). Although the scientific process can begin anywhere on the wheel, the easiest way to explain it is to start at the top with "Theory" and work our way around the wheel clockwise. Please note that although we introduce the steps of the wheel of science here, the remainder of the book goes into greater detail about each stage.

Figure 2.1   Scientific Process as a Recursive Process

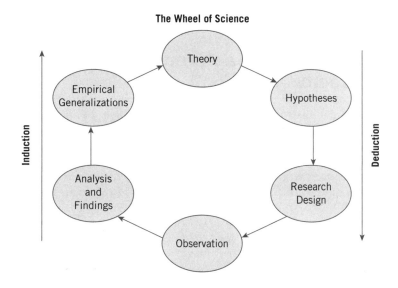

The Wheel of Science

Source: Adapted from Walter, 1971, *The Logic of Science in Sociology.*

Criminological **theory** provides a set of inter-related propositions (i.e., cause-and-effect statements that link unobservable concepts), assumptions, and definitions about how the world is expected to work or about how the people living in it are supposed to behave. For example, Cohen and Felson's (1979) routine activity theory suggests that when a motivated offender and a suitable target converge in space and time, and a guardian who is willing and able to prevent an incident from occurring is absent, a crime can occur. This is a popular theory for explaining why and when crime happens, and it forms the basis of many research questions. Research questions are the overarching question being addressed in a piece of research.

In some research, researchers develop hypotheses that they will also be testing in a piece of research. **Hypotheses** are statements (not questions) about expected relationships between variables. For instance, one may hypothesize that the more motivated offenders in an area, the higher the crime rates in that area. Although research questions are broad questions, hypotheses are the predictions that specific relationships or associations will be observed.

The next steps depicted in Wallace's wheel of science after establishing a research question and possibly hypotheses include (a) choosing an approach research methodology (i.e., Research Design) to answer the research question and test the researcher's hypotheses, and (b) collecting data (i.e., Observation) that will be analyzed as part of this process. With data in hand, the researcher then analyzes the data, develops findings to answer the research question and find support, or fails to find support for any hypotheses. Findings tend to raise more questions and influence our understanding of theory, which begins the cycle again.

This text is focused on this process. In this chapter, though, we begin with the first steps including research questions. We present information about *why* you need a research topic, and then we offer several sources for research topic ideas. Afterward, we discuss four primary purposes

Wheel of science: Diagram developed by Walter Wallace (1971) that illustrates the recursive nature of the scientific process of developing empirical knowledge.

Theory: Explanation about how things work. A set of interrelated propositions, assumptions, and definitions about how the world is expected to work living in it are supposed to behave.

Hypothesis: Testable statement about the relationship between variables.

or goals of research. By using the topic and the purpose of research selected, a discussion about the development of a research question follows. The chapter concludes with a discussion of common pitfalls associated with developing a topic, purpose, and research question, as well as ethical considerations to be aware of when engaging in these preliminary research steps.

Why Identify a Topic, a Purpose, and a Research Question?

This text presents the steps taken to conduct research in criminal justice and criminology to create new knowledge. The first step in conducting research includes selecting a research topic, identifying the purpose of the proposed research, and refining that information into a research question that will guide the research. In each of these steps, it is important that you as a researcher keep the broader purpose of what you are doing and why you are doing it—you are conducting research to create new knowledge. This requires a better understanding about what does and does not constitute research. Counterintuitively, this is most easily demonstrated by identifying and making clear what research is *not*. Research is *not* an unstructured, unguided, gathering or presentation of information or facts on some topic of interest. Research is *not* summarizing or synthesizing existing information or facts on some topic found by "Googling." An individual who is rearranging or compiling current knowledge on a topic is not engaging in research. Although some professors or teachers in your past may have referred to such activities as "research," these activities are not research; it may be a *part* of conducting research, but simply compiling information is not research. Why are none of those activities research? Because none of those activities are guided by a research question, require the collection and analysis of data, and ultimately lead to the creation of new knowledge. The steps outlined in this chapter show you how to take a topic and develop a research question that will guide the remainder of the research that ultimately leads to new knowledge. A research question is developed from a topic, and being guided by a research question is one distinction between research and nonresearch activities. This is why identifying a research topic is an important first step.

How to Identify a Research Topic

What is a **research topic**? A research topic is a subject about which you are intellectually curious, as well as a subject you are eager to investigate to develop greater knowledge. Being genuinely interested in a research topic is essential. Conducting research takes time and energy, and without a genuine interest in, and curiosity about that topic, it will be drudgery and a chore. In contrast, selecting a research topic of great interest makes research gratifying and enjoyable. To select a research topic, you should ask questions such as "What do I care about?" "What intrigues me?" "What would I like to learn more about?" and "What puzzles me?" With some curiosity, imagination, and a desire to learn, you will find fascinating and fun research topics.

If these questions do not result in the discovery of a research topic, the next section offers additional sources where ideas about research topics are plentiful. Keep in mind that these ideas or approaches are not mutually exclusive but rather several approaches can be used simultaneously to develop a research topic. We begin by considering published research.

Published Research

Published criminal justice and criminology research is a valuable resource for identifying topics of interest. A productive approach using extant research is to examine the titles of recently published articles. Consider, for example, some titles found in volume 33, issue number 2, of *Justice Quarterly,* published in 2016:

1. Wooldredge, J., & Steiner, B. Police Enforcement of Domestic Violence Laws: Supervisory Control or Officer Prerogatives?

2. Fox, K., Nobles, M., & Fisher, B. A Multi-Theoretical Framework to Assess Gendered Stalking Victimization: The Utility of Self-Control, Social Learning, and Control Balance Theories.

3. Stupi, E., Chiricos, T., & Gertz, M. Perceived criminal threat from undocumented immigrants: Antecedents and consequences for policy preferences.

An examination of these titles provides several potential research topics, including police enforcement, domestic violence, and gendered stalking. From reading these titles, you may realize you have an interest in police enforcement, the characteristics of domestic violence, or the prevalence of gendered stalking.

Another excellent place to search in journal articles is in the concluding sections of published articles. It is standard practice for a journal article to identify suggested topics for future research. Reading what published authors note is needed for future research is another way to identify a topic of interest.

In addition to examining titles and the recommended future research in published articles, you can read journal articles in their entirety. It is simply the case, *and this cannot be stated enough,* that the more you know about existing research on a topic, the more you will recognize what is *not* known about that topic. It may seem that there remains no stone unturned in the world of criminal justice and criminology research, but that is far from the truth. There is much that remains unknown, and much knowledge that can be enhanced. When consulting journal articles in the literature, pay special attention to the literature review where gaps in knowledge on a topic are generally explicitly identified. It may be that some identified gap is something of interest to you. This is exactly how the idea for the research on disadvantaged male youth and police relations conducted by Rod Brunson, another one of our featured researchers, was developed. In reading the literature, Brunson identified a lack of comparisons of youth and police relations between Black and White disadvantaged males. This made it challenging to know whether police youth interactions were a result of the disadvantaged neighborhoods or the race of the youth. It turns out that finding a high-crime, disadvantaged, predominantly White neighborhood was challenging, and as a result, the existing work focused primarily on Black neighborhoods (Brunson & Weitzer, 2009). Brunson and his colleague recognized that without the comparison between Blacks and Whites living in similarly disadvantaged neighborhoods, it was not possible to isolate whether poor police relations were a result of the high crime in an area (disadvantaged neighborhoods) or the race of the youth living in the neighborhoods. Seeing this gap in criminologists' understanding allowed Brunson and his collaborator, Ronald Weitzer, to compare experiences and perceptions across neighborhoods. In doing so, they found evidence that the key characteristic associated with quality of police relations was race, and not the crime rates of the disadvantaged neighborhoods. A result of recognizing this gap in the literature led to this timely and interesting finding that enhances the body of police-relations research.

Another featured researcher, Chris Melde, along with his collaborators, conducted research on gang members and fear that also stemmed from Melde's familiarity of the gang research literature (Melde, Taylor, & Esbensen, 2009). Melde recognized the ample evidence that indicates that gang members are far more likely to be violently victimized than nongang members. Yet, the literature also offers evidence that gang members join gangs because they allegedly provide safety and security. In gang members' words, as a member of a gang, others "got your back." Melde wondered, how can both of these contradictory phenomena be so?

Data codebook: Collection of all data gathered by a particular data set. Many criminal justice and criminology data codebooks are available online at no charge.

Exploiting this apparent inconsistency in our understanding of gangs led Melde and his collaborators, Finn-Aage Esbensen and Terrance Taylor, to this research topic.

Obvious gaps in the literature also led to Zaykowski's (2014) research of victim reporting of violence to the police. Zaykowski had long been interested in better understanding crime-reporting behavior and other forms of help-seeking among victims. She recognized that in this literature, the research focus was mainly on female victims, specifically on sexual and relationship violence. She felt it important to expand knowledge regarding victim reporting to include male victims as well as other types of crime experienced by females (beyond sexual and relationship violence). In these ways, Zaykowski was able to add knowledge to a criminologist's understanding about help seeking for male and female victims and for a broader range of crimes.

Featured researcher Rachel Boba Santos's knowledge of the literature, and her understanding about practical issues faced by police agencies given her background as a crime analyst, gave rise to her research topic on the effect of offender-focused, high-intensity policing on burglary and property theft in known suburban hot spots. Santos and her collaborator, Roberto Santos, surmised that because offenders tend to offend near their homes (but not too near their homes), the implementation of an offender-focused intervention (i.e., high-intensity surveillance and patrol) focused on multiple known offenders living in hot spots, should lead to a reduction of that crime type in that hot spot (Santos & Santos, 2016). This research contributes to our knowledge about both offender-focused intervention and place-based research. In addition, it demonstrates the usefulness of this approach in a suburban setting (most research focuses on urban crime) and for property crimes (most research focuses on violent crime). By understanding the research literature, and the practical needs of law enforcement, Santos and her collaborator developed a research topic that brought together multiple, and related, lines of inquiry. These are just a few ways in which existing research can offer a gold mine of ideas for identifying a research topic.

Data

Available data are an excellent resource for identifying research topics. What are data? Data are[1] pieces of information or evidence that can take a variety of forms such as numbers, words, observations, measurements, illustrations, recordings, and descriptions. Some data sets have a **data codebook** that identifies every characteristic or variable available in the data, and how it is measured. For example, a codebook may have a variable or characteristics named "School_Year" that is measured using six categories: freshman, sophomore, junior, senior, other, and unknown. Codebooks often have hundreds or thousands of variables found in the data set. For example, in the National Crime Victimization Survey (NCVS), a major source of crime victimization data in the U.S. data codebook, you can find an enormous assortment of characteristics related to criminal property and personal victimizations including data about the victim, offender, and incident. In the NCVS codebook, you can learn that data on weapons used, injuries sustained, police reporting, offender drug/alcohol use, and hundreds of other topics are available. You might find multiple codebooks for the same data for different years that reflect changes in data collected. In the case of the NCVS, new topics of interest have been added over time. In 2003, a variable designed to gather data about the victim's perception of whether his or her victimization was a result of a hate crime were added. In June 2005, a variable used to gather data was added about whether the victim of a crime was pregnant at the time of the incident. In June 2008, new variables designed to gather data on whether victims felt distress, worry, anger, violation, and so on were added. Any of these variables may prompt the recognition of a topic of interest.

---

[1] The word *data* is typically considered to be plural in scientific writing; thus, the phrase "data are . . ." is correct.

In some cases, examining a codebook prompts research ideas because of what is *not found*. Zaykowski noted that as a graduate student reading through the NCVS codebook, she was frustrated by the lack of variables available about victim behavior. In particular, she was interested in victim drinking or drug use at the time of the victimization. Although data on this topic are asked with regard to the offender in the NCVS, they are not asked with regard to the victim. This prompted Zaykowski to seek other data sets, as well as to consider gathering her own data on this research topic.

Many fail to recognize that they are surrounded by data. Data take on many forms, including words, actions, interactions, speech, text, and numbers. That was the case for the youth and police relations research conducted by Brunson. Brunson recognized he had access to young African American males in a high-crime, disadvantaged neighborhood, as well as to young Whites in a similarly disadvantaged place. Being able to interview these individuals to collect data on their experiences offered a key opportunity to conduct research that adds to our collective knowledge. The access and the trust Brunson established with the neighborhood youth in multiple neighborhoods over time allowed him to undertake this important study.

Theory

Criminal justice and criminological theories are sources of potential research topics. A theory comprises statements that explain a phenomenon. Theory is an explanation about how things work. Many argue that theory and research go hand in hand, and one is not of value without the other. For example, Cao (2004, p. 9) states that "[o]bservation without theory is chaotic and wasteful, while a theory without the support of observation is speculative." To some, theory is the starting point of the traditional research model, and that theory guides the entire research process. Conducting research using this model is respected, but there are practical reasons that nontheory testing research is conducted. For instance, some theories are so vague as to be difficult to confirm or disconfirm using research. In some cases, theories include elements for which there are simply no data available (or gathering those data is not feasible). In addition, the purpose of some research is to build theory versus to be guided by established theory.

© EyeJoy/iStockphoto.com

Many people falsely believe that data comes in the form of numbers only. The truth is that data are everywhere you look. For Rod Brunson, gathering information from individuals in an African American Barber Shop in St. Louis—a type of data—formed the basis for multiple research publications. Yes, interviewing people in their natural settings doing fun things can be research and provide valuable data. Where around you do you see data?

Valuable research has been conducted outside of the pure theory testing approach. In fact, none of our case study researchers engage primarily in theory testing. Their understanding of criminal justice and criminology is informed by theoretical perspectives, but each researcher describes him- or herself as a more applied and practical researcher. As Brunson notes, "it is important that scholars be well-versed in theory. However, I don't think that theory—or lack thereof—should restrict intellectual pursuits. Theory should be used as a framework and guide and not discourage further exploration of ideas." Theory and research are never fully divorced, however. Research that is not focused on theory testing is used to develop or enhance extant theory. Similarly, theory testing has yielded understanding that guides additional research.

Whether you are interested in traditional theory testing or other types of research, understanding theory leads to ideas about research topics. For example, routine activity theory identifies three necessary, but not sufficient, components for crime to occur: a capable guardian, a motivated offender, and a suitable target (see Figure 2.2). Although you may not test this theory directly, understanding the theory may lead you to ask, "What makes a guardian capable?" This may lead to a fruitful line of inquiry on this topic that intrigues you.

Requests for Proposals (RFPs)

In some cases, an organization will advertise the need for research on a specified topic. These types of requests frequently come in the form of a **request for proposals (RFP)**. Requests for proposals are formal statements asking for research proposals on a particular topic. Qualified researchers, or teams of researchers, submit an in-depth proposal for conducting research on that topic. The proposals are reviewed by experts, and none, one, or several of the proposals are funded. The federal government as well as state and local governments regularly publish requests for proposals. Carlos Cuevas, another one of our featured researchers, and his colleagues (Sabina, Cuevas, & Cotignola-Pickens, 2016) were able to secure a grant to fund the data collection that led to their study on Latino teen dating violence in this way. Although the RFP that had been posted requested research about teen dating violence only, Cuevas's team wanted to examine it, other types of violence, and the role that cultural influences play on victimization. Even though the topic of teen dating violence among Latinos was an area of interest to Cuevas prior to the government's RFP, the RFP offered Cuevas and his colleagues an opportunity to collect data that enabled them to conduct research that simply could not have happened without the grant funding. Together, an interest in the topic, familiarity with the fact that the literature had little information about experiences of Latinos, and the presence of an RFP led to a research topic and an opportunity to conduct research on this topic by Cuevas and his collaborators.

Peruse RFPs posted online to see whether they prompt research topics of interest for you. It may be surprising to see the variety of topics across RFPs. To see all current RFPs originating from the federal government, go to www.grants.gov. On this page, you can select RFPs from specific departments such as the Department of Justice. You can also go directly to a page of current RFPs posted by the Department of Justice at www.grants .gov/search-grants.html?agencyCode%3DUSDOJ. Aside from the federal government, private entities, local governments, nonprofits, and smaller organizations also post RFPs. For example, imagine yourself in your new role as an analyst at a research organization focused on criminal justice and criminology research. In this role, you would be constantly watching for RFPs to submit a proposal, and hopefully, you would be awarded grant funds to do research. In these cases, your research question is guided by the parameters of the RFP.

Personal Experiences

Personal experiences are another way to identify a research topic. Each of us has experienced or witnessed events that make us wonder about something. Perhaps you and a friend engaged in the same behavior, but your friend went to prison and you did not. This may lead to your interest in understanding variation in arrest or sentencing in the criminal justice system. Perhaps you have noticed that some people you know are given tickets for traffic violations when they are pulled over, yet others who engage in the same behavior get off with a warning. This experience may stimulate an interest in investigating variation in receiving traffic citations. An all too common experience is that a family member has experienced violence committed by an intimate partner. Given this, you might develop an interest in the ways that people cope with or respond to intimate partner violence or what leads some to become a perpetrator of intimate partners.

Figure 2.2 Routine Activity Theory

Theories offer explanations for how things work. Routine activity theory, developed by Cohen and Felson (1979), identifies three elements necessary, but not sufficient, to lead to macro changes in crime. In looking at this illustration, what types of research topics come to mind?

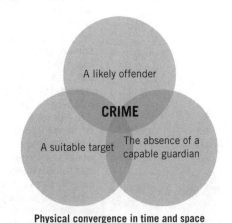

A likely offender

CRIME

A suitable target

The absence of a capable guardian

Physical convergence in time and space

A personal experience led to featured researcher Mary Dodge's idea to conduct research on prostitution stings where women law enforcement agents act as decoys (Dodge, Starr-Gimeno, & Williams, 2005). Dodge spends a fair amount of time in the field as a researcher with members of police agencies. Prior to starting this research, Dodge was engaged in a ride-along with officers and detectives while they focused on cracking down on prostitution. Part of Dodge's time was spent in the hotel room where police would arrest "johns" entering with prostitutes they quickly learned were law enforcement officers acting as decoys. Although Dodge wanted to interview the men being arrested for that research, it became apparent that men in handcuffs who are arrested for soliciting prostitution are not very talkative. Imagine you are the minister that was arrested in this situation. Would you want to talk about it? He certainly did not. It occurred to Dodge during this particular incident that no one had interviewed female police officers acting as crack-addicted prostitutes about their experiences as decoys. Dodge knew they would be willing to talk, and she did not think there was any research on this topic. This personal experience lead to the development of the highlighted research we follow in this book.

Personal experience was partially responsible for the hot spots research topic focused on by Santos (Santos & Santos, 2016). Santos's colleague, Roberto is a former law enforcement officer who is now an assistant professor at the same university. As an officer, he developed a new policing approach. As a team, they knew that some research takes into account certain crime patterns and places but that the research frequently fails to consider the role of offenders. Santos and her colleague recognized (from literature gaps) that there was a need to focus on offenders. Given these personal experiences, knowledge of the literature, and a well-timed RFP, Santos and her collaborator were able to develop a research topic on hot spots that was practical and applicable to law enforcement agencies.

Reading

Reading is an excellent source for finding interesting research topics. Consider *Coming Out from Behind the Badge,* which chronicles Greg Miraglia's (2007) experiences as a gay police officer. Given the hypermasculine culture of law enforcement, Miraglia recognized that coming out as a gay law enforcement officer would be ill advised while he was an officer. Reading about Miraglia's experiences may lead to a curiosity about the presence of LGBTQ officers in law enforcement or about changes in acceptance of LGBTQ officers over time.

Or consider reading about the colorful Art Winstanley. Art was a burglar specializing in safe cracking in the 1960s. What makes his story unusual is that he was also a Denver police officer, and he operated with a ring of burglars, most of whom were also Denver police officers. As told in *Burglars in Blue,* Winstanley (2009) began burglarizing Denver area businesses as a rookie. He and the other burglars would case a business during the day, chatting up store owners who freely shared information such as where the safe was located. By taking advantage of trusting business owners and the lack of technology available at the time, Winstanley would return later to burglarize the business. His partner would wait in the patrol car to monitor the radio (portable radios did not exist). If a call came over the radio about a burglar alarm going off where Winstanley was safe cracking, his partner would radio that he and Winstanley would investigate. By doing this, no one else showed up who could apprehend these crafty burglars. Winstanley was eventually caught and sentenced to prison after a safe fell out of the trunk of his vehicle as he fled a scene. Reading about Winstanley and his co-conspirators may prompt you to learn more about police officers who commit crimes, officers who serve time in prison, or changes and improvements in technology in law enforcement and the criminal justice system.

Courtesy of Greg Miraglia

Greg Miraglia served as a law enforcement officer before taking a role in higher education. Reading his book titled *Coming Out from Behind the Badge* offers many possible research topics.

Although research has focused primarily on the violent offending of individuals with mental illness, recently attention has been given to the violent victimization of this group. In addition to examining victimization of the persons with mental illness, attention is being given to the revictimization of these individuals. Research shows that persons with mental illness have a high risk of being victimized and that this increased risk may extend to revictimization as well. The researchers point to a single study that has investigated the revictimizaiton of persons with mental illness that concluded that revictimization trajectories vary by diagnosis, symptomology, and alcohol abuse. What remains unknown is how other individual characteristics influence the chances of revictimization. Policastro, Teasdale, and Daigle (2015) fill these gaps in our understanding by exploring differences, if any, in the trajectories of recurring victimization by victim's race. To do this, the research addresses the following research questions:

1. What types of within-person characteristics influence recurring victimization over time for each racial group?

2. Do the trajectories of recurring victimization of Black persons diagnosed with serious mental illness differ from the trajectories of White persons diagnosed with serious mental illness?

The sample used in this research by Policastro et al. (2015) was gathered via a stratified random sample of eligible patients discharged from in-patient psychiatric facilities at sites in Pittsburgh, Pennsylvania; Worcester, Massachusetts; and Kansas City, Missouri. Those eligible for being drawn in sample were between the ages of 18 and 40, English-speaking, and White or African American.

Participants had to be civil (not criminal) admissions to each facility and have a medical diagnosis of at least one of the following disorders: schizophrenia, depression, mania, schizophreniform disorder, schizoaffective disorder, dysthymia, brief reactive psychosis, delusional disorder, substance abuse/dependence, or personality disorder. The outcome variable of interest is whether the individual had been threatened, or had been victimized physically, with or without a weapon. The independent variables in this research includes drug use, alcohol use, social network, symptomology, use of violence, level of daily functioning, stress, homelessness, marital status, employment, socioeconomic status, and diagnosis.

After describing the sample, the researchers identified two major findings. First that the effect of alcohol abuse differed by victim's race. Alcohol abuse is associated with increased risk of revictimization for White persons with serious mental illness but not for Black persons with serious mental illness. The second major finding is that the trajectories of revictimization differed between Whites and Blacks. Specifically, the trajectory of revictimization declines for Whites but remains flat for Blacks. This research indicates that the lived experiences of mental illness are different among the Black population compared with among the White population.

The policy implications of this work points to the need for mental health care services for diverse populations and cultural sensitivity in their delivery. The results also suggest the need to ensure the accessibility of mental health treatment exists for underserved populations. With more mental health care providers in Black communities, the trajectory of revictimization may be changed.

Policastro, C., Teasdale, B., & Daigle L. E. (2015). The recurring victimization of individuals with mental illness: A comparison of trajectories for two racial groups. *Journal of Quantitative Criminology, 32*, 675–693.

Viewing

Viewing the evening news, documentaries, or movies, combined with curiosity, can lead to excellent research topics. In the previous chapter, there was a discussion about media depictions of violence against college students. These media portrayals focus primarily on sexual and relational violence, as well as primarily on female victims. This may lead you to wonder about other types of violence and other types of college student victims. Alternatively, it would not be unusual to be viewing a channel on the evening news that reports that each year more Whites are killed by police than are Blacks. Yet on another channel, you may see reports that Blacks are

more likely to be killed by police than are Whites. These seemingly contradictory statements may lead to an interest in police killings, changes of police killings over time, or the role of race in the criminal justice system. Each of these, and countless others, would make an interesting research topic.

Lectures and events where others speak offer a goldmine of research topics. Thinking back to the last lecture you attended, what topics come to mind?

Listening

Listening to presentations, speakers, and even general conversation can lead to interesting research topics. You may be in a lecture where the speaker is presenting information on general topic such as policing. What is conveyed in the lecture may prompt a specific interest in that topic. This is precisely how the idea to explore police impersonation was developed by Rennison and Dodge (2012). Rennison was teaching an Introduction to Criminal Justice class and had invited a police officer in to talk about his job. The officer shared traditional policing information but also informed students how they could distinguish a police impersonator from a legitimate officer. After hearing this, Rennison began wondering what the literature had to say about police impersonation. Ultimately, this curiosity lead to a publication by Rennison and Dodge on this topic.

Casual conversations are also excellent sources of ideas. One of the best things about annual professional conferences of criminologists and criminal justice professionals are the research projects that originate from casual conversations. Zaykowski, in a video interview conducted for this book, related how she was discussing victimization research with a colleague who studies capital punishment. This exchange led to a discussion about any potential overlap that may exist between the two areas. What came of this was the topic of how the changing role of victim rights (i.e., variation in victim impact statements in court) may lead to disparity in capital punishment sentencing across trials. A new research topic was born.

Working on Research Projects With Professors

There are often formal and informal opportunities to work with professors engaged in research. Recall our introduction of our featured researchers in Chapter 1. Cuevas and Dodge both included students to assist on the research we are following in this text. Both of Dodge's collaborators were students (Starr-Gimeno and Williams), and Cuevas' collaborator Cotignola-Pickens was a student. This is a valuable opportunity, and one you should jump at given the chance. At times there may be a posted request for student research assistants. Or it may be that a student contacts a professor and asks whether he or she can assist on a research project. Although these assistant positions may or may not be paid, and they may or may not allow you to earn course credits, the greater value of them is the research experience. In volunteering to assist with research, the student gains a deeper understanding of the process of research, and from that experience, he or she may discover several research topics. This is part of the way that Zaykowski (2014) developed a topic that focused on victim consciousness. As an undergraduate student, she was intrigued by a call for research assistants for a study of youth perceptions of the police. She had recently completed a service learning class where she and others tutored inner-city youth about the police and their communities. Eventually she reached out to a professor to discuss some research, and they began studying how youth interpret potentially violent encounters in the inner city.

Internet

The Internet offers endless opportunities to discover a research topic of interest. If perusing the Internet does not lead to a research topic of interest, you could simply search on the phrase "research paper topics in criminal justice" or "research paper topics in criminology," and thousands of possibilities will be returned. If you opt for this approach, remember to choose a topic you both care about and are curious about.

How to Identify the Purpose/Goal of Research

Once a research topic is identified, you the researcher must work toward taking a very broad and general topic and narrowing it. The goal is to shape it into a feasible research question. Topics such as recidivism, sentencing, victimization, reentry, and policing are very broad, and to construct a practical research question, narrowing is required. One step toward narrowing a broad research topic is to identify the **purpose of the research** you propose. The purpose of research can be thought of as the "goal" of the research. It is common to find in a research articles, "the purpose of this research is to . . ." or "the goal of this research is to . . ." or "the aim of this research is to . . ." This section identifies four major purposes or goals of research. Do you wish to *explore* something about a topic? *Describe* something about the topic? *Explain* something about the topic? *Evaluate* something about a topic? Or are several of these aims of interest?

Exploratory Research

Exploratory research is appropriate when little or nothing is known about a topic. The purpose or goal of exploratory research is to answer "What," "How," or "Where" questions: "What is it?," "How is it done?," or "Where is it?" Exploring or investigating a topic generates a deep understanding about that topic that was previously unknown. In addition to highlighting important features of the topic, exploratory research can identify characteristics that are unimportant and not worthy of future consideration. The prostitution research conducted by Dodge (Dodge et al., 2005) in which female undercover police officers acted as decoys was exploratory in nature. Why? Because at the time of this research, almost nothing was known about how female police officers serving as prostitution decoys viewed their work. There was only a bit of speculation in the literature that this type of role was not positive for the women. Dodge's research would later demonstrate this speculation to be incorrect.

Brunson's work on youth and police relations was also exploratory in nature (Brunson & Weitzer, 2009). These researchers found that much of the existing knowledge on police relations was based on research that focused on adults and not on youth. Because youth are more likely to have involuntary and adversarial contact with police, Brunson, in a phone interview conducted for this book, told us that he felt at the time it was important to examine these interactions in particular. In addition, he said that a goal of this explanatory research was to understand if police and youth interactions and perceptions differed among Black and White youth living in similarly disadvantaged neighborhoods. This exploration into youth and police relations offered knowledge on how race and neighborhood context influences youthful males' orientations toward the police.

Descriptive Research

Descriptive research describes a topic. A researcher may want to describe something such as the extent of victimization or offending among a particular population. Like exploratory research, descriptive research seeks to answer questions such as "What is it?" "What are the characteristics of it?" or "What does it look like?" Unlike exploratory research, descriptive research is more narrowly focused. This narrower focus on the topic is often possible because of knowledge gained from earlier exploratory research.

By using descriptive research, you can provide an even more detailed understanding about a topic of interest. This information is useful standing alone and can be informative for future explanatory research.

Explanatory Research

Explanatory research provides explanations about a topic and builds off of knowledge gained from exploratory and descriptive research to answer questions such as "Why is it?" "How is it?" "What is the effect of it?" "What causes it?" or "What predicts it?" Explanatory research is used to identify what characteristics are related to a topic, as well as what impacts, causes, or influences a particular outcome of a topic of interest. In addition, through explanatory research, you may try to understand how to predict outcomes of topics of interest.

Zaykowski's (2014) highlighted research about accessing victim services is explanatory in nature. In this research, she wanted to understand the role that police reporting plays in influencing victim services. Better understanding this relationship will provide better understanding of ways to assist those who have been victimized. Similarly, Melde and colleagues wished to understand and explain the associations (or lack of associations) between gang membership, fear of victimization, perceptions of risk of victimization, and self-reported victimization (Melde et al., 2009). Cuevas's research on Latino teen dating violence is also explanatory (as well as descriptive) in nature (Sabina et al., 2016).

Specifically, Cuevas's research team wanted to gain an understanding of rates of violence, risk of violence, and what characteristics are associated with violence against Latino teens.

Evaluation Research

Evaluation research is used to generate knowledge; nevertheless, it has a different focus. Evaluation research is the systematic assessment of the need for, implementation of, or output of a program based on objective criteria. By using the data gathered in evaluation research, a researcher like you can make recommendations about whether a program is needed, and offer evidence showing how one can improve, enhance, expand, or terminate a program. The assessment of a program can be conducted using any and all of the purpose described as well as research approaches and types of data described in later chapters in this text.

Santos' highlighted research is evaluative (and experimental) in nature (Santos & Santos, 2016). In her hot spots research, she and her colleague evaluated, using an experimental approach, an offender-focused, high-intensity intervention for nonviolent property crime offenders living in property crime hot spots. An additional element of this research is that it takes places in a suburban (vs. urban) community. The findings from this research are useful in informing prevention and deterrence strategies associated with property crime in suburban settings. Table 2.1 illustrates the type of research, purposes of research, and questions answered in one place.

Descriptive research:
Focused description of a topic that answers questions such as "What is it?" "What are the characteristics of it?" and "What does it look like?" It is similar to exploratory research, but it is narrower given knowledge gained by exploratory research.

Explanatory research:
Research that provides explanations about a topic by addressing question such as "Why is it?" "How is it?" "What is the effect of it?" "What causes it?" and "What predicts it?"

Evaluation research:
Applied systematic assessment of the need for, implementation of, or output of a program based on objective criteria.

Table 2.1 Types, Purposes, and Questions Answered in Research

Topic	Purpose	Research Questions Answered	Where Occurs	Subject Aware of	Methodologies Used
Exploratory Research	Explore something	What is it?	Natural setting	Possibly	Qualitative Research (Ch. 6)
		How is it done?	Office	No	Secondary Data Analysis (Ch. 9)
		Where is it?			
Descriptive Research	Describe something	What is it?	Natural setting	Possibly	Qualitative Research (Ch. 6)
		What are the characteristics of it?	Any location	Yes, voluntarily	Survey Research (Ch. 7)
		What does it look like?	Office	No	Secondary Data Analysis (Ch. 9)
		*More narrowly focused than exploratory research	Office	No	GIS and Crime Mapping (Ch. 10)
Explanatory Research	Explain something	Why is it?	Natural setting	Possibly	Qualitative Research (Ch. 6)
		How is it?	Any location	Yes, voluntarily	Survey Research (Ch. 7)
		What is the effect of it?	Any location	Yes, voluntarily	Experimental Research (Ch. 8)
		What causes it?	Office	No	Secondary Data Analysis (Ch. 9)
		What predicts it?	Office	No	GIS and Crime Mapping (Ch. 10)
		Is a program needed?			
Evaluation Research	Evaluate something	Does a program work?	Natural setting	Possibly	Qualitative Research (Ch. 6)
		Who uses this program?	Any location	Yes, voluntarily	Survey Research (Ch. 7)
		Is the program effective?	Any location	Yes, voluntarily	Experimental Research (Ch. 8)
		Does the program lead to unintended	Office	No	Secondary Data Analysis (Ch. 9)
		Should the program be stopped?	Office	No	GIS and Crime Mapping (Ch. 10)
		How can we make the program better?			

Gathering More Information and Refining the Topic

At this point, you should have an idea or topic about which you wish to explore, describe, explain, or evaluate. What is needed now is additional narrowing or focusing of the topic. For example, perhaps you are interested in studying the topic of *sentencing*. Specifically, you wish to *describe sentencing*. Describing sentencing is still a broad goal since subsumed under the heading of "describing sentencing" could be research that describes the history of it, important people who have changed the way sentencing is done, changes in sentencing over time, trends in sentencing, cross-national difference in sentences, race and gender in sentencing, and so on. Clearly, there is a need to continue to narrow the focus of this proposed research.

Narrowing or focusing the topic requires you to gather more information about the topic and purpose selected. This can be done in many ways including the methods described earlier to identify the topic initially. You can search on the broad topic and purpose "What is sentencing?" to focus your future research. You can discuss the broad topic and purpose with others. You can read more about this general topic and purpose. You can simply sit and ponder what it is about the topic and purpose that is of greatest interest to you. Is it to describe how gender influences sentencing? Maybe it is to describe how gender of the judge and the offender influences sentencing? Or perhaps you find you are interested in the role that race plays or income or in describing how the nature of the crime or the history of the offender is related to sentencing. Or perhaps policies such as "three strikes" may be of interest. Whichever approach is used, the goal is to narrow the focus of the research so it can be stated in a clear, concise, and feasible manner.

How to Construct the Research Question

You now have the information needed to state the purpose of your research, as well to develop the focused research question that will guide your research. Now you need to construct a formal research statement or research question that identifies the purpose, and the narrowed topic. For example, consider the sequence illustrated in Figure 2.3 regarding the sentencing example:

The purpose of this research is to describe sentencing. In particular, this aim of the research is to describe sentencing with an emphasis on the demographics of the offender. To accomplish this, the following research question serves as a guide: "How does sentencing vary in terms of the demographics of the offender?"

These sentences offer the purpose of the research (description), the primary topic of interest (sentencing), and the more focused topic of interest (demographics and sentencing). You should be able to see how these statements, culminating in the research question, offer boundaries, are clear, and will guide the remainder of the research endeavor.

It is important to recognize that the language used in describing the purpose of research is not highly rigid. For example, in consulting journal articles, you may not find sentences such as "The purpose of this research is to describe, or explore or explain . . ." Rather, researchers

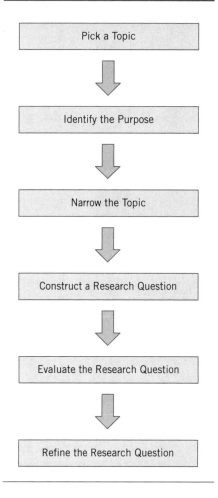

Figure 2.3 Example Research Statement and Question

Pick a Topic

Identify the Purpose

Narrow the Topic

Construct a Research Question

Evaluate the Research Question

Refine the Research Question

will identify their purpose using synonyms such as determine, investigate, effect, influence, examine, ascertain, identify, and so on. When reviewing the literature, you must understand the greater context of the purpose by reading more than a single statement.

Why Have a Research Question?

By now, the reason for having a research question should be evident. A research question is the impetus behind research, and it guides every step in the research endeavor. Based on what you have read in this book so far, it should be clear to you that the research question will drive all decisions about the design of the research, the way the data will be collected, and how those data will be analyzed as well. The research question establishes boundaries for, and focuses, the proposed research.

Evaluating the Research Question to Avoid Common Pitfalls

Once you have identified a research question (or questions), it is important to evaluate the research question to ensure it is practical and useful. It is not unusual to have to adjust or modify a research question early on in the research process, especially when you conduct your literature review (explored in Chapter 3). This section offers some ways to begin to evaluate the practicality and usefulness of a research question. Do not be alarmed if you find you must circle back and refine your purposes and research question given newly learned information. That is the norm. The following section identifies ways to evaluate your research question.

Is it a question, or does it imply a question? It may seem trite, but it is important that a research question be a question, or at least be a statement that implies a question. By implying a question, a statement must contain a verb such as *examine, explain, investigate,* or *describe.* A statement that does not imply a question cannot drive research. In research, the researchers pose a question and answer it. Consider the differences between these sentences:

- Does a victim's gender influence reporting violence to the police?
- Men report violence more than women.

The question, "Does a victim's gender influence reporting violence to the police?" asks something that allows a researcher to gather data, analyze it, and answer a question. The statement "Men report violence more than women" does not imply a question that can be investigated. It is a statement and a conclusion. There is nothing to study about this. This statement could be changed to the question "is the likelihood of reporting to the police different for male and female victims of violence?" That is a question that can be explored. Be certain that your research question is a question or, at a minimum, that it is a statement that clearly implies a question.

Is it feasible? Answering a research question must be feasible. That is, as a researcher you must have the time, money, and other resources needed to conduct the research and answer the research question posed. Consider this example: What policies and programs are most valuable to assist homeless ex-convicts across the United States? Is answering this question feasible? Probably not. Why? Because it would be exceedingly difficult to identify the location of all homeless ex-convicts in the United States. It would also be extremely resource intensive to gather data from them (or even a subset or sample of them). A researcher would need an army of assistants, the money to pay the assistants (and their expenses), and an enormous amount of time to gather the data needed to answer this question. If you do not have the resources, time, or information needed to undertake that research, the research question should be adjusted.

Is it interesting? Is the research question posed interesting? Will others be interested in the research, conclusions, and knowledge gained by answering it? Although there is no way to measure definitively whether a topic is "interesting," and not everyone will find every research question or topic interesting (think back to the criticism regarding Brunson's interest in youth and police relations), you should take the time to ponder this question. At a minimum, the researcher should believe the research question posed is interesting. If the researcher does not believe it is an interesting research question, it is going to be a long and painful research endeavor. Also, if you do not find the research question interesting, what makes you think anyone else will? Consider the following research question as an example. Is it interesting?

> What fabric is used for patrol officer uniforms?

At least on face value, this research question and the suggested descriptive research is not interesting, and answering it would not increase meaningful knowledge about policing or about uniforms. It might be better to consider other topics and purposes and then proceed.

Does it increase knowledge? The entire purpose of conducting research is to increase empirical knowledge and understanding about a topic. If a research question does not increase knowledge, then why conduct it? Why waste the resources needed to engage in research if it adds nothing to our existing understanding and knowledge about a topic? Consider the following research question:

> Are females or males more likely to be victims of rape in the United States?

Although understanding the role of sex in sexual victimization risk is valuable, there already exist volumes of research that have addressed this question and clearly established that females, compared to males, have a greater risk of being raped in the United States. Conducting research based on this research question today would likely lead to no *new* knowledge. As such, it is not advisable.

Is it too broad? It is important to craft a research question that is not overly broad. An excessively broad research question will be challenging, time-consuming, and possibly impossible to answer. Consider the following research question:

> What are the differences in economic, demographic, psychological, and social predictors of becoming a patrol officer, detective, sergeant, sheriff, federal agent, or judge compared to those entering noncriminal justice professions?

This research question is far too broad. In fact, you could take this single question and parse it into dozens of possibly useful and interesting questions. Such an overly broad question lacks feasibility and is ill-advised to pursue.

Is it too narrow? It is also important to craft a research question that is not too narrow. Research questions that are too narrow tend to be uninteresting, and generally, they fail to add knowledge on a topic of interest. Consider the following research questions:

> What are the motivations for working for a small prisoner reentry nonprofit in the metro Denver area during 2016?

> How many people graduated in Texas in 2014 with a PhD in criminology?

With regard to the first question, it is difficult to imagine how answering this question would be of interest or add to any particular knowledge base. A researcher could broaden the question by removing the size of the nonprofit and the locale to get "What are the motivations for working for prisoner reentry programs?"

The second question is astonishingly narrow (and boring). Answering this would take little more than a Google search or a peek in the *Statistical Abstracts*. There are no data to be gathered and no methodology to be considered. This sort of question is not suitable for research. Research questions that are too narrow must be broadened.

Research Questions From Our Case Studies

Let's consider some purposes and research questions found in the literature from our featured researchers. In Melde and colleagues' research (Melde et al., 2009), they sought to explain something about gangs. In particular, they wished to explain how gang membership is related to (a) self-reported victimization, (b) perceptions of victimization risk, and (c) fear of victimization. Melde and colleagues' stated purposes and three guiding research questions are therefore very clear:

1. What is the effect of gang membership on self-reported victimization?

2. What is the effect of gang membership on perceptions of victimization risk?

3. What is the effect of gang membership on the fear of victimization?

These three research questions address an interesting and contradictory set of findings in the literature. By investigating these questions, Melde and his collaborators moved our understanding of gangs and fear forward.

Brunson and his colleague (Brunson & Weitzer, 2009) published descriptive research focused on accounts of police relations with young White and Black males in St. Louis, Missouri, from the young males' perspectives. The purpose of this research is clearly indicated by the authors' statements that

> [t]his article examines the accounts of young Black and White males who reside in one of three disadvantaged St. Louis, Missouri, neighborhoods—one predominantly Black, one predominantly White, and the other racially mixed.

Brunson's research frequently focuses on the experiences and views of young African Americans regarding police relations. What are some interesting research questions on this topic you can pose?

Although there is no explicitly stated research question, the implied question is, "How do young Black and White males describe police relations across disadvantaged neighborhoods?" Brunson has long studied the topic of police relations with young males in disadvantaged communities. Given recent events in the United States, the public is more aware of the importance of this research topic and research questions.

Zaykowski's (2014) research is based on the knowledge that victims' access to and use of services is poor. Her research seeks to understand why that is. This explanatory work is clearly outlined in her purpose statement:

> The present study examined factors associated with victim service use including reporting to the police, the victim's demographic characteristics . . . the victim's relationship to the offender, and the victim's mental and physical distress. (p. 365)

Like many, Zaykowski opted to use a statement versus a research question to note her intentions. Although a research question was not presented, the question that guided her research, "What factors are related to victim service use?" is implied given the verb *examined*.

© Justin Sullivan/Getty Images

This research is interesting, feasible, and of great importance as it offers knowledge about what facilitates or hinders victim access the services they require.

Santos' research (Santos & Santos, 2016) is designed to evaluate the effectiveness of offender-focused strategies in long-term hot spots. Stated as a research question, her goal is to answer:

> Will an offender-focused intervention implemented for multiple offenders, or a particular type of crime, in a long-term hot spot lead to a reduction of that crime?

This question guides the rest of their research endeavor and adds to the literature in that it evaluates a new approach to crime prevention, does so in a suburban environment, and focuses on property crime.

The work by Cuevas and colleagues (Sabina et al., 2016) focused on Latino teen dating violence was guided by four stated goals, which can be phrased as these questions:

1. What are the rates of dating violence by victim gender?

2. What is the risk of experiencing dating violence over time?

3. Is dating violence victimization associated with other forms of victimization?

4. What cultural factors (e.g., immigrant status and familial support) are associated with dating violence over time?

Although the goals of their research were not posed in the form of questions in the original text, the implied research questions are clear and serve to guide the researchers as they engage in this important work. The strength of these research questions, and the care put into crafting excellent research questions, pays off in the rest of the research endeavor. Having a solid foundation to work from and be guided by matters. Your research is only as strong as the weakest part of it. For that reason, you want to ensure you have developed a strong and excellent research question.

Common Pitfalls When Developing Topics, Purposes, and Research Questions

Each step of research is plagued with potential pitfalls to be avoided. Developing a topic, purpose, and research question is not different. Many of the pitfalls are identified in the chapter, but it is useful to offer these reminders. First, develop a research question that is feasible. Many beginning researchers develop research questions that would take years and years to conduct (not even taking into account the funds that would be needed to accomplish it). Critically assess your research question in terms of whether it is doable in the time you have available. Consulting with more experienced researchers is useful for this. Also, know that no matter how carefully you plan, the research will always take at least 1.5 times longer as a result of unexpected things such as your institutional review board (IRB) being backed up, your proposed respondents being challenging to find, and other assorted surprises. None of these are project killers, but there is always something to slow a researcher down.

Also, a common pitfall seen in newer researchers is forgetting their research question. It is very easy to end up down an interesting rabbit hole thinking about all kinds of fascinating and related things. You must stop and ask yourself daily, "Is this helping to answer my research question?" If it is not, stop what you are doing and get back to the task at hand—answering the research question. Your research question provides the guardrails of your research. Some researchers even type out their research question and tape it to their computer monitor for a constant reminder of what their goal is.

Ethical Considerations When Developing Your Topic, Purpose, and Research Question

Ethical considerations must remain at the forefront during the research process, including the selection of a research topic and development of a research question. As noted in Chapter 1, the Nuremberg Code from 1947 (Office of History, National Institutes of Health, n.d.) and Belmont Report (National Commission for the Protection of Human Subjects of Biomedical and Behavioral Research, 1979) established the moral foundation that influences social science research conducted today. A research question, and the research that will be conducted to answer that question, must consider the three core principles coming from these historical documents. Individuals should be respected and treated as autonomous agents, researchers must focus on doing no harm (or at least minimizing it), and the possible benefits and harms must be distributed fairly among respondents.

Even with this guidance in place, unethical research has continued. Consider the core principle of beneficence, which is to do no harm (or to minimize to the extent possible) to study participants. Harm can take on a variety of forms including physical, psychological, legal, financial/economic, or social. One reason Milgram's teacher/learner study (conducted long after the Nuremberg Code was released) is considered unethical is that it inflicted psychological and emotional distress among the teachers participating in the experiment. In the journal article published on this study, Milgram (1963, p. 375) noted,

> Subjects were observed to sweat, tremble, stutter, bite their lips, groan, and dig their fingernails into their flesh. These were characteristic rather than exceptional responses to the experiment. One sign of tension was the regular occurrence of nervous laughing fits. Fourteen of the 40 subjects showed definite signs of nervous laughter and smiling. The laughter seemed entirely out of place, even bizarre. Full-blown, uncontrollable seizures were observed for 3 subjects. On one occasion, we observed a seizure so violently convulsive that it was necessary to call a halt to the experiment.

Figure 2.4 Balancing Respect for Persons, Beneficence, and Justice

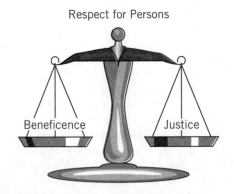

Respect for persons, beneficence, and justice have been required for many decades, yet unethical research has continued. What do you think it will take to finally stop unethical treatment of human subjects?

The initial Milgram experiments were conducted with observers hidden behind a one-way mirror. Observers remarked about the clear distress experienced by the teachers. One observer noted (Milgram, 1963, p. 377),

> I observed a mature and initially poised businessman enter the laboratory smiling and confident. Within 20 minutes he was reduced to a twitching, stuttering wreck, who was rapidly approaching a point of nervous collapse. He constantly pulled on his earlobe, and twisted his hands. At one point he pushed his fist into his forehead and muttered: "Oh God. let's stop it." And yet he continued to respond to every word of the experimenter, and obeyed to the end.

For years after the Milgram study, it was rumored that one of the "teachers" in the experiment committed suicide as a result of his participation in the study. It was believed that although this person had been told that no one had been hurt during a post-experiment debriefing, he was still distraught believing that he would cause pain to others, even when the learner begged him to stop. The urban legend suggests that because he was unable to forgive himself, he committed suicide. Although no evidence that this suicide occurred can be located, it does not take much imagination to believe it could occur. This type of harm must be considered when a researcher is developing a research question.

Today, the primary sources of guidance regarding behavioral science human subjects research originated in the U.S. Department of Health and Human Services (HHS). By building on the knowledge from earlier ethical regulations and rules, the HHS developed the Federal Policy for the Protections of Human Subjects in 1991. HHS regulations (Health and Human Services, 2009) include five subparts: A, B, C, D, and E. Subpart A, colloquially referred to as the Common Rule, outlines the fundamental procedures for conducting human subject research including the framework for IRBs and informed consent. Subpart B outlines requirements to ensure additional protections for pregnant women, neonates, and fetuses. Subpart C outlines additional protections for prisoners, and subpart D focuses on additional protections for children. Subpart E was added in 2009 and focuses on the registration requirements of IRB committees.

The Contemporary Role of IRB

The Common Rule, or subpart A, outlines the basic policy of protection of human subjects (see Table 2.2). Much of this document is devoted to identifying the membership and responsibilities of IRB committees. IRB committees are required to be diverse across a variety of dimensions. First, committees must have diversity in terms of member demographics, areas of expertise, and affiliation with the institutions. No committee can consist solely of men, women, or individuals of the same profession. Scientists and nonscientists must be IRB members, and at least one IRB member cannot be affiliated with the institution. The unaffiliated party is the "community member."

The Common Rule also identifies research that must be reviewed by an IRB. First, it defines a **human subject** as "a living individual." This indicates that work on cadavers does not have to be reviewed under the Common Rule. In addition, it defines **research** as a systematic investigation or examination that will contribute to generalizable knowledge. An example of an activity that does not seek to contribute to generalizable knowledge is an interview with a victim's advocate about the types of programs available to victims of violence. This type of activity does not contribute to generalizable knowledge and does not have to be reviewed by IRB.

The IRB committee must review many elements of proposed research and has the authority to approve, require modifications, or disapprove any proposed research. The committee ensures that risks to subjects are minimized, risks are reasonable in relation to benefits, and

Human subject: According to the Common Rule refers to a living individual.

Research: According to the Common Rule refers to a systematic investigation or examination that will contribute to generalizable knowledge.

Table 2.2 "The Common Rule"

45 CFR Part 46 Subpart A

Adopted by 18 federal departments and agencies

Department of Agriculture 7 CFR Part 1c	Department of Energy 10 CFR Part 745	National Aeronautics and Space Administration 14 CFR Part 1230
Department of Commerce 15 CFR Part 27	Consumer Product Safety Commission 16 CFR Part 1028	Agency for International Development 22 CFR Part 225
Department of Housing and Urban Development 24 CFR Part 60	Department of Justice 28 CFR Part 46	Department of Defense 32 CFR Part 219
Department of Education 34 CFR Part 97	Department of Veterans Affairs 38 CFR Part 16	Environmental Protection Agency 40 CFR Part 26
Department of Health and Human Services 45 CFR Part 46	National Science Foundation 45 CFR Part 690	Department of Transportation 49 CFR Part 11
Central Intelligence Agency*	Department of Homeland Security*	Social Security Administration*

*Denotes compliance with *ALL* subparts of 45 CFR part 46 but has not issued the Common Rule in regulations.

Vulnerable populations: Those that receive an additional layer of review when proposed to participate in research. According to Department of Health and Human Services (HHS) regulations, pregnant women, human fetuses and neonates, prisoners, and children are vulnerable populations. These populations are considered vulnerable in that they may be more vulnerable to coercion or undue influence.

the selection of research subjects is equitable. The committee also reviews to ensure the informed and voluntary consent of subjects is gained and documented. In addition, IRBs should make certain that consent is treated as an ongoing action. A person can withdraw consent at any time, and IRB committees ensure this is made clear. Consideration is given that data are maintained such that the privacy of subjects and confidentiality of data are ensured. All research protocols operating under the Common Rule are reviewed for these basic elements. Depending on the protocol, additional scrutiny may be given by the IRB.

To date, almost two dozen agencies and departments of the federal government, including the Department of Justice, have codified subpart A—the Common Rule—of the HHS regulations to protect against human subject abuses in research. The Department of Justice, a source of research funding for criminal justice and criminology research, is one of those adopting the Common Rule. Like many other federal agencies, however, the Department of Justice did not adopt subparts B, C, or D, which provides additional protections for three groups of vulnerable populations. Nonetheless, in choosing a research topic and developing a research question, it is important that a researcher take into account the use of vulnerable populations, whether codified or not.

Vulnerable Populations

Subparts B, C, and D of the HHS regulations identify three **vulnerable populations** that receive an additional layer of review when proposed to participate in research. Vulnerable populations outlined in the HHS regulations are pregnant women, human fetuses and neonates, prisoners, and children. These populations are considered vulnerable in that they may be more susceptible to coercion or undue influence.

Pregnant Women, Human Fetuses, and Neonates

In general, review of research using pregnant women, fetuses, and neonates is designed to provide extra scrutiny to ensure no harm comes from the research. For example, for research involving pregnant women and **neonates** (i.e., newborns; a nonviable neonate refers to a newborn who while living after delivery is not viable) (Health and Human Services, 2009), the oversight outlined in the Common Rule is required; in addition, all ten requirements must be met to allow for their participation in research. A few of the requirements that must be met are "(a) [w]here scientifically appropriate, preclinical studies, including studies on pregnant animals, and clinical studies, including studies on nonpregnant women, have been conducted and provide data for assessing potential risks to pregnant women and fetuses" and "(c) [a]ny risk is the least possible for achieving the results of the research" (Health and Human Services, 2009). "(h) No inducements, monetary or otherwise, will be offered to terminate a pregnancy"; "(i) [i]ndividuals engaged in the research will have no part in any decisions as to the timing, method, or procedures used to terminate a pregnancy"; and "(j) [i]ndividuals engaged in the research will have no part in determining the viability of a neonate." Research involving neonates is required to prevent the termination of the heartbeat and respiration and must ensure that there is no added risk to the neonate participating in the research (among other requirements).

Prisoners

Prisoners are specifically identified as a vulnerable population in HHS's regulations given their confinement and inability to express free choice. A prisoner is defined by these regulation as the following (Health and Human Services, 2009, §46.303 Definitions, para. 3):

> [A]ny individual involuntarily confined or detained in a penal institution. The term is intended to encompass individuals sentenced to such an institution under a criminal or civil statute, individuals detained in other facilities by virtue of statutes or commitment procedures which provide alternatives to criminal prosecution or incarceration in a penal institution, and individuals detained pending arraignment, trial, or sentencing.

Ex-prisoners are not considered a vulnerable population under subpart B. The additional scrutiny given research proposing to use prisoners results from a concern that because of incarceration, their ability to make a truly voluntary decision without coercion to participate as subjects in research is compromised. Additional requirements stipulate that the IRB committee include at least one prisoner or prisoner representative, and that advantages gained by participating in the research are not of such a magnitude as to make difficult the weighing of risks to the advantages. In addition, the research proposed must provide assurances that parole boards will not take into account research participation when making decisions about parole. Prisoners must be informed prior to consent that their participation will not have any effect on the probability of parole.

To protect prisoners even more, contemporary research can only involve one of four categories of research related to prisoners. The first category requires that a study examine the possible causes, effects, and processes of incarceration, as well as of criminal behavior. The second category of research involves investigations of prisons as institutions. Third, research focusing on conditions that particularly affect prisoners (e.g., diseases, victimization, and drug/alcohol abuse) is possible. And finally, research on policies or programs that would improve the health or well-being of prisoners is authorized.

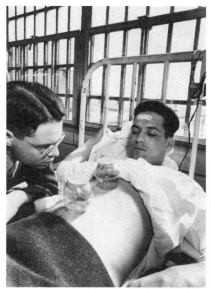

© AP Images/ASSOCIATED PRESS

This image from the Holmesberg Prison skin experiments illustrates the unethical nature of this work. Prisoners were unable to provide informed voluntary consent given the way the study was conducted. One finding out of this research led to Retin A which is widely used today to treat acne among other things. How might you have developed this same product without taking advantage of impoverished and imprisoned men?

Neonate: Newborn.

© baona/iStockphoto.com

Children, by definition, can only assent to participate in research. Why can't they consent? What characteristics are taken into account to ascertain if assent is necessary? Would you handle children in research differently? How?

Assent: Agreement by a child to participate in research that will likely benefit him or her. To gain assent, the child must be able to comprehend and understand what it means to be a participant in research.

Permission: Frequently, but not always, required by at least one parent when a child participates in research.

Unfortunately, the additional layers of review have proven necessary given that prisoners have been used in unethical studies in the past. In Chapter 1, some of the experiments conducted on prisoners in concentration camps were described. In the United States, there have been a shameful number of unethical experiments on prisoners as well. "All I saw before me were acres of skin. It was like a farmer seeing a field for the first time." These are the words of Dr. Albert Kligman who performed skin experiments on prisoners—primarily poorly educated people of color—confined at the Holmesburg Prison in Pennsylvania from 1951 to 1974. The prisoners referred to experimentation as perfume tests, but Kligman was conducting experiments using toothpaste, shampoos, eye drops, hair dye, detergents, mind-altering drugs, radioactive isotopes, dioxin (an exceedingly toxic compound), herpes, staphylococcus, and athlete's foot. Some prisoners had objects placed in incisions in their skins over time to determine the effects of these foreign bodies. This experimentation, lasting more than two decades, included injections and frequent painful biopsies. Kligman paid his subjects from $10 to $300 a day. Most prisoners at that time earned about 15 cents a day. Offering compensation of this magnitude made it questionable if prisoners' ability to voluntarily consent was honored. Given the poor information about the experiments the prisoners were given, and their circumstances as prisoners, it is clear no voluntary consent was given, or even possible.

Children

Subpart D of the HHS regulations identifies children as a vulnerable population. Children are defined as persons younger than 18 years of age (local laws may vary and may take precedence over the HHS definition of children. For definitions related to this vulnerable population, see 45 CFR 46.402[a-e]; HHS, 2009). Reviews of research proposing to include children must meet all requirements in the Common Rule as well as others. For example, in general, research using children must offer no more than a minimal risk. If the risk is greater, it must be demonstrated that the research will lead to generalizable knowledge about a disorder or condition. Because they are younger than 18, children are not able to consent to participation in any research. Rather, children are frequently asked to **assent** or agree to participate in research that will likely benefit them, with the assurance that the child can comprehend and understand what it means to be a participant in research. Assent requirements can be waived as per 45 CFR 46.408(a) by IRB committees if a consideration of the child's age, maturity, and psychological state indicate assent is not possible, and if the research offers direct benefit of health and well-being to the child. In addition to considering the need for a child's assent, an IRB committee will determine whether parental **permission** for participation is required. In most cases where parental consent is needed, permission from one parent or guardian is sufficient. In some situations, consent from both parents is required unless one parent has died, is incompetent, is not available, or there is not a second parent who has custody of the child.

A repeated theme is that these additional requirements have proven necessary given unethical research using children in the past. Consider the research of Farfel and Chisolm, researchers at Johns Hopkins University, with the approval of the university's IRB committee (Farfel & Chisolm, 1991). This research, sponsored by the Department of Health and Human Services, compared the effectiveness of traditional lead abatement procedures compared with modified abatement procedures during the 1990s. Interior lead paint was outlawed in 1978 by Congress, yet years later, many dwellings still had this paint including older inner-city rental housing in Baltimore where low-income tenants lived, and where this research took place. Lead paint is easily absorbed through the skin, and lead dust is especially problematic around doors and windows. Exposure to even a small amount results in permanent damage, especially to children less than six years of age. Lead toxicity has been associated with speech delays, aggressiveness, ADHD, learning disabilities, and criminal offending.

The five groups of housing units used in the study by Farfel and Chisolm (1991) were identified by the Baltimore City Health Department, which had records of dwellings in which children suffering from lead toxicity resided. One group of dwellings had never had lead paint. A second group included dwellings in which all lead paint hazards had been removed. The three other groups of housing units were contaminated with lead paint but differed in terms of the approach taken to remove the lead. The first group was treated with traditional abatement techniques including the scraping and repainting of peeling areas, as well as the addition of a doormat at the main entrance. The second group of homes was treated in the traditional way in addition to placing doormats at all entrances, installing easy-to-clean floor coverings, and covering collapsing walls with plasterboard. The third in the group of dwellings in abatement groups received the treatment the other groups received, plus replacement of all windows.

Researchers encouraged owners of these housing units to rent to parents with children between the ages of six months and four years old since brain development is very sensitive to lead exposure during this time. Parents living in these housing units were offered a financial incentive to participate in the study, which was portrayed as a study about how well different methods of renovation protected children from lead poisoning. Efforts were made to dissuade renters from leaving the units during the experiment.

During the two-year experiment, testing of the presence of lead in the housing units and testing of blood lead levels in the children were taken periodically. Some children who moved into these units were exposed to dangerous levels of lead, and their blood tests showed enormous increase in their blood level. In others, lead toxicity was reduced but remained at unhealthy levels. Yet the experiment continued, and children continued being exposed to lead.

When the details of this experiment finally came to light, lawsuits were filed, and judgment was harsh. One judge compared this study to the Tuskegee Syphilis Experiment, as well as to the Nazi medical experiments. Others continue to maintain that there were no ethical lapses with this research and that some children in the study experienced decreases in their lead toxicity over the course of the study.

Potentially Vulnerable Populations

Although subparts B, C, and D of the HHS regulations specifically identify pregnant women, prisoners, and children as vulnerable populations, it is incumbent on the researcher to consider what other groups may be potentially vulnerable. Vulnerable populations include any population that requires additional consideration and augmented protections in research. Consider the gathering of data for the National Crime Victimization Survey (NCVS). Like many social surveys, its methodology considers potentially vulnerable populations given the nature of data gathered. The NCVS identifies vulnerable populations as pregnant women, prisoners, and children, as well as "the elderly, minorities, economically or educationally disadvantaged persons, and other 'institutionalized' groups such as students recruited as research subjects by their teachers and employees recruited as research subjects by their employer/supervisor" (Winstanley, 2009, p. 40). For these groups, it is important to contemplate ethical considerations such as whether consent is informed and autonomous, research participation is free of coercion, and the language and presentation fit the needs of the particular population. What is considered a vulnerable population may differ depending on the topic and purpose of the research.

One **potentially vulnerable population** not identified in the NCVS documentation or HHS regulations are veterans. Although veterans are not a vulnerable population according to

Potentially vulnerable populations: Any population that may be more vulnerable to coercion or undue influence.

the HHS, the Veteran's Administration considers veterans as potentially vulnerable populations. The reasons stated for this are veterans' rigorous training to obey orders, willingness to sacrifice, as well as the potential for veterans to be suffering from post-traumatic stress and other disorders related to their status.

Given this, would it be ethical to conduct an investigation of suicide ideation among active military who are currently receiving help after an attempted suicide? This research was proposed by a graduate student who noted that this research could offer important information related to this topic including the role that demographics (e.g., age, income, race, ethnicity, and arm of the services) played in suicide ideation and attempted suicides. Would this type of research be wise? Ethical? Would asking these particular individuals to share their experiences offer information that was greater than the potential trauma it might invoke? In this real-world example, professors overseeing this student's work did not think it was an ethical line of inquiry for this population, and the student was encouraged to find another topic.

HHS regulations do not identify veterans as a vulnerable population, but the Veteran's Administration views them as potentially vulnerable. What make them potentially vulnerable? What other populations might be vulnerable in research settings? Why?

Exempt, Expedited, or Full Panel Review at the IRB

There are three types of research categories when submitting to IRB: exempt, expedited review, and full board review. **Exempt research** occurs when human participants conform to one of the categories from section 46.101(b) of 45 CFR 46 (HHS, 2009). This includes research using existing data, documents, or records in which the data offer no means to identify subjects. Work with the NCVS, like that conducted by Zaykowski (2014) in her victim services research is an example of exempt research. **Expedited review** of research does not mean that an IRB review will be conducted quickly. Rather, it means that the review of the research protocol will be done by the IRB chair and possible other committee members. Expedited review can only be used when the research involves no more than minimal risk, does not include vulnerable populations, and is not using deception. **Full board review** is required in all other types of research. In this instance, the research protocol is reviewed and discussed by the full IRB committee. Important elements considered such as informed consent is voted on by the full committee.

Exempt research: That which does not have information about respondents, is publicly available, and has no more than minimal risk.

Expedited review: Review by the institutional review board (IRB) committee chair (and perhaps one or two other members). This is not necessarily a fast review but one that does not require the full board.

Full board review: All research that is not exempt or expedited and requires the review of the full institutional review board (IRB).

Much of the research featured in this text went to full board review, and some required the additional scrutiny required given Subpart D regulations. Brunson, Melde, and Cuevas and their colleagues gathered data from youth that required additional scrutiny. The researchers report generally good experiences with IRB committees and approval. Many also note that others are frequently negative about IRB but that in general, a negative interaction involves a lack of preparation, organization, clarity, or thoroughness on the part of the researcher. The challenges described generally focused on individual IRB committees (which can vary institution to institution). An often repeated challenge was the lack of consistency across IRB protocol consideration, as well as a lack of institutional memory. A researcher can submit nearly identical protocols at two points in time resulting in two very different experiences. This may be a result of changing committee members or of a lack of expertise on a committee (e.g., lack of a researcher with expertise in gathering and using qualitative data, lack of familiarity of a particular methodology, and lack familiarity with the area of interest). With regard to working with juveniles, some researchers note that some committees make it easier to access delinquent or at-risk juveniles but make accessing so-called good kids very challenging.

Training in Protecting Human Subjects

If you are conducting research that will be reviewed by an IRB committee, your institution will likely require you to take training on the topic of human subjects research. Please note that you do not have to wait until you are submitting proposed research to the IRB to get trained. Most universities offer free training to faculty, staff, and students. In addition, anyone can access free human subjects online training through the National Institutes of Health (NIH), a federal collection of 27 institutes and centers engaged in biomedical research. Although the NIH training focuses primarily on medical and health research, this training is applicable to research in the social sciences given the similarities of research in the areas. For example, victimization, injury, and other topics of interest to criminologists and criminal justice professionals are also of great interest to health scientists. This overlap is further demonstrated as this training is based on the HHS regulations described earlier (HHS, 2009). To access the English version of this free training, go here: https://phrp.nihtraining.com/users/login.php. The Spanish version can be accessed here: https://pphi.nihtraining.com/users/login.php. To take this free course, a brief registration is required. The entire course is estimated to take three hours to complete and will cover some of the topics presented in this text. You can save work and return later so it is not necessary to carve out a three-hour block of time. Once the course is completed, a certificate is made available online to demonstrate your successful training in protecting human research subjects!

IRB Expert—Sharon Devine, JD, PhD

Sharon Devine, PhD, is a research assistant professor and chair of the Exempt/Expedited Panel and chair of the Social and Behavioral Panel for the Colorado Multiple Institutional Review Board (COMIRB) at the University of Colorado Denver Anschutz Medical Campus. Her research focuses on research ethics and evaluation of public health projects. She is currently examining the evaluations of various public health projects, specifically, training professionals engaged in clinical and behavioral interventions around HIV and STDs (funded by the Centers for Disease Control and Prevention), facilitating integration of family planning into STD clinics (funded by the Office of Population Affairs), and reducing teen pregnancy (funded by the Office of Adolescent Health).

Devine was a successful practicing attorney for years when she made the decision to pursue a master's degree in anthropology. During her master's course work, a professor identified her research skills and encouraged her to continue for a PhD, noting she would want to conduct her own research. Recognizing this opportunity, Devine closed her law practice and returned to school full time to pursue a PhD. Her fondness for research grew when she recognized that she could create new knowledge and make actionable recommendation that would have a positive impact on society. In the course of seeking her PhD, a professor was looking for a student volunteer to sit on the university IRB, so she volunteered. Since then, she earned her PhD and continued her work on the university IRB committee. Eventually, she was asked to sit on the newly devised Social and Behavioral Panel. Prior protocols had to go through the medical school IRB, which created great difficulties for social science researchers. Although she never thought, "Hey I want to be on an IRB committee," the opportunity presented itself and has taken her on a great path. Today she oversees all protocols coming through the system. This offers her a unique perspective on research and ethics.

Courtesy of Sharon Devine

Devine notes that IRB is important for several reasons. First, it offers an independent review of research design and procedures to ensure everything is ethical for human subjects. It is important that all be treated with dignity and respect, and having an independent body consider proposed research enhances the changes to treat research subjects appropriately. Second, it forces a researcher to plan his or her research and to be able to articulate that research plan, carefully. She comments on how she as a young researcher did not appreciate the need to really think out the methodology in advance. The IRB review helps ensure this and, in doing so, is respectful of human subjects kind enough to participate in our research. Third, seeing how researchers have handled themselves in the past indicates the need for some type of oversight.

Yet, Devine recognizes several challenges researchers face when they engage with the IRB. First, she recognizes that that IRB can come across as nit-picky. All researchers must understand that not only is it the university's responsibility to protect human subjects, but it is its responsibility to document that the reviews were conducted thoroughly. This care and consideration can come across to researchers as the IRB being difficult. Devine recognizes that some of the existing regulations are heavy handed for a fair amount of social science. She also would like to see the regulations simplified, while still focusing on the risk to subjects. A second challenge she sees is that a committee can at times lose focus. It is not the committee's responsibility to say, "I'd do this research differently," but to identify whether the methods, design, and protections as proposed are adequate to protect subjects. And a final challenge she identifies is working with students and junior faculty who have not been properly mentored about how to submit an IRB protocol. Devine offers examples of problems frequently seen in submitted research protocols:

- Failure to include appropriate level of detail in the submitted materials. It is not enough to say that you will conduct survey research. You must also submit the survey so that the IRB can review it, and the documentation is obtained.

- Protocols that are tone-deaf or cavalier about the proposed research. The subjects are human and deserve respect. Do not infantilize respondents or treat them with a lack of dignity.

- Application documents are internally inconsistent. If you note that you will interview 50 people in one area of the application, and 80 people in another area of the application, IRB approval will be delayed.

- Failure to complete the forms in full. You must fill in all blanks. Dr. Devine understands some questions asked on the applications are not clear, but the university is required to ask them. If a researcher does not understand the question, do not leave it blank. Rather, contact the IRB and ask what is needed.

- Failure to respond to prior comments. At times, a researcher is instructed to make particular changes, or to provide additional information, but they do not do so. Detailed records are kept in IRB, and this oversight will be noted.

Devine notes that building knowledge via research demands a lot of thought and that makes it different from general opinion polls, marketing surveys, and so on. Building knowledge frequently requires the help of others (i.e., research participants) and we owe it to them to treat them properly and to conduct research that will be rigorous and valuable. IRB is one part of that process.

Chapter Wrap-Up

This chapter presents the steps you should take to identify a research topic and research purpose. By using these elements, the chapter discusses ways to focus this information into a clear, concise, and feasible research question. As demonstrated, many sources are available from which you can develop an area of interest. Easy methods to evaluate the research question were discussed. Examples from our case studies were used to illustrate the variation in how researchers used their intellectual curiosity to develop a research question. As was shown, ideas came from a variety of sources. Table 2.3 in this chapter offers a

Table 2.3 Featured Research: Topics, Purposes, Research Questions, and IRB Approvals

Researcher	Topic	How Developed	Purpose	Research Question	IRB Approval
Rod Brunson	Racial variation in youth and police relations in disadvantaged urban neighborhoods	Gap in literature	Exploratory	What are differences in views of police relations of Black and White youth based on where they reside: a Black disadvantaged neighborhood, a White disadvantaged neighborhood, or a racially mixed disadvantaged neighborhoods?	Full board with additional scrutiny given focus on youth
Carlos Cuevas	Teen dating violence rates among Latinos over time	RFP combined with knowledge of gaps in the literature	Explanatory and Descriptive	(1) What are the rates of dating violence by victim gender? (2) What is the risk of experiencing dating violence over time? (3) Is dating violence victimization associated with other forms of victimization? (4) What cultural factors (e.g., immigrant status, familial support) are associated with dating violence over time?	Full board with additional scrutiny given focus on youth
Mary Dodge	Perspectives of female law enforcement officers acting as prostitutes in stings	Personal experience while on police ride-along	Exploratory	Explore how female police officers serving as prostitution decoys view this work.	Expedited
Chris Melde	Gangs and the apparent contradiction that they join gangs for safety, yet in gangs experience violence at higher rates	Untangling what appears to be a contradiction in the literature	Explanatory	(1) What is the effect of gang membership on self-reported victimization among adolescents? (2) What is the effect of gang membership on perceptions of victimization risk among adolescents? and (3) What is the effect of gang membership on the fear of victimization among adolescents?	Full board, with extra scrutiny given the focus on youth
Rachel Santos	Crime prevention by bringing together offender-focused and place-based literature	Knowledge of the literature	Situated between evaluation and experimental rsearch	Will an offender-focused intervention implemented for multiple offenders, or a particular type of crime, in a long-term hot spot lead to a reduction of that crime?	Expedited
Heather Zaykowski	Male and female reporting/help-seeking behaviors across multiple types of violence	Gaps in literature	Explanatory	To examine factors associated with victim service use including reporting to the police, the victim's demographic characteristics, the victim's injury, offender's use of a weapon, the victim's relationship to the offender, and the victim's mental and physical distress	Exempt

quick review of the featured researchers and research focusing on the topics in this chapter. You should become familiar with these journal articles as we will discuss them in detail throughout the book.

Although we have discussed our cases studies throughout this chapter, it is useful to consider each case study article with regard to the topics presented in this chapter. As Table 2.3 demonstrates, each case study focused on a different topic that was developed in a variety of ways. Purposes varied, and the research questions each researcher used reflect this. Note that in some cases, researchers used more than one research question to guide the research. This is acceptable and fairly common. This table also shows that each approach required varying scrutiny from the IRB committee. The varying scrutiny not only was based on the topic and research conducted but also on variation in university requirements.

In addition, this chapter focused on common pitfalls associated with setting the stage for your research. A major one is losing sight of the role of the research question. Answering it is why you are conducting research. Ethical considerations when moving through these initial steps in the research process were also highlighted. Information provided highlighted the influence of historical human subject ethical documents—the Nuremberg Code and the Belmont Report—on contemporary rules based on HHS regulations. Information on the subparts of the HHS regulations was also provided, bringing attention to vulnerable populations and the additional reviews such groups entail. Students were shown a place to take a free online human subjects research class, which will further hone their understanding of ethics in the research process. Dr. Devine, the Chair of the Social and Behavioral Panel IRB committee at the University of Colorado Denver Social and Behavior Panel IRB, also discussed her role on this committee. As she indicated, IRB is a serious undertaking, and many people work very hard to protect human subjects. In the next chapter, we review how research questions are used to guide and conduct a literature review. As will be seen, the literature review allows a researcher to polish and focus the research question even more. Once the literature review is completed, the planning of the nuts and bolts of the actual research begins.

Applied Assignments

1. Homework Applied Assignment: Identifying a Purpose and Research Question

Find **two** peer-reviewed journal articles from major journals that interest you. Using these two articles, please write a paper providing the following information for each article: Clear statement of the purpose of this research (Descriptive? Explanatory? etc.), clear statement of the research question, and basic summary of the research including the methodology used and research findings. What is your assessment of these findings? In addition, provide your assessment about any ethical

issues this research may have encountered and the ways the researchers dealt with them. Be prepared to discuss what you found in class.

2. Group Work in Class Applied Assignment: Developing and Assessing Research Questions

As a group, come up with three research questions. The first should be used to study something related to adolescent offenders. The second should be used to study something related to victims of sexual violence. And the final research question should be used to study something about incarcerated women. Be able to describe how you developed those research questions. What motivated you to narrow your topics to the ultimate research questions you developed? Evaluate each research question to ensure it is not too broad, too narrow, is interesting, and so on using the information in this text. Be able to identify the purpose of each research question (Descriptive? Explanatory? etc.). Given these research questions, do you see any ethical issues you may have to address before conducting this research? What are they? Why are they important? What type of IRB approval would you need to conduct this research? Prepare a table like Table 2.3 with your three proposed pieces of research indicated by the research questions

to share with the class. Be prepared to discuss what you found in class.

3. Internet Applied Assignment: Training in Human Subjects

Access the free online human subjects training offered by the National Institutes of Health (NIH; https://phrp .nihtraining.com/users/login.php). Once you have successfully completed your training, you will be awarded an online completion certificate. Please print out and provide that certificate to your professor/ instructor.

KEY WORDS AND CONCEPTS

Assent 52
Data codebook 34
Descriptive research 41
Evaluation research 41
Exempt research 54
Expedited review 54
Explanatory research 41
Exploratory research 40

Full board review 54
Human subject 49
Hypotheses 31
Neonates 51
Permission 52
Potentially vulnerable
  population 53
Purpose of the research 40

Request for proposals (RFP) 36
Research 49
Research topic 32
Theory 31
Vulnerable populations 50
Wheel of science 31

KEY POINTS

- A research topic is the general subject matter in which someone has an interest. Topics can come from a variety of places including the extant literature, data, theory, RFPs, Internet, and personal experiences.

- Purposes for research generally fall into four primary categories: exploratory, descriptive, explanatory, and evaluative. Any piece of research may have one, two, or more purposes.

- A research question guides the rest of the research process. Answering the research question is the goal of your research.

- Research questions should be interesting, seek to increase knowledge, feasible, not too broad, and not too narrow.

- Although important and influential, the Nuremberg Code and Belmont Report are considered historical documents in regard to human subjects research. Yet the intentions of these documents continue to influence today's research.

- The Federal Policy for the Protections of Human Subjects, developed by HHS in 1991, is an improvement on earlier attempts at stopping unethical research. Unlike earlier efforts, this policy ties compliance with funding.

- The Federal Policy for the Protections of Human Subjects contains five subparts: A (aka Common Rule), B, C, and D. Subpart E was added in 2009.

- Subpart A of the Federal Policy for the Protections of Human Subjects outlines the fundamental procedures for conducting human subject research including the framework for IRBs and informed consent. It is more commonly known as the Common Rule.

- Subpart B of the HHS regulations outlines additional protections for pregnant women, neonates, and fetuses; subpart C outlines additional protections for prisoners; and subpart D outlines additional protections for children proposed to participate in research. Subpart E focuses on registration requirements of IRB committees.

- Vulnerable populations are those that receive an additional layer of review when proposed to participate in research. Populations are considered vulnerable if they may be more susceptible to coercion or undue influence given their circumstances. According to HHS regulations, pregnant women, human fetuses and neonates, prisoners, and children are vulnerable populations. Researchers must be sensitive to other groups who are potentially vulnerable, such as veterans.

REVIEW QUESTIONS

1. Where are some good sources to find a good research topic?

2. What purpose does exploratory research serve? When is the best time to use it?

3. What is the purpose of descriptive research, and how does it differ from exploratory research?

4. Explanatory research answers many questions. What are some of them, and how are they different from other research purposes?

5. How does evaluative research differ from the other purposes? When is it best used?

6. Why is having a research question important?

7. What makes a research question a good research question?

8. What advantages do the HHS regulations have over early documents such as the Nuremberg Code and the Belmont Report?

9. What were some of the impetuses of subparts B through D of the HHS regulations?

10. Who are considered vulnerable according to HHS? Why is considering vulnerable populations important?

CRITICAL THINKING QUESTIONS

1. A student proposes the following research question for a class project: "What are the criminal backgrounds of older males entering the police academy in Cincinnati, OH?" If you were asked to provide feedback and evaluate this research question, what would you say?

2. A student proposes the following research question for a research project she wishes to conduct: "What influences explain whether children reveal they have been neglected, abused, or maltreated by their parent?" If you were asked to evaluate this proposed research, what feedback would you provide? What challenges do you foresee should this student go forward?

3. Research by Farfel and Chisolm in the 1990s investigated the effectiveness of a variety of lead abatement protocols. Some consider this research to be as unethical as the Tuskegee Syphilis Experiment. Yet others argue that some of the children in the experiments experienced a decrease in lead toxicity. In your opinion, was this or was this not ethical research? Use the principles of respect for persons, beneficence, and justice to justify your stance.

4. Subparts B through D of the HHS regulations identify several vulnerable populations. Do you believe other groups should be identified as vulnerable in additional subparts of the regulations? If so which groups would you specify and why? Do you believe that researchers will self-police and take into account potentially vulnerable populations? What evidence do you have of that?

5. Dodge hopes to conduct research on incarcerated female embezzlers. In particular, she would like to understand their motivations and compare them with motivations identified decades ago. What additional considerations will Dr. Dodge have to consider should she engage in this research? How might she demonstrate to the IRB that she has considered issues related to human subjects?

$SAGE edge™

SAGE edge offers a robust online environment featuring an impressive array of free tools and resources for review, study, and further exploration, keeping you on the cutting edge of teaching and learning. Learn more at **edge.sagepub .com/rennisonrm**.

CHAPTER 3

Conducting a Literature Review

Learning Objectives

After finishing this chapter, you should be able to:

3.1 Summarize what a literature review is, what it tells the reader, and why it is necessary.

3.2 Evaluate the nine basic steps taken to write a well-constructed literature review.

3.3 Conduct an electronic search using terms, phrases, Boolean operators, and filters.

3.4 Evaluate and identify the parts of an empirical research journal article, and use that knowledge to summarize a piece of research.

3.5 Identify and summarize the organizational approaches and writing strategy elements of MEAL that are useful when conducting a literature review.

3.6 Demonstrate an understanding of the ethics involved and the common pitfalls associated with writing a literature review.

Introduction

With a research question in hand, you are ready to conduct a literature review. This chapter provides the information needed to write a quality academic literature review. Although it is widely recognized that many students fear statistics, less acknowledged is that the fear, loathing, and dread of writing a literature review is equally if not more common. This apprehension should not be surprising. As Rachel Boba Santos, one of our featured researchers, notes, "[w]riting a literature review is easy with the right skills. In general, students have not learned how to write them, but when taught skills, they can do it well." This chapter offers those skills.

Before learning the skills needed to write a literature review, we want to acknowledge some realities about literature reviews. First, people frequently are not taught the *skills* needed to write a literature review. Writing a literature review is not instinctive, so without these skills, students are confused and stressed, and professors frequently are disappointed with the resulting work. Second, *why* you or other researchers need a literature review is rarely discussed, or when it is, it is quickly glossed over. With a full understanding about the purpose of a literature review, people are better able to accomplish them. Third, *what* a literature entails is rarely explicated. Too frequently, someone is expected to write a literature review when what is involved in constructing a literature review has not been explained to them. Fourth, clearly outlining the *steps* taken to construct a literature review is frequently incomplete or not provided at all. In short, why a literature review is needed, what a literature review is, and how to write one too frequently receive little, if any, attention in research methods texts. That is not the case in this book where we devote a full chapter to this important topic.

This chapter begins by identifying *why* a literature review is important, and it clearly describes *what* a literature is. The chapter then offers concrete *steps* taken to construct a literature review including identifying what sources are needed, how to find the sources, a systematic method to summarize and synthesize the sources, and organizational and writing strategies to produce an excellent literature review. Finally, pitfalls commonly found in literature reviews, as well as ethical considerations in the construction of a literature review, are discussed. The chapter closes with a discussion with Sean McCandless, PhD, an expert literature review writer, about best practices, common errors, and what makes literature reviews great.

Why Conduct a Literature Review?

A literature review is an important part of research that serves many purposes. Consider how our featured researchers responded to "Why is a literature review important?" Santos notes that "[t]he purpose of literature review is to tell the story of what is known about the topic and identify the strengths and weaknesses of that knowledge, including gaps our understanding. Gaps can be as simple as 'while there is a good study done, it is the only study done on this topic.'" Carlos Cuevas stresses that "[a] literature review lets the world know you have a clue on what you are talking about. It also provides the means to 'sell' the research proposed. It offers an opportunity to make the argument as to why the research I want to do is important." Rod Brunson contends, "A literature review situates the current study into the broader body of scholarship. It provides an understanding of related research that has been done, the populations research has focused on, and the context of prior studies. This highlights the contribution of the proposed study." Given these valuable reasons to conduct a literature review, it is not surprising that Brunson states that, "while you can technically conduct research without conducting a literature review, you really shouldn't. It makes no sense to do so–you may be planning on conducting a study that has been done, and this is something you could discover easily with a literature review."

Literature reviews provide an opportunity to learn what research has to say about a selected research question and topic.

A literature review presents an understanding, or a snapshot, of the overall state of the literature by surveying, summarizing, and synthesizing existing literature about the topic of interest. A well-constructed literature review identifies major themes associated with a topic, and it demonstrates where there is agreement, and disagreement, about that topic. The review identifies limitations of prior research, and it exposes gaps in our understanding about a topic, which indicate possible directions of future inquiry on the topic. A well-constructed literature review should situate the proposed research in the context of extant literature, and it should clearly identify how the proposed research will create new knowledge that enhances the existing knowledge about the topic. If a research question is the guardrails of our research, the literature review is the pavement on which we are traveling. Understanding what we know about a topic is critical to ensuring the research—whether done as a student at the university or during your career—increases our knowledge.

A Road Map: How to Conduct a Literature Review

This chapter describes the steps taken to conduct a literature review. Although the following sections provide detail on these steps, this initial section presents an overview, or a road map, of this process. As shown in Figure 3.1, the first step in conducting a literature review is to develop appropriate search terms using electronic search tools available in most libraries. The

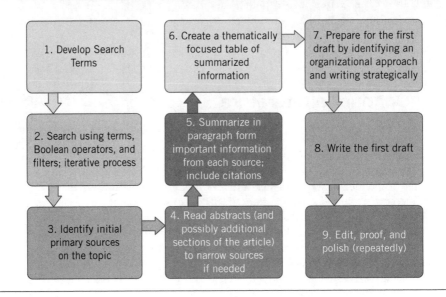

Figure 3.1 Road Map for a Literature Review

1. Develop Search Terms

2. Search using terms, Boolean operators, and filters; iterative process

3. Identify initial primary sources on the topic

4. Read abstracts (and possibly additional sections of the article) to narrow sources if needed

5. Summarize in paragraph form important information from each source; include citations

6. Create a thematically focused table of summarized information

7. Prepare for the first draft by identifying an organizational approach and writing strategically

8. Write the first draft

9. Edit, proof, and polish (repeatedly)

Original sources: Also known as "primary sources." They are primarily peer-reviewed journal articles. There are three basic forms of original source journal articles: peer-reviewed empirical journal articles, theoretical journal articles, and literature review journal articles.

Primary sources: Also known as "original sources." They are primarily peer-reviewed journal articles. There are three basic forms of primary source journal articles: peer-reviewed empirical journal articles, theoretical journal articles, and literature review journal articles.

Peer-reviewed journal articles: Published articles that were rigorously peer-reviewed before being published in an academic journal. These are an excellent source of information used in a literature review.

next two steps involve using these search terms, in conjunction with Boolean operators and filters, in an iterative process to identify the initial list of primary source journal articles for use in writing the literature review. Step 4 begins the process of selecting the final set of primary sources, and steps 5 and 6 describe how to summarize and synthesize the material.

The seventh step requires identifying the preferred organizational approach and writing strategy to construct the initial rough draft. The final step includes iterative editing, proofing, and polishing until the literature review is complete.

It is not uncommon to feel intimidated when embarking on writing a literature review. Rather than viewing it as one giant, daunting task, it is easier and more accurate to view it as a series of smaller, attainable steps as illustrated in Figure 3.1. Writing an excellent literature review does take some time and requires the writer to *think about* (not just compile) the source material. Before thinking about the material, however, you must find sources that you will use to construct the review. The next section focuses on sources and where to find them.

About Sources

A literature review is constructed using information from existing legitimate sources of knowledge. Identifying which sources are appropriate when writing a literature review can be puzzling. Furthermore, knowing where the sources can be found is sometimes challenging. What to do with the sources once they are gathered is a common source of trepidation by students. What to do if the research question has already been studied is a common question as well. The next sections clarify these concerns and questions.

What Are the Best Sources?

The best sources of information for constructing an academic literature review are **original sources** or **primary sources**. These primarily come in the form of **peer-reviewed journal articles**.

A peer-reviewed journal article means the research went through a rigorous review process by multiple experts in the field prior to being published in an academic journal. The editor of that journal managed the peer-review process by sending the manuscript (generally with no author-identifying information) to at least three research experts for a review. Each of the three experts scrutinizes the manuscript, and each submits a detailed review of the research making suggestions for improvements. They also provide their assessment of whether the manuscript should be rejected (common), be revised (i.e., the revise and resubmit, aka R&R), or accepted as is for publication (rare). The editor makes the final decision about the manuscript and then informs the original researcher of the decision. If the original author receives an R&R, he or she may revise the manuscript for additional peer review using the same process. Reviews can take months or years, so it is not unusual for a research contribution to take years from beginning to being rejected or, in some cases, published. The peer-review process, while imperfect, seeks to ensure that only the highest quality research contributions are published. In the criminology and criminal justice world, there are many peer-reviewed journals in which you can find valuable empirical research. Some are

> **Empirical peer-reviewed journal articles:** Type of original or primary source that is useful in constructing a literature review. This research is based on systematic observation and has undergone rigorous peer review prior to publication.
>
> **Empirical:** Type of research based on systematic observations, experimentations, or experiences.

American Journal of Criminal Justice

Crime & Delinquency

Criminal Justice and Behavior

Criminal Justice Review

Criminology

Criminology & Public Policy

Feminist Criminology

Homicide Studies

Journal of Contemporary Criminal Justice

Journal of Crime and Justice

Journal of Interpersonal Violence

Journal of Quantitative Criminology

Journal of Research in Crime and Delinquency

Justice Quarterly

Psychology of Violence

Punishment & Society

Sexual Abuse

Violence Against Women

Violence and Victims

A more extensive, but still partial, list of criminal justice and criminology journals can be found on the American Society of Criminology website: https://www.asc41.com/links/journals.html. Although some links on this webpage are chronically broken, it is easy to search on the name of journals of interest to gain access.

There are three common types of primary source journal articles: peer-reviewed empirical research journal articles, theoretical journal articles, and literature review journal articles. In addition, local and federal governmental reports, conference papers, and information from conference presentations are useful sources. The following sections describe several of these sources.

Empirical Peer-Reviewed Journal Articles

Empirical peer-reviewed journal articles are the most commonly used type of primary source used in the construction of literature reviews. **Empirical** indicates that the research was based on systematic observations, experimentation, or experiences. Empirical journal articles are written using a predictable structure (which we describe later in this chapter) in which the author (a) identifies a research question, (b) reviews the relevant literature, (c) describes in detail the methodology used and how the data were collected and analyzed, and (d) presents findings and conclusions.

Theoretical Journal Articles

Also valuable are peer-reviewed **theoretical journal articles.** A theoretical journal article does not present research (i.e., does not pose a research question, gather evidence, analyze it, and offer conclusions), but instead, it evaluates an existing theory, proposes revisions to an existing theory, or forwards a new theory. A theory comprises, most simply, ideas that *explain* something such as offending behavior, recidivism, or victimization. Theories tie together elements or characteristics to suggest how they work together. Depending on the research topic and research question, theoretical sources are important to include in a literature review. If the proposed research seeks to test social bond theory, for example, then the literature review needs to include information about what social bond theory is and how it has been, or how it could be, used to explain the research question posed. Theoretical journal articles can be found in any peer-reviewed journal. In addition, theoretical pieces are published in specialized theoretical journals such as *Feminist Theory* (http://fty.sagepub .com/), which is an international peer-reviewed journal focused on academic analysis and debate within feminism. Like empirical research sources, theoretical journal articles are peer reviewed, meaning they receive the same level of scrutiny during review that an empirical research article does.

Literature Review Journal Articles

Peer-reviewed literature review articles are also excellent primary sources to use when constructing a literature review. A **literature review journal article** presents, organizes, and synthesizes existing understanding about a topic. This is exactly the purpose of the literature review section in a research manuscript. Although literature review articles may appear in any journal, they are more likely to be found in specialized journals such as *Trauma, Violence, & Abuse* (http://tva.sagepub.com/) and *Aggression and Violent Behavior* (http://www.journals .elsevier.com/aggression-and-violent-behavior/). *Trauma, Violence, & Abuse* is a peer-reviewed published quarterly and is devoted to organizing, synthesizing, and expanding knowledge on all forms of trauma, abuse, and violence.

Finding a literature review journal article, especially a contemporary one, on the topic of proposed research offers an invaluable resource for constructing one's own literature review and for understanding the state of the field. Like the other types of primary sources, literature review pieces undergo rigorous peer review and assessment by experts in the field prior to publication.

Government Research and Reports and Policy Briefs

Additional valuable sources to use when writing an academic literature review are government reports and publications and policy briefs. In the world of criminology and criminal justice, this includes reports and documents from the Department of Justice and its many offices (Bureau of Justice Statistics, the FBI, National Institute of Justice, etc.), or private organizations such as RTI, Westat, and policy centers in universities. Many of these documents can be searched for and found at the National Criminal Justice Reference Service (NCJRS; https://www.ncjrs.gov/). Searching using key terms or phrases will identify research that does not appear in journals but is published by governmental statistical agencies. You may also go to a particular agency's website to access additional information. For example, the FBI website offers a section on reports on crime statistics at https://ucr.fbi.gov/. The Bureau of Justice Statistics offers statistics and reports on a broad selection of criminal justice related topics at http://www.bjs.gov/. Additional information about searching on websites is provided in the next section. You should also find out about local criminal justice agencies to ascertain whether their research would be of value to a proposed research project.

Avoiding Predatory Publishers and Predatory Journals

Once upon a time, a researcher could find a peer-reviewed journal article and be assured the research was quality. Unfortunately, the proliferation of predatory publishers and predatory journals muddied that. **Predatory publishers** are illegitimate publishers that take fees from unsuspecting authors. Some characteristics of predatory publishers are that they publish multiple journals, yet the publisher's owner is identified as the editor of every one of these so-called journals. These predatory publishers tend to not have an editorial board, and no academic credentials about the editor are made available. The predatory publishers also report fabricated **impact factors** (which are an indication of the journal's quality). Generally, the mission of the journal is not in alignment with the title of the journal. Jeffrey Beall of the University of Colorado Denver, who has compiled a list of these predatory publishers, estimates that from 2011 to 2017, the number of predatory publishers grew from 11 to 1,155.[1]

Peer-reviewed and published quarterly, journals such as *Trauma, Violence, & Abuse,* and *Aggression and Violent Behavior* are devoted to organizing, synthesizing, and expanding knowledge on all forms of trauma, abuse, and violence.

In addition to the predatory journals published by predatory publishers, standalone **predatory journals** are increasingly problematic. Predatory standalone journals engage in several nontraditional journal behaviors. For example, they charge authors a significant publication fee. Commonly this fee is not disclosed until the end of the process. Predatory journals frequently list real academics as members of editorial board, unbeknownst to those academics. In addition to including real academics without their permission on editorial boards, these predatory journals also include fictitious academics on the board. Like their predatory publishing counterparts, standalone predatory journals report fabricated impact factors and fabricated physical locations.

A troubling aspect of these predatory journals is that they describe themselves as peer reviewed when, in fact, they are not. As a result, articles of questionable value are published under these titles. Consider this peer-reviewed research piece, which had been submitted to the *International Journal of Advanced Computer Technology* (*IJACT*) in 2005. The peer reviewer's report was included along with the letter of acceptance for this work. In the peer-review report, the reviewer noted that the manuscript was "excellent." Authors Mazières and Kohler (2005) of Stanford University must have been surprised at the acceptance of their "research" given the title and complete manuscript was one sentence repeated thousands of times: "Get me off your #ucking mailing list." The authors were asked to submit $150 to the editor after its acceptance for publication. Beall estimates that between 2013 and 2017, predatory standalone journals increased from 126 to 1,294 (see Footnote 1 for source).

When searching for *legitimate* primary sources of information, you must ensure you are not using information from a predatory source. As noted in Footnote 1, until early 2017, one way to ascertain this is to consult a list of predatory publishers and journals created and maintained by Beall. Beall advocates the careful consideration of journals. You must first determine whether this is a trustworthy journal (versus assuming it is). The criteria described earlier offers ways to assess journals. These include asking yourself the following: Can you tell which professional organization is associated with the journal? Can you contact this organization easily if needed? Are the editorial policies and editors legitimate? Do you know any of the editors? Is actual peer review conducted (journals that publish within days of receiving a manuscript do not). Are there surprise publication fees? Is it clear how much publication

Predatory publishers: Illegitimate publishers of predatory journals. In general, elements of the publisher are fabricated (e.g., impact factor scores, editorial boards, journal holdings, peer-review, location of offices and office holders). Predatory publishers are not a source of quality academic information.

Predatory journals: Illegitimate journals that are in business to take fees from unsuspecting authors. In general, elements of the journal are fabricated (e.g., impact factor scores, editorial boards, peer-review, location of offices and office holders). Information taken from predatory journals should not be used in academic literature reviews.

---

[1]During the writing of the book, Beall suspended publication of his lists. This information has been pulled and published elsewhere, however. For instance, a copy can be found at http://beallslist.weebly.com/ .

Impact factors: Scores
assigned to journals
theoretically indicating
the journal's quality. The
higher the score, the
higher the quality.

fees are, if they exist? What is the timeline for publication? If a journal promises publication within days, avoid it. If after checking you find satisfactory answers to these questions, by all means use the article.

Only recently did the U.S. government take action against predatory publishers and journals. In 2016, the Federal Trade Commission (FTC) filed a complaint against the OMICS Groups, Inc., iMedPub, LLC, Conference Series, LLC, and Srinubabu Gedela (U.S. District Court, District of Nevada, 2016). The charges state that these organizations, under the control of their president and director Srinubabu Gedela, have deceived researchers about the predatory nature of the publisher by hiding publication fees ranging from hundreds to thousands of dollars. In addition, the charges allege that Gedela and his organizations falsely claimed the journals used rigorous peer review, had editorial boards of scholars, and advertised false impact factor scores. Researchers were pursued to submit articles, which were accepted days later. At the same time, pay was demanded. Many researchers attempted to withdraw their manuscript from consideration, realizing these publishers and journals were illegitimate. The organizations refused to allow the researchers to withdraw their work and, at times, published them. This is problematic as it is unethical for researchers to submit research to more than one journal at a time. In addition, it is unethical to publish the same research in multiple journal outlets. A researcher can't ethically walk away from predators and submit his or her research to a legitimate publisher once ensnared in their trap. Time will tell the outcome of the FTC complaint, but perhaps it will serve as a warning to predators.

Avoiding predatory sources means you are using quality literature to construct your literature review. Using these sources leads to a weak literature. If your research starts with a weak, wrong, or incomplete literature review, your entire research endeavor is compromised. Your research is only as strong as your weakest part, and you want to avoid the literature review being that weak link.

Inappropriate Sources

Predatory publishers and predatory journals are not the only inappropriate sources for use when constructing a literature review. Another inappropriate source for an academic literature review is Wikipedia. Wikipedia began in 2001 as an online encyclopedia that differed from traditional encyclopedia in that entries are written by a multitude of people. Entries can be updated or altered indefinitely (only some pages in Wikipedia are locked from editing). The open access nature of editing in Wikipedia suggests that the information found there may or may not be correct and that the information is subject to sabotage, and manipulation. In addition, Wikipedia does not report the elements of original research that is needed when writing an academic literature review such as the method, findings, and research questions. Although Wikipedia has several useful purposes, use of the information published there to write an academic research literature review is not one of them. This is not to say that Wikipedia is of no value. At times, a Wikipedia page lists primary source citations for a topic of interest. By using those citations, you can find original sources that are useful in writing a literature review. Taking what a Wikipedia page states about original sources, however, is risky as there is no guarantee that the information is accurate or legitimate.

For the same reasons, various information or summaries presented in textbooks, magazines, blogs, newspapers, other media, and nonacademic sources are not appropriate original primary sources for a literature review. These sources, at best, generally describe or summarize limited information from primary sources. These types of sources do not provide important details such as the methodology, the state of the literature, and the limitations of the research—information required in the construction of a literature review. Furthermore, it is not uncommon that these sources fail to accurately describe research and information from primary sources. Still, like a Wikipedia page, these sources may lead you to a primary source of information that would be useful in constructing a literature review.

Later in this chapter, we use police impersonation as an example of searching for literature while developing a research topic. Why focus on the topic of police impersonation? Media articles, although anecdotal, demonstrate that police impersonation places community members at risk for easy victimization. Police impersonation can affect the public's confidence in law enforcement, particularly if victims believe that an impersonation was a "legitimate" police action undertaken by a corrupt cop. In addition to damaging the public's trust in authority and undermining the reputation of legitimate police officers, impersonators may threaten officers' ability to do their work effectively.

To conduct this exploratory research, Rennison and Dodge (2012) were guided by three purposes:

1. Exploring police impersonation incident characteristics

2. Comparing police impersonation incident characteristics with national violent crime statistics

3. Identifying common themes found among impersonation events

To address these research questions, the researchers gathered 56 police case files originating from three metropolitan areas in the United States. To gather the data, the researchers relied on personal connections within agencies that expressed a willingness to provide data. Participating agencies were assured that identifying information about the departments and incidents would remain confidential. The impersonation events occurred from May 2002 to February 2010. The 56 incident files provide information on 63 offenders and 71 victims. A total of 45 case files were used in the qualitative analysis and include the initial police report complete with details about the incident, suspect(s), and victim(s).

To analyze the data, multiple approaches were used. First, the incident, offender, and victim characteristics were described using descriptive statistics. Second, these impersonation statistics are compared with statistics based on overall violent crimes (i.e., attempted and completed rape/sexual assault, robbery, aggravated assault, and simple assault) from 2002 to 2009 NCVS data restricted to crimes reported to the police only. Third, the 45 case narratives are aggregated and analyzed for major themes and content phrases. These qualitative data were first analyzed for general statements among categories of analogous events and then grouped into conceptual domains. Selected quotes representative of the major themes are presented as examples. The objective of the qualitative analysis is to provide a descriptive, in-depth narrative that assists in establishing a framework for future inductive, grounded theory development.

With regard to the first research purpose, the findings showed police impersonation incidents most often involve one victim, one offender, no witnesses, no weapon, and no injury to the victim. Although impersonation incidents occur most commonly on a highway/roadway/alley, about one fifth take place in/near the residence/home of the victim. Most of the 63 police impersonators in the sample were male, White non-Hispanic, and 31 years of age. Of the 71 victims of police impersonation, the findings show that victims are about equally split between males and females, about equally split between Hispanics and non-Hispanics, primarily White, strangers to the offenders, and about 31 years of age.

To address the second research question, comparisons were made with overall reported violence in the United States. The findings show that police impersonation incidents are more likely to involve one offender, be committed with no witnesses, and be less likely to involve an injured victim than overall violence. Impersonation events were equally likely to involve an armed offender as overall violent victimizations. Police impersonators are far more likely to be White and older than are general violent offenders from incidents reported to the police. Although overall violence and impersonation victims are similar in many ways, a major difference

(Continued)

(Continued)

was found when comparing the Hispanic origin of impersonation victims with overall violent crime victims. About half of all impersonation victims are Hispanic, compared with only about one in ten of overall reported violent crime victims.

The qualitative content analysis focused on the third research question that police impersonators are engaging in three primary activities: vehicle pull-overs, knock and talks, and harassment. The most typical impersonator incident involves an offender driving an unmarked car who uses a spotlight or red and blue flashing lights for a pull-over. A total of 13% of the cases involved knock and talk impersonations. The cases generally are motivated by attempts to gain entrance into a home for a variety of reasons. In about three in ten cases, the impersonators are seeking information or engaging in harassment. In these cases, the impersonators call the victim, identify themselves as an officer or a detective, and give a fake badge number to gain information. One collection agent, for example, claimed to be a detective and threatened to arrest the victim, who was behind on her car payments.

What sort of policy implications come from this work? First, the findings indicate that police impersonators may be easily deterred. In vehicle pull-over cases, most impersonators fled when the targeted victim was on the phone with 911 verifying the legitimacy of the stop. Additionally, potential victims who questioned the legitimacy of the stop and challenged the fake officer tended to avoid further victimization. Second, the findings indicated the need to better educate the public (as well as officers) that the practice of confirming that they are being pulled over by a legitimate officer is a reasonable action. Third, the role of fear of terrorism and out-groups or vulnerable populations in the public plays into the hands of impersonators. Particularly interesting are the disproportionate number of Hispanics victims in the sample. These findings are similar to existing historical research on impersonation against a vulnerable population. Previous research shows that in general Hispanics are less likely to contact the police compared with non-Hispanic Whites. The findings indicate that, in some areas at least, Hispanics are being targeted.

Rennison, C. M., & Dodge, M. J. (2012). Police impersonation: Pretenses and predators. *American Journal of Criminal Justice, 37,* 505–522.

Finding Primary or Original Sources

With an understanding about what is and is not an appropriate source of information, the next step in writing a literature review is to find the original sources. The best way to go about finding primary or original sources is using electronic search tools available at most libraries. With advances in technology, most anyone can access a library with excellent search capabilities whether in person or online. Given variability in tools available in libraries, it is not possible to describe the steps in accessing sources for every library. Therefore, it is strongly recommended that you get a tour of your library, including how to access and operate electronic search tools. In general, librarians are happy to demonstrate how to use their electronic search tools to conduct research. What follows are general steps taken to find these sources.

Develop Search Terms

1. Develop Search Terms

The first step in searching for primary sources is to identify some search terms. After spending considerable time in the previous chapter developing a research topic and research question, deciding on search terms should be easy: They are the topic of research. By way of example, let's consider a real example encountered when conducting research on police impersonation. The topic of the research is "police impersonation," which suggests that a reasonable starting point is to use two search terms in the initial search: *police* and *impersonation*. Conducting this search requires accessing the library's online search tool. The library's home page offers a place to input terms for a search. Typing in the two terms *police* and *impersonation* results in 58,427 sources. Reading or even skimming this many sources is unreasonable; therefore, you need a more refined or limited search. This initial search highlights an important strategy when searching for sources: Start with the narrowest search possible. Clearly a narrower search is needed in this example. Aside from using different terms, there are tools available that can assist.

Search Using Boolean Operators and Filters

2. Search using terms, Boolean operators, and filters; iterative process

There are two useful tools available to narrow (or broaden if needed) a search. The first tool involves Boolean operators, and the second involves filters. **Boolean operators** are used to connect or to exclude particular search terms or phrases. A **term** refers to a single word, whereas a **phrase** refers to a series of terms. For example, *police* and *impersonation* are terms, whereas "police impersonation" is a phrase. To identify a phrase, use quotation marks around the terms.

There are three frequently used Boolean operators: "and," "or," and "not." Using "and" to separate terms in a search will produce results for sources in which all of the search terms (police, impersonation) are present. In many search engines, the word "and" is implied when you enter terms. In other words, searching on "police and impersonation" is the same as searching on "police impersonation." Use the Boolean operator "or" to generate results containing at least one of the search terms or phrases. You would use the Boolean operator "not" when you do not want the results to contain the specified term.

Table 3.1 presents an assortment of searches for police impersonation sources using a variety of terms, phrases, Boolean operators, and quotation marks. Results shown in Table 3.1 make clear the importance of wisely choosing the Boolean operators and quotation marks. The results also demonstrate the iterative nature of searching for sources.

In the examples shown in Table 3.1, the searches did not deviate from using the terms *police* and *impersonation*. What did vary was the use of Boolean operators. It is important to keep an open mind about search terms. This raises a second important strategy, which is to use other related phrases or terms to generate additional potential sources. For example, and as shown in Table 3.2, when searching using the phrase "impersonation of police," 118 results for sources are identified. Not surprisingly, removing the quotations and searching on the three terms *impersonation of police* results in 58,426 results—an unwieldly and unworkable number.

Another tip in conducting a search is to consider literature in other fields. Just because an existing piece of research is not found in a criminal justice or criminology journal does not mean it is not useful. As Brunson notes, "searching for studies across disciplines can lead to useful research results. Do not be overly rigid in a search." In addition, if you are interested in a theoretical article or a review on a topic, include the term "theory" or "review" in the search. Searching is an iterative process so do not expect to search once and be finished. The goal is to find a workable number of relevant sources that represents the topic of interest. This takes some time and multiple attempts.

The second useful tool used to narrow an electronic search are filters. **Filters** place restrictions on the search. A search engine may not use the term *filter*, so look for a filtering process identified as "refine your search" or similar language. In general, there are many filters or refinements that can be made to a search. You can restrict the search in terms of type of media (journals, books, etc.), publication date, discipline (e.g., film, history, literature, etc.), language, and others. Most useful are filters for the type of source and dates of publication. Recall that an academic literature review should include primary sources, including empirical peer-reviewed journal articles, theoretical pieces, and literature reviews published as journal

Boolean operators: Connect or exclude particular search terms or phrases used in an electronic search. Use of Boolean operators enables the searcher to narrow or broaden a search for material.

Term: Single word used in an electronic search.

Phrase: Particular series of terms or words. Phrases used in electronic searches are identified using quotation marks.

Filters: Used in electronic searches to place restrictions on or refine a search. Common filters used are on the type of source needed (e.g., journal articles) and date range of publication (e.g., last five years).

Table 3.1 Search Results: Variety of Terms, Phrases, Boolean Operators, and Quotation Marks

Search Terms/Phrases	Number of Hits	What It Searched
Police impersonation	58,427	Sources with the terms "police" and "impersonation" in them.
"police" "impersonation"	58,427	Identical to the prior search
"police impersonation"	692	Sources with the phrase "police impersonation"
Police and impersonation	58,425	Sources with the terms "police" and "impersonation" in them.
"police" and "impersonation"	58,425	Identical to the prior search
"police and impersonation"	5	Sources with the phrase "police and impersonation."
Police or impersonation	58,340	Sources with at least the term "police" or "impersonation" in them.
"police" or "impersonation"	58,340	Identical to the prior search
"police or impersonation"	0	Sources with the phrase "police or impersonation."

Table 3.2 Search Results: Impersonation of Police

Search Terms/Phrases	Number of Hits	What It Searched
"impersonation of police"	118	Sources with the phrase "impersonation of police."
Impersonation of police	58,426	Sources with the terms "impersonation," "of," and "police."

articles. Electronic search engines in most libraries allow you to filter the search based on the type of source and journal article. Table 3.3 shows how the search results change when the police impersonation search is restricted only to journal article sources.

A rule of thumb when gathering sources for a literature review is to focus on contemporary sources. Contemporary sources are considered to be sources published in the previous five to seven years. Most library search engines allow a person to filter using publication dates. What if the police impersonation search was restricted to journal articles no more than seven years of age? Table 3.3 presents these search results. Filtering using dates can be a valuable approach in many instances, but you must consider the purpose of their literature review when using them. In some cases, a literature review may cover the topic of interest in a chronological or historical fashion. This type of literature review would suffer from using a filter based on publication date because foundational or classic research, which is older, will be missed. In addition, if you wish to review the theoretical underpinnings of a particular topic, it would not be wise to restrict the search to contemporary work only because the classic theoretical work probably occurred decades before.

The final search of police impersonation shown in Table 3.3 identified seven sources. Are these too few sources? To make that decision, you must read the titles of the identified sources to determine whether the sources are useful for examining, describing, and

Table 3.3	Restricting Search to Journal Articles Published in Last Seven Years	
Search Terms/Phrases	**Number of Hits**	**What It Searched**
Police impersonation	438	Journal articles published in the last seven years with the terms "police" and "impersonation."
"police impersonation"	7	Journal articles published in the last seven years with the phrase "police impersonation."

understanding police impersonation. Only two of the seven titles appear to focus on police impersonation research. Does this indicate there is little research on police impersonation, or does this indicate that a broader search is needed? To be sure, it is prudent to broaden the search.

One way to broaden this search is to focus on "impersonation," namely, by removing the focus on "police" to ascertain if additional results appear. A search of journal article sources that focused on impersonation and that were published in the last seven years results in 3,609 results. A quick examination of these titles indicates that many of the sources focus on biometric impersonation, female impersonation, online impersonation, and visual impersonation, not on police impersonation. You can even find information about Elvis impersonators! Given this information, you may conclude that there is little research available on police impersonation, and you may proceed with relevant sources already identified. In fact, this is exactly what happened when Callie Rennison and Mary Dodge (2012) conducted a literature review on police impersonation (although at that time, the only relevant source was a somewhat related master's thesis). It was also Dodge's experience when she conducted a literature review for her women decoy prostitution research (Dodge, Starr-Gimeno, & Williams, 2005). There was no existing literature examining it. All Dodge could find in the literature were related pieces that provided only speculation about women's views in these roles. As Dodge, who is also one of our featured researchers, notes that, if after searching thoroughly, you find little or no existing literature, "move forward with your research and the satisfaction that you were the first to think about the topic. This means you have a research imagination that allows you to come up with something different." Dodge's research was path-breaking in that way.

Saturation: Has several related meanings, one of which involves searching for sources for a literature review. In particular, it indicates the search for sources is complete because one finds no new information on a topic and the same studies and authors repeatedly are discussed.

Identify Initial Primary Sources

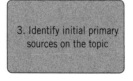

3. Identify initial primary sources on the topic

Using the search strategies described earlier should result in a list of initial primary sources on the topic of interest. At this point, you need to go through that list to determine which sources are irrelevant and should be discarded, and which will be used to write the literature review. The initial way to do this is to examine the title and abstract of each source.

A common question is as follows: "When do I know when to stop looking for sources?" Recall that the purpose of the review is to give a complete overview of the topic. **Saturation** is a term that has many related meanings, one of which is used by several of our highlighted researchers to indicate the search for sources is complete. Dodge states that it is time to stop searching for literature review sources when she "sees the same citations repeatedly. There is a point where it seems clear you've found it all–given ease of electronic data bases–you reach some type of information saturation." Brunson also noted, "When a person comes across the same authors, and same studies cited in numerous journal articles, saturation is reached and the

Abstract: First section of a journal article that provides, in a concise paragraph of approximately 150 to 250 words, the purpose, method, findings, and conclusions of the research.

search can be concluded." A frequent question is as follows: "How many sources does it take to accomplish that?" Santos notes, depending on the purpose of the review, "12 to 15 sources are minimum, but that it is more about the quality of the sources, not the quantity. In general, more recent research is better (last 5 years), but be aware that the first things that come up in a search is not necessarily the best research." What kinds of sources does it take to reach saturation? Heather Zaykowski finds that a literature review is complete when she reaches a "saturation in that the search is not revealing anything drastically new. She finds this occurs often when she has a mix of the 'classic' studies, and those that seem to have the biggest impact on the field (oftentimes understood by the number of citations, but not necessarily so), and current research (past five years)." Zaykowski's (2014) literature review provided a lot of relevant research but little on male victims who seek services, and little on female victims of nonsexual and nonrelational violence.

Cuevas knows it is time to stop searching for sources when he feels he has the material needed and can "make the argument for conducting the research nicely. Once there, I stop. I also ask, given the information in these sources, can I make an argument that the average person on the street can read and understand where I am going and why? If so, I have the sources needed." This was the case for his work on Latino teen dating. Although no one had been able to do the research Cuevas and his team did (Sabina, Cuevas, & Cotignola-Pickens, 2016), there was a rich literature focused on teen dating violence to inform his work. Being able to work with a manageable amount of literature requires the strategy used by Cuevas.

Read Abstracts to Narrow the List of Sources

4. Read abstracts (and possibly additional sections of the article) to narrow sources if needed

What do you do if you have refined a search to be as narrow as possible, yet you are still presented with a large number of potential sources (e.g., 692 sources)? This requires the use of an additional strategy to narrow the list of sources: Read the abstracts of each potential source. An **abstract** provides, in one concise paragraph (e.g., 150–250 words), the purpose, method, findings, and conclusions of the research. Abstracts should be visible online using the library search software. If after consulting the abstract it is clear the article is not one that should be used, remove it from the list of those saved for the literature review. If you cannot ascertain the article's relevance from the abstract, then consulting other parts of the complete journal article should make its value clear. The next section discusses the anatomy of an empirical journal article, which should allow for an efficient search of the article to aid in the selection of the final list of articles for the literature review.

The Anatomy of an Empirical Research Article

Those new to research frequently find it impossible to read and comprehend all of the primary sources gathered from a search. Fortunately, reading every word of every primary source is not necessary. As Dodge notes, a key to a successful literature review is "not to get caught up in the minutiae of each piece of research, especially the more sophisticated studies. You do not need to read every word of the journal article, rather, you need to see the big picture of what was done and how it relates to the proposed research." Zaykowski offers similar advice: "It is not always important to include minute details of each study. Instead think about the broader general takeaways, and provide one or two examples to support those takeaways."

With an understanding of the anatomy of an empirical research journal article, you can skillfully find key information about the research that will be used to (a) decide to keep or remove an article from consideration and (b) pull key information needed to write the literature review (described in a later step). Empirical research journal articles have a predictable structure. Understanding what type of information is found in each section assists in a more efficient consideration of each piece.

Journal articles begin with an abstract, which is commonly block justified so that it stands apart from the text in the journal article. The abstract provides a concise description of the research. In terms of being useful in constructing a literature review, the abstract should help you decide whether that primary source is relevant for the proposed literature review. Note the information conveyed in Dodge and colleagues' 164-word abstract describing the female police decoy research (Dodge et al., 2005). Reading Dodge's abstract is quick, easy, and gives a good idea about the topic and purpose of the research.

Abstract—Dodge et al. (2005)

Reverse police prostitution stings, which target men by using female police officers as decoy prostitutes, are becoming a common method in some United States cities for controlling the problem of solicitation for prostitution. The role of policewomen as decoys has received scant attention by scholars, though critics and traditional feminists view the practice as further evidence of the subjection and degradation of women in law enforcement. This article presents participant field observations of how reverse prostitution operations are conducted in Aurora, Colorado Springs, and Denver, Colorado, and qualitative interview data from 25 female police officers who discuss their experiences as prostitution decoys. The findings indicate that female officers view the decoy role as an exciting opportunity for undercover work, despite the negative connotations of acting like a whore. According to the officers who work as decoys, it adds excitement and variety and offers potential for other opportunities for advancement within the police department in contrast to the mundane duties often associated with patrol. (p. 71)

A second example of an abstract is found in Cuevas and colleagues' research on Latino teen dating (Sabina et al., 2016). Note the tremendous amount of information packed into the 155-word abstract.

Abstract—Cuevas and Colleagues (Sabina et al., 2016)

This study uses data from two waves of the Dating Violence Among Latino Adolescents (DAVILA) study and focuses on the 1) rates of dating violence victimization by gender, 2) risk of experiencing dating violence victimization over time, 3) association of dating violence victimization with other forms of victimization, and 4) association of immigrant status, acculturation, and familial support with dating violence victimization over time. A total of 547 Latino adolescents, from across the USA, aged 12-18 at Wave 1 participated in both waves of the study. Rates of dating violence were around 19% across waves. Dating violence at Wave 1 and non-dating violence victimization were associated with an elevated risk of dating violence during Wave 2. Cultural factors did not distinguish between dating violence trajectories, except for immigrant status and familial support being associated with no dating violence victimization. Overall, dating violence affects a large number of Latino teens and tends to continue over time. (p. 5)

Brunson's abstract is also clear, easy to read (Brunson & Weitzer, 2009).

Abstract—Brunson and Weitzer (2009)

Much of the research on police–citizen relations has focused on adults, not youth. Given that adolescents and particularly young males are more likely than adults to have involuntary and adversarial contacts with police officers, it is especially important to investigate their experiences with and perceptions of the police. This article examines the accounts of young Black and White males who reside in one of three disadvantaged St. Louis, Missouri, neighborhoods—one predominantly Black, one predominantly White, and the other racially mixed. In-depth interviews were conducted with the youths, and the authors' analysis centers on the ways in which both race and neighborhood context influence young males' orientations toward the police. (p. 858)

Key words: Major concepts of greatest importance found in a journal article. They are generally found on the first page of the article.

Introduction section of a journal article: First section of the text (after the abstract) that identifies the purpose of the research and why it is important.

In some cases, an abstract does not offer enough information to allow a decision to keep or discard the source. In those situations, you should consult other parts of, or sections of, the journal article. One place to consider is the list of key words. **Key words** are generally found on the first page of the journal article, frequently following the abstract. These are words designated by the author(s) that identify the main concepts of greatest significance in the publication. Reviewing them may offer information about whether the article will be useful in the writing of a literature review. Other more formal sections of journal articles are described next.

The **introduction section of a journal article** is the first "normal" body of text (i.e., not block justified). The introduction is generally not labeled as the "introduction," but instead usually the title of the paper appears at the top of that page. In terms of being useful in constructing a literature review, an examination of the introduction section provides information about the purpose or goal of the research, why it is important to study, and how it adds to the literature. This information should be useful in ascertaining whether the article will be useful in writing your literature review. In some cases, such as in Brunson's research (Brunson & Weitzer, 2009), a separate introduction section was not provided. Rather, the introduction blends with the review of the literature (see the next section).

Consider this text taken from the introduction section of the Santos' research on offender-focused police intervention (Santos & Santos, 2016). Reading just the first three paragraphs of the six paragraph introduction offers enough information about the research that you should be able to identify if this would be useful as a primary source in your proposed literature review.

Santos and Santos (2016) Introduction— Offender-Focused Police Intervention

Classical criminological research shows that a small number of offenders account for a disproportionate amount of crime (Blumstein et al., 1986). In recent years, police agencies and researchers have sought to develop data-driven methods to identify chronic offenders so that police can implement offender-focused strategies as one of the effective ways to reduce crime (Bureau of Justice Assistance, 2012; Jennings, 2006; Ratcliffe, 2008; Schaible & Sheffield, 2012; Telep & Weisburd, 2012). Simultaneously, criminologists have concluded that crime reduction strategies that focus on "place" are more effective than those that focus on people (Telep & Weisburd, 2012; Weisburd, 2015).

Nonetheless, criminology of place research consistently shows that offending is "tightly coupled" to place (Weisburd et al., 2012). Offenders commit crimes relatively close to where they live, and the farther offenders travel from where they live, the less likely they will commit crime (Bernasco & Block, 2009; Bernasco & Nieuwbeerta, 2005; Hesseling, 1992; Rossmo, 2000). Yet, there are currently few studies that rigorously examine the effectiveness of offender-focused strategies implemented by police in crime hot spots (Groff et al., 2015).

Consequently, this study is an effort to contribute to both offender-focused and place-based research by testing a prevention-oriented, offender-focused intervention while also accounting for place. The premise tested here is that if the offender-focused intervention is implemented for multiple offenders of a particular crime type living in a long-term hot spot of that crime type, there will be a reduction of that crime in the hot spot since the offenders are likely committing some of their crimes near where they live. (pp. 373–374)

The third section in an empirical research journal article is the literature review. The purpose of the literature review is to outline the state of the knowledge related to a topic at the time the piece was published. This section of the paper, although very important, does not offer much in terms of deciding whether it should or should not be used in constructing your literature review. Should a source be selected, however, the literature review is vital in that it describes valuable research that may inform your literature review.

The next section in an empirical research paper is the **method** section. This section outlines in detail the approach and strategies taken to answer the research question. This includes information on the source of the gathered data (e.g., sample), the approach taken to gather the data (e.g., survey, observations, and interviews), and the organizational and analytic techniques used to analyze these data. This section is of limited value for ascertaining whether the journal article is valuable for the construction of the proposed literature review unless the methodology used in the study is specifically related to your particular research question.

A **findings** section follows the method section and presents results from the data analysis. In this section, the findings and only the findings are offered. These results are used to answer the research question or questions. This section is of limited value for determining whether the source should be used to write your literature review. This section is of great value, however, if this piece is selected for your literature review.

A **discussion** section follows the findings section and places the findings into the context of the existing literature. In this section, the author discusses whether his or her results support the literature or deviate from it. The discussion generally avoids presenting statistics or findings such as themes or core meanings. Instead, it focuses on *interpreting* the findings presented. It points out limitations of the research, gaps that remain, and offers directions for future research. The findings section may be useful in determining whether this source is one that should be used to inform the proposed literature review. The discussion section definitely has important information should the source be used.

Sometimes there is a standalone **conclusions** section in a journal article. In others, it is combined with the discussion section. Conclusions sections are generally short and briefly summarize the overall conclusions of the research, including why the findings are important. In general, and to help readers better understand the key points of the article, it presents information found elsewhere in the article.

All peer-reviewed journal articles conclude with a list of **references.** In the reference section, every source cited in the body of the paper is listed with information needed to find and access that source. The references section is not useful in terms of deciding to keep or reject a primary source for use in a proposed literature review. In contrast, should you decide to use the article in constructing your literature review, the references offer valuable information about potential additional sources.

Throughout a journal article, including the reference section, the authors will adhere to a specific writing-style guideline. A commonly used style guideline in the criminal justice and criminology literature is APA. APA, an acronym for the American Psychological Association style, was created almost a century ago to standardize scientific writing in an effort to facilitate reading comprehension. APA presents guidelines and rules that dictate every element of a paper. With respect to the referencing, it includes how citations are handled both in text and in the references section, the required sections in a paper, heading formats, and punctuation. Without APA and other styles (e.g., MLA and *Chicago Manual of Style*), finding key information in scientific journal articles would be far more challenging. The sections described earlier are based on APA style. Please note that articles using a different style may deviate from this in some ways. You can buy a book on APA (2010), or you may access that information online at websites such as Purdue University's Online Writing Lab (OWL): https://owl.english.purdue .edu/owl/resource/560/01/. Style guidelines change on occasion, so you must ensure you are using the required edition, or at least the most current version. Once you have reviewed the abstracts (and possibly additional sections) of a journal article, what remains is a list of sources that will be used to construct the literature review. The next sections address how to take the sources, glean relevant information, summarize that information, and construct the literature review.

Method: Sections in journal articles that outline in detail the approach taken to answer the research question.

Findings: Section that reports the findings of a piece of research. In this section, the research questions are answered.

Discussion: Section found near the end of a journal article that follows the findings section. Discussion sections are used to discuss the findings and to place them into the context of the existing literature.

Conclusions: Found at the end of journal articles and are generally short sections that briefly summarize the overall conclusions of the research, and why the findings are important. In many cases, the discussion and conclusion sections are combined.

Reference: Section in journal article offers the full citation information for every source cited in the body of a journal article.

Writing the Literature Review

Using your final list of primary sources and your understanding of the anatomy of an empirical journal article makes you ready to summarize each primary source. The next sections describe strategies for doing so.

Summarize Each Original Source

> 5. Summarize in paragraph form important information from each source; include citations

A key step in constructing a literature review is to summarize each primary source in paragraph form using complete sentences. The summary should include several pieces of information. Many of those elements are listed here along with the likely location of this information in the original source:

- What is the article's full citation? This is found on the first page. The full citation should include author names, the year the piece was published, the title of the article, journal name and volume, and the page numbers where it appears.

- What is the purpose of the article? What is the research question? This information should be located in several places in the paper including the abstract, the introduction, and the conclusion sections.

- Why is the research important? What gaps are being addressed with this research? This information is commonly located in multiple locations such as the abstract, the introduction, and the conclusion sections.

- What is the theory used/tested (if any)? Not all research tests theory or is guided by theory. If the research in the source is guided by theory, then information about it should be mentioned in the abstract and introduction. In addition, some articles will have a standalone theory section.

- What sample was used? How was the sample obtained? How large is the sample? What are characteristics of the sample? Some of this information may be mentioned in the abstract, but a full accounting of the sample should be in the method section. In some cases, this information will be located in a subsection called "Sample" in the method section.

- How were data gathered? What years do the data cover? This information should be available in the method section.

- What are key definitions used? Although some key definitions may be offered in the introduction, all definitions should be described in the method section. In many cases, you will find a subsection labeled "Measures" in the method section that identifies definitions and measurement of key concepts. Identifying definitions in each piece is important because standardized definitions are not common across studies.

- What type of analytic technique was used? The analytic technique used to analyze the data may be mentioned briefly in the abstract. A full accounting of it will be found in the method section. In some cases, the Method section will have a subsection called "Analytic Technique" where this information is described.

- What are the findings? What was concluded from the data analysis? Findings and results are located in the Findings (also called "Results") section. The overall outcome may also be mentioned in the abstract as well as the discussion and possibly conclusion section.

- What additional key themes emerged? Did findings support extant literature? Did findings fail to support extant literature? Are particular characteristics important to consider (e.g., race or gender)? Answers to these questions should be located in the discussion section. In addition, you may identify themes that are not described in the article.

APA, an acronym for the American Psychological Association style, was created almost a century ago to standardize scientific writing in an effort to facilitate reading comprehension.

By using these questions as a guide, you can write a summary paragraph for each source. It is strongly recommended that the summary be written using complete sentences in paragraph form and that each sentence conclude with an in-text citation. (Consult APA or the style guide required to see how to construct in-text citations, or check out Purdue's OWL at https://owl.english.purdue.edu/owl/resource/560/02/ or https://owl.english.purdue.edu/owl/resource/560/03/). It is important to include the citation at the end of *each* sentence because later the sentences in the paragraphs will be disaggregated. Having the citation attached to each sentence means you will not have to try to figure out which article a statement came from later. Also, if you are pulling verbatim text from a primary source, it is *required* that quotation marks be placed around the copied text to indicate the statement is a direct quote. A direct quote will also require the page number(s) with the in-text citation or the paragraph number if it is an unpaginated source, such as a government brief. Failure to include page/paragraph numbers at this point would require revisiting the journal article or report to find where the quote is found. This is really time-consuming and tedious. In fact, there is strong reason to include page/paragraph numbers for each sentence in the paragraph. Although these page/paragraph numbers may be removed in the final version of the literature review, having them present will make referring back to the original piece for additional information or clarification easier if needed.

By using this strategy, summaries of two of our featured researchers' studies are presented: Heather Zaykowski's (2014) research on mobilizing victim services and Chris Melde and colleagues' (Melde, Taylor, & Esbensen, 2009) study on teen gang members. You should be able to identify the location in the original sources of each piece of information in the summaries. As a novice researcher, you may find some of the summarized elements such as sample type and analytic techniques unfamiliar. That is to be expected at this stage, but students are encouraged to summarize these elements as best as possible. Later portions of the text, additional courses, and greater familiarity with original sources will better familiarize students with these elements.

With these examples, how to summarize a primary source peer-reviewed journal article should be clearer. With some practice, and greater familiarity with the anatomy of journal articles, summarizing becomes faster and easier. Although summarizing may become faster and easier, it is important to *focus* on the material. Having a deeper understanding of the sources—versus simply copying and pasting sentences from the articles to a word processing program—will pay dividends later when you need to identify themes and synthesize all of the material.

Example Summary of Zaykowski (2014)

While the number of victim services have increased over time, victim use of these services remain poor (Zaykowski, 2014, p. 365). The purpose of this research is to examine variation in use of victim services by violent crime victims and to ascertain the effect of victim and incident characteristics, particularly the role of reporting on the police to seeking victim assistance (Zaykowski, 2014, p. 365). This research adds to the literature in two ways. First, unlike existing literature that has used small nongeneralizable samples, this research uses a national generalizable sample. Second, although extant research focuses on female victims, the present research will consider male victims and victim service access (Zaykowski, 2014, p. 365). This research does not test theory (no citation, just observation). The research used 2008–2011 NCVS data and was restricted to violent victimizations (as property crime victims were not asked about victim services; Zaykowski, 2014, p. 366). The final sample size was 4,746 violent victimizations (Zaykowski, 2014, p. 366). Help-seeking was ascertained based on respondent self-identification when asked, "Did you receive any help or advice from any office or agency–other than the police–that deals with victims of crime?" (Zaykowski, 2014, p. 367). Results include descriptives (means, standard deviations, and percentages) to describe the sample, as well as output from multivariate logistic regression (Zaykowski, 2014, p. 367). The findings show that victim services utilization differ across a broad variety of victim and incident characteristics including sex, race/Hispanic origin, marital status, bystander presence, and whether the violence was reported to the police (Zaykowski, 2014, p. 366). The results also indicate that victim service usage was more likely among sexual assault victims, females, and violence reported to the police (among others; Zaykowski, 2014, p. 367). In conclusion, Zaykowski (2014, pp. 367–368) finds that victims of intimate partner violence and family violence benefited the most from victim services.

Example Summary of Melde, Taylor, and Esbensen (2009)

"I got your back": An examination of the protective function of gang membership in adolescence. *Criminology, 47*(2) 565–594.

The purpose of this research is to better understand a contradiction in the literature (Melde et al., 2009, p. 566). On the one hand, research shows that youth gang membership and violent victimization are related (Melde et al., 2009, p. 566). On the other hand, gang members report joining gangs because they report that being a gang member reduces risk of violent victimization by others (including other gang members; Melde et al., 2009, p. 566). The research is guided by three research questions: "1) What is the effect of gang membership on self-reported victimization? 2) What is the effect of gang membership on perceptions of victimization risk? and 3) What is the effect of gang membership on fear of victimization?" (Melde et al., 2009 p. 566). This research increases our understanding of the "gang membership-victimization literature by incorporating subjective concepts of fear and perceived risk of victimization with traditional self-report measures of actual victimization" (Melde et al., 2009, p. 573). The authors are not testing a theory in this research (no cite—observation not discussed in the article). To investigate these research questions, Melde and colleagues (2009) used data from surveys administered to a nonrepresentative sample of 1,450 students in 15 schools in 2004–2005 (Melde et al., 2009, pp. 573–575). Gang membership was determined based on self-report of the student to the question: "Do you consider your group of friend to be a gang?" (Melde et al., 2009, p. 575). Students responding "yes" were coded as gang members (Melde et al., 2009, p. 575). The authors analyzed the data using basic descriptives to describe the sample (e.g., percentages, means, and standard deviations), and binomial and ordinary least-squares (OLS) regression analyses to address the three research questions (Melde et al., 2009, pp. 579–582). The findings indicate that when controlling for other factors, the effect of gang membership on victimization during the last three months was significantly increased for males, compared with for females (Melde et al., 2009, pp. 582–583). Nevertheless, the findings also show that gang-involved males do not perceive that they have a higher risk of victimization compared with females (Melde et al., 2009, p. 583). Furthermore, the results indicate that gang-involved males have a greater decline in fear of victimization than do females over time (Melde et al., 2009, p. 584). These results are consistent with prior literature, although prior literature relied on cross-sectional data versus the panel data used here (Melde et al., 2009, p. 584). Even though the findings are not generalizable, Melde and colleagues conclude that gang members provide youth with peace of mind and reducing their fear of violence, even if the reality is that victimization risk increases (Melde et al., 2009, p. 588).

Someone Has Already Focused on My Topic!

At times, while summarizing primary sources, you will discover that others have already addressed your topic and research question. Maybe even multiple parties have done so. Do not despair. As Zaykowski notes, a "literature review shapes the research question. If you have a research question in mind, then reading through the literature may indicate the need to revise the question." This is just part of the continuous circling back that research entails. It is also an example of a bump in the road that must be dealt with. Research is not purely linear, and bumps in the road are common.

How can reviewing the literature aid in refining a research question? First, reading about existing studies focused on the same research question should reveal gaps in our understanding that require additional attention. Perhaps the research question has been considered broadly but not for women, juveniles, Latinos, the poor, or single individuals. Second, understanding the details about the methodology used in prior work may indicate an opportunity to revisit the topic using improved or an alternative methodology. For example, someone may have studied a topic using a small, local sample, which means the findings may not accurately describe a larger population. It may be that the same research question can be addressed using a large national survey that has recently become available. Third, a review of the literature on a particular topic may reveal that our existing understanding about the topic is dated. This may indicate that a new examination of this old question can increase our current understanding of the topic. A new study focused on the same question may be possible using newer or improved data. Or the new study may take place in a different context than the extant work (e.g., following a major policy change such as the legalization of marijuana in several states). In addition, existing work may have used simplistic analytic approaches because greater computing power was not available at the time of the original research. It may be that reexamining this research question using more powerful analytic software available today will lead to an enhanced understanding of the issue. In short, if your topic has been studied, look for gaps in our understanding or ways that the work can be improved.

Thematically constructed literature review: Review focused on the ideas found in the literature, not on the particular articles or authors.

Create a Summary Table

> 6. Create a thematically focused table of summarized information

At this point, all primary sources have been summarized individually. Many new researchers make the terrible mistake of stringing their summary paragraphs together and calling it a literature review. Simply stringing the summaries together does not make an appropriate literature review. Aside from this style of literature review being absolutely *brutal* to read, others cannot easily identify the major themes, gaps in the literature, agreement and disagreement in the literature, and other important information. This type of literature review doesn't provide any of the critical information. Identifying this information requires a thematically focused *synthesis* of the material, not an individual-source/author focus. It is worth repeating that stringing together summaries is *not* a literature review. Don't do it!

The need for a **thematically constructed literature review** cannot be overstated. Cuevas makes the point elegantly with his advice about how to write an excellent literature review: "Try to paint a picture, try to tell the story, and make an argument, for why you are conducting the research. Think about the literature review as putting forth the idea. Get less hung up on who wrote what, and talk about the ideas and concepts. The point is more about the ideas and less about who did what." Keeping this in mind during the next steps will assist in constructing an excellent review. The next step toward that is creating a thematically focused table.

Making a summary table requires a researcher to move the sentences in each summary into a thematically focused structure. This is easily accomplished using a table with thematically labeled columns. The columns should correspond to the questions used in creating the individual summaries. For instance, the first column should focus on the purpose of the research. The second column should focus on the research question. The rows should also be labeled. The first row should be titled "main point" or "main statement." Each row after that should be labeled using the full citation for each original source used.

Next, you should copy and paste each sentence from each summary into the appropriate box. In other words, the column labeled "purpose" should include the copy-and-pasted (from the summaries written) purpose of each original source in that column. The column labeled "research question" should include the copy-and-pasted research question from each source in that column. An example of the structure of a summary is shown in Table 3.4.

The next task is to fill in the row of Table 3.4 labeled "main point/statement." To identify what the main point for each column/theme is, you must study and think about the information presented in that column. If you have to summarize in one or two sentences the nature of research about that theme, what would it be? These main point/statements are your own words. They can't be found in any other source.

For example, does the research question focus on the total population in each study neglecting a relevant subpopulation? A main point might be "Extant research has identified much about the relationship between X and Y, however, without exception, this research has focused on the total population. What is needed is an examination of females only." Or, "Research has identified several key predictors of dating violence among teens. Missing from the literature however is a focus on Latino teen dating violence." Is theory never used to study this issue? If so, a main point might be "A review of the literature indicates that all research conducted has been atheoretical in nature." Does the material in the sample column suggest that most research on the topic is based on small samples? If so, a main point might be "Existing examinations are focused only on small, local samples limiting our ability to generalize to larger populations." Is there disagreement or a lack of consistency about key definitions? If that is the case, then a main point might be, "A review of the empirical literature demonstrates tremendous variation in the definition of 'sexual violence' used across studies." Are there four major findings apparent in the literature? If so, a main point might be, "Evidence indicates four major findings including . . ." Table 3.5 offers nouns and verbs frequently used when constructing main points. Remember, the purpose of the main point statement is to identify an overall summary based on a synthesis of material found for each theme in the table. With the table completed, and the information synthesized, you have the elements needed to write the first draft of the literature review.

Table 3.4 Thematically Based Table

Thematically Based Table	Article Purpose	Research Question	Why Important	Theory	Sample Used	Sample Size	Data Info	Key Definitions	Analytic Technique	Findings	Additional Key Themes
Main Statement											
Original source 1											
Original source 2											
Original source 3											
Original source 4											
Original source 5											
Original source 6											

Preparing for the First Rough Draft

> 7. Prepare for the first draft by identifying an organizational approach and writing strategically

With the summary in Table 3.4 completed, you have the raw materials needed to write a first draft. Before doing so, it is important to have decided on an organizational approach and a writing strategy. Establishing the organization of the literature review and using a writing strategy will facilitate a strong first draft of the review.

Organizational Approaches

Recall that the purpose of a literature review is to give an overall view of the literature as it pertains to the proposed research. In addition, the literature review needs to make clear what addition to the literature the proposed research will make. Doing that is accomplished using one of two primary organizational structures: descriptive organization or chronological organization.

A **descriptive literature review** organization identifies and describes the major elements of a particular topic. It shares with the reader what is known about the topic currently. This type of review typically does not present how understanding about a topic has changed over time. For example, a descriptive literature review focused on victimization risk may discuss what is known today about risk including the important role of gender, race, and age of the victim. This literature review may be organized in the following way:

Introduction: Victimization Risk and Personal Characteristics

Subsection 1: Gender and Victimization Risk

Subsection 2: Race and Victimization Risk

Subsection 3: Age and Victimization Risk

Subsection 4: The Proposed Study and Why It Is Important

The organization of this literature review describes the currently identified main themes presented in subsections, followed by what the proposed research will add to our understanding and why it is important to conduct it. Subsections (with headings) are very useful in that they allow you to "organize the information and helps the reader," according by Zaykowski. After reading this descriptive format literature review, the reader will have a good understanding of what is known, as well as information on why the proposed research is important.

Table 3.5 Constructing a Main Point

To construct a main point, use the appropriate noun and verb in context

Noun	Some Form of Verb
Scholars	indicate(s)
Findings	show(s)
Results	demonstrate(s)
Researchers	identify(ies)
The authors	reflect(s)
Current understanding	suggest(s)
Research	argue(s)
The literature	note(s)
Evidence	find(s)
Studies	speculate(s)
	focuses on
	examine(s)

Descriptive literature review: Organization format for a literature review that identifies the major elements of contemporary understanding about a particular topic.

Another useful organizational approach is chronological. A **chronologically organized literature review** describes changes and growth in understanding of a topic over time. As the name suggests, you would describe earlier studies first, then more contemporary ones, and then a section identifying the proposed research and why it's important to conduct. For example, a chronologically organized literature review focused on violence against college women may discuss how our understanding of this topic has changed over time. This literature review may be organized in the following way:

Introduction: Understanding of Violence Against College Women Over Time

Subsection 1: Era 1—Foundational Studies: Mary Koss and Colleagues

Subsection 2: Era 2—Use of Nationally Representative Studies

    a. Mary Koss and Colleagues

    b. National Crime Victimization Survey findings

    c. Bonnie Fisher and Colleagues

Subsection 3: Era 3—Use of Large Nonrepresentative Samples

    a. Krebs and Colleagues—Campus Sexual Assault Survey

    b. Cantor and Colleagues—AAU Survey

Subsection 5: Era 3—Use of Individual Campus Climate Studies

Subsection 6: The Proposed Study and Why It Is Important

Using a chronological organization should identify changes in understanding of a subject over time. The change over time can be focused on the substantive changes in understanding, changes in methodological advances, or changes resulting from theoretical development. Which type of change over time is focused on is dependent on the purpose of the proposed research.

Should you decide to organize your literature review using a chronological methodological approach, you might offer a section discussing foundational methodology tools, followed by a section devoted to advanced methodologies that became available, and finally a section focused on current understanding using the most up-to-date tools. Presented in this fashion, a reader can see how *understanding* in the field has grown over time. Furthermore, it makes clear how the proposed research will build on what is currently known.

A word of caution—a chronological organization or any kind does not mean that a researcher should simply offer summaries of each author's research in the order in which they were published. Rather, the researchers must write the review based on major *periods of understanding* in the field. The periods are the topic, and the individual pieces of research are synthesized to provide support for what occurred in each time period. For instance, you may note that the initial research in the field pointed to the importance of considering gender. A later burst of research attention built on this knowledge by demonstrating the need to focus on race as well. And the most recent period of research makes clear the need to consider gender, race, and age simultaneously. The final section of the review may cover the proposed research, which seeks to examine age by noting it has been neglected in earlier work.

A Writing Strategy: MEAL

You should also be guided by a writing strategy. An easy to use and effective writing strategy that is often widely used by researchers is summed up by the acronym MEAL.[2] **MEAL** describes the strategy used not only for the entire literature review but also for each section in the literature review.

<u>M</u> signifies the *main point,* which should describe the current state of or quality of the literature overall. In addition, the first sentence (or sentences) of each subsection should identify the main point of that section. Note that the main points placed in the first row for each column in the summary table in Table 3.2 can be used for this purpose.

<u>E</u> indicates *evidence.* Evidence for the main point follows the main point statement. Evidence in an academic literature review comes in the form of information gleaned from primary source material. Note that the statements (with citations) in the cells of the summary table in Table 3.2 are used as evidence in the literature review.

<u>A</u> denotes *analysis.* After the presentation of evidence, you need to identify the take-away message from the section. That message may center on important examinations that are missing in the literature or on agreement or disagreement that needs to be highlighted. The analysis should tell the reader in a sentence or two the most important information he or she should have gained from reading this section.

<u>L</u> represents *linking.* Linking occurs in two ways. First, it refers to the need to include a statement that connects the subsection back to the overall main point of the literature review. Second, linking refers to including segues between sections. For instance, you may comment, "There is agreement among researchers on the role of X on Y. In contrast, there is little agreement when considering the role of W on Y as the following section shows." Linking in a literature review ensures that there is flow from one section to section and that the review is cohesive.

MEAL is a very useful tool, but it need not be used in an overly rigid way. You can use a MEAL-like structure and vary the parts. For example, an M-E, M-E, M-E, A, L is a common strategy. Note the elements of MEAL in this paragraph from Zaykowski's (2014) victim services research.

MEAL: Writing strategy in which one begins with a *m*ain point, offers *e*vidence, *a*nalyzes the evidence, and then *l*inks that material to the main point.

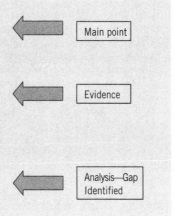

Victim assistance agencies have grown since the 1970s in response to increasing concern for victim's rights and health concerns (U.S. Department of Justice, 2012). Very few victims of violent crime, however, seek help from victim services (New & Berliner, 2000; Sims, Yost, & Abbott, 2005). This is particularly concerning because agencies play a critical role in addressing mental and physical health problems associated with criminal victimization and they also inform victims of their rights. The current study addresses two limitations in prior research (for a review, see McCart, Smith, & Sawyer, 2010). First, much of the literature on victim service usage is based on small samples that are not generalizable, and therefore may not be applicable to other regions. Second, although men are eligible for many victim services prior research has focused almost exclusively on women.

← Main point

← Evidence

← Analysis—Gap Identified

---

[2]The MEAL writing strategy proposed here was adapted for use in writing literature reviews by Sean McCandless.

The following are several paragraphs from a "cultural factors" subsection in Cuevas and his colleagues' literature review focused on Latino dating violence (Sabina et al., 2016). Note the use of MEAL and the clearly stated main point, evidence, analysis, and linkage in this example.

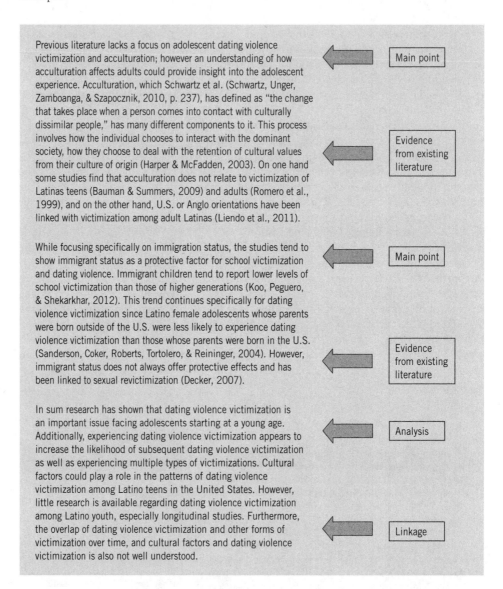

Previous literature lacks a focus on adolescent dating violence victimization and acculturation; however an understanding of how acculturation affects adults could provide insight into the adolescent experience. Acculturation, which Schwartz et al. (Schwartz, Unger, Zamboanga, & Szapocznik, 2010, p. 237), has defined as "the change that takes place when a person comes into contact with culturally dissimilar people," has many different components to it. This process involves how the individual chooses to interact with the dominant society, how they choose to deal with the retention of cultural values from their culture of origin (Harper & McFadden, 2003). On one hand some studies find that acculturation does not relate to victimization of Latinas teens (Bauman & Summers, 2009) and adults (Romero et al., 1999), and on the other hand, U.S. or Anglo orientations have been linked with victimization among adult Latinas (Liendo et al., 2011). — **Main point** / **Evidence from existing literature**

While focusing specifically on immigration status, the studies tend to show immigrant status as a protective factor for school victimization and dating violence. Immigrant children tend to report lower levels of school victimization than those of higher generations (Koo, Peguero, & Shekarkhar, 2012). This trend continues specifically for dating violence victimization since Latino female adolescents whose parents were born outside of the U.S. were less likely to experience dating violence victimization than those whose parents were born in the U.S. (Sanderson, Coker, Roberts, Tortolero, & Reininger, 2004). However, immigrant status does not always offer protective effects and has been linked to sexual revictimization (Decker, 2007). — **Main point** / **Evidence from existing literature**

In sum research has shown that dating violence victimization is an important issue facing adolescents starting at a young age. Additionally, experiencing dating violence victimization appears to increase the likelihood of subsequent dating violence victimization as well as experiencing multiple types of victimizations. Cultural factors could play a role in the patterns of dating violence victimization among Latino teens in the United States. However, little research is available regarding dating violence victimization among Latino youth, especially longitudinal studies. Furthermore, the overlap of dating violence victimization and other forms of victimization over time, and cultural factors and dating violence victimization is also not well understood. — **Analysis** / **Linkage**

This example highlights the very important use of main point statements leading off each section. This example also demonstrates the synthesized use of evidence that is presented based on the topic of interest (versus author focused). Although the text at the beginning of this section on cultural factors is not shown here, the concluding sentence in this section ties back to the earlier stated purpose of that section.

As noted, a well-constructed literature review uses MEAL in two ways. It structures the full literature review, and it is used to structure each subsection. When we return to an earlier example of a descriptively organized literature review, we see that a reader would expect to see MEAL in the following places:

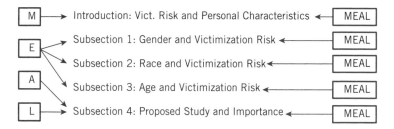

Write the First Draft

8. Write the first draft

At this stage, you have all the skills, strategies, and information needed to construct the first draft of your literature review. You have a table that has clearly identified main points and evidence (with citations) for each theme. You have selected the organization of the literature review as either descriptive or chronological. You have the understanding of using MEAL to organize this material using a main point + evidence + analysis + linkage approach. What remains is to put pen to paper (or fingers to keyboard) to aggregate these pieces in an orderly fashion. When writing the first draft, do not go for perfection in terms of every word used or every sentence typed. Focus instead on getting the overall structure and organization in place. You will devote time to editing, proofreading, and polishing the draft next.

Edit, Proof, and Polish

9. Edit, proof, and polish (repeatedly)

You should not expect to have a completed literature review with the construction of the first draft. Rather, a well-written literature review requires repeated edits, proofing, and polishing. When you feel you have completed the literature review, you should check it carefully to ensure you have included important elements that may have been lost (or never been included) such as main points, evidence, analysis, linkages, citations, quotations, and stylistic considerations. Another helpful strategy for proofing is to read your own paper aloud to see whether it flows. Reading your paper aloud forces you to focus on what is written, not on what you think was written. It is always good practice to ask someone who has not been working on the literature review to read it to ensure it is clear, flows well, and is free from error.

Common Pitfalls of Literature Reviews

Writing literature reviews takes time, focus, and patience. A part of the process is to verify that you have avoided some common errors. This section identifies several pitfalls that are found in literature reviews. These include not allowing enough time, constructing the review around authors and not themes, and a lack of organization and writing strategies.

Not Allowing Enough Time

A common pitfall encountered is not allowing enough time to write your literature review. You can see from this chapter that no step in writing a literature review is difficult. What is apparent, though, is that each step and the whole process take time. Writing a literature review cannot be done in a night or even two. You must set aside a good amount of time to search for and through potential primary sources. Time is needed to summarize each article.

Additional time and effort are required to create a summary table and to consider the material so that main points can be identified. Finally, writing the review takes time. Writing literature reviews is not a task that can be done well when rushed. To avoid this pitfall, allow adequate time to do a thorough and excellent job.

Failing to Focus on Themes

Although we warned against it earlier, and although professors warn students in classes, it is exceedingly common for students to construct a literature review focused on authors instead of on themes. A literature review that describes the work of one author after another, after another, is not a literature review. When each paragraph focuses on one piece of research and its author instead of on the substance of the topic, not only is it inhumane to ask someone to read it, but it is also extremely difficult to identify the overall state of the literature. A literature review that fails to synthesize the materials and present main points is not a literature review. To avoid this pitfall, ensure the review is thematically based, not author or individual research article based.

Lack of Organization and Structure

A third pitfall of writing literature reviews is to fail to organize and structure the material in a meaningful way. This chapter presented two useful formats for the review: descriptive and chronological. A well-constructed literature review will use one of these approaches. This chapter also presented information on the importance of MEAL as a writing strategy. MEAL is useful for the overall review, and it is useful for subsections in the review. If a review fails to identify main points, offer evidence, analyze the material, and link it to other sections of the review, the review is incomplete and poorly executed.

Quoting Problems

Common pitfalls in writing a literature review involve the use of quotes. As noted in this chapter, a literature review should focus on the ideas in the literature, not on what any specific author has written. For that reason, the excessive use of direct quotations should be minimized. Zaykowski shares, "Avoid using direct quotations—unless there is one or two that really are important in their original form. Too many quotations make it difficult to read and also isn't convincing to the reader that you have an original argument." Taken to an extreme, some writers over-quote by quoting multiple paragraphs and multiple pages of text. Zaykowski notes, "It is not okay to do this. Even though technically the writer is giving the author credit (assuming that the author is recognized), it is not enough of the writer's own thoughts. The writer didn't actually write anything, put into their own words, or in many cases interpret the quote's significance." When writing, the writer needs to include his or her own thoughts, and offering pages of quoted material fails in that regard.

Miscellaneous Common Errors

Beginning researchers make a few additional mistakes that are easily remedied. First, never type the title of an original source in the literature review. Similarly, never use the author or researcher's full name in the literature review. Many learning to write literature reviews construct needlessly bulky sentences similar to

In an article titled "'I Got Your Back': An Examination of the Protective Function of Gang Membership in Adolescence," authors Chris Melde, Terrance J. Taylor and

Finn-Aage Esbensen studied the "gang membership-victimization literature by incorporating subjective concepts of fear and the perceived risk of victimization with traditional self-report measures of actual victimization" (2009, p. 573).

The problem with this sentence is the presentation of the title, the full names of all the authors, and a direct quote. Rather, the title of the work should only be presented in the references. The authors' full names belong in the references as well. Only authors' last names belong in the text. Finally, the writer of the faux sentence used a quote when the writer's words would do. This sentence could be improved as

Melde and colleagues (2009) investigated the gang membership-victimization literature with an emphasis on the concepts of fear and perceived risk of victimization (p. 573).

Academic literature reviews should rarely if ever use the word *I*. *I* is not appropriate because the literature review is focused on what the literature offers, not on how the literature review writer accessed and worked with it. As an example, sentences such as "I found two articles focused on race and victimization. I summarized them and learned that . . ." should never be included. Rather, the point should be conveyed as "A review of the literature makes clear the importance of considering race when identifying victimization risk." The literature review is about the knowledge, not about the person reading the knowledge.

Similarly, academic literature reviews should not use the word *prove*. In social science research, you never *prove* anything. Rather, researchers conduct research and in doing so find evidence to support, or fail to find evidence to support, relationships, theories, and notions about how the world works. For this reason, never use the word *prove* and instead note that there is, or is not, evidence for whatever topic is at hand.

Failure to Justify the Need for the Proposed Research

Finally, a common error in literature reviews is the failure to conclude with a strong case for why the proposed research is important and needed. The proposed research may be filling a gap in the literature, focus on an ignored population or concept, use improved data or measures, use improved or more appropriate methodology, or myriad other reasons. Do not assume the reader understands or knows the justification. It is the researcher's responsibility to state clearly the justification for the proposed research.

Ethics and the Literature Review

Ethics are an important consideration during the construction and writing of a literature review. There are two major ethical considerations to consider when conducting a literature review: plagiarism and accurate portrayal of other's research.

Plagiarism

Although most people have a notion about what plagiarism is, most people are unaware of the fact that plagiarism is fraud and theft, and that it can be committed in many ways. Most simply, **plagiarism** is fraud and theft of another person's words, thoughts, ideas, or other creations (e.g., songs or artwork) and the presentation of that material as one's own. It is a highly unethical and immoral act that is no different than going to another person's home and

Plagiarism: Fraud and theft of another person's words, thoughts, ideas, or other creations (e.g., songs, artwork), and the presentation of that material as one's own.

stealing his or her money or items of value. Copying and pasting others' words verbatim—a practice also known as **cloning**—without citing the original author is the most widely recognized form of plagiarism. It is easily avoidable by using quotation marks around the verbatim text and properly citing the original author and source.

Less recognized is that plagiarism also includes summarizing or paraphrasing another's work without properly crediting them. Even if every word used in the summary or the paraphrase differs from the original text, failure to include proper citation is fraud and theft as the *ideas* of the original author are being passed off as someone else's.

Mosaic plagiarism is a form of plagiarism that occurs in multiple ways. One presentation of mosaic plagiarism is when a writer takes another person's text and replaces some words in the statement with synonyms. Failure to cite the original author in cases like *this is mosaic plagiarism* and is unethical. Even if a writer uses many synonyms, the ideas presented are still those of the original author, and the resulting text is theft. Another form of mosaic plagiarism occurs when a writer strings together verbatim fragments from multiple authors or sources without citing the original authors. Again, the issue is the theft of the ideas, not the words. Plagiarism is an unethical act that can (and should) result in negative consequences for the offender. One way to avoid this pitfall is to always cite and credit the original author. If ever in doubt, cite and credit the original author.

Why do people plagiarize? It could be because of a conscious decision to engage in unethical behavior that someone feels he or she can get away with. In contrast, many recognize that plagiarism comes from other motivations. Zaykowski believes the reasons some plagiarize are complex, although a common theme is because a student is overwhelmed by school, work, and family obligations. In some cases, plagiarism occurs because of sloppiness or disorganization on the part of the writer during the writing process. A person may type a sentence verbatim with the intention of citing the original author later. If the citation is forgotten, the result is plagiarism. The process outlined in this chapter offers an organized and systematic approach to writing a literature review that should minimize the possibility that a citation becomes lost or separated from the original idea. It is the writer's responsibility to remain organized to avoid plagiarism regardless of the causes.

Accurate Portrayal of Existing Research

An issue to be sensitive to in constructing a literature review is the misrepresentation of existing research. One way an original source is misrepresented is to rely on some other source material that offers a summary of an original source. There is no guarantee that any summary of an original source is correct. In fact, often it is incorrect. You can never be sure that an original source is accurately described in anything other than the original source. Failure to access the original source may save time but often at the cost of accuracy. Even though accessing the original source may take a little more time, the result is the security of knowing the description written about the original source is accurate.

At times, extant research is criticized unfairly and inaccurately. Although it is true that no research is perfect, and all research has limitations, ensure any criticism leveled is fair. First, remember that the writer is reviewing the research, not the author. Comments about an author or researcher being careless, or malicious, stupid, or clueless are always inappropriate. It seems this sort of advice is not needed, but experience demonstrates it is (this includes criticizing individuals on social media; it gets seen and shared).

Second, should someone criticize existing research for failing to use a particular analytic technique, they must be certain that the technique (and computing power needed for that technique) was available at the time the research was conducted. Remember, it was not until 1981 that the first widely used personal computer (PC) was developed (with a maximum of 10 KB of memory on the hard drive), and not until the late 1980s that the cost of PCs declined such that they could be found in many homes and offices. The widespread use of

SPSS* became available on a personal computer using DOS from 1984 to 1992. But it was not until 1992 to 1996 that SPSS was made available in a Microsoft® Windows™-based environment (SPSS Inc., 2009). Earlier analyses relied on mainframes and other time-intensive approaches. Prior to 1970, it could take up to 24 hours to get the results from *one* regression, assuming the researcher even had access to the required technology (Ramcharan, 2006). When finally obtaining those results, which were generally printed and made available in some other location, it was not uncommon to discover that an error was made, and the process had to begin again. Today, getting results from one regression is instantaneous on a laptop in a coffee shop, plane, or beach destination. Therefore, be cautious when criticizing earlier researchers for using basic analyses when it may reflect the most advanced technology available at that time.

A similar unfair criticism focuses on data. The advent of technology has enabled nationally representative surveys that simply were not possible in the not-so-distant past. Previously, researchers had to rely on easier to obtain, smaller, and local samples to conduct research. Similarly, you must be knowledgeable about the data by someone else before leveling unfair criticism. For instance, some criticize research using National Crime Victimization Survey (NCVS) data for failing to consider the immigration status of the victim. The fact is that the NCVS data do not, and never have, gathered information on respondents' immigration status. In addition, be cognizant that data change over time. Some also criticize the NCVS for failing to gather data on sexual assault. The NCVS underwent a massive redesign in 1992 (approximately 25 years ago), and one change made was that it started gathering data on sexual assault (and continues to do so). Yet, even today, some criticize the NCVS for not gathering data on sexual assault. It seems that those offering this critique are repeating it from old sources (and not accessing original sources) or that they simply lack knowledge about the data.

In sum, when describing existing literature and research, be accurate, access original sources, and be sensitive to changes in the field over time. In addition, be diplomatic. A person never benefits by implying (or stating clearly) that early research is poorly conducted or that earlier researchers were less than dedicated scientists working hard to understand something about our world.

Literature Review Expert— Sean McCandless, PhD

Sean McCandless, PhD, is an academic resources coordinator and instructor in the School of Public Affairs at the University of Colorado Denver. Prior to coming to the university, Sean worked as an editor, where literature writing skills were mandatory. Since his arrival at the university, Sean has taught a variety of courses at the undergraduate and graduate levels including English writing, public administration, and political science. He worked in academic writing centers for more than a decade and continues to guest lecture in numerous undergraduate and graduate classes on the topic of literature writing skills and APA style.

Courtesy of Sean McCandless

Sean credits his becoming a writing expert to being a huge *Star Trek* fan. As an 11-year-old, he developed and wrote three scripts that he submitted to *Star Trek* for consideration. At the time, the show allowed fans to submit speculative scripts. Of the three submitted, two were politely declined, but the third caught the eye of a producer who

*IBM® SPSS® Statistics / SPSS is a registered trademark of International Business Machines Corporation.

responded. The producer, not apparently recognizing he was corresponding with an 11-year-old, noted how much potential he saw in Sean's ideas and writing skills. This prompted Sean to write as much as possible, which eventually landed him a position in a university writing center. It was in this role that Sean honed his writing skills and developed the ability to teach others how to write literature reviews. Learning to teach writing literature reviews came not only from more writing but also from dissecting published literature reviews to understand their structure. After a short period of time, he became the go-to guy at the university for advice on writing literature reviews.

When asked about whether some people are naturally good writers and others are not, Sean comments that it doesn't matter. Sean strongly believes that anyone can be a good writer with the correct skills and environment. Regardless of one's background of natural skills, he argues that if a person learns the correct skills, and practices those skills, they will become a better writer or rewriter. In this, Sean agrees completely with author Robert Graves's statement, "There is no such thing as good writing. Only good rewriting." Being a natural writer is not relevant. Developing skills and practicing writing is relevant.

Sean has seen some common errors when working with students writing literature reviews. A major error is that students often do not know what the purpose of their writing is or what the purpose of a literature review is. Not surprisingly, Sean notes that without clarity in purpose, a writer will never have clarity in writing. A second common error is that students frequently cannot identify a main point at the level of the whole paper or at the level of a paragraph. It is not enough to offer a series of uncoordinated details in a paper; the writer must identify the main point. Sean notes this skill in summarizing complex information is one engaged in daily in other contexts. Think for example of someone asking, "How was your day?" Most people respond with a summary of the main points of their day: "Had a wonderful meeting with a new client and celebrated my anniversary out at a nice restaurant." This summary offers the main points of the day versus a litany of each activity, no matter how small, of the day.

To become a better writer, Sean recommends reading other literature reviews and dissecting them. Can the reader find the main points? The evidence? Linkages? Furthermore, Sean encourages new writers to practice summarizing complex material in a few sentences (i.e., practicing developing main points). This practice can be done by looking at other literature reviews or any type of writing such as movie reviews and newspaper stories. Identify how MEAL approaches work and how a failure to offer a framework does not.

Chapter Wrap-Up

By building on the material presented in the first two chapters, this chapter presents the steps and skills needed to write a literature review. Understanding these skills removes or minimizes the anxiety out of writing and constructing a literature review. As Cuevas notes, writing a good literature gets easier over time as the skills become more engrained and the literature becomes more familiar. The steps covered in this chapter include identifying what appropriate sources for a review are, where to find them, and how to avoid predatory journal pieces. Steps summarizing the original sources were offered, culminating in a table (Table 3.4) that has all of the information needed to write the review. In addition, two organizational approaches—descriptive and chronological—were presented. A very useful writing strategy—MEAL—was introduced and described to assist writers with writing the review. The chapter also provides information on common pitfalls to avoid when writing a literature review. In addition, the ethics associated with writing a literature review were highlighted, including plagiarism in its many forms and misrepresenting existing research. Finally, the chapter concludes with an interview with Sean McCandless, an expert literature review writer and academic resources coach. In this interview, Sean discussed his experience as a writing coach. In his

Table 3.6 Featured Research: Abstracts

Researcher	Articles	Abstract
Rod Brunson	Brunson, R., & Weitzer, R. (2009). Police relations with Black and White youths in different urban neighborhoods. *Urban Affairs Review, 44*(6), 858–885.	Much of the research on police–citizen relations has focused on adults, not youth. Given that adolescents and particularly young males are more likely than adults to have involuntary and adversarial contacts with police officers, it is especially important to investigate their experiences with and perceptions of the police. This article examines the accounts of young Black and White males who reside in one of three disadvantaged St. Louis, Missouri, neighborhoods—one predominantly Black, one predominantly White, and the other racially mixed. In-depth interviews were conducted with the youths, and the authors' analysis centers on the ways in which both race and neighborhood context influence young males' orientations toward the police.
Carlos Cuevas	Sabina, C., Cuevas, C. A., & Cotignola-Pickens, H. M. (2016). Longitudinal dating violence victimization among Latino teens: Rates, risk factors, and cultural influences. *Journal of Adolescence, 47,* 5–15.	This study uses data from two waves of the Dating Violence Among Latino Adolescents (DAVILA) study and focuses on the 1) rates of dating violence victimization by gender, 2) risk of experiencing dating violence victimization over time, 3) association of dating violence victimization with other forms of victimization, and 4) association of immigrant status, acculturation, and familial support with dating violence victimization over time. A total of 547 Latino adolescents, from across the United States, aged 12e18 at Wave 1 participated in both waves of the study. Rates of dating violence were around 19% across waves. Dating violence at Wave 1 and non-dating violence victimization were associated with an elevated risk of dating violence during Wave 2. Cultural factors did not distinguish between dating violence trajectories, except for immigrant status and familial support being associated with no dating violence victimization. Overall, dating violence affects a large number of Latino teens and tends to continue over time.
Mary Dodge	Dodge, M., Starr-Gimeno, D., & Williams, T. (2005). Puttin' on the sting: Women police officers' perspectives on reverse prostitution assignments. *The International Journal of Police Science & Management, 7*(2), 71–85.	Reverse police prostitution stings, which target men by using female police officers as decoy prostitutes, are becoming a common method in some United States cities for controlling the problem of solicitation for prostitution. The role of policewomen as decoys has received scant attention by scholars, though critics and traditional feminists view the practice as further evidence of the subjection and degradation of women in law enforcement. This article presents participant field observations of how reverse prostitution operations are conducted in Aurora, Colorado Springs, and Denver, Colorado and qualitative interview data from 25 female police officers who discuss their experiences as prostitution decoys. The findings indicate that female officers view the decoy role as an exciting opportunity for undercover work, despite the negative connotations of acting like a whore. According to the officers who work as decoys, it adds excitement and variety and offers potential for other opportunities for advancement within the police department in contrast to the rather mundane duties often associated with patrol.
Chris Melde	Melde, C., Taylor, T., & Esbensen, F. (2009). "I got your back": An examination of the protective function of gang membership	The threat of victimization has been regarded as a central feature in both the development and the continuation of youth gangs. Although many studies find the need for protection to be a common reason youth join gangs, recent literature suggests that gang members are at an increased risk of victimization. Given this seeming contradiction between expectations and reality, the current article examines the "objective" and "subjective"

(Continued)

Table 3.6 (Continued)

Researcher	Articles	Abstract
	in adolescence. *Criminology, 47*(2) 565–594.	dimensions of gang member victimization using panel data collected from youth between the ages of 10 and 16 years. Findings reveal that gang members report higher levels of actual victimization and perceptions of victimization risk than non-gang-involved youth. Gang membership is associated with reduced levels of fear, however. Overall, although gangs may not be functional in terms of actual victimization, they seem to decrease anxiety associated with the threat of future victimization.
Rachel Santos	Santos, R. B., & Santos, R. G. (2016). Offender-focused police intervention in residential burglary and theft from vehicle hot spots: A partially blocked randomized control trial. *Journal of Experimental Criminology, 12,* 373–402.	Objectives: To test an offender-focused police intervention in residential burglary and residential theft from vehicle hot spots and its effect on crime, arrests, and offender recidivism. The intervention was prevention-focused, in which detectives contacted offenders and their families at their homes to discourage criminal activity. Method: The study was a partially blocked, randomized controlled field experiment in 24 treatment and 24 control hot spots in one suburban city with average crime levels. Negative binomial and ordinary least squares (OLS) regression were used to test the effect of the presence of intervention and its dosage on crime and offender recidivism, and examination of average and standardized treatment effects were conducted. Results: The analyses of the hot spot impact measures did not reveal significant results to indicate that the treatment had an effect on crime or arrest counts, or on repeat arrests of the targeted or non-targeted offenders living in the hot spots. However, the relationships, while not significant, were in a promising direction. Conclusions: The collective findings from all four impact measures suggest that the intervention may have had some influence on the targeted offenders, as well as in the treatment hot spots. So, while the experimental results did not show an impact, they are promising. Limitations include large hot spots, the low case number, low base rates, and inadequate impact measures. Suggestions are provided for police agencies and researchers for implementing preventive offender-focused strategies and conducting studies in suburban cities.
Heather Zaykowski	Zaykowski, H. (2014). Mobilizing victim services: The role of reporting to the police. *Journal of Traumatic Stress, 27*(3), 365–369.	Victim assistance programs have grown dramatically in response to the victim's rights movement and concern over difficulty navigating victim services. Evidence, however, indicates that very few victims seek assistance. The present study examined factors associated with victim s service use including reporting to the police, the victim's demographic characteristics, the victim's injury, offender's use of a weapon, the victim's relationship to the offender, and the victim's mental and physical distress. Data came from a subset of the National Crime Victimization Survey 2008–2011 ($N = 4{,}746$), a stratified multistage cluster sample survey of persons age 12 years and older in the United States. Logistic regression models indicated that fewer than 10% of victims of violent crime sought help from victim services. Reporting to the police increased the odds of seeking services by 3 times. In addition, the odds of victims attacked by an intimate partner seeking services were 4.5 times greater than victims attacked by strangers. Findings suggest that additional exploratory work is needed in uncovering the mechanism of police involvement in linking victims to services. Specifically, do police understand what services are available to victims and why are police more likely to inform some types of victims about services more than others?

experience, he learned that everyone has the potential to be a great writer (because of rewriting) when exposed to the appropriate skills and environment. Although we have presented a fair amount of text from our case studies in regard to literature reviews, Table 3.6 offers each study's abstract. Notice the information that each abstract offers and how useful it is in identifying whether the article would be useful in a literature review you are writing.

In the next chapter, we shift gears and begin discussing the information necessary to design a study. This includes a discussion on concepts, definitions, measurements, and variables. The chapter discusses measurement as well as the advantages and disadvantages of different approaches to measurement. Like the previous chapters, a section is devoted to common pitfalls in the hopes that they can be avoided. And, of course, ethical consideration during the nuts and bolts planning of research is emphasized.

Applied Assignments

1. Homework Applied Assignment: Conducting a Literature Search

Using the same **two** peer-reviewed journal articles you used for your homework in Chapter 2, conduct a search for literature related to those articles. Be sure to use Boolean operators and filters. Present your findings in a series of tables (e.g., Table 2.2) shown in this chapter. Given searching is an iterative process, be sure to show all tables and results for each iteration. Be prepared to justify why you stopped your search when you did. Be prepared to discuss your findings in class.

2. Group Work in Class Applied Assignment: Summarizing Research Literature

As a group, select two articles from the following case studies: Dodge, Cuevas, Brunson, and Santos. Once your group has selected the article, summarize each article following the approach described in step 5 (see p. 78).

Remember to use the bulleted tips provided in step 5, and write in complete sentences. Be able to speak to why this approach would be useful in constructing a literature review. Next, create a thematically based table using the two selected articles based on the thematically based table presented in step 6 in the chapter. Be prepared to discuss and share your summaries in class.

3. Internet Applied Assignment: The Results of Plagiarism

Search the Internet to find three examples of people who lost their job, or were denied a high-profile position, because they plagiarized. Provide a summary of who they are, the jobs they had (or were seeking), and any reason they gave for the plagiarism. Provide details on the type of plagiarism they engaged in and why it was wrong. Describe the outcome of their unethical act and how you think it may affect them in the future. Please provide a paper addressing these topics to your professor/instructor.

KEY WORDS AND CONCEPTS

Abstract 74
Boolean operators 71
Chronologically organized literature review 84
Cloning 90
Conclusions 77
Descriptive literature review 83
Discussion 77

Empirical 65
Empirical peer-reviewed journal articles 65
Filters 71
Findings 77
Impact factors 68
Introduction section of a journal article 76

Key words 76
Literature review journal articles 66
MEAL 85
Method 77
Mosaic plagiarism 90
Original sources 64
Peer-reviewed journal articles 64

Phrase 71

Plagiarism 89

Predatory journals 67

Predatory publishers 67

Primary sources 64

References 77

Saturation 73

Term 71

Thematically constructed literature
review 81

Theoretical journal
articles 66

KEY POINTS

- A literature review presents an understanding of the overall state of the literature by surveying, summarizing, and synthesizing existing literature. Reviews identify major themes, demonstrate where there is agreement and disagreement, identify limitations of prior research, and expose gaps in our understanding about a topic. A well-constructed literature review places the proposed research in the context of extant literature, and it identifies how the proposed research will create and enhance existing knowledge.

- Writing a literature review can be intimidating, but with the appropriate skills, and a clear set of steps toward that end, anyone can write an excellent literature review.

- Sources used to construct a literature review, known as original sources or as primary sources, primarily come in the form of peer-reviewed journal articles, including empirical pieces, theoretical pieces, and review pieces. In addition, local and federal governmental reports, conference papers, and information from conference presentations are useful sources.

- Recent years have seen a proliferation of predatory publishers and predatory journals that are inappropriate sources for writing an academic literature review. Predatory publishers and journals are illegitimate entities that extort fees from unsuspecting authors.

- Searching for original or primary sources is easily accomplished using search tools, terms, phrases, Boolean operators, and filters. Searching is an iterative process that should begin with the narrowest search.

In addition, searches commonly should be restricted to journal articles published in the last five to seven years.

- Empirical journal articles are published using predictable sections making finding important information easy. Those sections include an abstract, introduction, literature review, the method, findings, discussion, and conclusion. All academic journal articles include references with full citation information.

- Summarizing each primary source and then disaggregating statements from the summaries into a summary table where main themes are identified and stated are important steps toward creating a thematically based literature review.

- Prior to writing the first rough draft, it is important that the writer identify which organizational approach taken (descriptive or chronological) and be familiar with the writing strategy identified as MEAL. By using MEAL, one offers a main point, evidence, analysis, and linkage across the literature review, as well as within each subsection.

- Two primary ethical concerns while writing a literature review are plagiarism and misrepresentation/unfair criticism of others' work. Plagiarism comes in many forms, but all have in common that a writer has passed off another person's work as his or her own without crediting the originator of that material. In a literature review, the work is being critiqued, not the researcher. Should a person level criticism about extant research, it is his or her duty to ensure it is fair criticism given the context and available tools at the time the work was conducted.

REVIEW QUESTIONS

1. What are the purposes of a literature review?

2. What are the nine basic steps in writing a literature review? Why are they important?

3. What are appropriate and inappropriate sources for use in writing a literature review?

4. What are predatory publishers and journals, and how can you know they are not using one?

5. What are Boolean operators and filters, and why are they useful?

6. What questions should you address when summarizing an original source?

7. What is a main point, and how is one developed? What role does a main point play in the construction of a literature review?

8. What is the anatomy of an empirical research journal article, and what information does each section offer?

9. What types of organizational approaches are useful in writing a literature review? What is MEAL, and why is it important?

10. What are the two types of plagiarism discussed in this chapter, and why are they unethical?

CRITICAL THINKING QUESTIONS

1. Another student in your class is working on a literature review on sexual violence. He finds some literature in a journal but feels it does not cover the topic well. He decides to include information found in an article published in *Playboy* magazine because he argues it is a better source for this topic. How would you advise him to proceed? Why would you suggest that? (This is based on an actual incident.)

2. A student in your class notes she has completed her literature review on police use of force. She asks you to proofread her paper prior to turning it in because it is worth 75% of her course grade. She wants to do well. When you read it, you notice that the literature review offers a series of paragraphs summarizing individual pieces of research. What would you advise her to do, and why?

3. You are working on a literature review and realize that you could use much of a paper you turned in to another professor in a different class last semester. Would it be ethical to copy and paste those sections out of the old paper and place them into the new paper? Why or why not? Would plagiarism software find this? What is the best way to handle a situation like this?

4. You are writing a literature review, and it turns out one of the articles you are reviewing was written by a professor you had at your previous college. Since you worked closely with him, you know he often cuts corners and holds some dated views of particular groups. In the review, you write, "It is no surprise Dr. Lazyguy failed to consider the role of race in the analysis given his personal beliefs about particular groups." Is this an appropriate or wise approach? Why or why not? What would be a better way to handle this?

5. You go home to discover someone has broken in and stolen artwork you created. Although your artwork may not be worth millions, it is yours and you worked very hard creating it. In addition, it represents a lifetime of your labor with art. A few weeks later, you are walking downtown and in a window is your artwork for sale. On the accompanying information sheet, it notes the art was created by someone else. How would this make you feel? Do you believe that plagiarism is the same type of theft and fraud? Why or why not? What punishment should be given the art thief? How would you punish a plagiarizer if you had that power?

$SAGE edge™

Designing Your Research

art 2 provided guidance on developing research questions and on constructing a quality literature review. With that foundational material in place, Part 3 begins zeroing in on necessary considerations related to gathering your data. These considerations include learning about identifying concepts of interest and how you will draw a sample from which your data will come. For some research, you must clearly identify the concepts of interest given your research question. You must then identify how those concepts will be conceptualized and operationalized into variables. These considerations involve contemplating levels of measurement, validity, and reliability. These steps are important in research design because, as noted, a piece of research is only as good as its weakest part. Care must be taken to avoid weaknesses at every step of your research. Once these decisions are made, you must address sampling—deciding from whom or what your data will be gathered. Many considerations are taken into account when contemplating sampling, including the nature of the sample, the size of sample, and the source of the sample. Drawing a quality sample is one step toward maximizing the quality of the data you will ultimately use to answer your research question. Once you have developed your research and sampling plan, it will be time to gather your data. Part 4 discusses many types of data that researchers gather.

Concepts, Conceptualizations, Operationalizations, Measurements, Variables, and Data

Learning Objectives

After finishing this chapter, you should be able to:

4.1 Summarize what a concept is, compare how it is related to a variable, describe how it is related to different types of research, and identify why it is important.

4.2 Define and describe conceptualization, including its importance in conducting different types of research.

4.3 Identify the role of operationalization and how it differs from conceptualization. Describe how operationalization and conceptualization differ when using quantitative and qualitative data.

4.4 Summarize what variables are, how they are related to concepts, and the role they play in research. Be able to describe the characteristics and types of variables used in research.

4.5 Define measures, and provide examples of measures you see in research. Identify how measures and data are related to one another.

4.6 Be able to list, compare, and contrast the four levels of measurement and how each is distinguished from the other. Evaluate why it is important to make these distinctions when conducting research.

Quantitative data: Numerical data. Research using quantitative data generally uses deductive reasoning.

Deductive reasoning: Approach in which the researcher begins with broad or general statements that are used to derive more specific statements. Used in research that begins more generally and works to more specificity. Commonly used in research using quantitative data.

Introduction

You now have a research question and a quality literature review; now you are ready to begin planning the details associated with your research. To do so, you must begin thinking about concepts, conceptualizations, operationalizations, measurements, variables, and data, and the role of each in your research. Regardless of the purpose of your research, you must consider these things. Nevertheless, how you think about these elements depends, in part, on the type of data you will ultimately need to collect.

Two Primary Types of Data: Quantitative and Qualitative

Two primary types of data are used in criminology and criminal justice research: quantitative and qualitative. Research using **quantitative data** uses numerical data to quantify something about a topic. With quantitative data, a person can understand how many offenders recidivated, the rate of offending in the past year, the number of female police officers that are employed full time, or opinions measured on a scale from one (dislike) to ten (like). In using these numeric data, a researcher then calculates statistics, and findings and conclusions are offered. Research based on quantitative data is generally conducted by using deductive reasoning. **Deductive reasoning** means that the researcher begins more generally and works to more specificity. Many of our featured case studies used deductive reasoning and quantitative data. One specific research question posed by Chris Melde and colleagues (Melde, Taylor, & Esbensen, 2009) was, "What is the effect of gang membership on self-reported victimization among adolescents?" To answer this, Melde et al., gathered numerical data on whether an adolescent was in a gang and whether he or she had been victimized. With those data, Melde and colleagues calculated statistics and offered conclusions. Melde and his collaborators went into this research with clear boundaries regarding the data they needed to answer their research question. Similarly, Carlos Cuevas and colleagues (Sabina, Cuevas, & Cotignola-Pickens, 2016) posed four research questions that identified the specific things they would gather data about, analyze, and offer a conclusion. Recall their four research questions:

1. What are the rates of dating violence by victim gender?

2. What is the risk of experiencing dating violence over time?

3. Is dating violence victimization associated with other forms of victimization?

4. What cultural factors (e.g., immigrant status, familial support) are associated with dating violence over time?

These questions show that Cuevas and his team needed to gather data on dating violence, gender, risk associated with dating violence, other types of victimization, and cultural factors. They were not interested in understanding whether some other unrelated thing such as vacation locations was important to consider. Rather, Cuevas and his colleagues worked within specific conceptual boundaries to answer their research questions.

Other scientific research uses qualitative data. Research relying on **qualitative data** is conducted using *non-numerical* data such as text from transcribed interviews, narratives, published documents, videos, music, photos, observations, body language, and voice intonation, to name a few. In thinking back to Mary Dodge's exploratory research on policewomen decoys (Dodge, Starr-Gimeno, & Williams, 2005), the literature provided no guidance except for speculation about how women view this work. Because of that, Dodge, another of our featured researchers, and her colleagues found the best approach would be to gather qualitative data via interview. By gathering qualitative data, they were able to learn a great deal about officers' views of being a decoy, fears associated with this role, and how to walk, dress, and behave to be convincing. Therefore, they would not be constrained to preconceived notions about the work. Rather, those engaged in the work could tell Dodge and her colleagues what was and was not important and meaningful. Qualitative data are generally conducted using inductive reasoning. **Inductive reasoning** means that a researcher begins more specific and works to greater generality. The researcher begins with specific observations, interviews, or other data collection and uses the data gathered to make general statements about the topic of interest. Research using qualitative data is frequently, but not always, used in an exploratory manner. Research relying on qualitative data does not have the goal of counting or quantifying a topic; instead, it's goal is to deeply and richly understand the topic and nuances about the topic.

Often, the decision to use a quantitative or qualitative data (or both) is guided by the research purpose and question (see Figure 4.1). If you know nothing or little about a specific topic, gathering qualitative data may be the best approach. The undercover officer sting research conducted by Mary Dodge et al. (2005) and the research by featured researcher Rod

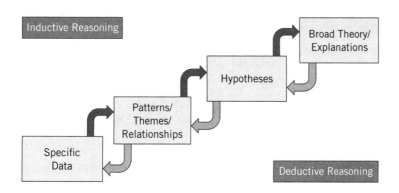

Figure 4.1 Inductive and Deductive Reasoning Illustrated

Brunson (Brunson & Weitzer, 2009) on adolescent youth perceptions and experiences with police both used this approach. In fact, Brunson and his colleague begin their literature review by noting that "most of the literature is quantitative, and it is important to complement these studies with qualitative research to document complex and nuanced citizen understandings of police practices. Only a handful of qualitative studies of either adults or youth exist" (Brunson & Weitzer, 2009, p. 861). Both Dodge and Brunson, along with their colleagues, gathered qualitative data to answer their exploratory research questions to gain a broad yet nuanced understanding of a topic. If, on the other hand, a fair amount of knowledge has accumulated about a topic and the goal is to explain something about it, then using quantitative data might be the best approach. Our featured researchers Heather Zaykowski, Carlos Cuevas, Chris Melde, and Rachel Boba Santos each used or gathered quantitative data to answer their research questions. Evaluation research frequently uses both quantitative and qualitative data. An evaluation may involve gathering numerical data to answer a research question. But it may also include gathering of non-numerical data in the form of interviews, focus groups, observing interactions, or studying documents to answer some other research question.

The decision about whether a researcher will use qualitative or quantitative data, or both, is important to make early in a research project. This is because the data required will influence how a researcher thinks about concepts, conceptualizations, operationalizations, and variables—the topics of this chapter—prior to gathering the data. For example, the qualitative data gathered are often used to identify the important concepts related to the topic of interest, gather an understanding about what their subjects (often people) identify as relevant concepts, as well as how the subjects define them (i.e., moving from the more specific to the more general). This approach entails being open to learning their subjects' views on important definitions, conceptualizations, and variables. In contrast, researchers intending to use quantitative data must identify the abstract unobservable concepts relevant to their research and describe how they will measure them using variables before gathering data.

The remainder of the chapter discusses these important elements. We begin by first identifying why careful consideration of these concepts, measurements, and variables are important. Then we describe each of these using examples. The chapter concludes with a discussion of ethics and common pitfalls, as well as with an interview with Brenidy Rice, who makes a living focusing on these elements of research while conducting and overseeing research for the state of Colorado.

Figure 4.2   Stages to Go From Concept to Variables

Concept
- Abstract

Conceptualization
- Definitions

Operationalization
- How to measure

Variable(s)
- Observable, empirical indicators used to gather data

Why Focus on Concepts, Conceptualizations, Operationalizations, Measurements, Variables, and Data?

Understanding concepts, definitions, measurements, and variables is important because without them a researcher simply could not conduct research. For the researcher gathering and using quantitative data, it would be difficult to systematically move from an unobservable abstract concept to measureable and observable variables. For the researcher gathering and using qualitative data, important information about a research topic may be overlooked and missed. Without an understanding of these elements of research, a researcher could not conduct research well.

To conduct research using quantitative data, a researcher has identified from the literature (and noted in the literature review) important concepts about which he or she needs to gather data. A critical step in this type of approach is to make those abstract concepts into measureable variables. To do so, researchers engage in several basic stages, moving from the abstract to the concrete. Figure 4.2 depicts these stages of identification of a concept, the creation of a conceptual definition, and a detailed plan for indirectly measuring that concept that results in a variable. After these stages, you can develop variables to gather data that serve as proxies for the concepts.

> **Concept:** Abstract, mental pictures of things that exist only in our minds. Examples include gender, victim, injury, recidivism, and rehabilitation.

What Are Concepts?

One of Zaykowski's (2014) research questions is as follows: What factors are associated with use of victim services? In particular, Zaykowski examines how things like reporting to the police, victim's demographics, the victim's relationship to the offender, and the victim's mental and physical distress are associated with the use of victim services. To answer her research question, she ultimately has to gather empirical data on each of these things. These things are **concepts** that are abstract, mental pictures that exist in our minds. They are not empirical (i.e., observable), tangible, and cannot be touched. Zaykowski noted in a video interview conducted for this book that "[w]hen we study victimization, victimization is a concept but one can't just say this is victimization, or that is victimization, a researcher must address what *exactly* they mean by victimization." We think about and communicate about our world and our research using concepts. Our ability to communicate using concepts is possible because individuals have a *general* agreement regarding the meaning of particular concept.

The focus on concepts differs slightly given the purpose of one's research. In exploratory research, a researcher is generally motivated to use the data to *identify* the concepts of importance. In descriptive research, a researcher frequently is already aware of the concepts of interest. Their ultimate goal is to *describe* what is known about concepts and how they are related or associated with one another. In explanatory and some evaluation research, a researcher is focused on identifying how some concepts *affect, influence,* or *predict* other concepts. Understanding that concepts are abstract mental images, and that research is focused on identifying, describing, or explaining how concepts are related, should make clear why these are the most basic building blocks of conducting research.

Examples of Concepts

Our case studies focus on several concepts in their research. Consider the work of Melde who focuses on concepts such as gang members, victimization, perceptions of victimization, victimization risk, adolescence, and perceived fear (Melde et al., 2009). Zaykowski's (2014) work points to several concepts of interest including police reporting, victim demographics, use of victim services, victim's distress, and so on. Consider Cuevas's research, which is focused on concepts such as cultural factors, dating violence, gender, Latinos, and other types of victimization (Sabina et al., 2016). The work of Santos focuses on concepts including hot spots, residential burglary, and offender-focused police intervention (Santos & Santos, 2016). Some of these abstract concepts are illustrated in Figure 4.3.

In contrast, Dodge's work needed to identify what the women who worked as prostitution decoys identified as important concepts (Dodge et al., 2005). Similarly, Brunson started his exploratory research on youths' views and experiences with police with little notion as

Figure 4.3 Several Case Study Concepts

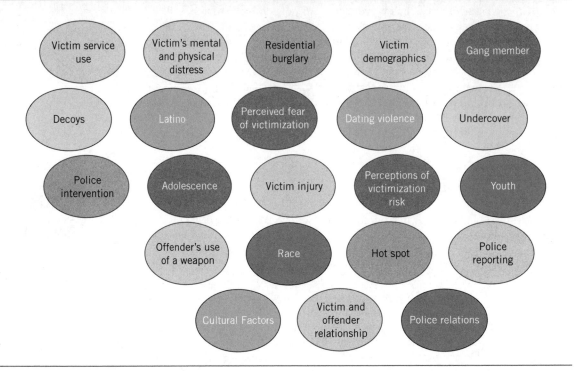

to what these youths thought were important concepts (Brunson & Weitzer, 2009). Beyond knowing that they wanted to compare experiences and perceptions of the youths in three neighborhoods, the researchers allowed many important concepts to be identified by the respondents during the interviews.

There is an endless number of concepts in criminal justice and criminology. Consider the examples of criminology and criminal justice concepts shown in Table 4.3. What characteristics do all concepts have in common? First, all concepts are abstract. Second, people in society have a *general* agreement regarding what concepts refer to. This general agreement about meaning allows individuals to communicate with one another about ideas and thoughts. Third, because they are abstract, concepts are not directly measurable.

Having generally agreed ideas about what abstract concepts refer to may be adequate to get along successfully in everyday life. It is not adequate when conducting research. Why? First, because concepts are not directly measureable, it is impossible to conduct research using concepts. Researchers who want to measure the concepts must use something measureable to represent the concepts. Second, although individuals may have a *general* agreement about what is meant by a concept, people do not share specific, detailed agreement about what is meant by each concept. You and those you know do not share the same specific notion about what constitutes an injury, intelligence, violence, an elder, kindness, happiness, a victim, or recidivism. Therefore, when conducting research using quantitative data, it is critical that the researcher clearly *define and identify the specific measureable elements of each concept* prior to gathering the data. When conducting research using qualitative data, it is critical to allow subjects to define the concepts they identify as important. The researchers' ideas about definitions may not match or even be close to how subjects view them. A great example of learning about definitions while gathering data (versus clarifying definitions prior to gathering data) is found in Dodge's research (Dodge et al., 2005). During Dodge's interviews, it was revealed

Figure 4.4 Understanding Research Using Quantitative and Qualitative Data

Research using qualitative data occurs frequently when a person wants to learn what concepts are important and how subjects define those concepts. The data dictate what the concepts are.

Research using quantitative data requires a researcher to identify the concepts and their conceptual definitions before gathering data. The definition guides exactly which data are gathered.

how decoy officers' defined being a successful decoy. A successful decoy is one who went barefooted, had messy/dirty hair, and a particular way of standing and walking. Other concepts and definitions were also revealed in Dodge's data gathering including sexual concepts such as "half-an-half" and "around the world" (see Dodge et al., 2005, for more information). For more understanding of research using quantitative and qualitative data, see Figure 4.4.

What Is Conceptualization?

As noted, a researcher cannot directly measure concepts because they are abstract. Yet, researchers are interested in understanding, exploring, examining, or investigating concepts and how they are associated or related to one another. To do so, *definitions* of the concepts must be identified. For the researcher using qualitative data, this means gathering data that provide insight into their subjects' definitions of important concepts. For example, in Brunson's research, the definition of "crooked cops" was revealed (and supported in other literature) and defined:

> Most Barksdale and Hazelcrest youth said that their communities were plagued by some "crooked cops"—a term frequently used (see also Carr, Napolitano, and Keating 2007). Martez observed, "They'll sell you crack, weed, X [ecstasy], and then will turn around and have you locked up." And David explained, "If somebody got pulled over and they had drugs and money on them, a lot of times the cops will search 'em and take the drugs and money and then lock 'em up. . . . They don't turn it in for evidence; they keep it for they self." "The undercover ones is crooked," Kyle observed. "The undercover ones get away with it because we can call the station up and report the [officers] in uniform, but we can't report the undercover ones" because their identities are often masked. (Brunson & Weitzer, 2009, p. 873)

In contrast, the researcher using quantitative data must develop *specific* detailed definitions of each concept of interest prior to gathering the data. In the parlance of research methods, the researcher using quantitative data develops a conceptual definition via conceptualization.

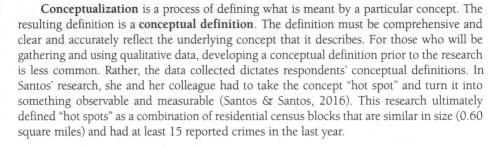

Conceptualization is a process of defining what is meant by a particular concept. The resulting definition is a **conceptual definition**. The definition must be comprehensive and clear and accurately reflect the underlying concept that it describes. For those who will be gathering and using qualitative data, developing a conceptual definition prior to the research is less common. Rather, the data collected dictates respondents' conceptual definitions. In Santos' research, she and her colleague had to take the concept "hot spot" and turn it into something observable and measurable (Santos & Santos, 2016). This research ultimately defined "hot spots" as a combination of residential census blocks that are similar in size (0.60 square miles) and had at least 15 reported crimes in the last year.

Example: Conceptualizing College Student

Consider the concept of "college student." How might you conceptualize this concept? In general, people have broad agreement as to who a college student is. Nevertheless, as should now be clear, there is no universally specific and shared definition about who a college student is. For that reason, as a researcher, you must conceptualize or define this concept to conduct research on it.

How would you conceptualize "college student?" Here are a few examples:

- Someone living on a university campus at a four-year university.

- People currently enrolled in any number of college courses whether online or in person.

- Individuals, 18 to 24 years of age, who have attended a university either online or in person, public or private, within the last six months.

- People who have graduated from high school and are obtaining additional education at a vocational school, community college, junior college, or four-year university.

Much research focused on college students defines them as persons age 18 to 24. Is this the best approach? Why or why not?

As these few examples indicate, there are *many* ways to conceptualize "college student." Each of these ways has ramifications about from whom data will be gathered. These four examples demonstrate that a researcher must think about several elements that make a college student. First, you must consider what is meant by a college or university. Does it refer to only a traditional brick-and-mortar four-year university? Or does it include community colleges and vocational schools? Must it be a public university? Or can it be private? Do religious universities count? Second, you must consider what is meant by student. Is there an age limit of who is a college student? Must someone be currently enrolled in courses, or can he or she have been enrolled in the last six months (or a year)? Must a person be enrolled at least part time, or must he or she be enrolled full time only? What if the student takes only online courses—is he or she a college student? Can a senior citizen taking an online course in ornithology from a university in state different from their residence be considered a college student? Is where a person lives related to one's status as a college student? Must a person live on a college campus in a dormitory to count as a student? What if someone lives at home with his or her parents? Which conceptual definition would you use to accurately define the concept of college student? Given this discussion, are you wondering how "college student" has been conceptualized in the research on college student sexual misconduct that is so prominent in the news these days? You should be because it might surprise you.

Keep in mind that there may be frequently used conceptual definitions of concepts identified in the literature. If appropriate, it is acceptable to build off this existing work and use that conceptualization. Nevertheless, the researcher must be careful to ensure that a selected existing conceptualization is appropriate for the research at hand. Just because a conceptual definition has been used does not make it the best conceptualization for every research application. Figure 4.5 offers an illustration of the conceptualization step.

Providing conceptual definitions is challenging. Yet, conceptualization is an important process, and a researcher must take the time to do it well. In the end, your research is only as good as its weakest element, and using poor conceptual definitions weakens the whole product. It also makes following steps in the research endeavor, including the next step of operationalization, more challenging. Having engaged in conceptualization, a researcher is one step closer to the next step: operationalization.

Must college students live on campus to be considered a college student? Do online students count? What of those taking a class at a nearby community college.

Figure 4.5 Conceptualization

What Is Operationalization?

For most planning on using quantitative data, the next step in the process is to specify exactly *how* you will measure the concept based on the conceptual definition. Identifying *how* you will measure each concept, being guided by the conceptual definition, is a process known as **operationalization**. Conceptualization focuses on developing specific definitions, operationalization focuses primarily on *how* a researcher will indirectly measure the concept. Although operationalization is engaged in primarily by researchers who will use quantitative data, researchers using qualitative data are interested operationalization in terms of how their respondents view the appropriate measurement of concepts. For instance, a respondent may note that they identify a bad police officer based on the way she drives or the language used. How respondents "measure" underlying concepts is of interest to researchers gathering qualitative data.

For researchers who will be using quantitative data, operationalization details the precise way in which they will measure the underlying concept. Will they use a survey question? Will they weigh something? Will they count something? Each of these are ways in which a researcher can operationalize a concept (or part of it). There are many ways to operationalize concepts, and the researcher must identify exactly how he or she will accomplish it.

Cuevas offers an excellent example regarding concepts and operationalization: someone says they are going to "travel to work." The concept of "travel to work" has shared meaning among people. Yet Cuevas notes that "traveling to work" can be accomplished in many ways, by taking different modes of transportation, by using different pathways, and so on. Operationalization refers to the *specific way* that person will "travel to work" by

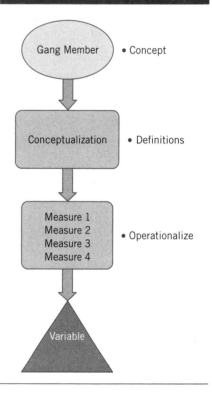

The role of victims in crime has remained unchanged, but what has changed is the way victims have been included in the criminal justice system. One way victims have been included in the system is the use of a victim impact statement at trial. Although many view victim impact statements as a win for victims (and their families), others have expressed fear that victim impact statements will lead jurors to make decisions in part based on judgments about the worth of victims. In this way, some believe victim impact statements will introduce an element of unfairness in trials. Regardless, victim impact statement are now a part of trials, but the question remains: Does the victim's socioeconomic status influence juror decisions? Existing research offers mixed findings. Schweitzer and Nunez's (2017) research addresses this question using multiple facets of socioeconomic status.

The specific purpose of Schweitzer and Nunez's research was twofold:

1. To examine whether victim impact statements affect sentencing decisions

2. To examine whether victim socioeconomic status information conveyed through a victim impact statement might influence jurors' sentencing decisions in capital murder cases

To conduct this research, 249 people were gathered in a sample using an online survey tool that offers a low-cost sample of subjects (Amazon's® MTurk™). Each subject completed a death qualification questionnaire that included three items that assessed whether participants were willing to give the death penalty and whether they would give the death penalty no matter what the circumstances. Only subjects who noted that they would give the death penalty if the circumstances warranted it were eligible to participate in the study. All participates listened to 35 minutes of audio of the sentencing phase of a capital murder trial. The evidence against the defendant was extremely strong. Subjects were told that the defendant had been found guilty of first-degree murder and that it was their role to sentence him. The subjects also learned that the defendant had been

on parole when he committed the murder and that he murder had occurred with additional felonies. The next part of the study involved the victim impact statements being given by the daughter of the murder victim. The daughter was varied in two primary ways: socioeconomic status and language. In terms of socioeconomic status, the daughter giving the victim impact statement was varied in terms of occupation (saleswoman at, or manager of, a furniture store), housing (mobile home versus house), type of vacation taken (camping or cruise), daughter's education (not mentioned or PhD), and occupation (flight attendant or college professor). Verbally, the daughter used language in terms of using *eh* or *you know,* and dropping the g at the end of words (e.g., I'm *goin* to the store) or using phrases such as *I think* or *I suppose* and more adjectives.

To analyze the data, a logistic regression was used to isolate the influence of socioeconomic status on a juror's sentence. With regard to the first purpose, the findings showed that victim impact statements do not bias jurors. In addition, the examination of the second research purpose suggests that victim information, specifically socioeconomic status conveyed through the reading of a victim impact statement, did bias jurors' sentencing decisions. Specifically, when the daughter was of lower socioeconomic status, the defendant was less likely to be sentenced to death. Defendants killing a middle socioeconomic victim were more likely to be sentenced to death.

The policy implications of this research suggest that the socioeconomic status of those giving the victim impact statement influence jurors' sentencing decisions. Judges must be made aware of this when deciding which portions of the impact statement should be allowed. In addition, an obvious policy consequence is that the use of victim impact statements may be called into question if additional research shows they have a biasing effect on sentencing especially in capital murder cases.

Schweitzer, K., & Nunez, N. (2017). Victim impact statements: How victim social class affects juror decision making. *Violence and Victims, 327*(3), 521–532.

identifying the streets and roads she takes, every turn she makes, and the type of vehicle used, the speed traveled, and so on. Santos offers an excellent example in terms of the concept of security. One way a researcher may conceptualize security is by lighting in an area. Operationalizing it means addressing the question, "What does this conceptualization mean in terms of gathering data?" For example, would you gather data on how bright lights are? Or would you measure where the lights are located? Perhaps you would measure how many lights there are? Or maybe simply whether there are any lights? These practical questions must be clarified during operationalization, so the researcher knows exactly what type of data to gather.

Concepts can be operationalized in myriad ways, and it is up to the researcher to identify precisely the way they are operationalizing each concept. First, you must identify the nature of each measure used to represent the underlying concept of interest. Is it a survey question? A count? Observation of behavior? Second, you must determine how many measures are needed to best measure the underlying concept. Often a variable is based on a single measure, yet other times, multiple measures are used. Zaykowski notes that in general, it is better to use multiple operationalizations because they can better capture the richness of underlying concepts. In the case of Zaykowski's (2014) featured research using the National Crime Victimization Survey (NCVS), she is constrained by the operationalizations available in these existing data (aka secondary data). Cuevas's work offers a great example of the use of multiple operationalizations for each concept to better capture concepts such as culture or victimization (Sabina et al., 2016). For instance, in Cuevas' study, the concept of victimization was operationalized by the use of the modified juvenile victimization questionnaire (JVC). The JVC gathers data on conventional crime, peer and sibling victimization, child maltreatment, and sexual victimization within the past year. There are 17 questions asked of respondents to see whether they had been victimized in the last year. If so, additional data are gathered on each attack such as whether the relationship to the perpetrator. Using 17 questions to get at a single concept offers a robustness to that operationalization. A third consideration is that you must identify the nature of how the data for each operationalization will be recorded. Will you note the presence or absence of the concept of interest? Or count how many times someone is victimized? Exactly what type of data will be recorded is an important consideration in operationalization. Once operationalization is concluded, the researcher will be working with variables. Therefore, the chapter now turns to variables, what they are, and how they are constructed.

Variable: Labels applied to measures used to represent the concepts of interest. Variables act as proxies for the abstract concepts they represent.

What Are Variables?

Variables are the labels for the observable and measureable counterparts of concepts. Variables act as proxies of the abstract concepts they represent. A researcher studies variables to understand the concepts, and a researcher investigates the relationship among variables to understand the relationship among concepts. This is possible because variables represent the observable measures used to gather data.

Variables are categorized based on the nature of the data collected. Before discussing the many types of variables, it is instructive to return to the research questions to better understand variables.

Revisiting Research Questions With a Focus on Variation

Recall that research questions guide the entire research enterprise. They are the question a researcher seeks to answer. Consider these research questions/objectives from some of our case studies:

Melde and collaborators (Melde et al., 2009): (a) What is the effect of gang membership on self-reported victimization? (b) What is the effect of gang membership on perceptions of victimization risk? (c) What is the effect of gang membership on the fear of victimization?

Brunson and colleague (Brunson & Weitzer, 2009): What are differences in views of police relations of Black and White youth based on where they reside: a Black disadvantaged neighborhood, a White disadvantaged neighborhood, or a racially mixed disadvantaged neighborhood?

For Melde, the concepts in his research questions indicate what he will gather data about. In contrast, Brunson's exploration, identifying and comparing concepts of interest within these three neighborhoods, is the goal of the research. Research seeks to identify or understand the importance of concepts, including relationships among concepts. Yet, the interest goes much deeper than that. Researchers are fundamentally interested in the *variation* in these concepts and in how the *variation* in one concept influences or is associated with the *variation* in another concept. For example, researchers are not interested in victimization per se; researchers are interested in variation in victimization experiences among those in the public. Why are some people victimized and others are not? Researchers are not interested in perceptions of the police per se; they are interested in variation in perceptions of police among Black and White youth.

Why place emphasis on variation? Variation is a fundamental element of research. The presence of variation can be used to establish a relationship among concepts. If concepts vary together, a researcher has evidence that the concepts may be related. If the concepts do not vary together, a researcher does not have evidence of a relationship among them. Because all people reside on planet Earth (to our best knowledge), it would not make sense to propose research asking whether the planet of one's residence is related to attitudes about police. Why? Because everyone lives on Earth, planet of residence is a constant and therefore cannot possibly account for any variation in attitudes toward police. If everyone has the same level of education, it would not make sense to study whether educational level is related to income. Why? Because educational level is a constant, meaning it cannot influence the variation in people's income. Given this newly identified emphasis on variation in and among concepts, it is useful to consider some research questions and what they really are asking.

Research question: Zaykowski (2014) asks: How does reporting to the police, the victim's demographic characteristics, the victim's injury, offender's use of a weapon, the victim's relationship to the offender, and the victim's mental and physical distress influence victim service use?

What is really being asked: How does variation in whether victims report to the police, variation in victims' demographic characteristics, variation in whether victims were injured, variation in whether offenders used a weapon, variation in victim–offender relationships, and variation in victims' mental and physical distress influence variation in seeking victim services?

Research question: Cuevas and colleagues (Sabina et al., 2016) ask: (a) What are the rates of dating violence by victim gender? (b) What is the risk of experiencing dating violence over time? (c) Is dating violence victimization associated with other forms of victimization? (d) What cultural factors (e.g., immigrant status, familial support) are associated with dating violence over time?

What is really being asked: (a) How do the rates of dating violence vary by whether a victim is male or female? (b) Does the risk of experiencing dating violence vary over time? (c) Is variation in dating violence victimization associated with variation in other forms of victimization? (d) Is variation in peoples' cultural factors (e.g., immigrant status, familial support) associated with variation in the amount of dating violence experienced over time?

Research question: Melde and collaborators (Melde et al., 2009) ask: (a) What is the effect of gang membership on self-reported victimization? (b) What is the effect of gang membership on perceptions of victimization risk? (c) What is the effect of gang membership on the fear of victimization?

What is really being asked: (a) How does variation in whether one is a gang member or not affect variation in amount of self-reported victimization? (b) How does variation in whether one is a gang member or not affect variation in perceptions of victimization risk reported? (c) How does variation in whether one is a gang member or not influence variation in level fear of victimization expressed?

Dependent variable: Type of variable that is the outcome of interest and focus of the research.

Research question: Brunson and his collaborator (Brunson & Weitzer, 2009) ask: What are differences in views of police relations of Black and White youth based on where they reside: a Black disadvantaged neighborhood, a White disadvantaged neighborhood, or a racially mixed disadvantaged neighborhood?

What is really being asked: How do the views of police relations among Black and White youths vary based on variation in neighborhood where they reside (a Black disadvantaged neighborhood, a White disadvantaged neighborhood, or a racially mixed disadvantaged neighborhood)?

Type of Variables: Dependent, Independent, and Control Variables

In general, three specific categories of variables are used in research: dependent variables, independent variables, and control variables.

Dependent Variables

Dependent variables are variables that are the focus of the research. Dependent variables represent the outcome of interest. It is variation in the dependent variable that many researchers using quantitative data are most interested in understanding. The basic question, "What causes the variation observed in the dependent variable?" drives a great deal of research using quantitative data. Because understanding the variation in a dependent variable (also referred to as DV) is an ultimate focus of this type research, it is also the primary focus in the literature review (refer back to Chapter 2). Let's consider the following hypothetical research questions.

Research question: Is educational attainment associated with recidivism?

In this example, the researcher seeks to understand what leads to or causes variation in recidivism (shown in the circle in Figure 4.6). In particular, the researcher asks what role variation in education level has on the variation in recidivism. This is illustrated in Figure 4.6.

In this depiction, the arrow indicates the direction of influence, and it always points to the outcome or the dependent variable. Notice how the researcher is *not* interested in what leads to variation in education level? Educational level is not the focus of this research.

This next example comes from the work of Zaykowski (2014). What is the dependent variable in this research?

Research question: How does reporting to the police, the victim's demographic characteristics, the victim's injury, offender's use of a weapon, the victim's relationship to the offender, and the victim's mental and physical distress influence the use of victim services?

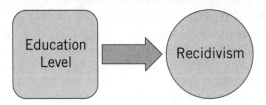

Figure 4.6 Effect Education Level Has on Recidivism

Education Level → Recidivism

Figure 4.7 Zaykowski's (2014) Research Question Illustrated

Demographics

Victim/Offender Relationship

Reporting to Police

Victim Distress

Seeking Victim Services

Independent variable:
Type of variable that is believed or hypothesized to influence, be associated with, or cause the variation in an outcome or dependent variable.

The dependent variable, or outcome of interest, in Zaykowski's (2014) work is variation in seeking victim services (shown in the circle in Figure 4.7). That is, as the arrows indicate, she wishes to understand what influences whether victims seek services. In particular, she focuses on how variation in reporting to police, demographics, victim–offender relationship, and victim distress influence whether a victim seeks out victim services. Zaykowski is not interested in understanding why reporting to police, demographics, victim–offender relationship, and victim distress vary, only in why seeking services varies. Zaykowski's research question is illustrated in Figure 4.7.

Note that the arrows in Figure 4.7 point to the outcome or the dependent variable. You might be wondering, what are these other variables such as victim distress or demographics if they are not dependent variables? What role do they play? Variables in this role are independent variables.

Independent Variables

Independent variables are variables thought to influence, be associated with, or cause the variation in an outcome or a dependent variable. The purpose of research is not to understand what causes variation in independent variables (also referred to as IVs). Rather, the purpose of research is to understand whether and how an independent variable is related to or causes the variation in the dependent variable.

What are the independent variables in the two examples? In the first example, focused on education level and recidivism, the independent variable is education level (shown as

Figure 4.8 Effect Education Level Has on Recidivism

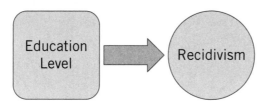

a square in Figure 4.8). This illustration indicates that the research seeks to understand or identify how variation in educational level (IV) influences, or is associated with, variation in recidivism (DV).

In the second example focused on victim services, Zaykowski identifies multiple independent variables including reporting to police, demographics, victim–offender relationship, and victim distress. These are shown in the squares in Figure 4.9.

Some researchers do not distinguish variables beyond independent and dependent variables. To those individuals, anything but the dependent variable is an independent variable. Nevertheless, it is common among criminal justice and criminology researchers to refer to a third category of variable: a control variable.

Control Variables

Control variables are a type of independent variable included in research to better highlight the role of an independent variable of interest. Control variables are also referred to as CVs. A research goal is often to understand the influence of the IV on the DV. For example, does (variation in) gender influence (variation in) income? In the example shown in Figure 4.10, the dependent variable is income, and the independent variable is gender.

Assume that based on this question, you gathered data of gender and income among a group of people, analyzed those data, and found that gender is related to income, and specifically that being male is associated with higher incomes. The work is published, but shortly after, the findings are criticized in this way: "This finding is meaningless because

Control variable: Type of independent variable included in research to better isolate the role of an independent variable of interest (frequently referred to as CVs).

Figure 4.9 Focus on Zaykowski's (2014) Independent Variables

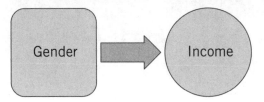

the researcher failed to consider, or take into account, educational attainment and years of experience in careers when conducting this analysis. Earlier research finds evidence that educational attainment and years of experience are related to gender and income. Without controlling for the influence of education or years of experience on income, this work cannot conclude the role that gender has on income."

This criticism indicates that to truly understand whether and how gender influences income, you must take into account—or *control for*—educational attainment and years of experience. By controlling for educational attainment and years of experience, you can better isolate the effect of gender on income (which is the purpose of the initial research). Consider the revised research question illustration in Figure 4.11.

The two control variables are shown as triangles. Analytically, independent and control variables are treated the same. The only difference in these variables is how the researcher labels and discusses them. Given the updated research question based on the illustration in Figure 4.11, you might still find that gender is related to income, and specifically that being male is associated with a higher income. Given the inclusion of control variables, however, the conclusion would be stated as "Gender is associated with income, even after taking into account—or controlling for—educational levels and experience in the field."

Figure 4.11 Focus on Control Variables

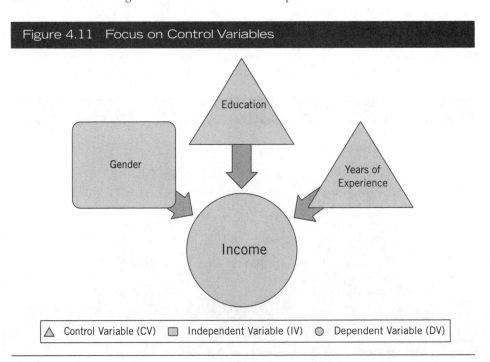

Memorizing IVs, DVs, or CVs—It Doesn't Work

Students frequently struggle with identifying variables as IVs, DVs, or CVs. A commonly attempted (but ill-fated) strategy is to try to memorize all independent, dependent, and control variables. Although seemingly a clever idea, this approach does not work. Why? Because a variable's role is dependent on the specific research in which it is found. For example, a variable such as income may serve as a dependent variable in one piece of research, may be an independent variable in some other research, and be a control variable in yet other research. Consider the three research examples in Figure 4.12.

Measure: Tools used to gather data that represent an abstract underlying concept. Data are gathered in the same way some tools in a garage are used.

In the first example, the researcher is focused on understanding the role of gender (IV) on income (DV), controlling for education and years of experience (CVs). In the second example, the researcher is focused on understanding the role of income (IV) on education (DV), controlling for gender and years of experience (CVs). Finally, the third researcher considers the role of education (IV) on years of experience (DV), controlling for income and gender (CVs). The role each variable plays is contingent on the research question of interest.

What Are Measures?

During operationalization, the researcher identifies the specific measure or measures used to measure the underlying concept. A **measure** is a tool used to gather data to represent an abstract underlying concept. Measures used in research are tools used in the same way some tools in a garage are used. You may use a measuring tape to gather data (i.e., how long something is) to represent an abstract concept (i.e., length). Alternatively, you might use a scale as a tool to measure the underlying concept of heaviness. Measures in research operate the same in that they are used to gather data to represent the underlying concept.

Measures can take many forms that must be identified during operationalization. For example, you might construct a survey with ten measures—or ten questions—on it. Or you might measure how often children act violently toward one another using observations as a measure. Or you might use questions during an interview as a tool to measure some underlying concept. You may use existing measures used by others found in the literature, or you may create your own. The following sections offer some examples of possible measures you can use during the operationalization of concepts.

Example: Measuring College Student

There are numerous ways to operationalize a college student based on the following conceptual definition: an individual who is 18 to 24 years of age, who has attended a university either online or in person, public or private, within the last six months. One option for operationalization is to gather data from all universities in the United States (i.e., online, in person, public, private, community college, four-year, etc.). In particular, by using those university records, you could identify current students or those who had attended in the previous six months from registrar records. With those records, you could identify individuals who were 18 to 24 years of age when they were enrolled in college. This would result in a plan to use a single measure, which would ultimately be used to gather data on this concept. A limitation of this approach is that universities could not reveal these data, given federal restrictions, unless every student provided permission to do so.

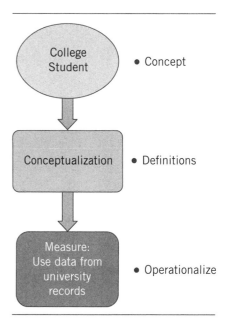

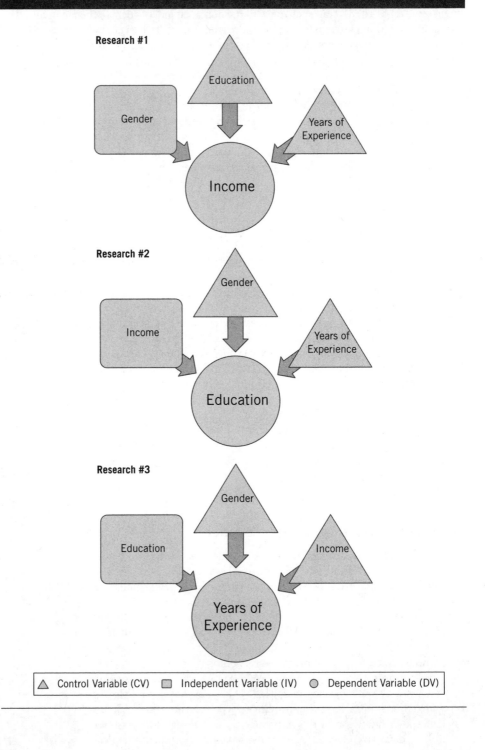

Research #1

Education

Gender

Years of Experience

Income

Research #2

Gender

Income

Years of Experience

Education

Research #3

Gender

Education

Income

Years of Experience

△ Control Variable (CV)   ▢ Independent Variable (IV)   ○ Dependent Variable (DV)

A second possible operationalization of college student (based on the conceptual definition) would be to conduct a survey of people in the United States. In that survey, you would include survey questions about the respondent's age, if he or she is currently enrolled in a college or university, or if the respondent was enrolled in a college or university in the last six months. Like all operationalization, this approach has some limitations. First, it can be expensive to conduct a national survey with enough respondents needed for an adequate amount of data. Second, it is especially challenging because those aged 18 to 24 make up a small proportion of the population, meaning you would need to make many calls before finding someone in the required age range.

A third operationalization option of college student is to use data that have already been gathered and available. For example, you could operationalize college student using data collected and available in the NCVS. The NCVS gathers data from individuals, 18 to 24 years of age, who have attended a college or a university in the prior six months. This operationalization and available measures align well with the conceptual definition.

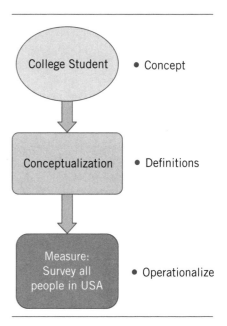

How Many Measures?

You could use a single measure or multiple measures to gather data that capture the meaning of an underlying concept. All else being equal, the use of multiple measures is advantageous. Why? Because in most cases, the full meaning of an underlying concept cannot be captured using one measure. Some concepts are complex enough that you *must* use multiple measures to as comprehensively as possible measure all dimensions of that concept. Take for example the idea of culture used in Cuevas's work (Sabina et al., 2016). One survey question would not comprehensively capture the meaning of culture. As a result, Cuevas and his team used multiple measures. Some researchers, especially those using existing data, may be constrained because of the availability of only one measure. For Zaykowski (2014), this meant that measuring the concept of victim services was limited to using a single question or measure to reflect that concept.

As an example, how might you measure the concept of a gang member? The conceptual definition of gang member for the purposes of this example is a person who is actively involved in a street gang, and is recognized by members of the gang as a member. How might you operationalize this? One option is to ask individuals whether they are gang members. This is simple and elegant, and is the approach used by Melde and colleagues (2009). Nevertheless, research shows that this approach may lead to false positives as many wannabe gang members claim membership when they actually are not gang members.

A second option is to ask known gang members who other gang members are. This is also simple and elegant, but it can be problematic if that gang member does not know all other members. A third approach could be to ask law enforcement who the known gang members are. This too is imperfect as law enforcement may only know of gang members who have tangled with the law. And a fourth way might be to identify gang members via observation of tattoos or articles of clothing depicting their membership. Again, this is not a perfect approach, but it should

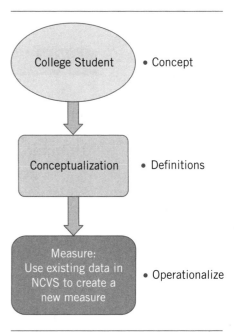

identify those showing this signs. This example demonstrates that any one of these approaches measures some, but misses other, elements of, the underlying concept of gang membership.

A fifth approach of measuring gang membership is to use multiple measures. Why not plan to use all four of these questions to measure the underlying concept of gang membership? You could operationalize gang membership such that an individual must be identified as a gang member for at least two of the four approaches to be considered a gang member. This offers an improved measurement of the concept. Figure 4.13 illustrates how operationalization may lead to the plan to use multiple measures to best measure a single concept.

What Are Data?

Throughout the chapter, we have relied on a general understanding about the meaning of data. Let's now offer a more specific definition of data. Data are the individual pieces of information—numeric or non-numeric—gathered and later analyzed to answer a research question. The word *data* is plural; *datum* is singular, therefore a researcher states that "data are" or "data were" rather than "data is" or "data was." As previously noted, data should vary to be useful in research. Consider the concept "Trust in Law Enforcement." To measure this, 16 people were asked whether they had contacted the police after a property or a violent crime in their lifetime. The data gathered are recorded in Table 4.1. The variable name used to reflect that measure is "Reporting to Police."

Notice how these data (yes/no responses) vary. Among the 16 individuals interviewed, 10 stated they had reported the victimization to the police. Notice also that in this case, the variable and the concept it represents do not share the same name. The concept is "trust in law enforcement," and the variable name is "reporting to police." In other cases, concepts and variables share the same name.

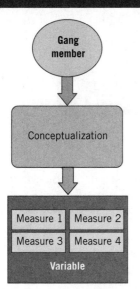

Figure 4.13 Operationalization Using Multiple Measures

Gang member

Conceptualization

| Measure 1 | Measure 2 |
| Measure 3 | Measure 4 |
Variable

Table 4.1	Data for "Reporting to the Police" Variable						
yes	yes	no	yes	no	yes	yes	yes
no	no	yes	yes	yes	no	yes	no

Attributes

A part of operationalization when one is gathering quantitative data is to identify the categories of data that will be gathered. The chapter has made clear that data must vary. The nature of the variation is determined by the attributes of the measures. **Attributes** are the categories of the data collected. These are also known as **response categories**. Examples of attributes make this concept clearer.

Imagine that a researcher has decided to conduct research on parolees. As a part of that research, the researcher is interested in the age of the parolee. During the operationalization stage of the research, the researcher identifies a variable named "age" and is trying to figure out what attributes or response categories he will use. One option is to use two attributes for the variable age: "juvenile" and "adult." Let's assume the researcher is using a survey administered to a group of parolees. On that survey, the age measure used to gather data on age may look like this:

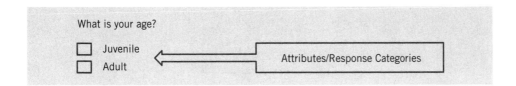

In this example, there are two response categories: juvenile and adult. A second option is to collect the data for parolee's age in this way:

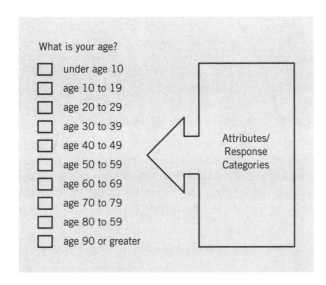

In this second example, there are ten attributes or response categories from which the parolee can chose. A third option is to gather data on parolee age in this way:

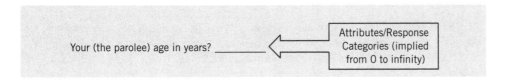

Another example involves a researcher operationalizing "weapon presence" during a violent crime. By using a variable called "weapon," the researcher has countless options in terms of attributes to represent weapon presence. One approach is

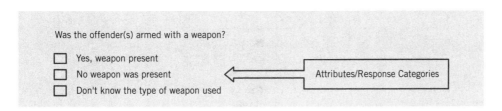

Or a greater number of attributes or response categories for collecting data on weapon presence is an option:

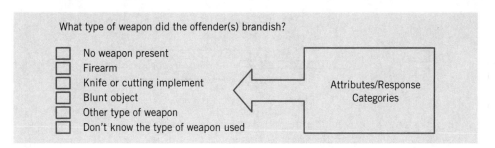

How do you know what the best attributes or response categories to use are? First, you must use enough options to allow every possible option for the question asked. Second, a variable's response categories or attributes must be different from one another so as to make clear which attribute is best for respondents to check. And third, you should gather the most data possible and practical. In other words, you need to pay attention to exhaustiveness, mutual exclusiveness, and levels of measurement. Each of these is discussed next.

Mutual Exclusiveness and Exhaustiveness

Certain considerations should be taken into account when selecting or identifying response categories. In situations in which only one attribute is to be selected by respondents, attributes should be mutually exclusive. **Mutually exclusive** means that the attributes offered do not overlap in meaning. A respondent should not struggle to understand which option fits. For example, consider these response categories for identifying marital status:

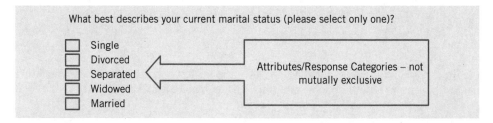

These attributes are not mutually exclusive. Why? Because a person can be single and divorced. In addition, a person can be married and separated. Without clear attributes to guide data collection, the resulting data will be fouled up. Consider these small changes to make these attributes mutually exclusive.

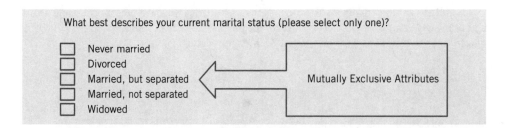

Given this change in attributes, a researcher can better gather data that accurately measure the variable (and underlying concept) of interest.

Another important characteristic for attributes is exhaustiveness. **Exhaustiveness** is the requirement that there be an attribute or response category for every possible response. This is illustrated with marital status again:

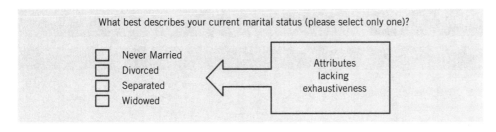

What best describes your current marital status (please select only one)?

- ☐ Never Married
- ☐ Divorced
- ☐ Separated
- ☐ Widowed

Attributes lacking exhaustiveness

In this example, a person who is married has no box to check. This list is not exhaustive. One way to ensure attributes are always **exhaustive** is to include an option such as the "other, please specify: _____" option. In this way, a full accounting of attributes can be gathered and good measurement is maximized.

Levels of Measurement

When using a research approach requiring quantitative data, a third important consideration in selecting attributes during operationalization is level of measurement. **Level of measurement** refers to the nature of the data gathered for a particular variable. Although multiple levels of measurement schemes are available, Stevens (1946) proposed a scheme that is widely used. This approach identifies four levels of measurement: nominal, ordinal, interval, and ratio. These levels are listed in an order of less information (nominal) to more information (ratio). You should strive to gather data offering the most information possible when you have a choice.

An easy way to remember the four levels of measurement is to remember the word "NOIR" (which translates to "black" in French). NOIR is an acronym comprising the first letter of each level of measurement (see Table 4.2). Each level of measurement is distinguished based on the presence or absence of these characteristics: ability to order attributes, equal distance between the ordered attributes, and, finally, presence or absence of a meaningful zero.

Nominal. **Nominal** measurement refers to attributes or response categories that differ in name only. Measurement of attributes at the nominal level has no inherent ordering between named categories or attributes, and the categories cannot be placed on a continuum with a meaningful zero. Because this measurement is only based on different categories, it is also referred to as a **categorical variable.** For example, consider the variable "type of violence" and these attributes: violent crime, and property crime. Two categories of type of crime have no inherent ordering and no meaningful zero. Another example is sex with the following attributes: female, male, other. Again, there is no ordering of these categories, and there is no meaningful zero. Many variables can only be measured at the nominal level including party identification, type of advocate, religious affiliation, types of rocks, and gender identity. If a variable can use attributes that can be measured at a higher level of measurement than nominal, it is recommended that you do so.

Ordinal. **Ordinal** measurement refers to named attributes of a variable that have an inherent order to them. In other words, ordinal refers to a level of measurement in which attributes can be rank-ordered. Variables measured using ordinal measurement indicate that the size between the categories is unknown and not equal. In addition, ordinal measurement is not associated with a meaningful zero. An example of ordinal measurement is class level at a university: freshman, sophomore, junior, or senior. These four categories represent four attributes that can be ordered from less to more university education. Nevertheless, you cannot state that the difference between a freshman and a sophomore is known or the same as the difference

Exhaustive: Desirable characteristic in response categories meaning every possible response option is offered.

Level of measurement: Nature of the data gathered for a particular variable.

Nominal: Level of measurement that indicates attributes or categories differ in name only. Nominal levels of measurement have inherent ordering between named categories or attributes, and the categories cannot be placed on a continuum with a meaningful zero. Variables with nominal levels of measurement are frequently called "categorical variables."

Categorical variable: Variables characterized by a nominal level of measurement.

Ordinal: Level of measurement that indicates that attributes of a measure have an inherent order to them. A level of measurement in which attributes can be rank-ordered.

Table 4.2 NOIR

		EXAMPLES
Nominal Data	Categories (no ordering or direction)	marital status, race of victim, state of residence, type of court, type of violence, type of weapon
Ordinal Data	Ordered Categories (rankings, order, or scaling)	university level (e.g., freshman, sophomore, etc.), levels of satisfaction (e.g., not satisfied to satisfied)
Interval Data	Equal differences between measurements but no true zero	temperature (e.g., Fahrenheit or Celsius), hours on a clock, IQ, GPA
Ratio Data	Equal differences between measurements, true zero exists	age, number of years in prison, years of education, annual household income, number of victimizations experienced

Complexity Increases →

between a sophomore and a junior, or between a junior and a senior. In other words, the distance between these ordered categories is neither clear nor equal. A widely used ordinal level of measurement are **Likert-type scales**. A Likert-type scale offers an ordered response format including attributes such as "very unsatisfied," "unsatisfied," "satisfied," and "very satisfied" to gather data on a variable. These attributes are ordered from least-to-most satisfied, yet you cannot know the difference between "very unsatisfied" and "satisfied" and whether this difference is equal to the difference between "unsatisfied" and "satisfied." There has been a long-standing controversy in the literature about the level of measurement of Likert-type scales as many use them as though they generate interval-level data. If you find that the difference or distance between each ordered category is known and equal, then they are working with interval-level measurement.

Interval. **Interval** level of measurement represents measurement of categories that can be rank-ordered and have known and equal differences between categories. These attributes, however, are not associated with a meaningful zero. A widely used example is the Celsius temperature scale. The distance between each degree on the scale is the same regardless of whether you are considering difference between 10 and 11 degrees or the difference between 45 and 46 degrees. Although this example has a zero value, it is an arbitrary point (i.e., zero degrees Celsius does not mean the "absence" of temperature measured on the Celsius scale), and you can use attributes below the zero mark in meaningful ways. For example, the difference between –3 and –4 degrees and between 18 and 19 degrees is equal. If you are using a scale with all the characteristics of an interval scale, but it also has a meaningful zero (i.e., the values lower than zero are not plausible), you are working with a ratio level of measurement.

Ratio. **Ratio** level of measurement has all the characteristics of levels of measurement described; plus, it has a nonarbitrary and meaningful zero. Many variables use ratio level of measurement in criminology and criminal justice research. In fact, any variable that is based on count data is ratio in nature. For example, asking how many victimizations a person experienced, how many children someone has, how many years were served in prison, and how many dollars' worth of goods were taken in a burglary all represent ratio levels of measurement. Zero is meaningful and nonarbitrary in that a person cannot have –4 victimization, –2 children, –13 years in prison, and –$3,499 worth of property taken during a burglary.

Collect Data at the Highest Level of Measurement Possible

A researcher should always strive to gather data at the highest level of measurement possible and practical. The level of measurement of variables determines the types of statistical techniques a researcher can use to analyze the data. Certain levels of measurement for a dependent variable determine which type of analysis you can use. Certain levels of measurement allow you to calculate a mean (e.g., average age; mean number of years of education), whereas other levels of measurement disallow it. You can always take data gathered at a higher level of measurement and collapse it to a lower level of measurement. On the other hand, you can never take a lower level of measurement and convert it to a higher level of measurement. Santos notes, "If you have a ratio level variable, you can do anything with it. You can always aggregate it to lower levels of measurement such as nominal or ordinal. However, you can never take nominal level data and convert it to ratio level. A researcher should develop their variables such that the get the maximal information and that is done by using ratio level data when possible."

Discrete and Continuous Variables

Another way a researcher might characterize a variable is as discrete or continuous. **Discrete variables** are measured using whole numbers only. Examples include number of offenders or bystanders. A person may have been assaulted by 1, 2, 3, 99, or 1,349 offenders in the presence of 1, 2, 3, or 199 bystanders. People cannot be assaulted by 1.37 offenders when 13.2 bystanders were present. Discrete variables differ from categorical in that it is a numerical measurement (e.g., number of times to prison), whereas categorical offers named measurement (e.g., offender). **Continuous variables** also use numerical measurement; nevertheless, the numerical measurement is not restricted to whole numbers. For example, weight in pounds may lead to responses such as 102.7 lbs, or 115.27 lbs, or 198.4582 lbs. A person could continue measuring this continuous variable if he or she had tools precise enough to add additional decimal points. These characteristics are important during data analysis because they indicate the analytic techniques a researcher can and cannot use.

The Role of Validity

This chapter has focused on the steps taken to move from abstract concepts to variables. A goal of these steps is for the measures and variables to correspond as accurately as possible to the underlying concepts they represent. An accurate measurement of the concept by the measures is associated with **validity**. Stated simply, in the general context of research, if a measure measures what it claims to measure, it is a valid measure. Measurement isn't precise. As Bollen (1989) indicated, validity can never be fully established, but researchers can provide evidence of the validity of any measure. That evidence can be gathered in several ways, as discussed next.

Face Validity

There are many specific types of validity researchers consider (more than will be covered here). The easiest to understand is face validity. **Face validity** indicates that a measure *appears* to measure the concept it is designed to measure. For example, if you are interested in measuring the concept of "age," you might ask individuals what their current age in years is. On its

Discrete variable: Additional way to describe interval- and ratio-level variables. These variables use numeric measurement and are restricted to only whole numbers.

Continuous variable: Additional way to describe a ratio or interval level of measurement. Continuous variables use numerical measurement and are not restricted to whole numbers. That is, they can be expressed using decimals (e.g., 1.3, 27.85, 1,079.453).

Validity: Sought-after characteristics in research that indicate that one's measures and variables correspond as accurately as possible to the underlying concepts they represent.

Face validity: Type of validity that indicates a measure *appears* to measure the concept it is designed to measure.

face, most would agree that this measure appears to be a valid measure. What if, instead, that same researcher asked individuals their horoscope sign to measure age? Most would agree this measure lacks face validity. Face validity is the crudest, simplest, easiest, and most subjective validity to establish. In reality, the measure may or may not accurately measure the concept of interest, but as long as it *appears* to do so, the measure has face validity.

Content Validity

A second type of validity is content validity. **Content validity** refers to whether the measures of a variable capture the meaning of the abstract concept given the conceptual definition. Suppose the concept of interest is "cybercrime" and a researcher defined it as "[a] crime in which a computer is the object of the crime (hacking, phishing, spamming) or is used as a tool to commit an offense (child pornography, hate crimes)" (Techopedia, 2017). To measure cybercrime offenses, a researcher develops a single measure used on a survey of individuals that asks, "Have you ever hacked someone else?" Given the conceptual definition offered, you can argue convincingly that this measure lacks content validity. Why? Because that particular measure only captures a small part of the conceptual definition. If someone answered "no" to that single measure, it only means he or she had not hacked someone else. The person may have phished, spammed, committed online hate crimes, or viewed, created, or distributed child pornography. To properly measure the full domain of cybercrime as defined, you would need multiple measures to do so. Bollen (1989) contended that the two primary ways to assess the presence of content validity are by using multiple measures and by consulting experts.

Criterion Validity

A third type of validity is criterion validity. **Criterion validity** is established when a measure corresponds to existing measures (aka criteria). For instance, imagine a researcher has a measure to ascertain whether someone experienced violent victimization that was reported to the police. Now imagine that the researcher has access to all police records to see whether those individuals actually did report the violence to the police. If there is a large degree of correspondence, the measure can be said to have criterion validity.

The Role of Reliability

Another attractive measurement quality is reliability. **Reliability** refers to whether the measure provides consistent measurement over repeated administrations (assuming no real change has occurred in the thing being measured). Reliability does not reflect the quality of a measure (it may be terrible); rather, it refers to the repeatability of the measure. Reliability should not be used to describe the value of a measure based on measurement of a single individual (or unit observed or measured). Rather, reliability is used to describe the quality of measurement taken across a group of individuals (or units observed or described).

A simple example of reliability involves a weight scale. Assume you needed to calculate the average or mean weight of all students in a classroom. The measurement tool you select is a weight scale. The average weight is calculated to be 130 lbs. Then that scale was used to calculate the average weight again. If the scale was reliable, you should expect that the average weight of the students is about 130 lbs. What if it is 178 lbs instead? And then 210 lbs? Then 120 lbs? That would be an unreliable measure.

Like validity, it is not possible to establish reliability with certainty; you can estimate it, however. Although the precise ways to estimate reliability are beyond the material presented here, the following discussion provides ways to think about it. **Inter-rater reliability** is the degree to which different raters or observers offer consistent assessments of the same phenomenon. Stated differently, inter-rater reliability is the degree of agreement between two raters examining the same phenomenon. The degree of agreement is the degree of reliability. A second type of reliability suitable for some types of measures is test–retest reliability. Evidence of **test–retest reliability** is found when the same measure, administered repeatedly, offers similar results (assuming no real change has occurred that would lead to different values from the second test). The weight example described earlier uses test–retest reliability.

Test–retest reliability: Way to establish the presence or absence of reliability by using the same measure repeatedly over time.

Reliability and Validity—Don't Necessarily Exist Together

Reliability and validity both focus on the quality and accuracy of measurement. Validity focuses on the measurement from abstract in-your-mind concept to the real-world, observable measure, whereas reliability focuses on the measurement that considers measurement quality of the same tool over time (see Table 4.3). Just because a measurement tool is valid does not mean it is reliable. Similarly, a measure that is reliable is not necessarily valid.

Table 4.3 Relationship Between Reliability and Validity		
	Reliability	
Validity	Valid, and reliable	Not valid, although reliable
	Valid, not reliable	Not valid, and not reliable

Overview of the Road From Concepts to Variables

This section presents the full process from concept to variables as presented in Figure 4.14. This figure illustrates how you can take a research question about a possible relationship of concepts at the conceptual level and study that relationship using variables. In this example, there are two concepts being studied: IQ and embezzler. In particular, the researcher seeks to understand whether there is an association between variation in IQ and variation in embezzling. Both IQ and embezzling are abstract concepts and not directly measureable. The researcher conceptualized these concepts resulting in two clear conceptual definitions. IQ is conceptualized as the relative intelligence of a person. Embezzler is conceptualized as whether someone had taken money or resources from a corporation illegally.

Based on the conceptual definitions, the researcher operationalized the definitions by describing *how* he or she would measure the abstract concepts. The researcher used standardized IQ tests to measure the underlying concept of IQ. The researcher opted to use a single measure or question in which a person self-identifies to capture the concept of embezzler, "Have you ever been convicted of embezzling from your corporation?" Are these measures perfect? No measures are perfect. IQ tests have been widely criticized as failing to account for things such as cultural difference, creativity, character, and morality. A person may lie about his or her embezzler status, or a person may have simply forgotten. It may be that for both concepts, multiple measures would be a better approach. For purposes of this example, only one measure for each concept is shown.

Having established these two variables (like the concepts, also labeled "IQ" and "embezzler"), the researcher selected eight people and obtained their IQ scores, and interviewed them to ascertain whether they had ever embezzled. As the table in Figure 4.14 shows, each of the eight people has an IQ and an embezzler score. The scores for both variables vary

Figure 4.14   From Concepts to Variables

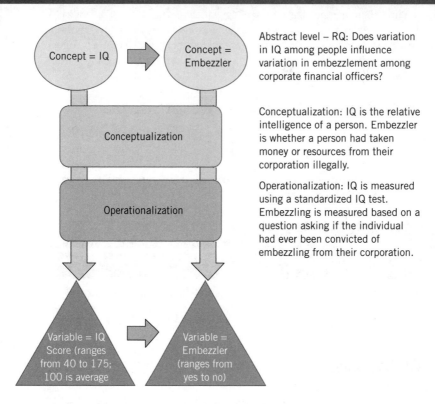

Abstract level – RQ: Does variation in IQ among people influence variation in embezzlement among corporate financial officers?

Conceptualization: IQ is the relative intelligence of a person. Embezzler is whether a person had taken money or resources from their corporation illegally.

Operationalization: IQ is measured using a standardized IQ test. Embezzling is measured based on a question asking if the individual had ever been convicted of embezzling from their corporation.

Research question: Is IQ associated with embezzling?

	Person 1	Person 2	Person 3	Person 4	Person 5	Person 6	Person 7	Person 8
Independent Variable (IQ):	110	110	110	90	80	120	145	101
Dependent Variable (Embezzler):	No	No	Yes	Yes	Yes	No	Yes	No

among the eight respondents. With these data, the researcher would use statistical techniques (covered in Chapter 12) to find evidence, or fail to find evidence, that variation in IQ scores is related to variation in embezzling.

Common Pitfalls in Concepts, Conceptualizations, Operationalizations, Measurements, Variables, and Data in Research Design

The most common pitfall when moving from concepts to variables is a general failure to understand the process, and why it is happening. It has been repeatedly stated (for this reason) that concepts and their relationships are the basis of interest in research. Yet, concepts of interest are abstract, meaning researchers must identify and use observable measures to *indirectly* study concepts. Those measures are used in research and described as variables. There may be one, two, or many measures used to create a variable.

A second common pitfall is to operationalize using a low level of measurement when higher level of measurement options exist. A frequent pitfall is for someone to use a nominal level of measurement when ratio-level data are easier to gather and offer more information. Santos notes that beginning researchers and students make this error often. When needing to gather data on lighting in an area, they will gather data at the nominal level—lighting is present yes/no. These nominal-level data tell the researcher little about lighting. Later when these developing researchers wish to present more information about lighting, they cannot. They learn that with the same amount of effort, they could have gathered more useful ratio-level data. Similar poor choices can found when seeking count data. A new researcher may identify only if something is present or not, versus counting it. When counting, a researcher can later offer means and conduct a broader range of analysis. With nominal-level data, the researcher has needlessly restricted his or her research. In general, it is good practice to gather data offering maximum information that presents the least respondent burden.

Labels can be a source of confusion resulting in pitfalls as well. Researchers give concepts and variable names. They may use the same names for concepts and variables, or they may use completely different labels. A researcher must be clear what he or she is speaking of when both the concepts and variables share names. It is useful to draw figures like those shown in this chapter—to have a clear understanding of the proposed relationship between concepts, between variables, as well as the relationships between the concepts and the variables in each research project.

Finally, a common pitfall found especially among new researchers is attempting to use concepts (or variables) that do not vary. An example is posing a question such as "Why don't old people commit crimes?" First, this is not a well-constructed research question (see Chapter 2). Second, "old people" does not vary. In addition, "not commit crimes" does not vary. Both are constants. A more appropriate approach is to construct a research question such as "How is age related to likelihood of committing crime?" With this new construction, a researcher has two concepts (age and crime commission) that each vary. Be certain to ask, "Does this concept vary?" and "Does this variable vary?" If they do not vary, then all the conceptualization and operationalization in the world cannot create a variable. Research focuses on variation (i.e., variables), not on constants.

Ethics Associated With Concepts, Conceptualizations, Operationalizations, Measurements, Variables, and Data

Ethics remain an important consideration at every stage of research. During this stage, a researcher must focus on engaging in this process ethically. It would be unethical to knowingly conceptualize and operationalize in such a way as to create variables and measures that poorly (or fail to) reflect the underlying concepts. A researcher must put in the time and intellectual effort to create measures and variables that are rigorous and accurate. Although no variable or measure is 100% valid, it is ethical to strive to produce as valid of variables and measures as is possible.

Attention must be paid to attributes. A researcher must offer the appropriate attributes for the research under consideration. Offering attributes that will lead to a desired outcome is unethical. Consider research examining intimate partner violence rates by marital category. Given a review of the literature, the researcher should provide multiple response categories or attributes including married, never married, divorced, widowed, and separated. Why is that? Because existing research shows that these categories are each characterized by very different rates of intimate partner violence. It would be unethical and misleading to opt to provide fewer categories that combine higher and lower rate groups such as never married, married (aggregation of currently married, separated and widowed), and divorced. Why is this misleading and unethical if done knowingly? Because married, separated, and widowed groups have wildly different rates (separated rates are very high, widowed rates are very low, and married rates are low but in between the two). By combining these three, the resulting rate is quite low because married individuals dominate the group and mask the very high rates found among separated people. Some with social agendas have done exactly that to encourage marriage, all the while failing to note the dangerously high rates among separated individuals (a period when risk of murder is greatest). Providing attributes to reach a desired outcome is unethical.

Similarly, using attributes to produce a wanted finding can occur with Likert-type scales. Likert-type scales should be balanced, and when they are not, findings are influenced. Consider this example:

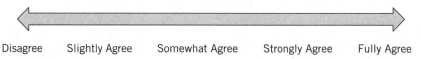

Disagree   Slightly Agree   Somewhat Agree   Strongly Agree   Fully Agree

In this example, by chance alone, the outcome is going to be that individuals agree with whatever they are being asked about. The better and more ethical approach is to offer balanced agree and disagree categories. Consider this superior option:

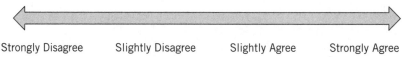

Strongly Disagree   Slightly Disagree   Slightly Agree   Strongly Agree

In moving from concepts to variables and associated measures, a researcher must strive for the best measurement. Recall a researcher is answering a research question. Setting up research to provide a desired answer is not ethical. Ensure the steps taken do not lead to a desired outcome, but rather, let the research offer evidence of what the truth is.

Concepts, Conceptualizations, Operationalizations, Measurements, Variables, and Data Expert—Brenidy Rice

Brenidy Rice is a problem-solving court coordinator with the state of Colorado's Judicial Department. In this important multidisciplinary role, Brenidy is involved in planning, conducting, evaluating, and implementing research on a daily basis, and she is working with a variety of other public service organizations such as probation, state public defendant's offices, state district attorneys' councils, and the office of behavioral health to do so. She is currently overseeing a large third-party evaluation of the state's problem-solving courts. The overarching goal of this evaluation is to determine the influence of these courts on recidivism, as well as the cost benefits of problem-solving courts. Her day-to-day work with such a variety of entities would not be possible without her understanding of the importance of concepts, conceptualizations, operationalizations, variables, and measurements. Brenidy notes, "I deal with research all the time. In this capacity I must be able to identify and evaluate if the research I am reading or studying is good research." She also notes that a part of that assessment is based on if the research had conceptualized and operationalized the concepts well. Another way Brenidy works with research is that she must be able to take research findings and convert them into the real world. This is complicated and requires an understanding of the materials discussed in this chapter.

Brenidy's undergraduate degree is in Spanish, and her master's is in public administration and policy. She started her career a dozen years ago working in social work with a nonprofit agency with court-involved families dealing with dependency, abuse, and neglect. In this role, she worked in her clients' homes. Although she recognized her work made a real positive difference in the lives or her clients, she wanted to help others on a larger scale so she changed jobs and was involved with the implementation of several problem-solving courts around the state of Colorado. This ultimately led her to where she is now. While in school, Brenidy did not realize the degree to which she'd use research methods and use them to be successful. There is no doubt her grasp of the skills described in this chapter built a structure for critical thinking and analysis that continues to be a key to her success.

Brenidy recognizes that research is especially important when it comes to problem-solving courts as their success is supported by a robust body of literature that is responsible for bipartisan support of the courts. This body of research, and Brenidy's ability to assess and convey that research to many types of parties, is responsible for gaining and maintaining resources needed to keep these courts going. She notes that individuals working in her field must understand existing research, emerging research, and how new findings may change or enhance what she and others are doing.

Understanding the role of concepts and how they are used in day-to-day research is critical in her success. For example, her office is currently working on a large federal grant focused on dependency and neglect of children. The overall purpose of this grant is to demonstrate the state's success in dealing with dependency and neglect cases. To do so, they first had to wrestle with the concept of success in this context. What is success? How should they define or conceptualize success? How will their office operationalize or measure this success (or lack thereof)? Currently, the office is using ten performance measures including quicker screening times for substance abuse and mental health assessments, whether a child remained in a home, and whether a child who was removed was returned or placed in a permanent home in a shorter period. These and other measures capture the underlying concept of success.

Another concept frequently encountered in Brenidy's work is recidivism. When challenged to reduce recidivism, they must first decide what recidivism means. What is the definition of recidivism? Is it based on a charge by a prosecutor? An arrest? A conviction? How much time goes by before a researcher should measure whether the subject has recidivated? Two years? Five years? Even a seemingly simple concept like recidivism can be challenging to conceptualize, operationalize, and use in research in a professional setting.

As someone who hires people out of college, Brenidy points to three critical skills beyond good research methods that applicants must have. First, she looks for excellent verbal skills. Employees must be able to communicate important information in a concise manner to different audiences. One audience may need details, and another audience may need a brief overview. Common pitfalls she sees in new applicants is the tendency to provide far too much information to the wrong audience (or vice versa). Also, she notes that in a professional setting, the presenter must understand the material being presented. She notes that a researcher cannot bulls**t professional audiences and that attempts to do so will destroy trust needed to be successful.

A second critical skill a researcher must have is strong written skills. She notes that too many college students with very poor writing skills apply for work and are turned away for that reason only. Brenidy commonly sees grammar and editing errors in applications, and these immediately makes those in the position to hire suspect of the candidate's entire body of work and skills in general. Like verbal skills, written skills must reflect an understanding of the audience the work is intended for. A researcher must know whether the audience will read one page, the first sentence of each paragraph, or require the finer details in a longer piece.

A third critical skill that applicants must have is the ability to engage in group projects. Brenidy notes that everything done in her office is a group project. Every member must pull his or her own weight, know his or her role, respect deadlines, and work with a diverse group of individuals who may use different styles. Those who cannot do this are not useful employees and will likely not be considered for hire.

Brenidy concludes by noting that understanding research, and translating research into programs and policies, is challenging. She recognizes that being able to do so are unique skills but they are extremely valuable. In fact, to be hired in her office, these skills are required. During interviews, candidates are given data and asked what recommendations can be made based on the data. This exercise looks to ascertain whether candidates understand basic research methods including an understanding of conceptualization, operationalization, and other topics described in this chapter.

Chapter Wrap-Up

This chapter presents the stages and skills needed to move from abstract concepts to measurable variables. These steps are crucial, and great attention must be given them to conduct strong and valuable research. Failure to address any of these foundational elements will result in weak research of questionable value. Variables are used to conduct analysis and answer research questions. The stages covered in this chapter include identifying concepts and how they vary. Next, the chapter presented what conceptualization is and why it is performed and important. By using the conceptual definitions resulting from conceptualization, operationalization was described and several examples were provided. These examples included identifying precisely *how* a researcher can indirectly measure—using one or multiple measures—each concept. Additionally, the chapter covered the variables including types of variables such as independent, dependent, and control variables. Attributes/response categories were also introduced, and the importance of multiple exclusiveness and exhaustiveness in relation to attributes were described. Relatedly, levels of measurement including nominal, ordinal, interval, and ratio were described as well as why these are important. In addition, validity and reliability, including types of each, were introduced and described. Each stage, and each element found in each stage, requires dedicated attention to maximize the value of the research conducted.

How did our case studies deal with the road from concepts to variables? Table 4.4 presents those items for each featured article. As shown, each piece of research dealt with different concepts, variables, and even the way they were handled during research. Finally, the chapter concludes with an interview with Brenidy Rice, a problem-solving court coordinator, who identifies the importance of these steps in her daily work. In the courts, understanding research and thinking deeply about concepts such as success and recidivism, and how to best operationalize them, is critical. In Chapter 5, the different types of samples and a variety of approaches for gathering samples are introduced and described. This chapter takes you one step closer to gathering data for your research.

Applied Assignments

1. Homework Applied Assignment: Conceptualization and Operationalization

Select three concepts used by either Cuevas, Santos, Melde, or Zaykowski in their research. After identifying those concepts, describe how each researcher conceptualized, and then operationalized, those concepts. What variables did they ultimately end up with? What measures were used to measure each concept? What are other ways that the researcher could have done this for each concept? Do you think that each measure used is valid? Why or why not? Be prepared to justify why you stopped when you did in your search. Be prepared to discuss your findings in class.

2. Group Work in Class Applied Assignment: Concepts to Variables in a Survey

As a group, you need five concepts to work with for this assignment. The first two are maturity and happiness. As a group, select three additional criminal justice or criminological concepts that interest you. As a group, describe in detail how you will conceptualize and operationalize each of those five concepts for use in a survey that will be printed and distributed. How will you ultimately measure each concept? What will your survey question look like

exactly? What will the response categories for each survey question include? Be sure to focus on mutual exclusiveness and exhaustiveness if applicable. What are the strengths of your measures? What are the limitations? Be prepared to discuss and share your summaries in class.

3. Internet Applied Assignment: Poor Survey Questions

Select a peer-reviewed academic journal article available online that includes independent and dependent variables. In your thought paper, you need to summarize the research conducted. Identify the dependent variable(s) (DVs) and how it is operationalized/measured. Specify all independent variables (IVs) used in this research and why they are important. Describe the way in which the researcher believes the IVs and DVs are related. Use an illustration to show the purported relationship among the variables. Discuss whether you think other independent variables should be included in their model and why. Identify any missing IVs and why you believe they were not included. What future research questions would these missing variables suggest to you? What were the conclusions of the research? Turn in the journal article with your thought paper.

Table 4.4 Featured Research: Hypotheses, Concepts, and Variables			
Researcher	**Hypotheses**	**Major Concepts**	**Primary Variables Used**
Rod Brunson	None	Police relations; Race; Youth; Urbanity - Given the nature of this research, a goal is to identify important concepts	Youths' attitudes toward the police, their personal experiences with officers, their observations of officers, and detailed accounts of their encounters. Identifying concepts that informs future work is a part of this exploratory research

(Continued)

Table 4.4 (Continued)

Researcher	Hypotheses	Major Concepts	Primary Variables Used
Carlos Cuevas	None	Dating violence; victimization; Latino; teens; Cultural factors	In research questions one through four, the variables are used in descriptive ways to offer estimates of rates of, and risk of, dating violence over time. In these instances, the variables do not serve as independent, dependent, or control variables. 2) In the case of the fourth research question, the dependent variable is dating violence over time, and the remaining variables (e.g., age, gender, SES, immigration, family support, etc.) served as independent variables of interest to demonstrate what cultural factors are associated with dating violence over time.
Mary Dodge	None	Decoys; Reverse prostitution stings–A part of the purpose of this research is to identify important concepts	This exploratory uncovered many concepts that may one day serves as variable in future research
Chris Melde	1) gang members would have higher levels of victimization and perceived risk of victimization than nongang members but 2) as one's actual and perceived risk of victimization increased, the fear of victimization was hypothesized to decrease as a result of youths' socialization into gang culture.	Gang members; Adolescence; fear of violence; perceived risk; actual victimization	(1) Gang membership: Independent variable for all three research questions (2) Actual victimization: Dependent variable for the first research question (3) Perceived risk of victimization: Dependent variable for the second research question. (3) Fear of victimization: Dependent variable for the third research question. (6, 7 & 8) Sex, race/ethnicity and age: Control Variables for all three research questions
Rachel Santos	Given offenders offend near where they live, the implementation of an offender-focused intervention focused on multiple offenders living in a long-term hot spot of a crime type committed by the offenders will lead to a reduction of that crime type in the hot spot.	hot spots; police intervention; offender	The analysis used the "presence of intervention (and its dosage)" as the independent variables. Dependent variables included were on crime and offender recidivism.

Researcher	Hypotheses	Major Concepts	Primary Variables Used
Heather Zaykowski	None	Victim services; reporting to the police	The dependent variable is whether the victim sought victim services. The independent variables used in this research include all remaining variables including demographics, incident characteristics, types of problems victims experienced, and mental and physical issues.

KEY WORDS AND CONCEPTS

Attributes 118
Categorical variable 121
Concept 103
Conceptual definition 106
Conceptualization 106
Content validity 124
Continuous variable 123
Control variable 113
Criterion validity 124
Deductive reasoning 100
Dependent variable 111
Discrete variable 123

Exhaustive 121
Exhaustiveness 120
Face validity 123
Independent variable 112
Inductive reasoning 101
Inter-rater reliability 124
Interval 122
Level of measurement 121
Likert-type scale 122
Measure 115
Mutually exclusive 120
Nominal 121

Operationalization 106
Ordinal 121
Qualitative data 101
Quantitative data 100
Ratio 122
Reliability 124
Response categories 118
Test–retest reliability 125
Validity 123
Variable 109

KEY POINTS

- Concepts are abstract notions residing in our minds about which society has general agreement. A researcher poses a research question using concepts. Ultimately, the researcher must be able to measure those abstract concepts, but he or she must go through several steps to do so indirectly. Those stages include conceptualization and operationalization that ultimately lead to variables. A researcher uses variables to conduct the research as proxies for the concepts.

- Conceptualization is the process of precisely and comprehensively defining each concept. Conceptualization focuses on definitions. The resulting conceptual definitions are used as guides for operationalization.

- Operationalization is the process of identifying how a researcher indirectly measures the underlying concepts. This includes identifying the nature of the measures that will be constructed, the number of measures used

for each concept, and the nature of data the measures will gather. In addition, operationalization identifies the variables that ultimately represent the concepts.

- Variables can be identified in many ways. One way is the role they play in a piece of research: dependent variables, independent variables, or control variables. Another way is based on the nature of the data gathered including categorical variables, discrete variables, and continuous variables.

- Variables and the data they gather must vary. Research cannot be conducted on constants.

- Levels of measurement identify something about variables as well. Specifically, they identify the nature of the data collected in terms of the degree of information gathered. These include nominal-, ordinal-, interval-, and ratio-level measures. In general, a researcher should opt to gather the highest level of measurement plausible.

- Attributes or response categories must be mutually exclusive and exhaustive for best measurement.

- As a researcher, you must strive to provide attributes that do not mask important

characteristics or that lead to a desired outcome. As a researcher, you are interested in what the research demonstrates, not in guiding the research to a desired outcome.

REVIEW QUESTIONS

1. What are concepts, and how are they related to research?

2. What is the goal of conceptualization? Why is it important?

3. What is the goal of operationalization? Why is it important? What is the difference between conceptualization and operationalization?

4. What are measures, and why are they important? Why would you want to use multiple measures?

5. What are variables? What characteristics should they have? Why?

6. What are attributes? What are they also called? How are they related to research?

7. What are the four levels of measurement? All else being equal, which level of measurement should you strive for? Why?

8. What are categorical, discrete, and continuous variables? How do they differ? Why does it matter?

9. What makes response categories or attributes mutually exclusive and exhaustive? Why is this important?

10. How are concepts related to variables? How is validity related to this? What does reliability refer to? Why are validity and reliability important?

CRITICAL THINKING QUESTIONS

1. A student wishes to examine the influence of personal characteristics of a judge on the outcomes of cases they hear in the courtroom. After a literature review, the student learns that race of the judge is found to be related to case outcome. How might the student conceptualize the race of the judge? How might you operationalize the race of the judge? Are multiple measures useful in this instance? What sorts of question(s) might the student ask, and what attributes would be best in this case? Why?

2. A professor shares some ongoing research with you. In it, she is examining the role of education on risk of violent offending. Which of these are the independent variable and the dependent variable? What might be some control variables you suspect would be important in this project? Why?

3. A student and you are working on a research project in class. The research question you've selected is, "How do personal characteristics influence the level of support for the LGBTQ community on campus?" One of the relevant concepts in this research taken from the literature is whether the individual is LGBTQ or not. Your colleague is proposing the operationalization of whether the respondent is

LGBTQ to include an observation (by you) based on how respondents dress. If you believe someone is LGBTQ given his or her attire, you are to mark that the person is. If you don't think so, given the person's physical appearance, then you are to mark that he or she is not. It is up to you to address the validity of this measure. What would you write? Is this a valid measure? What might be a better way to go about this?

4. Your roommate is working on a research project using a Likert-type scale. She is uses four response items for it, including Disapprove, Slightly Approve, Somewhat Approve, and Strongly Approve. You ask her why she selected those categories, and she responds that she knows that most people approve so she's making it easy for them to respond. She also mentions to you that because this is an interval-level measure, it is not a problem. What suggestions might you offer her in terms of this plan and her thoughts about her measure? Why is what she is proposing problematic? What is a better way to accomplish this?

5. You are studying with your study group for the upcoming midterm in research methods. One student has prepared a sheet that makes it easy for each of

you to memorize all the independent variables and dependent variables used in criminology and criminal justice research. You don't find this useful. Why is that? Can you offer several examples of why this approach would not be optimal for doing well on the exam?

6. It was noted in this chapter that although the public has general agreement about definition of concepts, they do not have agreement about the specific definitions. What are some examples that you have noticed? For example, what about religiosity? Patriotism? Elite? Educated? Poor? How might people disagree about these specific definitions, and why is acknowledging this disagreement important?

$SAGE edge™

SAGE edge offers a robust online environment featuring an impressive array of free tools and resources for review, study, and further exploration, keeping you on the cutting edge of teaching and learning. Learn more at **edge.sagepub .com/rennisonrm** .

Sampling

Learning Objectives

After finishing this chapter, you should be able to:

5.1 Describe what sampling is, and evaluate why it is an important part of conducting research.

5.2 Compare populations, samples, and censuses. Summarize how they are related, and the advantages and disadvantages of each.

5.3 Identify and describe the different types of units of analysis, and provide examples of each. Contrast units of analyses with units of observation.

5.4 Evaluate the differences between probability and nonprobability sampling. Be able to describe the advantages and disadvantages of each. Also, evaluate the different types of probability and nonprobability sampling approaches available to researchers.

5.5 Summarize the considerations that go into deciding how large a sample is needed when conducting research. Identify what problems arise when a researcher uses a sample that is too large or too small?

5.6 Summarize the ecological fallacy, and provide examples. Be able to provide examples of the problems associated with committing the ecological fallacy.

Inferences: Conclusions about the population based on evidence and reasoning about sample data.

Introduction

Chapters 1 through 4 focused on identifying why research is important, developing a research question, writing a literature review, and identifying the needed building blocks for conducting research. The next step in the research process is to identify and gather a sample from which data will be gathered and used to answer the research question. Sampling is a key stage that can make or break a perfectly designed research project. Understanding the types of samples one can gather, the advantages and disadvantages of each, issues that arise while sampling, and how to gather them are critical for you to be the best researcher you can be.

To present this important information, this chapter is structured as follows. First we describe why sampling is important. Next we define and provide examples of what exactly sampling is. We then compare and contrast it with censuses that are frequently misrepresented as samples (they are not samples). We discuss important concepts such as units of analyses and fallacies associated with these units. Next we turn to the specific approaches to sampling and the advantages and disadvantages of each. Finally, we address how large samples should be, ethical considerations, and pitfalls commonly seen in sampling. Finally, we hear from sampling expert Sam Gallaher, PhD, who uses sampling in his fascinating career. We think you'll find that sampling is a really fun part of conducting research. It takes you that much closer to your data. With your data, you can finally answer your research question!

Why Is Sampling Important?

Sampling is important because it allows us to conduct research. If you had to rely on gathering data from the complete population for every research question addressed, research would rarely happen. Sampling allows researchers to understand something about the larger population. In other words, using a sample allows a researcher to make inferences about the population from which the sample was taken. **Inferences** are conclusions about a population based on evidence and reasoning produced from a sample drawn from it. Sampling is critical. Our featured researchers reiterate this sentiment. For example, Rachel Boba Santos, in a video interview conducted for this book, states that "bad sampling negates the representation and confidence in the research itself. This is why it is very important to give sampling your full attention." Meanwhile, Carlos Cuevas finds that some are more thoughtful about it than others. He says that some researchers just look for the easy way to gather subjects, but that would be a mistake in many instances. As we have repeatedly noted, your research is only as good as the weakest part. If you are unsure about how to do this, take Heather Zaykowski's advice and ask an expert to help you. Don't let the weak link in your research be from poor sampling.

Population parameter: Summary of something in the greater population.

Sample statistics: Summaries of data gathered from a sample.

A goal of research is to understand something about a population. For example, Cuevas and colleagues wished to understand the rate of dating violence among Latinos in the population (Sabina, Cuevas, & Cotignola-Pickens, 2016). That rate in the population exists but is unknown. As shown in Figure 5.1, a **population parameter** is a numeric summary of something in a population such as the victimization rate. A population parameter may be the average age of *all* people in the population, the mean years someone spends in prison, the average number of children per household, or many other things. Because we generally do not know what the value of the population parameter is, we must do something to estimate that population parameter. We estimate a population parameter by drawing a sample and by calculating sample statistics from that sample. **Sample statistics** are summaries of data describing a sample. For example, you may gather a sample of high school students and calculate the average age of respondents. That average age is a sample statistic that summarizes the age of the students in the sample in one tidy numeric descriptor. That sample statistic is used as a best estimate of the population parameter. Other examples are that a researcher can calculate an estimate of the victimization rate among young Latinos, rates in which victims of violence access victim services, offending rates among women, or recidivism rates among juveniles, from a sample to learn about the population. In Zaykowski's (2014) research, she provided numerous population estimates, including that 76.1% of victimizations in which the victim accessed victim services were reported to the police compared with 48.0% of victimizations that were not reported to the police. Each of these statistics describes the sample, and those sample statistics are used to infer back to the larger population from which they came. In sum, a researcher gathers a sample from a population, calculates statistics using data from the sample, and then uses those statistics as an estimate of the unknown, but sought after, population parameter.

In other types of research using non-numeric data, a researcher does not focus on generating statistics. Still, this research uses a sample in much the same way: to learn something about the population from which the sample was taken. For example, featured researcher Rod Brunson and his colleague needed to compare perceptions and experiences of youth in three equally disadvantaged neighborhoods (Brunson & Weitzer, 2009). To do so, they interviewed 15 teen males in each of three disadvantaged urban neighborhoods to gather data about their experiences and perceptions of police relations. In using those data, Brunson and his colleague offered an understanding by comparing and contrasting experiences and perceptions of teens and police relations.

Sampling makes quality research and understanding about a population possible. Furthermore, sampling makes quality research affordable. If researchers could not gather data from a subset of the population, then most research would not happen given limitations on time, money, and other research-related resources. If samples did not make research feasible, knowledge about so many topics would be severely curtailed or nonexistent. Sampling, and sampling well, is important because any piece of research is only as good as its weakest part. After thoughtful and rigorous development of a research question, and planning about what data will be gathered, it would be disastrous to opt for a poor sampling approach that would call into question your research in its entirety. Conducting excellent research that adds to

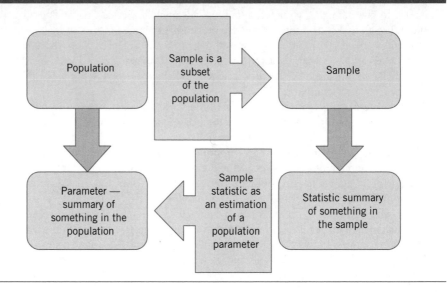

Figure 5.1 Relationships Among Populations, Parameters, Samples, and Statistics

Population

Sample is a subset of the population

Sample

Parameter — summary of something in the population

Sample statistic as an estimation of a population parameter

Statistic summary of something in the sample

Sampling: Selecting a subset of elements from the larger population.

Partial enumeration: Another term used for "sample": not all members of the population are included.

knowledge, aids in the generation of policy, improves the life of others, and assists in building and enhancing theory are all important reasons a researcher should strive to draw the best and most appropriate sample possible.

What Is Sampling?

Sampling is the process of selecting a subset of elements from the larger population. Data are gathered from the sampling units to understanding something about the population from which the sample came. Because the data are gathered from a subset of a population, sampling is also referred to as a **partial enumeration** . Let's consider sampling as it applies to some of our case studies. Consider the work of featured researcher Chris Melde and his colleagues and their three research questions (Melde, Taylor, & Esbensen, 2009):

1. What is the effect of gang membership on self-reported victimization among adolescents?

2. What is the effect of gang membership on perceptions of victimization risk among adolescents?

3. What is the effect of gang membership on the fear of victimization among adolescents?

Each of the three research questions is focused on the experiences and perceptions of adolescents. Given that, the population for this research includes all adolescents (operationalized by the researchers as people ages 10 to 16 years old). Given their goal of understanding these adolescents, Melde and his team could gather data from every adolescent in the United States or the world to answer the research questions. But it would be time-consuming, expensive, and likely impossible to gather data from every 10- to 16-year-old person needed to conduct this study. In lieu of that approach, Melde et al. used an existing data set (that

Esbensen originally collected; Melde was a team member of the original evaluation) that included a sample of adolescents—a subset of the population elements—from which to gather data. The ultimate sample of adolescents provided data, allowing Melde and his collaborators to analyze those data, generate findings, and make conclusions about a larger population of adolescents from which the sample was taken.

Populations and Samples

Researchers are interested in understanding something about a population. Depending on the research question

Some researchers focus on understanding something about groups or organizations such as gangs.

of interest, a population can include elements such as people, organizations, geographic areas, or other things. Although the term has been used repeatedly already, a definition of population has not been offered. A **population** is the collection of all elements that, when aggregated, make up that complete collective. Figure 5.2 offers one example of a population. In this example shown, there is a population of pterodactyls. In total, this population is composed of eight elements or of eight individual pterodactyls. **Elements** are the individual parts that when aggregated form a population. Researchers are ultimately interested in understanding something about the population they study.

Population: Collection of all elements that, when aggregated, make up that collective.

Zaykowski (2014) was interested in understanding what influences victims to seek out victim services in a population of criminal victimizations. Cuevas and his collaborators were interested in understanding something about dating violence among the population of Latino teens (Sabina et al., 2016). Brunson and his colleague wished to examine the views of police among a population of male teens in disadvantaged neighborhoods (Sabina et al., 2016). And Santos and her colleague sought to understand something about how police intervention influences crime in a geographic region (Santos & Santos, 2016). Although hot spots were not sampled (they were constructed across the full geographic region of interest and divided into experimental and control groups), Santos and her colleague did sample offenders to target in these areas. Sampled offenders included those who were convicted and on active felony probation with a prior burglary arrest, and nonviolent convicted offenders on felony probation for drug offenses. Zaykowsi, Brunson, Santos, and Cuevas—like most researchers—do not have the time, money, and other necessary resources to gather data from every element of a population when conducting research. The population may be too large. The population elements may be dispersed across an enormous geographic region. Or it could be that a full accounting of each element in the population is unknown or unavailable. As Santos notes, "[t]here is frequently no way you can look at everything in a population. It is not realistic. This is the reality of research." When gathering data from each element of the population is not feasible, which is most of the time, researchers use a sample. The research is then conducted on the units that compose that sample. The findings from the sample are then frequently used to infer back to the population from which the sample was drawn.

Elements: Individual parts that when aggregated form a population.

Census or a Sample?

Researchers use data from a sample of units to understand the population. At times, however, a researcher is working with a population that is small enough, or easy enough to access, that they can gather data about every element in the population. When the researcher is

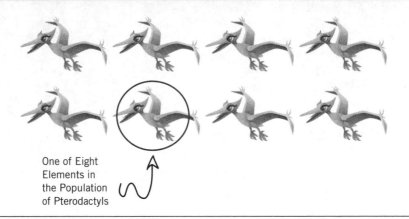

Figure 5.2 Population of Pterodactyls in this Chapter

One of Eight
Elements in
the Population
of Pterodactyls

Census: Gathering of data from a collective that includes every element of the population.

Full enumeration: Another term used for a census because all members of the population were used to gather data.

gathering data from every element in the population, a census (rather than a sample) is being conducted. A **census** is the gathering of data from a collective that includes every element in the population. Because data are taken from every element in the population, a census is also referred to as a **full enumeration** of the population. Using the data gathered from the census, a researcher can address a research question. Whether you are using a sample of population elements, or a census, the purpose of each is the same: gathering data to answer a research question and better understand the population.

Census Advantages and Disadvantages

Censuses offer a major advantage in that they provide complete data about the population. Although this is a major advantage, they are also characterized by disadvantages, making their use less common. The biggest disadvantage of a census is that it is resource intensive, often to the point of being impossible. First, gathering data from a census generally requires an incredible amount of time. Imagine gathering data from a census of all people in North America. How long would this take? Given that, would using a census be feasible? Second, and relatedly, gathering data from a census generally requires using a large staff, which is expensive. Third, and related to the first two, gathering data from a census is costly. Gathering for a census data costs money, and researchers generally do not have the financial backing required to gather data from a census. Finally, a major disadvantage of gathering data from a census is that identifying every element in a population may not be possible. For example, if you needed to gather data about every homeless person in the nation, can this be done? Are all homeless identified? Are many of them hiding? Is there a list of every homeless person available? How about a list of all teens living in an urban disadvantaged neighborhood? Does this list even exist? If you have access to a census and are not limited by resource constraints, conducting a census is ideal. Too often, however, resources are constrained, and a list of all elements in the population is unavailable, meaning you must opt for a sample instead. Happily, using samples can be as informative as a census under certain conditions.

Sample Advantages and Disadvantages

Samples are advantageous in that they are generally less expensive to work with and generally require less time to gather data needed. Some types of samples can closely represent the population from which it was drawn. A **representative** sample is one that accurately represents or reflects the population from which it came. When this is the case, a researcher can generalize the findings from the research based on the sample to the population from which the sample was taken. To be clear, a researcher rarely has a perfectly representative sample, although that is the goal. **Generalizability** means that the findings from research using a sample can be used to understand something about the population from which the sample was taken. Stated differently, generalizability means a researcher can use findings from a sample to make statements about the population. Both representativeness and generalizability are highly sought-after characteristics in many research projects.

The greatest disadvantage of a sample is that, except in rare circumstances, samples do not reflect the underlying population 100% accurately. Although you can gather a sample in such a way that it is highly representative of the population it is intended to represent, a perfectly representative sample is usually impossible. Santos shares that even when researchers thinks they have a perfectly representative sample, they likely do not. That is the reality of research; it is never perfect. There are several ways that a sample may not reflect the underlying population. Some are described in the following subsections.

Sampling Error

As noted, samples rarely perfectly represent the population from which they were drawn. The difference between the sample and the population is known as **sampling error**. All samples have some degree of sampling error. For samples using numeric data, sampling error is the difference or the error between sample statistics and population parameters. Given that a sample does not contain all data from every member of the population, then statistics from any sample are not going to be exactly equivalent to the corresponding population parameters. Sampling error is inversely related to sample size. This makes sense since as a sample size increases, it has more information about the population (hence, the smaller sampling error). On the other hand, as sample size decreases, the sample has less data and sampling error increases. Figure 5.3 illustrates how sampling error relates to sample size.

In scenario A, a researcher wishes to estimate the average age of people in the population of 80 people. A sample of 79 people was drawn, and the average age (the sample statistic) is 47 years. How reasonable do you think it is to suspect that this sample statistic based on the sample size of 79 (out of a population of 80) would accurately reflect the population parameter age? Given that the sample almost perfectly reflects the population from which it was drawn, it is reasonable to believe that there is *little sampling error* present. The little error that exists stems from the fact that one population member is not represented in the sample.

In scenario B, the scenario is the same except that the researcher selected a sample of one (out of a population of 80) to understand the average age of the population. In this example, we see the sample statistic for age is 14 years. Given that the sample is so small, there is a great deal of sampling error present. This sample statistic is much different from the age in the population, which we know is 45 years. A small sample will do a poor job informing about the population from which it was taken.

As this example demonstrates, sample size is related to sampling error. All else being equal, the larger the sample size, the smaller the sampling error. More data from a larger sample is equivalent to less error or deviation between a sample statistic and a population parameter—less sampling error. There is one way to eradicate sampling error (although other types of error may be present), and that is to use a census. This is generally not a realistic option, as described earlier. More realistically, a researcher can use approaches to minimize sampling error. First, as a researcher, you can gather a larger sample. A way to minimize sampling error is by selecting a sample that accurately reflects or represents the diversity of the population. Failure to use a representative sample will lead to greater sampling error. A third way sampling error is minimized is by conducting research on a homogenous

Representative: Desirable characteristic of a sample that indicates it accurately represents or reflects the population from which it came.

Generalizability: Desirable characteristic of findings from research indicating that the results from a sample can be applied to the larger population from which the sample was taken.

Sampling error: Error between sample statistics and population parameters.

Scenario A—Population of 80; Sample Size of 79
Population parameter for average age = 45; Sample statistic for average age = 47.
Very small sampling error

Sample

Scenario B—Population of 80; Sample Size of 1
Population parameter for average age = 45; Sample statistic for average age = 14.
Large sampling error

Bias: Describes a sample that fails to include a particular type of individual or particular groups found in the population.

Biased sample: Indicates that the sample fails to include a particular type of individual or some groups found in the population.

population. Generally, researchers do not have the ability to choose the characteristics of their population, but it is important to recognize that a more homogenous population is associated with less sampling error. Identifying the precise amount of sampling error associated with any sample is beyond the scope of this book, but it is important to recognize what sampling error is and how it affects research.

Bias

Another way a sample can be imperfect is through bias. **Bias**, or a **biased sample**, indicates that the sample fails to include a particular type of individual or some groups found in the population. Figure 5.4 illustrates this problem. In this example, there is a population of 21 kids in which 14 kids have crew cuts and 7 have ponytails. A sample of 7 kids was

drawn into a sample—all of whom have crew cuts. This sample is biased because none of the kids with ponytails is included in the sample. The findings from research using this biased sample would not generalize well to the population and would be characterized by more sampling error than expected. In reality, very few samples are completely unbiased. A more realistic goal for researchers is to select a sample in which any bias is so small that the sample closely approximates the population.

Unit of Analysis

An important concept to consider when sampling is the unit of analysis. A **unit of analysis** is the what, or who, that is being studied and analyzed for a particular piece of research. It is the unit being studied, and the level of social life the research question is focused. For example, in featured researcher Mary Dodge and colleagues' exploration of undercover women working john stings, her unit of analysis—the who or what being studied—was an individual (i.e., policewomen; Dodge, Starr-Gimeno, & Williams, 2005). In Zaykowski's (2014) research on accessing victim services, the who or what being studied was victimizations. For Cuevas and colleagues, an individual was the who or what being studied (i.e., Latino youth; Sabina et al., 2016). Santos's unit of analysis comprised the offenders being targeted for intervention (Santos & Santos, 2016). As these examples suggest, several categories of units of analysis are used in criminology and criminal justice research. In the broadest sense, they are individuals, groups and organizations, geographic areas, and social artifacts and interactions.

Individual

The most common unit of analysis used in criminology and criminal justice research is the **individual**. A large proportion of research in criminal justice and criminology is interested in analyzing and understanding something about people. Likewise, many of our featured researchers fall into this category. Chris Melde and colleagues focused on understanding adolescent individuals (Melde et al., 2009). And Rod Brunson and colleague focused on individuals who are male teens (Brunson & Weitzer, 2009), whereas Dodge and colleagues focused on understanding female undercover police officers (Dodge et al., 2005). In each case, and in a great deal of criminal justice and criminology research, the unit of analysis is the individual. Individual units of analyses can take on many forms, depending on the research: victims, college students, offenders, judges, parole officers, parolees, police officers, prisoners, university

Unit of analysis: What or who that is being studied and analyzed in a particular piece of research. It is the unit being studied and the level of social life that the research question is focused on. These sometimes differ from the unit of observation.

Individual: Most common unit of analysis used in criminology and criminal justice research that indicates that the who or what being studied is an individual. This could be any person in the population or specific individuals such as students, offender, or law enforcement officers.

Research in Action
Low Self-Control and Desire for Control: Motivations for Offending?

When people think of crime, they generally think of street crimes such as robbery, assault, or homicide. Yet, another common type of equally damaging crime, although much more challenging to define, is white collar crime. Craig and Piquero (2016) use the National White-Collar Crime Center's definition of white collar crime to compare the similarities and differences between street-level and white-collar offending. That definition is "Illegal or unethical acts that violate fiduciary responsibility or public trust, committed by an individual or an organization, usually during the course of legitimate occupational activity, by persons of high or respectable social status for personal or organizational gain." In particular, the researchers used two personality traits—low self-control and desire-for-control—to predict intentions to commit embezzlement, credit card fraud, and shoplifting.

Craig and Piquero offer two hypotheses they test in this research:

1. Low self-control will predict intentions to engage in embezzlement, credit card fraud, and shoplifting.

2. High desire for control will predict intentions to engage in embezzlement and credit card fraud among those with low self-control but will not predict shoplifting.

To explore this topic, the researchers used vignettes on a convenience sample of criminology courses at a university. Ten undergraduate courses were surveyed, and from them, 298 surveys were completed. The response rate equated to 54%. The vignettes used included three hypothetical scenarios of different offenses: two white-collar crimes and one minor property crime. One involved a scenario in which an individual embezzled $250 from the organization where he worked. A second vignette described an individual engaged in $30 credit card fraud. In addition, the third vignette involved a person committing minor shoplifting. After the subjects in the sample read these vignettes, they offered their likelihood of engaging in each act. In addition, the subject answered questions from two personality scales. The first scale gathered data on desirability of control, and the second gathered data on low self-control.

The researchers used regression to isolate the effects of both desirability of control and low self-control on the likelihood of committing each of the three acts. The findings indicated that those with low self-control would be more likely to embezzle, commit credit card fraud, and shoplift. These findings support Hypothesis 1. Furthermore, this finding offers support for the notion that both street-level criminals and white-collar criminals are guided in part by low self-control.

The findings failed to support the second hypothesis. Specifically, the findings found exactly the opposite of the hypothesis: that high desire for control would predict intentions to engage in embezzlement and credit card fraud among those with low self-control but would not predict shoplifting. Instead, respondents with higher self-control and a desire to have control over their life circumstances were less likely to report offending intentions than were those with lower desire-for-control.

White-collar crime costs the public greatly, and understanding what motivates offenders is important. This study, along with the research that came before it, offers some understanding of the role of low self-control and the desire for control on three types of offenses. The findings did not uniformly support the hypotheses and indicate the need for additional research on this topic. With greater understanding about white-collar crime motivation, the public can be saved from the ill effects of this behavior.

Craig, J. M., & Piquero, N. L. (2016). The effects of low self-control and desire-for-control on white-collar offending: A replication. *Deviant Behavior, 37,* 1308–1324.

administrators, children, teens, and so on. Using individual units of analysis means that the findings from the research apply to individuals, not to groups, organization, areas, or other social products.

Groups or Organizations

A second category of unit analysis used in criminology and criminal justice research is the **group** or **organization**. Although less common, some researchers focus on understanding something about groups or organizations such as police departments, fraternities, Girl Scout troops, gangs, extreme athlete organizations, Facebook® groups, married couples, and so on. For example, a researcher may be interested in learning whether bystander intervention programs affect fraternity attitudes toward stopping violence. In this example, fraternities are the units of analysis. Another researcher is interested in understanding how police departments differ in terms of adherence to rape myths, making the police departments the unit of analysis. Research based on groups or organizations explains something about groups or organization. This research does not inform about the people in those groups, the locations of the groups, or anything else except the groups and organizations.

Geographic Regions

A third major category of unit of analysis is geographic region. **Geographic regions** as units of analyses may include city blocks, census tracks, cities, counties, states, or countries. An example of research using the geographic unit as a unit of analysis would be research on three-strikes policies among the states. In this example, the unit of analysis is states. Researchers may decide to gather data from a census—a full enumeration—of the states, or they may decide to draw a sample of states—a partial enumeration. To complete the research, the researchers could gather legislative data from each state, newspaper articles about the policies, or interview the attorneys general in each state. Santos and colleague conducted research focused on geographic regions (Santos & Santos, 2016). The hot spots were then placed in an experimental and a control group (see Chapter 11 for more information); nevertheless, offenders (i.e., individuals) living in the hot spots were the actual unit of analysis. In their work, the geographic region of interest was hot spots. By using census tracks, the researchers constructed hot spots, which became a subject of the research. Research based on geographic regions explains something about geographic regions. This research does not inform about the people living in those geographic regions, groups or organizations in those regions, or anything else except the geographic regions.

Social Artifacts and Interactions

The final category of units of analysis is **social artifacts**, including **social interactions**. Social artifacts include tangible social products such as opinion pieces in newspapers, books, movies, commercials, social media posts, songs, vehicles, mug shots, and other such items. Social interactions refer to intangible social products such as crimes, victimizations, offenses, divorces, legislative meetings, and court cases. For example, Zaykowski's (2014) research attempts to understand the variation found in seeking services among a sample of victimizations.

A piece of research may include multiple research questions, each of which focuses on a different unit of analysis. For example, a piece of research may include a research question

Group: Unit of analysis used to indicate that the who or what being studied is a group. For example, a Boy Scout troop is a group that may be the who or what being studied. Treated the same as organizations.

Organization: Unit of analysis used to indicate that the who or what being studied is an organization. For example, fraternities and sororities are organizations that may be the who or what being studied. Treated the same as groups.

Geographic regions: Units of analyses and the who or what being studied. These may include city blocks, census tracks, cities, counties, states, or countries.

Social artifacts: Units of analyses and the who or what being studied. These include social products such as opinion pieces in newspapers, books, movies, commercials, social media posts, songs, vehicles, mug shots, and other such items.

Social interactions: Type of unit of analysis—or the who or what being studied—that includes interactions such as victimization, marriages, and aggression.

focused on individual units of analysis, but it may also include a research question focused on households as the unit of analysis (a group). Each research question has a unit of analysis associated with it. One unit of analysis is not better than another. Which unit is best to use is dependent on the research question being asked. It is important to understand what the unit of analysis is, as that it is what is being studied. In addition, that same unit of analysis is what the findings apply to. To apply findings for one unit of analysis to some other unit of analysis leads to invalid conclusions.

Unit of Analysis Versus Unit of Observation

Units of analysis were carefully defined as those units—the who or what—about which the research is focused. A related concept is the unit of observation. A **unit of observation** is the unit from which data are collected to answer a research question focused on the unit of analysis. In some research, the unit of analysis is the same as the unit of observation. For instance, recall that in Dodge's research on undercover policewomen acting as decoys (Dodge et al., 2005), the units of analysis is individuals, specifically undercover policewomen. The data about undercover policewomen come from individuals: the policewomen. In Dodge's research, the unit of analysis (undercover policewomen) and the unit of observation were the same—undercover policewomen. Similarly, Cuevas and colleagues' unit of analysis and unit of observation were the same: Latino youth (Sabina et al., 2016).

In other cases, the unit of analysis and unit of observation are not the same. For example, Zaykowski's (2014) unit of analysis was victimization, but the unit of observation was individuals. That is, she was interested in what happens in regard to a victimization (unit of analysis), but the information about what happens was gathered from individuals (i.e., victims; unit of observation). People were interviewed about the different victimizations they experienced. Santos and colleague's research had a different unit of analysis and unit of observation (Santos & Santos, 2016). The unit of analysis as described comprises offenders residing in hot spots. Santos and colleague's data about these offenders were taken from existing crime data, which are social artifacts. Another common example found in criminal justice research focuses on police departments. In this scenario, the unit of analysis—the unit about which the research is focused—is police agencies (a group or organization). Nevertheless, you cannot interview a police agency or have a police agency fill out a survey. Rather, the researcher uses a unit of observation to gather data *about* the police agencies. The unit of observation may be crime reports available online, newspaper articles, interviews of the police chiefs, or surveys completed by an administrative official in each agency. These examples highlight that the unit of analysis is not necessarily the same thing as the unit of observation.

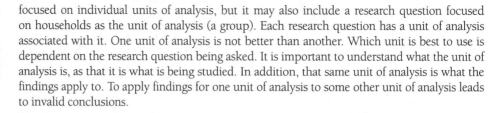

Ecological Fallacy

Understanding about units of analysis is important for many reasons, including avoiding making logical errors. Not only is the unit analysis the who or what that the research is about, it is the who or what the results of the research apply to. Applying findings from research focused on one unit of analysis to a different unit of analysis leads to reasoning errors and invalid conclusions. An error in reasoning related to the unit of analysis is the ecological fallacy. The **ecological fallacy** (Robinson, 1950) is an error in reasoning that occurs when a researcher applies conclusions related to a group or organization to an individual.

Assume a researcher conducted research and discovered that the average IQ at all-women schools is higher than the average IQs at all-male schools. Does this mean that all women have higher IQs than men? No. Suggesting that based on research on schools would be committing the ecological fallacy. The error is concluding that every individual woman has the *average* characteristic of the group of women. Recall that the research used schools as the unit of analysis and generated an average IQ for the school. The erroneous statement that women—all women—have higher IQs than all males is not supported by this research. Even in light of the findings about average school IQs, there will be some variation among the people in the schools. A researcher will be able to find women with lower IQs than men and vice versa.

Another example is that a researcher finds that offending rates in census blocks on the east side of a river are much greater than the offending rates on the west side of the river. In this example, census blocks are the units of analysis. The researcher discovers that someone reporting on her work states the conclusions as "People living on the east side of the river offend more than those on the west side of the river." This conclusion is an example of the ecological fallacy, and this statement is not supported by the analysis. The analysis offered findings on census blocks, and the fallacy assumes that all individuals living on the east side of the river are characterized by the *average* offending rate of the area. The incorrect conclusion takes findings from a large geographic region and applies it to individuals, which is inappropriate.

There are many reasons that the findings at a nonindividual unit of analysis do not translate to the individual unit of analysis. It may be that the census blocks on the east side of the river are populated and that those on the west side are unpopulated (leading to differences in offending rates). It could be that one family on the east side of the river commits thousands of offenses—enough to lead to a high offending rate in those census blocks—while all other people in those areas live crime-free lifestyles. The point is that it is a fallacy, and just plain wrong, to attribute findings to individuals based on conclusions about a nonindividual unit of analysis.

> **Individualist fallacy:** Also known as "reductionism" or as "reductionist fallacy." It is a reasoning error that occurs when a researcher applies conclusions based on research using an individual unit of analysis to a group or an organization.

Individualist Fallacy

Another error in reasoning related to unit of analysis is the **individualist fallacy**, also known as reductionism or the reductionist fallacy. The individualist fallacy occurs when a researcher applies conclusions based on research using an individual unit of analysis to a group or organization. This fallacy, identified by Alker (1969, p. 78), involves ascribing to the group the characteristics of an individual. In Alker's words, the individualist fallacy occurs when a person tries "to generalize from individual behavior to collective relationships." An example of the individualist fallacy would be to believe that all women who attend an all-women's school are brilliant because the five women attending an all-women's school you surveyed for some research had IQs in the top 1 percentile. Concluding that all in a woman's school are brilliant because of results from an individual or individuals is the individualist fallacy.

Choosing a Sampling Approach

What is the best sample? How do you choose the best sampling approach? The best sample and approach is the one that best allows you to answer the research question. Exactly how that is accomplished depends on the research project of interest. When we look back at the work of Melde and colleagues who focused on adolescents (Melde et al., 2009), imagine if Melde and his team opted for a sample of four adolescents from a holiday party at his house. From these four adolescents, they gathered data, and from those data, they produced findings. Are there better ways to develop a sample to gather data to from? Yes. Why? Because at least in this hypothetical scenario, the method in which faux-Melde and team gathered their sample of adolescents—easy-to-access people in Melde's family sharing a holiday meal with him—made them unlikely to reflect the larger population of adolescents. There are better ways for faux-Melde and team to approach these particular research questions, especially given the development of this topic in the literature.

Yet choosing easy-to-access adolescents is exactly the approach used by Brunson and colleague because in that case, it was the most appropriate approach available (Brunson & Weitzer, 2009). They had a small population (young males in those three neighborhoods) and no master list of young males from which to work. This meant using community organizers in local recreation centers to point to likely subjects was their best option. In some cases, using multiple approaches is desirable. Dodge et al. (2005) needed to interview a sample of women law enforcement agents who had worked undercover in prostitutions stings. To find these 25 women, they used both convenience sampling and snowball sampling. Cuevas and colleagues' sample was gathered using probability approaches (Sabina et al., 2016). First, subjects were drawn into the sample by using national random digit dialing (RDD) in high-density Latino neighborhoods. Second, telephone numbers were selected at random from a sampling frame of Latino surnames. **Random digit dialing (RDD)** is an approach used to gather subjects for a sample (when data gathering occurs over the phone) by generating telephone numbers at random. In using this approach, Cuevas and colleagues produced a sample that is representative of adolescent Latinos in the nation. Furthermore, their findings will be generalizable to the larger population of adolescent Latinos. Therefore, the best sample and approach depends on many elements of the research as the remainder of the chapter demonstrates. Using a well-constructed sample for research means the difference between having findings that are useful and having findings that are not useful at all.

A researcher can use many sampling methods to obtain a sample, and which method is best is contingent on a variety of factors, including the research question, and on knowledge about the population. Resource availability is also a consideration because different approaches require more or less time, money, staff, and other considerations. In general, there are two major approaches of sampling: probability and nonprobability. Also, a variety of specific types of probability and nonprobability sampling approaches are used. Figure 5.5 illustrates the variety of probability and nonprobability sampling approaches used in criminology and criminal justice.

Probability Sampling

Probability sampling refers to the process of selecting a sample from a population in which every population element has a known, nonzero chance of being selected. Probability sampling requires the presence of a **sampling frame**, which is a comprehensive list that includes all elements of the population. The elements listed in the sampling frame are **sampling elements**. Depending on the research question, a sampling frame

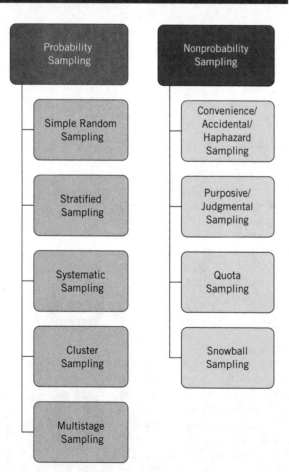

Figure 5.5   Probability and Nonprobability Approaches

could be a list of all students in a school, all governors in the nation, all prisons in the state of Texas, all prisoners in a prison, and so on. From this sampling frame, a researcher draws the desired number of sampling elements to construct the sample. Access to a 100% complete and accurate sampling frame may not always be possible, but getting a sampling frame as close to perfect is the goal. Researchers have to at times be creative about finding sampling frames. Unfortunately there is no "sampling frames r us" online warehouse. Cuevas and colleagues' research needed a sample of Latino youth (Sabina et al., 2016). To gather their sample, they used two probability approaches. First, through RDD, telephone numbers were generated in what were known to be high-density Latino neighborhoods. In addition, additional subjects were drawn into the sample by using a sampling frame of Latino surnames.

Drawing names out of a hat is one simple random sampling approach.

A researcher can use several types of probability sampling approaches, including simple random sampling, stratified sampling, systematic sampling, and cluster sampling. These approaches are not mutually exclusive and may be used in combination. In all cases, the probability sampling described as follows is done without replacement. **Sampling without replacement** indicates that any sampling element can appear only once in a sample. Should, during the selection of elements in a sample, an element be selected a second (or third, or fourth, etc.) time, a researcher should not add that element to the sample a second time, but the researcher should simply ignore that selection and move on with the sample selection. Each of the commonly used approaches to probability sampling is described next.

Simple Random Sampling

Simple random sampling is a type of probability sampling in which each element in the population has a known and equal probability of being drawn or selected into the sample. This is the only type of probability sampling with that characteristic, as the sampling elements in others approaches do not have equal probability of selection. To gather a sample using simple random sampling, you first need to identify the desired sample size. Then, you need to select sampling elements at random until the desired sample size is achieved.

The classic example of simple random sampling is putting the name of every sampling element in a population on a slip of paper and then drawing the slips of paper out of a hat one at a time until the sample size needed is reached. Names drawn from the hat are those selected for the sample. Another simple random sampling approach would be assign a unique identification number to every sampling element on the sampling frame and then using a random number generator (e.g., http://stattrek.com/statistics/random-number-generator.aspx) available on the Internet, or a table of random numbers, selecting elements into the sample. For example, a random digit generator may first randomly generate the number "37," which means the 37th element listed on the sampling frame would be in the sample. The random digit generator may next generate the number "173," meaning the 173rd element on the frame would be included in the sample. Disregard any number randomly generated multiple times and proceed. This process continues until the desired sample size is reached.

Simple random sampling produces samples with several desirable qualities. First, this approach is simple to use given a sampling frame. Second, simple random sampling works with large and small samples. Third, simple random sampling results in samples that nearly perfectly represent the population from which it was drawn. Simple random sampling is also limited in some ways. One disadvantage of simple random sampling is that complete sampling

Sampling frame:
Comprehensive list that includes all elements of the population. It is from the sampling frame that probability sampling selects the sampling elements.

Sampling elements:
Individual items found on sampling frames. Specific sampling elements are selected for samples.

Sampling without replacement: Any sampling element can appear in a sample only once. Should, during the selection of a sample, an element be selected a second (or more) time, a researcher should simply move on with the sample selection.

Simple random sampling:
Type of probability sampling in which each element in the population has a known, and equal, probability of being drawn or selected into the sample.

Systematic sampling:
Probability sampling approach in which the sample is constructed by selecting sampling elements from a sampling frame using a sampling interval.

Sampling interval:
Number, or the distance between, each sampling elements selected to be in a systematically drawn sample. Stated differently, a researcher picks every *n*th element from a sampling frame for inclusion in the sample.

1-in-*k* method: Most commonly used systematic sampling approach that is based on the formula $k = N / n$.

Periodicity: Potential issue when using systematic sampling approaches that refers to a pattern hidden in the sampling frame. Periodicity occurs when a characteristic relevant to the study being conducted is found in the sampling frame and when that characteristic appears on a cyclical basis that matches the interval used in systematic sampling.

frames are frequently not available. For many research questions, it is difficult or impossible to identify every element of a population. Second, simple random sampling is often expensive and not feasible in practice. For example, imagine you have a complete sampling frame from which to draw a sample but the population elements are dispersed over a huge geographic area such as the United States. If you need to access each element in the sample for an in-person interview, using simple random sampling would not only be time-consuming, but it would also be costly (travel expenses) and resource intensive in other ways. As a result, although simple random sampling has desirable qualities, it may not be the best choice for large populations, especially when they are dispersed widely.

Systematic Sampling

Another probability sampling approach is systematic sampling, which some argue is the most used type of probability sampling. **Systematic sampling** constructs a sample by systematically selecting sampling elements from a sampling frame based on a sampling interval. A **sampling interval** is a number or the distance between each sampling element selected. Stated differently, a researcher picks every *n*th element from a sampling frame for inclusion in the sample. Although several types of systematic sampling approaches are available, this text focuses on the most commonly used approach referred to as the **1-in-*k* method.** The 1-in-*k* method is based on the following basic formula:

$k = N / n$

k = sampling interval

N = population size; total sampling elements on the sampling frame

n = total sample size desired; number of sampling units required

Imagine a researcher who has a population size (*N*) of 144. He or she requires a sample size (*n*) of 12. To determine the sampling interval, the researcher uses the formula to find:

$k = N / n$

$k = 144 / 12$

$k = 12$

This basic calculation indicates a sampling interval of 12 is required. Next, the researcher must identify a starting point in the sampling frame. This is selected by randomly selecting a starting point from 1 to *k* or in this example from 1 to 12. Assume the researcher randomly selected the number 4 as the starting point. To draw the sample, the researcher selects the 4th element into the sample. They next select the 16th element (the 12th element from the starting point, which is 4 + 12 = 16), and then the 28th element (16 + 12 = 28), the 40th element (28 + 12 = 40), and so on. This continues until the researcher has the desired sample size of 12.

Systematic sampling offers the advantage of being easy to use. A disadvantage of this approach is that there may be a pattern hidden—or **periodicity**—in the sampling frame. Any hidden pattern in the frame might lead to a biased sample. An example of periodicity is if a researcher were selecting a sample of apartments in a high rise for use in a study. The researcher is given a complete list of all apartment numbers that serves as a sampling frame. The numbering of apartments on the frame indicates both the floor on which the apartment is found and the location (and type) of the unit. For example, apartments 410, 420, 430, and 440 are located on the fourth floor as designated by the first number (**4** 10, **4** 20, **4** 30, and 4 40). Because the apartment number ends in a zero, a researcher knows these are corner (i.e., more expensive and much larger) units in the building. If the researcher worked with a sampling interval such that only these larger, and more expensive, corner units were drawn into the sample, bias would be an issue. Similarly, if the sampling interval selected was such that a unit number ending with zero was never drawn into the sample, the sample would be similarly biased. One approach to dealing with this issue would be to ensure the sampling frame list itself is in random order.

Stratified Sampling

Another approach to probability sampling is the use of stratified sampling. **Stratified sampling** is an approach in which the sampling frame is first divided into mutually exclusive and exhaustive subgroups meaningful to the research being conducted. From each **strata** or subgroup, random sampling is then conducted. This approach ensures groups/characteristics on which the strata are based are accurately represented in the population. Note that the word *stratum* is singular and that the word *strata* is plural—the stratum is; the strata are. Figure 5.6 offers an illustration of stratified sampling.

A classic example of stratified sampling involves drawing a sample from a population of high school students. Imagine a researcher wishes to interview a sample of 100 students from a local high school, and it is vitally important for that particular piece of research that she has a sample that accurately represents the four classes (freshman, sophomore, junior, and senior). Her first step would be to construct strata of the four classes. The strata indicate that 30% of the population of students are freshman, 25% are sophomores, 25% are juniors, and 20% are seniors. The researcher next randomly selects 30 students from the freshman stratum (which corresponds to 30% of the population of students), 25 students from the sophomore stratum (which corresponds to 25% of the population of students, 25 students from the junior stratum, and 20 students from the senior stratum. After using this approach, the researcher has a sample of 100 students in which the class level of students perfectly reflects the population on that characteristic.

Stratified sampling produces samples with a desirable characteristic: a sample that offers representation of the population on key characteristics. In fact, stratified sampling produces samples that are more representative than samples generated using simple random sampling. In this way, the use of stratified sampling minimizes sample bias on key characteristics as those subgroups in the population are neither over- nor underrepresented. Like all things, however, stratified sampling has some disadvantages. It is not an approach that can be used for all research projects. First, a researcher must have a sampling frame in order to use it. Second, stratified sampling requires the sampling frame to have enough information that allows each sampling element be placed in only one stratum. Third each element must be placed in only one stratum. Although some population characteristics make placing each element in one stratum easy (e.g., class in high school), others characteristics are not as easily subdivided.

Cluster Sampling

In many cases, researchers do not have a sampling frame of the sampling elements required. Even though they may not have the needed sampling frame, they may have access to a sampling frame where groups or clusters of these elements are located. For instance, researchers may wish to gather data from people in a city. They may have a sampling frame of all housing unit addresses in a city but not a list of all people. When using cluster sampling, they first draw a probability sample (i.e., simple random, systematic, etc.) of all housing units in the city. Second, the researchers might interview one person in each sampled housing unit to gather data. **Cluster sampling** is a probability sampling approach where groups or clusters (where

Stratified sampling: Probability sampling approach that requires the sampling frame to be first divided into mutually exclusive and exhaustive subgroups meaningful to the research. The second step is to independently and randomly sample from each stratum.

Strata: Subdivisions or subgroups of the sampling frame created in stratified sampling.

Cluster sampling: Probability sampling approach where groups or clusters (where a researcher will find the units of observation needed for the research) are first sampled, and then each unit within each cluster is used to gather data.

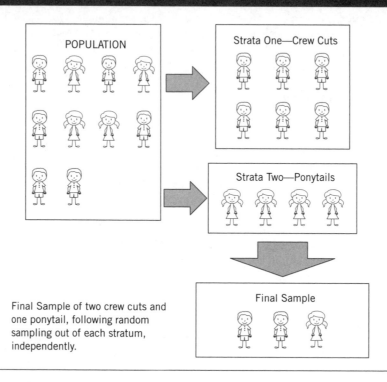

POPULATION

Strata One—Crew Cuts

Strata Two—Ponytails

Final Sample

Final Sample of two crew cuts and one ponytail, following random sampling out of each stratum, independently.

Cluster: Part of cluster sampling that refers to a sampling element where a researcher or more of the desired units of observation are found or associated.

researchers will find the actual sources of data needed for the research) are first sampled, and then each unit within each cluster is used to gather data. **Cluster**, in this context, refers to a sampling element where one or more of the desired sources of data are found or associated. Clusters take on many forms such as states, cities, universities, schools, housing units, census blocks, counties, and so on.

Cluster sampling can also be used in cases where a researcher may have the sampling frame, but gathering data from each unit drawn into sample is too costly or impossible for other reasons such as geographic dispersion. By using cluster sampling, the units from which the data are taken are clustered, meaning the time and money used to access these units is diminished. It would be faster, cheaper and easier to draw a sample of cities (clusters of people) and then to interview individuals in person in a restricted number of cities than it would be to interview people randomly dispersed throughout the nation.

Cluster sampling has wide applicability, and many benefits, and for that reason is widely used. One benefit is that it saves time, money, travel, and other research-related expenses. Second, it can be used in situations where you do not have a sampling frame of the units from which the data will be gathered. This scenario is not uncommon, especially when you need data from individuals. A third benefit is that it easily used for large populations, especially those dispersed over a broad geographic region. Like all approaches, cluster sampling has some drawbacks. Each unit from which data will be taken does not have an equal chance of being drawn in the sample (although their chance of selection is greater than zero, and known). This may lead to issues of representativeness of the population. For this reason, a larger sample is advisable (and cost effective) when using cluster sampling. Figure 5.7 provides an illustration of cluster sampling.

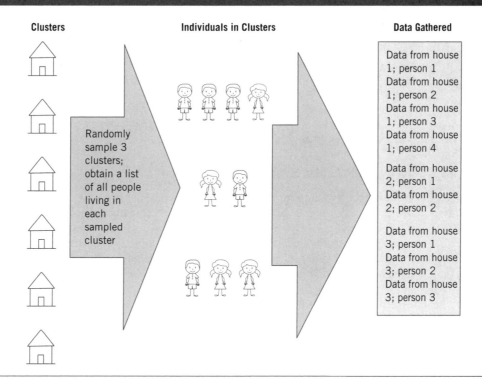

Multistage Sampling

At the beginning of the section on probability sampling, it was noted that a researcher can use probability sampling techniques separately or in conjunction with one another. **Multistage sampling** is not really a probability sampling approach but instead refers to the use of multiple probability sampling techniques to draw a sample. For example, a researcher may first randomly sample housing units (first stage; sampling a cluster of housing units) and then randomly sample those living in each selected housing unit (second stage). Another example of a multistage approach would be to collect a random sample of clusters (schools; stage 1), then stratify the students in selected schools based on a class-level example (stage 2), and then randomly select students to interview in each class level (stage 3).

National Crime Victimization Survey (NCVS) data, the data used by Zaykowski (2014) in her research article, are gathered using a stratified, multistage cluster sampling approach. In the first stage, geographic regions in the United States are stratified to ensure those living in rural and urban areas are represented in the data. Failure to engage in this stratification may lead to an overrepresentation of urban areas. In the second stage, strata are further subdivided into four frames that designate the areas: housing units, housing permits, group quarters, and other areas. In the third stage of sampling, clusters of approximately four housing units (or their equivalents) are selected from each stratum. And finally, all people 12 years of age or older are interviewed in each selected household about their experiences with crime victimization. Use of a stratified, multistage cluster sampling approach leads to a sample that is representative, findings that are generalizable

Multistage sampling: Not really a probability sampling approach, but instead it is the use of multiple probability sampling techniques to draw a sample. For example, a researcher may first randomly sample housing units (first stage; sampling a cluster of housing) and then randomly select people to interview in each of the selected clusters.

(after postsampling adjustments), and makes the NCVS data collection feasible and much more affordable than other approaches available.

Use of a multistage approach is advantageous especially when a researcher seeks data from geographically dispersed units when face-to-face contact is required. It is cost effective and requires fewer research resources. Furthermore, the use of sampling in stages offers the researcher a great deal of flexibility in drawing a probability sample. There are countless ways you could construct a multistage approach making it useful in many contexts. Use of a multi stage approach is limited in that it means the resulting sample is not perfectly representative of the population from which it came because of the unequal probability of selection inherent in its nature. You can use postsampling procedures such as weighting to correct for this; in its unadjusted form, however, the data are not representative of the underlying population from which it originated.

Nonprobability Sampling

Nonprobability sampling refers to selecting a sample from a population in which some members of the population have a zero chance of being drawn into the sample. In addition, the probability of being selected into a nonprobability sample is unknown. A nonprobability sample is constructed using respondents or other elements that have a particular characteristic of interest. That characteristic may be simply that the case is accessible, is a sex offender, or was a police officer who was imprisoned for burglary. For these reasons, research based on a nonprobability sample cannot be generalized to any larger population. Furthermore, research using nonprobability samples cannot be used to answer research questions estimating population parameters.

Although nonprobability samples are limited in some ways, they are very useful for conducting research. First, much research simply cannot be conducted using a probability sample because sampling frames are not available. For example, without nonprobability samples, the field's understanding of topics such as police impersonators, prostitutes, drug dealers, armed robbers, pedophiles, shoplifters, active robbers, and sex traffickers would be zero as no sampling frame is available for these groups. Second, using nonprobability samples allows you to conduct a pilot study before engaging in costly probability sampling approaches. A **pilot study** is a small-scale study conducted to ensure study procedures work as designed. Nonprobability sample based research also offers the opportunity to pretest a newly constructed survey instrument before fielding it to a large and costly probability sample. This is exactly the approach taken by Koss and her colleagues (1982) when studying rape measures. Initially, she used a nonprobability sample in her ground-breaking research focused on the measurement of rape. Koss gathered data from students at the institution where she was part of the faculty to better understand this phenomenon. Later, Koss and others gathered a probability sample and administered the survey to extend our understanding of this topic.

Several types of nonprobability sampling approaches are frequently used in criminal justice and criminology research including convenience sampling (aka accidental or haphazard sampling), quota sampling, purposive or judgmental sampling, and snowball sampling. Researchers frequently use multiple approaches to gather a sample for a single research question.

Convenience, Accidental, Availability, or Haphazard Sampling

Convenience sampling is a nonprobability sampling approach in which a sample is gathered simply based on convenience and ease of finding the elements from which the data will be gathered. Although primarily referred to as "convenience sampling," some researchers also use the phrases **availability sampling**, accidental sampling, and haphazard sampling to refer to this approach. For example, some research is conducted on a sample of students enrolled in Introductory Sociology courses. Or a convenience sample may be selected by stopping people who are shopping in the mall.

Convenience sampling was one of the sampling approaches used by Dodge and her collaborators to gather a sample of 25 women officers who had served as decoys during john stings (Dodge et al., 2005). (Dodge and colleagues also supplemented their sample of women with some snowball sampling, which is described later in the chapter.) These particular subjects were selected because Dodge knew them, knew they were undercover policewomen who had worked as decoys during john stings, and knew she could easily access them. Gathering a sample of women in general, policewomen in general, or even undercover policewomen would not be useful for Dodge's purposes. Why? Because Dodge needed a sample of undercover policewomen *who had participated in john stings* because only they could provide the data needed to address Dodge et al.'s exploratory research questions.

Convenience sampling has multiple advantages. First, it is (obviously) convenient and easy. Second, convenience sampling takes little time. Third, convenience sampling tends to be inexpensive. For these reasons, they are excellent ways to conduct preliminary research to test hypotheses, generate hypotheses, pretest new measures or survey instruments, or pilot other activities. Disadvantages include that the sample is biased and nonrepresentative of the population from which it is taken (unless you are extremely fortunate and just so happened to select a sample that is representative and unbiased). In addition, as mentioned, the findings based on convenience sampling are not generalizable to any larger population, meaning findings must be interpreted with great caution. For these reasons, some argue that research using convenience samples lacks credibility. Figure 5.8 offers an illustration of convenience sampling.

Quota sampling:
Nonprobability sampling approach in which a researcher gathers cases for the sample that have specific characteristics such as urban, suburban, and rural households. This is roughly the nonprobability sampling equivalent to stratified sampling.

Quota Sampling

Quota sampling is a nonprobability sampling approach in which a researcher gathers cases for the sample based on specific characteristics they possess. For example, a researcher may want a sample that reflects the racial proportions in the nation. They know that the population in the United States is currently 64% White, 12% Black, 16% Latino, 5% Asian, and 3% other racial categories. Knowing this, and wanting a sample of 100 individuals, the researcher enters a large Introduction to Psychology class and asks the first 64 White students, 12 Black students, 16 Latino students, 5 Asian students, and 3 students who appear to be biracial, American Indian, or some other race they encounter to complete a survey. Although the sample is still based on nonprobability sampling, the racial characteristics in the sample were selected using quotas. In some ways, quota sampling can be thought of as the nonprobability sampling equivalent to stratified sampling.

The benefits of this approach are that the sampling elements are selected based on desirable characteristics. Second, there is diversity in the sample on the identified characteristics.

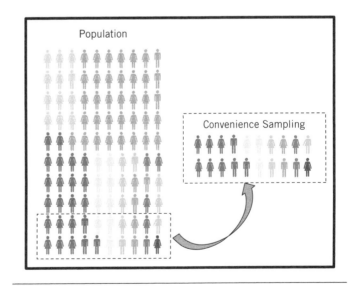

Figure 5.8 Example of Convenience Sampling

Population

Convenience Sampling

Purposive sampling:
Nonprobability sampling approach in which the sample is selected based solely on a particular characteristic of the case. Samples gathered using this approach are selected because the respondents have particular information needed to conduct the research.

Snowball sampling:
Nonprobability sampling approach in which current respondents are asked for contact information of others having the needed characteristics to participate in the study. Also called "networks," "chain referral sampling," or "reputational sampling."

In this way, quota sampling is better than convenience or haphazard sampling. Another advantage are those found in convenience sampling: Quota sampling is cheap, fast, and easy. The disadvantages are also the same as those characterizing convenience sampling. Even with the added diversity in the sample on the selected characteristics, the sample remains biased and nonrepresentative of the population from which it was selected. Just because the sample has racial diversity (in this example), you cannot know with certainty that the subjects used in the quota sample are representative of all people with the same race in the population. The findings of research based on a quota sample lack generalizability to any larger population.

Purposive or Judgmental Sampling

Purposive sampling is a nonprobability sampling approach in which the sample is selected based solely on a particular characteristic of the case. Samples gathered using this approach are selected because the respondents have particular data needed to conduct the research. In other words, respondents or subjects are selected because they have a particular characteristic relevant to the research such as occupation or where they live. Certain steps are required to conduct purposive sampling. First, a researcher must identify the characteristic that makes a researcher eligible to be in the sample. Second, the researcher must attempt to identify all possible subjects with that characteristic. Third, the researcher must strive to contact all individuals with that characteristic. Finally, the researcher should gather the needed data from those individuals. If a researcher merely reaches out to convenient cases of respondents with the named criteria, a researcher is engaging in convenience sampling.

This was the sampling approach taken by Brunson and colleague in their study on adolescent males living in three study neighborhood sites (Brunson & Weitzer, 2009). They approached counselors working in community organizations and asked that they identify young males for participation in interviews for the study. It was not enough for the researchers to find any young male; they required young males who lived in one of three disadvantaged neighborhoods who were at risk of delinquent activities. These characteristics made these young men more likely to have contact with police. Using this strategy, they were introduced to 45 youth for the study.

One advantage of purposive sampling is that it allows an in-depth examination of a topic. This makes this approach suitable for difficult-to-reach special populations. Although this approach is not as fast and easy as other nonprobability approaches, it is still relatively fast and easy to use a purposive sampling approach. It saves money as well as other research resources and allows the researcher to gather pertinent data with little delay. A researcher does not waste time with a probability sample where many or most of those sampled will not have the characteristics of interest. It is surgical-strike sampling in that a researcher homes in on those subjects with the most to offer.

The disadvantages of purposive sampling are the same as those described for the other nonprobability sampling approaches. Although efforts are made to identify all subjects with the desired characteristic, without a sampling frame, a researcher cannot state with certainty that the sample used for the research is representative of the greater population. Like the other nonprobability approaches, research based on a sample using purposive sampling is not generalizable, so the results obtained should not be treated as generalizable. An additional concern with purposive sampling is the potential for researcher bias. A researcher may unknowingly turn away potential respondents for a variety of reasons and, in doing so, bias the findings. Even with these limitations, purposive sampling enables a lot of research on topics that may not be accessible to research using other approaches.

Snowball Sampling

Margin of error: Maximum expected deviation expected between a sample statistic and a population parameter.

A specific type of purposive sampling approach is snowball sampling. **Snowball sampling** is a nonprobability sampling technique that gathers the sample based on referrals. Subjects are selected given a particular characteristic of interest. Once one or a few subjects are identified, they are asked whether they know others with the characteristics of interest that the researchers can contact. Then those referrals are asked for additional referrals. This approach is also called network sampling, chain referral sampling, or reputational sampling. In theory, a researcher stops when no new referral names are provided. Dodge and her colleagues used convenience sampling to gather their sample of undercover female officers. Yet, Dodge and colleagues also supplemented their convenience sampling strategy with snowball sampling. So not only did Dodge identify subjects she knew could provide needed data; she and her collaborators also relied on referrals from those subjects to find additional study subjects. By using two sampling strategies, Dodge gained access to more subjects than either single approach would have provided separately.

Snowball sampling has the same advantages and disadvantages noted for purposive sampling. An additional concern when using snowball sampling is that in addition to any researcher bias that may be present, subjects are located via referral, and bias among those referring might also be present. Again, although imperfect, excellent research has resulted from snowball sampling including the research described here.

Table 5.1 presents a summary of the different approaches to sampling, the advantages and disadvantages of each, as well as any issues related to the relative cost of each approach.

How Large Should My Sample Be?

Perhaps the most common question about sampling focuses on how large a sample should be. When does a researcher stop gathering subjects? When is a sample too big or too little? The answer is not very satisfying, unfortunately, as a researcher needs as big a sample as possible to conduct rigorous research. Yet, getting too large a sample is costly, time-consuming, and will bring no additional advantage to the research. These are not simple questions to answer because the size of a sample is contingent on many things including the type of research being conducted, the nature of the population, and the resources a researcher has available.

Purpose of the Research

If a researcher is conducting research on a topic in which all members of the population have a desired element (e.g., an opinion), then a smaller sample size is required. For example, if a researcher seeks to gather opinion data on a topic such as politics, the environment, or the six types of baby seals in the artic, from the population of Denver, Colorado, or even the United States, a smaller sample is needed. Why? Because everyone has an opinion, meaning everyone interviewed will provide data. In an instance like this, by using a random sampling approach, a researcher needs a smaller sample size to achieve a smaller margin of error. **Margin of error** is the greatest expected difference between a sample statistic and a population parameter. A reasonable margin of error for research on opinions or things in which all members of the population offer data is from ±2.5% to ±3%. A researcher can calculate the needed sample size given the desired margin of error desired using this formula (Niles, n.d.):

$$\text{Margin of error} = 1 \, / \, \text{square root of the sample size}$$

Table 5.1 Commonly Used Sampling Approaches, Advantages, Disadvantages, and Cost Considerations

Sampling Approach	Definition	Advantages	Disadvantages	Relative Cost
Simple Random Sample	Probability sampling approach in which each element in the population has a known, and equal, probability of being drawn or selected into the sample.	1. Simple to use 2. Works well with large and small samples. 3. Results in samples that nearly perfectly represent the population from which it was drawn.	1. Requires a sampling frame. 2. Can be expensive.	1. More expensive than nonprobability Sampling approaches. 2. Can be quite expensive if the population is dispersed over a large geographic area and in-person data gathering is planned. 3. Can be less expensive if data gathering is via the Internet or phone
Systematic Sampling	Probability sampling approach in which a sample is drawn by systematically selecting sampling elements from a sampling frame based on a sampling interval. A sampling interval is a number, or the distance between, each sampling element selected. In this approach, the researcher picks every nth element from a sampling frame for inclusion in the sample.	Simple to use.	1. Requires a sampling frame. 2. May lead to a biased sample if there is periodicity in the sampling frame.	1. More expensive than nonprobability sampling approaches. 2. Can be expensive if the population is dispersed over a large geographic area and in-person data gathering is planned. 3. Can be less expensive if data gathering is via the Internet or phone.
Stratified Sampling	Probability sampling approach in which the sampling frame is first divided into mutually exclusive and exhaustive subgroups meaningful	1. Produces samples that are representative of the population on key characteristics. In fact, stratified sampling produces samples that	1. Requires a sampling frame. 2. Sampling frame must have information on characteristics needed to stratify. 3. Each element must be present in only one stratum.	1. More expensive than nonprobability sampling approaches. 2. Can be expensive if the population is dispersed over a large geographic

	to the research being conducted, and random sampling is conducted independently within each subgroup. In stratified sampling, those subgroups of the population are known as strata.	are more representative than samples generated using simple random sampling. 2. Minimizes sample bias on key characteristics, as those subgroups in the population are neither over- nor underrepresented.		area and in-person data gathering is planned. 3. Can be less expensive if data gathering is via the Internet or phone.
Cluster Sampling	Probability sampling approach where groups or clusters (where a researcher will find the actual sources of data needed for the research) are first sampled, and then each unit within each cluster is used to gather data.	1. Has wide applicability. 2. Efficient and saves time, money, travel, and other research-related expenses. 3. Can be used when the researcher does not have a sampling frame of the units from which the data will be gathered.	1. Each unit from which data will be taken does not have an equal chance of being drawn in the sample (although their chance of selection is greater than zero, and known). This may lead to issues related to precision and representativeness of the population. 2. Requires a larger sample and not recommended for a smaller population.	1. More expensive than nonprobability sampling approaches. 2. Can be expensive if the population is dispersed over a large geographic area and in-person data gathering is planned. 3. Can be less expensive if data gathering is via the Internet or phone. 4. Less expensive than other nonprobability sampling approaches.
Multistage Sampling	Multistage sampling is not a type of probability sampling approach but instead refers to the use of multiple probability sampling techniques are used in two or more stages.	1. Useful when gathering data from a sample that is geographically dispersed and face-to-face contact is required. 2. Efficient and cost effective requiring fewer	Results in a sample that is not perfectly representative of the population from which it came as a result of the unequal probability of selection inherent	1. More expensive than nonprobability sampling approaches. 2. Can be expensive if the population is dispersed over a large geographic area and in-person data gathering is planned. 3. Can be less expensive

(Continued)

Table 5.1 (Continued)

Sampling Approach	Definition	Advantages	Disadvantages	Relative Cost
		research resources. 3. Offers the researcher a great deal of flexibility in drawing a probability sample.	in its nature (this can be accounted for using postsampling procedures such as weighting).	if data gathering is via the Internet or phone. 4. Less expensive than other nonprobability sampling approaches.
Convenience Sampling/ availability sampling/ accidental sampling/ haphazard sampling	Nonprobability sampling approach where a sample is gathered simply based on convenience and ease of finding the sources of data. Although primarily referred to as convenience sampling, some use the phrases availability sampling, accidental sampling, and haphazard sampling to refer to this approach.	1. No sampling frame needed. 2. Convenient and easy to use. 3. Takes little time. 4. Is inexpensive.	1. Resulting sample is biased and nonrepresentative of the population from which it is taken (however, drawing a representative sample is not always the goal). 2. Findings based on the sample are not generalizable to any larger population, meaning findings must be interpreted with great caution (but this may not be the goal). 3. Some argue convenience samples lack credibility.	Cheaper than probability sampling approaches.
Quota Sampling	Nonprobability sampling approach in which a researcher gathers members of the sample based on specific characteristics they possess. For instance, one gathers a sample of 50% women and 50% men.	1. No sampling frame needed. 2. Diversity in the sample exists based on the characteristics used for the quota. 3. Fast, cheap, and easy to use.	1. Resulting sample is biased and nonrepresentative of the population from which it is taken (however, drawing a representative sample is not always the goal). 2. Findings based on the sample are not generalizable to any larger population, meaning findings must be interpreted with great caution (but this may not be the goal).	Cheaper than probability sampling approaches.

Purposive Sampling	Nonprobability sampling approach in which the members of a sample are selected based solely on particular information they possess that is needed to conduct the research. For example, one gathers a sample of only women who have been undercover prostitutes in john stings (Dodge et al., 2005).	1. Sampling frame not needed. 2. Allows for an in-depth examination of a particular topic. 3. Excellent for difficult-to-reach or find populations. 4. Relatively fast and easy to use. 5. Relatively inexpensive.	1. Resulting sample is biased and nonrepresentative of the population from which it is taken (however, drawing a representative sample is not always the goal). 2. Findings based on the sample are not generalizable to any larger population, meaning findings must be interpreted with great caution (but this may not be the goal). 3. Potential for research bias in those selected in the sample.	Cheaper than probability sampling approaches.
Snowball Sampling	Nonprobability sampling technique that gathers the sample based on referrals of others.	1. Sampling frame not needed. 2. Allows for an in-depth examination of a particular topic. 3. Excellent for difficult-to-reach or find populations. 4. Relatively fast and easy to use. 5. Relatively inexpensive.	1. Resulting sample is biased and nonrepresentative of the population from which it is taken (however, drawing a representative sample is not always the goal). 2. Findings based on the sample are not generalizable to any larger population, meaning findings must be interpreted with great caution (but this may not be the goal). 3. Potential for research bias in those selected in the sample. 4. Those referring subjects may be biased negatively affecting the sample.	Cheaper than probability sampling approaches.

Table 5.2	Sample Sizes and Margins of Error
Required Sample Size	**Margin of Error**
800	3.54
900	3.33
1000	3.16
1100	3.02
1200	2.89
1300	2.77
1400	2.67
1500	2.58
1600	2.50
1700	2.43
1800	2.36
1900	2.29
2000	2.24

Saturation: Has several related meanings, one of which involves searching for sources for a literature review. In particular, it indicates the search for sources is complete because one finds no new information on a topic and the same studies and authors repeatedly are discussed.

Replication: Repeating of a piece of research.

Table 5.2 offers sample sizes calculated with this formula to arrive at associated with margins of error. This table demonstrates that when dealing with opinions or similar things, a researcher needs a smaller sample size to achieve a smaller margin of error.

Second, this formula and Table 5.2 demonstrate that the sample size needed for a particular margin of error is *not dependent on the population size*. Look again at the formula: The population size is not a part of it. That means that a sample size of 1,100 individuals, based on random sampling (and no refusals), will provide statistics within ±3% points from the true population value. Similarly, a randomly drawn sample of 1,600 is enough for findings with minimal error (±2.5%). A researcher would need a randomly drawn sample of 1,600 people in Denver to provide a statistic within ±2.5% of the true population parameter. Alternatively, a researcher would need a randomly drawn sample of 1,600 people in the state of Colorado to provide a statistic within ±2.5% of the true population parameter for Colorado. Likewise, a researcher would need a randomly drawn sample of 1,600 people in the United States to provide a statistic within ±2.5% of the true population parameter for the United States.

In contrast, the sample size needed to conduct research examining rarer events is much larger. This type of research is more common in the criminal justice and criminology disciplines. For example, if one's purpose is to estimate the amount of violent victimization occurring in the nation in one year, as is done with the NCVS, a far larger sample than 1,600 is required. Why? Because violent victimization is rare, meaning not everyone drawn in a random sample will have been a victim of violence. The sample size need must take into account the majority of those who have not been victimized. Therefore, a researcher would need to gather an enormous sample in order to have enough victimization cases to offer reasonable estimates of victimization that would be generalizable to the larger population. Consider that in 2015, NCVS data were based on data from 95,760 households and 163,880 people. Even with such large sample sizes, there were 1,023 violent victimizations revealed by the survey during the year, most of which were simple assaults (635). If a researcher wanted to investigate only female victims, young victims, or inner city males, the needed sample size of victimizations would need to be far larger. Although this text cannot go into the intricacies of sample size, it is important to recognize that the topic of the research is highly related to the sample size needed.

Type of Research

Related to the purpose of the research is the type of research conducted. The use of a probability versus a nonprobability sample will affect the needed sample size. Gathering a sample using probability methods tends to require larger sample sizes compared with gathering a sample using nonprobability methods. If a researcher seeks to generate findings that are generalizable back to the population, a larger sample is need compared with when generalizability is not a goal. Consider the work of Dodge and collaborators (Dodge et al., 2005). Their research used a sample size of 25 subjects for their work on women decoys. How did Dodge et al. know to stop their sample with 25 subjects? According to Dodge, she stopped pursuing additional subjects because of saturation. **Saturation** in this context refers to the point at which there is no new data gathered from new subjects. Saturation also indicates that replication of the research should not reveal additional information. **Replication** refers to the repeating of a piece of research. Research findings should remain the same when the study is replicated.

Brunson and his collaborator gathered a sample of 45 adolescents for the study on youth perceptions and interactions with police in disadvantaged neighborhoods (Brunson & Weitzer, 2009). Their sample of 45 is a bit larger than the one used by Dodge and colleagues (sample size = 25; Dodge et al., 2005), but given their need to have an adequate number of subjects (15) from each of the three neighborhoods, a larger sample was required. The researchers capped the number of participants for each neighborhood at 15 because they found they had reached saturation and no new information was being uncovered in the later interviews. Had Brunson and his colleague only been interested in what was happening in one neighborhood, a sample of 15 would have been sufficient.

Nature of the Population

Another consideration when thinking about needed sample size is the nature of the population. Is the population varied or heterogeneous in ways related to the research topic? Or is the underlying population homogeneous? If the research seeks to add to our understanding of a heterogeneous population, a larger sample size will be needed to accurately capture the diversity found in that population. In contrast, a homogenous population will require a smaller sample size since there is little diversity that must be captured by the sample.

Resources Available

Sample sizes are also contingent on resources available. It is a fact that researchers have limited resources available. Although a researcher may desire a sample size of 2,000, he or she may not have the time or finances to work with a sample of that size. The realities of research are a part of the research endeavor. Robert Groves, a methodology expert, and colleagues (2004) provided excellent advice when it was noted that when it comes to selecting a sample size, it is easier to determine what not to do versus what to do. Groves and his colleagues implored people not to use a sample size just because some other research used that sample size. As the information presented in this section should make clear, other research may involve differences not readily apparent. Just because the Gallup® polls interview 1,000 people does not make that the appropriate sample size for anyone else. Thinking about your research purposes, your population, your approach, and the other elements of your project should help you settle on the best sample size for your needs.

Finally, just because a sample is large does not always make it a good or even representative sample. The most important quality of a sample is not its size but *how* the data are collected. If the purpose is generalizability, then samples drawn using probability sampling approaches are better. A small representative sample is better than a large nonrepresentative sample if generalizability is the goal. Keep in mind that a huge nonrepresentative sample is still nonrepresentative. If generalizability is not an important issue for a particular research project, but a deeper and richer understanding of a particular topic is, then a smaller sample drawn using nonprobability methods may be the best option.

Common Pitfalls Related to Sampling

Sampling well is critical to conducting excellent research. Even though it may seem easy in some ways, there are several pitfalls one must be aware of when sampling. Some were introduced in the chapter but are worth repeating here.

Ecological and Individualist Fallacies

Although not pitfalls of sampling specifically, both the ecological and individualist fallacies point to the requirement that a researcher know which unit of analysis he or she is using and apply the findings to that unit only. Applying findings from one unit of analysis to another leads to errors in reasoning. The ecological fallacy occurs when a researcher applies conclusions based on a group or an organization to an individual. The individualist fallacy occurs when a researcher applies findings from an individual unit of analysis to a group or organization. Being clear about the unit one is working with will go a long way to prevent making either of these errors.

Generalizing Findings That Are Not Generalizable

Whether findings of research are generalizable depends on the sample used. A common error made by those who consume, propose, and produce research is to interpret all findings as being generalizable to the greater population. In Chapter 1, we discussed the many reports about statistics purporting to indicate that large proportions of female students are raped on college campuses. By returning to those examples, a review of the methodology of Krebs, Lindquist, Warner, Fisher, and Martin's (2007) Campus Sexual Assault survey and Cantor and colleagues' (2015) AAU survey of 27 institutions of higher education demonstrates that the statistics in question are based on nonprobability samples of all universities. The selection of the two universities in Krebs et al.'s and the 27 IHEs in Cantor et al.'s work came from a nonprobability sampling approach. For that reason, the findings from both pieces of research (as clearly noted by the authors) are not generalizable to any population beyond the universities participating. Although some continue to report this incorrectly, it is up to you as a perceptive and informed researcher to recognize this limitation. It does not mean the research is without merit—in fact, it has a lot of merit.

Ethics Associated With Sampling

When sampling, a researcher should use the sampling approach that is required given the particular research project of interest. Knowingly selecting a sampling approach that is not appropriate for purposes of a research project is not acceptable and should not be done. Gathering the appropriate type of sample for the research purposes and goals is an ethical obligation of all researchers.

Although this chapter has demonstrated that identifying the perfect sample size is not always possible, a researcher must make every effort to take into account the issues described in this chapter. Consider that using too large a sample is unethical because it wastes resources (and often people's time) with no gain in data. A researcher should engage in research that burdens respondents and participants as minimally as possible. This falls under the "do not harm" umbrella of human subjects. It is also incorrect to stop gathering subjects for a sample prior to reaching saturation if that is the goal of the research. A researcher must commit to gathering as many subjects as is required to reach that point.

Other, more obvious ethical considerations are to use the sampling approached approved by the institutional review board (IRB). If a researcher gains IRB approval to sample individuals 18 years of age and older in a setting but does not ensure that juveniles are kept out of the sample, that researcher is engaging in unethical research. As noted in an earlier chapter, certain groups have additional human subjects review, and yet other groups should be approached carefully, even if additional IRB scrutiny is not mandated.

Sampling Expert—Sam Gallaher, PhD

Courtesy of Samuel Gallaher

Sam Gallaher, PhD, is the data analytics and methodology specialist at the Auditor's Office of the city and county of Denver, Colorado. His work at the Auditor's Office includes three primary responsibilities. First, through audits, he adds assurance that taxpayer money is being spent wisely. Second, Gallaher also uses these audits to search for risks to the city (risks include the potential for being sued) as well as to assess whether those groups being audited are meeting their stated objectives (generally defined by the City Charter or outlined in strategic plans). Finally, his role includes searching for and setting up processes to minimize the risk of fraud or abuse. Each of these responsibilities requires an understanding of sampling.

Prior to the Auditor's Office, Gallaher worked as an industrial and manufacturing engineer who conducted research on systems that made fiberglass. The goal of this work was to increase understanding in how changes in a system affected production. Even though Gallaher enjoyed this work, he decided to return to the university to learn additional research skills so he could apply his systems knowledge to social issues. He felt that the combination of social research and systems knowledge could help guard against unintended negative consequences of social policy.

Gallaher's entre into the Auditor's Office was both out of necessity and because he was ready for a change. He was completing his dissertation, working as a research assistant and lecturer, but he needed to earn more money to deal with accumulating student debt. He found the Auditor's website and recognized that what auditors do is the same as researchers. They use quantitative and qualitative analyses and are methodical in their approach. Their work requires they identify a purpose, conceptualize and operationalize measures, collect data, conduct analyses, and report their findings. He was attracted to government auditing so that he could conduct research in the real world and have more a direct impact on society than he could have through traditional research.

A vital part of the work Gallaher does involves sampling. He offers two major reasons sampling is important. First, according to Gallaher, it is rare that a researcher is in a position to gather data from a population. Either a researcher cannot identify the population or they do not have the time or financial resources to gather data from the population. As a result, sampling makes Sam's auditing work possible. A second major reason that sampling is important, according to Gallaher, is that using particular techniques minimizes biases, which means better outcomes. He frequently uses stratification and then random selection from within each group in his sampling to reduce the chance of biases in his findings. Stratification forces Gallaher to identify meaningful differences within a population and then to collect data from within each group, which then creates a sample that more accurately reflects the variation in the population from which the sample was drawn. This technique is particularly helpful when the true variation or error rate of a population is unknown. Audit work may include examination of contracts for compliance, checking revenues and expenditures, measuring departmental performance, or evaluating information system access and data entry rules. Each of these approaches can use sampling given that Gallaher and the other auditors have limited resources to examine processes that could include hundreds or thousands of transactions, decisions, or rules.

Sam encourages students to take the time to understand sampling given its broad use in public and private entities. He finds that sometimes new researchers struggle with clearly defining their population. This step is critical for obtaining the best sample from it. In addition, he finds that new researchers frequently fail to fully understand that population, especially in terms of important variation in it. Understanding that variation enables a researcher to more strategically use stratification. Even with a full understanding of a population and important variation in it, Gallaher encourages students to be prepared for times when a researcher cannot conduct a textbook sample. When asked how often that occurs, he notes the reality of research is that a textbook sample never occurs! This means a researcher must be flexible in dealing with issues that inevitably arise in research, being clear of important variation a researcher can use to strengthen samples, and understanding the importance role of sampling and how it affects research.

Chapter Wrap-Up

This chapter presents information about sampling—what it is and why it is important. Sampling is the process of selecting a subgroup of elements from a population. Research is conducted using data gathered from a sample, and findings from this work are used to infer back to the population from which the sample came. As noted, all sampling approaches are not the same, and which sampling approach is best is contingent on many characteristics of the research as well as on the availability of resources. Two types of sampling approaches were described: probability and nonprobability sampling. Probability sampling includes approaches in which sampling elements have a known, nonzero chance of being selected in the sample. This is an important characteristic as it means the sample is representative of the population from which it came, and the findings that come from the sample are generalizable to the greater population. Although probability sampling approaches have many desirable qualities, not all research is suited for probability sampling. In this case, many methods of nonprobability sampling were discussed. Nonprobability refers to the process of selecting a sample from a population in which some members of the population have a zero chance at being selected in the sample. In addition, the probability of any element being selected into a nonprobability sample is unknown. Nonprobability sampling is useful in many ways, including for pretesting research procedures, and for gaining a very in-depth understanding of a particular topic. In addition, it allows research on a population for which there is no sampling frame or comprehensive list of all elements in the population. This chapter also discussed many important elements associated with sampling such as units of analysis, units of observation, censuses, and considerations about needed sample sizes. Common pitfalls such as the ecological fallacy and the individualist fallacy were discussed.

Table 5.3 offers some information about each of our case studies in regard to sampling. This matrix presents each featured researchers' population of interest, sampling elements, type of sampling engaged in, and units of analysis and observation. The table shows how varied sampling can be, and why it is important for you to carefully think through your sampling plan. Drawing a good sample for your purposes is critical in producing the best piece of research you can. In addition, as Sam Gallaher, PhD, noted, in careers using sampling, understanding how it works and when one approach is preferred over another is the difference in being successful or not in your role. As an analyst in an auditing agency, Gallaher showed how he uses sampling skills every day. He notes that sampling well is one step required for generating useful, accurate findings that have real practical implications both in and out of the academic sector. By using rigorous sampling, he and his colleagues guard against waste of taxpayer dollars.

After this chapter, the text switches gears to the different types of data that researchers collect and use to answer research questions. We begin by discussing qualitative data collection. This includes a presentation of what qualitative data are, why qualitative data collection is important, and the benefits and limitation of this approach.

Applied Assignments

1. Homework Applied Assignment: Sampling Without a Budget

Select either Dodge or Brunson's research for this assignment. In your paper, outline exactly the sampling plan they used. Indicate the advantages and disadvantages of their respective approaches. Now, pretend you have an unlimited budget. Describe how you would replicate their research using a different sampling approach. Why is your approach better? What does it gain that the approach used by the researcher does not? Be sure to discuss the population, sampling elements, sampling approach used, units of observation and analysis, and other important elements in your plan. Be prepared to discuss your findings in class.

2. Group Work in Class Applied Assignment: Developing a Sampling Plan for a Survey of Students at Your University

Your group has been hired by your university to survey students about their satisfaction with the university. At this stage, you need to develop a detailed sampling plan. With your group, identify the population of interest, population, sampling elements, sampling approach used, units of observation and analysis, and other important elements in your plan. Be sure to consider how you will deal with a variety of students, including those who are part-time, full-time, online only, on-campus only, night students only, and those taking both online and in-person courses. How will you deal with students who are taking one semester off, as well as with those who just started at the university this semester? Will you include people who both work at the university and take classes? What are the advantages of your approach? Who is left out, and how might their absence affect the findings of your research? Be prepared to discuss and share your summaries in class.

3. Internet Applied Assignment: Poor Survey Questions

You have been hired to conduct a study comparing the advantages of a larger versus a smaller sample. To make this comparison, you gather two samples. The first sample should consist of 15 people. The second sample should consist of 1 person (you). Once identified, gather data from all subjects regarding the number of friends they have on Facebook. Once you have the data for your 16 subjects, calculate the average number of friends in each sample. The average, or mean, is calculated by adding all the scores in a sample and dividing by the number of subjects in that sample. The mean number of friends in the sample of one person (you) is simply your number of friends you have on Facebook. If someone does not use Facebook, record a 0 for his or her average number of friends. Once you have your data and average number of friends on Facebook, write a paper. In that paper, describe your sample. What type of samples did you use? How did you gather the subjects for your samples? How large were your samples? What are the advantages and disadvantages of your samples? Will your results be representative of any population? Will your results be generalizable to larger populations? Next, present a table showing the data for each subject in your samples (you do not need to use their names; you can simply identify them as subject 1, subject 2, etc.). In looking at the two values (i.e., statistics) for the samples, what do you conclude? Would you be more willing to believe your sample of 1, or the sample of 15? Why or why not? If you had more time, how might you alter your sampling strategy to draw a sample representative of those attending your college, and to draw a sample of a rival university to compare the number of friends? Turn in your paper and be prepared to share your findings and thoughts with the class.

Table 5.3 Featured Research: Population and Sampling Considerations

Researcher	Population	Sampling Element	Type of Sampling	Sample Size	Unit of Analysis	Unit of Observation	Qualities of the Sample
Rod Brunson	Adolescent males in three neighborhoods.	Adolescent males.	Purposive sampling. Counselors working in community organizations were asked to identify and approach young males who were known to live in the neighborhood study sites for participation in the study.	45 male adolescents living in three neighborhood study sites. Respondents ranged in age from 13 to 19 (average age was 16).	Individuals (Adolescent males).	Adolescent males in three study site neighborhoods.	Sample is not representative of any larger population. Findings are not necessarily generalizable to any larger population.
Carlos Cuevas	All adolescent Latinos in the nation.	Latino adolescents.	Probability sample using two sampling frames. First, sampling of high-density Latino neighborhoods was conducted. Also, randomly selected telephone numbers from a list of Latino surnames were drawn into the sample. Numbers answered were asked whether there was an adolescent Latino in the household. If yes, they were offered the opportunity to participate. If there were more than one eligible adolescent Latinos in the household, the one with the next/ most recent birthday was selected to participate in the interview.	1,525 Latino adolescents in Wave 1 of the survey; 574 households in Wave 2 (both adolescents and their caregivers were interviewed).	Individual (Latino adolescents).	Latino adolescents.	Sample is representative of adolescent Latinos in the nation. Findings are generalizable to the larger population of adolescent Latinos.

Mary Dodge	Women law enforcement officers who had worked as decoys in prostitution stings.	Women law enforcement officers who had worked as decoys in prostitution stings.	Convenience sampling plus some snowball sampling as officers referred the researcher to co-workers for participation.	25 female officers; ages ranged from 30 to 41 years with 4 to 16 years of policing experience. Had participated in 5 to 20 decoy stings with an average of 10 stings per officer.	Individual (female undercover police officers).	Female undercover police officers.	Findings are not necessarily generalizable; Sample not necessarily representative of larger population of female undercover officers.
Chris Melde	250 schools that offered a "school-based law-related" education program. Found that 18 schools met the evaluation criteria for eligibility.	Schools participating in a select program.	Purposive sample of schools in the nation that offered a particular education program.	15 schools in 9 cities in four states participated in the evaluation research. All students in classrooms in the grade in which the program was taught were given pre- and post-tests.	Individual (adolescent students in schools using a program).	Students.	Sample is not representative to youth population in general; nevertheless, the sample is representative of students in participating schools using the program. Findings are not generalizable to all youth in the genial population, but the findings are generalizable to the youth attending the schools participating in the program.

(Continued)

Table 5.3 (Continued)

Researcher	Population	Sampling Element	Type of Sampling	Sample Size	Unit of Analysis	Unit of Observation	Qualities of the Sample
Rachel Santos	Noncommercially zoned hot spots.	Hot spots.	Type of random sampling for experimental studies with fewer than 50 cases was used: partially blocked randomization.	Total of 48 hot spots; 151 targeted offenders.	(1) Hot spots and (2) offenders.	Crime data from crime analysts in the law enforcement agency.	Representative of the crime data in this jurisdiction.
Heather Zaykowski	All noninstitutional housing units in the United States.	Housing units.	Probability sampling. Stratified, multistage, cluster sampling of housing units in the United States.	$n = 4,746$ victimizations.	Social Artifact/ interactions (victimizations).	Individuals (victims of violence).	Sample is representative of all persons age 12 years or older living in housing units in the United States. Findings are generalizable to the sample population.

KEY WORDS AND CONCEPTS

1-in-k method 150
Availability sampling, 154
Bias 142
Biased sample 142
Census 140
Cluster 152
Cluster sampling 151
Convenience sampling 154
Ecological fallacy 146
Elements 139
Full enumeration 140
Generalizability 141
Geographic regions 145
Group 145
Individual 143
Individualist fallacy 147
Inferences 136

Margin of error 157
Multistage sampling 153
Nonprobability sampling 154
Organization 145
Partial enumeration 138
Periodicity 150
Pilot study 154
Population 139
Population parameter 137
Probability sampling 148
Purposive sampling 156
Quota sampling 155
Random digit dialing (RDD) 148
Replication 162
Representative 141
Sample statistics 137
Sampling 138

Sampling elements 149
Sampling error 141
Sampling frame 149
Sampling interval 150
Sampling without replacement 149
Saturation 162
Simple random sampling 149
Snowball sampling 156
Social artifacts 145
Social interactions 145
Strata 151
Stratified sampling 151
Systematic sampling 150
Unit of analysis 143
Unit of observation 146

KEY POINTS

- Sampling is selecting a subset of elements from the larger population.

- Sampling is important because it allows researchers to understand the population.

- Researchers calculate statistics based on the sample to infer about the value of population parameters. Sample statistics are summaries of data gathered from the sample. A population parameter is a summary value of the same thing in the population. An example is the mean or average age of individuals in a sample to understand what the average age in the population is.

- All samples are imperfect. One way that samples are imperfect is they have some degree of sampling error. Given that a sample does not contain all data from every member of the population, then statistics from the sample are not going to be exactly equivalent to the population parameters.

- Probability sampling refers to the process of selecting a sample from a population in which every population element has a known, nonzero chance of being selected. Examples include simple random samples, systematic sampling, cluster sampling, stratified sampling, and multistage sampling. Nonprobability sampling refers to the process of selecting a sample from a population in which some members of the population have a zero chance at being selected in the sample. In addition, the probability of being selected into a nonprobability sample is unknown. Nonprobability sampling includes approaches such as convenience sampling, quota sampling, purposive sampling, and snowball sampling.

- A unit of analysis is the what, or the who, that is being studied and analyzed in a particular piece of research. It is the unit being studied, and the level of social life the research question is focused. Several broad categories of units of analysis are used in criminology and criminal justice research. They are individual, groups and organizations, geographic areas, and social artifacts and social interactions.

- Ecological fallacy is an error in logic where a researcher applies conclusions based on a group or an organization unit of analysis to an individual. This fallacy assumes all individuals in a collective are characterized by the larger collective's average characteristic.

REVIEW QUESTIONS

1. What is sampling, and why is it important?

2. What are the two major categories of sampling? Why would a researcher use a probability sample versus a nonprobability sample or vice versa?

3. What are some common types of probability sampling approaches used in criminal justice and criminology research? What are the advantages and disadvantages of each?

4. What are some common types of nonprobability sampling approaches used in criminal justice and criminology research? What are the advantages and disadvantages of each?

5. What is a census compared with a sample? When is it best to use one versus the other?

6. What is sampling error, and how can a researcher minimize it? How can a researcher totally eliminate sampling error?

7. What are sample statistics? Why are they calculated? What are population parameters? How statistics and parameters related?

8. What are units of analysis? What types of units of analysis are there? Why is it important to identify the unit of analysis for research questions?

9. What is a unit of observation? How does it differ from a unit of analysis? What error or fallacy arises when a researcher fails to pay attention to the unit of analysis?

10. What should a researcher consider when deciding on a sample size? What are the issues associated with too large a sample? What are the problems with too small a sample?

CRITICAL THINKING QUESTIONS

1. You have just completed some research with your professor. In this research, you and your professor concluded that the neighboring county—Adams County—has a DUI rate three times greater than the other surrounding counties. The school newspaper picks up this finding and reports the people living in Adams Country are more likely to be alcoholic and drive while drunk. Your professor has asked you to draft a letter to the paper outlining why what they reported is not correct. What will you include in that letter as evidence that their reporting inaccurately portrays your research findings?

2. Your classmate is conducting research for a research methods class project. She has interviewed every police officer in the local police department about their perceptions of offenders and what they believe is needed to minimize recidivism. She keeps referring to the group she interviewed as a sample. You argue it is not a sample but a census. Who is correct, and why?

3. You wish to conduct a study on the emotional toll of being a parole officer. To do so, you want to gather a representative sample of parole officers in the nation whom you will interview. To so this, you begin by randomly select 15 states to be in sample. Then you create a list of all counties (or parishes) in those 15 states, and from that list, you randomly select 15 counties (or

parishes) in each state. Next, you compile a list of all parole officers in those selected 15 counties (or parishes). Finally, you randomly select 15 parole officers in each of those areas to interview. Which type of sample design is this an example of? What are the advantages and disadvantages of this approach? How might a researcher generate a sample of parole officers in other ways?

4. You want to interview police officers who shot and killed someone in the line of duty for a research project. What type of sampling approach would be best for this type of project? What are the advantages of going with the approach you selected? Are there other approaches that would work as well?

5. A classmate is working on his senior project. After a long period, he obtained IRB approval to interview 15 individuals with severe cognitive disabilities about victimization experiences they have. The subjects all reside in a local assisted-living facility given their extreme vulnerability. Through casual conversation, you discover that your classmate actually interviewed 25 people and asked several questions beyond what his IRB protocol listed. Why would this be a problem? What would you do with this information? What would you recommend to your classmate?

Collecting Your Data

At this point, you are ready to gather data to answer your research question. As this section of the text will demonstrate, there are many types of data a researcher can gather. Which types of data are best depends on the research question posed as well as on considerations such as available time and resources. Chapter 6 covers how to gather qualitative data using approaches such as interviews, focus groups, observations, and content analysis. Gathering and using qualitative data appropriately is a skill that serves researchers well. Chances are you have taken many surveys, and possibly have even created some. Chapter 7 identifies best practices for creating surveys to gather data. Being able to construct well-designed surveys is a useful skill used in many careers today. When new researchers think of research, they often envision experiments. You may even be familiar with placebos and control groups. Chapter 8 covers gathering data via experimental research as well related approaches such as pre-experiments, quasi-experiments, and natural experiments. Many researchers rely on the use of secondary data to conduct research. Secondary data are data that have been collected by others but are available for use and are described in Chapter 9. Chapter 10 presents information about a newer (although not as new as many suppose) type of data based on location. How to gather and use mapping data is covered in that chapter. The final chapter in this section, Chapter 11, differs a bit from the others. Rather than focusing on a type of data, it describes research with a different purpose: evaluation research. Evaluation research uses all types of data to answer specific questions about a program or policy. Evaluation research is widely used in the "real world," meaning that an understanding of it opens up many career opportunities for you. If you go on to conduct your own research, work on a project with others, or only become a lifelong consumer of findings from research, understanding the different types of data and associated approaches used to answer research questions will benefit you. Recall the whole purpose of research is to answer a research question. Once you have collected your data, you have everything you need to analyze the data and answer your question.

6

Research Using Qualitative Data

Learning Objectives

After finishing this chapter, you should be able to:

6.1 Identify what makes qualitative data different than other types of data. Compare qualitative data to quantitative data, including the advantages and disadvantages of each.

6.2 Evaluate when the use of qualitative data is most appropriate.

6.3 Compare and contrast different approaches to gathering qualitative data including interviews, observation and field research, and document analysis, and the advantages and disadvantages of each.

6.4 Describe the basic steps to organizing and analyzing qualitative data, and what tasks are accomplished during each step.

6.5 Identify what makes ethics important when gathering qualitative data using examples from the classic cases of unethical research.

6.6 Summarize the common pitfalls associated with gathering and using qualitative data.

> **Qualitative research:** Uses non-numeric data to answer what are frequently exploratory research questions designed to provide detailed and nuanced understanding of a topic. Qualitative research is not focused on counting, quantifying, or measuring anything about a topic.

Introduction

This chapter focuses on collecting qualitative data to conduct research. Research using qualitative data, often called **qualitative research**, was briefly introduced in Chapter 4 as research that uses non-numeric data to answer what are frequently exploratory and descriptive research questions designed to provide detailed and nuanced understanding of a topic. Research using qualitative data is often not constrained by fixed notions of any element of the topic, and it is much like embarking on an adventure with no preconceived notions about what will be learned, what will be shown to be important, what will be shown to be irrelevant, and so on. Patton notes that qualitative research is useful in generating new concepts, explanations, findings, hypotheses and theories from the gathered data. Patton (2015, p. 311) describes the nature of qualitative research well as "[q]ualitative inquiry is rife with ambiguities. There are purposeful strategies instead of methodological rules. There are inquiry approaches instead of statistical formulas. Qualitative inquiry seems to work best for people with a high tolerance for ambiguity."

Contrast the goals of research using qualitative data with those of research using quantitative data that were also introduced in Chapter 4. Research using qualitative data is concerned with comprehensively *understanding* the topic—something that all the counting of something in the world cannot do. In contrast to research using qualitative data, research using quantitative data uses numeric data to answer what are often more narrowly defined research questions. The stark differences in qualitative and quantitative data have led to qualitative based-research often being described as "not research using quantitative data." Defining qualitative data in terms of how they are not quantitative data oversimplifies and disregards the distinct and valuable nature of qualitative data. Both types of data are valuable.

To better understand qualitative data and ways to collect it, this chapter is structured as follows. First, we discuss why you as a researcher would conduct research using qualitative data. In addition, we provide insight into the basics associated with collecting qualitative data. We describe clearly what are qualitative data as well as the advantages and disadvantages of these data. Next, we provide the major stages of conducting research using qualitative data including sampling considerations, recording the data, and analyzing the data. A discussion about the pitfalls common with using qualitative data, and ethical considerations associated with them, is also presented. Finally, we hear from Carol Peeples, a self-described qualitative researcher who founded and runs a consulting business specializing in collecting and analyzing qualitative data.

Why Conduct Research Using Qualitative Data?

Why would a researcher use qualitative data to conduct research? In short, because qualitative data are ideal for answering many research questions that seek to reveal a comprehensive understanding about a topic. By using qualitative data, you can glean an understanding about what is important and the meaning of symbols, body language, and rituals related to a particular topic. By using qualitative data, you can identify important patterns, themes, feelings, and core meanings associated with a topic. This type of rich, nuanced understanding cannot be garnered with all the quantitative data in the world. Much of what a researcher may be interested cannot be understood in quantifiable terms. If you are seeking knowledge about more than the quantifiable elements of a topic, research using qualitative data is ideal (see Figure 6.1).

> Research using qualitative data is concerned with comprehensively understanding the topic—something that all the counting of something in the world cannot do.

One of our featured researchers, Carlos Cuevas, revealed to us during a video interview conducted for this book that he finds that many students believe that conducting qualitative research is faster and easier to do. Cuevas wants to dissuade everyone from this notion. Qualitative inquiry is not faster, and it is not easier. As Cuevas notes, it is "differently" time-consuming and "differently" challenging. The biggest reason why someone should conduct

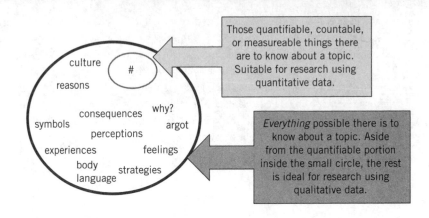

Figure 6.1 Abstract Topic and What Can Be Learned About It

Those quantifiable, countable, or measureable things there are to know about a topic. Suitable for research using quantitative data.

Everything possible there is to know about a topic. Aside from the quantifiable portion inside the small circle, the rest is ideal for research using qualitative data.

culture
reasons
consequences   why?
symbols   argot
perceptions
experiences   feelings
body   strategies
language

research using qualitative data is because it is the best way to answer their research question. Although Cuevas and colleagues' highlighted research did not include gathering qualitative data (Sabina, Cuevas, & Cotignola-Pickens, 2016), he recognizes the value of this approach, and the challenges associated with it.

Patton (2015, p. 13, Exhibit 1.2) identified seven specific purposes of qualitative inquiry (see Table 6.1). First, research using qualitative data illuminates meaning by investigating, analyzing, and interpreting how people construct and attach significance to their experiences, as well as by identifying implications of those experiences. Mary Dodge, another featured researcher, and her colleagues' research on female officers working as decoys in police prostitution stings does exactly this (Dodge, Starr-Gimeno, & Williams, 2005). Dodge found that some literature had speculated that a policewoman posing as a decoy would feel degraded and humiliated. Other speculation suggested that policewomen acting as decoy prostitutes are objectified and marginalized by their colleagues. The fact remained that until Dodge and colleagues conducted their study using qualitative data, no one knew for sure because no one had bothered to ask policewomen engaged in this activity how they felt and the meaning that was attached to their experiences. Findings from Dodge et al.'s data gathered using interviews demonstrated that women officers shared dichotomous views about this work. On one hand, they expressed feelings of disgust with the role-playing and with the clientele. On the other hand, they expressed feelings of excitement about the opportunity to work undercover, to have a break from patrol, and to advance their career. Importantly, this undercover work represented one of the few opportunities female officers had to gain the undercover experience needed to move up to more coveted roles in law enforcement ranks.

Second, research using qualitative data allows you to study how things work. By using qualitative data, a researcher can gain an understanding about how human phenomenon occurs, as well as about the effect on those participating in it. Dodge et al.'s (2005) interviews of female decoy officers provided insight into how decoys needed to look, what they needed to wear (or not wear), and how they needed to posture themselves. Some officers noted they had to change their stances because they could not stand like an officer. Decoys had to change the way they made eye contact, chewed gum, and other seeming mundane things. In addition, decoy officers learned they were more effective decoys if they did not bathe and instead showed up dirty with ratty clothes on. In some cases, decoys found great success at

Table 6.1	Patton's Seven Contributions of Qualitative Inquiry
1.	Illuminate meaning and implications
2.	Study how things work and the effect of those things
3.	Capture stories about perspectives and experiences
4.	Provide insight into how systems function
5.	Provide rich understanding of context
6.	Give meaning to unintended consequences
7.	Enable comparisons of similarities and differences to identify patterns and themes across cases

Source: John W. Creswell. 2013. 3rd edition. *Qualitative Inquiry and Research Design: Choosing Among Five Approaches.* Sage Publications.

attracting johns when they wore no shoes. Johns were not trusting of prostitutes who were neat, clean, and pretty.

Third, research using qualitative data captures stories about people's perspectives and experiences. In some qualitative research, you can offer an in-depth case study of a person, group, organization, or community. This is precisely the purpose of featured researcher Rod Brunson and colleague's study on police relations with adolescents (Brunson & Weitzer, 2009). Gathering qualitative data from the sample of 45 youths—15 in each neighborhood—Brunson illuminated the ways that race affects police interactions and perceptions. The findings indicated that although the neighborhoods were similar, the experiences and perceptions of the youths were not. White youth had less troubled relationships and more positive views of officers than Black youth. This is not surprisingly since the in-depth interviews indicated that police treatment of residents were less problematic in the White neighborhood, worse in the Black neighborhood, and somewhere in between in the mixed-race neighborhood. Black youths reported more personal experiences with police abuse in terms of unwarranted stops, verbal abuse, physical abuse, racial bias, and corruption (e.g., particular officers who sell drugs or take bribes). In addition, they reported more vicarious reports of the same.

Fourth, Patton (2015) stated that research using qualitative data can provide insight into how systems function and into the consequences of those systems on people. Indeed, this was at the core of Brunson and colleague's research (Brunson & Weitzer, 2009). Through interviews with youth in these neighborhoods, the researchers learned how the system worked differently for Blacks and Whites. The system differs for Blacks compared with Whites in terms of interactions and perceptions. Blacks overwhelmingly received negative police attention (detained, searched, arrested) when engaging in law-abiding behavior.

Fifth, research using qualitative data can provide rich understanding of context, including how and why the context matters. In addition, context provides deeper meaning about actions or beliefs. In Brunson and Weitzer's (2009) work, an attempt at holding the environmental context constant was made since the three neighborhoods used in the study were equally disadvantaged. By doing this, the research held constant the role that a disadvantaged neighborhood has on the outcome. In that way, the influence of race could be better identified. The researchers found evidence that as the context of the neighborhoods changed, so did the way police engaged members of the community. Respondents noted that as a neighborhood gained a larger percentage of Black residents, policing became more aggressive and abusive.

Based on research on female decoys provided, one may hypothesize that policewomen acting as decoys have higher job satisfaction than policewomen not engaged in this activity.

Open-ended questions: Designed to give the respondent the opportunity to answer in his or her own words. These are similar to essay questions on exams. Open-ended questions are ideal for gathering qualitative data.

Sixth, research using qualitative data offers an understanding of unanticipated consequences. The open-ended nature of qualitative investigations provides an understanding of both the planned and unplanned consequences of an event or phenomenon. Brunson and Weitzer's (2009) examination of youth and police relations identified important consequences. Because of negative interactions with officers, those in Black communities expressed a desire that police stay out of their neighborhoods unless they were specifically called. Black youth, given their experiences and perceptions, were cynical regarding police and had no confidence in law enforcement.

Finally, a seventh specific contribution of research using qualitative data is that it enables a researcher to identify similarities and differences, as well as to identify patterns and themes across cases. In short, if one's purpose is to gather information on topics about which very little is known, then an approach using qualitative data is ideal. If one's purpose is to understand very deeply the nuances of a topic, including characteristics of thoughts, feelings, opinions, symbols, motivations, descriptions of, and purposes related to topics, then an approach using qualitative data is ideal.

In addition, and not identified by Patton (2015) in that list, conducting research using qualitative data provides valuable information and understanding that allows researchers to develop hypotheses and propose theory that can guide additional qualitative as well as quantitative inquiry. Based on what Dodge and colleagues' (2005) research on female decoys provided, she may now hypothesize that policewomen acting as decoys have higher job satisfaction than policewomen not engaged in this activity. In later research, Dodge could test that hypothesis by constructing a survey with measures of the concept of "job satisfaction." She could then distribute those surveys to a probability sample of policewomen in the nation. By using responses to the survey, Dodge could then use those survey data to determine whether she has support for her hypothesis or not—are those working as decoys characterized by higher job satisfaction compared with those who do not? With enough qualitative data gathered, Dodge could propose a theory that could then be tested and enhanced using both quantitative and qualitative data. By using what is learned from qualitative inquiry, researchers develop relevant questions, response categories, hypotheses, and so on that can be addressed through qualitative, quantitative, or both types of data simultaneously.

And finally, our featured researchers such as Carlos Cuevas, Rachel Boba Santos, and Heather Zaykowski point to the complementary nature of qualitative and quantitative inquiry. All agree that studies using both qualitative and quantitative approaches at the same time are ideal. Use of both types of inquiry—a *mixed-methods* approach—provides statistics, as well as information that provides both context and meaning to those statistics. They are not competing approaches but complementary approaches.

What Is Research Using Qualitative Data?

Broadly, qualitative data are data that are non-numeric in nature. This includes text from transcribed interviews with people, narratives, published documents, videos, music, photos, observations, body language, and voice intonation to name a few. These types of data convey the qualities of the topic of interest. Qualitative data are gathered with an open mind. During interviews, it means using open-ended questions. An **open-ended question** is one in which the respondent is not asked to pick from a predetermined set of response categories but can instead answer using his or her own words. In contrast, a **closed-ended question** is one in which the response categories are provided and the respondent must choose among the option given only. In closed-ended questions, respondents are often asked to "check a box." An analogy that helps clarify open- and closed-ended questions is found on exams. Imagine an exam composed of 10 essay-type questions. Students are asked to use their own words to answer each question in a paragraph or more. This is an open-ended exam question. In contrast, a closed-ended question is similar to a multiple-choice question on an exam. In this case, students must pick from the options provided. A student cannot provide additional detail but must check a box or fill in a bubble (see Figure 6.2).

Stages of Research Using Qualitative Data

The remaining part of the chapter discusses methods used to gather qualitative data in greater detail. Before moving on, it is instructive to think of the big picture when it comes to gathering qualitative data. Like all research, this begins with a research question. Consider both Dodge et al.'s (2005) and Brunson and Weitzer's (2009) work. After developing a research question, both groups turned to the literature to gather an understanding of what was currently known regarding their topics. Dodge and colleagues learned there was virtually nothing in the literature about the topic of policewomen serving as decoys beyond conjectures about how they might feel. Brunson and colleague found a richer existing literature that suffered from an important gap: no detailed comparisons of Black and White youths living in similarly disadvantaged neighborhoods. This knowledge helped guide them to pursue interviews to fill this gap and enrich our knowledge of the topic.

Their next need was to identify a sampling strategy to gather the qualitative data required to answer their research questions. The most feasible sampling strategy depended on several things. Will the data be gathered directly from a person? From observations? From participation in the topic? From existing documents? Answering these questions provided direction regarding the next steps in their research. In both examples, the researchers opted to interview individuals. Knowing this allowed them to move forward with their sampling strategy. The remaining steps used to conduct qualitative research included specifying their sampling strategy, gathering their data, organizing the data, analyzing the data, and making conclusions that are shared (see Table 6.2). The postsampling steps are described in the remainder of this chapter.

Figure 6.2 Examples of Open-Ended and Closed-Ended Questions

Closed Ended Question:
How much time do you spend studying?
A) 1–8 hrs B) 9–18 hrs C) >18 hrs

Open Ended Question:
Tell me about your study habits. . . .

Source: http://housemadisonedm310.blogspot.com/2015/06/blog-assignment-4.html

Closed-ended question:
Type of survey question that requires respondents to select an answer from a list of response categories.

Table 6.2 Basic Stages of Research Using Qualitative Data
1. Developing a research topic and question
2. Consulting the literature to gain any insight on the topic or related topics that may be useful
3. Identifying the best way to gather data—observation, interviews and fieldwork, or document examination (to name a few)
4. Sampling or gaining access to sources of data
5. Gathering data
6. Organizing data
7. Analyzing data and developing conclusions
8. Reporting findings

Coding: Coding can refer to converting a respondent's answers into a numerical value that can be entered into a database. In qualitative data analysis, it is the process of attaching labels to lines of text so that the researcher can group and compare similar or related pieces of information.

Benefits and Limitations of Research Using Qualitative Data

Like all approaches and elements of research, qualitative data have both benefits and limitations. In general, a major benefit of qualitative data is that they allow the researcher to gather in-depth, detailed, and nuanced data that result in a comprehensive understanding of a topic of interest. Access to details and deeper understanding of a topic may be the greatest benefit of qualitative research. A second benefit of qualitative data is that they enable a researcher to study a difficult-to-reach group. For instance, by using qualitative data, developing detailed knowledge about gang members, shoplifters, active robbers, and prostitutes is possible. Third, the nimbleness of approaches used to gather qualitative data represents a major advantage in that a researcher can immediately incorporate new information during data collection. For example, a researcher can prompt respondents for more detail during an interview. A fourth advantage of qualitative data is the focus on context. Without a focus on context, meaning is lost. Qualitative data can be used to identify, value, and give meaning by focusing on context. Fifth, qualitative data are frequently less expensive (in terms of money but not necessarily time) than other approaches to gather. For instance, surveying a probability sample in the nation over the phone requires time and people that costs money. Although gathering qualitative data also requires time and people, the data are often gathered at lower financial costs.

Qualitative data have some limitations that must be acknowledged. First, the quality of research based on qualitative data is highly contingent on the skills of the researcher (this can be a criticism of all research approaches). Second, even though being as objective as possible is desirable, it is impossible for a researcher to be 100% objective whether they are using qualitative or quantitative data. Nevertheless, some approaches used to gather qualitative data make objectivity extra challenging. Becoming a part of the topic of interest is inevitable to some degree, meaning a qualitative researcher must constantly guard against the loss of objectivity, and the presence of bias. Fourth, gathering qualitative data is more time-consuming than many other approaches given the sheer quantity of data gathered. Gathering in-depth information through interviewing, observing, participating in the topic, and examining documents to gather data takes time. Once a researcher has those data, organizing and analyzing it is frequently slow-paced. Transcribing interviews takes time. **Coding** the data—the process in which data are ordered and arranged into categories based on manageable and important themes or concepts—takes time. Ensuring reliability of coding takes time. Synthesizing the data takes time. Working with qualitative data may be less expensive in terms of money, but it is more expensive in terms of time.

© Image Source/Getty Images

The presence of an interviewer, and knowing one is being watched, can change a respondent's behavior.

Fifth, research findings based on qualitative data are not generalizable to a larger population if the data were gathered from a nonprobability sample (and they frequently are). When this is the case, the findings of that research should not be used to make inferences about the larger population. Although the lack of generalizability is a commonly leveled critique against research findings based on qualitative data, it is also the case that the purpose behind much inquiry using qualitative is not to provide generalizable findings. Research does not have to be generalizable to be valuable. The more apt criticism may be that some individuals mistakenly treat research findings from qualitative data gathered from a nonprobability sample as generalizable.

A sixth commonly cited criticism of research using qualitative data is that the data tend to be gathered from small samples. This may be the case, and in some instances, it may be a weakness in a particular piece of research. Nevertheless, in other cases, given the purpose of the work, gathering qualitative data from a very large sample is not needed. Doing so may be inefficient and wasteful, and it does not generate additional information. Saturation, or reaching the point where additional cases do not lead to additional information, is far more important. Saturation may be reached with very few cases, or it may be reached with ten times the number of cases. The size of the sample is not as important as the quality of the sample. Finally, in some approaches used to gather qualitative data, the presence of the researcher can influence the topic being studied. It is not uncommon for people to change their behaviors when they are aware they are being watched or observed during the course of research.

Considerations: Research Using Qualitative Data

Inquiry designed to gather qualitative data frequently has some characteristics that differ from other types of inquiry. First, as noted, qualitative inquiry is conducted by analyzing non-numerical data that are generally collected in natural settings to answer what are frequently an exploratory or descriptive research question. Second, gathering qualitative data involves approaches that are flexible and immediately responsive to information learned. After learning of a new piece of information, a researcher can immediately probe for greater understanding while collecting these data. **Probing** can take on many forms, but it always includes questions such as "Say what you mean by [term]," or "Why was that important to you?" or "It sounds like you are saying ". . ." Is that a fair summary or what you mean?" or "Tell me more about that," or "What was your motivation for doing that?" or "Have your feelings about it changed over time?" to gain insight. Dodge and her collaborators (2005) interviewed undercover policewomen to understand what major concepts are, how the women engaged in this work defined elements of the work, what their feelings were about the work, how body language was important, and many other aspects of the role. As they learned new things about being a decoy, they could immediately follow up on those topics, including questions in interviews that had not taken place yet. Such flexibility and responsiveness during qualitative data collection represents a major strength of research using this approach. Third, qualitative inquiry is generally characterized by broad, open-ended research questions that generally focus on "why" or "how" things occur. They do not concern themselves with questions focused on "how many" or "how often." Fourth, qualitative inquiry is unconcerned with clearly identifying variables, attributes, conceptual definitions, or operationalization *prior* to data collection. Rather, qualitative inquiry—especially exploratory projects—is used to reveal, identify, or deeply understand what the participants view as important variables, concepts, attributes, definitions, and operationalizations. Finally, qualitative inquiry frequently uses inductive reasoning. In fact, another one of our featured researchers, Chris Melde, believes that the use of inductive reasoning is a major distinction between much qualitative and quantitative inquiry (see Figure 6.3).

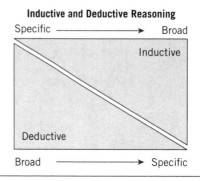

Figure 6.3 Inductive Reasoning Moves From the Specific to the Broad, Whereas Deductive Reasoning Does the Opposite

Inductive and Deductive Reasoning

Specific ⟶ Broad

Inductive

Deductive

Broad ⟶ Specific

Note: Generally, but not always, qualitative research involves inductive reasoning.

Probing: Subtle phrase or follow-up question that interviewers use to encourage survey participants to elaborate on previous responses.

Inductive Reasoning

In Chapter 4, we briefly introduced inductive and deductive reasoning. Inductive reasoning is an approach in which a researcher gathers a lot of specific data from interviews, observations, or examination of documents, and after analysis, the researcher develops a broad understanding, meaning, generalizations, themes, hypotheses, or even theories. In Brunson and colleague's (2009) work on youth relations with law enforcement, qualitative data from interviews were used to develop broad themes surrounding physical abuse, corruption, and unwarranted stops that led to broad, meaningful generalizations. Use of inductive reasoning means use of minimal assumptions when engaging in the research. Instead, inductive reasoning involves allowing the specific data gathered to tell a broad and general story. It is an approach that is open ended, a sort of journey in which the researchers are uncertain where the data gathering will lead them.

Although research using qualitative data is predominantly conducted using inductive reasoning; it is not universally so. For some, qualitative inquiry uses both inductive and deductive reasoning. Consider a scenario in which a researcher used inductive reasoning to uncover important themes such motivations of police impersonators. Once these motivational themes were established, that same researcher may use a deductive reasoning approach—one in which the researcher begins with broad or general statements to move to the more specific to develop additional research questions. This approach means the researchers constantly check the themes and core meanings they develop against the data gathered. They could use deductive reasoning to confirm the authenticity of these themes by testing and affirming the presence of them using additional qualitative data. Figure 6.4, which was also presented in Chapter 4, offers an illustration of the differences in inductive and deductive reasoning.

Sampling Considerations

Sampling was introduced in Chapter 5 by noting that there are two primary approaches to sampling: probability and nonprobability sampling. There we described probability sampling as the process of selecting a subset of elements from a population in which every population element has a known, nonzero chance of being selected. This sampling approach requires the presence of a comprehensive list of all members or elements of the population of interest. The second approach to sampling described is nonprobability sampling, which gathers a subset of the population without the presence of a comprehensive list of population members. By

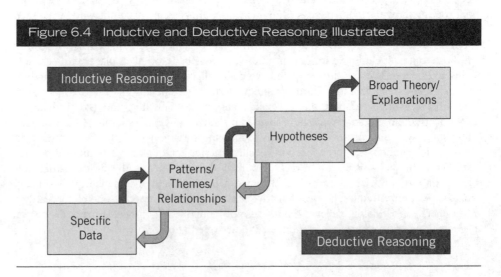

Figure 6.4 Inductive and Deductive Reasoning Illustrated

using nonprobability sampling, some members of the population have a zero chance of being selected into the sample, and the probability of being selected into a nonprobability sample is frequently unknown. A nonprobability sample is constructed using respondents or members that have a particular characteristic of interest relevant to the research problem or possibly because they are conveniently located.

Research using qualitative data frequently, but not always, uses nonprobability sampling approaches, especially when the research focuses on interviewing or gathering information from people. This should make sense given that much of qualitative inquiry explores a topic that has never been studied or has received little research attention. This usually means there are no comprehensive sampling frames or population lists from which sampling elements can be gathered. Several approaches to gathering qualitative data such as snowball sampling (see Figure 6.5, next page) were introduced in Chapter 5. More are discussed here.

A useful sampling approach when gathering qualitative data not discussed in Chapter 5 is maximum variation sampling. **Maximum variation sampling** refers to a purposeful sampling approach in that subjects are selected to maximize or increase the variation or heterogeneity of relevant characteristics in the sample. Rather than seeking some sort of representativeness in the sample, the goal is to seek maximum variation in the sample. This allows insight into how a topic is viewed and processed by subjects in a variety of settings under a variety of conditions.

Another useful approach when gathering qualitative data not discussed in Chapter 5 is theoretical sampling. **Theoretical sampling** is useful for gathering data with the purpose of developing grounded theory. Theoretical sampling is accomplished using an iterative approach where the researcher simultaneously "collects, codes and analyses his data and decides what data to collect next and where to find them, in order to develop his theory as it emerges" (Glaser & Strauss, 1967, p. 45). By using this approach, researchers can gather new information on emerging theoretical concepts from their sample that informs who the next needed sample subjects are based on the insight they can provide on the topics of interest. Throughout the process of theoretical sampling, the researcher asks, "What groups should I next gather data from, and why?"

As with any sampling, the researcher must identify the unit of analysis. A unit of analysis is the what, or who, that is being studied and analyzed in a particular piece of research. In both Dodge et al.'s (2005) exploration of undercover policewomen working john stings, and in Brunson and Weitzer's (2009) examination of youth relations with law enforcement, the units of analysis (and units of observation) were individuals. Although both of these case studies included individuals as the unit of analysis, other research gathering qualitative data may use different units such as police agencies, states, or counties, which present additional considerations.

For instance, qualitative inquiry based on document examinations use social artifacts such as books, movies, commercials, videos, meeting minutes, social media posts, newspaper articles, or songs as the unit of analysis. Consider a researcher who is interested in understanding how newspapers portray victims and offenders based on their race or age. To do that, the investigator might gather a comprehensive list of all newspapers in the nation. From that, they may draw a random sample from that list. This would result in a probability sample. A similar approach may be taken for gathering a sample of all nightly newscasts or episodes of a particular television series. A better sampling strategy depends on the purpose of the research and on the resources available to the researcher.

Sample Size

How large of a sample is needed to conduct research based on qualitative data? It should come as no surprise that the answer is "it depends." It depends on the topic and the resources. It depends on the nature of the groups of interest. Are those in the groups homogeneous? Then a smaller sample will do. Are those in the group wildly different from one another? Then a

Maximum variation sampling: Purposeful sampling approach in that subjects are selected to maximize or increase the variation or heterogeneity of relevant characteristics in the sample.

Theoretical sampling: Theoretical sampling is accomplished using an iterative approach where the researcher simultaneously collects, codes, and analyzes data and then by using that information decides what data to collect next.

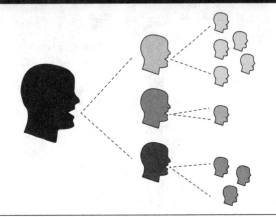

Figure 6.5 Illustration of Snowball Sampling—Using Current Respondents to Identify Others Who Could Be Interviewed

Note: Recall from Chapter 5 that snowball sampling is one type of nonprobability sampling approach in which current respondents are asked for the contact information of others having the needed characteristics to participate in the study.

Triangulation: Use of multiple methods, researchers, theory, or data—different "lines of action" to conduct a study.

larger sample is needed. If a researcher's purpose is to understand something deeply, it may be that a smaller sample is needed. It is the case that there is an inherent trade-off between breadth and depth of a topic. If someone is interested in gathering information needed for a deep understanding, then a smaller sample size is required. If you are focused on a broader understanding (with less depth), then a larger sample size may be warranted. One thing is certain, a researcher should be seeking a sample that as reasonably as possible represents the population of interest and is large enough to result in saturation. In the words of both Brunson and Dodge, when interviewing more people, or examining more documents, or making additional observations fails to expose additional information or meaning, you have an adequate sample size. Depending on the topic, saturation may be obtained with a sample of 10. In other cases, it may be a sample size of 50 or 100. It simply depends.

Approaches Used to Gather Qualitative Data

Many approaches are available for gathering qualitative data, many of which are shown in Table 6.3 (Creswell, 2013, pp. 8–10, Table 1.1). As this table indicates, providing an exhaustive accounting and description of each approach goes far beyond this chapter and text. Those who are interested in conducting research using qualitative data should consult the recommended readings found at the end of this chapter, seek out research methods courses devoted specifically to qualitative data at your university, and read existing research based on qualitative data for additional information. Nonetheless, this chapter provides basic information that enables you to begin gathering qualitative data.

The main approaches used to gather qualitative data can be categorized into three major categories: interviews, observations and fieldwork, and document examinations (see Figure 6.6). Interviews are used to gather qualitative data from a single individual, a small group, or a larger group such as a focus group. Observations and fieldwork involve the researcher going into the field to observe the topic of interest, as well as to participate or engage with the topic to some degree. Data are collected based on experiences in the field. Finally, document examination is used to gather qualitative data from existing written or electronic documents.

Although some research using qualitative data is conducted using only one of these strategies, it is beneficial for a researcher to use multiple approaches to address a single research question. This technique, known as **triangulation**, is the use of multiple methods, researchers, theory, or data to conduct a study (Denzin, 1978). In the words of Denzin, triangulation is a researcher using different lines of action. By using multiple approaches, data, or research approaches, a researcher can strengthen the conclusions in her study. For example, by using triangulation, you can use qualitative data from interviews, observations, and document analysis to answer a research question. Alternatively, as a researcher, you may opt to use multiple researchers to collect, organize and analyze the data. This goal is not just to use multiple lines of action but also to use the multiple lines of action together to remove threats to validity associated with any single line of action. By using triangulation, then, you can strengthen evidence used to support your conclusions.

Table 6.3 Qualitative Approaches Mentioned by Authors and Their Disciplines/Fields

Authors	Qualitative Approaches
Jacob (1987)	Ecological Psychology
	Holistic Ethnography
	Cognitive Anthropology
	Ethnography of Communication
	Symbolic Interactionism
Munhall & Oiler (1986)	Phenomenology
	Grounded Theory
	Ethnography
	Historical Research
Lancy (1993)	Anthropological Perspectives
	Sociological Perspectives
	Biological Perspectives
	Case Studies
	Personal Accounts
	Cognitive Studies
	Historical Inquiries
Strauss & Corbin (1990)	Grounded Theory
	Ethnography
	Phenomenology
	Life Histories
	Conversational Analysis
Morse (1994)	Phenomenology
	Ethnography
	Ethnoscience
	Grounded Theory
Moustakas (1994)	Ethnography
	Grounded Theory
	Hermeneutics
	Empirical Phenomenological Research
	Heuristic Research
	Transcendental Phenomenology

(Continued)

Table 6.3 (Continued)

Authors	Qualitative Approaches
Denzin & Lincoln (1994)	Case Studies
	Ethnography
	Phenomenology
	Ethnomethodology
	Interpretative Practices
	Grounded Theory
	Biographical
	Historical
	Clinical Research
Miles & Huberman (1994)	Interpretivism
	Social Anthropology
	Collaborative Social Research
Slife & Williams (1995)	Ethnography
	Phenomenology
	Studies of Artifacts
Denzin & Lincoln (2005)	Performance, Critical, and Public Ethnography
	Interpretive Practices
	Case Studies
	Grounded Theory
	Life History
	Narrative Authority
	Participatory Action Research
	Clinical Research
Marshall & Rossman (2010)	Ethnographic Approaches
	Phenomenological Approaches
	Sociolinguistic Approaches (i.e., critical genres, such as critical race theory, queer theory, etc.)
Saldaña (2011)	Ethnography
	Grounded Theory
	Phenomenology
	Case Study
	Content Analysis
	Mixed Methods Research

Authors	Qualitative Approaches
	Narrative Inquiry
	Arts-Based Research
	Autoethnography
	Evaluation Research
	Action Research
	Investigative Journalism
	Critical Inquiry
Denzin & Lincoln (2011)	Design
	Case study
	Ethnography, participant observation, performance ethnography
	Phenomenology, ethnomethodology
	Grounded theory
	Life history, *testimonio,*
	Historical method
	Action and applied research
	Clinical research

Interviews: Conversations between the researcher and an individual or a group of individuals. Interviews can be conducted with a single individual, in pairs, in small groups, or in slightly larger groups such as a focus group. Interviews also represent a type of survey mode that involves the researcher (i.e., the interviewer) directly engaging with the survey participant during the data collection process.

Interviews

Interviewing people has resulted in a rich body of research findings in the criminology and criminal justice literature. **Interviews** are conversations between the researcher and the subject or a group of subjects. Interviews can be conducted with a single person, in pairs, with small groups, or in slightly larger groups such as a focus group. Interviews allow the collection of detailed information about a topic based on the experiences of the respondents. They provide depth and nuance unavailable through other approaches, and they are extremely nimble as they allow researchers to tailor the interview to the specific respondent's opinions, experiences, and comments. Interviews allow the researcher to follow up immediately on information by probing more deeply about topics based on what is learned from the respondent. Remember that the goal of the interview is to gather data that will be used to answer the research question. The more in-depth and clear information you can gain from the respondent, the better the research.

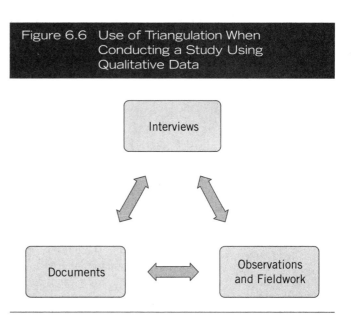

Figure 6.6 Use of Triangulation When Conducting a Study Using Qualitative Data

Note: Triangulation means using multiple methods, researchers, theories, or data to accomplish the research. For example, one might use interviews, document review, and observation/fieldwork.

Interviews can be unstructured and exploratory in nature. **Unstructured interviews**, also called ethnographic interviewing, are conducted conversationally and are based on very few, broad, guiding questions that provide a basic framework to the interview. An unstructured interviewing approach allows the researcher to gather data about the topic based on the respondent's experiences and perceptions. Respondents can share with the researcher what is important, versus the researcher asking the respondent about what the researcher believes is important. By using broad questions to guide the interview, the respondent is free to reply at length, in detail, about his or her experiences or thoughts.

Interviews allow the collection of detailed information about a topic based on the experiences of the respondents.

Alternatively, an interview can be semistructured, which better enables the researcher to compare responses across individuals or groups, as well as to address specific hypotheses since every respondent is asked some of the same questions. **Semistructured interviews** are ones in which all respondents are asked the same set of questions. By asking the same questions across respondents, the researcher can compare responses. Although questions are posed to every respondent, a semistructured interview still allows for and requires follow-up questions, as well as probing on interesting responses given. How did Dodge and her colleagues gather their data? Dodge and her collaborators used semistructured interviews to gather data from policewomen decoys. Although a complete list of questions used during these interviews is not provided in their published article, it is likely Dodge and colleagues (2005) asked the undercover officers things such as "Can you tell me about the most recent time you acted as a decoy prostitute in a sting?" and "How did acting as a decoy make you feel?" and "How did others view you when you were acting in this role?" Additional probing follow-up questions or requests to expand on respondent comments are the norm in unstructured interviews.

Unstructured interviews:
Also called "ethnographic interviews." They are conducted conversationally and are based on very few broad, guiding questions that provide a basic framework to the interview.

Semistructured interviews:
Interviews in which all respondents are asked the same set of questions. Still allows and requires follow-up questions and probing on interesting responses given.

Brunson and Weitzer's (2009) interviews were also semistructured given that the research focused on police relations (experienced and perceived) between the young men across three neighborhoods. Each adolescent male interviewed was asked the same questions, which allowed for comparisons of data across neighborhoods. Some questions included asking broadly about how police officers spoke to them, about police stops, any physical interactions, and corruption by officers. Although all respondents were asked the same questions, each were also asked questions specific to their responses. This flexibility in interviewing to gather qualitative data is a major strength.

Whether you use unstructured, or more structured, interviewing depends on the purposes of the research being conducted. Is the goal of the research exploratory given little to nothing is known about the topic? If so, an unstructured exploratory interview is useful. On the other hand, is there a body of knowledge available on the topic that lacks depth and nuance that can only be gathered using interviews? If so, you may opt for a semistructured interviewing approach. This was the case for both Brunson and Weitzer's (2009) and Dodge et al.'s (2005) work. Some literature related to each topic was available, but it did not answer some basic and important questions about the topics. Answering their research questions benefited greatly by using semistructured interviews to gather their data.

Individual Interviewing

Qualitative research frequently includes interviews with an individual. Individual interviews are generally in-depth conversations about the topic of interest, and they may last from 30 minutes to several hours. Interviews can be conducted in person, over the phone, or using a videoconferencing software such as Skype® or Zoom®. In general, in-person interviews are ideal because they allow establishing rapport and trust between the respondent and the researcher. In addition, in-person interviewing allows the interviewer to see and record important body language and other nonverbal responses of the respondent. Although at times unavoidable, telephone interviews are less desirable. Interviewing over the phone inhibits the development of trust and rapport, and the researcher is not able to observe and record important nonverbal cues of the respondent.

Interviews conducted in person should be conducted in a place of comfort for the respondent and can include a research facility or office, a home, or a public location like a park. It is good practice to record an interview. In fact, unless prevented, a researcher should always record the interview. Not only does this allow the researcher to be "present" during the interview (versus furiously writing notes); it also allows the interview to be transcribed later ensuring accurate gathering of the data. Having these transcribed notes are invaluable, and many researchers combing through transcripts find patterns or important elements that escaped them during the interview. Recording an interview should only be done with the respondent's permission. In some cases, the institutional review board (IRB) may disallow recordings if the topic is too sensitive. Some locations disallow recording, such as interviews conducted in jails or prisons. Special care must be taken to ensure that any recording is protected to honor any promised confidentiality.

In any research interview, it is important to phrase questions in such a way that the respondent cannot offer only a "yes" or "no" answer. Given that the purpose of an interview is to gather deep meaningful information, any question leading to one-word responses is inefficient. In addition, it is critical that the researcher never pose biased or emotionally laden questions that lead only to socially desirable responses. For example, it would be inappropriate to ask a female decoy officer, "How can you live with yourself acting like a prostitute and getting decent, family men arrested?" A researcher's personal views about a topic have no place in an interview. Remember, the goal is to learn about the topic, not to inadvertently share what a researcher thinks about a topic.

Focus Groups

Although single-person interviews are a common approach used in criminology and criminal justice research, there are instances in which it is desirable to interview a group of individuals simultaneously. Known as a **focus group**, these collections of people involve the discussion of a predetermined set of short, clear, and nonbiased questions. Even though sources vary in terms of details, it is commonly believed that focus groups should include up to ten individuals who are strangers, yet similar demographically (to facilitate safe sharing of ideas and opinions). The key to a successful focus group is not as much the absolute number of participants but to have a group that is large enough to facilitate group discussion but not so large as to drown out some voices. Ideally, about eight questions are asked during a focus group to allow for detailed discussion. Focus groups generally last from 45 minutes to 2 hours and are conducted by a moderator who not only guides and nurtures the discussion but also ensures the environment is open and accepting. Moderators are also expected to encourage opinions, ideas, and thoughts from all participants. Although hearing from each participant is important, it is the group discussion that is really wanted. This group interaction can offer additional depth to a topic that individual interviews cannot. An advantage of a focus group is that respondents who hear others' thoughts can be cued about their own views. It is also the moderator's responsibility to use follow-up questions to probe when needed. As with individual interviews, focus groups are traditionally, and ideally, held in person, in a private and comfortable location. Nevertheless, given increased technology, focus groups can also be held by videoconferencing or by using other technologies. In-person focus groups offer the same advantages as in-person interviews. In addition, like individual interviews, recording (with the permission of the focus group members) is desirable to ensure accurate gathering of data, as well as for in-depth later analysis.

Focus group: Collections of people involved in the discussion of a predetermined set of short, clear, and nonbiased questions.

Observation and Fieldwork

Observation and fieldwork: One of three primary forms of qualitative research that involved the researcher going into the field to observe, and possibly participate in, the topic of interest.

Participant observation: Combination of observation with some degree of participation by the researcher.

Role conceptions: Four roles a researcher can take while engaging in field research and observation. They include (1) complete observer, (2) observer as participant, (3) participant as observer, and (4) complete participant.

Ethnography: A type of systematic qualitative research in which the researcher's goal is to gather a comprehensive and holistic understanding of the culture, environment, and social phenomenon associated with a group or with individuals in a group. Ethnography involves a researcher immersing herself into a culture for a prolonged period.

Going native: Phrase devised by Gold (1958), occurs when the field researcher actually becomes the role he or she is playing and is no longer able to observe the situation with any objectivity.

A second commonly used approach to gathering qualitative data is observation and field research. **Observation and fieldwork** entails the researcher going into the field to observe and, possibly, participating in the topic of interest. This approach allows the researcher to be engaged in the natural setting and processes of the topic of interest. Observation is a useful approach to gathering qualitative data because systematic observation of behaviors or activities as they actually occur enables a more accurate and nuanced description of reality in contrast to asking individuals or surveying people about their behaviors and activities. When asked about behaviors and activities, respondents can distort reality with socially desirable responses, or they can forget important things. Observation generally occurs in a natural setting, versus in a laboratory, an office, or other controlled environments. In the natural setting, the researcher can observe the environment, context, and full behaviors and actions. Observation is especially useful when the objects of interest cannot express themselves (e.g., toddlers) or may not wish to share their actions (e.g., deviants).

Purely observational studies are useful, yet unusual. More commonly, observation is used in conjunction with some interaction or participation with the topic subjects. **Participant observation** refers to the combination of observation with some degree of participation by the researcher. Four frequently described types of participant observation are illustrated in Figure 6.7 using a continuum of role conceptions developed by Junker (1952) and later expanded upon by Gold (1958).

Four **role conceptions** identify the exact nature of the field researcher's engagement with the topic of interest. They are (1) complete observer, (2) observer as participant, (3) participant as observer, and (4) complete participant. Participant observational studies are often (but not always) associated with ethnography. **Ethnography**, which originated in anthropology, is a systematic research approach used to gather qualitative data in which the researcher's goal is to gather a comprehensive and holistic understanding of the culture, environment, and social phenomenon associated with a group or individuals in a group. Ethnography involves a researcher immersing herself into a culture for a prolonged period. In ethnography, the perspective of the researcher is that of subject(s) of the study and not the perspective of how the larger society views the subject(s).

Regardless of the role conception you use to conduct your research, there are hazards you must be aware. First, a researcher must guard against compromising his or her objectivity. It is a researcher's responsibility to maintain, to the best of his or her ability, objectivity regarding the topic of study. Researchers must work not to become overly invested in, or overly repelled by, the individuals or groups being investigated. A researcher's goal is to observe without making value judgments and to report simply on the environment, behaviors, activities, and beliefs of the individual or groups observed objectively. Should you as a researcher become overly invested in or enamored by a group or individual being observed, you will have "gone native." **Going native**, a phrase devised by Gold (1958), occurs when the researcher actually becomes the role he or she is playing and is no longer able to observe the situation with objectivity.

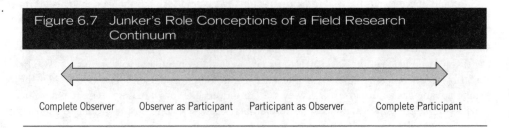

Figure 6.7   Junker's Role Conceptions of a Field Research Continuum

Complete Observer   Observer as Participant   Participant as Observer   Complete Participant

During the 1800s and 1900s, racial/ethnic minority groups have been tied to illicit drug use. The Chinese were depicted to be the primary opiate users, African Americans were considered "cocaine fiends." More recently, poor urban African Americans and Hispanics were identified as crack users during the mid-1980s, and poor rural Whites were portrayed as the primary meth users. Not only were connections made between race/ethnicity and drug use, but these relationships were portrayed as moral panics that occur when the majority perceives one social group or type of activity as threatening the stability of society. Moral panics include five elements that serve as indicators a moral panic has taken hold of a society: concern, hostility, consensus, disproportionality, and volatility. Cobbina (2008) noted that until her research, few studies encompassed the five conceptual components of moral panic to examine how such panic is created over drug abuse. Furthermore, Cobbina found that little attention had been given to the role of race and class to the development of moral panic over drug scares.

To address these gaps in the literature, Cobbina is guided by two research questions in this exploratory research:

1. Does the race and class of crack cocaine and methamphetamine users shape the print media's representation of these drugs?

2. Do media depictions affect the official response?

To address these research questions, Cobbina conducted a content analysis of four major newspapers from 1985 to 1987 (focuses on crack) and 2001 to 2003 (focuses on meth). The four newspapers used were the *The New York Times,* the *Chicago Tribune, The Washington Post,* and the *Los Angeles Times.* Cobbina searched the archives of each print media source between 1985 and 1987 using the keyword "crack cocaine" within the title and text and again between 2001 and 2003 using the keyword "methamphetamine" within the title and text. This search resulted in a total of 124 newspaper articles in the sample. In each sampled article, Cobbina searched for explicit mentions as well as for implicit proxies for race and socioeconomic status.

For example, for coding purposes, Cobbina constructed categories of race and class based on terms such as African American, White, working/lower class, and middle/upper middle class. "Urban" and "inner city" were used as euphemisms for African American; "rural" was used to signify White. Common neighborhood descriptors used by reporters were "poor," "impoverished," "ghetto," "less affluent," "crime ridden," and "drug infested" to signify working or lower class; and "affluent" and "elite" were typically offered as neighborhood descriptions signifying middle and upper class.

The research shows that race and class play a role in shaping the media's depictions of crack cocaine and methamphetamine. Crack is described as a problem primarily afflicting impoverished African American communities, and when White middle-class or affluent users purchase crack, they are profiled as victims of the drug instead of as criminals. Methamphetamine use is depicted as a problem among poor rural Whites. When middle- or upper-middle-class individuals are referenced as methamphetamine users, they are depicted as hardworking mothers attempting to fulfill multiple errands—victims of the drug.

With regard to the second research question, Cobbina found that the print media representation of crack cocaine does affect official response. In general, articles on crack were two times more likely than meth articles to express the need for harsher crime control policies and resulted in calls for more "get tough" policies, an increased war on drugs, more mandatory prison terms, and increased use of three strike laws. In contrast, print media representation of meth uses focuses on the public health issues and ways to help these victims.

Cobbina offers no policy implications of this work given its exploratory nature and limited sample. She calls for additional research on the topic, including the inclusion of immigrant status in further examinations.

Cobbina, J. (2008). Race and class differences in print media portrayals of crack cocaine and methamphetamine. *Journal of Criminal Justice and Popular Culture, 15*(2), 145–167.

Complete participant:
Role conception in which the researcher keeps hidden his or her true identity and purpose from those being observed. The researchers' goal is to interact in this natural setting as naturally as possible to gather data and meaning.

Participant as observer:
One of four role conceptions in which the researcher and his or her primary contact(s) in the field are the only ones aware of the researcher's actual role and purpose for the observation. While the researcher's role is known to a select few, the researcher engages with the group as a member or a colleague.

Hawthorne Effect:
Identified in 1953, refers to possible impact on behavior of those who are aware they are being observed and studied. It is a type of reactivity meaning that individual will hide or exaggerate behaviors when he or she is aware of being observed.

A second issue related to fieldwork relates to ethics. Even with IRB approval, researchers must consider if they believe the study they wish to engage in is ethical. Can someone voluntarily consent to participate in a study if they are not even aware they are being observed? Although the IRB does not require informed consent when observational studies are conducted in public areas where people have no expectation of privacy, and where harm to the subject will be minimal, is it always the right thing to do? What if you wish to observe and report on sacred religious ceremonies taking place in a large, public park? Alternatively, what if the topic of interest includes potentially disturbing activities? Or what if the behaviors that are observed and later reported about lead to psychological or emotional harm to people or other beings who were observed? It is the researchers' responsibility to answer these questions for themselves, and not to rely solely on the IRB's green light.

Complete Participant

Research using a **complete participant** role means that the researcher hides his or her true identity and purpose from those being observed. The researchers' goal is to interact in this natural setting as naturally as possible to best gather information and meaning. A researcher may dance as a topless dancer in a club to learn about dancers, customers, and the environment in which they interact. Or a researcher may join a gang. Alternatively, another researcher may obtain a job as a probation officer. In these cases, the researcher would not reveal the real purpose of his or her being in the club, the gang, or the probation office. This approach is unmatched in providing access to the information desired, and the people of interest, in their natural environment of interest. Although excellent at providing rich, in-depth information, acting as a complete participant has limitations. First, the risk of going native is greatest when the researchers actually become members of, and identify with, the individuals and group being observed. If going native occurs, the researchers' objectivity is compromised, and the research findings become questionable. Protecting oneself from going native is challenging. Gold (1958, p. 220) stated it well when he noted that "[w]hile the complete participant role offers possibilities of learning about aspects of behavior that might otherwise escape a field observer, it places him in pretended roles which call for delicate balances between demands of role and self." The second concern with this approach is that of ethics. As noted, you as the researcher must consider the ethical considerations with this approach beyond what the IRB allows or disallows. Those being observed are being duped. Is this ethical? Discussions with experienced mentors who have confronted these issues are recommended.

Participant as Observer

Research in which the researcher is a **participant as observer** occurs when the researcher and the primary contact(s) in the field are the only ones aware of the researcher's actual role and purpose for the observation. The researcher then engages with the groups as a member or as a colleague. Acting as participant as observer, the researcher must first make contact with and develop a good relationship with an informant. This informant assists the researcher in terms of gaining access to the group, individuals of interest, and group's environment. Given this approach, most of the individuals encountered are unaware of the researchers' purposes and real identity.

This approach is effective in gaining access to information, people, and environment of interest, yet it has challenges. First, it requires lying, misleading, and betraying the trust of those being observed. This raises the question of participants freely and voluntarily consenting to participating in the research (they cannot). Still, should the researcher be open and honest about his or her role and purpose, the behaviors of those being observed will likely change. The **Hawthorne Effect**, identified in 1953, refers to possible impact on the behavior of those who are aware they are being observed and studied. The Hawthorne Effect suggests that people will react by hiding or exaggerating behaviors when they are aware they are being observed. Researchers continue to study and debate all aspects of the Hawthorne Effect (McCambridge, Witton, & Elbourne, 2014). Some consider the Hawthorne Effect as nothing more than a well-known and glorified anecdote. Others argue there is no single Hawthorne Effect but multiple effects. Others debate the degree to which the Hawthorne Effect influences behavior. Although the scientific examination of this effect rages on, it is prudent for a researcher to at least be cognizant of the possibility that observing behavior will lead to a subject's reaction.

Observer as Participant

In some cases, the researcher acts as **observer as participant**, meaning the researcher's presence and purpose is known by those being observed. Even though all know the purpose of the researcher, the duration of the observation is brief, and any interaction between the observer and the topic is minimal. The overall goal of the researcher is to play a neutral role, while observing a topic in its natural environment. Given the very limited interaction between observer and topic of interest, going native is not a major threat. Nevertheless, given that individuals know they will be observed, there is a risk that their behavior may not be as it would be if they were unaware they were being observed. In addition, given the minimal contact between researcher and the topic of interest, there is an increased risk that the researcher will misunderstand the topic, people, or behaviors or that she or he will miss important information needed to understand the topic of interest well.

Complete Observer

In this role of a **complete observer**, the researcher only observes, and does not participate, or conduct interviews at all. The role of the observer is to observe and to take meaning from what is seen. Those being watched are unaware they are being watched. By using this approach, the researcher does not have to worry about the potential of the Hawthorne Effect; nevertheless, the possibility of misinterpreting behaviors, actions, and the environment is great. In addition, observing others without their knowledge, while ethical from an IRB standpoint when the individuals are in locations where privacy could not be expected (e.g., a park), is still troubling to many. It is clear those being watched cannot consent to participate. Yet, for some research topics, acting as a complete observer may be the only way to gain access to the people and group of interest. In addition, covert participation and observation may represent the only way to gather the information sought. Before engaging in research involving a lack of openness, you should discuss this with experienced mentors.

Documents

Qualitative data are not only gathered by interviewing and observing people. Qualitative data are also gathered by examining and analyzing documents. **Document analysis** refers to a systematic collection, review, evaluation, synthesizing, and interpretation of documents to gain meaning and understanding, regardless of whether the document is printed or available in electronic form. Documents include numerous sources of text, and images including cartoons, advertisements, books, letters, maps, public records, scripts, meeting minutes, and so on.

Bowen (2009) provided five specific functions of document analysis. First, the examination of documents provides data and information on the context in the form of text and images in which research participants operate. Second, document analysis offers insight into topics that need additional investigation, situations that require observation, and questions that need to be asked. A third valuable function of document analysis is that it offers research data that are not available using other approaches. Document analysis may be the best way

Observer as participant: One of four role conceptions available for field research. The researcher's presence and purpose is known by those being observed. While all know the purpose of the researcher, the duration of the observation is brief, and any interaction between the observer and the topic is minimal.

Complete observer: Role conception in which the researcher only observes, and does not participate, or conduct interviews at all. The role of the observer is to observe and to take meaning from what is seen. Those being watched are unaware of the presence of the researcher.

Document analysis: Systematic collection, review, evaluation, synthesizing, and interpretation of documents to gain meaning and understanding, regardless of whether the document is printed or available in electronic form.

to gather data when details have been forgotten or events or behaviors cannot be observed. Fourth, documents offer insight into changes and development of an organization, its environment, and those in it. Finally, document analysis can be used to verify findings or corroborate evidence obtained from other approaches or sources.

Document analysis involves three major iterative steps according to Patton (2015). First, the researcher skims, or superficially examines, the documents. Second, the researcher thoroughly reads the documents identifying data in the form of excerpts, quotes, paragraphs. Finally, the researcher organizes the data into themes, categories, and case examples, allowing interpretation. Interpretation leads to the identification of broad patterns, themes and meanings. By following this process, the researcher gains empirical knowledge and a deeper and richer understanding about the topic.

Document analysis, like all approaches, offers advantages and disadvantages. One advantage is that document analysis is less time-consuming than approaches such as interviews and observations. A second advantage is the increasing availability of documents, especially online. Today, you can access a rich selection of documents online without having to gain the favor of gatekeepers. If you have Internet access, one can access a multitude of documents. Associated with less time-consuming and ease of availability is that document analysis is cost-effective. You can use existing documents versus engaging in an expensive data collection effort of some other type. Another advantage of this approach is that the documents are exact and do not change over time, making them useful for repeated reviews without changes to the content within them.

Document analysis is also limited. First, the documents available may not have the detailed information needed for the research purposes. Second, the documents available may not represent the full accounting of the topic. Some documents may have been made available, whereas others were not. Third, available documents may not be accurate, and knowing if they are accurate or not may be challenging. Finally, in some cases, there may be no available documents making this approach to gathering qualitative data unfeasible. Although these challenges are significant, document analysis still offers insight into an organization, group, or entity that other approaches cannot.

Content Analysis

A fair amount of qualitative data comes from content analysis. What exactly is content analysis? It turns out there is no widely agreed-upon definition of **content analysis**. Many argue that content analysis refers to searching text to count recurring words or themes. This view may be the most pervasive and is best described by Neuendorf (2002, p. 10) as a summarizing, quantitative analysis of messages that relies on the scientific method, including attention to objectivity/intersubjectivity, a priori design, reliability, validity, generalizability, replicability, and hypothesis testing. The approach championed by Neuendorf and others is based on a complementary approach in which both qualitative and quantitative data are gathered. This type of content analysis leads to quantitative data in that it codes and counts the words, sentences, paragraphs, meanings, or illustrations in the content. Yet this type of content analysis can also be used to gather qualitative data in that it also examines and analyzes the context and narrative.

Some argue that content analysis is a descriptive study of human communications resulting in both quantitative and qualitative data. Others indicate that content analysis refers to activities involving the analyzing of text versus observations. According to this view, content analysis includes those activities outside of observation. Yet others argue that

© artisteer/iStockphoto.com

content analysis is qualitative data reduction in which one makes sense out of a volume of text by identifying patterns to develop major themes, which ultimately leads to the identification of core meanings. Although disagreement exists regarding the specifics about the meaning of content analysis, all definitions used indicate that content analysis is a process of organizing data that can be words, sentences, paragraphs, and illustrations into meaningful groupings. From those groupings, there does appear agreement that content analysis is at least the collection and analyzing of non-numeric information that leads to the development of inferences pertinent to the research question.

> **Field notes:** Field notes should include everything a researcher observes. The researcher uses words to describe the environment, time, weather, sounds, smells, and sights in as much detail as possible.

Recording Qualitative Data

Like all data, qualitative data need to be recorded. Given qualitative data are non-numeric in form, recording them can be done using multiple techniques. The most basic, and extremely useful, data recording technique used in qualitative inquiry is **field notes**. Regardless of the type of approach used during qualitative inquiry, field notes are necessary and valuable. What goes into field notes? Everything. A researcher should use his or her words to describe the environment, the time, the weather the sounds, the smells, and the sights. Notes must include as much detail as possible. Data reduction, or condensing those notes, occurs after the field notes are taken. At the stage of writing field notes, no detail is too small, and no occurrence is too unimportant to be included. Notes are not restricted to words. Notes can and should include drawings, maps, and sketches to gather as much detail as possible.

Taking field notes is invaluable, but doing so can also be challenging for multiple reasons. First, it is unlikely that a researcher can take notes during some approaches. For example, if you the researcher are looking down and writing while in the field, you are missing behaviors, body language, speaking, actions, and observations. For this reason, many researchers opt to write their notes after an interview, observation, or fieldwork (document analysis is different in that the researcher can jot down these other details such as environment, sights, and smells, while examining the documents). It is important to write the notes as soon as possible to avoid forgetting details in order to maximize your ability to get all details committed to paper (or computer document). For instance, after an interview or a focus group, the researcher should immediately spend time writing extensive and detailed field notes. After an interaction with a person or group in the field, you should immediately create pages of field notes about the interaction. When writing field notes, take care to keep the identities of any subjects safe. This may mean never using a real name or using a code name. Should your field notes get lost or fall into the hands of a nonresearcher, you must ensure your respondent's confidentiality (if promised) is kept.

Although field notes are a necessary way to record qualitative data, they can and should be augmented with other means of recording data. For instance, a researcher benefits greatly by also using a video or an audio recorder. Recorders are useful for capturing details a researcher may miss in writing field notes. Having recordings (audio or video) is really useful. Going over these recorded data can often reveal patterns or important elements or themes that escaped the researcher's attention initially. Nevertheless, like all things, audio and video recordings have some disadvantages, including being distracting to the people being studied, having the potential to break down, or otherwise requiring the researcher's attention (e.g., changing a battery or tape) when their attention should be squarely on the research topic.

> At the stage of writing field notes, no detail is too small, and no occurrence is too unimportant to be included. Notes are not restricted to words. Notes can and should include drawings, maps, and sketches to gather as much detail as possible.

Even with this potential technical difficulty, audio or video recordings are necessary especially if one is conducting long, complex interviews when the participants' words are important.

Organizing and Analyzing Qualitative Data

Once you have gathered your data in the form of field notes, audio tapes, video tapes, documents, or some combination thereof, what do you do next? Organize those data. This means different things depending on the different types of data. With field notes, organization means ensuring your field notes are legible, edited, and corrected. Recorded data should be transcribed, corrected, and edited. All data must be organized such that the researcher can move through the voluminous data swiftly and efficiently to glean meaning.

Once data are organized, analysis becomes the primary goal of the research. To be clear, analyzing qualitative data begins as soon as the first data are collected because the researcher is watching for patterns or relationships even then. It is at this point where no additional qualitative data are being collected, that the major task of organizing the data and analysis is the focus. Analyzing requires the researcher to reduce, condense, or code the large volume of data into broader categories or themes. In other words, you as a researcher must take a lot of specific information and from it develop broad categories and themes. This is an iterative process where coding leads to themes that are then reviewed for additional refinement of codes. Ideally, multiple researchers should engage in the coding process of qualitative data independently to look for regularities and patterns in the data. A specific description of how to analyze qualitative data is not easily described given the many types of qualitative data available. Even a review of published qualitative research tends to offer little more than a very brief description of how the researcher analyzed his or her data. This is the case for both Dodge et al.'s (2005) and Brunson and Weitzer's (2009) research. They described their data analysis approaches, in part as follows:

> Dodge and colleagues: "Each interview was taped with the subject's consent and then transcribed verbatim for qualitative data analysis. Major themes were extracted and grouped into conceptual domains based on generalised statement content (Glaser & Strauss, 1967; Schatzman & Strauss, 1973)." (p. 76) . . .

> Brunson and colleague: Youth were interviewed and recorded. The tapes of the interviews were transcribed and analyzed by the authors. The analysis included selecting statements that illustrated themes consistently found throughout the data. The quotes used were not atypical. Each author independently coded the data and subsequently categorized it into themes and subthemes (see methods section).

A specific way to analyze qualitative data is using grounded theory. **Grounded theory** is a systematic methodology that leads to the construction of theory through the coding and analysis of qualitative data. In addition to using qualitative data to develop themes, you can use these data to develop theory via grounded theory. This is the approach taken by Brunson and Weitzer (2009) in their exploration of adolescent and police relations in urban neighborhoods as noted in their text:

> The data analysis was conducted with great care to make certain that the themes we discovered accurately represented young men's descriptions. This was accomplished using grounded theory methods, by which recurrent topics were identified along with less common but important issues (Strauss, 1987). Each author independently coded the data and subsequently categorized it into themes and subthemes. (p. 864)

Grounded theory analysis involves three coding steps according to Strauss (1987): (1) open coding, (2) axial coding, and (3) selective coding. **Open coding** refers to a researcher reading the complete set of raw data multiple times to organize and summarize the data (whether they are words, sentences, paragraphs, illustrations, etc.) into preliminary groupings of analytic categories. The goal of open coding is to focus on the specific data and assign labels or codes identifying major themes. For example, for Brunson, it is plausible that some preliminary analytic categories identified centered on verbal interactions, and physical interactions between law enforcement and youth given these are the focus of subsections in their findings.

The second stage of coding using grounded theory is axial coding. During **axial coding**, the researcher focuses on the preliminary analytic categories or labels developed during open coding to identify relationships between the categories. The attention during this stage is not on the raw data but is focused on the summarized labels of the raw data.

Finally, the third stage of coding in grounded theory is selective coding. During **selective coding**, the researcher reviews all raw data and the previous codes or labels with few purposes in mind. First, the researcher makes comparisons and contrasts among themes or labels developed. Returning to Brunson and Weitzer's (2009) research, it is probable that during the selective coding stage, the researchers selected typical quotes illustrating differences in experiences and perceptions between the White and Black youth interviewed. A second purpose of selective coding is to identify overarching and broad variables that describe connections and relationships among some of the labels or themes. An illustration of these coding steps used in grounded theory is provided in Figure 6.8.

Once the data are condensed or reduced into broader themes, interpretation is required. Many options of interpretation are available, and which option is used is dependent on the specific research goals of the work. Interpreting qualitative data is a process that "involves abstracting out beyond the codes and themes to the larger meaning of the data" (Creswell, 2013, p. 187). It can be accomplished by asking, "What do these data mean?" "What is the big picture here?" and "What does this tell me about the topic being studied?"

Open coding: Refers to a researcher reading the complete set of raw data multiple times to organize and summarize the data into preliminary groupings of analytic categories.

Axial coding: In this step, the researcher focuses on these preliminary analytic categories or labels to identify relationships between the categories. The attention during this stage is not on the raw data but on the summarized labels of the data.

Selective coding: In this coding step, the research reviews all raw data and the previous codes or labels for several purposes. First, the researcher makes contrasts and comparisons among themes or labels. Second, during this secondary stage, the researcher identifies overarching and broad variables that describe connections and relationships among some of the labels or themes.

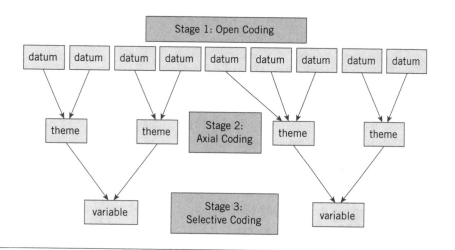

Figure 6.8   Simplified Example of the Three Stages to Coding Qualitative Data When Using Grounded Theory

Stage 1: Open Coding

datum datum datum datum datum datum datum datum datum

theme theme Stage 2: Axial Coding theme theme

variable Stage 3: Selective Coding variable

One way of interpreting the data is to identify relationships and patterns among the codes and themes. This also includes the researcher offering explanations and drawing conclusions. In other cases, a researcher will count the frequency of codes found in the data analyzed. This is frequently the approach taken when a researcher is engaged in content analysis. For others, the goal is more focused on the meaning versus on the quantity of any code found. A researcher can also contextualize the themes and relationships identified given the existing literature. A researcher may ask him- or herself, "Are these codes and themes found in the literature?" and "Do these codes and themes offer greater understanding to what is in the literature?" A researcher can also interpret the data by making contrasts and comparisons by asking, "How do the codes and themes compare to one another?" and "Are there meaningful contrasts?" In addition, the researcher could suggest some hypotheses that come from the data such as suggesting one particular group is more (or less) likely to support police than another group. Finally, interpretation is accomplished by visualizing the data using tables, figures, and illustrations. Graphics are excellent ways to understand and convey information. These additional steps in analyzing, interpreting, and visualizing qualitative data make clear that coding data and identifying themes are not necessarily the only, or the last, steps of research based on qualitative data.

Examples of Qualitatively Derived Themes: Brunson and Weitzer's (2009) Research

Brunson and his colleague used grounded theory to identify themes in their research on male youth experiences and perceptions of police relations. Six themes emerged from their research that indicate that when "holding neighborhood socioeconomic context constant, race makes a difference in how youth are treated by police and in their perceptions of officers." (p. 879). The six themes that led the researchers to offer this conclusion were following:

1. **Unwarranted stops**. Several respondents noted they had been stopped without cause. Black teens noted this happened regardless of their behavior (suspicious or not) and felt that they were stopped without reason frequently. White youth respondents noted they were stopped less and were stopped only under three specific conditions: (1) while in the company of young Black males, (2) when in racially mixed or majority-Black neighborhoods, or (3) while dressed in hip-hop apparel. White teens recognized that Black teens were treated differently and more harshly.

2. **Verbal abuse**. All teens noted that officers frequently were discourteous to them, used inflammatory language or racial slurs, and name-called those they stopped. Both Black and White teens were well aware that Black teens bore the brunt of this poor police behavior. All teens recognized that Black teens endured verbal abuse more often and in harsher ways.

3. **Physical abuse**. Although most police interactions did not result in any serious physical harm, the teens reported that excessive force was used on numerous occasions. This physical abuse included shoving, punching, kicking, and the use of mace. In addition, some teens were taken to other neighborhoods and released—behavior by the police that can place the teens in very dangerous or lethal circumstances.

4. **Corruption**. All the teens knew of some corrupt cops engaging in bribery, stealing from the teens, planting drugs on teens, and other reprehensible activities. No teen portrayed the entire police department as corrupt, however. The teens recognized that only a few individual officers conducted themselves in this way.

5. **Biased policing.** That idea that policing was biased (based on race) was held by all of the teens. Moreover, most teens believed that residents of White communities fared much better as a result of this bias.

6. **Police accountability.** The teens uniformly believed that there was little accountability among poorly behaving officers in the department. The young men noted that supervisors and other officers know of police misconduct, but they consistently fail to address it.

Computer-Assisted Qualitative Data Analysis (CAQDAS)

Software for analyzing qualitative data has been available for almost 40 years. These programs, known as **computer-assisted qualitative data analysis (CAQDAS)**, are useful in many ways; nevertheless, they are not a panacea. Some individuals mistakenly believe that CAQDAS programs can do the analysis and interpretation of qualitative data, but that is simply not the case. As Saldaña (2011) noted, the researcher, not the software or even the actual data, develops the research findings. Although CAQDAS does not produce findings, it does do many useful things. First, CAQDAS provides a means to store, transcribe, code, and interpret data. In addition, CAQDAS enables the researcher to quickly search and find wanted text, data, and codes. In this way, qualitative software is an organizational tool, not a thinking tool. Regardless of whether you use any of these available software programs, it is still incumbent on the researcher to code the data, make sense, and interpret both the information provided by the software as well as the information not provided by the software. CAQDAS, although a useful tool, is a long way from replacing the researcher using qualitative data.

Advantages and Disadvantages of CAQDAS

Even though CAQDAS cannot do everything for the researcher, it offers several benefits. First, CAQDAS offers time savings. The storage and search features of these programs offer a great deal of time savings for the researcher, especially when dealing with a huge amount of qualitative data. Qualitative software includes coding and linking tools that provide additional time savings to the researcher. Given the time-intensive nature of organizing and analyzing qualitative data, this is a real plus. Second, these software programs offer a way to efficiently organize and store data. In addition, CAQDAS programs have useful search functions making finding text, data, and codes fast and easy. Searches frequently offer the ability to find similar words (to the one searched), similar spellings of a word being searched (to deal with typographic errors), and similar meanings. In addition, some CAQDAS products offer the ability to conduct a Boolean search. An additional advantage of qualitative software is their visualization capabilities. For example, the researcher can visualize the data using tables, maps, network diagrams, and illustration relationships among codes and themes. Visual depictions of data and their meaning are useful for revealing additional insights to the researcher. Finally, an advantage of some computer-assisted qualitative software analysis programs is that many are available online for free.

Like all things, qualitative data software has some disadvantages that are important to consider. First, many of these programs are not easy to learn. Second, many researchers are uncomfortable with the notion that the machine develops codes, and how it does this is unclear. Many researchers prefer to develop their own codes. Although a researcher can change codes, doing so takes time and effort. Given the difficulties associated with most CAQDAS programs, several researchers using qualitative data opt to conduct their analysis the old-fashioned way—using their brains only.

Common Pitfalls in Research Using Qualitative Data

Loss of Objectivity—Going Native

A researcher using qualitative data (or quantitative data) must always be on guard against a loss of objectivity. All researchers seek to remain objective, as well as to observe, analyze, describe, report, present findings, and make conclusions without the use of value judgments or personal biases. This is more challenging when conducting research using qualitative data as the researcher is closer, at times physically closer, to the topic of interest. When a researcher actually becomes the role he or she is playing (or observing), and is no longer able to observe the situation with objectivity, trust and confidence in the researcher is lost.

Consider Dodge et al.'s (2005) work on women serving as undercover prostitutes during stings. What if Dodge and her colleagues answered their research question in a completely different way? What if Dodge and her colleagues had themselves dressed as prostitutes and brought clients back to the hotel room to be arrested? What if after having done so, they developed deep empathy for the female officers who do this work and deep resentment about the men picking them up? What if that experience altered Dodge and colleagues description of those engaging in this activity? How might having been a participant in the research, versus interviewing those who had, affected Dodge's research findings? If being a participant leads to a loss in objectivity and alterations in views of the research topic, then the researcher would be described as going native. Going native means a loss of the objectivity needed to observe and describe these situations.

Ethics Associated With Research Using Qualitative Data

A qualitative researcher has a tremendous responsibility in that in doing their research, he or she is developing a relationship with respondents or participants. It is imperative that a researcher take the care needed to protect the well-being of respondents and participants and treat them with the respect they deserve. As noted by Sanjari, Bahramnezhad, Fomani, Shoghi, and Cheraghi (2014, "Abstract," para. 3), researchers using qualitative data "face ethical challenges in all stages of the study, from designing to reporting. These include anonymity, confidentiality, informed consent, researchers' potential impact on the participants and vice versa." In addition, researchers must fiercely protect respondents' privacy and avoiding misrepresentations in their findings.

Researchers must decide, even beyond what the IRB allows, if the parameters of the relationship established with the participant are ethical. Should a researcher take a fully covert role in their research, he or she must consider the ethics associated with the deception inherent in this approach. The researcher must consider that engaging in a 100% covert role means that respondents cannot voluntarily participate. This is also a consideration when a researcher has opted to be less than fully honest and open with participants who may not know that this person they are dealing with is a researcher who is conducting research.

Researchers must also keep the well-being of their subjects at the forefront of their research. As ethical rules stipulate, a researcher must minimize any harm done to subjects. Respondents are freely giving of themselves for the benefit or research, and they deserve a researcher's full respect, zero judgment, complete care, and consideration. Judgments cannot be made regarding behavior or thoughts shared by respondents, no matter how personally challenging they may be to the researcher. Participants must be made comfortable and not traumatized as a result of the researcher's activities. This includes questioning of subjects. For instance, a researcher may ask about sexual violence, intimate partner violence, homicide, commission of child abuse, or any myriad of very sensitive topics. Should the researcher's questioning become harmful to the respondent, it is the researcher's obligation to stop the process and do what is needed to assist the respondent. For many research topics, it is advisable that an advocate be made available (or be present). No research is worth damaging another person (or being).

In addition, as a researcher, you must make every effort to protect respondents' privacy and confidentiality. This means stopping an interview to erase identifying data from tape recordings (as Brunson and colleague, 2009, had to do during their research) if needed. It means destroying or protecting records that could lead to respondent identification. It is the researcher's responsibility and ethical obligation to take great care with records so that the data gathered and respondents' identities are always protected.

The call to do no harm also extends to researchers. Researchers must not only consider the well-being of the respondents but of those engaging in any portion of the research. Honoring this was evident in Santos and Santos's (2016) research, although it was not based on qualitative inquiry. Given potential danger in making repeated contacted with known felons in Santos and Santos's research, only certain members of the research team interviewed these targeted offenders. It was deemed a potential safety issue for some members of the research team to make these contacts.

Finally, it is the researcher's responsibility to present findings that are accurate. It may be tempting to fail to share unflattering information about a topic or respondents. It may be tempting to emphasize only positive findings. Nevertheless, failure to offer a complete description is unethical. The findings presented must be complete and accurate.

Qualitative Data Research Expert—Carol Peeples

Carol Peeples is the founder and CEO of Remerg, a social cause company that produces remerg.com, a website for people coming out of jail and prison in Colorado. The organization's goal is to reduce recidivism by connecting people to the resources and information they need to succeed. Peeples developed Remerg with the vision of using the Internet to fill the informational gaps around systemic reentry efforts and the community brick and mortar organizations.

Before founding Remerg, Peeples was a K–12 teacher, mostly in private international schools. After moving to Colorado in 1999, she took a part-time job as a GED teacher in a prison for a community college program. Later, she began teaching college English composition classes in the same facility. She notes that "getting to know prisoners as their teacher was transformative as I'd really never thought about the issue of incarceration before this time. The greatest impact was the feeling that our prisons were full of a wasted resource—human beings—and I wanted to do something about it." Given that, she founded a voting project designed to educate people with a criminal record about their voting rights, researched and wrote a statewide guide for people coming out of prison for a criminal justice advocacy organization, worked as an advocate, and returned to the university and earned her MPA in public policy. When she began her MPA, she had no idea about the important role that research using qualitative data would play in the success of her career and organization.

Courtesy of Carol Peeples

Peeples finds that research using qualitative data is an approach that allows individuals to learn more about an issue. In her work, focus groups and personal interviews are extremely valuable because people share things society would never learn about otherwise. At Remerg, she conducts many one-on-one interviews to identify what people need when they are released from prison. Her favorite locations for these interviews are coffee shops. In addition, she moderates focus groups to learn about what information is useful and needed on the Remerge website. She wants to ensure the website is not only useful but easy to navigate.

Although research focused on gathering and using qualitative data is invaluable in her day-to-day work, there are challenges associated with it as well. Peeples recognizes that "in the criminal justice world, people want something that's 'evidence based,' which is a good thing since I'd like to see government dollars used more wisely." Nevertheless, gathering evidence-based data can be challenging when using only qualitative data. In general, providing evidence based on both qualitative and quantitative data is preferable.

Peeples points to several crucial skills needed when gathering and using qualitative data. First, the researcher must be a good listener. The interviewer must give people time to respond and share their thoughts. If the researcher talks too much, participants in focus groups and interviews lose their interest in helping. Being perceptive is another critical skill when gathering and working with qualitative data. Researchers must notice if the interviewee is comfortable with the rest of the group members. They must ask if the interviewee is distracted. Does the person feel threatened? A perceptive interviewer may need to come back to an interview question or two if a conversation goes off-track. Finally, although it cannot be taught in a book, Peeples stresses the importance of actually caring about the topic and the person interviewed. Why should anyone share his or her story with a researcher? Respondents must know that the researcher genuinely cares about them and the topic of interest.

Peeples argues that it is important that a researcher respect their subjects and anticipate how to make them comfortable. A researcher must "realize if the respondent is tired after a long day, or maybe they are hungry. Bring snacks and drinks to a focus group and make participants as comfortable as you would company in your own home. If you are meeting them for an interview in a coffee shop, pick up the tab. Finally, thank them! They gave of themselves to help you." Peeples believes that incarceration and reentry is one of the most important public policy issues facing society today given its impact on people, families, communities, and public dollars. By using qualitative data, she strongly feels like she and her organization are making a difference in people's lives as well as in society.

Chapter Wrap-Up

This chapter offered information about qualitative research. Qualitative data are concerned with comprehensively *understanding* a topic. Qualitative inquiry is fundamentally exploratory in nature in that the researcher engages in a project with no preconceived notions about what will be learned, what will be shown to be important, what will be shown to be irrelevant, and so on. It is generally not conducted with predetermined definitions, measures, operationalization, and so on. Rather, collecting and using qualitative data is a means to understand widely held definitions, meaningful measures, and appropriate operationalization. According to Patton (2015), qualitative inquiry seems to work best for people with "a high tolerance for ambiguity."

The chapter noted that although many approaches are used to gather qualitative data, the three most frequently used approaches are interviews, observations and fieldwork, and document examinations. Interviews are used to gather qualitative data from a single individual, a small group, or a larger group such as a focus group. Observations and fieldwork gather data by going into the field to observe the topic of interest. It may also entail participating in or engaging directly with the topic. Finally, document examination is an approach used to collect qualitative data from written or electronic documents.

Table 6.4 Featured Research: Purposes, Research Questions, Sampling, and Analysis Considerations

Researcher	Purpose	Research Question	Type of Sampling	Sample Size	Qualities of the Sample	Methodology Used to Gather Data	Type of Data Analysis
Rod Brunson (Brunson & Weitzer, 2009)	Exploratory	What are the differences in the views of police relations of Black and White youth based on where they reside: a Black disadvantaged neighborhood, a White disadvantaged neighborhood, or a racially mixed disadvantaged neighborhood?	Purposive sampling. Counselors working in community organizations were asked to identify and approach young males who were known to live in the neighborhood study sites for participation in the study.	45 male adolescents living in three neighborhood study sites. Respondents ranged in age from 13 to 19 (average age was 16).	The sample is not representative of any larger population. The findings are not necessarily generalizable to any larger population. The purpose of research does not require either as it is exploratory in nature.	Qualitative research using in-depth interviews lasting about one hour each with male adolescents living in three highly disadvantage neighborhoods in St. Louis, MO.	Each interview was recorded, and the tapes were transcribed and analyzed by the authors. Themes were extracted, and typical quotes were highlighted to represent those themes.
Mary Dodge (Dodge et al., 2005)	Exploratory	Explore how female police officers serving as prostitution decoys view this work.	Convenience sampling plus some snow-ball sampling as officers referred the researcher to co-workers for participation.	25 female officers; ages ranged from 30 to 41 years with 4 to 16 years of policing experience. Had participated in 5 to 20 decoy stings with an average of 10 stings per officer.	The findings are not necessarily generalizable; The sample is not necessarily representative of a larger population of female undercover officers. The purpose of the research does not require either as it is exploratory in nature.	Qualitative research using semistructured interviews in respondent's homes, coffee shops, and offices; lasted about 60 minutes; taped and transcribed; focused on experiences as a decoy, difficulties associated with the role and assignment, personal views on prostitution, and the dynamics surrounding the interactions with johns on the street.	Transcriptions were used to extract themes where they were grouped into conceptual domains based on generalized statement contents.

Methods of gathering qualitative data frequently, but not always, are based on nonprobability sampling approaches, especially when the research focuses on interviewing or gathering data from people. This is because qualitative inquiry often does not have the benefit of a comprehensive population list of sampling elements available. Although this results in findings that are not generalizable, it is important to remember that generalizability is not necessarily the goal of qualitative research. Not having widely generalizable findings does not make the research less useful or valuable.

Two of our featured researchers gathered qualitative data for their research—Dodge and Brunson. Table 6.4 offers details about their research as it relates to the qualitative data they gathered and analyzed to address their research questions. This table shows important differences between the two pieces of research although they both used qualitative data. For example, their research questions, methodology used to gather the data, and samples differed. As is custom, we emphasized the common pitfalls and ethical considerations of conducting qualitative research. Finally, we heard from Carol Peeples and the use of qualitative data in her private organization focused on assisting those recently released from prison. In this capacity, Peeples uses many qualitative data gathering approaches such as interviews, and focus groups.

The next chapter, Chapter 7, focuses on data gathered using surveys. Survey research is a widely used approach in academia, public, and private entities. Although it may seem easy to construct and field a survey, Chapter 7 will offer best practices to assist you in developing and fielding an excellent survey that will result in quality data.

Applied Assignments

The materials presented in this chapter can be used in applied ways. This box presents several assignments to help in demonstrating the value of this material by engaging in assignments related to it.

1. Homework Applied Assignment: Assessing Research Using Qualitative Data

Select two peer-reviewed journal articles that describe research using qualitative data. Using Table 6.4 describing our case studies as a guide, create a table for your two articles. Be sure to clearly articulate the purpose and research question in each piece. Identify the type of sampling used, the sample size, and other qualities of the sample. And in the table, identify the methodology used to collect the data and the type of data analysis used. After completing your table of the two articles, write a paper that describes each as well the advantages and disadvantages of this approach. What other approaches can you envision to answer the research question? What future research does each article suggest to you? Be prepared to discuss your findings in class.

2. Group Work in Class Applied Assignment: Field Observation as a Group

Your group needs to enter the field as "complete observers." As a group, and with the permission of your professor, you need to go to an open area (park), coffee shop, diner, shopping mall, bus station, or somewhere you can observe people interact. Ideally, the site you choose will be somewhere your group is interested in and easily accessible. Your goal is to observe anything and everything at your location, assuming you know nothing.

Data you can gather can include (it is useful to delegate responsibilities among the group members):

- Describing the interactions occurring in the setting, including who talks to whom, whose opinions are respected, how decisions are made

- Noting where participants stand or sit

- Examining interactions from a perspective of comparing those with and without power, men versus women, young versus old, majority versus majority, and so on

- Counting persons or incidents of observed activity that would be useful in helping one recollect the situation, especially when viewing complex events or events in which there are many participants

- Listening carefully to conversations, trying to remember as many verbatim conversations, nonverbal expressions, and gestures as possible

- Noting how things at your location are organized and prioritized, as well as how people interrelate and what the cultural parameters are

- Providing a description of what the cultural members deemed to be important in manners, leadership, politics, social interaction, and taboos

- Describing what is happening and why

- Drawing a map of the place

- Sorting out the regular from the irregular activities

- Looking for variation to view the event in its entirety from a variety of viewpoints

These data should be gathered using field notes. As a group, summarize your field notes. What do the data mean? What surprised you when doing this assignment? Does your observation suggest any research questions for later analysis? Be able to report your findings to the class.

3. Internet Applied Assignment: Gathering and Analyzing Online Qualitative Data

You have been hired as a researcher to explore university mission statements from 10 universities. Find at least 5 public and 5 private universities for inclusion your sample. In a paper, you need to identify your purpose and research question. You must identify how you will select your ten universities for study. Next, after using and analyzing these qualitative data, identify themes. What findings emerge? Are there differences in public and private universities? Any other patterns you can discern? What future research does your analysis suggest? Write a qualitative research paper that describes what you did, your methodology, your findings, and your conclusion. Be prepared to share your findings with the class.

KEY WORDS AND CONCEPTS

Axial coding 197
Closed-ended question 179
Coding 180
Complete observer 193
Complete participant 192
Computer-assisted qualitative data analysis (CAQDAS) 199
Content analysis 194
Document analysis 193
Ethnography 190
Field notes 195

Focus group 189
Going native 190
Grounded theory 196
Hawthorne Effect 192
Interviews 187
Maximum variation sampling 183
Observation and fieldwork 190
Observer as participant 193
Open coding 197
Open-ended question 178
Participant as observer 192

Participant observation 190
Probing 181
Qualitative research 174
Role conceptions 190
Selective coding 197
Semistructured interviews 188
Theoretical sampling 183
Triangulation 184
Unstructured interviews 188

KEY POINTS

- Qualitative research uses non-numeric data to answer what are frequently exploratory research questions using inductive reasoning to provide detailed and nuanced understanding of a topic.

- Research using qualitative data is especially good at providing a deep, nuanced understanding of a topic with an emphasis on the context. In general, it provides information on everything nonquantifiable about a topic.

- Qualitative data come from interviews, observations and field research, and document analysis. In each of these categories, there are additional variants of qualitative research.

- Qualitative data are non-numerical in nature and includes things such as narratives, published documents, videos, music, photos, recordings, observations, body language, voice intonation, and other aspects of a topic.

- Triangulation is the use of multiple methods, researchers, theory, or data to conduct a study. In the words of Denzin, research that has been triangulated offers "different lines of action." By using triangulation, a researcher can offer strengthened evidence supporting the conclusions.

- Interviews can be face to face or over video or audio technology. They can be conducted one on one, in small groups, or with focus groups. Regardless of the style, a researcher should pose broad questions to the subjects and be prepared to use follow-up probes to gather more data.

- As per Gold (1958), role conceptions represent the four roles a researcher can take on during field research that indicates the degree of participation and observation taken on by the researcher. They include complete observer, participant observer, observer as participant, and complete participant. As a researcher, you must pay attention to the possibility of the Hawthorne Effect, as well to the ethical considerations that come along with participant observation.

- Document analysis refers to a systematic collection, review, evaluation, synthesizing, and interpretation of documents to gain meaning and understanding, regardless of whether the document is printed or available in electronic form. Content analysis is one type of document analysis that focuses on the analysis of non-numeric data to develop inferences pertinent to the research question. There is no agreement on the precise definition of content analysis, but most agree it has characteristics of both qualitative and quantitative research (i.e., counts or quantifies non-numerical data).

- Sampling for qualitative research generally uses nonprobability approaches such as convenience, purposive, or snowball sampling. The sample should be large enough to reasonably represent the population of interest and result in saturation. The size of the sample is less important than the quality of the sample.

- After gathering qualitative data, the research must spend time organizing the data. After that, analysis can take place. Although analysis is widely varied (and frequently not detailed), it generally consists of coding that involves three stages according to Glaser and Strauss (2012): open coding, axial coding, and secondary coding.

- Even though qualitative data analysis software is available, it is only a tool. Whether software is used or not, the research must still make sense of, organize, synthesize, and condense the data to meaningful generalizations.

REVIEW QUESTIONS

1. What is qualitative research, and how does it differ from quantitative research?

2. What are qualitative data, and how do they differ from quantitative data?

3. What are the advantages and disadvantages of qualitative research approaches? What research questions are most appropriate for qualitative research?

4. What are the three primary types of qualitative research? What are the advantages and disadvantages of each?

5. When would a researcher use unstructured versus structured interviews? When would a researcher opt for one-on-one interviews versus focus groups?

6. What are the responsibilities of a moderator?

7. What are the four types of role conceptions? What are the advantages and disadvantages of each? What ethical considerations and research issues are associated with each?

8. What is content analysis? Is it quantitative or qualitative in nature? Why? What sorts of documents can be analyzed in document examination?

9. What are ways a researcher can record qualitative data? What is the most important? Why? Is it best to use only one recording method? Why or why not?

10. What are the three general steps involved in qualitative data analysis? What occurs at each of these stages?

CRITICAL THINKING QUESTIONS

1. A student proposes a research project with the following research question: "What are the important symbols and rituals in the Aetherius Society?" To address this research question, the students propose using data from the U.S. Census to calculate statistics about this society. How might you counsel this student? Is this the best way to answer that question? Is it even possible to answer the research question using Census data? What are some other options that a student should consider?

2. You wish to study parents who routinely use corporal punishment when disciplining their children. Although your research is exploratory in nature and you are open to learning about this approach in general, you specifically hope to gain an understanding as to how they justify this form of punishment, when they use it, and how they maintain trust with their child after this punishment. Given what you have learned in this chapter, how might you conduct this research? Would you reveal the purpose of your research to the participants you select. Would any type of Hawthorne Effect be a concern? Would the respondents have informed consent? Would their participation in the research be fully voluntary? What are the advantages and limitations of the methodology you propose?

3. You have been hired as a moderator to conduct an extremely important focus group to gather data on the rights of students accused of misconduct on college campuses. What specifically are your responsibilities during the focus group as the moderator? In the middle of the focus group, one individual repeatedly raises his voice in anger and tells the other group members they are losers and pansies. You notice that a few other focus group members have not offered any information. How, as a moderator, should you handle this? What is your goal in dealing with one unruly focus group member? What are your concerns about the quiet focus group members? What prompts might you use for each of these focus group members to ensure success?

4. You have designed qualitative research that explores the motivations, environment, and culture surrounding the Masons. A part of this research involves interviewing 15 Masons from the local Lodge. Your respondents will be obtained via convenience and snowball sampling beginning with your neighbor who is a Mason. A friend sees your design and tells you that the proposed research is no good because the sample size is small, nonrepresentative, and the findings will not be generalizable to the larger population of Masons in the nation. Is your friend correct? Why or why not? How might you defend your research design against his criticisms?

5. A student in your research methods class is conducting quantitative research using a bit of data available online for her class project. You are gathering your own data using face-to-face interviews to learn about the nuances associated with the same topic that your classmate is examining. Your classmate begins taunting you for conducting "easy" qualitative research since, as she says, you are "just talking to a bunch of people." Is qualitative research easier than quantitative research? Why do you say that? Is quantitative research better than qualitative research? Why or why not? What are some suggestions you might make to your classmate regarding both of your lines of inquiry?

$SAGE edge™

SAGE edge offers a robust online environment featuring an impressive array of free tools and resources for review, study, and further exploration, keeping you on the cutting edge of teaching and learning. Learn more at **edge.sagepub .com/rennisonrm**.

Survey Research

Learning Objectives

After finishing this chapter, you should be able to:

7.1 Describe how surveys are used in contemporary criminal justice research, the ways in which they are commonly administered, and the strengths and weaknesses associated with each delivery method.

7.2 Provide examples of some "principles" for developing good survey questions.

7.3 Compare different tactics for constructing good survey questionnaires, and highlight common pitfalls that should be avoided.

7.4 Evaluate why online surveys have grown in popularity in recent years, and articulate some of the challenges associated with using them.

7.5 Compare and contrast "confidentiality" and "anonymity" as it pertains to survey research.

7.6 Evaluate the ethical challenges researchers face when conducting surveys.

Introduction

Surveys are everywhere. You can hardly go to a restaurant, shop, or class without being asked to fill in a survey. The ubiquity of surveys means it is likely you have participated in many surveys over your lifetime. You may have even tried your hand at creating and fielding a survey or two in the past. Be warned, however. Just because you *can* create and administer a survey does not mean you *should!* As with most things that are worth doing right, creating and administering surveys that produce accurate and reliable data—data that can be used to advance our empirical knowledge on crime and justice issues or to inform criminal justice–related programs and policies—requires a particular skill set that can only be achieved through training and practice. A theme in this text is that one's research is only as good as its weakest part. Destroying well-designed and important research using poor surveys would be a shame, especially when you can use the material in this chapter to begin learning how to create good surveys.

The aim of this chapter, therefore, is not to make you an overnight expert in survey research. Instead, the goal of this chapter is to equip you with the basic knowledge, skills, and abilities needed to become a good survey researcher. To that end, the chapter begins by explaining what surveys are and how they are commonly used in criminology and criminal justice research. Next, we provide details on the specific types of surveys used to answer research questions, providing information about the strengths and weaknesses associated with each survey mode. This information is followed by tips on how to construct good questionnaires, with particular emphasis on how to avoid common mistakes when creating survey questions. We also discuss certain ethical considerations associated with survey research. We conclude the chapter with an interview with survey research expert Bridget Kelly, who is the project coordinator at the University of Nevada Las Vegas's Cannon Survey Center.

Why Conduct Survey Research?

When it comes to collecting original data, the most common approach used in the social sciences, including criminology and criminal justice, is survey research. Why? There are several good reasons to conduct surveys. Given the fact that surveys are everywhere, it should be clear that having survey methodology skills are valuable in the workforce. One of our featured researchers, Rachel Boba Santos, during her video interview conducted for this book, commented that when she teaches about surveys and survey construction, students repeatedly tell her that those skills are the most valuable they learned in school. Not only do her students find them valuable for honor's theses, master's theses, and capstones, but also these students find that these skills lead to jobs.

Nevertheless, there are many other reasons to conduct surveys. First, surveys when created properly can be an incredibly efficient method for collecting vast amounts of data from large groups of individuals. For example, a researcher can use an online survey tool such as Qualtrics® or SurveyMonkey® to distribute surveys to thousands of e-mail addresses. A second reason why surveys are so popular and widely used is that they can be administered through a variety techniques or modes, each with specific strengths and weaknesses. This flexibility is one reason that surveys are used for all research purposes. Third, surveys are also easy to use for repeated measurement. By using the same survey, or instrument, a researcher can gather data on a topic to measure how it has changed over time. A fourth reason why one should consider using survey research is that it is cost effective. Distributing surveys tends to be far less time intensive and more cost effective than other methods of gathering data, such as face-to-face interviews. Fifth, for some sensitive topics, a survey offers the respondent a way to share data without having to tell it directly to a person. The level of anonymity makes it feasible to ask about many topics that may not be easily learned through the use of other data collection methods. Simply put, researchers use survey research because it is often the most appropriate methodology to efficiently, effectively, and inexpensively answer research questions.

> This chapter provides tips on how to construct good questionnaires, with particular emphasis on how to avoid common mistakes when creating survey questions.

Survey: Instrument, or tool, used to gather data. The survey includes questions that are either open-ended or closed-ended and can be administered in multiple ways.

Items: Questions contained on a survey instrument.

Survey research: Research methodology that involves gathering qualitative and quantitative data from a sample of survey participants, known as "respondents", using a survey instrument.

Respondents: Individuals participating in a survey.

Questionnaires: Written, printed, or electronic survey instruments that a respondent fills out on his or her own.

What Are Surveys?

Surveys are tools or instruments used to gather data on a variety of topics. Surveys are composed of several questions or **items**. Items are the questions asked in a survey. **Survey research** is a research methodology that involves gathering qualitative and quantitative data from a sample of individual survey participants, known as **respondents**, using a survey instrument. Most broadly, surveys come in two forms: questionnaires and interviews.

Questionnaires refer to written, printed, or electronic survey instruments that respondents fill out themselves. The respondent may receive the questionnaire in the mail, it may be distributed in person, or it may come to the respondent via the Internet. Alternatively, maybe you received a link in an e-mail that directed you to an online survey that you filled out yourself. Some individuals have taken surveys on laptops given to them by researchers even. This type of survey is useful for gathering data using both open- and closed-ended questions. As a college student, you have probably received a paper or online survey questionnaire used to evaluate a

© Camrocker/iStockphoto.com

Unlike questionnaires, interviews represent a type of survey that involves the researcher (i.e., the interviewer) directly interacting with the survey participant, during the data collection process.

Interviews: Conversations between the researcher and an individual or a group of individuals. Interviews also represent a type of survey mode that involves the researcher (i.e., the interviewer) directly engaging with the survey participant during the data collection process.

professor or class that you were enrolled in. Regardless of the form the survey takes, if you fill out a survey yourself, you are engaged in a questionnaire-type survey.

Unlike questionnaires, **interviews** represent a type of survey that involves the researcher (i.e., the interviewer) directly interacting with the survey participant during the data collection process. Most often, it is the field representative that guides the participant through a structured questionnaire comprising mostly close-ended questions. The field representative fills in the survey based on the respondent's answers. Interviews are a bit more flexible than questionnaires, given they can be semistructured or unstructured. During semistructured and unstructured interviews, survey participants are free to express themselves in a more personal (and often more private) manner versus only responding to a set number of questions with fixed response categories. These types of surveys are often useful in situations when the researcher is collecting sensitive data. Interviews can be conducted over the telephone, in person, or via video conferencing. Regardless of the type of survey a researcher uses, both are valuable ways to gather quantitative and qualitative data of interest from respondents. Surveys can be used to answer research questions related to every type of empirical research study: exploratory, descriptive, explanatory, and evaluation. Given the flexibility and usefulness of survey research, it is not a surprise that in our featured case studies, almost all of them used survey methodology to gather quantitative and qualitative data.

General Steps in Survey Research

Before we move on to more detailed information related to survey research, it is useful to consider the survey research process. An examination of this process shows how in each step there is information that informs one's decision about how to gather data. Will it be a questionnaire or a survey? Will it be administered in person, via e-mail, or by handing out surveys. The first step in all research, including survey research, is to develop a research purpose and research question. This step is important because the purpose and question helps to inform whether one will use a questionnaire or an interview. If research is purely exploratory, an unstructured or a semistructured interview may be the way to go. This allows the flexibility to follow up with respondents immediately when new information is learned. If the purpose is explanatory, it may be appropriate to use a questionnaire with a fixed number of items. In the following sections, we will provide greater information about how survey research can be used in the four purposes we consider in this text: exploratory, descriptive, explanatory, and evaluative. The purpose and research question also informs how one will handle concepts, conceptualizations, and operationalization. For example, if one is seeking to gather data on a topic that is associated with a rich literature, then using a questionnaire may be best. This is because the research can identify the concepts of interest, conceptualize them, and operationalize them into survey items on a questionnaire. The questions or items on the questionnaire should correspond to concepts of interest. On the other hand, if the research is fully exploratory on a topic in which little is known, then an unstructured or semistructured interview may be best. In this way, the researcher can learn from his or her respondents about key concepts, how respondent define these concepts, and the best ways they might be measured in the future. Developing a sampling plan is the next major step. Depending on resources, and on the nature of the sample (is there a sampling frame available?), one may adjust the way the way the survey is distributed.

For example, if there is a sampling frame of e-mail addresses available, then using an online survey might be the best approach. If the sample desired is hard to find and no sampling frame is available, however, the approaches available may be more limited. Interviews may be best in these situations. Alternatively, if this population gathers in a single place, a researcher may be able to distribute surveys. There are many ways a survey can be distributed that will be discussed in this chapter. After distribution of the survey, the data must be gathered and analyzed, and the research question must be answered. Throughout the development of the research methodology, the research uses information to decide on the best approach. Let's now turn to the many purposes of research and how survey research can be used for each.

Surveys Across Research Purposes

As indicated, surveys are useful across all research purposes. This is in part why they are the most popular form of gathering data in the social sciences. In this section, we consider how surveys are used across purposes with an emphasis on your case studies to demonstrate this flexibility.

Surveys and Exploratory Research

Recall from Chapter 2 that exploratory studies are useful when researchers know little or nothing about a topic. Exploratory research is especially useful when the researchers seek to answer "what," "how," or "where" questions. Throughout the text, we have described how featured researcher Rod Brunson and his colleague's study of young Black and White males residing in disadvantaged St. Louis, Missouri, neighborhoods was an example of an exploratory study (Brunson & Weitzer, 2009). What we have not yet shared is that this research also benefited from survey research as one means to collect their data. Brunson explained that the use of face-to-face interviewing allowed the researchers to build confidence and trust with the respondents. After this trust was established, the researchers used self-administered survey questionnaires to obtain general information from participants. Then during the face-to-face conversations, researchers were able to delve deeper into important issues and topics, allowing for more detailed and qualitatively rich data to be collected.

The law enforcement prostitution decoy research conducted by featured researcher Mary Dodge and colleagues is also exploratory research (Dodge, Starr-Gimeno, & Williams, 2005). Like Brunson and colleague (Brunson & Weitzer, 2009), Dodge et al. used multiple methods to gather their data, including a survey. Dodge et al.'s approach differed from that of Brunson and colleague in that they administered the survey to their respondents during face-to-face interviews conducted at participants' homes, their offices, and coffee shops. Dodge et al. asked respondents questions from the survey that consisted of preplanned open-ended survey questions designed to examine experiences as a decoy, difficulties associated with the role and assignment, personal views on prostitution, and the dynamics surrounding the interactions with Johns on the street. Dodge et al.'s study participants never saw her data collection instrument; and by administering their survey this way, they were able to gather the same data from all respondents. They were also free to deviate from the survey to ask other questions based on responses. Dodge et al. chose to use this less structured, or semistructured, interview format for their surveys to allow the female officers to elaborate on their responses and to reflect more deeply on the events they experienced.

Surveys and Descriptive Research

Recall that descriptive research allows researchers to describe phenomenon so they have a more detailed understanding of it. Brunson and Weitzer's (2009) research highlighted that

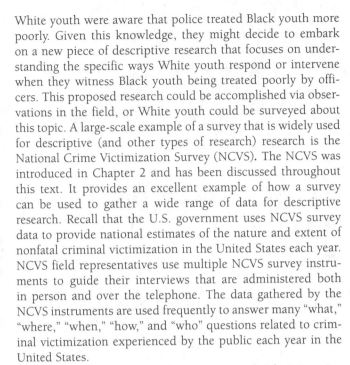

U.S. Department of Justice
Office of Justice Programs

Bureau of Justice Statistics

Law Enforcement Management and Administrative Statistics, 2000: Data for Individual State and Local Agencies with 100 or More Officers

Personnel

Expenditures and pay

Operations

Community policing

Policies and programs

Equipment

Computers and information systems

The LEMAS survey is used to gather data from state and local law enforcement agencies that employ 100 or more sworn officers (i.e., large law enforcement agencies).

Law Enforcement Management and Administrative Statistics (LEMAS): National survey sponsored by the Bureau of Justice Statistics (BJS) that gathers data from state and local law enforcement agencies that employ 100 or more sworn officers (i.e., "large" law enforcement agencies).

White youth were aware that police treated Black youth more poorly. Given this knowledge, they might decide to embark on a new piece of descriptive research that focuses on understanding the specific ways White youth respond or intervene when they witness Black youth being treated poorly by officers. This proposed research could be accomplished via observations in the field, or White youth could be surveyed about this topic. A large-scale example of a survey that is widely used for descriptive (and other types of research) research is the National Crime Victimization Survey (NCVS). The NCVS was introduced in Chapter 2 and has been discussed throughout this text. It provides an excellent example of how a survey can be used to gather a wide range of data for descriptive research. Recall that the U.S. government uses NCVS survey data to provide national estimates of the nature and extent of nonfatal criminal victimization in the United States each year. NCVS field representatives use multiple NCVS survey instruments to guide their interviews that are administered both in person and over the telephone. The data gathered by the NCVS instruments are used frequently to answer many "what," "where," "when," "how," and "who" questions related to criminal victimization experienced by the public each year in the United States.

The **Law Enforcement Management and Administrative Statistics (LEMAS)** survey is another national survey that is widely used for descriptpve research. The Bureau of Justice Statistics (BJS) sponsors the LEMAS survey, which is conducted, or fielded, every 3 to 4 years. **Fielded** means that the survey has been distributed or launched and data are being collected. The LEMAS survey is used to gather data from state and local law enforcement agencies that employ 100 or more sworn officers (i.e., large law enforcement agencies). Self-administered survey questionnaires are mailed to a representative from each law enforcement agency who provides organizational and administration data on the LEMAS surveys. Data collected during the survey administration includes agency responsibilities, operating expenditures, job functions of sworn and civilian employees, officer salaries and special pay, demographic characteristics of officers, weapons and armor policies, education and training requirements, computers and information systems, vehicles, special units, and community policing activities.

Surveys and Explanatory Research

Explanatory research, also introduced in Chapter 2, is an approach that provides explanations about a topic and builds off knowledge gained from exploratory and descriptive research. Explanatory research is used to identify what characteristics are related to a topic, as well as to identify what impacts, causes, or influences a particular outcome or topic of interest. In addition, through explanatory research, a researcher may try to understand how to predict outcomes or topics of interest. Surveys are a valuable tool for gathering data for explanatory purposes.

Although the NCVS is widely used to describe topics related to criminal victimization in the United States, NCVS data are also used widely for explanatory research. For example, featured researcher Heather Zaykowski's (2014) research analyzed NCVS data to estimate the likelihood that crime victims would access victim services. Specifically, she focused on better understanding the role that police reporting plays in influencing victims accessing services. These NCVS data, gathered via surveys administered on the phone and during face-to-face interviews, allowed her to do so. Featured researcher Chris Melde and colleagues' study is also explanatory, given their goal to explain associations (or lack thereof) between gang membership, fear of victimization, perceptions of risk of victimization, and self-reported victimization (Melde, Taylor, & Esbensen, 2009). Data used to answer Melde et al.'s research questions were collected from self-report surveys that involved students at sampled schools answering questions as they were read aloud by a researcher. Consent forms were sent to the students' parents, and only those students whose parents gave consent were allowed to complete the questionnaires. The ethical protocol was in place to protect the children, especially their privacy, and all students' data collected during the study remained confidential. Overall, 72% of students sampled participated in the surveys, which took about 40 to 45 minutes to finish.

Finally, featured researcher Carlos Cuevas and colleagues' research on Latino teen dating violence is another example of explanatory (and descriptive) research made possible by survey research (Sabina, Cuevas, & Cotignola-Pickens, 2016). Along with most of the other case studies used throughout this textbook, Cuevas and colleagues used survey research as their primary data collection method. Specifically, Cuevas and his team used data gathered from the Dating Violence among Latino Adolescents (DAVILA) survey to answer their research questions. In fact, Cuevas and his colleague Sabina were the ones who originally collected the DAVILA data. DAVILA data were collected during telephone interviews. Because the focus of the DAVILA study was on Latino students, interviews were conducted in English and Spanish. The DAVILA was a **longitudinal data** study. That means the survey was fielded twice to measure changes over time. Approximately 40% of participants who completed a survey at Wave 1 (i.e., time 1) completed surveys at Wave 2 (i.e., time 2).

Fielded: Term used to mean that a survey has been distributed or administered and data are being collected.

Longitudinal data: Data collected from the same sample at different points in time.

Surveys and Evaluation Research

Surveys are also widely used in evaluation research. The purpose of evaluation research is to assess many facets of policies or programs. In this context, surveys are used to generate empirically based evidence in support of (or against) some element of a policy or program. For example, two online surveys were used recently by researchers in Queensland, Australia, who evaluated the effectiveness of two rapid action policing (RAP) hubs—a new policing strategy introduced in some Queensland communities (Ransley, Hart, & Bartlett, 2017). During the RAP evaluation study, two surveys were created and administered through an online survey solution called Qualtrics. The researchers carefully constructed the questionnaires using open-ended and closed-ended questions, attitudinal scales, and other types of questions made possible using online and Web-based surveys. One of the two surveys was sent to Queensland Police Service (QPS) stakeholders (e.g., representatives from the local city council, fire department, and ambulance service) who had regular contact with RAP officers and officials. A separate online questionnaire was administered to a sample of community business leaders. The results from both online surveys were used to determine whether the RAP hubs worked and to guide policy and procedures related to the wider adoption of RAP throughout Queensland.

Surveys are the most popular way to collect original data in criminology and criminal justice research, in part, because they can be used for any research purpose (i.e., exploratory, descriptive, explanatory, and evaluation research). In addition, they are desirable because they are useful when the unit of analysis is the individual or individuals representing groups, agencies, or organizations. By understanding the broad value of survey research, you can now focus on the best way to distribute the survey.

How Are Surveys Distributed?

We opened this chapter by noting that surveys are a popular research methodology used in criminology and criminal justice research in part because they are versatile. Part of that versatility relates to the variety of ways a researcher can distribute surveys. Stated differently, surveys are versatile given the variety of **survey modes.** Four primary survey modes or means of distribution are available for surveys: mail or written, phone, face-to-face, and online or mobile surveys. The choice of which type of survey mode is best to use in any research project is influenced by many factors. Influential factors include the research purpose and goal, the amount of time a researcher has to field the survey, the amount of money the researcher can spend, and other resources (such as availability of Internet or laptops used). In addition, each survey mode has particular strengths and weaknesses that must be considered. Each is discussed next.

Mail/Written Surveys (Postal Surveys)

When you think of a survey, you probably think of answering a series of questions on a form or document and returning the completed form back to the person or organization that distributed it. **Mail and written surveys** are a mode of surveying that involves providing a written survey to an individual. This survey can be sent via the mail or handed out in person. Since the respondent is the person responsible for completing the survey (i.e., no one else is with the respondent to assist in completing it), the survey is considered a self-administered questionnaire. A **self-administered questionnaire** is a survey administered either in paper or in electronic form that a survey participant completes on his or her own.

Advantages

There are many advantages of a mail/written survey. First, because an interviewer is not present during a self-administered survey, there is no chance of interviewer bias. **Interviewer bias** can occur if the survey participant is influenced by the presence or actions of an interviewer or field representative. Imagine you are filling out a survey in the presence of an interviewer,

© MarkHatfield/iStockphoto.com

and you check a box noting you had taken a drug. As a response to that, the (unprofessional and poorly trained) field representative shakes his or her head in disgust. This may cause you to go back and change your answer or to answer later questions differently to avoid the representative's judgment. Alternatively, imagine you are filling out a survey focused on whether you had hired a prostitute. Imagine the field representative or interviewer looking at you during this survey is a woman who looks like your mother. Might that affect your answer if you had hired a prostitute? If something about the field representative, whether appearance or behavior, affects your responses on the survey, interview bias is present. Interview bias distorts the outcome of the interview, affects the data gathered, and ultimately affects the results of the study.

Another advantage of a mail/written survey is that they can be distributed across a massive geographic study area at a low (to moderate) cost. The cost of a mail survey can increase, however, based on the length of the questionnaire (i.e., the number of survey pages), whether return postage is prepaid and return envelopes are provided, and whether other strategies designed to reduce survey nonresponse are implemented.

Disadvantages

Mail or written surveys are imperfect and characterized by disadvantages as well. A disadvantage of a mail or written survey is that it requires the researcher or someone on the research team to take the completed surveys, code the responses, and enter the codes for every completed survey into a database. Coding, as introduced in Chapter 6, refers to converting a respondent's answers into a numerical value that can be entered into a database. In addition, when a mail or written survey includes open-ended questions with short answers provided by respondents, their answers must be typed into a database for later analysis. These steps are not only time-consuming, but they also represent a point in the research process where error can be introduced through inaccurate coding and text entry. A second disadvantage associated with mail or written surveys is that it is vulnerable to survey nonresponse. **Survey nonresponse** occurs when sample respondents who choose to complete and return surveys differ in meaningful ways from those who are selected in the sample, but do not complete and return the survey. When this occurs, the data may be biased, and ultimately the finding of the study may be compromised. Survey nonresponse is measured using response rates. **Response rates** are the proportion of surveys returned relative to the total number of surveys fielded. The response rate is generally described as a percentage and is calculated using this basic formula:

$$\frac{\text{\# completed surveys returned}}{\text{\# surveys distributed}} \times 100$$

For example, if you mail out 100 surveys, but only 10 are completed and returned, your response rate is 10%. Historically, mail or written survey response rates are low (e.g., 10% to 15%). This is markedly less than the response rates associated with other survey modes. As a researcher, you need to keep this in mind if you plan to mail out surveys to your sample. You need to draw a large enough sample to ensure you have enough data taking into account the likely survey nonresponse.

Low response rates for mail surveys are not a foregone conclusion. Researchers have spent decades studying ways to increase mail survey response rates (i.e., decreasing nonresponse). No other researcher is more closely associated with survey research—and the strategies used to maximize response rates—than Don A. Dillman. As an expert in survey methodology at Washington State University, Professor Dillman has written extensively on ways to minimize survey nonresponse. His book *The Tailored Design Method* is considered the "go-to book" for those interested in conducting high-quality self-administered questionnaires. By following his advice, you may be able to get response rates as high as 80% (Dillman, Smyth, & Christian, 2009).

Besides survey nonresponse, other sources of nonresponse biases exist. Some of those sources of nonresponse bias researchers have control over, but other sources they do not. By using many of the ideas developed by Dillman and colleagues, Daly, Jones, Gereau, and Levy (2011) identified several of the most common reasons why survey nonresponse occurs. One major reason is that the intended respondent never received the survey sent to him or her. Alternatively, it may be the respondent received the survey, but for a variety of reasons, he or she did not complete or return the instrument. An accounting for these nonresponse influences is presented in Table 7.1.

In addition to the threat of nonresponse bias caused by low participation rates, other important shortcomings are associated with self-administered questionnaires. In the case of

© claudiodivizia/iStockphoto

When using self-administered mail surveys, researchers must try to avoid other threats to data quality.

Survey nonresponse: When sample respondents who choose to complete and return surveys differ in meaningful ways from those who are chosen but do not participate in the survey.

Response rate: Way to measure the success of a survey and, subsequently, how well the participants represent the larger population they are intended to reflect. Rates are typically reported as the percentage of all eligible subjects asked to complete a survey and are computed by dividing the number of participants by the total number of eligible participants and by multiplying that proportion by 100.

Table 7.1	Reasons Why Mail Surveys Are Not Received by Participants, Completed by Participants, or Returned to Researchers (Daly et al., 2011)
No contact was ever made because . . .	**Contact was made, but participant refused to participate because . . .**
• there was not enough postage • the wrong mailing address was used • bulk mail was delayed or not delivered by the post office • the survey was intercepted and disposed of by a family member, significant other, or other household member (i.e., roommate)	• no return address was provided • no postage-paid return envelope was provided • the survey instructions are unclear • the survey is too long or complicated • the participant mistrusts the confidentiality assurances • no/too little incentive was offered to participate • the research topic is unappealing • participant isn't interested • the survey is lost among other "junk" mail

Recall bias: When the survey participant's responses to questions lack accuracy or completeness because they are unwilling or unable to "recall" events or information from the past.

Recency effects: Stems from question ordering on a survey. This question-order effect occurs when the ordering of questions on a survey influences responses given to later questions.

Question-order effect: When the ordering of questions on a survey influences responses given to later questions.

mail surveys, the researcher never truly knows who completes the questionnaire. Although the mail survey might have been addressed to a particular household respondent, nothing can guarantee that the addressee is the person who completed it. Similarly, even though the absence of an interviewer eliminates the chances of interviewer bias, not having an interviewer present while the respondent completes a survey means that the respondent cannot get help if he or she is confused by a question, needs aid in understanding or interpreting instructions, or seems to lose interest in completing or returning the questionnaire. All of these circumstances can affect data quality and ultimately the results of the study.

When using self-administered mail surveys, researchers must try to avoid other threats to data quality. Recall bias and recency effects are two examples of problems that can occur when researchers gather data using mail surveys. Both of these forms of error threaten the validity and reliability of data, which were discussed in earlier chapters. **Recall bias** occurs when the survey participant's responses to questions lack accuracy or completeness because they are unwilling or unable to recall events or information from the past. Recall bias is not uncommon. Think back to something that has occurred to you such as having a car stolen, your house broken into, a marriage dissolved, or a heart broken. Have you ever found yourself describing this as having happened more recently than it did? Maybe you told someone that your car was stolen two months ago. When you stop and think about it, you may realize that it was stolen six months ago (time flies). **Recency effects**, on the other hand, stem from question or item ordering on a survey. This **question-order effect** occurs when the ordering of questions on a survey influences responses given to later questions. Perhaps you are taking a survey that asks about a time you felt discriminated against. You answer and describe such an event. The next question on the survey is as follows: "Do you believe discrimination is a problem?" Chances are this question ordering affects responses to the second question. Researchers must pay attention to the ordering of their questions to avoid recency effects.

Online and Mobile Surveys

Increasingly, researchers are disseminating self-administered questionnaires online, as well as through mobile applications (i.e., apps). Cuevas goes as far as suggesting that the days of traditional phone surveys are numbered and that methods such as online and mobile surveys do a better job of maximizing the success of survey research. **Online surveys** and **mobile surveys** are offered to respondents online via a desktop computer, laptop, Apple® iPad™, smartphone, or other mobile device. Many researchers design their surveys to ensure their surveys can be taken using any of these devices.

Advantages

Web and smartphone technologies offer a faster (and often less expensive) alternative to collecting survey data than do traditional mail surveys. As with self-administered mail or written surveys, the absence of an interviewer eliminates the threat of interviewer bias.

In addition, constructing questionnaires for online/mobile surveys is much faster, cheaper, and easier than is creating a physical questionnaire. With an online or mobile survey, there is no need to print forms, stuff envelopes, pay for postage, or sit around waiting for questionnaires to be returned. In addition, online and mobile surveys do not require anyone to code or enter data from the actual survey into a database. This means data-entry errors are eliminated because survey participants' responses are recorded directly into a data file once the participant submits his or her survey. In addition, the data file can easily be exported from the survey software company's website, or directly onto the researcher's computer, at any time during the study. Online and mobile surveys are also convenient survey modes as they allow respondents to answer questions according to their own pace, chosen time, and preferences. And in some cases, finding respondents is made easier because many companies provide access to samples, or **survey panels** of respondents, at an additional cost.

An additional advantage of online and mobile surveys is that they can easily be tailored for specific subgroups of respondents using **skip-and-fill patterns** or conditional logic statements. A skip-and-fill question is a type of survey question in which questions asked are contingent on answers to previous questions. Imagine you program your online or mobile survey to begin by asking the participant whether he or she has any siblings (i.e., Question 1). If the answer to Question 1 is "No," then you do not need that respondent to be asked Question 2 (how many siblings do you have?). Given that, the researcher creates a skip-and-fill routine in survey software to "skip" Question 2 if the answer to Question 1 is "No." The software will then automatically record (i.e., "fill") a "Not Applicable" answer for Question 2 for people who noted in Question 1 that they have no siblings.

Example of Skip-and-Fill Pattern in a Survey

Question 1: Do you have any siblings that are currently alive?

- Yes
- No

Question 2: How many?

- 1
- 2
- 3
- 4
- More than 4

Question 3: What is your current zip code? (Enter your 5-digit zip code.)

In addition to all of the advantages of online and mobile surveys described earlier, there are certain characteristics specific to *mobile* surveys that set them apart from *online* surveys.

Online survey: Mode of survey research whereby a questionnaire is delivered to an eligible participant via the Internet and completed on a personal computer, usually through a Web browser.

Mobile survey: Mode of survey research whereby a questionnaire is delivered to an eligible participant via the Internet and completed on a smartphone or tablet, usually through a Web browser or a mobile application (i.e., app).

Survey panels: Existing samples that a researcher can pay to get access to.

Skip-and-fill patterns: Also known as "conditional logic statements." A type of survey in which the questions asked are contingent on answers to previous questions.

> Question 2 is asked *only* if the answer to Question 1 is "Yes"; otherwise, Question 2 is skipped, and "Not applicable" is automatically recorded as the answer, based on a "skip-and-fill" routine set up in the online/mobile survey software by the researcher.

Perhaps the most notable difference is that surveys administered on mobile devices can be used in Ecological Momentary Assessment (EMA) studies. An **Ecological Momentary Assessment (EMA)** is a unique type of survey methodology designed to collect data that have greater **ecological validity**. In this context, ecological validity refers to data that more accurately reflect the real world. For example, historically, studies on fear of crime use self-administered mail questionnaires to gauge individuals' perceptions of crime, especially violent crime like assault or robbery. Ironically, however, participants are often asked to complete these types of surveys in the comfort, safety, and security of their own homes. Surveys on fear of crime can collect data with greater ecological validity if they are administered to participants during their everyday routine activities, in other words, while they are out and about in the "real world."

EMA and other EMA-like techniques are used in research that focuses on the daily processes of individuals, and they share four common characteristics. First, EMAs are used to collect data from individuals in real-world environments. Second, they focus on the individual's actions, behaviors, or attitudes that are temporally proximate (i.e., feeling the research participant has "in the moment"). Third, they typically are triggered by predetermined events, at predetermined times, or at random times during the day, using complex triggers available in many mobile survey software solutions. Finally, EMAs are administered to subjects repeatedly over an extended period. Compared with online surveys, EMAs delivered as brief mobile surveys gather data from individuals while in their natural settings. Therefore, they can produce information with greater ecological validity than data collected from survey modes.

Ecological Momentary Assessment (EMA) is unique type of survey methodology designed to collect data that have greater ecological validity.

Disadvantages

For all that is good about online and mobile surveys, many disadvantages are associated with these survey modes. As with self-administered mail surveys, the absence of an interviewer means that no one is able to assist the participant if he or she needs help or encouragement to complete the survey. Another disadvantage of online and mobile surveys is that they are not suited to study certain samples of the population. For example, it would be inappropriate to choose an online survey mode if you were interested in collecting data from senior citizens regarding elder abuse or victimization. A mobile or online survey may be a questionable mode if the population of interest includes those in rural communities who may not have access to Internet services. Problems with access to the Internet, familiarity with using web browsers, and issues related to text size might adversely influence response rates.

Finally, survey fraud is something that researchers must consider before conducting an online or mobile self-administered survey. **Survey fraud** occurs during online and mobile surveys when participants sign up to be part of a survey panel just for the incentives offered. Those committing this fraud have no interest in a study and may not even meet the criteria set forth by the research to be eligible for the study. These fakes (and losers) complete questionnaires with little to no interest in topic. As a result, their responses can bias results. Despite these limitations, online and mobile surveys represent powerful survey modes that are growing in popularity and use.

Telephone Surveys

Telephone surveys are a common interview modality used to collect original survey data. Telephone surveys are less expensive to administer and offer quick data collection. Telephone surveys are also inexpensive and efficient when you need to gather data from a large number of people or from a sample of individuals living across a large geographic area. In addition, telephone surveys are characterized by higher response rates.

Random digit dialing (RDD), as discussed in Chapter 5, is a commonly used method of accessing potential respondents in a telephone survey. Prior to RDD, a researcher had to access a sampling frame of phone numbers in the area of interest. This sampling frame had limitations in that unlisted numbers and cell phone numbers were not listed on the frame. Plus, some homes had multiple phone lines making their chances of participating in the survey higher than others. In addition, some numbers may have been disconnected since the construction of the sampling frame. With random digit dialing. researchers no longer had to rely on tangible sampling frames like phone books. Rather, RDD generates telephone numbers at random that are called to find respondents to take the survey. RDD is increasingly important as more and more households have stopped using landlines and use only cell numbers for communication (see Figure 7.1). According to the Centers for Disease Control and Prevention's National Health Interview Survey, about half of U.S. households no longer have a landline in their home (Blumberg & Luke, 2015). Despite this rising figure, and especially with the use of RDD, telephone surveys still offer researchers a powerful way to collect survey data. This is especially the case when a researcher needs data from groups of the population that may not have access to the Internet or who live in remote areas.

Regardless of the way the participant was reached on the phone, historically, telephone surveys were conducted by a field representative who would ask questions and record responses on their paper-and-pencil survey instruments. Increasingly, however, telephone surveys are conducted using **computer-assisted telephone interviewing (CATI)** systems. CATI operates such that the interviewer on the phone is guided through the survey by prompts on a computer. Responses are entered directly into the computer. CATI systems allow survey data to be collected even more quickly and easily from a sample population than do traditional telephone survey techniques, especially when they involve random digit dialing. In addition, the step of coding and entering data later, and the associated errors, is removed from the process.

Telephone surveys: Common interview modality used to collect original survey data over the telephone.

Computer-assisted telephone interviewing (CATI): Computerized system that guides the interviewer through the survey on a computer. The system prompts the interviewer about exactly what to ask.

Figure 7.1 Graphs of Cell Phone Usage by U.S. Adults and Corresponding Increase in Surveys Conducted via Cell Phone by the Pew Research Center

As more Americans go mobile, Pew Research Center will conduct more survey interviews via cell phone

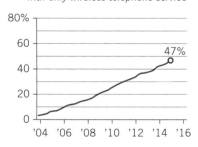

% of U.S. adults living in households with only wireless telephone service

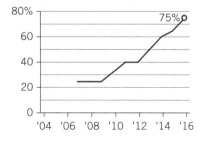

% of interviews conducted on cell phones in typical Pew Research Center surveys

Source: As more Americans go mobile, Pew Research Center will conduct more survey interviews via cell phone. Pew Research Center, December 10, 2015.

CATI systems that are used in contemporary telephone surveys are straightforward. First, an administrator working directly on a research project or with a research team sets up the system. This process usually involves creating an electronic version of the survey instrument that is uploaded to the CATI system. This uploaded survey will be displayed on trained interviewers' computer monitors to guide them during the telephone interview. Like online and mobile surveys, CATI software allows the researcher to customize questionnaires based on the answers provided during each telephone interview. The second step when using a CATI system is for the sample population's telephone numbers to be fed into the CATI system. Several companies now sell "phone lists" that have been verified for the purpose of survey research. CATI can also be used with RDD. Third, data collection begins when the CATI system is activated. This means that the CATI system automatically dials potential participants' phone numbers and prompts interviewers (displays exactly what they should say to the person on the phone) to begin a survey when a call is answered. Data gathered from respondents is recorded into a CATI database by the interviewer, in real time. Finally, once a survey is finished and the call ends, the interviewer waits for the CATI system to connect them to the next eligible participant. This process repeats itself each day, during designated times of the day/days of the week, until the data collection period is over.

Advantages

An advantage of telephone surveys is that they are quick and easy. It takes little effort to dial a number (or to allow a computer to dial that number) and to speak to someone who answers. If no one answers, it takes little effort to dial the next number (or to have a system dial for the interviewer). A second advantage is that telephone interviews are cheaper. There is no postage, or envelopes, or return envelopes to pay for. Telephone surveys are advantageous in that people are more likely to respond to a live human being on the other end of the phone compared with a mail survey. Because trained interviewers oversee the data collection process, the number of response errors or incomplete surveys is less than self-administered surveys. Having that human interaction is important and pays off in terms of response rates and data collected. Finally, a telephone survey allows the respondent to ask for clarification about questions. Interviewers should be trained to deal with the most common questions raised. Answering respondents' questions means potentially gathering more data or reducing nonresponse. Telephone surveys also offer participants the opportunity to be involved with a data collection project and remain anonymous. This may facilitate more honest answers to survey questions.

Disadvantages

Like all approaches and every element of research, nothing is perfect. One disadvantage of telephone surveys is that they are intrusive. Often, the best time to reach someone at home (i.e., the time of day when someone is most likely to answer the phone) is also the time of day when people least want to participate in a survey (i.e., dinnertime). For this reason, telephone surveys must often be short, which means they can be constrained by the amount of data they can collect. Similarly, telephone surveys require short and clear questions. The respondent does not have the advantage of being able to read and re-read a question. This may limit what can be asked of respondents. Many people also screen their calls. In other words, they will not answer a call unless they know who is calling them. Since most CATI systems have "blocked" outbound numbers, many calls made from them simply go unanswered because the person receiving the call does not want to answer a call from a blocked number. An increasing issue is that those answering the phone may mistake a survey call as a sales call. Individuals are unlikely to engage a salesperson and may mistakenly terminate a call with a researcher. Like any approach involving an interviewer, interviewer bias may be an issue.

Face-to-Face (In-Person) Interviews

Face-to-face interviews, also referred to as in-person interviews, represent another popular survey modality. A face-to-face interview is similar to a telephone survey in that the interviewer engages the participant while the survey is being completed. Unlike telephone surveys, face-to-face interviews are conducted with the interviewer present. As a result, several things must be considered before choosing face-to-face interviews as a survey methodology, if they are to be used successfully.

The interviewer is critically important to the success of face-to-face interviews. A good interviewer can help assure a successful survey by assisting participants with challenging questions, confusing instructions, or when the participant becomes tired or disinterested in completing the survey. Well-trained interviewers can also probe respondents to get more in-depth and complete answers to questions. Probing, as we saw in Chapter 6, refers to a subtle phrase or follow-up question that interviewers use to encourage survey participants to elaborate on previous responses. On the other hand, interviewers have the potential to negatively affect face-to-face surveys. For example, if survey participants do not identify with an interviewer because they are over- or underdressed, respondents can be put off, refuse to participate, and increase nonresponse rates. Similarly, if a survey interviewer does not understand the project or design and layout of the questionnaire, stumbles over questions, or appears to lack basic interviewer training or practice, then data quality and the overall success of the project will suffer. In short, an interviewer can make or break face-to-face interviews.

> **Face-to-face interviews:** Also referred to as "in-person interviews." They represent another popular survey modality in which the interviewer asks the respondent questions and records the respondent's answers.

Advantages

There are several advantages to conducting face-to-face interviews. Compared with other survey modes, in-person interviews can produce more accurate and reliable information. For example, no one might ever know if a woman participating in a self-administered mail survey answers "male" for a questions that asks about her sex, but providing similar (inaccurate) data during an interview can be more difficult with someone present. The presence of an interviewer can also help reduce survey fraud because interviewers can better screen those who want to participant but do not obviously meet eligibility requirements. Other survey modes are not as well suited as face-to-face interviews to pick up on participant's verbal and nonverbal cues. Similarly, participants' emotions and behaviors can easily be identified and recorded during an in-person interview. Finally, compared with other survey modes, face-to-face interviews tend to produce higher response rates even though the surveys are often longer.

Disadvantages

The biggest downside of in-person surveying is cost. Training interviewers requires a considerable amount of money. Once interviewers are trained, they will be spending a considerable amount of time in the field collecting data. Time is money, which means the costs of completing a single face-to-face interview are more than in any other survey mode. In addition, data quality might be an issue, although this is highly dependent on the quality of the interviewer. Some people have a natural ability to conduct face-to-face interviews, whereas others do not. It is unlikely that an entire interviewing staff will all have great survey-taking skills. If some are poor, then data quality may suffer (not to mention a good bit of the research budget will have been wasted on that interviewer's training).

> Another problem associated with face-to-face interviews is that unless you have a gigantic budget, they can only be administered if a study involves collecting data from a relatively small sample.

Another problem associated with face-to-face interviews is that unless you have a gigantic budget, they can only be administered if a study involves collecting data from a smaller sample. It would simply take too much time (and money) to conduct interviews otherwise. Related to this limitation is data entry. Unlike some other survey modes, data collected during face-to-face interviews must either be manually entered into a data file or transcribed from tapes or other recoding mediums. Transcription services and paying someone to enter data is an additional cost related to face-to-face interviews. If a research project requires collecting high-quality and detailed data from a smaller group of people and the research team has the time and money to train an effective interview team, then conducting face-to-face interviews might be the best survey mode option.

With this foundational information, we next present information on designing your own survey.

Designing Your Own Survey

Perhaps you have decided that survey research is the best way to gather original data to answer your research question. A key component of creating a survey includes the survey questions and the survey layout.

Survey Questions

Survey questions must be clear, relevant, and unbiased. Using clear and concise survey questions can mean the difference between success and failure. Survey questions are used to gather the specific data needed to answer your research question. Zaykowski (2014) wanted to understand the role that police reporting had on accessing victim services. Had she designed her own survey, she would have needed to include a question asking whether the respondent had reported the victimization to the police, questions identifying whether someone had been a victim, as well as a question asking whether the respondent had accessed victim services (among others). Every survey question on a survey should correspond with specific concepts for which you need data. Asking about more than is necessary increases the respondent burden. **Respondent burden** refers to the effort needed in terms of time and energy required by a respondent to complete a survey. As a researcher, you must minimize respondent burden in all ways possible.

A way to ensure you have excellent survey questions is to use language that is understandable. A rule of thumb is when surveying adults, to use language an eighth grader could understand. If you are surveying younger people, like much of Melde et al.'s (2009) research, you must ensure the language used is understandable for the sample. Something that researchers can do is use existing research questions or use focus group feedback to ascertain whether your language is appropriate for the sample. You do not always have to start from scratch as Zaykowski notes. Look around at existing surveys for question wording that you can use. Aside from these general recommendations, there are other more technical things to be focused on when writing survey questions. When Zaykowski teaches about research methods, her students are tasked with writing good survey questions that are understandable, not double-barreled, lacking loaded language, and reflecting attention to levels of measurement. These and other types of survey questions are described in more detail next. Open- and closed-ended questions are two general types of questions that are useful in survey research. Although these were introduced in Chapter 6, recall that an open-ended question is designed to give the survey participant the opportunity to provide an answer in his or her own words. Conversely, a close-ended question is a type of survey question that requires respondents to select an answer from a predetermined list of response categories. Response categories are a list of options available from which a respondent selects an answer. In creating your survey, you must also focus on the need for your response categories to be mutually exclusive and exhaustive. These concepts were introduced in Chapter 4. Exhaustive response categories mean every possible response option is offered. Mutually exclusive response categories mean that the responses do not overlap in any way. Something else introduced in Chapter 4 was the idea of levels of measurement. Be sure to use the highest level of measurement possible to gain as much information as possible when writing survey questions.

Surveys should also avoid including double-barreled questions. A **double-barreled question** asks about more than one issue in a single question so that it is unclear what part of the question the respondent is responding to. Let us say, for example, a questionnaire contained the following question:

How strongly do you agree or disagree with the following statement:

The police in my neighborhood protect and serve the community:

- Strongly agree

- Agree

- Disagree

- Strongly disagree

- Undecided

The problem with this double-barreled question is that it is asking about both police protection and police serving. If a respondent checks the "Agree" response, do they agree that police both protect and serve? What if a respondent feels the police *protect* but don't *serve* or vice versa? How are they to answer this question? A far better approach is to break this question into two questions on the survey: one question asking about protection, and one question asking about serving. The researcher must construct questions that are not loaded or leading. A **loaded question** or leading question is one that contains a controversial or unjustified assumption that leads a respondent to answering in a particular way that may not reflect their true feelings. For example, it is unlikely that the following question would produce valid responses or useful data because it is a leading question:

Do you agree with most bleeding-heart liberals that minor drug offenses should not result in jail time for those who are convicted, despite the fact that police are on the streets working hard every day to keep you safe from these criminals?

There is nothing wrong with including a question on a survey that is designed to ascertain respondents' attitudes about how to respond to drug offenses. To produce meaningful results, however, the question should not contain loaded phrases such as "bleeding-heart liberals" or evoking the image of police fighting to make you safe from these criminals. A better way to ask this question is simply, "Do you believe that minor drug offenses should result in jail time?" A real example of a problematic way to ask an important concept is included in Cuevas and colleagues' study (Sabina et al., 2016). In particular, they needed to learn whether respondents were documented. Although this may seem a direct way to get that information, this is a threatening approach especially given the study was funded by the U.S. Department of Justice. Asking directly would have resulted in respondents stopping the survey or the gathering of inaccurate information. Instead, Cuevas and his team used a more creative (and less intimidating) approach involving other questions. Specifically, they asked whether someone had a green card, if they had a visa, if they were a refugee, and

Double-barreled questions: Questions that ask about more than one issue in a single question. This makes it unclear which part of the question the response refers to.

Loaded questions: Questions that contain a controversial or unjustified assumption that leads a respondent to answer in a particular way that may not reflect his or her true feelings. Also known as a "leading question."

similar questions. If the respondent responded no to all of those questions, they were coded as undocumented.

A matrix is an efficient and useful means of gathering data in a survey. A **matrix question** includes multiple closed-ended questions sharing the same response categories. Note that six questions are asked, and each is answered using the same response categories in Table 7.2.

Dillman, Smyth, and Christian's (2008) comprehensive list of principles for writing good survey research questions is in Table 7.3.

A great approach to writing survey questions is shared by Cuevas who stresses the importance of understanding the type of data that particular questions will produce. He says that it is not uncommon for a researcher to develop survey questions that they think are "good" but then go to enter the data collected from those questions into a data file only to realize that the questions did not produce the kind of data they envisioned or needed. Cuevas says being able to think about how the data that particular questions will produce is the key. In addition, Cuevas is a fan of holding focus groups to consider survey questions. Using the thoughts of people similar to those in the sample can provide additional insight into what is a good or a poor performing question.

Table 7.2   Matrix Question About Support or Opposition of Drone Use by Law Enforcement That Was Created in Qualtrics

Do you SUPPORT or OPPOSE the use of aerial drones by police in the following situations:

	Strongly Support	Support	Oppose	Strongly Oppose	Undecided
International Border Patrol (e.g., monitoring immigration activities)					
Detecting Traffic Violation (e.g., speeding, reckless driving)					
Monitoring Highway Accidents or Traffic Flow					
Search and Rescue Operations (e.g., finding missing/injured persons)					
Monitoring Political Protest or Civil Unrest (e.g., protests over working conditions, public policies, social issues)					
Crowd monitoring at Large Public Events (e.g., sporting events, concerts)					
Tactical Operations for Officer Safety (e.g., active shooting situation, bomb scares)					
Crime Scene Photography (e.g., evidence gathering)					
Deterring Criminal Activities in Open Public Places (e.g., using drones to patrol high crime areas)					
Locating or Apprehending Fugitives (e.g., suspect on the run)					
Monitoring of Offenders under House Arrest (e.g., probation)					

Source: Miethe et al. (2014).

Table 7.3 Dillman et al.'s (2008) 19 Principles for Writing Survey Questions

Principles	Problem	Solution
Use simple words	Candid, leisure, rectify, courageous	Honest, free time, correct, brave
Use as few words as possible	Do you strongly agree, agree, neither agree nor disagree, disagree, or strongly disagree with the following statement?	To what extent to you agree or disagree with the following statement?
Use complete sentences	Your city? _____ (City)	In what city do you live? _____ (City)
Use precise estimates	• Never • Rarely • Occasionally • Regularly	• Not at all • A few times • About once a month • 2–3 times a month • About once a wee • More than once a week
Use response sets that increase respondent's ability to provide accurate information	How many times did you visit Starbucks during the past year? _____ (No. of Visits)	How many times did you visit Starbucks during the past year? • None • 1–10 • 11–20 • 30–40 • 41–50 • 50+
Use "balanced" response sets	• Strongly agree • Somewhat agree • Agree • Somewhat disagree • Strongly disagree	• Strongly agree • Agree • Disagree • Strongly disagree • Undecided
Use "undecided," which is different from a "neutral" response, at the end of a response set	• Strongly agree • Agree • **Undecided** • Disagree • Strongly disagree	• Strongly agree • Agree • Disagree • Strongly disagree • **Undecided**
Use "unbiased" comparisons	In your view, which of the following is most responsible for juvenile delinquency? • Video games • Irresponsible parents • Bad school policies	In your view, which of the following is most responsible for juvenile delinquency? • Video games • Parents • Schools

(Continued)

Table 7.3   (Continued)

Principles	Problem	Solution
Include both sides of an attitude scale	How much do you agree with the following statement . . . ?	How much do you agree or disagree with the following statement . . . ?
Avoid using "Choose all that apply" questions	Which activities does your child enjoy participating in after school? (Please choose all that apply).	Use a matrix question/answer format
Use mutually exclusive response sets	How many speeding tickets have you received in the past 12 months? • 0 • 1–3 • 3–6 • 6–9 • 10 or more	How many speeding tickets have you received in the past 12 months? • 0 • 1–2 • 3–5 • 6–9 • 10 or more
Use strategies to improve recall	A 12-month retrospective victimization survey	A 6-month retrospective survey
Use reasonable time periods as references	How many times in the past 3 years have you had contact with the police?	How many times in the past 6 months have you had contact with the police?
Use accurate wording	In the past year, have you been caught and fined by the police for a DUI?	In the past year, have you been caught and ticketed by the police for a DUI?
Use response sets that allow for comparisons with existing data	Do you own or rent your current residence? • Own • Rent	Is this house, apartment, or mobile home: • Owned by you or someone in this household with a mortgage or loan? • Owned by you or someone in this household free and clear (without a mortgage or loan)? • Rented for cash rent? • Occupied without payment of cash rent?
Avoid double negatives	Do you favor or oppose not allowing firearms to be carried on college campuses?	Do you favor or oppose allowing firearms to be carried on college campuses?
Avoid double-barreled questions	How much do you agree or disagree with the following statement: The police in my neighborhood are fair and respectful when dealing with the public.	How much do you agree or disagree with the following statement: The police in my neighborhood are respectful when dealing with the public.
Soften the impact of questions that might be considered "objectionable"	What was your total household income in 2017? $_____ (Total income)	What was your total household income in 2017? • $10,000 or less • $10,001 to $25,000 • $25,001 to $50,000 • $50,001 to $75,000 • More than $75,000
Don't make the respondent "do math"	Last year, what percentage of crimes in your city do you think resulted in a conviction?	For every 100 crimes in your city last year, how many do you think resulted in a conviction?

Source: Dillman, D. A., Smyth, J. D., & Christian, L. M. (2008). *The Tailored Design Method* (3rd ed). Hoboken, NJ: Wiley.

Design and Layout

Demographic questions:
Questions that ask about basic characteristics of the person such as gender, age, race, ethnicity, income, and so on.

Survey instruments need to be attractive, uncluttered, easy to follow, and have instructions that are clear and concise. This is especially the case for self-administered instruments. The instrument must *make* the respondent want to fill it out, and it must be easy to complete. Having a physically appealing survey is important. This means not cramming in too many questions and directions, making an instrument cluttered. White space is needed so the survey is attractive to the eye. The survey must include clear and concise directions, and the placement and ordering of questions must be thoughtful.

The *flow* of a survey should be easy to follow and make sense. Is it easy to move from one question to the next? Or is it easy to get confused as to what questions you are supposed to be answering. Good survey flow is easy to accomplish using automated telephone surveys using CATI systems or with online/mobile survey given the ease of incorporating skip patterns. This is a bit more of a challenging goal to accomplish with self-administered mail surveys. If you find your self-administered mail survey is very complex, you need to reassess if it would be better administered using interviews. This is precisely what the NCVS does. The instruments and their flow are far too complex for respondents to follow on their own.

For example, consider the 2010 U.S. Census, which used a self-administered questionnaire aimed at enumerating the entire U.S. population. The phrase "Start here" was written in bold and italic font in the upper left corner of the first page, using a font point much larger than the rest of questionnaire. This makes it easy for the respondent to know where to start. The Census questionnaire was also uncluttered, with easy-to-follow instructions, and introduced each section or block of questions with a brief explanation of what sort of data were being collected. These are good practices and are strategies that will also help maximize the likelihood that all questions will be answered, that they will be answered correctly, and that the participant will complete and return his or her completed census.

All sections in a survey should include breaks that inform the respondent about the topic covered in the next section. For example, if a researcher wants to obtain demographic data from self-administered survey participants, questions to gather these data should (a) be offset by a block of text introducing the demographic questions section, and (b) limit the questions only to those that are meaningful to the study:

> We conclude our survey with a few demographic questions. These questions will help us understand how closely our sample resembles the population it is intended to represent and will also allow us to control for some of the individual characteristics related to criminal victimization. Please provide us with an answer to every question.

If you do not need to know about someone's race, age, or income, then do not ask for that information. Ask only the questions needed to gather data to answer the research question to reduce respondent burden.

The ordering of questions on the instrument is important. If a survey is being administered by an interviewer, it is best to start with demographic questions because they are easy to ask, nonthreatening, and allow the parties to build rapport. **Demographic questions** ask about basic characteristics of the person such as gender, age, race, ethnicity, income, and so on. Once rapport is established, the survey can move into the substantive questions. In contrast, demographic questions should be asked last in self-administered surveys. Why? Because it is important to immediately "hook" the respondent by asking an interesting question—one he or she wants to read and answer. Demographic questions are never great hooks on self-administered surveys.

Layout is especially important when it comes to mail/written surveys to maximize response rates. Self-administered mail/written surveys often consist of multiple pages. Best

All law enforcement agencies desire to have a good relationship with the community and public they serve. The current study by Bradford, Stanko, and Jackson (2009) conducts secondary data analysis of data collected from the British Crime Survey (BCS) and a community survey conducted by the Metropolitan Police Service (MPS; London). The aim of the study was threefold. First, the researchers aimed to document historical trends in public confidence in police, especially among those who had personal contact with law enforcement. Second, the researchers tried to identify factors correlated with positive public opinions of the police. Third, the investigators argued how MPS could use survey data to help improve the way in which police handled interactions with the public so that public attitudes could be improved.

The researchers answered their first research question by producing simple descriptive statistics and visually displaying information about public contact with police, using a series of line graphs. The data they described were secondary data produced from the BCS conducted from 1988 to 2006. In particular, the researchers examined historical trends of people's contact with police. Data collected during a similar period were also described, and presented as a series of bar charts, that described the levels of *dissatisfaction* with police and the type of contact with police that participants had with law enforcement (i.e., self-initiated, police car stop, or other police-initiated contact). Comparing historical trends in contact with and attitudes of police allowed the researchers to answer their first research question.

Conducting secondary data analysis from the Metropolitan Police's Public Attitude Survey (PAS) allowed the researchers to answer their second research question. Specifically, they examined data produced from the PAS to identify correlates to attitudes supportive of police.

The results of the researchers' analyses of the BCS data revealed that during a 20-year period (i.e., 1988 to 2006), public contact with police in England and Wales steadily declined, especially since 2000. Declines in police–public contact were consistent across all types of contact, including self-initiated, contact as a result of victimization, and police-initiated contact.

The results of analyses of BCS data also revealed differences in the levels of dissatisfaction with the police among survey participants. For example, since 2000, those who self-initiated contact with the police were the most dissatisfied, and the levels of dissatisfaction had steadily increased. Based on these data, the researchers concluded that during face-to-face interactions, it will be more difficult for police to improve opinions than to undermine them, but they used data from the MPS PAS to develop ideas about how the police could do just that.

The results of analysis of the MPS PAS showed that it matters how police treat people, especially those who come to them for help and assistance, and if these individuals are treated well, the levels of public satisfaction are likely to increase. The researchers place particular importance on the way with which officers communicate with people.

The researchers concluded their study by answering their third, and final, research question. They did this by synthesizing their first two findings and offering the police recommendations for developing policies around incidents involving contact with the public. Specifically, they suggested that people could be classified as one of four types of Londoner: the supporters, the contents, the needy, and the demanding. Furthermore, the authors suggested that the police incorporate this information in policies and procedures related to dealing with the public. In doing so, they could likely see an increased level of public satisfaction with police, especially among those with whom they have contact. They conclude their paper by explaining, "The provision of such information may reassure that the police are taking the matter seriously, or justify what might otherwise be seen as arbitrary and unjust behaviour."

Bradford, B., Stanko, E. A., & Jackson, J. (2009). Using research to inform policy: The role of public attitude surveys in understanding public confidence and police contact. *Policing, 39*(2), 139–148.

practices suggest that when a questionnaire spans more than one page, the instrument should be printed on a single 11" × 17" piece of paper and folded into a booklet, making a total of four pages, rather than on multiple four pages stapled together. Be aware that respondents often miss what is printed on the back of pages, so alerting them to the fact that questions are on the back of pages is a good practice. Other recommended strategies associated with design and layout best practices include the following:

- Ask one question at a time.

- Minimize the use of question matrices (see the next section).

- Use large/bright symbols to identify the starting point on each page.

- Consistently identify the beginning of each subsequent question.

- Number questions consecutively and simply, from beginning to end.

- List answer categories vertically instead of horizontally.

- Place answer spaces consistently to the left or right of the category labels.

- Use simple answer boxes for recording of answers (see the next section).

- Vertically align question subcomponents across questions.

- Place instructions for determining eligibility for responding to a section or other major efforts to redirect respondents inside navigational guides rather than in a freestanding format to increase the likelihood they will be read.

- Ensure the font is large enough to easily read Place more blank spaces between the questions than between subcomponents of the questions.

- Use dark print for questions and light print for answer choices.

- If special instructions are essential, write them as a part of the question statement (see the next section).

- Use of lightly shaded background colors as fields on which to write all questions provides an effective guide.

- When lightly shaded background fields are used, identification of all answer spaces in white helps to reduce item nonresponse.

- Use shorter lines to prevent words from being skipped.

- Words and phrases that introduce important but easy-to-miss changes in respondent expectations should be visually emphasized consistently but sparingly.

Pretesting of Survey Instruments

Once the survey is completed, but before the actual fielding of a survey, it is imperative that researchers pretest or pilot their instrument. A survey pretest or pilot, as introduced in Chapter 5, is used to identify problems with a survey before it is fielded to the sample of respondents. Santos emphasizes the value of survey pilots. In her work with police departments, she and her collaborator, created and piloted surveys to ensure the instrument was working as intended (Santos & Santos, 2016). To conduct a pretest, the researcher asks a small group of people to complete the survey instrument. These survey guinea pigs can help to reveal errors or issues with instructions, wording, formatting, or skip-and-fill

Notification letters: Letters mailed to those in the sample to alert them that they will be receiving a survey.

Incentives: Used in survey research when eligible participants are given something of value in return for their participation.

Confidentiality: When the researcher knows and can identify individual respondents but promises to keep that information private.

Anonymity: Refers to situations where the researcher cannot link the data gathered to the respondent or does not gather identifying information about the respondent.

logic (or display logic for electronic questionnaires that can be corrected before the actual fielding of the survey). Imagine learning of a major problem with the instrument during the actual fielding. This avoidable error may mean the loss of critical information, poor response rates, and just bad data. Given your research is only as strong as the weakest part, failure to pretest your instrument means the difference between an expensive disaster resulting in useless data and good data.

Survey Administration

The instrument is designed and tested; now it is time to administer the survey. Administering your survey requires three major steps. First, you need to contact potential survey participants and alert them that a survey is coming. Next, you need to field the survey. And finally, you need to follow up with those who have not completed and returned it. The next sections focus on these three steps.

Notification Letters

In general, once the survey is ready to be fielded, you must engage the potential participants with a notification letter. Their first contact for a written/mail survey should come in the form of a notification letter. **Notification letters** are simply letters mailed to those in the sample to alert them that they will be receiving a survey. Notification letters are effective tools for increasing response rates. In the 2010 U.S. Census example, a notification letter explaining why the survey was being conducted, why it needed to be completed, and how to complete and return it was sent to all residential households a few days prior to the questionnaire arriving. Dillman (2000) recommends that mail/written survey notification letters be sent a few days to a week before the survey is fielded.

Notification letters should include several pieces of information, including the following:

1. Title of and purpose of the research project

2. Name and contact information of the primary researcher or chief investigator

3. Name of the agency or organization sponsoring the project

4. Whether **incentives** (i.e., rewards or inducements for participating) are being offered for participation

5. Information about how the data will be used, how the results of the study can be accessed or obtained once the project is over, and the safeguards in place to protect participants' information

Notification letters should disclose whether participants' identities and data would be kept confidential or anonymous. Recall that **confidentiality** refers to when the researcher knows and can identify individual respondents but promises to keep that data private. In contrast, **anonymity** refers to situations where the researcher cannot link the data gathered to the respondent or does not gather identifying data about the respondent. Survey data cannot be both confidential and anonymous. In some cases, different people on the research team have access to confidential, whereas others have access to anonymous data. For example, Zaykowski worked on a project focused on gathering data from young people. Individuals at the organization administered the surveys and could tie respondents to the data (i.e., confidential). Then the organization stripped all identifying information out of the data so that when Zaykowski received it to work with, it was anonymous.

For a recent survey administered to law enforcement personnel, Santos explains that she told potential survey participants that their responses could not be linked back to them to assure officers that they could be open and honest about answering questions. This means that the data Santos gathered were anonymous. No one, not even Santos, could tie responses back to individual respondents. To further ensure that the data provided could not be tied back to a particular individual, Santos did not ask about the responding officer's race, sex, or number of years at the agency. This further guaranteed anonymity.

A critical part of the notification letter is to explain why it is important for participants to complete the survey, and how to return a survey. As a researcher, you are asking respondents for their valuable time and views. You must convince them that sharing *their* thoughts and information is important. Making the survey easy to return is critical. Providing preaddressed, postage-paid envelopes assists in this aim. The notification letter (and any correspondence) with potential survey participants should also include personalized salutation (e.g., "Dear Mrs. Jackson") and a signature block that contains a real-looking signature (i.e., not a signature that looks photocopied). Research shows that when surveys (both mail and Internet/web surveys) use presurvey notification letters like these, response rates increase.

Survey processing:
Process of converting survey responses into useful data via coding so they can be analyzed.

Fielding the Survey

Once potential participants have been notified, Dillman (2000) recommends the survey be disseminated a few days (up to a week) after the notification correspondence has been sent.

Follow-Up to Nonresponders

Finally, the administration of most surveys will require follow-up and reminders for those who fail to complete and return their surveys. Research shows that follow-up reminders increase response rates. A follow-up letter should include a plea to complete the survey with a replacement survey (or link to the survey). The timing of correspondence differs slightly for mail/written and online surveys. As shown in Table 7.3 for written/mail surveys, Dillman (2000) recommends that the first of three reminders to those who have not completed and returned the instruments be sent out two weeks from the fielding of the survey. A second reminder should be sent two weeks after that. In addition, the final reminder should be sent eight weeks after the survey was fielded. For Web surveys, the timing is compressed in that what takes a week via mail, takes a day via the Web. Thus, the first reminder should be sent via e-mail two days after the survey was fielded. The second and third should be sent four and eight days after fielding, respectively. At the same time reminders are sent, thank-you notices should be sent to those who participated. Thank-you notes are extremely important. Respondents took time to assist in your research, and they are deserving of your gratitude.

Survey Processing and Data Entry

Processing survey data is an often overlooked, albeit important, part of conducting survey research. **Survey processing** refers to taking the survey responses and converting them into useful data via coding. The different survey modes require different levels of time and energy to process collected data. Thinking about this step during the design phase is necessary to minimize the burden of survey processing and data entry in the survey research process.

A strength of online and mobile surveys is that the data collected using these modes are captured in real time. This means that there is no need for survey processing or data entry, which translates into savings in time, money, and reduction of errors. If you are using a system that captures data, however, you may still need to extract or transfer that data to the analysis program you will use. It may be that the analysis techniques provided by the data

Table 7.4 Timing of Survey Correspondence (Crawford, Couper, & Lamias, 2001; Dillman, 2000)

Correspondence	Mail	Online
Notification Letter	Few days to one week before the survey is distributed	N/A
Invitation/Cover Letter (included with the questionnaire)	N/A	N/A
Postcard/Thank-you/Reminder	2 weeks	2 days
Reminder Letter	4 weeks	4 days
Reminder—Final Contact	8 weeks	8 days
Survey Closing Notice (Web only)	N/A	10 days

Source: Crawford, Scott D., Mick P. Couper, & Lamias, M. J. (2001). Web surveys: Perceptions of burden. *Social Science Computer Review, 19*(2):146–162; Dillman, D. A. (2000). *Mail and internet surveys: The tailored design method.* John Wiley & Sons, Inc: NY.

gathering software you are using are sufficient for their needs. Depending on the software used, this could be easy or challenging. Be prepared for it either way.

When it comes to self-administered questionnaires, other types of technology and simple design features integrated into the instrument can help ease the burden of data processing and entry. Some software companies offer optical readers and scanning systems that can be used to read responses directly from self-administered questionnaire forms that are created with their proprietary software. When completed surveys are returned, a member of the research team simply feeds the instrument into the scanner, and since the forms were created with the scanner vendor's own software, data are captured from the form and populated into a database. This assumes, of course, that the participant followed the instructions for properly completing the survey (i.e., filled in bubbles instead of circling answers, used the correct writing implement, did not damage the form, etc.). Other data such as the questionnaire number, a participant's home address, and other confidential data can also be "embedded" on a survey using a QR code or bar code so that surveys can remain confidential while appearing to be anonymous, thereby instilling greater confidence in participating.

Some interviews can have very high data processing and entry costs associated with them, whereas others can have lower costs. For example, if a research study uses telephone interviews and those interviews are administered via a CATI system, the data processing and entry will be on par with online and mobile surveys. Nevertheless, if telephone interviews are conducted where the interviewer is required to record responses on a survey form, then the data processing and entry costs will be more in line with that of a regular self-administered mail survey. Face-to-face interviews, however, are nearly always more costly than other survey modes in terms of the costs associated with data processing and entry. This is because face-to-face interviews, especially those that are unstructured, are often recorded. Under these circumstances, the recordings must be transcribed. This is often done professionally and at an added cost.

Easy-to-Use Survey Software

At the beginning of this chapter, we warned our readers that just because they *could* create and administer surveys did not mean they *should!* Moreover, even though we have provided guidance and strategies for choosing an appropriate survey mode, developing clear and concise survey questions, and constructing high-quality questionnaires, you may feel overwhelmed or intimidated at the thought of creating your first survey. Fear not! There is an abundance of survey software available to those who want to try their hand at survey research. Many of these software programs are very good, following most of the guidelines (or enabling you to follow them) we have presented in this chapter. Obviously, these programs are primarily available online. We discuss the three most common platforms available: SurveyMonkey, Qualtrics, and LimeSurvey. Because these three solutions are among the most common, there is a good chance that you will, assuming you haven't already, use one to help develop or administer a survey one day. Developing these survey research skills has real-world applicability!

SurveyMonkey

SurveyMonkey is a popular online survey platform that was introduced in 1999. SurveyMonkey is an easy-to-use online software development and administration platform that also allows some basic statistical analysis and report generation-based data collected from completed questionnaires. For basic purposes, SurveyMonkey requires little training. Free licenses are available, but they have limited functionality. If a researcher needs greater functionality, basic plans start at around $30 per month. It may be that your university has a contract with SurveyMonkey, so before you pay any money to access it, check with your university to see whether you can use it free.

SurveyMonkey allows people to construct an instrument by using more than a dozen different types of survey questions (i.e., open-ended, close-ended, matrix, etc.). Survey instruments are also customizable so that they can include a logo to make it appear like it was sent from your organization. SurveyMonkey's surveys can be administered online, on iOS, or on Android mobile devices; printed and used during interviews; or presented as a self-administered questionnaire. For online and mobile surveys, you can program SurveyMonkey to contact participants at certain times of the day or days of the week, issue reminders to participants who have not completed and returned their questionnaire (when the survey is not anonymous), and view data in real time as surveys are returned. With online/mobile SurveyMonkey surveys, there is no need for data entry, as data are entered into an exportable data file automatically as questionnaires are returned. The online SurveyMonkey interface can also be used to run basic data analysis. Alternatively, data can be downloaded directly from the SurveyMonkey website for use in more advanced analysis software. Finally, SurveyMonkey offers researchers ways to target their audiences by making available for purchase survey panels. Many say that SurveyMonkey is easy to use, especially for those with limited technical expertise. Nevertheless, SurveyMonkey's primary goal is to make money, and the more "bells and whistles" that you want to incorporate into a survey, the more you will have to pay to do so.

Qualtrics

Qualtrics is another popular research software company based in Provo, Utah, and founded in 2002. Qualtrics is a paid software solution, although your university may allow you free access to it. The Qualtrics platform is easy to use, offering a "drag-and-drop" interface that lets researchers quickly add advanced online survey options and analysis features to questionnaires. Similar to SurveyMonkey, Qualtrics allows researcher to build surveys that can be used online or on mobile devices, printed and used as self-administered questionnaires, or administered during telephone or face-to-face interviews. Online and mobile surveys can be administered to survey participants via their e-mail address by providing them with a direct link to the survey.

Do you **SUPPORT** or **OPPOSE** the use of aerial drones by police in the following situations:

	STRONGLY SUPPORT	SUPPORT	OPPOSE	STRONLY OPPOSE	UNDECIDED
International Border Patrol (e.g., monitoring immigration activities)	○	○	○	○	○
Detecting Traffic Violation (e.g., speeding, reckless driving)	○	○	○	○	○
Monitoring Highway Accidents or Traffic Flow	○	○	○	○	○
Search and Rescue Operations (e.g., finding missing/injured persons)	○	○	○	○	○
Monitoring Political Protest or Civil Unrest (e.g., protests over working conditions, public policies, social issues)	○	○	○	○	○
Crowd Monitoring at Large Public Events (e.g., sporting events, concerts)	○	○	○	○	○
Tactical Operations for Officer Safety (e.g., active shooting situation, bomb scares)	○	○	○	○	○
Crime Scene Photography (e.g., evidence gathering)	○	○	○	○	○
Deterring Criminal Activities in Open Public Places (e.g., using drones to patrol high crime areas)	○	○	○	○	○
Locating or Apprehending Fugitives (e.g., suspect on the run)	○	○	○	○	○
Monitoring of Offenders under House Arrest (e.g., probation)	○	○	○	○	○

Source: Miethe et al. (2014).

A wide variety of survey questions can be used in a Qualtrics survey. Figure 7.2 shows some types of questions that are available, including open-ended (i.e., text entry—useful for gathering qualitative data), close-ended (i.e., multiple choice), and matrix questions (i.e., matrix table) options. More sophisticated questions like Heat Map questions or questions that allow users to identify locations on an "on-the-fly" map can also be incorporated into a Qualtrics survey. The characteristics of each question can be tailored, including being able to quickly and easily change the number of response categories on close-ended questions and modify preformatted response labels to response options. In Qualtrics, the researcher can "pipe" in text from one question directly into another to streamline the data collection instrument, while appearing to personalize the questionnaire to individual respondents. For example, if a question on a Qualtrics survey was used to identify whether a participant had previous contact with a law enforcement officer, the participant's answer could be used in subsequent questions or response sets so that the survey would appear as though it were tailor-made for the particular respondent. It might look something like this:

Question 1: Last month, did you have direct contact with any officers from the Gold Coast or Townsville rapid action police (RAP) team?

- Yes, the Gold Coast RAP
- Yes, the Townsville RAP
- No

Question 2: On average, during the past 12 months, how often have you personally had contact with the police from the ${q://QUESTION1/ ChoiceGroup/SelectedChoices} RAP?

The part of Question 2 that reads, **${q://QUESTION1/ChoiceGroup/Selected Choices}**, is code used by Qualtrics to automatically identify the response given in Question 1 and to insert it seamlessly into the question text, assuming that one of the two "Yes" responses was provided. A logical skip statement could also be added to Question 2 that would only make it visible to participants who did *not* answer "No" to Question 1. Strategies such as these are common in online survey software solutions, like Qualtrics. They allow researchers to create dynamic, streamlined survey instruments that adapt survey participants' responses.

LimeSurvey

LimeSurvey is another popular online survey software solution, but it is very different from SurveyMonkey and Qualtrics. The main difference is that LimeSurvey (formerly PHPSurveyor) is that it is a free and open-source online survey application. LimeSurvey is written in a scripting language called PHP, which is especially suited for Web development and can be embedded into a website via HTML. It also uses the popular MySQL database (or sqlite, PostgreSQL, or MSSQL databases). As a Web server-based software application, LimeSurvey allows users using a Web interface to develop and publish online questionnaires, collect responses, create statistics, and export the resulting data to other applications.

The saying "You get what you pay for" holds true when it comes to LimeSurvey. Although it is open-source software (i.e., it is free), there are very few "bells and whistles" integrated into the base software. Furthermore, the administrator's interface is somewhat clunky and sometimes difficult to navigate (Figure 7.3). Different question types are available, but if the researcher wants to customize a survey instrument, it may require a good bit of programming knowledge and other technical skills. It is possible to incorporate new source code into LimeSurvey to meet the specific needs of a research project, but a researcher will (a) require some level of programming knowledge to do this or (b) be able to access, download, customize, and install existing code from GitHub (https://github.com/LimeSurvey/LimeSurvey) or a similar source code repository. Although LimeSurvey is more difficult to use, it is important to know about it.

Figure 7.3   LimeSurvey Administrator Interface

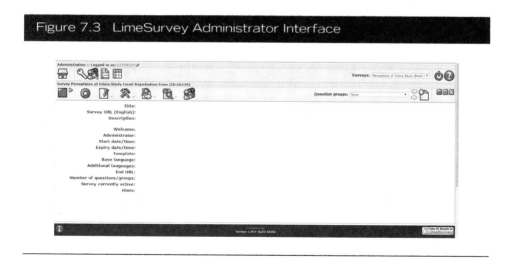

Common Pitfalls in Survey Research

Many common pitfalls are associated with survey research. Generally, most of these problems can be avoided if you use the information provided in this chapter. The main piece of advice is to pretest your instrument. Many research projects have failed when researchers skipped this step only to learn they had a skip pattern in their survey that skipped all respondents to the end of the survey without gathering any data. We have also seen surveys fail when the researchers forgot to include a question that would provide key data for the research project (e.g., data on the dependent variable). You do not get a second chance to survey your respondents, so make sure your survey works properly by pretesting.

Aside from pretesting, it is imperative that you review all your survey questions with a critical eye. Ensure your questions are clear and easily understandable. It is recommended that you use language that an eighth grader can read and understand. Avoid jargon and acronyms. Ensure you do not have any loaded, leading, or double-barreled questions. Ensure your response categories are mutually exclusive and exhaustive. Also, please make sure you use a readable font size. This means it is *at least* 12-point font. In addition, fonts should be plain and easy to read. If a respondent struggles to read the type, he or she will throw out the survey.

Another consideration for online surveys is programming them to require a response before moving to the next question. Respondents will get frustrated if you force them to answer all questions. A frustrated respondent is a respondent who will not complete your survey. Although a forced response might be necessary at times, generally it is not and should be avoided.

Ethical Considerations in Survey Research

Ethical considerations are omnipresent when research is conducted, including research that involves the use of surveys. Like all types of research, eligible participants must be informed about the research project before consenting to participate. Steps need to be taken to assure proper care and control over data collected from respondents, including identifiable data, if a survey is not anonymous. Moreover, the benefits of conducting a survey must be greater than the burden caused by administering it. For in-person interviewers, researchers have an ethical responsibility to ensure the safety and security of members of the interviewer team.

One issue that is especially relevant for survey research is the decision to incentivize participants. There is nothing that *prohibits* the use of incentives in survey research. When incentives are incorporated into the research protocol, however, their value must not be so great as to be "the deciding factor" for the participant. In other words, the incentive cannot be so valuable that the participant would essentially suffer a financial harm or undue burden if he or she decided *not* to participate. For example, during the first phase of the Arrestee Drug Abuse Monitoring Program (ADAM; 1998–2003), free candy bars were offered to jail inmates for participating in a survey about their past drug and alcohol use. The candy bars were allowed to be used to reward volunteers for their participation in the ADAM project because they were considered not to be so valuable that the inmates would "suffer" if they did not participate in the survey. Instead, they were valuable enough to increase the number of volunteers likely to participate without creating a harm or burden for the participants/nonparticipants.

Proper care and control over data collected from respondents is another aspect of survey research that requires careful consideration. For example, if a survey is confidential and individual identifiable data are obtained from participants, then those data must be protected so that the respondent's information is never disclosed to unauthorized persons. Procedures in place for the care and custody of participants' data must be described in detail in the researcher's institutional review board application. In addition, the researcher must describe how all survey data will be stored securely after it has been collected, the length of time it will be stored, and how it will be destroyed once the study has ended. It is very easy today with the widespread use of laptops to carry around survey data. This is inappropriate and unethical considering the risk of losing the data this presents. Data must be stored in a safe and secure place. On a researcher's laptop is not a safe place unless one uses encryption. **Encryption** is a process in which data and information are encoded making unauthorized access impossible.

In certain situations, ethical consideration must address more than the protection of survey participants and the data collected from them. For example, researchers that hire interviewers to conduct face-to-face interviewers must have ethical protocols in place to ensure their safety and security. Risk to interviewer safety can range from minor threats such as verbal harassment or threating looks or gestures to more dangerous situations that can include physical violence. Therefore, survey researchers carefully consider where and when face-to-face interviews will be conducted as a way of keeping interviewers (and interviewees) safe. Depending on the situation, conducting a face-to-face interview in the middle of the afternoon and at a local coffee shop or library may be chosen instead of an alternative time and place in an effort to keep interviewers safe. Without such protocols in place, there is a good chance that an institutional review board will not approve a research application when the study involves face-to-face interviews.

Encryption: Process in which data and information are encoded making unauthorized access impossible.

Surveying Expert—Bridget Kelly, MA

Bridget Kelly is the Cannon Survey Center's project coordinator at the University of Nevada, Las Vegas (UNLV). Kelly studied criminal justice for her Bachelor's and Master's degrees, and is currently studying for her Doctorate in criminology and criminal justice at UNLV. She began pursuing research-oriented work as a graduate student by assisting her professors with a variety of criminal justice research projects and was first exposed to the work carried out by the Center while studying survey research in her research methods course. Kelly and her classmates visited the Cannon Center to learn more about surveys. At that time, she couldn't have imagined that someday she would be the Center's project coordinator—the primary person responsible for a variety of tasks in all phases of survey projects managed by the Center.

© R. Marsh Starks/UNLV Photo Services

On behalf of the Center, Kelly serves as the point of contact for clients through all phases of a research project. Center clients typically include University faculty, local government agencies, and local businesses. To assist clients with research projects that involve surveys, the center provides survey design consultation, project management, data collection, data entry (for surveys collected on paper), data analysis, and report preparation. The most common projects held by the center are telephone surveys, Internet surveys, and data entry from previously collected paper forms. Occasionally, the center collects data by mail or in person as an intercept survey, particularly in clinic settings. The Center employs a team of part-time interviewers, many of them undergraduate students, shift leads, a supervisor that oversees the call center, and a project coordinator.

By using the principles outlined in this chapter, Kelly collaborates with clients in the initial preparation phase to determine the ideal administration mode and sampling design, balancing best practices in research methods with feasibility constraints. She assesses the goals and resources of the client, and together, they decide who will be surveyed and how they can best be reached (e.g., in person, by phone, by e-mail, or by postal mail). Sometimes the client comes prepared with a contact list consisting of phone numbers or e-mail addresses of the target population to be surveyed. Other times, Kelly will assist the client by obtaining a sample of telephone numbers or access to an online panel of prerecruited research participants. For telephone surveys, Kelly helps the client to determine whether an RDD sample of mobile and landline phone numbers or directory-listed sample of only landline phone numbers is better for the needs of the study.

Once the survey mode and sample are determined, Kelly works with clients to design the survey instrument with the appropriate question format, response options, and skip logic, again using the principles outlined in this chapter to avoid common pitfalls. Once the survey instrument is prepared as a document, Kelly programs the survey into a CATI system for phone surveys or into an online platform such as Qualtrics for Internet surveys. This involves entering the question-and-response option text, as well as setting up behind-the-scenes logic to determine the order in which questions and responses are presented, or whether they are presented at all (e.g., when a question does not apply based on an earlier response). For phone surveys, this provides the interviewers with a script to read, as well as with any supplementary interviewer instructions.

Before data collection begins, the surveys are pretested. During data collection, Kelly monitors the progress of the study and uses CATI functions to ensure an optimal flow of sample records through the system so that potential respondents are attempted at varying times and days of the week in order to reach them at a time when they are able to answer and willing to participate. For Web surveys, she strategically articulates and times a series of reminders to be sent via e-mail to nonrespondents to boost participation. To ensure data quality for phone and Internet surveys, she monitors the data and any feedback from respondents or interviewing staff to ensure that study protocols are followed and easy to follow, and to ensure that any concerns are addressed as needed. She provides updates to clients regularly regarding progress and any issues that arise in the field, and she communicates any additional feedback or clarification from the client back to the staff.

Once the survey data are collected, Kelly exports the database into Microsoft® Excel™ or a similar format to be analyzed. For many clients, Kelly prepares a report of results that demonstrates the number and percentage of responses to each question with tables and graphs. She also provides a brief explanation of each result to highlight the most common responses or unexpected results. Seeing the results of a survey is a rewarding conclusion to survey work because this reveals the much-needed insight that prompted the project in the first place.

In her role, Kelly has worked with many students and has studied survey research as both an undergraduate and a graduate student. From the combination of these perspectives, she offers three "words of wisdom" to students interested in conducting surveys: be *patient,* be *attentive,* and be *persistent.*

Chapter Wrap-Up

In this chapter, we introduced readers to survey research. We described how surveys are used in contemporary criminal justice research, including how they have been used in exploratory, descriptive, explanatory, and evaluation research using the case studies we have used throughout this text. We offered insight into the self-administered questionnaires and interviews, discussing the strengths and weaknesses of mail, online, mobile, telephone, and face-to-face surveys. We explained the importance of constructing an effective survey instrument and provided guidelines for doing so. We also discussed different types of survey questions that can be incorporated into survey instruments and offered some best practices for creating survey questions that are likely to produce valid and reliable survey data. In addition, the chapter described information on some of the common survey software used today to construct and administer questionnaires. We concluded the chapter with a discussion of several of the common pitfalls associated with survey research—most of which can be avoided with survey pretesting. In addition, ethical considerations associated with survey research, including the ethical issues associated with incentivizing eligible participants, the care and custody of survey data, and protecting interviewers that are part of the survey research team were discussed. Finally, we heard from survey research expert Bridget Kelly who uses these skills every day in her job. As her example shows, surveys skills are useful and can lead to a rewarding career with a bit of patience, attentiveness, and persistence.

Table 7.5 shows how widely used survey research was for our case studies. As the table demonstrates, only Santos did not use survey research for her study (Santos & Santos, 2016). Among those who did use survey research, a variety of approaches were taken. Brunson used both interviews (face-to-face) and questionnaires (self-administered) to gather data for his study on youth experiences and perceptions of police relations (Brunson & Weitzer, 2009). Cuevas and his colleagues used data gathered via telephone interviews in the Dating Violence Among Latino Adolescents survey (DAVILA; Sabina et al., 2016). Dodge relied solely on face-to-face interviews to gather data from her subjects (Dodge et al., 2005). Melde and his collaborators gathered data from their adolescent sample using self-administered questionnaires (Melde et al., 2009). Finally, Zaykowski's (2014) research used data gathered for the National Crime Victimization Survey, which is administered using two modes of interviewing: in person and over the phone. As our case studies show, survey research is versatile and allows many approaches for gathering data. This means you can personalize your approach to best suit the needs of your research as well as your sample.

In the next chapter, we shift gears and discuss experimental research. This is the type of research that students enter the class feeling they know most about. Much of that understanding is from so-called experiments they have conducted over time or have seen in the movies. In that chapter, we discuss what makes an experiment an experiment and how they can inform our understanding of the world.

Table 7.5 Featured Research: Survey Types and Modes Used		
Articles	**Survey Type**	**Survey Mode**
Rod Brunson	Interview and Questionnaire	Face-to-Face interviews followed up by self-administered paper-and-pencil questionnaires.
Carlos Cuevas	Interviews - Dating Violence Among Latino Adolescents (DAVILA)	Telephone
Mary Dodge	Interview	Face-to-face
Chris Melde	Interview	Face-to-face
Heather Zaykowski	Interview - National Crime Victimization Survey	Telephone and face-to-face

Applied Assignments

The materials presented in this chapter can be used in applied ways. This box presents several assignments to help in demonstrating the value of this material by engaging in assignments related to it.

1. Homework Applied Assignment: Bad Survey Questions

Find a survey used in a peer-reviewed, published academic journal article in criminal justice or criminology. In your thought paper, describe the purpose of this *survey*. What is your overall assessment of the instrument? Identify two poorly asked questions, and identify why you believe they are poorly constructed, given the material presented in this chapter. Describe how you would improve these questions. What value would you place on data gathered using these two questions? Given what you have learned in this chapter, how would you improve the instrument? Why would your way be better? Turn in the instrument, the article that used it, and your thought paper. Be prepared to discuss your findings in class.

2. Group Work in Class Applied Assignment: Constructing Excellent Survey Questions

As a group, select three of our case study articles. Pretend your group has been hired to write a short survey to gather data that would be useful for these articles. As a group, write 10 survey questions including response categories that you believe would gather additional data that our case study researchers could use to answer their research question(s). Be sure to use the best practices described in this chapter to write questions that will likely produce valid and reliable data. Make sure you also include appropriate response categories for your questions. Be able to point to the concepts that each survey question is measuring. Be able to describe what type of data each survey question would gather (quantitative or qualitative) and the levels of measurement that each question would produce (e.g., nominal, ordinal, interval, or ratio). Discuss the strengths of your measures, as well as their limitations. Be prepared to discuss and share your work with the class.

3. Internet Applied Assignment: Constructing a Survey

Use the survey questions that your groups developed in the second assignment to build a questionnaire on SurveyMonkey. Be sure to provide the informational boxes described in this chapter, and make the survey attractive. After you have created your survey, pretest it on a friend to work out any bugs. Once your survey is complete, print it out to turn in. Include with your printed survey a paper describing your 10 questions and the concepts they are measuring. In addition, describe the type of data each question gathers in terms of qualitative and quantitative, as well as the levels of measurement of the data you would gather with the questions. Describe any issues you faced and how you overcame them. Include any changes you made to your questions and response categories after the survey was pretested.

KEY WORDS AND CONCEPTS

Anonymity 230
Computer-assisted telephone interviewing (CATI) 219
Confidentiality 230
Demographic questions 227
Double-barreled questions 223
Ecological momentary assessments (EMA) 218
Ecological validity 218

Encryption 237
Face-to-face interviews 221
Fielded 213
Incentives 230
Interviewer bias 214
Interviews 210
Items 209

Law Enforcement Management and Administrative Statistics (LEMAS) 212
Loaded questions 223
Longitudinal data 213
Mail and written surveys 214
Matrix question 224
Mobile survey 217
Notification letters 230

Online survey 217
Questionnaires 209
Question-order effect 216
Recall bias 216
Recency effects 216
Respondent burden 222

Respondents 209
Response rate 215
Self-administered questionnaire 214
Skip-and-fill patterns 217
Survey 209
Survey fraud 218

Survey modes 214
Survey nonresponse 215
Survey panels 217
Survey processing 231
Survey research 209
Telephone surveys 219

KEY POINTS

- Surveys research is the most common approach used in criminology and criminal justice to collect original data because it can be an incredibly effective and efficient method for collecting vast amounts of data from large groups of individuals, and because surveys can be administered using a variety techniques.

- In survey research, data are collected either from self-administered questionnaires or during interviews. Mail, online, and mobile surveys are types of self-administered surveys, whereas interviews are conducted over the telephone or face to face. These different survey modes can be used to collect data for exploratory, descriptive, explanatory, or evaluation research projects.

- There is no "one-size-fits-all" approach to designing an effective survey instrument. Nevertheless, all questionnaires should be designed and administered in such a way as to increase response rates and minimize inaccurate answers to questions that result from poor question wording or interviewing. This means that survey researchers must be mindful of how the design and layout of a questionnaire, its administration, and the processing and entry of the instrument once it is returned must be considered.

- Surveys should have good "flow," which can come from asking one question at a time, minimizing the use of matrix questions, listing answer categories vertically instead of horizontally, using dark print for questions and light print for answer choices, and vertically aligning question subcomponents across questions.

- In general, presurvey notification letters should contain the title of the research project, the name and contact information of the chief investigator, the name of the agency or organization sponsoring the project, whether incentives are being offered to participants, information about how the data will be used, how the results of the study can be accessed at the end of the project, and the safeguards in place to protect participants' information.

- Survey research questions also must be clear, relevant, and unbiased questions, and much free and paid software is available to help those interested in conducting survey research, including LimeSurvey, SurveyMonkey, and Qualtrics.

- Ethical considerations need to be given when conducting survey research. Of special interest is the use of incentives as well as the protection of the survey data. Finally, for in-person interviewers, researchers have an ethical responsibility to ensure the safety and security of members of the interviewer team.

REVIEW QUESTIONS

1. Why is survey research a popular research method in the field of criminology and criminal justice?

2. What are the different modes in which surveys are conducted? Describe the strengths and weaknesses of each.

3. How can survey research be used in an exploratory research project? Explain.

4. How can survey research be used in a descriptive research project? Explain.

5. How can survey research be used in an explanatory research project? Explain.

6. How can survey research be used in an evaluation research project? Explain.

7. What are some ways an interviewer can help improve interview response rates? What are some ways an interviewer can cause increases in interview nonresponse?

8. What are some ways a questionnaire can be designed to help increase completion/response rates?

9. Why are incentives used in survey research? When should they be avoided, and why?

10. In survey research, what is the difference between anonymity and confidentiality? What are some other ethical considerations of survey research that must be considered before administering surveys or conducting interviews?

CRITICAL THINKING QUESTIONS

1. As part of a research team, you have been asked to give your thoughts on which survey mode should be used on an upcoming data collection project. Before offering your advice, ask the lead researchers a few questions about the project. What kind of questions do you think you should ask her before making your recommendation? Why?

2. Suppose you want to conduct a survey or jail inmates and are worried about low participation rates. You decide you want to encourage eligible participants to complete a survey by offering an incentive. What type of incentive do you think would be inappropriate to offer inmates? Why? What type of incentive do you think would be appropriate to offer inmates? Why?

3. Create three questions that could be included on a survey of college students, aimed at helping answer research questions related to better understanding the associations between lifestyle/risk behavior and personal victimization. Create the three questions as open-ended questions, and then create the same three questions as close-ended questions? Is one approach better than the other? Explain.

4. You are leading a research project that involves face-to-face interviews. The interviews will be used to collect data from self-identified "head of household" (i.e., a person living in a sampled household who can answer questions about everyone currently living in the residence) that is living in one of 500 randomly sampled residences. The aim of the study is to understand the nature and extent of criminal victimization experienced by the population of residents that the sampled household members represent. What are some strategies you could use to increase the likelihood that the interviews will be completed? What are some things you will want to avoid?

5. What are some strengths and weaknesses of online surveys or mobile surveys? Give an example of a research study where an online or mobile survey could be a better choice of survey mode than other potions. Given an example of a research study where an online or mobile survey could be a worse choice.

6. Go online and do a quick search for a free online survey website that will allow you to create and print a brief questionnaire consisting of five to ten questions (on any topic). Pretest your survey instrument by giving a printed copy of it to another student in your class. Ask for feedback. Did your classmate identify any problems with your survey? If so, what were they? How might the problems that your classmate identified have adversely affected your survey had it not been piloted? If your questionnaire was going to be administered as a self-administered mail survey, what other aspects of the research project should you consider but that your classmate could not provide feedback on?

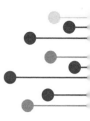

CHAPTER 8

Experimental Research

Introduction

For many researchers, a goal of research is to identify **causal relationships** between variables. That is, many researchers seek to find evidence that the variation in one variable is *caused* by (at least in part) the variation in another variable. Identifying a causal relationship between variables is the purpose of experimental research because it can provide evidence of if and how one variable affects, causes, influences, or predicts another variable. Conducting experiments is useful for many research projects, and it is useful in conjunction with other approaches. This is how one of our featured researchers, Heather Zaykowski, uses experimental research: in combination with other approaches such as interviews and survey research.

This chapter provides information about conducting experimental research. Many students feel they know what experimental research is—after all, you may have grown up on a diet of experiments in the media. What you will learn in this chapter is that what you have been told is an "experiment" probably is not. This chapter begins with a discussion of *why* a researcher would engage in experimental research. Then we discuss the many types of experiments used in criminology and criminal justice research, including true experiments, pre-experiments, quasi-experiments, and natural experiments. We describe validity and reliability as they are concerns of experimental research. The chapter also provides information about the pitfalls and ethics associated with experimental research. Before moving to the next chapter, we also hear from experimental research expert Chris Keating, PhD. Keating is a great example of how research methods skills including experimental research skills are desired and valuable in a variety of careers.

Learning Objectives

After finishing this chapter, you should be able to:

8.1 Describe and evaluate the characteristics of true experimental research designs. Indicate why true experiments are described as the "gold standard" of experimental research designs.

8.2 Assess the criteria for establishing a causal relationship among variables. Identify how these criteria are related to true experiments.

8.3 Describe internal validity and external validity, and compare the two. Identify why internal and external validity are important considerations in experimental research.

8.4 Compare the true experimental, pre-experimental, quasi-experimental, and natural experimental designs. Identify important ways they differ and what that means about claims of causality.

8.5 Explain and compare the advantages and disadvantages of each type of experimental design and internal and external validity threats of each.

8.6 Explicate the role that ethics play in conducting experimental research. What elements of ethics are most important to consider in conducting experimental research.

Causal relationship: Purpose of experimental research because it can provide evidence of if and how one variable affects, causes, influences, or predicts another variable.

Why Conduct Experimental Research?

A common goal of criminology and criminal justice research is to identify the causal relationships between variables. That is, an objective in some research is to find evidence that the variation in one variable is *caused* by (at least in part) the variation in another variable. Identifying a causal relationship between variables is precisely the purpose of experimental research that seeks to identify or explain how one variable affects, causes, influences, or predicts another variable. Recall that featured researcher Rachel Boba Santos and colleague's research (Santos & Santos, 2016), investigated whether an offender-focused, high-intensity intervention in hot spots focused on felon offenders led to a reduction of crime in those areas. In part, to conduct their analysis, Santos and colleague used experimental research. Demonstrating causation is also a goal in a great deal of evaluation research that attempts to identify whether a program or policy is causing the desired changes in an outcome of interest. Given the overlap between experimental research and much of evaluation research, it is not surprising to find Santos and colleague's research uses both approaches. Experimental research—frequently referred to as the gold standard for establishing causality and the topic of this chapter—is one way a researcher can identify causation, or how an independent variable affects, influences, predicts, or causes the variation in a dependent variable.[1]

What Is Causation?

Experimental research is a research approach that is useful for identifying a causal relationship between variables. Featured researcher Carlos Cuevas, as a psychologist, cut his teeth on experimental research. As time has gone on, Cuevas's work has taken him in different directions, however. Still, Cuevas noted, in his video interview conducted for this book, that although experimental research may not be appropriate for all types of criminal justice research, it is his hope that more social scientists take advantage of it as a way to conduct research. Cuevas's wish is becoming a reality. Before describing how a researcher can identify causation, it is important to define causation. **Causation** exists when variation in one variable causes, or results in, variation in another variable. Three criteria must be met before a researcher has evidence of a causal relationship: temporal ordering, association, and a lack of spurious relationships. Without all three criteria, causation is not present.

The first requirement for establishing a causal relationship between variables is temporal ordering. **Temporal ordering** requires that the variation in the independent variable occurs *prior* to the variation in the dependent variable. If a causal relationship between years incarcerated and risk of recidivism exists, then the number of years incarcerated (the independent variable) should occur before the opportunity to recidivate does (the dependent variable). The temporal requirement should make sense in that something that happens today cannot have possibly *caused* something that happened yesterday. Something that happened today may be related to, or associated with, something that occurred yesterday, but it cannot have *caused* it. The number of years served in prison cannot be *caused* by one's future educational attainment. A decision to rob a store today cannot have been *caused* by the loss of income next week. Without establishing the temporal ordering requirement, you cannot claim that the variation in an independent variable

A cause-and-effect relationship being investigated by criminologists and criminal justice practitioners is the influence of high school drop outs on being sentenced to prison. This cause-and-effect relationship has major ramifications on our society.

---

[1] A second way is using statistical techniques to control for the influence of variables aside from the one of interest.

causes the variation in a dependent variable. The temporal ordering requirement may be the easiest of the three criteria to establish, and it is easy to do in experimental research given the control of the researcher. Although a necessary element of causality, the presence of temporal ordering is not sufficient to claim causality between two variables. A researcher must also offer evidence of an association between variables, as well as a lack of spurious relationships.

Association between variables is another criteria needed to demonstrate causation. **Association** means that the values in the independent variable and the values in the dependent variable move together in a pattern, or they are correlated. The association between variables may be linear, curvilinear, or some other pattern. A linear association between variables is found when increases in the values of the independent variable occur with increases in the values of the dependent variable. Another linear association between variables is found when the values in the independent variable are associated with decreases in the value of the dependent variable. A nonlinear association is another type of relationship found between variables. Age is frequently associated with outcomes in a curvilinear fashion. For example, as age increases, values in a dependent variable initially increase until some point when values begin decreasing. Patterns of association or correlation come in many forms, and a comprehensive discussion of all of them is beyond the scope of this text. The important point is that two variables must move together in a pattern for there to be an association between them. Some examples of associated variables are shown in Figure 8.1.

Like the temporal ordering requirement, establishing an association between variables alone is not sufficient to demonstrate causality between variables. In addition to the temporal ordering requirement and association, a researcher must also rule out the influence of a third variable. In other words, a researcher must rule out the influence of a spurious relationship.

The third requirement for establishing causality is ruling out the presence of a spurious relationship between the independent and the dependent variable. A **spurious relationship** is an apparent relationship between independent and dependent variables when in fact they are not related. Spurious relationships can occur via confounding factor or intervening variable. A **confounding factor** is a third variable that causes the independent and dependent variables to vary. Although initially one may think that the independent variable is making the dependent variable vary, what is happening with a confounding variable is that it is making the independent and dependent variables vary. In reality, the independent and dependent variables are unrelated. Failure to consider the presence of a confounding factor may lead a researcher to conclude erroneously a causal relationship between the independent and dependent variables. A spurious relationship may also result when an intervening variable is at work. An **intervening variable** is a variable that is situated in time between the independent and dependent variables. When an intervening variable is operating, the independent variable does not cause the dependent variable, but instead the independent variable causes the intervening variable to vary, and the intervening variable causes the dependent variable. Figure 8.2 illustrates spurious relationships resulting from a confounding factor, and spurious relationships resulting from intervening variables.

Association Is Not Causation

Association, or correlation, is not the same as causation. As described earlier, association means that variables vary together. For example, you likely notice that bird singing is associated with flowers blooming. You might also recognize that drinking a lot of coffee

Understanding cause and effect means that we can better control phenomenon. For example, if we better understood what leads to an increase in crime rates, we could better control crime rates.

Association: One of three criteria needed to establish causation, which is found when the values in the independent variable and the values in the dependent variable move together in a pattern.

Spurious relationship: Relationship among variables in which it appears that two variables are related to one another, but instead a third variable is the causal factor.

Confounding factor: Third variable at work in a spurious relationship that is causing what appears to be a relationship between two other variables.

Intervening variable: Variable that is situated between the two other variables in time, creating a type of a spurious relationship.

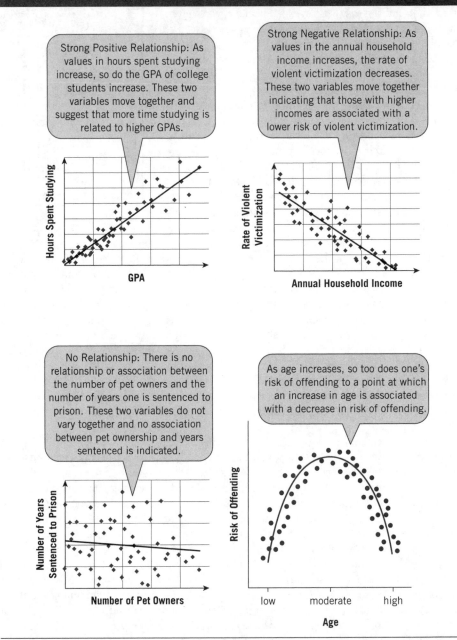

Figure 8.1   Examples of Associated or Correlated Variables

Strong Positive Relationship: As values in hours spent studying increase, so do the GPA of college students increase. These two variables move together and suggest that more time studying is related to higher GPAs.

Strong Negative Relationship: As values in the annual household income increases, the rate of violent victimization decreases. These two variables move together indicating that those with higher incomes are associated with a lower risk of violent victimization.

No Relationship: There is no relationship or association between the number of pet owners and the number of years one is sentenced to prison. These two variables do not vary together and no association between pet ownership and years sentenced is indicated.

As age increases, so too does one's risk of offending to a point at which an increase in age is associated with a decrease in risk of offending.

Source: Used with permission. Copyright © 2017 Esri, ArcGIS Online, and the GIS User Community. All rights reserved.

Note from the authors: This figure is found here: http://resources.esri.com/help/9.3/arcgisengine/java/ GP_ToolRef/Spatial_Statistics_toolbox/regression_analysis_basics.htm.

Figure 8.2   Examples of Spurious Relationships

W

X   Y

A spurious relationship
between X and Y due to
a confounding factor W

X ⟶ W ⟶ Y

A spurious relationship between
X and Y due to an intervening
variable W

is associated with earning higher grades. Although each of these pairs of variables is associated, additional work is needed to suggest that these pairs of variables are causally related. To establish causality, a researcher needs to offer evidence of appropriate temporal ordering of the variables, a lack of spurious relationships, and association between the variables. Only with this evidence can you state with certainty that the variables are causally related.

Causation is vital to understanding our world. Given its importance, understanding experimental research designs is crucial to understanding our world as well. If through experimental research you can find evidence of a causal relationship between two variables, then you have information that may allow you to influence the outcome variable. For example, if we have knowledge about what causes an increase in offending risk, then through manipulation of the causal factor, we can reduce offending risk. Understanding causal relationships offers the possibility of knowing how to influence myriad things including recidivism, crime rates, risk of victimization, police misconduct, diversity in the criminal justice system, bias in sentencing, restorative justice outcomes, effectiveness of education, and so on. In short, using experimental research to establish causality between variables offers the opportunity to improve our world and the lives of people in it.

Establishing causality is important. Without it, we are left to make assumptions about the role of something on some other. We are often left to using anecdotal evidence. As featured researcher Chris Melde notes, "people often think they see an effect, but we know that how people think, or what they think they see is not always accurate. Someone might attribute an outcome to a treatment when it actually does not exist." Furthermore, Melde states that, "our gut instinct and interpretation of processes is not as robust as we like to think it is." Although Melde's highlighted research does not include experimental research (Melde, Taylor, & Esbensen, 2009), he has engaged in a great deal of experimental work. Melde knows that experimental designs help to guard against this human error. Finally, Zaykowski warns students that many people use the terms *causation* and *association* imprecisely. They are different, and those differences are important.

© Adam Sandiford/asandiford.com

Just because some
things are associated
doesn't imply any sort
of causal relationship.

What Is Experimental Research?

Most students enroll in a research methods class with some notion of what experiments are given unforgettable exposure to them in the media. Consider the classic 1931 movie *Frankenstein* where scientist Henry Frankenstein experiments with the reanimation of lifeless bodies. After success reanimating animals, Henry decides to reanimate a human body. To do this, he stitches together various body parts gathered from numerous corpses to conduct his biggest experiment ever. He is successful in reanimating the body—Frankenstein's monster—but almost immediately, things go terribly wrong. The monster accidently kills a little girl (among other things), and eventually, Frankenstein is killed in a burning building.

Alternatively, consider the experiments highlighted in the classic movie *The Fly* (versions available in 1958 and 1986) in which scientist Seth Brundle developed telepods that can transport a person (or other beings) through space from one telepod to the another. When Seth feels he has finally worked out all the kinks to teleportation, he hops in to transport himself across the room. Unfortunately, unbeknownst to Seth, a fly is buzzing around in the telepod with him. Bad news! The transportation is successful in that Seth arrives in the other telepod, yet because he was transported with a fly, their molecular makeup is jumbled and Seth begins to transform into a (nasty looking) fly!

More recently, the movie *Supersize Me* highlights an experiment. In the documentary, Morgan Spurlock experimented with his own body to determine the influence that eating three McDonalds meals every day for a month would have on his body. A part of his experiment required him to supersize the meal if the McDonalds clerk asked him if he wanted to do so. In addition, Spurlock foregoes exercise during that month. Prior to beginning the 30-day experiment, multiple doctors (a general practitioner, a cardiologist, and a gastroenterologist) run tests demonstrating that Morgan is outstandingly healthy. A dietician/nutritionist and an exercise physiologist also assess Morgan and conclude he is exceedingly fit. After the 30-day experiment, Morgan is again tested by the physicians and finds that his health declined dramatically during the period.

Although the experiments depicted in the movies generally end badly with the creation of monsters, death, carnage, and high blood pressure, luckily, experiments conducted in criminology and criminal justice tend have tamer outcomes. What accounts for these radical differences? A part of the difference may be because what we see in movies are not true experiments. Why is that? That is because true experiments have particular characteristics that allow a researcher to establish causality among variables. You might be asking yourself, "What about the Stanford Prison Experiment? That didn't turn out so well." You are correct—it did not turn out so well! How did all these normal people very quickly turn on the prisoners? How did this so-called experiment end so badly? How can it be that this experiment resulted in monsters wearing Ray Bans® and khaki shirts? Consider a question posed by Cuevas as you read this chapter—was the Stanford Prison Experiment an experiment at all? An argument can be made that although this work is called an experiment, it has none of the important characteristics of experiments. Something to keep in mind, as emphasized by Zaykowski, is that experimental research is not always conducted in a laboratory setting. The numerous types of experimental approaches show that they can occur anywhere. We next turn to defining true experiments and describing those very important characteristics.

True Experiments

A **true experiment** is an approach to research that has three defining characteristics: (1) at least one experimental and one control group, (2) random assignment to the experimental and control group, and (3) manipulation of an independent or a **predictor variable** (i.e., treatment) by a researcher. Research that includes these three criteria is a true experiment. Santos and Santos's (2016) research is an excellent example of a true experiment. In this research, Santos and her collaborator used 24 treatment (or experimental) and 24 control geographic areas, a type of randomization (recommended for low sample sizes), and researcher control of the treatment administration. The purpose of this research was to identify whether the treatment—intensive policing—led to a reduction of crime in hot spots in the experimental group. The next section discusses each element that makes up a true experiment.

Experimental and Control Group

True experiments have at least one experimental and one control group. The **experimental group** is the group of subjects or other units of analysis that receives the treatment during the experiment. In contrast, those subjects or units of analysis in the **control group** do not receive any treatment. Why do this? We use control and experimental groups to compare what happens when a treatment is applied. The control group shows what happens with no treatment, and the experimental group shows what happens with treatment. After administration of the treatment, posttests are administered to allow the researcher to measure whether any differences between the two groups were found. Santos and Santos's (2016) research made use of control and treatment groups in the form of hot spots. Once the hot spots were identified, they were placed into either the control group or the experimental group. This work on a policing intervention treatment in hot spots offered a perfect opportunity to ascertain whether this increased police intervention would influence crime rates in the treatment hot spots. Figure 8.3 shows the treatment and control groups used in Santos and colleague's research.

Experimental group: Group of subjects or other units of interest that receives the treatment in experimental research.

Control group: Group of subjects or other units of interest that does not receive any treatment during experimental research.

Figure 8.3 Crime Map Taken From Santos and Santos's (2016) Featured Research Shows Areas in the Geography of Interest

Source: Santos, R. B. & Santos, R. G. (2016). Offender-focused police intervention in residential burglary and theft from vehicle hot spots: A partially blocked randomized control trial. *Journal of Experimental Criminology, 12,* 373–402. With permission of Springer.

Random Assignment

Random assignment: Characteristic of a true experiment in which subjects or units of interest are randomly placed in an experimental or a control group. The random nature of the assignment maximizes the chances that the experimental and control groups are equivalent.

Confounders: Variables that the researcher seeks to control or eliminate in experimental research.

Matching: Randomization technique that eliminates the possibility that differences between subjects based on the matching variables can affect results.

How did Santos and her colleague (2016) choose which geographic areas would be in the control or treatment group? Santos randomly assigned each hot spot into either the treatment or the control group. The **random assignment** or randomization of subjects or units of analysis to the experimental and control groups is a defining characteristic of a true experiment. Random assignment of subjects is critical because it generates theoretically equivalent groups. Groups are considered equivalent because possible confounders are also randomly assigned. **Confounders** are variables that can affect the outcome of research. For example, gender, income, population density, and percentage of single-headed households could be confounders in research. By using random assignment of subjects, these characteristics are randomly distributed into the control and experimental groups. As McCall noted with regard to experiments in 1923, "[j]ust as representativeness can be secured by the method of chance . . . so equivalence may be secured by chance provided the number of subjects to be used is sufficiently numerous" (as quoted by Campbell & Stanley, 1963, p. 2). McCall referred to this as the groups being "equated by chance." Because the experimental and control groups are equivalent, and potential confounders are randomly assigned, a researcher can theoretically conclude that any difference between the two groups is the treatment. Random assignment allows the researcher to better isolate the effect (if any) of the treatment.

Matching in True Experiments

A useful approach to randomization in true experiments is the use of matching. **Matching** is a randomization technique that eliminates the possibility that differences between subjects based on the matching variables can affect results. Next we describe two commonly used types of matching: paired-matching and block matching.

Paired-matching or a matched pairs design is a matching approach used in true experiments that requires that the researcher create pairs of subjects based on relevant characteristics that are identified prior to the experiment. For example, pairs of individuals may be matched based on sex, age, years in prison, or income. Geographic areas may be matched on characteristics such as percentage of female-headed households, crime rates, or other characteristics. Once pairs are established, one unit in the pair is randomly assigned to the experimental treatment, and the other unit is assigned to the control group. The experiment is then conducted. The researcher has certainty that the experimental and control groups were equivalent on those matching variables.

You may be interested in conducting research on a treatment designed to reduce the risk of offending. Nevertheless, research indicates that offending risk is associated with several demographic characteristics. To conduct true experimental research on this topic and to control for those demographic characteristics, you as the researcher would select subjects and create pairs based on the demographics. Then one person in each pair would be randomly assigned to an experimental or a control group. By using this approach, the only remaining characteristics associated with the outcome (risk of offending) that should differ between each of the two people in the matched pair should be exposure to the treatment. The use of matched pairs controls for relevant characteristics (e.g., sex, age, income, and marital status) in better ways than does random assignment.

Block matching is another useful matching technique that includes the creation of subgroups of subjects

> ### Figure 8.4 Example of Matched Pairs for Use in True-Experimental Research
>
> Two women, both age 32, divorced, earn $22,000 annually
>
>
>
> assigned to experimental group   assigned to control group

based on block variables. **Block variables** are variables the researcher believes will affect response to the treatment. For example, a researcher may be aware that subjects' sex influences the way subjects respond to the treatment. Given that, the research blocks the subjects based on sex. The experiment is then conducted independently on each block (in this example, sex). Thus, for the female block, subjects are randomly assigned to either the experimental or the control group. Similarly, for the male block, subjects either are randomly assigned to either the experimental or the control group. The experiment is then conducted separately for each block. By conducting the experiment on two groups or blocks, the researcher has controlled for the effect of the characteristic making up the block.

For example, imagine a researcher is conducting research on the effect of a policy used to reduce recidivism. Research indicates that college students and noncollege attenders respond to this policy (the treatment) differently. The researcher gathers a sample of 400 individuals—200 of whom are attending college and 200 of whom are not. The researcher creates two blocks based on the college-attending status of the individuals. The block of 200 college students is then randomly assigned to a control and an experimental group. Similarly, the block of 200 noncollege attenders is randomly assigned to a control and an experimental group. The experiment is then conducted separately for each group. When conducted this way, the researcher can investigate whether the treatment causes an outcome with certainty that one's college attending status is not affected by the outcome.

Thinking about Santos and Santos's (2016) research, exactly what type of randomization was used to assign randomly each hot spot into either the treatment or the control group? First, they had to identify the hot spots. Hot spots refer to geographic areas that are characterized by high crime rates. But how did they define hot spot? In that research, hot spots were identified as clusters of census blocks totally about .6 square miles. Each hot spot was consistent in terms of numbers of reported crimes and geographic and social environment. Next, Santos and Santos identified three blocks: low crime per offender, medium crime per offender, and high crime per offender. Next, by using the block matching discussed earlier, half of each block was assigned to either the control or the treatment group. Then, with this approach, and some additional statistical tests to ensure similarity between the control and the treatment group, they began the experiment confident that the randomization process was successful.

Paired-matching: Also called "matched pairs design." It is a matching approach used in true experiments in which the researcher creates pairs of subjects or units of interest based on relevant characteristics that are identified prior to the experiment. Once pairs are established, one unit in the pair is randomly assigned to the experimental group, and the unit other is assigned to the control group.

Block matching: Type of matching used in some true experiments that includes the creation of subgroups of the subjects or units of interest based on a block variable. The experiment is then conducted separately on each block. By conducting the experiment on two groups or blocks, the researcher has controlled for the effect of the characteristic making up the block.

Figure 8.5 Example of Using Block Matching When Conducting Research

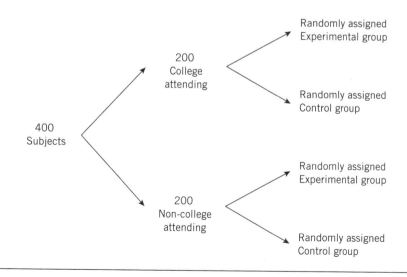

Block variables: Those variables the researcher believes will affect response to the treatment. Block variables are used to create blocks used in block matching.

Manipulation of an independent variable: One of three characteristics of true experimental research. The control or manipulation of the independent variable must be done by the researcher.

Treatment: Researcher's manipulation of the independent variable.

Gold standard: Phrase used to describe true experimental research designs given their ability to establish causality.

Taking great care in defining and measuring hot spots and the randomization of the hot spots into experimental and control groups was imperative to maximize the rigor of this work by Santos and her colleague (2016). A theme of this text is that one's research is only as strong as its weakest part. By taking their time to clearly define, and carefully randomize, the researchers were able to maintain the integrity of their work. This is an important consideration because as Cuevas notes, too often, experimental researchers fail to account for, or think about, the specific nuts and bolts of conducting research. Santos and her colleague used a carefully thought-out design, and they followed this plan. This means they are able to have the confidence in the strength of their design.

Researcher Manipulation of Treatment

A third characteristic of true experimental research is that it includes the researcher's control or **manipulation of an independent variable**. The manipulation of the independent variable is also referred to as the **treatment.** By controlling the treatment, a researcher can better isolate any effect of the treatment on the outcome. For instance, the researchers implemented a treatment—in this case of Santos and Santos (2016), intensive policing—in the experimental hot spots. The control group of hot spots did not receive the treatment but continued to be policed in the traditional ways. The experimental group received the treatment, which was offender-focused intervention carried out by law enforcement officers. Santos and colleague managed the application of the treatment by managing two officers engaging in high-intensity policing. What did the intensive policing entail? First, each of the two detectives repeatedly contacted each sampled offender or family member in the treatment groups in a friendly way. The detectives would ask whether the offender had any information about crimes that had recently been committed in the area. In addition, the detectives conducted curfew checks and encouraged the offenders about the importance of following their probation rules. The detectives visited the offenders and their families on random days. In addition, contact by the detectives was made by phone. The message of these intensive interactions was to influence the offender's perceptions of their risk of being caught should they commit additional crimes. Activity in the control group hot spots remained unchanged from normal policing protocols. Given the use of this protocol, Santos and Santos could later measure to see whether intensive policing influenced crime rates (one of four dependent variables) in the geographies of interest.

True Experimental Designs

True experiments are frequently described as the **gold standard** in experimental research because they help to establish causality. Although experiments offer many advantages that will be identified in this chapter, experiments are not the panacea that some claim. Given the practical challenges of true experimental research, it may be that its claims of superiority is overstated. Why is that? For one, the notion of the role of randomization for solving the causal inference problem is a myth according to Sampson (2010). One of our other featured researchers, Rod Brunson, reiterates this point when he notes that in theory, conducting a true experiment is easy (and can appear to be the gold standard), but in reality it is much more difficult to actually accomplish it. A researcher can plan all day, but it all may go sideways the minute the experiment begins. This means that conducting true experiments requires vigilance by the researcher, great care in planning, and attention to detail. Cuevas agrees when he states that true experiments may be the gold standard in theory, but in reality, they are silver or nickel-standards because experimental research is hard to do. Cuevas continues that although being able to pull off gold-standard experimental research is challenging, it must be our goal. Another featured researcher, Mary Dodge, believes that this challenge of executing a perfect experimental design into practice may be a reason that more experimental research is not conducted. Although her featured research in this text did not include experimental research (Dodge, Starr-Gimeno, & Williams, 2005), she has conducted many experimental projects especially earlier in her career. Dodge understands the challenges with it. Even though experiments are easy to design, experimental research is far more difficult to execute. Brunson agrees in that researchers should not drop their guard when it comes to experiments. Experiments require the same critical eye that other approaches do. Although we should all aim for perfection, no research is perfect. We strive for perfection, but it is difficult or impossible to obtain. Despite this imperfection, though, Sampson argues that experiments are "an essential part of the methodological tool kit of criminologists, and I would hope to see more, not fewer, field experiments—especially at the group level" (Sampson, 2010, p. 490) The following sections describe some more commonly used true experimental designs that researchers should be familiar with. All are characterized by at least one control and one experimental group, randomization into those groups, and a researcher's control over the treatment.

Two-Group Posttest-Only Design

One commonly used true experimental design is the two-group posttest-only design. The **two-group posttest-only design** incorporates a randomly assigned experimental group (RE) and a randomly assigned control group (RC). The researcher manipulates the independent variable (i.e., administers the treatment) and administers it to the experimental group. Finally, there is a comparison of measures of the dependent variable (i.e., posttests) after the treatment to assess any differences. If there are any differences between the posttest measures, it is presumed that they are a result of the treatment. In other words, this comparison of posttests can help to identify whether the treatment caused any change in the outcome. Illustrated, the two-group posttest-only design looks like Figure 8.6.

Although a strong design, a two-group posttest-only approach has a slight limitation. In particular, although random assignment to a control and an experimental group theoretically results in equivalent groups prior to the treatment, in reality, there may be some differences between the experimental and control groups that could influence the outcome. Because of that, you cannot know with full certainty what portion of any differences found between the posttest measurements are a result of the treatment or of preexisting differences between the groups.

Consider this experimental research conducted by Melde and colleagues (Melde et al., 2009) that highlights the limitation of two-group posttest-only. This research focused on a school-based violence project designed to reduce victimization. The project introduced a program (i.e., treatment) designed to reduce victimization. Melde and colleagues did this and found that when comparing the pre- and posttreatment victimization rates among the experimental groups, the treatment seemed to reduce victimization! Victimization rates in the treatment group *did* decrease. You may at first think that this offers evidence of a treatment effect. Yet, the important role of the control group must be taken into account. What Melde and others discovered was that the rates of victimization went down in the control group as well. What they found was that as students age, victimization decreased, and this happened

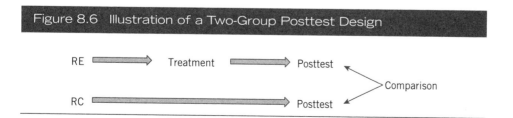

Figure 8.6   Illustration of a Two-Group Posttest Design

RE ⟹ Treatment ⟹ Posttest

RC ⟹ Posttest

Comparison

in the both the experimental and control groups. The use of control groups guarded against what would have been an erroneous finding. One way to guard against this possibility is to use both pretest and posttest measurement of the dependent variable as Melde and colleagues did. That is the approach is described next.

Two-Group Pretest–Treatment–Posttest Design

The two-group pretest–treatment–posttest design improves on the two-group posttest design by including a pretest. Not surprisingly, given it is a true experiment, the **two-group pretest–treatment–posttest design** uses randomly assigned control and experimental groups, and manipulation of the independent variable (i.e., treatment) by the researcher. This test enables multiple comparisons. Because the researcher can compare pretest measurements, they can assess whether the experimental and control groups are equivalent prior to any treatment. If the groups are not equivalent, then adjustments to the groups can be made to ensure this equivalence, or this difference, can be accounted for after the treatment. When comparisons of posttest values are made and differences are identified, the researcher can offer evidence of a causal relationship between the independent variable (the treatment) and the dependent variable. In addition, this design offers the researcher an idea about how both the control and the experimental group changed from pre- to posttest. If he or she finds the control group changed over time, the research can identify why that is. If it had to do with subjects getting hungry, then he or she should expect the same change to occur in the experimental group. The question then becomes how much change did the experimental group experience beyond the control group. Illustrated, the two-group pretest–treatment–posttest design is shown in Figure 8.7.

Because the two-group pretest–treatment–posttest design is a true experiment, and incorporates both a pre- and a posttest, the design is regarded as the most rigorous experimental design available. This is the design used by Santos and her colleague (2016). Rather than conducting one true experiment, however, they conducted four experiments because they used four outcome measures. Why use multiple measures? Because as the researchers noted, each measure had its strengths and limitations. These measures are the following:

1. The count of residential burglary and theft from vehicle reported crimes in each hot spot

2. The count of all arrests for each targeted offender

3. The count of burglary, theft, and drug offense arrests in each hot spot of individuals who live in the hot spot

4. The ratio of burglary, theft, and drug offense arrests per individuals arrested who live in the hot spot.

Figure 8.7   Example of a Two-Group Pretest Treatment Posttest Design Used in Research

RE Pretest ➡ Treatment ➡ Posttest

Comparison

RC Pretest ➡ Posttest

Comparison

Comparison

Comparison

The value of each of these measures was calculated prior to the treatment (i.e., the pretest measures) using data available at the local law enforcement agency. Then posttest measures were taken after the treatment period. The findings from this research offered mixed findings. First, in turning to the first outcome, the results of the experiment did not indicate that the intensive policing program led to lower counts of residential burglary and theft from a vehicle. Santos and Santos (2016) do note that the tests were suggestive of the beneficial impact of the intensive policing, but it just did result in a large enough difference to conclude an effect. More research with a larger sample of hot spots is recommended. The findings from the other three experiments also failed to indicate causality. Each experiment had limitations (all research has limitations), however, and Santos and her colleague discuss them in their journal article.

It is important to note that although this design is rigorous, it is not without potential issues. A potential issue of the two-group pretest–treatment–posttest design is precisely because of the presence of the pretest. In particular, that subjects are given the pretest may affect their response to the treatment, and that could affect the findings and jeopardize the generalizability of the findings. Even though this was not an issue with the work of Santos and colleague's (2016) research (given the subjects were not aware of either the pre- or posttests), it is of concern in other types of research. We discuss the generalizability of experimental findings later in this chapter.

Solomon Four Group Design

One answer to whether treatment is affected by the presence of a pretest, and to minimize the effect of any confounding variables, is to use the **Solomon Four Group** design. In using this approach, a researcher randomly assigns members of the sample to one of four groups:

1. A pretest, treatment, posttest group

2. A pretest, no-treatment, posttest group

3. A treatment, posttest group

4. A no-treatment, posttest group

The first two groups (1 and 2) are identical to those found in the two-group pretest–treatment–posttest. The next two groups (3 and 4) are included to better identify whether the presence of a pretest influenced the outcome measures.

In using these four groups, several assessments or comparisons are made. The four comparisons in the two-group pretest–treatment–posttest are made for the same reasons as described earlier. The Solomon Four Group test includes four additional comparisons. First, by measuring for any differences between the posttests in groups 1 and 2, the effectiveness of the treatment given the presence of a pretest can be identified. If the researcher finds a difference in this comparison, they can conclude the presence of the pretest had an effect. Next, by measuring for any differences between the posttests in groups 3 and 4, the effectiveness of the treatment without a pretest can be identified. The Solomon Four Group design is illustrated in Figure 8.8.

Given this approach is characterized by the strengths of a true experiment, that it includes a pretest and a posttest, and that it can identify any influence of the presence of a pretest on the treatment, it is considered one of the most rigorous designs available for a true experiment. This approach guards against threats to both internal and external validity. It guards against threats to internal validity in that it offers all the necessary components to identify causality. It also guards against threats to external validity in that it allows an assessment of the treatment as it would occur in the real world where pretests are not the norm. Although it is the gold standard, true experiments must still be assessed for threats to both the internal

Solomon Four Group: True experimental design that includes four randomly generated groups of subjects. It has all the benefits of a two-group pretest–treatment–posttest design; plus it offers information about whether the results were affected by the presence of a pretest.

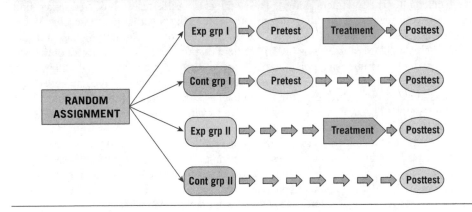

Figure 8.8   Solomon Four Group Design

A rigorous researcher is always on the lookout for threats to internal and external validity.

Internal validity: Related to the degree to which a researcher can conclude a causal relationship among variables in an experiment. Internal validity is often at odds with external validity.

and the external validity. In addition, a researcher must focus on reliability. The next sections introduce important issues related to validity and reliability.

Validity

Regardless of the design or approach taken when conducting research, researchers must be sensitive to threats to their work. As noted in earlier chapters, your research is only as strong as its weakest component. For this reason, when conducting any experimental research, one matter of concern is the validity of the research. In Chapter 4, we introduced the concept of validity in terms of variables accurately capturing the essence of an abstract concept it is designed to represent. In this section, we introduce you to some other important types of validity. There are two primary types of validity of concern: internal validity and external validity. **Internal validity** refers to the degree to which a researcher can conclude a treatment effect. In other words, can the researcher be reasonably sure that any change in the experimental group is a result of the treatment? In general, true experiments are characterized by high internal validity given the researcher's control. The presence of randomness in constructing the control and experimental groups, and the manipulation of the independent variable (i.e., treatment) by the researcher, makes for a highly controlled experiment. This in turn leads to high internal validity for true experiments.

A researcher must also be attentive to external validity. **External validity** is related to the generalizability of the experimental findings to other people in others situations and other environments. A researcher must ask, "Do the findings apply to the larger population of interest in the 'real world,' outside of a highly controlled experimental world?" Internal and external validities are frequently at odds with one another. Brunson notes it is one challenge associated with experimental research. The researcher must keep an eye on both. Another issue that Brunson emphasizes is that given the controlled nature of experiments, it is questionable how the findings translate into the real world. The real world is not characterized by rigorous controls found in experiments, but it is far messier.

Internal Validity Threats

Internal validity allows a researcher to claim a causal relationship. In their iconic book, Campbell and Stanley (1963) identified several types of threats to internal validity of experimental research. This section introduces some of these threats, although it does not offer a comprehensive list of them. It is important to recognize that one or many internal validity threats may be present. Understanding what threatens internal validity of experiments is the first important step in guarding against them.

Experimental Mortality

Experimental mortality is a potential threat to the internal validity of experimental research and occurs when subjects from either the control or the experimental group drop out of the research at differential rates for reasons related to features of the study. If experimental attrition is related to key elements of the study, it becomes unclear how much of the experimental outcome is a result of the treatment or of the differential attrition. A researcher must spend time contemplating whether there were differences in those who dropped out of the experiment and those who remained in the experiment that are relevant to the study. For example, assume a researcher is conducting a study on a new treatment designed to reduce recidivism. If the treatment group experiences attrition as a result of the challenges of engaging in the treatment, then those remaining in the experimental group are those who find the treatment easier to accomplish. Given that, any difference in posttests may be a result of the treatment, but some is because of the treatment and others is because the treatment group consisted only of those finding the treatment easy to engage in. This experimental mortality threatens the internal validity of the experiment, making it difficult to assign a causal effect between the treatment and the outcome.

© Konstantin Zavrazhin/Getty Images

Experimental mortality is a threat to the internal validity of an experiment. When experimental mortality is present, it is difficult to know if the outcome of the experiment is due to the treatment or due to the loss of subjects.

History

History is a threat to the internal validity of experimental research and refers to the occurrence of a specific event during the course of an experiment that affects the posttest comparisons between the experimental and control groups. A researcher must ask whether some event occurring during the course of an experiment may cause a change in subjects that would affect the experimental outcome. If so, history is a problem. For example, imagine an experiment with the purpose of testing if increased police presence leads to higher perceptions of safety among residents. The researcher randomly assigns police districts in a jurisdiction to experimental and control groups. The experimental group districts receive a treatment of doubled the normal police presence, and the control group districts continue receiving the same level of police presence. Now imagine that in the middle of the experiment, there is a protest in the jurisdiction. During the course of the protest, the police clash with the public, and several members of the public are injured and arrested. In addition, substantial property damage results. How might this event affect the posttest measures of perceived safety among subjects? It stands to reason that having this historical police–public clash occur in the midst of the experiment will influence the internal validity of the experiment, but it will be unclear how much of any posttest differences found will be a result of the increased police presence (i.e., the treatment) versus the effects of clash.

Melde is currently involved in research focused on schools in Michigan. This includes areas in Flint, Michigan, which have been terribly affected by drinking water with dangerously high levels of lead (recall our earlier discussion about the very real dangers of lead exposure). During the course of this experiment, some schools started getting safe drinking water through the tap (versus only bottled water). How might Melde and his colleagues account for this in their study? Might the introduction of safe water and some of the schools affect test scores? Will this influence the attitudes of children in the study? Will this history event present a threat to the validity of his research? You can bet that Melde and colleagues will be keeping data about the water issue to control for its effects in this experiment as best as possible.

Instrumentation

Instrumentation is a threat to internal validity that refers to the possibility that instruments used in an experiment may affect measurement and the ultimate posttest comparison between control and experimental groups. Instruments take on many forms. Instruments may be a mechanical instrument such as a weight scale, survey instruments (and questions on them), or human observers who gather data or score subjects in an experiment. The researcher must ask whether the precision of the instrumentation used has changed in the course of the experiment. If so, instrumentation may be at play. For example, imagine an experiment uses a breathalyzer to measure blood-alcohol content. What if during the course of the experiment, the breathalyzer's calibration changes. This would affect measurements and the conclusions of the experiment. You may erroneously conclude a causal effect between an independent and a dependent variable when, in reality, the only thing that may have changed was the instrument's calibration. A researcher must strive to conclude that any differences seen in posttest comparisons are a result of the treatment, not of the instrumentation.

Maturation

Maturation is a potential threat to the internal validity of experimental research that refers to the natural changes that happen to subjects participating in experimental research. A researcher must ask whether during the course of the experiment, something occurred to the subjects with the passage of time that would affect the outcome. Subjects in an experiment may get tired, hungry, or impatient. In addition, for longer term experiments, a researcher must be aware of changes in subjects such as aging. For example, imagine an experiment designed to understand whether a new approach to teaching improves math ability. The experiment is designed to last eight hours. Let us assume the researcher failed to consider the subjects would get hungry during the course of the day. As a result, subjects rushed through posttests because they were hungry (and crabby). This suggests that posttest measurements reflect not only any change resulting from the treatment but also changes resulting from hunger. Researchers must guard against the effects of maturation.

Selection Bias

Yet another potential threat to the internal validity of experimental research is selection bias. **Selection bias** refers to important differences between the control and the experimental group that exists when they are randomly assigned to control and experimental groups. Even though the random assignment of subjects to experimental and control groups minimizes the threat of selection bias, the threat must be considered especially when working with small samples. If either the control or the experimental group disproportionately includes subjects characterized by a confounding factor, then any treatment effect found may be in whole or part a result of this confounding factor instead of the treatment. A researcher must spend time contemplating whether there are differences between the control and the experimental group such as a willingness to participate, attitudes, or personality characteristics that may affect the outcome of the research.

Statistical Regression

Statistical regression is a threat to the internal validity of experimental research using subjects selected for participation based on extreme scores. **Statistical regression** refers to the tendency for extreme scores to move toward the mean over repeated measures. This threat requires a researcher to consider whether a change in a score during the course of an experiment is a result of the treatment or whether it is a result of the natural tendency of extreme scores to move toward the mean. Imagine an experiment in which subjects with scores in the bottom 2 percentile of the SAT are selected for a study. The purpose of this experimental study is to ascertain whether a new technique designed to improve study habits can improve students' SAT scores. Now imagine the experimental findings demonstrate that the new studying technique improved students' SAT scores dramatically. The posttest comparisons show dramatic increases. Nevertheless, the researcher must consider that an alternative explanation for the improved SAT score is regression to the mean. It may be that the new studying approach did improve performance on the SAT. A plausible alternative explanation—a threat to the internal validity of the research—is that of statistical regression. (Note that another plausible explanation may be a testing effect that is described next). Researchers must recognize that these SAT scores may have improved in part or wholly as a result of the tendency for extreme scores to move, or regress, toward the mean.

Testing

Testing is a threat to internal validity that refers to the effect of taking one test on the results of taking the same test later. In terms of experimental research, this means the researcher must be aware that the act of taking the pretest may affect a subject's performance on the posttest. Some students are aware of the testing affect because they have experienced it. Consider the SAT or GRE. Have you been told to take the SAT or GRE multiple times because you did poorly your first attempt? Why? Because it is widely recognized you are

Selection bias: Potential threat to the internal validity of experimental research that refers to differences that may exist between the control and experimental group unbeknownst to the researcher.

Statistical regression: Threat to internal validity of some experimental research where groups have been selected for participation in an experiment based on extreme scores that refers to tendency for extreme scores to move toward the mean over repeated measures.

Testing: Threat to the internal validity of an experiment that refers to the effect that taking one test can have on another; the results of a later test. In terms of experimental research, this means the researcher must be aware that the act of taking the pretest may affect one's performance on the posttest.

© skynesher/iStockphoto.com

When an experiment involves repeated testing, statistical regression is a threat to the internal validity of the experiment.

"Your son, running screaming from the real world, is home."

likely to earn an improved score on the second (or third) exam by simply retaking it. The change in your score is not totally a result of additional studying, but it is also the effect of testing. If there is a change during the experiment, the researcher must ask whether that change is a result of the treatment or of testing (or some combination of both).

External Validity Threats

External validity is the ability to generalize experimental research findings to the population of interest in the "real world." Campbell and Stanley (1963) identified multiple external validity threats that researchers must consider. The generalizability of findings from experimental research is threatened when the treatment or the independent or experimental variable is contingent or dependent on other factors. For this reason, the types of external validity threats are generally described as interactions between the experimental or the treatment variable and some other feature. Like the section on internal validity, this section is not comprehensive in terms of the many potential threats to external validity. Readers seeking additional information on threats to external (and internal) validity are encouraged to access the resources listed at the back of this chapter.

Interaction of Selection Biases and Experimental Variables

The **interaction of selection biases and experimental variables** is an external validity **testing threat** that results from the interaction between some features of the sample and the treatment resulting in nongeneralizable findings. A researcher considering the possibility of this threat must consider whether there is something about those in the experiment such as willingness to volunteer for an experiment that makes them unlike those in the general population. For example, consider research focused on a treatment designed to reduce the negative psychological effects of witnessing violence. The researcher gathers a sample of volunteers to engage in this research. All volunteers are given a pretest to measure the negative psychological trauma resulting from witnessed violence. Half of the volunteers randomly are placed in an experimental group, and the other half are placed in a control group. The treatment designed to reduce psychological trauma is administered to the experimental group. A posttest is then administered to both groups to ascertain whether there is a difference in trauma experienced between the two groups. Imagine the findings show those in the treatment group now register significantly lower levels of trauma. The researcher may conclude that the treatment was effective in reducing trauma. This may be true for those selected for the experiment, but do those findings apply to the larger population of interest? Is it that those who are likely to volunteer for experimental research on trauma differ in important ways from those who do not volunteer? If there are selection biases, then the external validity of the experimental findings is jeopardized.

Interaction of Experimental Arrangements and Experimental Variables

The **interaction of experimental arrangements and experimental variables** refers to how the artificially controlled situations in which experiments are conducted may jeopardize the

External validity refers to the ability to general findings from experimental research into the real world versus the controlled environment of a lab or other artificial setting.

Interaction of selection biases and experimental variables: Threats to the external validity of experimental research resulting from the sample used in experimental research.

Testing threat: Threats to the external validity of experimental research due to the use of pre- or posttests that may lead subjects to respond differently or to be sensitized in unnatural ways to the treatment during the course of the experiment.

Interaction of experimental arrangements and experimental variables: Threats to the external validity of experimental research that refers to how the artificially controlled situations in which experiments are conducted may jeopardize one's ability to generalize findings to a nonexperimental setting.

©Andrew Toos/Cartoonstock.com

The first drug court in the nation was established in Miami, Florida, where innovative approaches to treating those in criminal court includes using a more informal, supportive, nonadversarial approach. One approach used included the use of acupuncture as a part of the drug treatment regimen (White, Goldkamp, and Robinson, 2006). Over time, this "Miami Model," including acupuncture, has been implemented elsewhere in the United States. Although there has been research focused on the effectiveness of drug courts more broadly, no research had been conducted on the effectiveness of acupuncture in these drug courts. The purpose of this research is to examine the effectiveness of acupuncture in a drug court setting.

To conduct this research, White et al. focused on a drug court in Clark County, Nevada, more commonly referred to as Las Vegas, Nevada. The Clark County drug court was an early adoption of the Miami Model, and it normally requires it participants to receive auricular acupuncture at a specific clinic five days a week. Drug court participants typically remain in this initial state of treatment for 30 days or until they produce five clean urine specimens. After that, acupuncture is recommended but not required. Struggling participants can be ordered to resume acupuncture by the judge later in the program.

The research by White et al. included an experimental and a quasi-experimental element. The experimental approach included 336 newly admitted drug court patients who were randomly assign into one of two groups: a nonacupuncture control group and a treatment or an experimental group that receives acupuncture. Those assigned to the control group received relaxation therapy as the treatment alternative. The experiment lasted six months. In addition, a quasi-experimental element included the researchers using existing records to examine the influence of acupuncture on outcomes. This study found that the more acupuncture participants received, the more likely they were to be rearrested or terminated from the program. This finding is not surprising given the use of additional acupuncture to participants who are struggling.

This did demonstrate the need for an experimental design, where participants would be randomly assigned to acupuncture and nonacupuncture groups.

The findings from the experiment showed few differences in the outcomes between the acupuncture and the control groups. As is the nature of research, however, especially true experiments, a few issues were encountered. The first major issue concerned the ethical problem of denying a presumably beneficial treatment to half of the drug court participant population. Given this concern, the drug court officials required that participants who requested acupuncture receive the treatment, regardless of random assignment. In addition, when couples entered drug court together, court officials required they be in the same group. Third, court officials also required those in the control group to receive relaxation therapy (versus nothing). These changes affected the true experimental nature of the design. First, random assignment was not used. Second, the experiment compared the effect of two interventions with no control group. As noted by the authors, "unless an experimental design is implemented perfectly, it is difficult to disentangle the effects of acupuncture from all of the other influences on treatment outcomes" (p. 59). Furthermore, they noted that "the problems with treatment integrity in this study are by no means unique, and in fact they are fairly common in criminal justice field experiments" (p. 59).

The policy implications of this work include that acupuncture participants did as well and certainly performed no worse than those receiving relaxation therapy. This opens up other possibilities for treatment among drug court participants. In addition, this research points to the need to conduct additional research in which a true experimental design is used.

White, M., Goldkamp, J., & Robinson, J. (2006). Acupuncture in drug treatment: Exploring its role and impact on participant behavior in the drug court setting. *Journal of Experimental Criminology, 2*(10), 45–65.

Interaction of testing and experimental variables: Also known as the **reactive effects of testing**, it is a threat to the external validity of an experiment that results from subjects responding differentially to the treatment or being sensitized to the treatment in ways that affect the findings.

Reactive effect of testing: Also known as the "interaction effect of testing." It is a threat to the external validity of experiments that result from subjects responding differentially to the treatment, or being sensitized to the treatment, in unnatural ways affecting the findings.

Reactivity threats: Threats to external validity that refer to how the novelty of participating in research, and being aware that one is being observed during the experiment, influences one's behaviors and views.

Reliability: Refers to consistency of measurement. This includes the quality of measurement taken across a group of subjects over repeated administrations (assuming no real change has occurred), as well as consistency of findings from an experiment conducted repeatedly under the same conditions. In this case, reliability helps establish validity.

ability to generalize findings to a nonexperimental setting. As noted, a feature of experimental research is the control of the experimental situation that assists in a researcher's ability to isolate the effect of the treatment on the outcome. Although important for isolating the effect of the treatment, these same controls on the situation affect the external validity of the findings. A researcher must question whether the artificial environment of an experiment is affecting the findings such that the same outcome would not be found in the "real world." For example, in an experiment, the researcher takes great care to ensure the control and experimental groups are exposed to identical situations. The degree of lighting, temperatures, locations, noise, and other parts of the situation are identical during the experiment. A limitation of this is that in the real world, people are exposed to a variety of situational characteristics. This researcher must ask whether variation in lighting, noise, temperature, or myriad other situational characteristics would affect the experimental outcome. If so, the external validity of the research is questionable.

Interaction of Testing and Experimental Variables

The **interaction of testing and experimental variables**, also known as the **reactive effects of testing**, and the interaction effect of testing, is another way in which the external validity of experimental research can be threatened. In experimental research, the use of pre- or posttests is common. In the real world, however, people are not normally tested during the course of the day. It is plausible then that the use of tests during an experiment may lead to subjects responding differently to the treatment or to being sensitized to the treatment in unnatural ways affecting the findings. It may be that the causal relationship found in an experiment exists only when pretests are used. Alternatively, it may be that the causal effect found in an experiment is found only when posttests are used. On the other hand, it may be true that the causal effect is measured only when both are used. The result is the same—if the presence of tests during the experiment affects the outcome of the experiment, the claim of causality may not be generalizable to the larger population of individuals of interest.

Reactivity Threats

Another threat to the external validity of experimental research is known as **reactivity threats**, which refer to instances in which the novelty of participating in research, and being aware of being observed during the experiment, influences the subject's behaviors and views. In normal life, individuals are not reacting to observation or a part of an experiment. The Hawthorne Effect, introduced in Chapter 6, is one kind of reactivity that may affect the external validity of an experiment. Should subjects alter their behaviors or views because of the novelty of participation in an experiment, then the generalizability of the findings can be called into question.

Reliability

In Chapter 4, we introduced the idea of **reliability** as consistency of measurement. Reliability in the context of experimental research is the same: the notion that repeated experiments by others under the same conditions should result in consistent findings. Zaykowski notes that it is important to recognize that in an experimental setting, reliability is not an indicator of a perfectly designed experiment, but it demonstrates an experiment that produces consistent findings when repeated under the same conditions. In addition, according to Zaykowski, it means getting the same findings with different populations. Offering evidence of reliability bolsters a researcher's claim of validity of an experiment. In others words, with evidence of reliability of experimental findings, a researcher has evidence of valid findings.

Beyond True Experiments

Although true experimental designs are considered the gold standard of research design, it is often challenging, or impossible, to meet the criteria needed for true experiments. For example, a researcher may not be able to control perfectly the administration of the treatment for logistical or ethical reasons. One challenge is that in much research, the researcher relies on someone in a participating organization to administer the treatment. Imagine a community organization that should be randomly choosing youth to administer a particular treatment designed to minimize the risk of joining a gang. Alternatively, imagine an experiment in which police officers are asked to administer treatment of warning versus arrest to every third person disturbing the peace they contact. The community organization worker may choose to provide the treatment to the youth he or she feels would most benefit from it (versus those randomly selected in the experimental group). Or some police officers may feel they know who needs to be arrested versus warned without regard to the whether the person contacted was the third. Melde has been involved in experimental research in which those charged with administering the treatment failed to follow protocol. Melde finds that often administration of treatment based on randomization "is a shock to the system and takes a lot of trust in the researchers. Many organizations do not seem to want that commitment." When the treatment protocol is not followed precisely, the findings of the experiment are jeopardized.

Alternatively, it may be that a researcher cannot randomly assign subjects or units of interest to a control or experimental group. Melde notes that this is a trust issue as well. As researchers, Melde notes, we are always dependent on people and organizations to participate. Although there are always many people and organizations that are willing to participate, it takes only a few who refuse to collapse the entire experiment. Melde has found through his career that people frequently do not like, trust, or understand the purpose of randomization. They find it threatening. Getting buy-in from all engaged in an experiment is important. Even though books like this one offer the seemingly easy ingredients to meet the gold standard in research, it is clear that because universal buy-in is challenging, it is difficult to conduct these studies in reality.

Whenever any of the three characteristics of true experiments—randomization, an experimental and control group, and researcher control of administration of treatment—is missing, a person cannot conduct a true experiment. When this is the case, what is a researcher to do? In these all-to-common situations, researchers have less rigorous options. The following sections describe some research designs that are available when one or more of the three true experiment criteria are not feasible. We begin with the weakest of options by describing pre-experimental research designs.

Pre-Experimental Research

Similar to experiments highlighted in movies like *The Fly*, **pre-experiments** are not true experiments because they are not characterized by the three defining characteristics of true experiments. Frequently, pre-experiments lack control and experimental groups, lack random assignment to control and experimental groups, and lack researcher control of the treatment. Because most pre-experimental designs include only one group, they are also sometimes referred to as single-group experiments. Because pre-experiments frequently involve only one group, pre-experiments do not allow the comparison of tests between the control and the experimental group, which is something that Stanley and Campbell (1963, p. 6) view as a basic requirement of conducting science. Pre-experiments also frequently lack manipulation of an independent variable by a researcher. It is important to recognize that pre-experimental designs are plagued with major issues. It is not possible to discern whether any alleged causal relationships found based on these designs are a result of the treatment, or of a host of other confounding factors. Although pre-experiments have little scientific value, they may be useful for exploratory purposes prior to committing resources to a more rigorous experiment. In this way, pre-experiments offer a cost-effective and timely method to ascertain whether future experimental research is warranted.

Even though pre-experimental designs are discussed in this chapter on experiments, it is a stretch to refer to them as experiments given they frequently have more in common with movie "experiments" than with true experiments. We review pre-experiments next with the strong warning for new researchers to avoid designing experiments like these. Similarly, as critical consumers of information, you should avoid accepting evidence from pre-experimental research.

One-Shot Case Design

A **one-shot case design** is a pre-experimental design including one group that experienced some type of treatment (not administered by the researcher) believed to have been related to some outcome. The researcher compares the findings of the posttest with the personal expectations of the measurement had the treatment not been administered. This design is illustrated as

Treatment ➡ Posttest

Given what has been described earlier in true experimental designs, the problems associated with the one-shot case design should be obvious. This design is problematic in that it does not include random assignment to a control or experimental group. In addition, it only includes one group. This means that the ability of the researcher to isolate the effect of a treatment via a comparison of measurement of the experimental and control group is missing. This design is also lacking in that it does not include the manipulation of the independent variable by the researcher. The control of the situation by the researcher is a key feature that gives rigor to experimental work. In sum, a one-shot case design lacks all three criteria of true experiments, making it difficult to dismiss alternative influences on the outcome. This calls into question any causal claims based on this research design. As a result, it is not surprising that the one-shot case study has weak internal validity.

One-Group Pretest–Posttest Design

The one-group pretest–posttest design is a pre-experimental design that offers slightly more rigor than the one-shot case study. In the **one-group pretest–posttest design**, the researcher uses only one group (no comparison group) and no randomization. Any changes indicated by the pre- and posttest are assumed to have resulted from the treatment. This design is illustrated as

Pretest ➡ Treatment ➡ Posttest

Because of the pretest and posttest in this design, you may believe they can attribute any change measured to the treatment. In reality, any claim of causality based on this design would be suspicious because this design offers no control over confounding factors that can and do influence outcome measures. For that reason, the internal validity of the one-group pretest–posttest design is poor. In addition, external validity is also problematic.

Static-Group Comparisons

Unlike the other pre-experimental designs described, a **static-group comparison design** includes a control group and an experimental group. Still this pre-experimental design lacks random assignment of subjects to the experimental and control groups. This design also lacks researcher control of treatment administration. In addition, this approach is weakened by the lack of pretesting.

E ⟹ Treatment ⟹ Posttest

C ⟹ Posttest

Given the limitations of this design, internal validity is weak because without random assignment to the experimental and control group, any changes measured cannot be stated confidently to be in whole or part a result of the treatment. Rather, confounding factors may be at play. Like all pre-experimental designs, the internal and external validity of the static-group comparison design is poor.

Quasi-Experimental Research

As described earlier in this chapter, there are instances when random assignment to a control or an experimental group is not possible. Fortunately, in these cases, quasi-experimental research designs are an option. **Quasi-experimental research** designs, also called nonran-domized designs, are used when random assignment to a control or experimental group is not possible, impractical, or unethical. Without the benefit of random assignment, valuable attributes found in true experiments are unavailable in quasi-experimental work. The lack of randomization and the loss of associated properties is why Don Campbell referred to quasi-experiments as queasy experiments.

In criminology and criminal justice research, random assignment to control and experimental groups is frequently impossible, impractical, or unethical. Consider research examining how experiencing child abuse influences future victimization risk. It would be unethical to randomly assign children to a control group and an experimental group (who would then be abused—the treatment). It would be unethical to use a true experimental design to study the influence of heroin addiction on future criminality given that would entail randomly assigning some people to an experimental group where they would be forced to become addicted to heroin.

Because random assignment is not often possible or practical does not mean research that cannot use randomization are not valuable. Happily, research designs are available that accommodate this issue.

For some important experimental research, random assignment to a control and an experimental group is not possible. For example, we cannot randomly assign children to an experimental group (receives abuse) and control group (no abuse) to better understand the results of child abuse.

Nonequivalent Groups Design

The most commonly used quasi-experimental design is the **nonequivalent control groups design**, which uses two nonrandomly generated groups that are thought to be similar. The researcher controls the treatment in this design and includes a control and an experimental group. A way to minimize the lack of randomization is to assign similar subjects to a control and an experimental group. Then the experiment is conducted. For example, a researcher may choose census tracts that are similar in nature, or classrooms that are similar in nature, and implement a nonequivalent groups design. This type of design can be illustrated as follows:

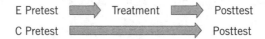

E Pretest ⟹ Treatment ⟹ Posttest
C Pretest ⟹ Posttest

An advantage of this design is that it allows experimental research to be done when random assignment to an experimental and control group is not possible. Nonetheless, this approach has some limitations. Internal validity is jeopardized as a result of selection bias. The researcher may not be able to completely control for selection biases. Internal validity is threatened because the researcher is not able to control for potentially confounding variables that could affect the outcome. External validity can be acceptable because this design occurs in a more natural and less controlled setting. Nevertheless, threats to the external validity such as testing still pose a threat.

Before-and-After Design

Less widely used is the before-and-after design. The **before-and-after design** is a quasi-experimental design that has no random assignment and no comparison group. It does include a pretest and a posttest. This design is illustrated as follows:

Pretest ⟹ Treatment ⟹ Posttest

This design has marginal internal validity given the inability to control for confounding factors making claims of causality challenging. In addition, external validity is also poor.

Natural Experiments

© gwflash/iStockphoto.com

Exposure to lead paint offers an opportunity to investigate its influence on offending.

Natural experiments represent an additional approach that has been used increasingly in recent years as researchers take advantage of opportunities arising in the real world. **Natural experiments** occur outside of laboratories or other artificial locations in the natural world (hence, their name), and they have several attractive qualities. First, natural experiments include both a control and an experimental group. Nevertheless, natural experiments do not allow a researcher to assign subjects to the experimental and control groups. Rather, the assignment to the experimental and control groups occurs naturally. In fact, researchers may not be aware of the mechanism that places a subject in a treatment or a control group or if it was random. Researchers tend to treat the sorting into the two groups as if it occurred randomly. Although natural experiments include a treatment, it does not allow the researcher to control the administration of the treatment. It too occurs naturally. Although a natural experiment shares several characteristics of quasi-experiments, they differ in the researcher's assignment to the control and experimental groups. In quasi-experiments, the researcher has control of this assignment. In natural experiments, assignment to control and experimental groups occurs naturally without the input of the researcher.

Natural experiments are a useful approach when controlled experimentation is difficult or impossible to implement. For instance, through the use of a natural experiment, a researcher could assess the causal influence of lead paint exposure on offending risk as an adult. Clearly, a researcher should not randomly assign children to experimental groups where they would be exposed to lead paint. Yet, a researcher could find subjects who had lived in lead-painted households as a child and compare their adult offending risk with others who had not been exposed to lead paint.

Natural experiments: Occur outside of laboratories or other artificial locations and in the natural world. Natural experiments have a control and an experimental group, but they do not include randomization or researcher control of the treatment.

Common Pitfalls in Experimental Research

Like all research, experimental research must be undertaken with great care and attention to detail. As Dodge has stated, experimental research is challenging to execute. This section addresses some pitfalls that are associated with experimental research. When conducting experimental research, a researcher *must* select the most rigorous design available. Ideally, you can engage in a true experiment using both pre- and posttests or, even better, a Solomon Four Group design. Using a less rigorous design when better options are available is something to be avoided.

A common pitfall in experimental research is claims of causality when the criteria for them are not present. Merely pointing to the proper temporal ordering, association between variables, and a lack of spurious relationships is not enough. This potential pitfall is related to failure to consider threats to internal validity. Has the researcher considered in addition to the causal criteria whether there was experimental mortality that may have affected one's ability to claim causality? Did the researcher address history? Instrumentation? Potential selection biases and other threats? Claiming causality requires more than the presence of three criteria of causality.

Attention to the sample and sample sizes is important in experimental research. Like any research, care must be taken to gather a sample that is representative of the population of interest if possible. In addition, the researcher must gather a sample that is large enough to work with. Too small a sample decreases a researcher's ability to find a significant difference when one exists in the population. Concluding no difference presents problems if this finding is only a result of a small sample size. This clearly has repercussions for generalizing nonfindings to the larger population. In addition, Santos notes that not having a large enough sample size could mean the difference between a successfully completed experiment and one that fails before completion. Santos recommends that researchers and students familiarize themselves with G-Power Software. This is a free, open-source software available on the Web. Although a discussion about how to use G-Power is beyond the scope of this text, you should be familiar with this resource should you find you have a sample size problem.

Treatment of experimental and control groups deserves special attention and is an area of great challenge for experimental researchers. Inadvertently treating the two groups differently (aside from the administration of the treatment) is easy to do, but it will influence and bias findings. A researcher must take great care to ensure both groups are treated equivalently with the exception of the treatment. One way that this can be done is to leave the randomization task to a third party who will not share the outcome with the subjects or the researcher. This blind approach helps to ensure that the random assignment really is that and that the researcher does not accidentally treat one group differently from the other.

Another way that random assignment in experimental research offers special challenges is getting buy-in from potential subjects. Melde recognizes that in some of his research, including that conducted in schools, those in charge of agreeing to participate frequently want assurances that they will (or will not be) in the experimental group. Given what you have learned in this chapter about the importance of random assignment, the problems with that should be clear.

Right to service: Instances in which a subject is denied potentially beneficial treatment in an experiment.

As Melde knows, and conveyed to use during a video interview, "Randomization is key. It is through randomization that we can conclude that all the other unobservable factors are mute."

Another potential error stems from matching. Should a researcher choose to employ matching as a technique, he or she must be certain the matching is based on relevant confounding factors. Failure to do so means that relevant factors may be overlooked, potentially biasing the findings. In addition, the researcher must pay attention to how matching affects the sample. In some cases, the use of matching means the loss of much of the sample that cannot be matched. Attention must be given to how the sample loss may affect the experiment.

Melde finds that a problem that many students studying experimental research has is confusing randomization with the random person on the street. As noted, placing subjects in control and experimental groups randomly means that every subject has an equal chance of being placed in one or the other group. This is *not* the same as conducting research on the random person found on the street. Administering treatment to random people encountered is not a technique used in experimental research. Random selection also does not mean "without a plan." Randomization means the allocation of subjects into control or experimental groups based on a rigorously designed plan.

Cuevas, Dodge, and Santos all point to a major pitfall of experimental research. Specifically, they find that even experienced researchers at times fail to focus on the nuts and bolts of experimental research. First, the researcher must offer a detailed plan about each step. Second, the researcher must follow these carefully devised plans. Third, the research must be prepared for challenges to pop up. Dodge points specifically to difficulties in getting subjects to participate. Too often beginner researchers, and even experienced researchers, fail to appreciate the seemingly mundane elements of the research design. This lackadaisical approach is guaranteed to lead to a poor outcome. And a poor outcome weakens the entire research enterprise.

Ethics and Experimental Research

When conducting experimental research, the researcher must keep ethical considerations at the forefront of every step of the experiment. As in all research, care must be taken that subjects engaged in any experiment do so voluntarily. This means that subjects can withdraw their consent at any time. Attrition from subject loss has ramifications for the experimental design including potential issues with too low of sample sizes affecting the ability to find differences, and mortality issues affecting the internal validity of the work. Although attrition presents challenges to experimental research, it is imperative that subjects not feel pressured to remain in a study they want to disengage from.

Experimental research should be designed to minimize any harm to the subjects, third parties, or researchers. In some types of experimental research where the withholding of treatment may be construed as harmful, this is known as a subject's **right to service**. If the experiment means that some subjects (control group) do not receive treatment that may have beneficial effects, it can be argued that harm ensures. Recall that harm can be physical or psychological. Would recognizing that you are not receiving potentially beneficial treatment cause you psychological distress? Researchers must consider things like this to ensure harm is minimized. Relatedly, Melde cautions against being stuck in the idea that a control group subject gets nothing at all. Being in a control groups does not mean that subjects are kept in some sort of isolation with no interaction or exposure to programs at all. It may be that that those in the control group continue getting treatments that they normally received before the experiment began. Alternatively, it may be that those in the control group get some other type of attention that helps them. As Melde stated to us, "[t]oo often control groups are talked about as the absence of everything. That is not the case. Those in this group may still get some services especially if they are particularly vulnerable." Santos has seen the same in her research. Namely, in an experiment, the treatment group is receiving a treatment, but the control group does not get anything new. This is different from the control group being deprived of anything. This design can be used to gain buy-in from decision makers. A researcher can say, "The treatment group gets this treatment, and once we are able to establish it offers benefits, then the control group will receive it too." It is not about depriving the control group.

Perhaps the trickiest ethical element of much of experiment research is associated with fully informed consent. Why is that? Because experimental research often requires deception. Subjects may be deceived in terms of the full purpose of the research when knowing that purpose may affect findings. In addition, subjects are deceived in terms of knowing the complete procedures used in the experiment. For example, it cannot be revealed if the subject is in the control group or the experimental group. It also cannot be shared if the subject is receiving the treatment or a placebo. This lack of disclosure may be necessary to protect the rigor of the experiment, but it may raise questions about fully informed consent.

Finally, the researcher must be honest about whether the experiment should continue. For instance, if it appears the treatment is not providing benefits and in any way harming the subjects, then the experiment must be stopped. Think back to the Stanford Prison Experiment outlined in Chapter 1, which was shut down early given the harm experienced by those in the experiment. In addition, if it becomes clear the treatment is offering great benefits and continuing the experiment will not add valuable data, it should also be halted and the treatment should be given to the control group. The researchers must ask themselves, "Is it ethical to continue this? Can I ethically finish the experiment?"

Figure 8.9 Use of an Experimental and a Control Group in Experimental Research

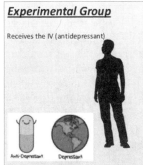
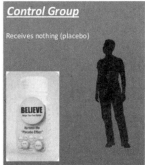

Experimental Research Expert—Chris Keating, PhD

Chris Keating, PhD, is the president and founder of Keating Research, Inc. based in Telluride Colorado. Prior to founding Keating Research, Keating earned an undergraduate degree in political science at Northwestern University and a PhD in economics from the University of Illinois. Although he initially thought he would become a professor, Keating moved to Colorado and put his research skills to use at private firms focused on marketing, customer satisfaction, effective messaging, and political campaigns. To date, Keating has accumulated 21 years of experience based on hundreds of successful polling research, survey research, experimental research, and focus group research projects for candidate, initiative, and issue campaigns. Today his portfolio primarily consists of campaign and issue-based research.

Experimental research is used to assist Keating Research clients who want to understand whether a particular mode of advertising or messaging influences voters' positions on issues or candidates. This is an important area of study because candidates generally do not have many financial resources, and assisting candidates in spending their scarce resources effectively is vital to successful campaigns. Recently, Keating assisted a client to investigate whether regular mail is an effective way to communicate about a ballot measure among likely voters.

To address that research question, Keating gathered a voter universe to serve as a sampling frame of households with likely voters from the geographic region of interest. From this sampling frame, households were randomly selected for participation in the study. Next, the households were randomly placed in the experimental or the control group to maximize the probability that the two groups were equivalent. Next, Keating Research mailed pieces of literature to the households in the treatment group, while households in the control group did not receive any mail pieces. After administration of the mail treatment, Keating Research completed telephone interviews among 1,000 households in the treatment group and 1,000 in the control group, and by using a survey instrument, staff members assessed whether those receiving the mail pieces had different opinions compared with the households in the control group. In particular, subjects were asked on a scale of 0 to 100 how favorable they were toward public officials in their district. A comparison of survey results between the control and experimental groups indicated statistically significant differences between the treatment and control groups. The results of the experiment suggest that the use of mail pieces remains an effective means of communicating with likely voters.

Keating has an important piece of advice for students studying research methods in general and experimental research specifically: Focus on developing and honing attention to detail. Keating finds that many fail to pay attention to detail resulting in flawed work products and damaged reputations. Keating notes that paying attention to detail is a learned skill that a researcher must focus on. For example, when conducting research, the researcher must ensure he or she has the proper sampling frame. Researchers must ensure that assignment to control and experimental groups is random. As a researcher, you must then verify that the control and experimental groups are equivalent (to maximize internal validity of the research). Attention to detail at every step of research design is imperative, and without it, the resulting research is worth little. Students should recognize that it is far more important to design and conduct research precisely with attention to detail than it is to design and conduct research quickly. Keating notes that even though no research is perfect, as a researcher, you must strive for perfection. Keating's life offers evidence that the research methods skills presented in this text are useful in and out of academia. In using these researcher methodology skills, you too can contribute to society in general, and you can do so while living, hiking, and cross-country skiing in a beautiful setting.

Chapter Wrap-Up

This chapter presents foundational information on experimental research. This included what experimental research is, and why it is important. The relationship between causality and experimental research was introduced as well as the criteria for establishing causality. This chapter also presented information describing multiple types of experimental research, including true experiments, pre-experiments, quasi-experiments, and natural experiments. For each type of experimental research, several specific designs, including the advantages and disadvantages of each, were presented. These experimental research designs are shown in Table 8.1 in reference to the criteria for causality.

The chapter also focused on an important consideration for experimental research: internal and external validity. Both internal and external validity were defined, and the relationship between the two were described. In addition, several specific types of internal validity

Table 8.1 Characteristics of Experimental Designs

		Types of Experimental Designs and Their Features		
Design	Randomization	Control and Experimental Groups	Researcher Control Over Treatment	Pretests and Posttests
True Experiments				
1. Two-group posttest only	Yes	Yes	Yes	No
2. Two-group pretest–treatment–posttest	Yes	Yes	Yes	Yes
3. Solomon four group	Yes	Yes	Yes	Yes – doubly so
Pre-Experiments				
1. One-Shot Case Study	No	No	No	No
2. One-Group Pretest–Treatment–Posttest	No	No	No	Yes
3. Static Group	No	No	Yes	No
Quasi-Experiments				
1. Nonequivalent Groups	No	Yes	Yes	Yes
2. Before-and-After	No	No	Yes	Yes
Natural Experiments	As-if randomization	Yes, occurs naturally without researcher influence	No	No

and external validity threats were presented. Understanding these threats enables readers to be alert for these problems.

Some overarching themes of this chapter are that true experimental research is considered by many the gold-standard design in part because it can provide evidence of causality. Also, true experiments are not impervious to problems. Those problems come in the form of poor designs, threats to internal and external validity, failure to execute a well-designed experiment, and a lack of attention to detail. An experimental research expert, Chris Keating, PhD, offered ways in which experimental research is used outside of academia. Some of his work focuses on political campaigns and policy issues using experimental research. Keating's work demonstrates that research methodology skills are useful beyond academia. In addition, Keating's work shows that research methodology can be used in a wide variety of substantive areas beyond criminal justice and criminology. Not only that, Keating's life indicates that someone like you can use these skills to help others and live an enviable lifestyle.

Two of our case studies used experimental design in their featured research: Santos (Santos & Santos, 2016) and Melde (Melde et al., 2009). Table 8.2 summarizes some experimental elements of their research. As this table shows, experimental research comes in many variations making it an excellent choice for many research projects. In the next chapter, the text addresses the topic of secondary data analysis. In this chapter, what secondary data analysis is and the types of data available for this work are described.

Researcher	Type of Experiment Used	Control and Experimental Groups?	Random Assignment?	What Was Treatment?	Researcher Control of Treatment?	Posttest?
Chris Melde	Quasi-experimental; Nonequivalent groups design	Used paired-matching of classrooms	Classrooms were matched but not randomly. Teachers had already chosen to teach the curriculum in many locations. Those classrooms would then be matched with another classroom at the same grade level.	Exposure to a school-based, law-related education program	No. Researchers evaluated the treatment through both a process and an outcome evaluation (see Chapter 11 on evaluation researcher for more information)	Yes, six months later
Rachel Santos	Two-group pretest–treatment–posttest design	Used block matching of geographic hot spots	Yes	Intensive policing	Yes	Yes, 9 months later

Table 8.2 Featured Research and Characteristics of Any Experimental Designs Used

Applied Assignments

The materials presented in this chapter can be used in applied ways. This box presents several assignments to help in demonstrating the value of this material by engaging in assignments related to it.

1. Homework Applied Assignment: Movie Experiments

Select one of the following movies that feature an experiment (some of these are violent so choose carefully):

- *The Belko Experiment* (2016)

- *The Fly* (1986)

- *The Incredible Hulk* (2008)

- *To Search for a Higher Being, the Island of Dr. Moreau* (1996)

- *My Little Eye* (2002)

- *Reanimator* (1985)

After watching the movie you selected, write a paper with the following information. First, offer a summary (in your own words) of the movie. In that summary, describe the experiment featured in that movie. Include the type of experiment the movie portrays (e.g., true experiment, quasi-experiment, etc.) Next, write a section that analyzes the experiment shown in the movie based on the information in this chapter. For example, describe the control groups used, when measurements are taken, etc. Next, outline what would need to happen for the movie to portray a true experiment. Be sure to include information regarding ethics (e.g., voluntary participation, etc.). Be prepared to discuss your findings in class.

2. Group Work in Class Applied Assignment: Designing a True Experiment

As a group, pretend that you have been hired by your university to conduct a true experiment designed to answer the following research question: Does mandatory training of all students on an annual basis about the university's antiviolence policy reduce violence against students at the university? In your plan, you need to identify your population, how you will select subjects for your true experiment, and how many subjects you need. Include additional information on sampling given what you have learned in this class. Next, identify the type of experimental design you will use. Include what exactly you will measure and how often you will measure it. What are advantages of your research design? What problems might your research design encounter? How will you overcome those issues? Be prepared to discuss and share your summaries in class.

3. Internet Applied Assignment: Describing a Real Experiment

Access the webpage for the *Journal of Experimental Criminology* (https://link.springer.com/journal/11292). Find an article that you are interested in. Next, write a paper about this article. Begin the paper with a statement of the purpose of the research and why it is important research. Provide some information about the literature, and how this research will add to the literature. Next, provide details on this experiment. What type of experiment is it? What are the advantages and disadvantages of that type of experiment? Describe the control and experimental groups, the treatment and how it was administered, and the findings. Did they answer their research question? What issues of validity and reliability are present? What would you do differently if you could work with the authors on a replication of this work? Turn in a copy of the journal article with your thought paper.

KEY WORDS AND CONCEPTS

Association 245
Before-and-after design 266
Block matching 251
Block variables 252
Causal relationships 243
Causation 244
Confounders 250
Confounding factor 245
Control group 249
Experimental group 249
Experimental mortality 257
External validity 257
Gold standard 252
History 258
Instrumentation 258
Interaction of experimental arrangements and experimental variables 260
Interaction of selection biases and experimental variables 260

Interaction of testing and experimental variables 262
Internal validity 257
Intervening variable 245
Manipulation of an independent variable 252
Matching 250
Maturation 258
Natural experiments 267
Nonequivalent control groups design 266
One-group pretest–posttest design 264
One-shot case design 264
Paired-matching 251
Predictor variables 248
Pre-experiments 263
Quasi-experimental research 265
Random assignment 250
Reactive effect of testing 262

Reactivity threats 262
Reliability 262
Right to service 268
Selection bias 259
Solomon Four Group 255
Spurious relationship 245
Static-group comparison design 264
Statistical regression 259
Temporal ordering 244
Testing 259
Testing threat 260
Treatment 252
True experiment 248
Two-group posttest-only design 253
Two-group pretest–treatment–posttest design 254

KEY POINTS

- Experimental research is one way a researcher can identify causation, or how an independent variable affects, influences, predicts, or causes the variation in a dependent variable.

- Causation exists when variation in one variable causes, or results in, variation in another variable and is demonstrated with temporal ordering, association, and a lack of spurious relationships.

- A true experiment is an approach to research that has three defining characteristics: at least one experimental and one control group, random assignment to the experimental and control group, and manipulation of an independent or a predictor variable (i.e., treatment) by a researcher.

- Internal validity refers to the degree to which one can conclude causal relationships based on experimental research. Threats to internal validity include things like experimental mortality, history, instrumentation, selection bias, testing, and statistical regression.

- External validity is related to the generalizability of the experimental findings to other people in other situations and environments. This includes interactions of elements of the research with the independent variable. Internal and external validity are frequently at odds with one another.

- Pre-experiments are not true experiments because they are not characterized by the three defining characteristics of true experiments. In general, they do not include control and experimental groups, they lack randomization, and they lack researcher control over the administration of the treatment. In general, pre-experiments should be avoided.

- Quasi-experimental research designs, also called nonrandomized designs, are used when random assignment to a control or experimental group is not possible, impractical, or unethical. The lack of randomization and the loss of associated properties is why Don Campbell referred to quasi-experiments as queasy experiments.

- Natural experiments occur in the natural world and include a control and an experimental group. Nevertheless, natural experiments sort subjects into the control and experimental groups naturally with no control by the researcher.

REVIEW QUESTIONS

1. What characteristics do true experiments have that make them powerful?

2. What are the criteria required to establish causality?

3. How are causation and association related? How are they different? Why does it matter?

4. What are pre-experiments, and what are their limitations? When would one use a pre-experiment?

5. What characterizes quasi-experiments, and how do they differ from true experiments?

6. What is internal validity? What are some threats to internal validity, and why?

7. What is external validity? What are some threats to external validity, and why?

8. What is a natural experiment, and how does it differ from other experimental designs?

9. Under what circumstances would one use a quasi-experimental design versus a natural experiment?

10. What types of pitfalls and ethical considerations are associated with experimental research? How might a researcher avoid them?

CRITICAL THINKING QUESTIONS

1. You wish to demonstrate a program you have established to ensure bystander intervention is effective at increasing bystander intervention on a college campus. How might you go about demonstrating a causal relationship between the intervention and the bystander intervention? What design would you use, and why?

2. You have an interest in understanding how exposure to violence as a child is related to victimization risk as an adult. How might you go about investigating this? What design would you use, and why? What might be threats to internal and external validity of your design?

3. Your boss is considering how to implement a new program to improve employee morale after reading about it online. Your boss asks your opinion about the proposed program. You go to the study used to support this new program and find it was based on a one-shot case study. What does this suggest to you? What do you recommend to your boss about adopting it? Do you recommend the new program be adopted? Why or why not?

4. You have spent the last year planning a new study for your capstone project. Finally it all comes together and you have subjects in the control and experimental groups. The subjects in the control group learn that they are not getting any treatment and object. They feel they are being denied the benefits offered by the treatment. What do you do? How might this event jeopardize your experiment? What will you do?

5. Your classmate is completing her dissertation. She has gathered a sample of 100 individuals, 50 of whom were in the experimental group and 50 of whom were in the control group. At the time she contacts her subjects for posttests, she learns that 35 subjects in her experimental group and 4 in the control refuse to continue. What issues does this raise in her study? What does this mean for her findings? What should she do? Why?

6. Cuevas asks whether the Stanford Prison Experiment was really an experiment at all. Thinking back to the Stanford Prison Experiment, introduced in Chapter 1, which of these characteristics of a true experiment is present in this work? Are there control and experimental groups? Was randomization into a control and experimental group used? What about the researcher's control of a treatment? What research design in this chapter best describes this work? Should it be called an experiment? Why or why not? Do you see elements of other research approaches? If so, what are they? Why do we call this an experiment?

$SAGE edge™

SAGE edge offers a robust online environment featuring an impressive array of free tools and resources for review, study, and further exploration, keeping you on the cutting edge of teaching and learning. Learn more at **edge.sagepub .com/rennisonrm**.

CHAPTER

9

Research Using Secondary Data

Learning Objectives

After finishing this chapter, you should be able to:

9.1 Define research using secondary data and compare it with research using primary or original data. Identify when one approach is preferable to the other. Articulate the advantages and disadvantages of each.

9.2 Describe what criminal justice and criminology data are available at the Inter-university Consortium for Political and Social Research (ICPSR) and how to access those data.

9.3 Identify some of the federal, state, and local sources of secondary data available to you as well as how to access them. Compare the advantages and disadvantages of each of these sources of secondary data.

9.4 Compare strategies for reporting findings produced from secondary data compared with that produced from original data.

9.5 Explain some of the common pitfalls associated with using secondary data and reporting findings from secondary data analysis.

9.6 Evaluate the ethical considerations associated with using secondary data in particular.

Primary data collection: Also known as "original data collection." When research methodologies are used in the collection of original data.

Introduction

Up to this point in our textbook, you have learned about stages of conducting research, including literature reviews, research design, sampling, and so on. We then moved to descriptions of different ways to gather data that can be used to answer your research question. The last two chapters focused on collecting *original* data to answer specific research questions and to accomplish specific research goals. Chapter 7 discussed gathering original qualitative data, or non-numeric data, which are useful in answering many research questions. Chapter 8 described experimental and related research that is useful for gathering original data. When researchers use these methods to collect original data, they are engaged in **primary data collection,** also known as original data collection.

In this chapter, we shift gears. When conducting research, it is common for some to use primary data collected by some other person or group, to test new hypotheses, or to answer new research questions. When you use and analyze data collected by someone else, you are engaged in **secondary data analysis**. One of our featured researchers, Rod Brunson, in his video interview conducted for this book, highlights the fact that even researchers like him who primarily conduct research with qualitative data still use and benefit from secondary data. He notes they can be used in a mixed-methods approach (using multiple approaches). And Brunson uses existing data to triangulate findings he has arrived at through qualitative data. As has been stated throughout the text, the use of multiple approaches is an ideal one. Secondary data use is no different. Mary Dodge, another featured researcher, who, like Brunson, focuses primarily on research in which she collects her own qualitative data, agrees—secondary data are useful for adding to findings reached using other approaches.

This chapter offers information about using existing data, secondary data, to answer your research question. To do this, the chapter begins by clarifying why researchers use existing data. After answering the why question, we move toward a more in-depth presentation about what secondary data are, including many commonly used examples of secondary data.

We also identify where these data can be accessed and downloaded online. Afterward, we provide a brief description of how to present findings from second data analysis, and some of the common hazards that should be avoided when conducting secondary data analysis. In particular, we discuss specific ethical considerations and common pitfalls associated with using secondary data to answer your research question. The chapter wraps up with an interview about secondary data analysis with Jenna Truman, PhD. Truman works as a statistician with the Department of Justice, at the Bureau of Justice Statistics (BJS), in the National Crime Victimization Survey (NCVS) Unit. As noted, we begin our discussion of secondary data in the next section by answering the simple but important question, "Why conduct research using secondary data?"

Secondary data analysis: Research methodology that involves the reanalysis of data collected by someone else, for some other purpose, to answer a new research question or to test a new research hypothesis.

Why Conduct Research Using Secondary Data?

Secondary data represent a critically important information resource for researchers. Without secondary data, huge bodies of literature and our subsequent understanding about many criminal justice topics would not exist. As many chapters in this book demonstrate, gathering original data can be time-consuming, very expensive, and require huge resources in terms of people, computing equipment, transcription services, and so on. Given these costs, secondary data analysis is an attractive alternative to primary data collection methodologies. In short, secondary data analysis saves time, money, and other valuable resources; it provides an option to investigate very large data sets that a single researcher may not be able to collect on his or her own; and it provides the opportunity to investigate myriad criminal justice topics.

For example, the availability of secondary data, like data from the National Crime Victimization Survey (NCVS), allows researchers like Heather Zaykowski to analyze nearly five decades worth of criminal victimization data so she can conduct her research with no data collection costs. She simply downloads NCVS data from the Internet. Access to secondary data, like those found in the Dating Violence among Latino Adolescents (DAVILA) data, also enables researchers to study important victimization topics focused on Latino adolescents; again, at with no data collections costs. Featured researcher Carlos Cuevas and his colleague Chiara Sabina, collected DAVILA originally, and it exists now online so that others may use it for their own research purposes (www.icpsr.umich.edu/icpsrweb/NACJD/studies/34630).

So much secondary data exist that are readily available right now that if you knew where to look, you could go online, download data collected by other researchers, and run statistical analysis on these data in less time than it would take to finish reading this chapter. Accessing existing data for secondary data analysis is just that easy. Given the volume of data that is being collected in contemporary society, and how accessible these data are, coupled with the speed (instantaneously) at which it can be disseminated, you should be able to see why it makes sense for researchers to consider research using secondary data as an option for answering research questions. In fact, with these benefits, featured researcher Rachel Boba Santos encourages students and junior faculty she knows to consider strongly focusing solely on research using secondary data early in their careers. In addition, being adept at using secondary data makes one marketable outside of academia. This is exactly how Santos first used secondary data. She worked as a crime analyst using existing data in a law enforcement agency before earning her PhD and becoming a professor.

Aside from the saving resources, researchers opt to engage in secondary data analysis because available data often include very large samples and are collected using sound (and often complex) methodological techniques. Again, data collected for the NCVS provide an excellent example. Recall that in Chapter 1 we explained that the NCVS is an ongoing survey of a nationally representative sample of about 169,000 people, age 12 or older, living in U.S. households. The NCVS is a federally funded data collection program, which is designed to gather data on hundreds of variables related to victims, offenders, and incidents of nonfatal crimes against persons and property. No other source of victimization data is available with this level of detail, so researchers interested in conducting victimization research are able to study myriad victimization topics quickly, easily, and inexpensively by using existing NCVS data. Great attention has been given to the design and administration of the NCVS since its inception in the early 1970s. Time and time again, it has been shown that the NCVS produces accurate and reliable data about nonfatal violent victimization in America. Given the high quality of NCVS data, it is unlikely that a researcher could conduct his or her own study that produced "better" victimization data than what is currently available. Therefore, researchers like Zaykowski (and the authors of this text) interested in doing victimization research often conduct secondary data analysis of NCVS data. This is done because the data set is large, of high-quality, nationally representative, and easily accessible online.

Finally, the breadth of data that can be found in existing secondary data sources may be unmatched by what researchers can collect on their own. This is often the case because the federal government has funded many of the studies that have produced data that can be used in secondary data analysis; and when it comes to funding research, few can match the funding power of the federal government. This means that more data can be collected during these primary data collection efforts than what could have been collected if a researcher conducted a study on his or her own, without funding from the government. In other words, the adage "You get what you pay for" holds true when it comes to many of the available data sets that researchers use for secondary data analysis—those data may be free to you, but a lot of money went into their creation. Again, the NCVS provides an excellent example.

What Are Secondary Data?

Answering research questions does not always require collecting original data directly from or about research subjects. Instead, answering research questions can be accomplished using existing data collected in a previous study. These existing data are known as secondary data. Use of secondary data is a popular approach because it can produce new empirical knowledge without the time and money associated with collecting original data. Two of our case studies provide examples of the value of using secondary data to answer new research questions.

Santos and colleague's research on hot spots and high-intensity policing on known felons was conducted using secondary data collected by the Port St. Lucie Florida Police Department (Santos & Santos, 2016). The pretests and posttests of the experimental and evaluation research were based on police data. Four impact measures using police data were used:

1. The count of residential burglary and theft from vehicle reported crime in each hot spot

2. The count of all arrests for each targeted offender

3. The count of burglary, theft, and dug offense arrests in each hot spot of individuals who live in the hot spot

4. The ratio of burglary, theft, and drug offense arrests per individual arrested who live in the hot spot

The purpose of the intervention of high-intensity policing was to put the felons in the experimental groups on notice they were being watched. It stands to reason then that over time, the counts of each of these measures should decrease compared with those of the control hot spots where policing was unchanged. This research would not be possible without the use of the secondary data at the police department. Although the availability of these data in other jurisdictions varies, it points to the need to be creative when thinking about where secondary data are and when building relationships so that you can access data should you learn they exist.

Zaykowski's (2014) research used completely different secondary data to examine what increases the odds that crime victims will use victim services. She answered these questions by analyzing a subset of the NCVS data collected between 2008 and 2011. Those data included variables she needed to answer her research questions including whether victimizations were reported to the police, victim's demographics, the victim's relationship to an offender, the victim's mental and physical state, and whether the victim accessed services.

Zaykowski (2014) followed a series of steps to begin her study that were consistent with the typical stages of research presented in Chapter 1. For example, she began by developing her research questions and reviewing the existing literature. Instead of designing a study that required her to collect original data, however, she knew her study could be successfully completed using existing NCVS data. In other words, her research design did not require her to collect new data from crime victims across the nation. She knew that data existed already in the form of the NCVS. Zaykowski also knew those NCVS data were available at no cost to her through the Inter-university Consortium for Political and Social Research (ICPSR), located at the University of Michigan. To gain access to these data, all she needed to do was create a free account and agree to ICPSR's terms of use. You can go there now to see the vast amount of secondary data they house (https://www.icpsr.umich.edu/icpsrweb/). She was also aware that her university's institutional review board (IRB) would support her using NCVS data for her research because the data are de-identified, and she knew she would be able to apply for an expedited IRB review.[1]

Zaykowski was convinced that using secondary data was the best way to go about answering her research questions. Knowing certain characteristics of the NCVS program and about the data collected during NCVS interviews supported her decision. She knew, for example, that the NCVS program

- produces high-quality data because, in part, trained interviewers are used to conduct each survey;

- draws a nationally representative sample of people 12 years if age or older, living in U.S. households, which meant her findings could be generalized to the broader population;

- produces very high response rates, which meant problems associated with survey nonresponse would not likely be an issue;

- could provide her with more robust data about crime victims than other existing data could, like official police data, because incidents that are both reported and not reported to police are identified;

- includes multiple variables associated with victims, offenders, and nonfatal criminal incidents, thereby making it possible for her to answer all of her research questions; and

---

[1]At the time of her study, Zaykowski's university's policy required *all* research of any kind to be reviewed, including secondary data. If the same study was conducted today, according to Zaykowski, it would not be reviewed at all because it would not fall within the regulatory definition of research involving human subjects (see the section titled "Ethics Associated with Secondary Data Analysis" for more details).

- have been used in previous studies to generate knew empirical knowledge; in other words, she knew that using NCVS data for secondary data analysis was an established and acceptable approach to conducting research.

After Zaykowski received confirmation from her university's IRB committee that her research was exempt from full review, she proceeded to visit the ICPSR website, registered, agreed to the terms of use, found the NCVS data she needed, downloaded it, and began answering her research question using these secondary data. Her (2014) analysis of the existing NCVS data involved examining nearly 5,000 records to predict the likelihood a person would seek help from victim services after personally experiencing criminal victimization.

By using secondary data, Zaykowski's (2014) research identified several significant predictors of victim service usage, including victimizations involving female victims and sexual assaults. That is, when a victimization involved a female victim, victim service use was more likely. Furthermore, when a victimization involved a sexual assault, victim service access was more likely. Zaykowski also discovered that victim services are more likely to be used when a crime is reported to the police, and when more than one offender is involved in an incident. In addition, she discovered using secondary data that victims who had job problems and physical distress are more likely to contact victim services than those that do not. Some of the findings produced by Zaykowski's study reaffirmed results found in other studies, but some of her findings represented new knowledge. Collectively, her investigation into victim service usage made an important contribution to our field. In addition, it did not require her to collect original data, meaning her research was accomplished more cheaply, quickly, and robustly.

Frequently Used Secondary Data

In relating Zaykowski's story, we described how the NCVS data were obtained from the Interuniversity Consortium for Political and Social Research or ICPSR. The ICPSR data archive is just one of many places researchers can go to get access to existing data that can be used in projects involving secondary data. We discuss how to access data files located at ICPSR in the following section, along with some of the kinds of data available and commonly downloaded. We also identify other resources that are less well known and used in criminal justice and criminology research. You can access any of these sources of secondary data for use in answering many of your research questions.

ICPSR

ICPSR is located on the campus of the University of Michigan, in Ann Arbor. ICPSR was established in the early 1960s; and at that time, it had no permanent staff, 25 member institutions, total revenues of less than $70,000, and only one data archive. Over the next 15 years, the consortium grew to more than 200 member institutions, with a budget of more than $1.3 million. ICPSR also employed more than 60 staff members. In 1978, the National Archive of Criminal Justice Data (NACJD) was established at ICPSR.

The National Archive of Criminal Justice Data (NACJD) is a specialized data archive sponsored by the Bureau of Justice Statistics (BJS), National Institute of Justice (NIJ), and the Office of Juvenile Justice and Delinquency Prevention (OJJDP). The purpose of the archive is to preserve and distribute crime and justice data for secondary data analysis. These data come from federal agencies, state agencies, and investigator-initiated research projects. Currently, 12 subject areas make up the NACJD archive:

- Attitude surveys

- Community studies

- Corrections

- Court case processing

- Courts

- Criminal justice system

- Crime and delinquency

- Official statistics

- Police

- Victimization

- Drugs, alcohol, and crime

- Computer programs and instructional packages

In addition to this accessible criminal justice secondary data, ICPSR provides online resource guides that offer detailed information about some of the more complex and frequently accessed data collections that help facilitate the use of data housed at the archive for secondary data analysis. More recently, the website incorporated a useful online data analysis system that allows users to conduct analyses on selected data sets without having to download the data onto their own computer or without having access to statistical analysis software. Figure 9.1 shows the online data analysis interface, analyzing crime data from the Uniform Crime Reporting program that are archived at ICPSR.

Figure 9.1 Online Data Analysis Interface, Analyzing Crime Data From the Uniform Crime Reporting Program That Are Archived at ICPSR

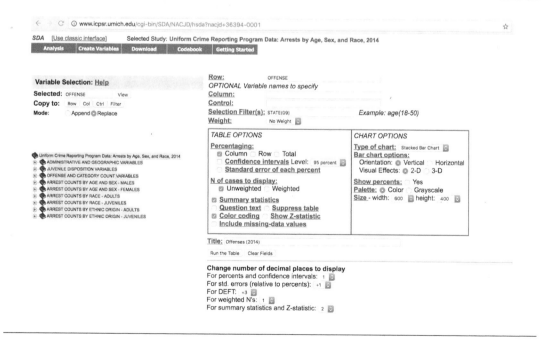

Today, ICPSR has more than 750 member organizations, more than 100 staff members, and operates on revenues of greater than $17 million. During the past several decades, the number of special topic archives housed at ICRSR has also increased. These archives now include the Substance Abuse and Mental Health Data Archive (SAMHDA), Data Sharing for Demographic Research (DSDR), Project on Human Development in Chicago Neighborhoods (PHDCN), the National Addiction & HIV/AIDS Digital Archive Program (NAHDAP), NCAA Student-Athlete Experiences Data Archive, and the National Archive of Data on Arts & Culture (NADAC).

Not only does ICPSR offer secondary data, and information about those data; it also helps to develop quantitative and qualitative analytic skills among students and social scientists through various workshops and seminars. The ICPSR Summer Program in Quantitative Methods of Social Research is one of the more popular programs offering many workshops. For example, in 2015, 81 courses, taught by 101 instructors from across North America and Europe, were offered through ICPSR's Summer Program. Participants included students, faculty, and researchers from more than 40 countries, 300 institutions, and 30 disciplines. Although ICPSR does not offer as many qualitative workshops and seminars, it does offer some. For example, you can take a class in Process Tracing in Qualitative and Mixed Methods Research in the same summer program. To learn more about ICPSR and to become registered so that you can access data housed in its archives, visit https://www.icpsr.umich.edu/icpsr-web/ICPSR/.

The main role of ICPSR, however, is to archive political and social research data. Accessing these secondary data is simple and straightforward. First, your university, government organization, or other institution must be an ICPSR member institution by paying a subscription fee. The fee is based on the size of an organization, and it can cost more than $17,000 each year for large universities and colleges. Once your university or organization is a member, however, you will have free access to ICPSR data archives. You can find out whether your university or college is a member institution by checking to see whether it is listed at www.icpsr.umich.edu/icpsrweb/membership/administration/institutions.

If you are affiliated with a member institution, three basic steps can be followed to conduct secondary data analysis using ICPSR data: (1) accessing the ICPSR archive, (2) finding the data you need to answer your research question, and (3) downloading these data onto your local hard drive. Accessing ICPSR data archives requires a new user to create a MyData account. The MyData account will permit you to download data available only to ICPSR members. Once an account is created, you can log in to the archive. All users of the archive must also agree to terms of use outlined by ICPSR. On subsequent visits, users may log in to ICPSR using their Facebook® or Google® account that is affiliated with their university or organization via third-party authentication.

Step 2 of the process for conducting secondary data at ICPSR involves finding the specific data you need to answer your research question. ICPSR offers several different ways for finding data once a registered user has logged on. You can browse for data by topic, data collection themes, geography, or series name (e.g., NCVS). Data can also be queried based on when it was released (i.e., searching for data released in the last week, month, or year). Alternatively, data can be searched for by how often they are downloaded or by which countries are using ICPSR data. In other words, researchers can limit their search for data to the most frequently downloaded data found in ICPSR archives. When searching for data on the archive, do not forget some of the strategies presented in Chapter 3 that relate to using Boolean operators and filters. These strategies can help you find just what you are looking for more quickly and easily even at ICPSR.

The third and final step in obtaining data housed at ICPSR for use in research using secondary data involves downloading data files from the archive to your local hard drive. Figure 9.2 is a screenshot from the ICPSR archive. It shows some of the options available to users who want to download the FBI's UCR data from 1980. Notice that different subsets of the data can be downloaded in different formats for use on a variety of statistical software programs

Figure 9.2 Different Data File Types That Can Be Downloaded From ICPSR That Contain Information From the FBI's UCR Program

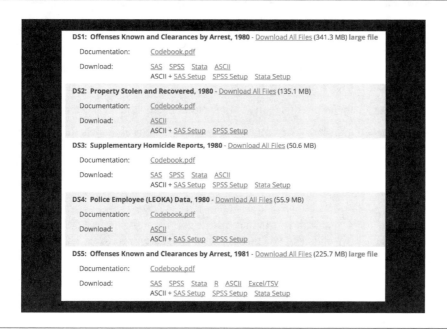

Figure 9.2 Different Data File Types That Can Be Downloaded From ICPSR That Contain Information From the FBI's UCR Program

(including SPSS™, SAS®, STATA™, R, Excel™, and ASCII). Import files for SPSS, SAS, and STATA are also available. These software programs are discussed in greater detail in Chapter 12. Finally, **codebooks** that provide documentation on how the data files are structured, the variables contained in the data set, and the coding of specific variables is available for download for each of the data sets. These data and their supporting documents and files can be downloaded individually or as a compressed file onto a user's local hard drive. Once they are, the user can then begin his or her secondary data analysis—that is, the analysis of these secondary data.

Codebook: Documentation for a data set that explains how the data files are structured, how the variables are contained in the data set, and the type of coding of specific variables is also available for each data set.

Federal Statistical System (FedStats)

Secondary data files can also be found on sites other than ICPSR. The Federal Statistical System website called FedStats is a useful example. FedStats was launched in 1997 and offers open access to a wide range of statistical data generated from the federal government. What makes FedStats attractive to many researchers is that they do not need to know in advance which federal agency is responsible for collecting or producing the data. More than 100 federal agencies feed data into FedStats, and users of the site can easily search it using basic search terms like "crime," "population," and "health" to find data that they can use to conduct secondary data analysis.

If a federal agency is a recognized U.S. Statistical Program and reports annual expenditures of at least $500,000 in one or more of the following categories, their data are available through FedStats:

- Planning of statistical surveys and studies, including project design, sample design and selection, and design of questionnaires, forms, or other techniques of observation and data collection

- Training of statisticians, interviewers, or processing personnel collection, processing, or tabulation of statistical data for publication, dissemination, research, analysis, or program management and evaluation

- Publication or dissemination of statistical data and studies

- Methodological testing or statistical research

- Data analysis

- Forecasts or projections that are published or otherwise made available for government-wide or public use

- Statistical tabulation, dissemination, or publication of data collected by others

- Construction of secondary data series or development of models that are an integral part of generating statistical series or forecasts

- Management or coordination of statistical operations

- Statistical consulting or training

That these data are available to you should make sense because your tax dollars are used to collect these data. They belong to you the taxpayer. The easiest way to access nearly 200,000 data sets provided through FedStats is to visit www.data.gov.

U.S. Department of Justice

One primary contributor to FedStats is the U.S. Department of Justice (USDOJ), whose mission is to "enforce the law and defend the interests of the United States according to the law, to ensure public safety against threats foreign and domestic, to provide federal leadership in preventing and controlling crime, to seek just punishment for those guilty of unlawful behavior; and to ensure fair and impartial administration of justice for all Americans" (USDOJ, n.d., "Our Mission Statement"). In executing its mission, the USDOJ produces data that are often overlooked by academics and other researchers studying important topics related to criminal justice and criminology. Nevertheless, the USDOJ provides a comprehensive list of open data it provides free to the public. For example, you can access data on these topics:

- Longitudinal Perspective on Physical and Sexual Intimate Partner Violence Against Women

- List of the civil rights matters recently addressed by the Federal Coordination and Compliance Section of the Department of Justice's Civil Rights Division

- Americans with Disabilities Act (ADA) Regulations

- Annual Parole Survey, 2000

To obtain any of these data, requests must be made to the agency's contact overseeing a program or project's data. Contact names and e-mails are listed with each data set. A full list of the USDOJ's open data sets as well as contact name and contact information can be viewed at https://www.justice.gov/data/.

Federal Bureau of Investigation (FBI)

When researchers look for criminal justice and criminology data to conduct secondary data analysis, the two agencies they most often turn to are the Federal Bureau of

Investigation (FBI) and the Bureau of Justice Statistics (BJS). Researchers go to the FBI for data because they manage one of the most well-known data collection programs in our field: the Uniform Crime Reporting (UCR) Program.

The UCR Program is a local, state, tribal, and federal law enforcement program that provides one of the two national measures of crime in the United States. UCR data are voluntarily submitted to the FBI from law enforcement agencies throughout the country. Data are submitted to the FBI either through a state's UCR Program, or they are submitted directly to the FBI from a law enforcement agency. Today, the UCR program gathers crime reports from approximately 17,000 (of the more than 18,000) law enforcement agencies from all states, the District of Columbia, and some U.S. territories. Furthermore, the UCR Program describes crime occurring in almost the entire nation. The purpose of the UCR Program has always been to serve the needs of law enforcement agencies. Over the past several decades, data from the UCR Program have become one of the country's leading social indicators and offer researchers a rich source of information about crime reported to the police. Thousands of researchers (including students) have seized on this opportunity throughout the years. For example, the Uniform Crime Reporting Program Data [United States]: 1975–1997 is one of the most frequently downloaded data sets from ICPSR. According to the ICPSR website, in 2016, more than 14,000 files in this data series were downloaded from the archive. This may not be surprising given the amount of data collected under the umbrella of the UCR Program. Many of those data collection efforts are described in the next section.

Summary Reporting System (SRS aka UCR). When the UCR Program began, it collected crime data. Over time, as the program began gathering other types of data, what was originally called the UCR data was renamed the Summary Reporting System to distinguish it from the umbrella program sharing the same name. The Summary Reporting System (SRS) primarily offers *counts* of each type of in-scope crime. These include murder and non-negligent manslaughter, rape, robbery, aggravated assault, burglary, larceny/theft, motor vehicle theft, and arson. The SRS was not designed to gather data on characteristics of the crimes, crime victims, or offenders, although some exceptions existed. SRS data, for example, includes these details: whether a rape was completed or attempted, whether a burglary involved forcible entry, type of motor vehicle stolen, and whether a robbery involved a weapon. Even though these data are valuable, the lack of additional details for all SRS crimes is a limitation of these data. More recent data made available under the UCR Program offer more detail.

Supplementary Homicide Reports (SHR). If your research focuses on murder or non-negligent manslaughter in the United States, then the Supplementary Homicide Reports (SHR) are a good source of secondary data. Although the FBI has long collected data on murder, it was only in 1976 that detailed data from this program were gathered and archived. The SHR provides detailed data on murder (both justifiable and not), including the victim's age, sex, and race; the offender's age, sex, and race; weapon type (if any); victim–offender relationship; and the circumstances that led to the murder. The patterns uncovered by these data have been used to identify trends in murder, and in the development of policy recommendations focused on murder, like the pattern shown in Figure 9.3.

National Incident-Based Reporting System (NIBRS). The important data gained by gathering details of homicide in the SHR made clear the need to gather details for nonfatal

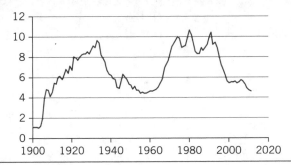

Figure 9.3 Trend in Murders and Non-Negligent Homicides per 100,000 Inhabitants

Source: Data are based on annual estimates of homicide from previously published versions of *Crime in the United States*. Data for 1989 to 2008 reflect updated homicide estimates from *Crime in the United States, 2008*. Data for 2009 and 2010 reflect updated homicide estimates from *Crime in the United States, 2010*.

crimes as well. Those details are now available in the National Incident Based Reporting System (NIBRS). This data collection effort was introduced in the mid-1980s and gathers detailed incident data about crimes in the SRS. These additional data gathered include the nature and types of crimes committed during each incident, victim(s) and offender(s) characteristics, type and value of stolen and recovered property, and characteristics of arrested individuals. The NIBRS also offers data on new offense categories of crime, including "crimes against society." Crimes against society consist of drug/narcotic offenses, pornography/obscene material, prostitution, and gambling offenses. NIBRS presents quantitative and qualitative data that describes each incident and arrest.

The modernization, enhancements, and improvements found in NIBRS over the SRS have resulted in data that better serve the needs of its primary constituency—law enforcement. Even though law enforcement officers are the primary focus on these data, NIBRS data have been valuable to policy makers and other researchers regarding victimization risk.

Law Enforcement Officers Killed and Assaulted. Yet another excellent FBI source of data is found in the Law Enforcement Officers Killed and Assaulted (LEOKA) data set. The purpose of this UCR Program collection is to provide law enforcement managers, trainers, and personnel data needed to improve officer training to prevent death and serious injury of law enforcement officers. These data include information on incidents resulting in the assault and killing of on-duty officers. Details gathered as part of LEOKA data include the circumstances of the incident, such as the type of call answered, type of weapon used, and details about the type of patrol the officer was on at the time of the incident.

Hate Crime Statistics. By using data gathered in the UCR Program, the FBI publishes an annual hate crime statistics report. This congressionally mandated publication originated from the Hate Crime Statistics Act of 1990. Since then, additional congressional acts have extended the data collection and have expanded protected groups. In 1996, this became a permanent annual data collection effort. Today, by using data from the hate crime file that can be downloaded at ICPSR, you can answer research questions focused on hate crimes. Given that these data are collected in the UCR Program, it should come as no surprise that the hate crime data on murder and non-negligent manslaughter, rape, aggravated assault, simple assault, intimidation, arson, and destruction, damage, or vandalism of property, are voluntarily submitted to the FBI by state and local law enforcement agencies. Hate crime data available as part of the UCR program include the number of incidents, offenses, victims, and

The process by which offenders choose their victimization targets, whether they are persons or property, is an area of interest for many researchers. Johnson, Summers, and Pease (2009) tested a popular explanation for residential burglaries: the boost hypothesis. Specifically, they tested whether the boost hypothesis explains both residential burglary and theft from motor vehicle (TFMV) in the "short run" (i.e., when typical circumstances of the locales are evident). They referred to this type of boost account of burglaries as "offender foraging." Six research hypotheses were tested:

H1: Burglary will cluster in space and time.

H2: Sharing similar motivations to burglary, theft from motor vehicle offenses (TFMV), will cluster in space and time.

H3 and H4: Burglaries (or TFMV) offenses detected by the police occurring close in space and time are more likely to be cleared to the same offender(s) than other pairs of crimes of the same type.

H5: If there is evidence of offender versatility across the two offense types of interest, incidents of burglary and TFMV will cluster in space and time.

H6: If H5 is supported, pairs of detected burglaries and TFMV offenses occurring close to each other in space and time will be those most likely to be cleared to the same offender(s). If H5 is unsupported but this hypothesized pattern is evident, this would suggest that the patterns are the result of a detection bias rather than of offender foraging strategies.

To answer these questions, the researchers conducted secondary data analysis of recorded victim and crimes incident data recorded by the police. Space–time clustering was identified using sophisticated analytic tests developed in the field of epidemiology, designed specifically to determine space–time patterns in the spread of disease. To determine whether patterns of offending supported Johnson et al.'s foraging hypotheses, they developed a contingency table for both crime types that showed the likelihood the same offender was involved in both incidents that were identified in the cotangent models. This information was presented by specific day/time intervals (i.e., the percentage of near repeat burglaries that occurred within 14 days and within 100 meters of each other).

The results of Johnson et al.'s analyses of the BCS data revealed that during a 20-year period (i.e., 1988 to 2006), public contact with police in England and Wales steadily declined, especially since 2000. Declines in police–public contact were consistent across all types of contact, including self-initiated contact as a result of victimization and police-initiated contact.

In line with previous research, there was clear evidence of space–time clustering for both residential burglaries and for thefts from motor vehicles (i.e., more crimes occurred near to each other in space and time than would be expected). Furthermore, their results suggested that there were no associations between the timing and locations of incidents examined (i.e., for either burglaries or TFMV) other than that which could be explained by their general distribution in space or time. Finally, repeat burglary victimizations detected by police were almost always cleared to the same offender, and a similar pattern was observed for TFMV. In summary, the results of the researchers' investigation supported their hypotheses, collectively, providing support for theories of offender foraging.

The authors suggest that their findings have clear implications for the forecasting of crime locations and detection strategies, which could be supportive of law enforcement agencies' efforts to fight crime. They argue that their findings extend the knowledge about crime forecasting by earlier work, showing that the generation of crime forecasts that consider when and where crimes occurred in the past improves predictive accuracy relative to standard methods of crime hot spot analysis (for both residential burglaries as well as for theft from motor vehicles).

Johnson, S. D., Summers, L., & Pease, K. (2009). Offender as forager? A direct test of the boost account of victimization. *Journal of Quantitative Criminology, 25*(2), 181–200.

offenders in reported crimes that were motivated in whole or in part by a bias against the victim's perceived race, religion, sexual orientation, ethnicity/national origin, or disability.

Cargo Theft Statistics. A part of the UCR Program entails gathering detailed data on cargo theft. According to the FBI (2015), cargo theft is

> the criminal taking of any cargo including, but not limited to, goods, chattels, money, or baggage that constitutes, in whole or in part, a commercial shipment of freight moving in commerce, from any pipeline system, railroad car, motor truck, or other vehicle, or from any tank or storage facility, station house, platform, or depot, or from any vessel or wharf, or from any aircraft, air terminal, airport, aircraft terminal or air navigation facility, or from any intermodal container, intermodal chassis, trailer, container freight station, warehouse, freight distribution facility, or freight consolidation facility. For purposes of this definition, cargo shall be deemed as moving in commerce at all points between the point of origin and the final destination, regardless of any temporary stop while awaiting transshipment or otherwise. ("What is cargo theft?" para. 1)

Cargo theft data, and reports focused on it, are recent. They became a topic of interest because of the economic nature and the risk of terrorism associated with these crimes. Cargo theft data collection was mandated by the USA Patriot Improvement and Reauthorization Act of 2005. These data are collected using NIBRS, and the first FBI report on the topic was published in 2013.

These secondary data sets are only some of what the FBI offers. Because data needs change over time, you should expect to see data collection efforts change as well. Returning to the FBI.gov website, as well as other sources of data described in this chapter, will help you stay up to date on available secondary data that you can use in your research.

Bureau of Justice Statistics (BJS)

The Bureau of Justice Statistics (BJS) is another valuable resource for secondary data that you can access easily. In 1965, it was recognized that the nation needed additional data on crime, data that were not limited only to that which was reported to the police. Commissions considering the need for additional data recommended the establishment of a national criminal justice statistics center in 1968. In response, the Law Enforcement Assistance Administration (LEAA) was established. The LEAA, which later was renamed the Office of Justice Programs (OJP), housed the National Criminal Justice Information and Statistics Service (NCJISS). The NCJISS became the Bureau of Justice Statistics in 1979, with the passage of the Justice System Improvement Act. The mission of NCJISS—and later BJS—is to gather and analyze crime data, publish crime reports, and make available this information to the public, policy makers, media, government officials, and researchers.

BJS publishes data regarding statistics gathered from the 50,000 agencies that comprise the U.S. justice system. Much of these data are made available, usually through ICPSR's NACJD, for secondary data analysis. BJS also maintains more than 30 major data collection series. Periodically, the Bureau receives authorization to conduct special data collections in response to programmatic, policy, and legislatives needs for the department, the administration, Congress, and the criminal justice community. Statistics from these data are published annually on criminal victimization from data collected through the National Crime Victimization Survey (NCVS) program. Other annual publications produced from data that BJS collects (and are available publicly) include populations under correctional supervision from data collected through its National Corrections Reporting program, and federal criminal offenders and case processing statistics from its Federal Justices Statistics program. A list of all the Bureau's data collection series can be found at www.bjs.gov/index.cfm?ty=dca and include, but are not limited to the following (BJS, 2017):

Annual Probation Survey and Annual Parole Survey

- Collects data from probation and parole agencies in the United States on an annual basis

Arrest-Related Deaths

- A component of the Deaths in Custody Reporting Program (DCRP); it is a national census of all manners of arrest-related deaths and includes all civilian deaths that occurred during, or shortly after, state or local law enforcement personnel engaged in an arrest or restraint process

Capital Punishment

- Provides an annual summary of inmates admitted to and removed from under sentence of death (including executions) and of statutes pertaining to capital punishment and annual changes to those statutes

Census of Federal Law Enforcement Officers

- Collects data from all federal law enforcement agencies with arrest and firearms authority

Census of Jail Inmates

- Conducted approximately every five to seven years, it provides information and data on supervised populations, inmate counts and movements, and persons supervised in the community

Census of State and Local Law Enforcement Agencies

- Provides data on all state and local law enforcement agencies operating nationwide

Emergency Room Statistics on Intentional Violence

- Collects data on intentional injuries, such as domestic violence, rape, and child abuse, from a national sample of hospital emergency rooms

Human Trafficking Reporting System

- Developed in 2007 to collect data on alleged human trafficking incidents from state and local law enforcement agencies

Law Enforcement Management and Administrative Statistics

- Conducted periodically since 1987, the program collects data from more than 3,000 general-purpose state and local law enforcement agencies, including all those that employ 100 or more sworn officers and a nationally representative sample of smaller agencies

National Corrections Reporting Program

- Collects offender-level administrative data annually on prison admissions and releases, year-end custody populations, and parole entries and discharges in participating jurisdictions

National Crime Victimization Survey

- Serves as the nation's primary source of data and information on nonfatal property and personal criminal victimization in the United States

National Judicial Reporting Program

- Provides detailed information and data on felony sentencing from a nationally representative stratified sample of state courts in 300 counties

National Prisoner Statistics Program

- Produces annual national- and state-level data on the number of prisoners in state and federal prison facilities

National Survey of DNA Crime Laboratories

- Provides national data on publicly operated forensic crime laboratories that perform DNA analyses

Police-Public Contact Survey

- Provides detailed data on the characteristics of persons who had some type of contact with police during the year, including those who contacted the police to report a crime or were pulled over in a traffic stop

Survey of Campus Law Enforcement Agencies

- Provides data describing campus law enforcement agencies serving U.S. 4-year universities or colleges with 2,500 or more students

Survey of State Criminal History Information Systems

- Collects data used as the basis for estimating the percentage of total state records that are immediately available through the FBI's Interstate Identification Index (III) and the percentage that include dispositions

Survey of State Procedures Related to Firearm Sales

- Collects data about the state laws, regulations, procedures, and information systems related to sales and other transfers of firearms that were in effect as of June 30 of the collection year

The U.S. Bureau of the Census, which is part of the U.S. Department of Commerce, collects data for most of the statistical series that BJS sponsors.

U.S. Department of Commerce

The U.S. Department of Commerce (USDOC) was established in 1903 as the U.S. Department of Commerce and Labor. Today, its primary task is to create jobs, promote economic growth, encourage sustainable development, and improve standards of living for all Americans. The department's mission is "to promote job creation, economic growth, sustainable development, and improved standards of living for Americans" (USDOC, n.d., para. 2). In achieving this goal, the USDOC generates a substantial amount of data related to economic conditions and demographic characteristics of the labor force. These data are used for business and government for decision making and for helping to set industrial standards. Researchers in criminal justice and criminology can also use these data for conducting secondary data analysis. Of particular interest to them are data produced from the U.S. Census Bureau.

Census Bureau

You have probably heard of the U.S. Bureau of the Census, which is more commonly referred to as the Census Bureau. You have likely heard of the Census Bureau because it is the federal agency responsible for producing data about the American people and its

US Department of Commerce

economy. In particular, the U.S. Census Bureau is the federal agency in the United States responsible for administering the decennial census, which is used to allocate seats in the U.S. House of Representatives based on states' populations. In addition to the decennial census, the Census Bureau conducts several surveys, including the American Community Survey and the Current Population Survey. Researchers often look to these comprehensive data sets about individuals and the communities in which they live when conducting secondary data analysis. For example, Cuevas says he often uses census data in writing grant applications to help make arguments about where the people he wants to study are located and that there is a sufficient number of potential research participants in those locations to study.

The American Community Survey (ACS). The American Community Survey (ACS) is the largest survey (only the U.S. Census, which is not a survey, is larger; the NCVS is the second largest survey conducted by the Census Bureau) that the Census Bureau manages. The survey is administered to more than 3 million people living in America every year, collecting data on income and education levels as well as on employment status and housing characteristics. After the data are collected, the Census Bureau aggregates responses with previously collected data one, three, or five years prior to produce several sets of estimates. First, it produces one-year estimates for areas of the country with a population of at least 65,000. Second, it produces three-year estimates for areas with at least 20,000. Finally, it produces five-year estimates for all census administrative areas called block groups, respectively.

Block groups are a geographic area used by the Census Bureau for aggregating population data; a population of 600 to 3,000 people typically defines a single block group. ACS are available online through at American Fact Finder (https://factfinder.census.gov/) and include data on both people (e.g., age, sex, education, and marital status) and housing units (e.g., financial and occupancy characteristics). This website can be queried to find population figures about specific geographic areas, based on data collected by the Census Bureau, including data collected from the ACS. In addition, data can be downloaded from the site onto a researcher's local drive so he or she can use it for secondary data analysis.

The Current Population Survey (CPS). The Current Population Survey (CPS) is another survey administered by the Census Bureau. The CPS is smaller than the ACS. It is a monthly survey of approximately 60,000 U.S. households sponsored by the Bureau of Labor Statistics. Its primary aim is to gauge the monthly unemployment rate in the United States, providing one of many indicators of the economic health of the nation. Information related to individuals' work, earnings, and education are available in the CPS data. Survey supplements are also commonly used as part of the CPS to measure other topics of interest to the nation, such as data on child support, volunteerism, health insurance coverage, and school enrollment. Researchers conducting secondary data analysis can access data produced from the CPS at the Integrated Public Use Microdata Series (PUSM), the world's largest individual-level population database. The IPUMS website is located at https://www.ipums.org.

Geospatial Data

The data available for the secondary data analysis already discussed thus far in this chapter represent the tip of the iceberg with respect to what is out there. There are thousands of data sets that researchers can access and download quickly and easily through the Internet. The challenge for those wanting to use existing data to conduct secondary data analysis is finding data files that contain the variables you need to answer your specific research question(s). Increasingly, research in criminal justice and criminology is focusing on the spatial and temporal characteristics of crime, and many of those who are interested in this topic turn to existing **geospatial data** to help support their research projects.

Block groups: Geographic area used by the Census Bureau for aggregating population data that is typically defined by a population of 600 to 3,000 people.

Geospatial data: Data containing spatially referenced information (e.g., the latitude and longitude coordinates) included as part of all the data contained in a data set.

Geospatial data have spatially referenced information (e.g., the latitude and longitude coordinates of a particular point or an administrative area such as a census block, block group, or tract) included as part of all the data contained in a data set. Geospatial data are particularly useful in that it allows researchers to consider the importance of time and place as they relate to their research question. A more detailed look at the use of geospatial data is considered in the next chapter.

In addition to the decennial census, the ACS, and the CPS, the Census Bureau produces geographic data files that can be used in secondary data analysis. They have provided these data for more than 25 years through their Topologically Integrated Geographic Encoding and Referencing (TIGER) program. TIGER products are extracted from the Census Bureau's TIGER database, which contains geographic features like roads, railroads, rivers, and legal and statistical geographic areas (e.g., census block groups). The Census Bureau offers several file types and an online mapping application to support analysis of TIGER data. For example, Figure 9.4 shows income data mapped by county for 2015. Some of the different types of data that can be downloaded from https://www.census.gov/geo/maps-data/data/tiger.html include the following:

TIGER/Line Shapefiles

- Can be used in most mapping projects and are the Census Bureau's most comprehensive data set. They are designed for use with geographic information systems and can be useful in various crime-mapping projects. Chapter 10 covers **Geographic Information Systems (GIS)** in greater detail, but it can be defined as a branch of information technology that involves collecting, storing, manipulating, analyzing, managing, and presenting geospatially referenced data.

TIGER Geodatabases

- Useful for users needing national data sets on all major boundaries by state.

TIGER/Line with Selected Demographic and Economic Data

- Compiles data from selected attributes from the 2010 Census, 2006–2010 through 2010–2014 ACS five-year estimates and **County Business Patterns (CBP)** for selected geographies. CBP data contain annual economic information by industry and can be used to support studies that consider economic activity of small areas as part of their research question.

Cartographic Boundary Shapefiles

- Provide small-scale (limited detail) mapping projects clipped to shoreline. Designed for thematic mapping using GIS.

TIGERweb

- Can be used for viewing spatial data online or streaming to your mapping application.

Although data available from the TIGER program are generally not primary data that have been used to answer a particular research question, like NCVS or UCR data, they do represent existing data that can be used by researchers conducting studies that use secondary data analysis. It is especially true for studies interested in some aspect of criminal justice and criminology that are focused on identifying or explaining spatio-temporal patterns in data.

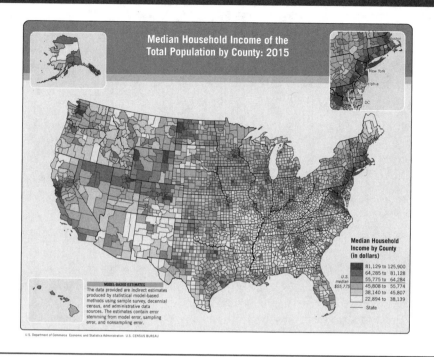

Median Household Income of the Total Population by County: 2015

Median Household Income by County (in dollars)

81,129 to 125,900
64,285 to 81,128
55,775 to 64,284
45,808 to 55,774
38,140 to 45,807
22,894 to 38,139
U.S. median $55,775
State

MODEL-BASED ESTIMATES
The data provided are indirect estimates produced by statistical model-based methods using sample survey, decennial census, and administrative data sources. The estimates contain error stemming from model error, sampling error, and nonsampling error.

U.S. Department of Commerce Economic and Statistics Administration U.S. CENSUS BUREAU

Source: U.S. Census Bureau, Small Area Income and Poverty Estimates (SAIPE) Program, Dec. 2016.

Center for Disease Control and Prevention

A useful, but often overlooked, source of secondary data is the Centers for Disease Control and Prevention (CDC). Violence is a public health issue, and for this reason, the CDC gathers data valuable to criminal justice researchers. The CDC is a part of the Department of Health and Human Services and is located just outside of Atlanta, Georgia. Of particular interest is the National Center for Injury Prevention and Control found in its Office of Noncommunicable Disease, Injury and Environmental health. The CDC has come a long way since its participation in the Tuskegee Syphilis Experiment that ended in 1972 (see Chapter 1 for details). Today, the CDC gathers data on violence, although the 1996 Dickey Amendment stated that "none of the funds made available for injury prevention and control at the Centers for Disease Control and Prevention may be used to advocate or promote gun control." Even though this avenue is not one that is examined at the CDC, it does provide useful information and data on other types of violence, including elder abuse, sexual violence prevention, global violence, suicide prevention, and child abuse and neglect (to name some). The CDC's violence prevention webpage can be accessed here: https://www.cdc.gov/violenceprevention/index.html

A particularly useful CDC data source is the National Vital Statistics System (NVSS) program, which provides data on vital events including deaths (but also births, marriage, divorces, and fetal deaths). Mortality data, including that on homicide, from the NVSS are a widely used source of cause-of-death information. It offers the advantages of being available for small geographic places over decades, allowing comparisons with other countries. For example, Table 9.1 provides the numbers taken from death certificates of assaults leading

Table 9.1 Numbers of Assaults Leading to Death for All People, for Males, and for Females

	Both Sexes			Males			Females		
Cause of Death	Number of Deaths	Percent Total Deaths	Rank	Number of Deaths	Percent Total Deaths	Rank	Number of Deaths	Percent Total Deaths	Rank
Assault (homicide) (X 85-Y09,Y87.1)	15,872	0.6	17	12,546	0.9	15	3,326	0.3	22
Assault (homicide) by discharge of firearms (X93-X95)	11,008	0.4	—	9,278	0.7	—	1,730	0.1	—
Assault (homicide) by other and unspecified means and their sequelae (X85-X92,X96-Y09,Y87.1)	4,864	0.2	—	3,268	0.2	—	1,596	0.1	—

Source: Kochanek et al. (2016).

to death for all people, for males, and for females. These secondary data show that in 2014, 15,872 people in the United States died from an assault: 12,546 were male, and 3,326 were female. Homicide by assault was the 17th leading cause of death in the country in 2014. Although these represent just a few of the data available, all data can be accessed and downloaded at https://www.cdc.gov/nchs/data_access/vitalstatsonline.htm.

Also available is an online tool that allows you to gather data instantly. This tool named CDC WONDER is found here https://wonder.cdc.gov/controller/datarequest/D76. Using it, you can gather data from the DCD about the underlying cause of death from 1999 to 2015. You can restrict those data by geographic regions, demographics, days and months. Until 2013 the FBI did not gather data on the Hispanic or Latino origin of homicide victims nationally. Before then, this was the only location one could find homicide numbers for Hispanics.

State Statistical Agencies

Statistical Analysis Centers (SACs) are state agencies created by legislation or Executive Order that gather state-level data to better understand criminal justice topics in that state. SACs are like BJS but at the state level. In other words, state SACs collect, analyze, and disseminate criminal justice data, but they do it at the state level, not at the national level like BJS. State SACs can be located in universities, within other state agencies, within not-for-profit organizations operating at a state level, or within a State Administering Agency (SAA). An SAA is a state agency responsible for distributing formula grant funds or grants that are noncompetitive and based on an existing formula for allocation, from the U.S. Department of Justice's Office of Justice Programs (OJP) to agencies within the SAA's state.

Currently, 48 of the 50 states have a SAC. It's up to each state government to decide whether it wants to establish a SAC, and not all states have done so. The two exceptions are Texas and North Carolina (see Figure 9.5). SACs are important agencies to keep in mind given they frequently are looking for people with research methodology skills. They can be an excellent place to begin your career. A comprehensive list of state SACs, which includes contact information for each state SAC director, can be found at www.jrsa.org/sac.

If you as a researcher are interested in analyzing data collected at the state level or produced from a state project, then you may find the information you are looking for at

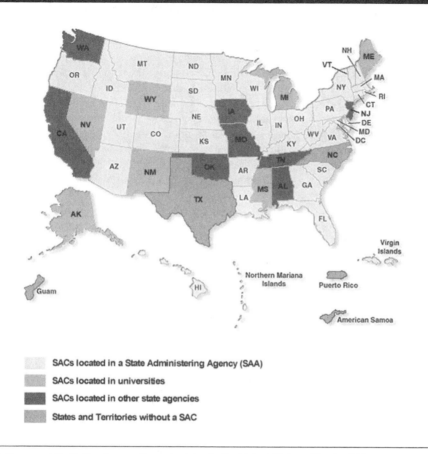

SACs located in a State Administering Agency (SAA)

SACs located in universities

SACs located in other state agencies

States and Territories without a SAC

Note: Texas and North Carolina are the only states in the United States without a SAC.

your state SAC. For example, the Arizona SAC is run out of the Arizona Criminal Justice Commission (www.azcjc.gov). The Arizona SAC facilitates the sharing of information and data about Arizona's criminal and juvenile justice systems. It shares data with policy makers, practitioners, researchers, students, and the public through their Community Data Project. These data can be used in studies involving secondary data analysis that are specifically focused on issues in Arizona or projects that have been administered through Arizona's SAC. Other state SACs operate similarly. SACs are actually great places to work as well, so keep them in mind when you are looking to begin a career with your methodological skills.

Local Statistical Agencies

Finally, secondary data analysis can be based on data obtained from local governments or local government agencies. The amount and type of data available locally varies by place. Links to local governments, by every state in the country, can be found on the USA.gov website (https://www.usa.gov/local-governments). For example, following the link on this site to Colorado's local government can lead users to demographic profiles of the state's general population and housing characteristics, by the state's cities and towns (https://demography .dola.colorado.gov/census-acs/2010-census-data/#census-data-for-colorado-2010). These data are based on 2010 U.S. Census data and can be downloaded from the American Fact Finder website, but if a researcher is interested in these data specifically, then it may be faster to go directly to Colorado's Division of Local Government for data (https://www.colorado .gov/pacific/dola/division-local-government).

A particularly useful source of local data can be found at police agencies' websites. For example, Kansas City, Missouri, homicide and monthly crime data and statistics can be found on the police department's website located at http://kcmo.gov/police/homicide-3/ crime-stats/#.WUR212jys2w. Similarly, UCR data for San Bernardino, California, are available on their police department's website at https://www.ci.san-bernardino.ca.us/cityhall/police_ department/crime_statistics/default.asp. It's important to remember that local agencies sometimes offer more data online than they submit to the FBI, so it is worthwhile looking at your local police department's webpage. Although the amount and quality of data available differ by agency, this is a great place for students and researchers to find data on crime-related topics in their community.

This book cannot possibly cover all local sources of crime and criminal justice data available online. We encourage you to use an online search engine to get a better sense of what's out there that is related to your area of interest to your particular areas of interest. For example, if you are interesting in researching courts, then search on "courts" and "data" and "<your state's name here>." If you are interested in conducting research on corrections, do the same. With minimal effort, you can find an amazing amount of data available for you to use.

Disadvantages of Using Secondary Data

Secondary data offer an amazing opportunity to conduct research quickly, efficiently, and inexpensively. Although they offer so many benefits, like all things research, analysis involving secondary data has some disadvantages. When you use secondary data, you must be aware of these issues to avoid making a mistake that could jeopardize the quality of your research. One major disadvantage to using secondary data is that the available existing data may not be able to address your specific research question. For example, if your research question focuses on how a person's immigration status is related to their victimization risk, you may be thinking the NCVS would be an ideal data set to use. Although the NCVS is huge and has thousands of variables, it does not gather data on people's immigration status. Imagine your research question focuses on whether students enrolled in a college or university part time have victimization rates that differ compared with their full-time counterparts. Where might you go for these data? Again, the NCVS seems like a good source, but it does not differentiate between full- and part-time students. These data are not collected during NCVS interviews. If these were your research questions, you would have to keep searching for other possible existing data, or devise a plan to collect your own data.

A second issue to be aware of when conducting secondary data analysis is that existing data may not code variables or have the response categories you need for your research project. The example about full- and part-time students in the NCVS is a good example of this problem. Although the NCVS gathers data on whether a person is a college student, it does not code the responses in more than a nominal (i.e., "Yes" or "No")

Imagine your research question focuses on whether students enrolled in a college or university part-time have victimization rates that differ compared to their full-time counterparts. Where might you go for these data?

way. Another example of this possible shortcoming in existing data concerns age. Perhaps your research question focuses on how each year of age is related to recidivism risk. Perhaps you have found a source of data on recidivism that codes respondents' age in an ordinal fashion (e.g., in categories of 0–10 years, 11–20 years, 21–30 years, etc.). Because these data are coded this way, your research question cannot be answered with these data. If a study wanted to use existing data to conduct secondary data analysis, the way in which variables are originally coded may limit (or even prohibit) its utility. In conducting secondary data analysis, you must ensure that the variables you need to answer your research question are coded in a way that is appropriate for your project.

A third limitation to be aware of when considering using secondary data is that a researcher must understand (as best as possible) how the original data were gathered.

"So things are good, stuff is OK, and I reiterate my request for more specific data."

In conducting secondary data analysis, you must ensure that the variables you need to answer your research question are coded in a way that is appropriate for your project.

Just downloading a codebook and using a variable are not enough. Because a researcher conducting secondary data analysis did not participate in the planning and execution of the primary data collection process, they may not be able to know exactly how or why it was collected the way it was originally collected, which is another disadvantage. If you are using secondary data, you must look for literature that describes how the data were collected and some history about it. This may indicate that you can use it, but we need to issue a caveat about it. For example, when we discussed some of the FBI data collections, we noted that the purpose of these data collection efforts was to inform law enforcement. It was not intended that they be used in ways that many researchers use them. That is okay in some circumstances but not in others.

For instance, some researchers use the SRS to estimate criminal victimization it the United States. This is okay as long as it is acknowledged that those data only represent what is reported to the police. We know that a lot of crime is never reported to the police. This issue illustrates that a researcher conducting secondary data analysis needs to try to understand all he or she can about the quality of the existing data used, including how seriously the data might be affected by problems such as low response rates or respondents' misunderstanding of specific survey questions. In other words, if the researcher conducting secondary data analysis was not present during the data collection process, he or she has to determine independently the overall quality of the data to be used and must decide, based on this information, whether it is suitable for his or her investigation. Much of this methodological information should be available, but it may not always be. If you cannot find information in writing, contact the agency collecting it and ask to talk to an expert on the data there. If you share what you are considering doing with the data, the agency can offer advice as to the feasibility of your project.

Finally, it is often that secondary data do not provide nuance about topics. Dodge finds this to be true in much of her research. Dodge has worked with others on projects that include secondary data. Nevertheless, she finds that using secondary data to supplement what is learned through qualitative data leads to the richest research. In addition, Dodge finds that looking at studies using secondary data highlights gaps in the literature she can fill conducting research using qualitative data. Brunson reiterated this point by noting to us, "I may be able to use secondary data to learn about the frequency of police stops, but generally I cannot find any information about the nature of the stop." In studies of procedural justice, like Brunson conducts, the key is what happened during the stop, not that a stop happened necessarily.

Reporting Findings From Secondary Data Analysis

When reporting results from studies based on the use of secondary data, you should always include some basic information about the data used in your analysis. This includes reporting how the data were obtained, and how they are capable of answering your study's research question(s). This is exactly the kind of information Zaykowski (2014) included when she reported her findings about the use of victim services by crime victims, using data from the NCVS. Here is a direct passage from her journal article to illustrate:

> Data for this study came from the National Crime Victimization Survey (NCVS; 2008–2011) incident files (U.S. Department of Justice, 2013), which were de-identified datasets available through the Interuniversity Consortium for Political and Social Research (ICPSR). The data are available to researchers by creating a free account and agreeing to the ICPSR's terms of use. The Institutional Review Board of the University of Massachusetts-Boston approved this research. The survey years 2008 through 2011 contained information about mental and physical health and related consequences of victimization that were not available for earlier surveys. The surveys were stratified multistate cluster samples of approximately 50,000 households each survey year that included non-institutionalized persons age 12 years and older living in households across the United States. Because the design was not a simple random sample, there is some variation in the probability of selection in addition to non-sampling error. The response rate for the NCVS averaged over 95%. Surveys from 2008 through 2011 were combined into one dataset. (pp. 365–366)

There are several things this first paragraph contains worth noting that you should emulate should you use secondary data. First, Zaykowski (2014) identified that the primary data were collected as part of the NCVS program. Second, she stated that these data were obtained directly from ICPSR. Third, Zaykowski explained that she received IRB approval for using the NCVS for this research. Fourth, she included specific information about characteristics of the NCVS data that conveys to the reader some of the reasons it is appropriate to use to answer her specific research question. Information about the NCVS data presented in the article continued with the following passage. Keep in mind that Zaykowski did not gather these data, yet she reports about how the data were originally collected. This information is only available by reading documentation associated with the NCVS, as well as information on variables included in the codebook:

> Trained researchers conducted in-person interviews with all members in each sampled household using a screening questionnaire. This screening questionnaire asked subjects about demographic information and about events that may have happened to them in the past 6 months. For example, subjects were asked "has anyone attacked or threatened you in any of these ways: With any weapon, for instance, a gun or knife . . . ? With anything like a baseball bat, frying pan, scissors, or stick . . . ?" If subjects had experienced any of the situations, they were then asked to complete an additional questionnaire for every incident. The incident questionnaire asked subjects where the incident occurred, how well they knew the perpetrator, how the perpetrator attacked the victim and if any weapons were used, what injuries the victim received, how the crime affected the victim's mental and physical health, what type of help the victim sought including if the incident was reported to the police, if there was anyone else present at the scene of the incident,

and the victim's relationship to the offender. The trained interviewer determined, based on this information, into which crime category the incident fit. (p. 366)

This next paragraph conveys additional information about the quality of the NCVS data and how some of the variables used in the study were measured. When findings from secondary data analysis are reported, this level of detail about the data being used helps the reader contextualize results from the secondary analysis. In other words, details about data quality help convince the reader that their use is justified. Zaykowski (2014) also includes information specific to the number of cases used in her analysis and the criteria used for selecting them. This is valuable information about the NCVS sample. Recall in our earlier chapter on sampling, we discussed the value of representativeness; Zaykowski has noted that her study uses both a representative sample of persons age 12 years and older in households and that her research is based on a large sample. In part, this information is presented so that someone else can replicate her study:

> The dataset of 27,795 cases contained both property and violent crime victims. Only victims of violent crime, however, were asked if they sought assistance from a victim service agency. Therefore, the sample was limited to victimization by violence (sexual assault/rape, physical assault, and robbery). Included cases significantly different from excluded cases (i.e., property crime victims) in that a greater proportion of violent crime victims were black/African American, male, not married, had lower household incomes, and were younger in age ($p < .10$). Subjects whose household income was unknown were retained in the sample through a dummy variable (compare with Kaukinen, Meyer, & Akers, 2013). Subjects with missing data were excluded from the analysis using listwise deletion ($n = 330$). The final sample included $N = 4,746$ cases of whom few sought services (7.8%). (p. 366)

Although this paragraph has some more advanced technical information in it, notice that it demonstrates the need for researchers—whether a student, a professor, or an analyst working outside a university setting—to include specific information about the data he or she used to conduct secondary data analysis. When you are conducting research using secondary data, you should include important information such as the:

1. Identify the project or program undertaken to collect the primary data.

2. Explain how the primary data were obtained from those who collected it.

3. Include a statement about whether they have received IRB approval to use the primary data.

4. Provide a justification for why the primary data are being used instead of other existing data.

5. Identify the unit of analysis.

6. Discuss which variables from the primary data are focal variables and how they were measured.

7. If the entire primary data set is not used, explain why and how the subset of data was extracted, including details of the final sample size and how missing data were handled.

By providing these details, readers can more easily draw conclusions about whether it is appropriate for a researcher to conduct secondary data analysis on a particular existing data set.

Common Pitfalls in Secondary Data Analysis

Not unlike the other research methodologies discussed in previous chapters, researchers must think carefully before engaging in secondary data analysis. Secondary data analysis is subject to many pitfalls. Some challenges associated with using this particular research methodology can threaten the overall quality of a research project, which threatens the overall quality of your research. This section addresses the most common pitfall associated with secondary data: forcing the data to be what they aren't.

In discussing secondary data analysis, many researchers will express concern over the fact that not being part of the original research team can pose serious problems when working with existing data. Santos says it is the biggest pitfall associated with working with secondary data. She explained during a video interview conducted for this textbook that "[i]t boils down to trying to change the data to adapt to your research question, or changing your research question to adapt to the data. In other words, sometimes researchers can't truly test what they think they are testing when they use secondary data; when researchers try to adapt existing data to their own research question, it simply makes the existing data too watered down." As Santos stated, it can get "ugly." Brunson shared similar concerns during a phone interview. He said that when researchers and students use secondary data, they are not intimately knowledgeable about the data, compared with the researcher who collects his or her own original data. The users of secondary data do not always understand the way the data were gathered, why certain questions were asked, and why other questions were omitted. Brunson noted that users of secondary data often "don't understand how decisions about how questions were asked and the data gathered were made; and how these decisions impact the overall quality of the existing data." In short, he noted, "Users of secondary data inherit the short comings of the decisions made by the original research team. Without knowing everything there is to know about the data and how it was collected, chances are that it will not be used in the way it's should be."

GIVE ME A MOMENT TO FIND UNBIASED DATA THAT SUPPORTS CALLING YOU AND YOUR IDEA STUPID.

© Tom Fishburne/Marketoonist.com

© marketoonist.com

In discussing secondary data analysis, many researchers will express concern over the fact that not being part of the original research team can pose serious problems when working with existing data.

Not surprisingly, Cuevas echoed this concern about secondary data. He believes that too often researchers think that "just because they can read a data codebook up and down, look at every variable, and look at the data documentation, researchers have a good sense of the data; but they don't." During his video interview, he noted, "It's one thing to know how the sausage was made, but it's another thing to actually make the sausage. The process of making the sausage is what matters." Cuevas also thinks there is a bit of a "round-hole-square-peg" problem with secondary data analysis. He believes that researchers often try to make variables in existing data reflect the concepts they are interested in studying, when often they do not, and suggests that when this occurs, secondary data analysis becomes a potentially misleading and poor methodology. Dodge dealt with these data issues most recently on an internal project using police use-of-force data. She was provided data from a law enforcement agency that she felt looked wrong. She did not feel the data she had been provided really constituted police use-of-force data regardless of how it was labeled. A second request was made for additional data, and those data still looked wrong. Somehow, in the course of Dodge's research and trying to understand exactly what data the agency had, the media got ahold of the same data and reported about them as police use-of-force data. They were wrong. Unfortunately, the questions surrounding these secondary data stemmed from issues about what the data actually referred to. Cuevas offers a good strategy for researchers to avoid the common pitfalls associated with secondary data analysis: Research must "stay in their lane" and not use a variable for purposes far removed from its original purpose. Santos and Dodge both have been called in on projects where an organization needed its data analyzed, yet the organization did not even have a codebook describing its data. Both researchers were faced with a puzzle about what the variables were, what the data and variables were supposed to represent or measure, what the data actually represented, and even what the codes for the response categories were. To say these projects are challenging is an understatement.

Dodge identifies a final pitfall associated with secondary data: that it can often be rife with missing data. **Missing data** refer to when there are no data recorded for a particular variable. Missing data come in two broad forms. First, it can refer to when a person was supposed to include information and did not do so. These are nonresponses. For example, you may be asked on a survey to provide your annual household income but opt to leave that answer blank. That is missing data. It can also refer to not applicable responses. For example, a survey asks how many children live in your home. Assuming you have none, the survey then skips you to a question focused on something unrelated. For those who noted they had children living in the home, the survey then asks how many males and female children live in the home. When we look at the resulting data, the person with no children in the home would not have a value recorded for the sex of children in the home. This would appear as not applicable missing data. A problem with some secondary data is that they include a large amount of missing data raising challenges with analyzing the data. Understanding if what is missing is truly missing, versus not applicable missing, is important to know and often not clear with some secondary data.

> **Missing data:** When no data are recorded for a particular variable.
>
> **Public use data:** Data that are prepared with the intent of making them available to anyone (i.e., the public).

Ethics Associated With Secondary Data Analysis

Many universities and institutions acknowledge that some research projects involving secondary data analysis may not meet the definition of "human subjects" research; and therefore, they may not require IRB review. Nevertheless, some secondary data analysis projects do require IRB approval. This section of the chapter is designed to provide guidance on IRB policies and procedures that could be applied to projects using existing data. Despite this information, researchers conducting secondary data analysis on existing data must always have their host university or institution make the final assessment on whether IRB review is necessary. In other words, researchers should not assume that just because they are using secondary data that they are *always* exempt from the IRB review process.

Although projects that involve secondary data analysis do not involve interactions or interventions with humans, they may still require IRB review. Typically, IRB review is required for secondary data analysis when the data being used meet the definition of human subject data, as defined by 45 CFR 46.102(f): *living individuals about whom an investigator obtains identifiable private information for research purposes* (Health and Human Services, 2009). When the analysis of existing data does not meet this definition, however, IRB review usually is unnecessary.

In general, secondary data analysis research is exempted from IRB review most often because the definition of human subject data is not met. This is typically the case with most public use data. **Public use data** are data that are prepared with the intent of making them available to anyone (i.e., the public). These data are not individually identifiable, and therefore, analysis would not involve human subjects. As a result, most IRB committees would recognize that the analysis of these de-identified, publicly available data would not constitute human subjects research and would not require their review. If a public use data set is manipulated in some way, however, say by merging it with another public use data set, and the creation of this new data set could identify individuals, then IRB review of the study would likely be required.

If subjects' private information were contained in an existing data set that was being used in a secondary data analysis study, then an IRB committee would likely deem it as research involving human subjects and require a review. In this situation, private information is information provided by research subjects during the original study for specific purpose of participating in that research and that the subject reasonably expects will not be made public (e.g., a medical or a school record). On the other hand, private information does not include data that may have been made available (or could be made available) publicly (i.e., university faculty members' salaries). If an existing data set does not contain "private information," then secondary data analysis using it would not likely require IRB review.

Even if primary data sets contain private information that could identify specific research subjects, the identifiable information is often stripped from the file when the data are archived. For example, many of the data sets archived at ICPSR have been **de-identified**, or stripped of all identifiable information so that there is no way it could be linked back to the subjects from whom it was originally collected. In this scenario, "identifiable information" means the identity of the subject is known or may be readily ascertained by the investigator. When researchers conducting secondary data analysis on existing data, and the existing data contain identifiable information about the original research subjects, then the secondary data analysis project will likely require IRB approval prior to commencing.

In summary, federal regulations on human subjects research protections (45 CFR part 46) specify six categories of research that may be exempted from IRB review, one of which applies specifically to existing data (i.e., Category 4). Research involving the collection or study of existing data, documents, and records can be exempted under Category 4 of the federal regulations if (a) the sources of such data are publicly available or (b) the information is recorded by the investigator in such a manner that subjects cannot be identified, directly or through identifiers linked to the subjects. Typically, however, researchers must still apply to their university/institution's IRB committee for them to make the final determination regarding whether their proposed secondary data analysis project is, in fact, exempt from IRB review. In other words, it is not the researcher who makes the final determination as to whether his or her secondary data analysis project is exempt from IRB review.

Finally, at times, research agencies and organizations provide primary data files to researchers to conduct secondary data analysis and these files are provided with specific restrictions regarding their use and storage. It is common for those data to contain identifiable information or several variables that if combined with one another could enable the researcher to identify the original research subjects, even though this is not the researcher's intent. In these scenarios, researchers will generally not be exempt from IRB review and will be required to receive IRB approval before conducting secondary data analysis on the existing data.

The U.S. Department of Health and Human Services (HHS), Office for Human Research Protection, offers a series of flowcharts to help researchers determine whether their research falls under the umbrella of "human subject" research and, as such, requires ethics approval to undertake. Figure 9.6 shows the decision chart for researchers wanting to use existing data for secondary data analysis. All of HHS's Human Subject Regulations Decision Charts are located at https://www.hhs.gov/ohrp/regulations-and-policy/decision-charts/.

Secondary Data Expert— Jenna Truman, PhD

Jenna Truman, PhD, is a statistician at the Bureau of Justice Statistics (BJS). She is in the Victimization Statistics Unit at BJS and works primarily on the National Crime Victimization Survey (NCVS). Her current research and work

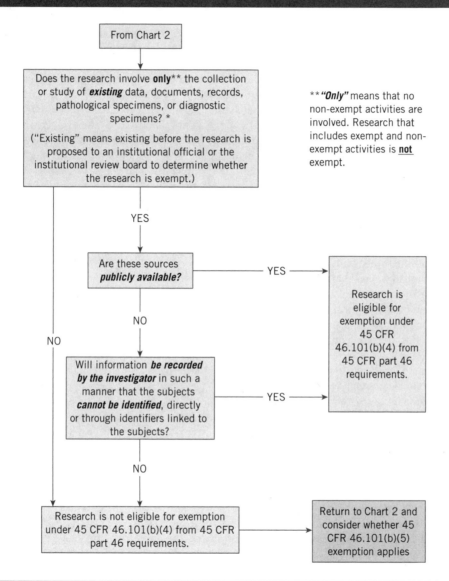

Figure 9.6 Health and Human Services, Office for Human Research Projection's Decision Chart for Research Involving Existing Data

From Chart 2

Does the research involve **only**** the collection or study of *existing* data, documents, records, pathological specimens, or diagnostic specimens? *

("Existing" means existing before the research is proposed to an institutional official or the institutional review board to determine whether the research is exempt.)

** *"Only"* means that no non-exempt activities are involved. Research that includes exempt and non-exempt activities is **not** exempt.

YES

Are these sources *publicly available?*

YES

NO

NO

Will information *be recorded by the investigator* in such a manner that the subjects *cannot be identified*, directly or through identifiers linked to the subjects?

YES

Research is eligible for exemption under 45 CFR 46.101(b)(4) from 45 CFR part 46 requirements.

NO

Research is not eligible for exemption under 45 CFR 46.101(b)(4) from 45 CFR part 46 requirements.

Return to Chart 2 and consider whether 45 CFR 46.101(b)(5) exemption applies

focuses on victimization patterns and trends, stalking victimization, domestic violence, firearm violence, and the measurement of demographic characteristics using the NCVS. As a statistician at BJS, she is tasked with a number of responsibilities including survey design, data collection, data analysis, writing reports, presenting analysis, overseeing the Office of Management and Budget clearance process for data collections (think IRB clearance), and project management. Most recently, she has been involved in the redesign and data collection of the Supplemental Victimization Survey on stalking victimization, implementing the addition of new demographic items to the NCVS, and the redesign of the NCVS instruments.

Truman never thought she would end up making a living working with secondary data. Initially, she wanted to be an archeologist (like Indiana Jones!). As she got a bit older, she decided she wanted to be a lawyer, but an internship in high school demonstrated to her that it was not the career for her. She then fell in love with sociology as an undergrad, which led her to pursue her graduate degree. After receiving her MA in applied sociology, she made the decision to pursue her PhD in sociology. As a PhD student, she had the opportunity to be the project manager for the department's research lab (Institute for Social and Behavioral Sciences). There, she gained experience in survey research. Between this experience, learning about all of the applied research that was being done outside of academia, and learning that she did not love teaching, she decided that she wanted to pursue an applied research job after finishing graduate school rather than an academic position at a university. She was aware of BJS's work throughout graduate school as she had read BJS reports and had even used the stalking supplement data for her dissertation. Therefore, she knew BJS as a place that she would look at to apply when she went on the job market. She was fortunate enough that BJS had an opening when she was finishing school. She applied, interviewed, and got the job! She feels fortunate that everything worked out as it did and recognizes having research methods skills was a part of her success.

Truman knows that many times in research it is not possible for researchers to collect their own data, and this is where secondary data analysis can be helpful. Depending on the research question, there may be existing data that could be used to examine it. There is a plethora of data out there for researchers and students to use, including many national data collections from the federal government. Secondary data analysis is also beneficial from a cost perspective because a researcher is saving from spending any data collection costs. In addition, many of the large-scale data collections that exist have a variety of variables and were collected with varying methodologies.

Truman notes that when students or researchers consider using secondary data analysis, it is vital that they seek to understand how the data are collected, what variables and response categories are included in the data, and if and how the data should be weighted. In her capacity at BJS, she speaks to many data users about the NCVS to answer questions and provide necessary documentation. For federal data sources, like the NCVS, there are typically data codebooks and user's guides or other documentation publicly available. Truman states that it is essential that users use those resources to be sure that they are analyzing the data appropriately. It is also important to understand the population of study so that you are making appropriate conclusions. Although the available resources for secondary data analysis may be numerous, one challenge is finding the right data to answer your research question. It is possible that the data may not have the exact measure that you need or that the variables are coded differently than you would like.

Truman has some words of advice for students. First, they should focus on understanding both the benefits and challenges of secondary data analysis. Students should be aware of how to find possible data sources for their research, and once data are found, they should make the effort to understand the data file, the collection process, variables, and appropriate methodologies. Students must understand that each data set might require a different level of statistical skill to analyze it. For example, working with a **longitudinal** compared with a **cross-sectional data** file may require more advanced statistical skills. Another important skill for students is to be able to be critical of and evaluate the secondary data they are using. Overall, a broad understanding of secondary data analysis is an important skill to have and would be a valuable asset for various research organizations, academia, and the federal statistical system.

Chapter Wrap-Up

This chapter introduces and describes research using secondary data. We began the chapter by defining why a researcher would use secondary data, and what it is. The chapter provided insight into how secondary data differ from primary or original data. We introduced you to several sources of criminal justice and related secondary data that can be used to answer your research questions, including the Interuniversity Consortium for Political and Social Research (ICPSR). We also described several data sets available for secondary data analysis from the FBI, BJS, and other organizations. In addition, we described how to access those data. We concluded the chapter by identifying key strategies for reporting findings from secondary data analysis, the most common pitfall associated with using secondary data, and we highlighted some ethical concerns related to secondary data analysis. Research using secondary data is a popular and efficient way to conduct research assuming the data available suit your research question. In our case studies, Santos (Santos & Santos, 2016) and Zaykowski (2014) benefited from existing data. Cuevas was on the original team that gathered the DAVILA data, and it remains available for others to use. Being on the original team collecting DAVILA offers some advantages to Cuevas who understands the details of the data and how they were collected. Melde also worked with the team that collected the data he used for his highlighted research (Melde, Taylor, & Esbensen, 2009), which came from an evaluation of the Teens Crime, and the Community and Community Works Program. He too has a richer understanding of these data, which benefits his research. Still, when using these data, Cuevas and Melde, like everyone else, must be sure not to stretch the data too far from its original intention. Today, each of these data sets is available for researchers like you to use. Santos benefited from using data available at a law enforcement agency. Many may not consider the local police or sheriff's office as a source of data, but they are. Furthermore, much of their data are available online. And Zaykowski used the NCVS data, which have been available for decades. Table 9.2 highlights some of the features of each of our case studies in which secondary data was used to conduct the research. In this table, we again see the diverse ways in which one can conduct research, even when all are using secondary data.

In the next chapter, we introduced geographic information systems (GIS) and crime mapping and analysis. In that chapter, we will explain why researchers and practitioners use these types of data to study crime and other crime-related problems. We provide a detailed description of GIS and present several techniques and methods commonly used in crime analysis and mapping. We also provide an overview of how results from GIS and crime mapping and analysis should be presented cartographically, as well as identify common pitfalls and ethical considerations associated with this type of methodology.

Table 9.2 Featured Research: Characteristics, Sources of, and Generalizability of Data Used

Researcher (Article)	Data Used	Characteristics of the Data	Source	Representative?	Are Findings Generalizable?
Carlos Cuevas (Sabina, Cuevas, & Cotignola-Pickens, 2016)	Dating Violence Among Latino Adolescents (DAVILA) 2010–2012.	The Dating Violence among Latino Adolescents (DAVILA) study assessed the victimization experience of a national sample of 1,525 Latino adolescents living in the United States. Trained professionals from an experienced survey research firm conducted the interviews over the phone in either English or Spanish, from September 2011 through February 2012.	Sabina, Chiara, and Carlos Cuevas originally collected these data. They are now available at ICPSR (ICPSR 34630-v1) funded by a grant from the U.S. Department of Justice. Office of Justice Programs. National Institute of Justice.	Of 12- to 18-year-old self-identified Latinos.	To 12- to 18-year-old self-identified Latinos.
Chris Melde (Melde, Taylor, & Esbensen, 2009)	An existing data set that is part of an evaluation of school-based, law-related education program called the Teens Crime, and the Community and Community Works Program.	Three waves of data. This document is a research report submitted to the U.S. Department of Justice. This report has not been published by the Department. Opinions or points of view expressed are those of the author(s) and do not necessarily reflect the official position or policies of the U.S. Department of Justice. 6 from a sample of students in 15 schools, in nine cities, in four states had been collected. The student questionnaire, while developed specifically to test the effectiveness of the CW program, contained several questions that allow for exploration of important issues of criminological and policy interest.	Data were collected to evaluate the Teens, Crime, and the Community and Community Works (TCC/CW) program.	Only of the classrooms that offered this law-related education program. Not representative of students across the nation.	Only to the classrooms that offered this law-related education program.

Rachel Santos (Santos & Santos, 2016)	Port St. Lucie, Florida, Police Department data used focuses on crimes and offenders. Data used included residential burglary counts and locations, residential theft counts and locations, those arrested for residential burglary or theft from vehicle, also those on felony probation with a prior burglary arrest, and nonviolent convicted offenders on felony probation for drug offense. Additional information used by researchers includes a criminal résumé and demographics of each targeted offender.	The crime data include only those crimes reported to the police.	Port St. Lucie, Florida, Police Department.	Yes, of reported crimes in the geographic areas/ hot spots.	Yes, to the geographic areas/ hot spots.
Heather Zaykowski (2014)	National Crime Victimization Survey data.	Interviews all persons age 12 or older in a housing unit in the United States about criminal vicitmization. Interviews are conducted throughout the year. In-sample housing units are interviewed every six months for a total of 2.5 years.	Sponsored by the Bureau of Justice Statistics in the Department of Justice. Collected by the U.S. Census Bureau.	Yes, of persons age 12 and older living in a housing unit in the United States.	Yes, to persons age 12 and older living in a housing unit in the United States.

Applied Assignments

Materials presented in this chapter can be used in applied ways. This box presents several assignments to help in demonstrating the value of this material by engaging in assignments related to it.

1. Homework Applied Assignment: Value of DAVILA at ICPSR

Go to the ICPSR website and open an account. Find the 2010–2013 DAVILA data archived by Cuevas and Sabina. Based on the documentation available there, write a paper that provides the following information about these data:

- Explain, in detail, how these original data were obtained.

- Describe and assess the sample. Is it representative? Is it large? Small? How would you feel about using these data in your own work?

- Provide a section identifying why these data are important—what they offer that other data do not.

- Identify the unit of analysis in these data. Is it offenders, states, victims, victimizations, incidents, etc.?

- With the codebook, select four substantive variables that are of interest to you. Describe what each variable is and how it is coded. Describe what level of measurement the coding of these variables represents. Identify advantages or disadvantages of these coding schemes.

Conclude your paper with a section describing ways you see these data could be useful in terms of potential future research that could be conducted using these data. Be prepared to share your paper and findings with the class.

2. Group Work in Class Applied Assignment: Using Secondary Data

The U.S. Bureau of Labor Statistics (BLS) provides extensive economic indicator data on the Internet for regions, states, and cities. Go to the BLS webpage, which offers statistics by location: http://stats.bls.gov/eag/. Click on four states and find the unemployment data for the most recent year available for each one. Your goal as a group is to identify how the four states compare. In making these comparisons, you need to identify the following:

- What is your unit of analysis?

- Describe the data set you are using, including how it was gathered, its advantages, and disadvantages.

- Identify the unemployment rate for each state.

- Draw a figure that shows the differences in unemployment rates across the four states.

- Describe what these findings suggest to you. Provide some hypotheses about what may account for any similarities or differences in unemployment rates by state.

- Did these findings surprise you? How? If not, why?

- What further research is suggested, given your findings?

Be prepared to report your findings to the class.

3. Internet Applied Assignment: Accessing Secondary Data Research on the Internet

You have been hired as a researcher to conduct research on murder in the state where you were born (if you were not born in a state in the United States, chose a state of your liking). In particular, your client wants you to answer whether the murder rate in that state has increased, decreased, or stayed stable the last five years for which there are data. Your client is paying you big bucks for this information, so you want to get it right. Because you are a junior researcher, you ask a colleague with more experience what to do. She suggests you access the FBI's violent crime data tables (of which murder is a part) and the CDC WONDER online. Based on the data available at each of these locations, write a report for your client. In your report to your client (needed for payment), you need to state the purpose of your task. You then need to describe the data you used to address this client's need. Include a description about how the data were collected and the advantages and disadvantages of the data. Next, provide the rates (per 100,000 people) for the last five years for your state. Provide a figure in your paper to illustrate the trend in murder for the state that you are focused on.

Note the discrepancies in the FBI and the CDC data. You need to share your thoughts about what might be behind these discrepancies (thinking back to Chapter 1 when we discussed some reasons good data collection systems can differ). Finally, clearly articulate your conclusions based on these data. Be sure to thank your client for the work, and express your hope that the client will send additional consulting jobs your way. Be prepared to share your findings with the class.

KEY WORDS AND CONCEPTS

Block groups 291
Codebook 283
Cross-sectional data 305
De-identified data 302

Geospatial data 291
Longitudinal data 305
Missing data 301
Primary data collection 276

Public use data 301
Secondary data analysis 276

KEY POINTS

- Use of secondary data is a popular approach to conducting research that involves reanalyzing existing data, collected by other researchers, to answer new research questions.

- The biggest advantage to conducting research using secondary data is that it saves time, money, and other resources.

- Researchers conducting secondary data analysis are constrained by the questions that were asked during the primary data collection, how key concepts were measured, and the collected data were categorized within these measures.

- Established in 1962, the Interuniversity Consortium for Political and Social Research (ICPSR) maintains and provides access to a vast archive of social science data for research and instruction. ICPSR is located at the University of Michigan.

- ICPSR maintains the National Archive of Criminal Justice Data (NACJS), which is a specialized data archive sponsored by the Bureau of Justice Statistics (BJS), National Institute of Justice (NIJ), and the Office of Juvenile Justice and Delinquency Prevention (OJJDP).

- FedStats was launched in 1997 and offers open access to a wide range of statistical data generated by the federal government.

- Under the Uniform Crime Reporting (UCR) Program, the FBI provides access to many data collection efforts that can be used in secondary data analysis, including the Summary Reporting System (SRS), the National Incident-Based Reporting System (NIBRS), the Supplementary Homicide Reports (SHR), Law Enforcement Officers Killed and Assaulted (LEOKA), and Hate Crime Statistics.

- The Bureau of Justice Statistics (BJS) collects, analyzes, publishes, and disseminates data on crime, courts, prisons, jails, law enforcement officers, criminal offenders, victims of crime, the operation of justice systems at all levels, and other topics related to criminal justice. These data are useful for research using secondary data.

- The Census Bureau is a part of the U.S. Department of Commerce responsible for conducting the decennial census and other government surveys that are of use for those conducting secondary data analysis.

- Data used in secondary data analysis projects can be obtained from state and local agencies as well as from the federal government. Those agencies include SACs, police departments, court administrators, and other agencies.

- Projects that use secondary data analysis often are exempt from IRB review because no new data are being collected from human subjects and data are publicly available. You must verify with your IRB to see whether your secondary data analysis project requires review.

REVIEW QUESTIONS

1. What is secondary data analysis, and how does it differ from research involving primary data collection?

2. What are some advantages to conducting secondary data analysis?

3. What are some disadvantages to conducting secondary data analysis?

4. How can researchers obtain secondary data files through ICPSR?

5. What kinds of data useful for secondary data analysis can be obtained from the Bureau of Justice Statistics/ National Archive of Criminal Justice Data?

6. Where can researchers access geospatial data that can be used in secondary data analysis projects?

7. What are some state and local agencies that provide secondary data to the public?

8. What is the name of your state's Statistical Analysis Center (SAC), and where is it located? If your state does not have a SAC, what is the nearest SAC to your location? What type of data and reports does that SAC offer?

9. Why is it important to for a researcher to justify why a particular data set was used in his or her secondary data analysis study?

10. Why are most studies involving secondary data analysis exempt from IRB review?

CRITICAL THINKING QUESTIONS

1. Develop a research question that you think could be investigated using existing data, and then go to ICPSR's website. What is your research question, what data set(s) archived at ICPSR do you believe can be used in a secondary data analysis project to answer it, and what problems do you think you might encounter using these existing data?

2. Go to the Census Bureau's American Fact Finder website located at https://factfinder.census.gov/faces/nav/jsf/pages/guided_search.xhtml. Enter your zip code in the search box to retrieve data about your area. What sort of information about your area that was produced from this search is available for you to use, what are the sources of these data, and how could these data be incorporated into a research project using secondary data analysis?

3. Compare and contrast the data available from three different state Statistical Analysis Centers (SACs). Why do you think that the kinds of data available from the SACs are less consistent?

4. Identify any existing data set that you think could be used to answer a research question that was going to be based on secondary data analysis. Explain how you would access these data for the project, justify their use, identify the unit of analysis and the specific variables that you would use to answer your question, and explain why you think these data may/may not be exempt from IRB review.

5. Suppose you are given access to an existing data set for a proposed secondary data analysis project. The existing data come from your faculty advisor's inmate

survey research project conducted last year. The data consist of coded survey responses, and the advisor will retain a key that can link the data to individually identifiable data. You will extract only the data you need for your project, however, without including any identifying data and without retaining your advisor's linking codes. Do you think that the use of these data constitutes human subjects research, or do you feel that your project would qualify for IRB exempt status?

⑤SAGE edge™

SAGE **edge** offers a robust online environment featuring an impressive array of free tools and resources for review, study, and further exploration, keeping you on the cutting edge of teaching and learning. Learn more at **edge.sagepub .com/rennisonrm**.

GIS and Crime Mapping

Learning Objectives

After finishing this chapter, you should be able to:

10.1   Describe how GIS and crime mapping techniques are used in contemporary criminal justice research in both the academic and nonacademic settings.

10.2   Assess examples of the different types of crime analysis conducted in law enforcement agencies and the specific problems and methods commonly used with each approach.

10.3   Explain the role of GIS and crime mapping techniques in academic research, including how crime analysis is used to forecast crime and victimization risk and to identify temporal patterns in crime data.

10.4   Compare the three most common metrics for assessment of the predictive accuracy of prospective crime hot spot maps.

10.5   Identify the five required elements that must be included on a map when crime analysis information is presented cartographically.

10.6   Evaluate some of the ethical challenges researchers face when conducting research using GIS or crime mapping, as well as the common pitfalls that must be avoided when conducting crime analysis.

Introduction

Not everyone enjoys looking at a wall of data or a table full of statistics. For some, examining data in tables does not offer clear answers to research questions. Given the choice, would you rather look at a big table of numbers or a figure or map that represents the same data? It is always the best policy to present your data in a way that makes it easy to understand. This is the idea behind geographic information systems (GIS) and crime mapping. With geospatial data, you as a researcher can illustrate data on a map in ways that allow you to answer your research questions. Introducing and describing GIS and crime mapping techniques used in criminal justice and criminology research is the purpose of this chapter.

To introduce GIS and crime mapping, the chapter is structured as follows. First, we address the question of why anyone would use GIS and crime mapping techniques to conduct criminological research. Understanding why these methods are used and why they are important helps to place the rest of the information shared here into context. We then offer an in-depth discussion of what GIS is, which includes the role of data, technology, application, and people. We then turn to articulating what crime mapping and analysis is. This discussion includes several different types of analysis that can be done within this particular area of research; we then provide insight into the use of these techniques in academics research, that is, the use of crime analysis to create empirical knowledge. Next, we move to describing common pitfalls when using these methods and the ethical considerations that you should be aware of. Finally, we conclude the chapter with an interview of a crime-mapping expert Henri Buccine, research coordinator at Rutgers University's Center on Public Safety. At the end of this chapter, you should have a sufficient introduction to GIS and crime mapping that will hopefully encourage you to seek additional courses in the subject. Like all of the material in the text, having GIS and mapping skills is useful when looking for a career. These skills are in demand, and the need for them in governmental, public-sector, and private-sector organizations is only growing.

Why Conduct Research Using GIS and Crime Mapping Techniques?

Presenting data in a way that is easy to understand is important. For example, the weather map shown in Figure 10.1 is something that most everyone reading this text can understand without much explanation. Most of you will look at this map of geographic data in the United States and recognize that the dark gray areas represent places experiencing high temperatures, and the light gray areas are experiencing lower temperatures. Differences in temperatures are illustrated through

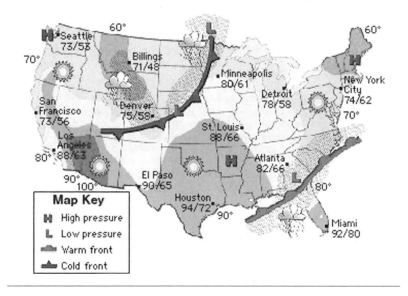

Figure 10.1 Simple Weather Map That Conveys Information About Weather Conditions Across the United States Visually

the use of tones and intensity of color on a map. The notion of crime mapping in criminal justice and criminology is the same: presenting geographic data that clearly and easily demonstrate crime and justice information in space. GIS and crime mapping allows researchers to present their data and findings in an easy-to-understand way.

Although many view this use of maps to illustrate crime and justice information as new and revolutionary, in fact, it began more than a century ago. The origins of contemporary crime mapping and analysis techniques can be traced back to the early 1800s and the works of Belgian mathematician Adolphe Quetelet and French lawyer André-Michel Guerry. Guerry, who spent much of his career focusing on the relationship between "moral statistics" and crime, demonstrated the effectiveness of crime mapping and analysis in a presentation to the French Academy of Science in 1832. By using frequency data (how often something has happened), also known as count data, and a series of choropleth maps, Guerry illustrated spatio-temporal changes in the levels of crime and suicide across French districts. In this context, spatio-temporal refers to space and time. A **choropleth map** is a thematic map that uses shaded or patterned areas in proportion to the measurement of a variable being displayed on the map. The variables displayed on a map can represent any number of different variables, such as crime rates, population density, or per-capita income.

Interest in mapping variations in sociodemographic characteristics of communities continued in Europe through the 19th century and is reflected in the publications of Joseph Fletcher and Charles Booth (see Figure 10.2). Much of this work laid the foundations upon which many students, researchers, and practitioners develop their ideas about the geographic distribution of crime and delinquency.

alchetron.com

André-Michel Guerry. Guerry, who spent much of his career focusing on the relationship between "moral statistics" and crime, demonstrated the effectiveness of crime mapping and analysis in a presentation to the French Academy of Science in 1832.

Along with André-Michel Guerry, Adolphe Quetelet is credited with the origins of crime mapping.

Choropleth map: Type of thematic map that uses shaded or patterned areas in proportion to the measurement of the statistical variable being displayed on the map, such as population density or per-capita income.

Even though GIS and crime mapping has a long history, it continues to be used only by a few criminal justice and criminology researchers, although those ranks are growing. Consider our featured researchers, for example. Mary Dodge, Rod Brunson, Chris Melde, Carlos Cuevas, and Heather Zaykowski have not personally used GIS or crime mapping in their research. Yet, each noted to us that as the application of this approach grows, it may be a valuable approach for use in their areas of interest.

Today, law enforcement agencies throughout the country routinely rely on geographic information systems (GIS), using various crime analysis and mapping techniques to examine the locations of, and to combat, crime. The results from a recent Bureau of Justice Statistics (BJS) survey show that more than 87% of the nation's largest law enforcement agencies have personnel—crime analysts—designated specifically to crime analysis duties and that more than a third of large agencies provide direct access to crime maps produced by crime analysts via the Web. Other uses of GIS among law enforcement analysts include monitoring and tracking sex offenders, geographic profiling, and identifying crime hot spots. In short, law enforcement agencies all over the world have identified GIS as a valuable tool for addressing the multiple facets of fighting crime. This widespread use of personnel focused on GIS and the advances in modern computing technology means that possessing GIS and mapping research skills can make you a desirable candidate for many excellent career opportunities.

In conjunction with the increased use of crime mapping and analysis among law enforcement agencies, a growing number of applied and scientific publications examining the use and role of GIS and mapping within the field of criminal justice and criminology have been published. For example, some of the leading journals in the field of criminology such as the *Journal of Quantitative Criminology, Criminology, Justice Quarterly,* the *Journal of Research in Crime and Delinquency,* and the *British Journal of Criminology* have released several articles on crime mapping and analysis over the past several years. Similarly, the publication of prominent reports and recently published books also suggests strongly that crime mapping and analysis have come of age. In fact, one of our featured researchers, Rachel Boba Santos, has written a text focused specifically on crime analysis with crime mapping (Santos, 2017). That text is in its fourth edition, indicating its usefulness and popularity. In short, crime mapping and analysis is here to stay.

Crime mapping and analysis has strong theoretical grounding, well-developed techniques used to analyze these data and increasingly widespread implementation both in and out of academia. For these reasons, it is common for researchers to use GIS and mapping techniques as a research methodology, especially when their research question or questions focus on spatial or temporal patterns. Not surprisingly, given her expertise, an example of this is Santos and colleague's research (Santos & Santos, 2016), which directly addresses spatial and temporal issues of crime. In her featured research, Santos and her colleague tested whether an offender-focused police intervention in residential burglary and residential theft from vehicle hot spots was effective at reducing crime, arrests, and offender recidivism. When you read that article, you should have noticed their use of a map to depict the different experimental and control hot spots used in the study.

What Is GIS?

Although we briefly defined GIS earlier in the text, it warrants further discussion. GIS means different things to different people. For example, Rhind (1989, p. 322) defines GIS as

> a system of hardware, software, and procedures designed to support the capture, management, manipulation, analysis, modeling, and display of spatially referenced data for solving complex planning and management problems.

Figure 10.2   Section of Charles Booth's "Poverty Map" in 1889

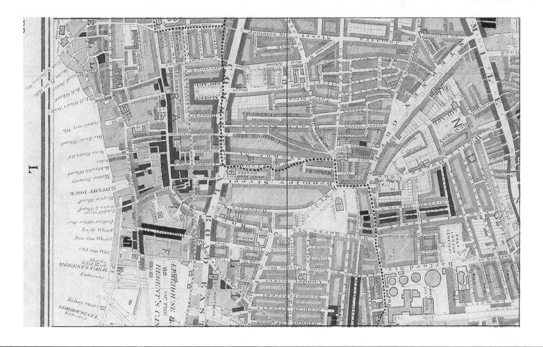

Note: The map shows an area of East End, London, where streets are colored to represent the economic class of residents.

A slightly different definition of GIS is offered by the U.S. Geological Survey. The USGS (2007) defines GIS as

> a computer system capable of assembling, storing, manipulating, and displaying geographically referenced information (that is data identified according to their locations). (para. 1)

Spatial data: Data that have geographic coordinates associated with a corresponding physical location. The coordinates associated with spatial data are the key.

In this text, we define geographic information systems (GIS) as a branch of information technology that involves collecting, storing, manipulating, analyzing, managing, and presenting geospatially referenced data. To better understand what GIS is and how it is used to study criminal justice and criminology topics, it can be best thought of as an approach to processing data that consists of four interrelated parts: (1) data, (2) technology, (3) application, and (4) people. Each of these components is discussed next.

Data

Data comprise one of the four parts of GIS. GIS data differ from other types of data gathered and used in criminal justice and criminology research in that GIS data contain or can be linked to spatial or geographical data. **Spatial data** include data that have geographic coordinates associated with a corresponding physical location. The coordinates associated with spatial data are important. For example, if we administered an online survey to a sample of university students and we asked them to provide us with their home address as part of the data we collected, we would have collected data about where the students live. Nevertheless,

Vector data: Type of geospatial data used to represent the characteristics of the real world in one of three ways: as points, lines, or polygons.

Raster data: Type of geospatial data represented as a matrix of cells (i.e., pixels) that is organized into rows and columns, like a grid.

simply providing an address lacks the spatial coordinates, or reference of the latitude and longitude coordinates, that correspond to the addresses. If we assigned spatial information (i.e., latitude and longitude coordinates) to the students' home addresses that were collected from our survey, then we would have converted the original (nonspatial) survey data (i.e., home address) into geospatially referenced or geographic data. This allows us to illustrate where on a map our respondents live. Now imagine we gathered geospatial data (with coordinates) about where a criminal victimization occurred. With these geospatial data, we now have where the victimization occurred on a map.

In general, two types of spatial data are used in GIS: vector and raster data. Most people are familiar with vector data; nonetheless, many may not be aware of vector data by name.

Vector data are geospatial data that represent characteristics of the real world on a map. Vector data do this in one of three ways: points, polygons, or lines. Figure 10.3 is an example of vector data used to produce a map that represents geographic information about the location of registered sex offender homes in Pinellas County, Florida. The sex offenders' homes are shown on this map using georeferenced points (i.e., pins labeled "O"). In addition, this map illustrates a georeferenced point representing the location of a home near a school (i.e., the pin labeled "H"). Point vector data are illustrated using a pin because these locations represent a single point or discrete location on a map. These point data are overlaid on a map image showing an area of Pinellas County, Florida, that also includes surrounding waterways. These waterways are symbolized as the solid gray areas in the bottom left corner and are georeferenced as polygons. Finally, major street networks are also symbolized on the map using vector data; in this case, they are georeferenced lines. Streets run across the area of the county that is visible on the map and look exactly as you would expect—as lines on a map. Combined, points, lines, and polygons are three types of vector data used in GIS to depict characteristics of the real world.

Raster data represent a second type of geographic data used in GIS. In general, a **raster** is a matrix of cells (i.e., pixels) that are organized into rows and columns, like a grid. This grid is overlaid on a study area. Unlike vector data, each raster cell contains a value that represents some aspect or characteristic of the data being depicted on a map. For example, each raster cell may have the number of crimes that occurred in that cell area. Or it may offer the number of sex offenders living in that area. Although each cell contains a value, those data are not shown in the grid. Instead, the values of the data in the cells are illustrated using colors and shade intensity.

Figure 10.4 shows a crime hot spot map, based on the known incident locations of motor vehicle thefts in Austin, Texas, occurring in 2007. In addition, the locations of motor vehicle thefts recorded in 2008 are depicted on the raster map as points (i.e., vector data). On this hot spot map, the raster cells are visible as little squares (i.e., grid cells). Some raster cells are shaded dark gray to show the most highly concentrated clusters of motor vehicle thefts in

Figure 10.3   Map of Sex Offenders' Residential Locations, and the Location of an Elementary School, in an Area of Pinellas County, Florida

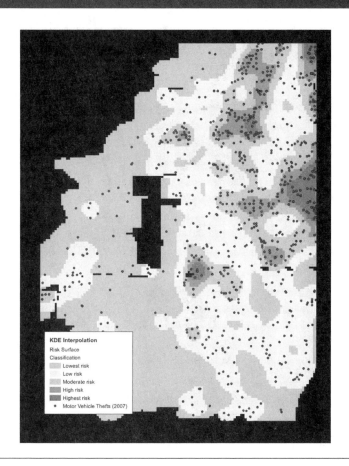

2007. Conversely, the light gray raster cells on the map show the areas in Austin that correspond with significantly less auto theft clustering. These particular raster data were used to determine or forecast where similar crimes were likely to occur the next year.

Data stored and depicted in a raster grid can represent a multitude of real-world phenomena such as temperature, elevation, crime rates, traffic stops, homicides, poverty, or spectral data such as satellite images and aerial photographs. Raster data are commonly used in criminal justice and criminology research to depict a continuous crime risk surface or hot spot map, where each raster cell corresponds with the relative intensity (i.e., heat) of crime concentration or risk elevation, just like the weather map shown in the beginning of this chapter.

Raster: Matrix of cells (i.e., pixels) that are organized into rows and columns, like a grid. This grid is overlaid on a study area. Unlike vector data, each raster cell contains a value that represents some aspect or characteristic of the data being depicted on a map.

Technology

Technology is one of four primary components of GIS, and it is at the heart of GIS. Technology in the GIS context consists of both hardware and software. Hardware is the physical

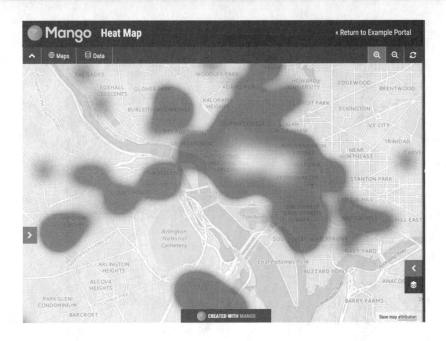

Figure 10.5 Heat Map Shows the Concentration of Starbucks® Coffee Shops in the Washington, D.C., Area, Using a Commercial Online GIS Software Company Called Mango®

equipment that makes up a geographic information system, and it includes servers, client workstations, back-up hard drives, and a local area network connecting them all. It is all of the equipment that someone can see, touch, move, and feel. In contrast, software is the technology that is *not* visible, and it includes the programs used in crime analysis. For example, Microsoft® Word™ is the software you might use on your laptop (which is the hardware). Esri® ArcGIS™ and Pitney Bowes® MapInfo™ are two of the most notable commercial GIS software applications. Some open-source geographic information system (GIS) programs also exist, including QGIS, MapWindow GIS, and GRASS GIS. Most GIS software applications are processor intensive, meaning that the hardware used has to have sufficient computing power to support the required software.

Increasingly, companies and organizations are leveraging the power of the Internet and integrating traditional GIS software applications with Web hosting capabilities. What this means is that the processor-intensive requirement is being shifted from a researcher's personal hardware to the Cloud. By making this shift, the researchers' hardware resources are freed up, but they can still develop maps, produce maps, and analyze the data. For example, Esri's ArcGIS Online is a complete, cloud-based mapping platform that allows users to make and share maps. These maps can be presented online and viewed through Internet browsers, including smartphone or tablet browsers. Similarly, a company called Mango allows users to create Web map applications quickly and easily, without the need for expensive programmers, servers, software licenses, or support personnel. Figure 10.5 illustrates a sample hot spot map produced on the Mango online platform. This particular example illustrates the concentration of Starbucks locations in the Washington, D.C., area.

Application

Application is the third of four primary components of GIS. The application component of GIS refers to the way in which it is used. Lo and Yeung (2002) suggest that the application of GIS is best understood when viewed from three perspectives: areas of applications, nature of applications, and approaches to implementation. For example, local and municipal governments (area of application) use GIS to support public safety and law enforcement (nature of application) by conducting spatio-temporal analysis of crime, to deploy personnel, and for agency management and administration (approach to implementation). This is just one of many applications of GIS in contemporary society, but it provides an excellent example of its "application" in criminal justice and criminology.

People

Like the application component of GIS, the people component—the fourth and final component of GIS—can be best understood from three perspectives: the specialists, the users, and the consumers. In geographic information systems, the specialist takes on many roles and responsibilities. The specialist can be responsible for developing applications for GIS users and consumers. Specialists can take on the role as project manager or as systems designer. Alternatively, the GIS specialist can oversee database administration or computer programming jobs that support GIS projects. Depending on the specialist's level of expertise, a crime analyst working in a law enforcement agency can be thought of as a GIS specialist. These are just some of the many careers available to people with GIS skills.

The GIS user takes on slightly different roles and responsibilities in a geographic information system. The GIS user is the person or organization that requests support from GIS specialists to provide services to the GIS consumer. GIS users can be public planners, engineers, scientists, or lawyers, for example. This might be someone from the Mayor's office that requests a crime map from an agency's GIS specialist. In short, the GIS user is someone who relies on GIS for conducting business, providing goods or services, or supporting decision-making processes. Santos, during her video interview for this book, pointed to the GIS specialist as playing an important role in preparing grant proposals, for example. In this capacity, the specialist can help create maps used to demonstrate that the research team knows where the issues are and how bad the problem is, as well as indicate that the research team knows what it is talking about. Combined, this information can be depicted clearly and concisely using maps, which helps get funding.

Finally, GIS consumers represent another type of GIS people. Consumers use information produced from GIS users in their everyday lives to check the weather, property values, traffic conditions, or crime in their community. They may use GIS information to plan a trip, to find a good place in the city to be entertained, or to identify a good plumber closer to their home. As a GIS consumer, you may have even relied on geographic information systems to find a good place to live, near campus, while studying at your university. The GIS consumer is the end user of geographic information systems. The skills of the GIS specialist and GIS user directly determine how useful and easy to understand a GIS product is for the consumer.

To summarize, GIS is a field of information technology that deals specifically with the collection, storage, manipulation, analysis, management, and presentation of geographical data. GIS consists of four distinct parts, including data, technology, application, and people. The "people" part of GIS can be the specialists who develop applications, administer databases, or manage a GIS project. GIS users, on the other hand, use GIS as a way to provide goods or services to consumers of GIS information. GIS consumers use geographical information in their everyday lives, including when they query the weather forecast, plan a trip, or check for crime hot spots or sex offenders living in their neighborhoods. GIS plays an important role in criminal justice and criminology research, and the remainder of this chapter focuses on how

Crime mapping: Research methodology used to identify spatio-temporal patterns in crime data.

Crime analysis: When used in geographic information systems (GIS), it refers to spatial analysis methods used on crime data to understand where and when events occur so that patterns can be systematically identified and reduction and prevention strategies implemented.

Administrative crime analysis: One of three types of crime analysis performed by law enforcement personnel, typically involving long-range projects that are internal to the agency.

GIS is used in our field, from both a practitioner and an academic perspective. We begin by providing a thorough discussion of crime mapping and analysis.

What Is Crime Mapping and Analysis?

Crime mapping is a research methodology used to identify spatio-temporal patterns in crime data. In the context of GIS, spatio-temporal refers to space and time. Practitioners, students, and academic researchers often want to map crime problems, and they do this with GIS. For most law enforcement practitioners, **crime analysis** involves conducting spatial analysis on crime data to understand where and when crime occurred. Knowing these patterns assists in identifying crime problems that can help facilitate solutions for reducing or preventing crime in the future. Agencies can also use crime analysis to evaluate the success of these crime-fighting programs and strategies. Crime analysts engage in many activities including reviewing all police reports to identify patterns as they emerge. By analyzing data, crime analysts can assist the agency in answering the who, what, when, where, how, and why of crimes. Crime analysts in law enforcement agencies conduct crime analysis that is administrative, tactical, or strategic in nature. In contrast to academics using crime mapping, crime analysts are supporting the needs of law enforcement agencies. Administrative, tactical, and strategic crime analysis is described as follows.

Administrative Crime Analysis

Administrative crime analysis is one of three types of crime analysis performed by law enforcement personnel, and it typically involves long-range projects. The work of administrative crime analysist tends to be internal to the agency. Common practices associated with administrative crime analysis include providing economic, geographic, and law enforcement information to police management, city hall, city council, and neighborhoods, citizen groups, or the media. Administrative crime analysis involves specific analytic techniques that can include the following:

- Districting and redistricting analysis

- Patrol staffing analysis

- Cost–benefit analysis

- Resource deployment for special events

Administrative crime analysis does *not* include typical administrative tasks that are not analytic in nature. For example, administrative crime analysis does not include tasks such as preparing leaflets for police events or performing basic technology support. Although results produced from administrative crime analysis are often the same results that are produced from the other analytic approaches, Santos suggests that information chosen for presentation in this type of crime analysis "represents only the tip of the iceberg of the complete analysis. The purpose of the presentation and the audience largely determine what analysis is presented."

Law enforcement agencies routinely post information produced from administrative crime analysis on their websites in the form of community bulletins, interactive Web-based maps, or agency reports. For example, Figure 10.6 shows the Denver Police Department's online crime map, where users can query the locations and times of many types of crimes in the agency's jurisdiction.

Source: https://www.denvergov.org/content/denvergov/en/police-department/crime-information/crime-map.html

Tactical Crime Analysis

In addition to administrative crime analysis, law enforcement personnel including crime analysts conduct tactical crime analysis. **Tactical crime analysis** emphasize collecting data, identifying patterns, and developing possible leads so that criminal cases can be cleared quickly. Tactical crime analysis usually involves analysis of individual, incident-level data associated with specific events (e.g., robberies, motor vehicle thefts, residential burglaries, etc.) that are believed to be part of a crime series, committed by a single individual, or group of individuals.

Crime analysts engaged in tactical crime analysis often produce reports containing time series (i.e., analysis of data that are linked by time) or point-pattern analysis (i.e., analysis of discrete points) depicted in charts, graphs, maps, or a combination of each. This information can then be used tactically to address known crime problems within an agency's jurisdiction and is often incorporated into a broader, agency-wide policing strategy such as CompStat (COMPuter STATistics). **CompStat** is an organizational management approach used by police departments to proactively address crime problems. It does so by using data and statistics—with a heavy emphasis on crime analysis and mapping—to identify surges in crime that are then targeted with enforcement. CompStat began

Tactical crime analysis:
Type of crime analysis used in law enforcement that emphasizes collecting data, identifying patterns, and developing possible leads so that criminal cases can be cleared quickly.

CompStat: Organizational management approach used by police departments to proactively address crime problems, which relies heavily on crime analysis and mapping.

in the New York City Police Department, but it has since been adopted by law enforcement agencies throughout the world.

Most of the data used in tactical crime analysis are produced from the law enforcement agency's records management system, which includes crime incident report data. That is, when someone calls into the police department about a crime, or an officer makes a stop or witnesses a crime, data from that incident are collected. By using data representing all incidents known to the police, the following types of tactical crime analysis are common:

- Repeat incident analysis

- Crime pattern analysis

- Linking known offenders to past crimes

Since tactical crime analysis almost always involves examining crimes that are a part of a series of criminal events, criminal profiling or criminal investigative analysis is often considered to be part of tactical crime analysis.

In summary, tactical crime analysis is a crime analysis technique that describes and conveys information about crime patterns efficiently and accurately so that criminal cases can be cleared quickly. This may involve the reviews of available crime data gathered from arrest reports, field interview reports, calls for service, trespass warnings, and other available sources of data. This approach allows the tactical crime analyst to identify how, when, and where criminal activity has occurred on a daily basis.

Strategic Crime Analysis

Unlike the other two approaches, **strategic crime analysis** is a crime analysis technique that focuses on operational strategies of a law enforcement organization in an attempt to develop solutions to chronic crime-related problems. Chronic means that something—in this case, crime-related issues—is ongoing and persistent. Furthermore, spatial analytic techniques used in strategic crime analysis differ somewhat because they usually focus on analysis of geographic units such as an agency's jurisdiction, census tracts, patrol districts, or beats, instead of on individuals or crime series. Often, the aim of strategic crime analysis is to focus on cluster analysis to produce information that can be used for resource allocation, beat configuration, identification of nonrandom patterns in criminal activity, and unusual community conditions. **Cluster analysis** is a technique that involves the identification of similar types of crime that clump together in space or time.

The process of strategic crime analysis often begins with data pulled from an agency's records management system. In addition, this type of analysis also incorporates other data sources derived from a variety of quantitative and qualitative methods. Some specific types of strategic crime analysis techniques can include the following:

- Trend analysis

- Hot spot analysis

- Problem analysis

In summary, strategic crime analysis provides law enforcement agencies with the ability to offer more effective and efficient service to the community. Figure 10.7 is an example of a crime hot spot map for Henderson, Nevada, used in strategic crime analysis showing the concentration of propane gas tank thefts. Hot spot analysis for this particular type of theft was conducted because it was believed that gas tank bottles could be used in terrorist activities

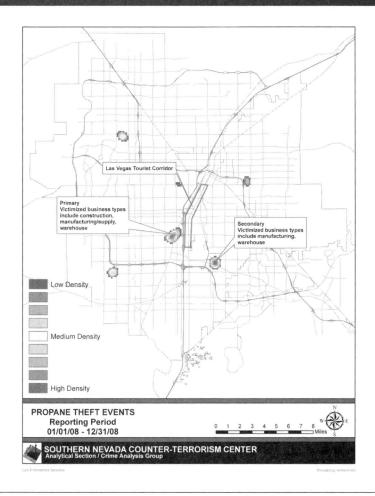

and the agency wanted to develop a better strategy for addressing the particular problem. Crime hot spot mapping is one of the most common forms of strategic crime analysis used in law enforcement today.

Crime Analysis in Academic Research

Academics, and in turn students, may think of crime analysis in ways that are slightly different from how practitioners and crime analysts in agencies such as police departments think of crime analysis. To academics, crime analysis is often viewed as a research methodology that can be used to answer research questions, as well as to test criminological theories, specifically, those theories that attempt to explain when and why crime occurs (e.g., crime pattern theory, routine activities theory, social disorganization theory, etc.). Academics also use crime analysis to develop new techniques used to identify crime patterns, as well as to improve existing methods, which allows them to advance new ways of thinking about where and when crime occurs, and the victims and offenders involved in criminal activity. Academics may also apply crime analysis techniques as a research methodology to assess the efficacy of various crime prevention or reduction policies and programs, including the case study research discussed in this text conducted by Santos. Recall that Santos and her colleague used this approach to test the efficacy of an offender-focused intervention strategy, implemented using a randomized control trial, based on crime hot spot analysis (Santos & Santos, 2016).

Crime Hot Spot Mapping

Hot spot mapping: Various, advanced, spatial-statistical methods and techniques that use the known locations of recorded crime incidents to identify nonrandom, high concentrations of crime events within a study area.

Just like there are different ways in which crime analysts investigate crime, academics also use numerous crime analysis techniques. One of the most popular crime methods used by academics and their students involves crime hot spot mapping. **Hot spot mapping** uses advanced spatial-analytic methods and techniques to map the known locations of recorded crime incidents. In doing this, hot spot maps illustrate nonrandom, high concentrations of crime events within a study area. Even researchers like Cuevas, who has not done crime hot spot mapping, find this kind of analysis cool and interesting. Cuevas, in his video interview for this book, also said he sees ways in which using hot spot mapping in the future could inform his research on youth and Latinos, specifically.

A wide range of different methods and techniques has emerged to characterize crime hot spots. Although we do not provide an in-depth discussion of each one in this textbook, interested readers should consider the comprehensive review conducted by Eck, Chainey, Cameron, and Wilson (2005). In general, existing approaches to retrospective (i.e., looking backward in time) crime hot spot identification fall into one of three categories:

1. **Global statistical tests.** These tests focus on the spatial clustering of crimes across an entire (i.e., global) study area. This approach often involves the calculation of statistics such as mean center, standard deviation distance and ellipse, and global tests for clustering such as the Nearest Neighbor Index, Moran's I, and Geary's C statistic.

2. **Hot spot mapping techniques.** These techniques focus on the analysis of point pattern data and include the use of K-means clustering, thematic mapping using enumeration areas, quadrat mapping, and kernel density estimation techniques.

3. **Local indicators of spatial association statistics.** These indicators are used to assess the existence of clusters *within* an entire study area (i.e., locally) and include the Gi and Gi* statistics.

Although these three categories are not discussed in detail in this text, you should know that even though these techniques serve a somewhat different purpose, they all can be used to characterize crime hot spots in an effort to develop a better understanding of where criminal or other criminological incidents cluster in space.

As noted in the previous section, crime hot spot mapping is also a popular crime analysis approach among practitioners, and crime analysts commonly use many of these hot spot methods. Nevertheless, research undertaken by academics has resulted in significant advances in these techniques and methods, which in turn has improved the way crime analysts apply them. Perhaps the most noteworthy of these advancements has resulted in a method designed to aid law enforcement agencies to proactively administer crime prevention strategies by using crime hot spot maps. This approach to crime analysis is commonly referred to as predictive policing.

Predictive Policing

The Rand Corporation defines **predictive policing** as "the application of analytic techniques–particularly quantitative techniques–to identify likely targets for police intervention and prevent crime or solve past crimes by making statistical predictions" (Perry, McInnis, Price, Smith, & Hollywood, 2013, p. xiii), The idea that crime can be "predicted" is based on two related assumptions: (1) Crime is not randomly distributed in space and time, and (2) the nonrandom distribution of crime is a reflection of systematic behavior patterns of potential offenders and victims, both of whom are influenced by the physical environment in which they live and interact. Academic researchers studying crime patterns have developed two of the most well-known predictive policing algorithms used by law enforcement agencies today: PredPol® and HunchLab™.

PredPol bills itself as "The Predictive Policing Company" and claims its software is more than just a hot spot tool. Created by academics from UCLA and Santa Clara University, PredPol develops crime forecasts based on the following:

1. Location of historical crime data

2. When the crimes occurred

3. Type of crime that was committed

Algorithms developed by PredPol researchers are applied using a method originally developed form the field of seismology called self-exciting point process modeling. **Self-exciting point process modeling** is analogous to the aftershocks of an earthquake. In the context of crime, think of an increase in likelihood of a second crime following an initial crime within a particular area. Every six months, PredPol models are updated with new crime data to allow the model to produce a more accurate forecast. Law enforcement agencies in Los Angeles, California; Hagerstown, Maryland; and Orange County, Florida, have used PredPol reportedly to reduce crime in their jurisdictions. They reduce crime by allocating resources in areas they believe will likely experience more crime in the future.

Working with academics from Rutgers University and Temple University, software development company Azavea® created another popular software product used in predictive policing: HunchLab. Law enforcement agencies feed the HunchLab algorithm cartographic data, including data that define an agency's jurisdiction, divisions, and beats. They also provide data such as calls for service or crime location information. HunchLab then processes that information to produce prospective (i.e., future) crime hot spot maps, like the one shown in Figure 10.8. This information can then be used in targeted crime prevention efforts. HunchLab is used in Philadelphia, Pennsylvania, and Miami, Florida, and it is being tested by the New York City Police Department.

Recently, Jerry Ratcliffe and other researchers from Temple University developed a free predictive policing software application called PROVE. Similar to commercial products like PredPol and HunchLab, PROVE uses past crime event data, combined with long-term crime indicators, to model the likelihood of future crime, and it maps these data as a prospective crime hot spot map. According to the developers, PROVE "enables police departments and other agencies across the country to use geocoded crime data in combination with freely available census data to create micro-spatial estimates of future criminal activity at the local level. The output of the utility is a simple map of statistically significant areas of high risk" (see https://www.hunchlab.com/tools/prove/). Figure 10.9 shows a prospective hot spot map produced from the PROVE algorithm. Areas shaded the darkest gray on the map indicate locations that are significantly more likely to experience crime in the future, based on the PROVE predictions.

So, how well do these types of forecasting approaches work? At this point in our discussion of predictive policing, it should be noted that there are many ways that practitioners and researchers assess the quality of crime forecasts. The three most common approaches to

Predictive policing: Application of analytic techniques to identify likely targets for police intervention and prevent crime or solve past crimes by making statistical predictions.

Self-exciting point process modeling: Analogous to the aftershocks of an earthquake. In the context of crime, think of an increase in likelihood of a second crime after an initial crime within a particular area.

Figure 10.8   Screenshot of a Crime Forecast Produced by Azavea's
            Hunchlab

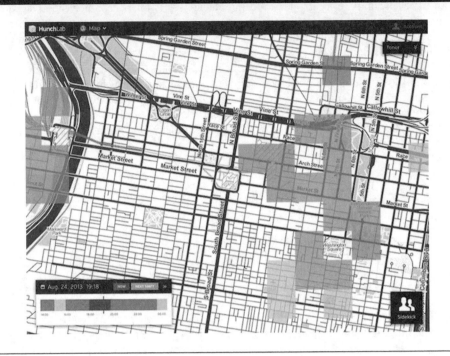

Hit rate: Measure of predictive accuracy used in predictive policing, which is defined by the number of crime incidents that actually fall within a predicted crime hot spot, based on past crime events. The hit rate is expressed as a simple percentage that ranges from 0% to 100%.

Predictive accuracy index (PAI): Used to assess the quality of prospective hot spot maps that is calculated as the ratio of the hit rate to the proportion of the study area that has been in a hot spot in the past. A higher PAI value reflects greater predictive accuracy.

Recapture rate index (RRI): Metric used to determine the quality of crime hot spot predictions. The RRI is based on the ratio of hot spot density for the present time and the previous time, standardized for changes in the total number of crimes in each year.

evaluating prospective crime hot spot maps include the hit rate, predictive accuracy index, and recapture rate index. Most often, these three metrics are used in combination to provide a robust picture of the predictive accuracy and reliability of a prospective crime hot spot map.

A **hit rate** is a measure of predictive accuracy of prospective crime hot spot maps. Hit rate is defined by the number of crime incidents that actually fall within a predicted crime hot spot, based on past crime events. The hit rate is expressed as a simple percentage that ranges from 0% to 100%. A higher hit rate corresponds to greater predictive accuracy of the forecast. The main limitation of the hit rate is that it can be artificially increased simply by making hot spots cover more of the study area. Nevertheless, increasing the hot spot coverage and the subsequent increase in hit rate would come at the expense of an agency's ability to patrol a larger hot spots.

In addition to the hit rate, a **predictive accuracy index (PAI)** can be used to assess the predictive accuracy of a prospective hot spot map. The PAI is calculated as the ratio of the hit rate to the proportion of the study area that is a hot spot in the past. For example, you may have 580 of 1,531 crimes fall in forecasted hot spot areas, which yields a hit rate of 0.3788 (i.e., 580 / 1,531 = 0.3788 or about 38%). If the total area of the forecasted hot spots was 68 km^2 and the total study area was 1,035 km^2, then the PAI would be 5.77 (i.e., 0.3788 / [68 / 1,035]). Like the hit rate, a higher PAI value reflects greater predictive accuracy. The PAI controls for the size of the hot spots, which overcomes the primary limitation of a hit rate.

Finally, the **recapture rate index (RRI)** is another metric used to determine the quality of crime hot spot predictions. The RRI is based on the ratio of hot spot density for the present period and the previous period, standardized for changes in the total number of crimes in each year. By building on the previous example used to calculate the PAI, if the PAI at Time 1 was

5.77 and the PAI at Time 2 was 4.87, the RRI would be 1.18 (i.e., 5.77 / 4.87). An important difference between the PAI and the RRI is that the RRI considers time to be an important factor in predicting crime hot spots because it relies on two PAIs in its calculation: a historical PAI (Time1) and a current PAI (Time2).

Risk Terrain Modeling

Academics have also developed forecasting techniques similar to, but distinct from, those associated with predictive policing. Perhaps most noteworthy of these methods is called **risk terrain modeling (RTM)**. RTM was developed by Joel Caplan and Les Kennedy at Rutgers University, in collaboration with Eric Piza at SUNY. RTM takes a slightly different approach to predictive crime analysis. Instead of simply using past locations of crime events to inform decisions about where crime will occur in the future, RTM uses a more holistic strategy that is strongly guided by criminological theory.

RTM is a forecasting process that identifies the spatial influence of multiple factors found in the environment that are associated with elevated risk of criminal victimization. Existing criminological theory (e.g., routine activities theory, opportunity theory, and crime pattern theory) is used to inform decisions about factors that are used to model an area's risk patterns. For example, Paul and Patricia Brantinghams' (1999) crime pattern theory suggests a high concentration of crime will cluster within small geographic areas (i.e., crime hot spots), and that these areas of elevated risk of victimization are best characterized as one of three different kinds of places: crime generators, crime attractors, or crime enablers.

Risk terrain modeling (RTM): Crime analysis technique used to identify risks that come from features of a landscape. RTM models how these risk factors are co-located to result in unique behavior settings for crime.

© Jeremy Waller. Reprinted with permission.

A bus stop in Henderson, Nevada that is near a shopping plaza but designed within materials that allow for increased visibility.

Crime generators: Places that attract large numbers of both offenders and victims, such as shopping malls, sporting events, parades, and other festivities.

Crime attractors: Places that are attractive to offenders simply due to the nature of the activity that occurs at that particular location.

Crime enablers: Locations that have little or no regulation of behavior. The lack of control increases the likelihood for crime to occur.

Crime generators are places that attract large numbers of both offenders and victims, such as shopping malls, sporting events, parades, and other festivities. Some areas, such as bus/subway interchanges or huge "park and ride" parking lots, may become crime generators as a result of the large number of people that come and go. These locations have a high number of criminal incidents simply because of the sheer volume of people interacting in one area. Large numbers of potentially unprotected targets mingle with motivated offenders, creating many opportunities for crimes to occur.

One possible solution to curbing crime at this type of hot spot is to increase the level of protection, possibly through increased police or security presence or through environmental design strategies. For example, the photo (left) shows a bus stop location in Henderson, Nevada. The stop is located in close proximity to a shopping plaza. The bus stop seating area is enclosed in metal mesh to increase visibility and reduce risk of victimization for those waiting for public transportation.

Crime attractors are a bit different than crime generators. Crime attractors are places that are attractive to offenders simply because of the nature of the activity that occurs at that location—offenders are looking to have a good time and not actively searching out a potential target to victimize. Conversely, a crime attractor location is known to provide many criminal opportunities and motivated offenders are drawn to these locations to commit crimes. Areas with open-market drug sales, bar districts, large unsecured parking areas, or known prostitution strolls would be examples of crime attractors. To reduce crime at these locations, offenders must somehow be discouraged from coming to the location.

Crime enablers are locations that have little or no regulation of behavior. The lack of control increases the likelihood for crime to occur. According to Clarke and Eck (2005), changes in the level of guardianship may be abrupt (such as when the services of a bouncer at a bar are eliminated) or may be gradual over time, as the level of monitoring slowly erodes. Because of the unsavory reputation, many victims tend to avoid going to these locations. Unknowing or unwitting attendees tend to put themselves at high risk because there are fewer targets for the motivated offenders to prey on. Crime may be reduced at these locations by reinforcing the level of guardianship—one of the three core concepts related to routine activities theory.

Ideas about elevated victimization risk that are found in crime pattern theory are applied to prospective crime hot spot mapping produced by RTM. Specifically, researchers combine separate risk map layers, made up of various crime generators and attractors, using kernel density estimation (KDE) to produce a composite risk terrain map. The RTM map shows the presence, absence, or intensity of all risk factors at every location throughout the landscape, simultaneously. Clustering of illegal activity in particular areas is explained in RTM by the unique combination of risk factors that make these areas opportune locations for crime. Clustering occurs when the potential for or risk of crime results from all the factors found at these places. Figure 10.10 is an example of an RTM map showing areas of elevated risk of assaults against police, involving firearms, throughout Chicago.

One feature of RTM that makes it especially appealing is the Risk Terrain Modeling Diagnostics Utility (RTMDx). This software allows researchers or practitioners to enter geolocated crime data and location data for selected features (i.e., risk factors) that are found in the community (e.g., bars, bus stops, schools, etc.). Once the user specifies outcome variables (e.g., street robbery locations), the utility then measures the spatial correlation between where the crimes have occurred and where they are in relation to different features

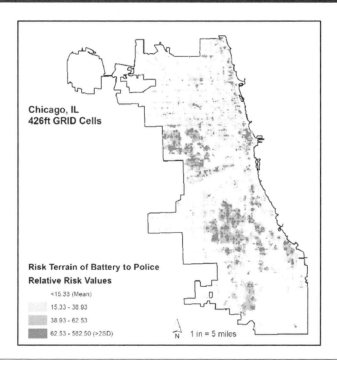

Chicago, IL
426ft GRID Cells

Risk Terrain of Battery to Police
Relative Risk Values

<15.33 (Mean)
15.33 - 38.93
38.93 - 62.53
62.53 - 582.50 (>2SD)

1 in = 5 miles

of the environment. The educational version of RTMDx can be downloaded for free at www
.rutgerscps.org/software.html. RTM and the research team from Rutgers have received a
growing number of awards and accolades in recent years, demonstrating RTM's utility and
popularity within the academic and practitioner communities.

Aoristic Analysis

Aoristic analysis is another crime analysis technique developed by the academic community and used by academics and practitioners to study crime patterns. Unlike the methods
discussed previously in this chapter, aoristic analysis is focused on identifying temporal, or
time-dependent, patterns in crime data. Specifically, **aoristic analysis** is a statistical method
used for determining the 24-hour rhythm of crimes when the exact time of crime event is
unknown. Jerry Ratcliffe of Temple University developed aoristic analysis and first characterized it as a way to estimate "the probability that an event occurred at a location within given
temporal parameters" (2000, p. 670). The following illustration provides a better explanation
of this particular crime analysis technique.

Suppose you had data on ten burglary incidents and wanted to identify temporal patterns in the data by using aoristic analysis. To begin with, you realize that one of the distinct
characteristics of burglaries is that it is a type of crime where the victim often does not know
exactly when it occurred. Instead, a victim has an idea of approximately when the crime was
committed, based on a time span or time interval. This time span is derived from the time
that someone was last at his or her residence *before* it was burglarized to the time someone
arrived back at the home *after* the criminals stuck—these times could also be established by a

Aoristic analysis: Crime
analysis method used for
determining the 24-hour
rhythm of crimes when the
exact time of crime event
is unknown.

neighbor or someone else not residing at the property (i.e., a witness). Therefore, each of the ten hypothetical burglaries used in this example has a "start" time and an "end" time, instead of an exact time the crime occurred.

Next, imagine that the "start" and "end" times for each of the ten hypothetical burglaries were plotted along a number line, which depicts every hour of the day, at one-hour intervals. If the ten burglaries used in this example were timed as in Table 10.1, then we would start our aoristic analysis by determining the proportion of each of the ten events that falls within each hour interval, according to the entire event time span.

This approach is fairly obvious for an incident like Burglary 3 or Burglary 4 in Table 10.1 since these events span only one one-hour interval. For example, we are 100% certain that Burglary 4 occurred between 9:00 am and 10:00 am; and therefore, the proportion of the event allocated to this one-hour time interval would be "1." Similarly, Burglary 2 spans two intervals (i.e., the 11:00 am and 12:00 pm interval); thus, each interval would be allocated a value of 0.5, which represents a 50% chance that the incident occurred during each hour.

When this approach to proportioning burglary events across one-hour intervals is completed for each of the ten hypothetical incidents presented in Table 10.1, the information in Table 10.2 is derived.

Finally, the next step in aoristic analysis it to sum the proportions of burglary events that were allocated to each one-hour interval in Table 10.2. From this information, one would then produce a chart that depicts the "intensity" of burglaries over time. For example, Figure 10.11 shows a bar chart with the hypothetical burglary data used in this example to depict the temporal patterns derived from our aoristic analysis. The hours of the day are plotted along the x-axis and the "temporal weight" of the ten burglaries on the y-axis. This example of aoristic analysis is very simplistic and does not go into some of the details that must be followed to produce more accurate results. For example, incident time spans often begin on one day and carry over into the next. Furthermore, the use of whole-hour intervals is also uncommon (i.e., it is more common to use 15-minute intervals). Nevertheless, it provides a simple explanation of how this technique is performed.

Although producing an accurate aoristic crime pattern can be tricky, there are many websites that can assist. For example, a Microsoft Excel™ spreadsheet that allows data to be

Table 10.1   Ten Example Burglaries

Incident #	Sometime After	Sometime Before
Burglary 1	08:00	14:00
Burglary 2	11:00	13:00
Burglary 3	16:00	17:00
Burglary 4	09:00	09:30
Burglary 5	07:00	17:00
Burglary 6	08:00	12:00
Burglary 7	22:00	02:00
Burglary 8	22:00	08:00
Burglary 9	13:00	21:00
Burglary 10	10:00	14:00

Table 10.2 Proportioning of Burglary Events Across One-Hour Intervals for Ten Hypothetical Incidents

Hour	Burglary ID									
	1	2	3	4	5	6	7	8	9	10
1							.25	.10		
2								.10		
3								.10		
4								.10		
5								.10		
6								.10		
7					.10			.10		
8	.17				.10	.25				
9	.17			1.0	.10	.25				
10	.17				.10	.25				.25
11	.17	.50			.10	.25				.25
12	.17	.50			.10					.25
13	.17				.10				.13	.25
14					.10				.13	
15					.10				.13	
16			1.0		.10				.13	
17									.13	
18									.13	
19									.13	
20									.13	
21										
22							.25	.10		
23							.25	.10		
24							.25	.10		

entered into cells that will conduct the analysis automatically is available for free download at PoliceAnalyst.com (http://policeanalyst.com/revisiting-aoristic-analysis/). Similarly, Michael Townsley of Griffith University in Australia has developed a ShinyApp website that will conduct aoristic analysis automatically from crime data contained in a simple Excel spreadsheet. The data need to contain (a) Start Date (in dd/mm/yy format), (b) Start Time (in HH:MM:SS format), (c) End Date (in dd/mm/yy format), and (d) End Time (in HH:MM:SS format). Once

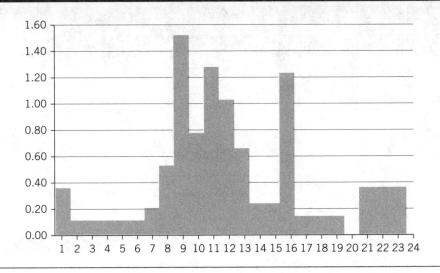

Figure 10.11 Temporal Patterns of 10 Burglaries Identified Using Ratcliffe's (2000) Aoristic Analysis

Boost account: One of two explanations of the repeat victimization phenomenon. It suggests that repeat/near repeat victimization is a result of the same offender returning to where he or she succeeded at committing the initial offense because the initial offense increased the offender's perception of reward and decreased the risk (i.e., "boosted" his or her confidence).

Flag account: One of two explanations of the repeat victimization phenomenon. The flag account suggests it is the characteristics of the person/target that entice potential offenders but that these characteristics remain constant over time.

the analysis is complete, a bar chart like the one in Figure 10.11 is produced. The website is located at https://crime-analysis-apps.shinyapps.io/aoristic_strict_formating/.

Repeat Victimization and Near Repeats

Repeat victimization (RV) and near repeat victimization (NRV) are patterns commonly identified in crime data. RV and NRV are phenomena whereby the likelihood of victims (i.e., people) or targets (i.e., places) of crime to be victimized more than once is greater than the likelihood of someone/place being victimized for the first time. Two explanations have been offered to better understand RV/NRV patterns. First, the **boost account** suggests that RV/NRV is a result of the same offender returning to where he or she succeeded at committing the initial offense. The boost account explanation is based on optimal foraging theory, which suggests a simple risk–reward assessment of the situation: Time and effort (and risk of apprehension) should be diminished, while benefit and reward should be maximized. An alternative explanation of RV/NRV is the **flag account**. The flag account suggests the characteristics of the person/target entice potential offenders. Note that these characteristics remain constant over time. Simply put, the boost account explains the RV/NRV phenomena in terms of the behavior of the offender, whereas the flag account explains it in terms of the characteristics of the target or victim.

The most common approach to identifying RV/NRV patterns in crime data is through the application of the Near Repeat Calculator. Developed by Jerry Ratcliffe at Temple University, the Near Repeat Calculator can be downloaded for free at www.cla.temple.edu/cj/center-for-security-and-crime-science/projects/nearrepeatcalculator and can be distributed for educational purposes at no cost. Figure 10.12 is an image of the Near Repeat Calculator interface, where the user provides a crime data file (in .csv format—available in Excel™) that contains three simple characteristics for each crime event: the latitude coordinate, the longitude coordinate, and the date of the incident. Next, the user sets four parameters that guide the analysis: the spatial bandwidth (e.g., 400 ft), number of spatial bands (e.g., 4), temporal

Figure 10.12 Near Repeat Calculator Interface

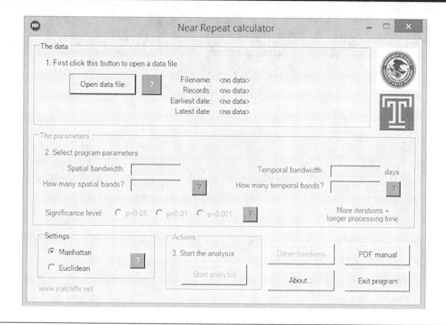

bandwidth (e.g., 14 days), and number of temporal bands (e.g., 13). The researcher can also set the significance level for statistical testing, choosing between $p = .05$, $p = .10$, and $p = .01$. Levels of significance for statistical testing are discussed in greater detail in Chapter 12.

The first two parameters, spatial bandwidth and spatial bands, are used to determine whether spatial patterns exist in the data. To make observed spatial patterns in the data easier to interpret, they are disaggregated into distance bands (i.e., spatial bands). For example, if each block in a study area is about 400 feet, then a spatial bandwidth of 400 ft might be appropriate. This will allow the user to understand the output in terms a certain number of blocks, which would be a reflection of a feature (i.e., city blocks) found in the urban landscape. In addition, the number of spatial bands is used to quantify how far RV/NRV patterns in the data are expected to extend. If, for example, RV/NRV patterns are believed to extend 1,600 ft and a distance band is set at 400 ft, then the number of spatial bands would be set at 4 (4 bands × 400 ft bandwidth = 1,600 ft distance). In short, the spatial distance, divided by the spatial bandwidth, produced the number of spatial bands used in the analysis.

The temporal bands and bandwidths use a similar logic, but they are applied to identify temporal patterns in the data. The temporal bandwidth refers to the length of time after a crime occurs that the program will "search" for repeat incidents. This parameter can be set at number of days (i.e., 7 days, 14 days, 21 days, etc.). Bandwidths commonly used in previous research included one week, two weeks, and one month. Finally, you must determine how long to continue to search for patterns (i.e., how many days) and divide this temporal distance by the number of temporal bandwidths to establish the number of temporal bands to use in your analysis. This is comparable to how the number of spatial bands is determined (e.g., 13 bands × 14-day bandwidth = 6-month period).

When output from the Near Repeat Calculator is produced, distances are reported as either straight-line distance (i.e., Euclidean distance or as the crow flies) or grid-based distance (i.e., Manhattan distance and imagine walking blocks in Manhattan), which is used

Most predictive policing efforts aim to proactively forecast *crime*, but the study by Daley et al. (2016) offers a unique twist to this process. This study involved an innovative application of RTM, testing whether it can be used to develop a prediction model of child maltreatment. Specifically, the researchers wanted to examine the, "cumulative effect of environmental factors thought to be conducive for child maltreatment" in the City of Fort Worth, Texas, by using RTM.

Researchers began their study only after a hospital IRB conducted a full review of the study proposal. The IRB approved the entire research study, including the collection and analysis of all data. Then, existing data from (a) the Fort Worth Police Department, (b) the Texas Alcoholic Beverage Commission, and (c) the Department of Family and Protective Services were obtained and entered into the Risk Terrain Modeling Diagnostics (RTMDx) professional utility for analysis.

Factors believed to increase the risk of child maltreatment, including the commission of aggravated assaults, robberies, murders, domestic violence, narcotics crimes, the presence of gangs and street prostitution, along with runaways, households living under the federal poverty line, and the presence of bars and nightclubs with a license to serve alcoholic beverages past midnight were included in the analysis. Analysis of these data in the RTMDx utility involved a regression process to determine the best-fitting risk terrain model, which was based on a Negative Binomial type II model that retained six of the initial ten risk factors.

Specifically, the RTMDx utility examined the geographical distributions of all entered risk factors and created risk maps (i.e., a choropleth map) for each factor. All locations that were either within a certain distance of points or exhibited a significant density of points were coded as one for having elevated risk, and all other locations were coded as zero. The RTMDx algorithm then identified the best-fit prediction model through a series of regression analyses using the statistical software R. The best-fitting model was displayed on a rasterized cell map that showed the aggregate risk score for each raster cell dependent on how many of the included risk factors exhibited elevated risk levels within it, using ArcGIS 10.3.

To test model fit, the resulting 2013 RTM model was overlaid with the actual locations of substantiated occurrences of child maltreatment A total of 52% of all future cases were accurately predicted in the 10% of highest risk cells, and almost all observed incidents were located in cells that were predicted to have an elevated risk. To examine the performance of RTM against a traditional hot spot (HS) model, a corresponding hot spot analysis was conducted based on 2013 data from just the Department of Family and Protective Services (i.e., child maltreatment cases). The results showed that the RTM model outperformed the traditional hot spot prediction model using kernel density estimation (KDE) by more than 10% (i.e., the percentage of cases accurately predicted by RTM was greater than the percentage of cases accurately predicted by KDE). These findings will enable future interventions designed to reduce cases of child maltreatment to optimize the allocation of scarce prevention and treatment resources in narrowly confined, highest need locations.

Daley, D., Bachmann, M., Bachmann, B. A., Pedigo, C., Bui, M., & Coffman, J. (2016). Risk terrain modeling predicts child maltreatment. *Child Abuse & Neglect, 62*, 29–38.

to reflect street networks. These distances are reported in a simple RV/NRV table, where the columns of the table are associated with time (i.e., temporal bandwidths) and the rows of the table are associated with distance (i.e., spatial bandwidths). Each cell of the table indicates the likelihood of another victimization occurring at that time/distance, following an initial incident, and those that are significantly higher than expected likelihoods of repeat victimization (or near repeat victimizations) are color coded for easy identification.

Geographic Profiling

Another popular crime analysis technique that involves identifying patterns of offending is **geographic profiling**. Geographic profiling is a method for identifying the most probable area in which a serial offender lives. This information is gathered using known locations of crimes that are believed to be committed as part of a series of the offender's linked events. Developed by Kim Rossmo at Simon Frasier University's School of Criminology in Canada, geographic profiling was originally intended for use in identifying serial rapists and murderers:

> Geographic profiling focuses on the probable spatial behaviour of the offender within the context of the locations of, and the spatial relationships between, the various crime sites. A psychological profile provides insights into an offender's likely motivation, behaviour and lifestyle, and is therefore directly connected to his/her spatial activity. Psychological and geographic profiles thus act in tandem to help investigators develop a picture of the person responsible for the crimes in question. (1997, p. 161)

At the heart of geographic profiling is the idea that serial offenders are less likely to commit offenses very near to their homes and that offenders will not travel too far to commit additional crimes.

At the heart of geographic profiling is the idea that serial offenders are less likely to commit offenses close to their homes, and that offenders will not travel too far to commit additional crimes. These journey-to-crime assumptions were used to create the original geographical profiling formula, developed by Rossmo (1997): the distance decay function. Hot spots identified by Santos and her colleague (Santos & Santos, 2016) in their evaluation of offender-focused intervention strategies implemented in Port St. Lucie, Florida, were constructed, in part, based on the distance decay function (i.e., offenders were more likely to reoffend close, but not too close, to their home residence).

Commercial geographic profiling software can be purchased from ECRI, a company co-founded by Rossmo. Free software is also available that can conduct geographic profiling, such as CrimeStatIV (https://nij.gov/topics/technology/maps/pages/crimestat.aspx). When used to analyze crime data, geographic profiling results in output that is similar in appearance to a hot spot map (i.e., the output is a raster surface data layer). Unlike a hot spot map, however, the geographic profiling map associates the "hottest" part of the map with the locations of where a serial offender is most likely to live, visualized in three dimensions.

Geographic profiling: Crime analysis method used for identifying the most probable area in which a serial offender lives, based on the known locations of crimes that are believed to be committed as part of a series of linked events.

Reporting Findings From GIS and Crime Mapping Studies

Many researchers have long careers without ever having used crime mapping. Nevertheless, that may be changing. Brunson acknowledges that he has seen an increased interest in GIS and crime mapping among students. In his phone interview conducted for this book, Brunson noted that students really want to "strengthen their technical skill set; a growing and beneficial skill set for students to make sure they're as masterful as they can be." Knowing how to report findings from GIS and crime mapping studies is an important skill in studying crime for them to master. Again, skills like these make students marketable.

The ways in which researchers and analysts report findings from GIS and crime-mapping studies will vary, depending on the topics investigated and the methodologies used. Typically, results are reported in graphical (i.e., charts and graphs) or in tabular form. Most often, however, findings are conveyed cartographically as maps. When findings are produced as maps, the map is the center of attention. When presenting findings using a map, there are map elements or parts of a map that should always be included.

First, all maps used to convey research findings need a title. A good map title conveys the general theme of the map or findings to the reader. A title should be clear, concise, and include information about the area represented and a date range if applicable. The title should also be the first place that a reader looks on the map, so it should not be hiding or tucked away in a corner of the page. A title can have a subtitle but only if it adds additional, relevant information that will help the reader better understand what is being presented on the map.

Second, all maps used to convey research findings must also contain a **map legend** or key. Map legends explain what symbols on the map represent. The different types of vector data, for example, contained on a sex offender map presented previously in this chapter (see Figure 10.3) should all be included in a map legend, if this map were being used to present findings about sex offenders' proximity to schools. Without a map legend containing all the symbols reflected on the map, the map reader could make erroneous conclusions about the research findings presented or fail to understand the findings altogether.

It is important to note here that raster maps, like those used to convey results of hot spot maps (see, for example, Figure 10.4), should also contain a legend. Typically, raster data layers are symbolized using color ramps. On a crime hot spot map, a color ramp that goes from green to red to reflect low to high crime densities across the entire study area, respectively. One of the more common ways to break apart the different categories of a color ramp is to base the categories on **standard deviation** units, that is, the average distance something is from the mean value. When this approach is taken in crime hot spot mapping, the "hottest" of hot spots can by symbolized as the red areas that are more than two standard deviations above the average crime cluster (i.e., significantly high clustering). Using standard deviations (which are discussed in greater detail in Chapter 12) to break the color ramp into different sections will also keep the number of categories to a minimum. A good rule of thumb to follow is to have no more than seven color categories in a color ramp.

Third, all maps should have a north arrow. **North arrows** should be included with maps that convey crime analysis results displayed cartographically because they orient the map for the reader. In addition to orienting the reader directionally, all maps should include a **scale bar**—the fourth required element of a map—which orients the map reader with respect to distance. Scales indicate how much a distance on a map (e.g., 1") represents in the real world (e.g., 10 kilometers). Like north arrows, most mapping software will give the map creator several different scale-bar templates to choose from, and it is up to the researcher to choose the one that works "best" with the map he or she has created. Just be sure that the map scale bar is in the metric that most map readers are familiar with. In other words, if most of the map readers who will see your results are American, use feet or miles as the scale bar metric. On the other hand, if most users are European, it is best to use meters or kilometers.

Finally, maps containing the results of crime analysis or GIS studies must contain a citation or credit. The citation or credit identifies who created the map, when it was created, and acknowledges the assistance of those who supported the project, including agencies that may have provided the analyst or researcher with data needed to produce the map.

Common Pitfalls in GIS and Crime Mapping Analysis

Like any part of research, there are particular pitfalls to be avoided. GIS studies and crime mapping and analysis research is no different. In terms of GIS and crime mapping, there are two hazards that one must focus on geocoding nonspatial data and the modifiable areal unit (MAUP) problem.

Geocoding

Addresses are the most common way that location is conceptualized in geographic information systems. To use data containing address locations (e.g., crime data), the address must be converted to a feature on a map (i.e., a point location). That is, the addresses must be given spatial reference. The process of assigning spatial reference to nonspatial data is called **geocoding**. Geocoding involves assigning an XY coordinate pair to the description of a place (i.e., an address) by comparing the descriptive location-specific elements to those in reference data that have existing spatial information associated with it.

The geocoding process can be thought of as a process that can be broken into three steps. Step 1 involves translating an address entry for a nonspatially referenced location. Step 2 involves searching for that address in a separate, spatially referenced data set. The third and final step involves returning the best candidate or candidates (i.e., match or matches) as a point feature on the map that reflects the spatial location of the address.

One of the main challenges to accurate geocoding is the availability of good reference data, and the most widely employed address data model used in the geocoding process is street networks. Geocoding an address using street network reference data is referred to as street geocoding. Street geocoding is commonly used in criminal justice and criminology studies, but other types of geocoding exist, including geocoding to parcel reference data and address point reference data. Nearly all commercial GIS products (e.g., ArcGIS) provide geocoding services capabilities. Figure 10.13 provides a conceptual diagram of the geocoding process when addresses are street geocoded.

Certain quality expectations must be met for the results of a geocoding process to be considered good. That is, the overall quality of any geocoding result can be characterized in three distinct ways: completeness, positional accuracy, and repeatability. Completeness refers to the percentage of records that can reliably be geocoded and is commonly referred to as the match rate. Positional accuracy refers to how close each geocoded point is to the actual location of the address it is intended to represent (see, for example, Figure 10.14). Finally, repeatability indicates how sensitive geocoding results are to variations in the input address, reference data, matching algorithms of the geocoding software, and the skills and interpretation of the analyst. Geocoding results are considered to be of high quality if they are complete, spatially accurate (i.e., valid), and repeatable (i.e., reliable). Collectively, geocoding quality research clearly demonstrates that errors in geocoding can be substantial, and when they are, they can adversely impact findings and conclusions based on spatial analytic results.

> **Geocoding:** In GIS and crime analysis, it is the process of assigning an XY coordinate pair to the description of a place (i.e., an address) by comparing the descriptive location-specific elements of nonspatial data to those in reference data that have existing spatial information associated with it.

Modifiable Areal Unit Problem (MAUP)

In many of the crime mapping and analysis examples discussed in this chapter, the locations of points of interest (e.g., crime events) are symbolized as a single point on a map. Often, however, spatial analysis requires that discrete point locations be aggregated to larger units of analysis. For example, crime incident points are often aggregated to census blocks, block groups, patrol beats, or some other meaningful unit of analysis so that the number (or rate) of crimes per that area can be studied. Geographers have long warned of the problems that arise when point-based

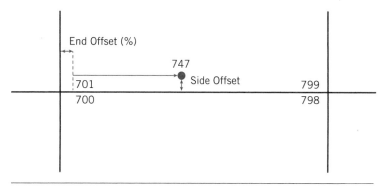

Figure 10.13 Conceptual Diagram of the Algorithm Behind Street Geocoding

Note: The location of an address is placed on a street segment based on linear interpolation along the street segment within the street number range for the segment.

Figure 10.14   Positional Accuracy Illustrated

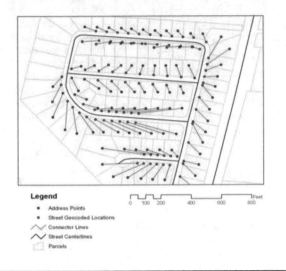

Legend
- Address Points
- Street Geocoded Locations
- Connector Lines
- Street Centerlines
- Parcels

Note: Pairs of dots correspond to the address point location and street geocoded location of a crime incident. The line connecting each pair of dots represents the positional error measured in Euclidean distance between the two locations.

measures of spatial phenomena, like crime, are aggregated to larger areal units. This phenomenon has become known as the **Modifiable Areal Unit Problem (MAUP)**.

MAUP is formally defined as "a problem arising from the imposition of artificial units of spatial reporting on continuous geographical phenomenon resulting in the generation of artificial spatial patterns" (Heywood, Cornelius, & Carver, 2002, p. 8). For example, by definition, an administrative boundary represented as a census block, block group, or tract can contain several households. Each household represents a discrete location and can be associated with demographic information collected from residents during a particular data collection project (e.g., the decennial U.S. Census or the American Community Survey). When these point-based data are aggregated to blocks, block groups, or tracts so that the effects of some social process on a particular outcome can be estimated, models may produce biased estimates because of the arbitrary scale of the spatial unit. This means that findings produced from crime analysis and mapping may be influenced by the mapmaker's decision about how best to represent discrete point data when using larger units of analysis.

Ethical Considerations in GIS and Crime Mapping Research

Modifiable Areal Unit Problem (MAUP): In geographic information systems (GIS), it is a problem arising from the imposition of artificial units of spatial reporting on continuous geographical phenomenon, which results in the generation of artificial spatial patterns.

When GIS and crime mapping research is undertaken, many ethical issues must be considered. These considerations often relate to the balance between personal privacy and the integrity of results. Based on information already presented in this text, you should know that a researcher wanting to conduct spatial analysis on crime event locations would need to get his or her research approved by the university's institutional review board (IRB). The IRB would likely require that any results produced by the researcher's project not expose the location of where an individual victim lives (or any other personal identifying information such as his or her name). We have also discussed in this chapter how different methods of geocoding data can affect data quality, such as positional accuracy. Similarly, we have described how aggregating point data to larger units of analysis may introduce additional problems (e.g., MAUP) and how a single approach to understanding a problem (e.g., crime hot spots) can be studied using a variety of techniques and methods that could produce inconsistent results. As you can see, this is quickly becoming a tricky balancing act.

The ethical tightrope between protecting crime victims' privacy and producing results that are accurate and unbiased is not limited to just academics. Crime analysts must also consider these ethical issues. For example, many law enforcement agencies make their crime incident data available to the public on the Internet in an effort to provide greater transparency. Often this is accomplished through the publication of interactive crime maps that are available on the Internet (see, for example, Figure 10.6). To protect the privacy of crime victims, discrete point data representing the locations of where incidents occur are often "masked." One way to do this is to round address house numbers to the 100-block (i.e., a crime that occurred at 123 Main St. would be reported and shown on the Web-based map as 100 Main St.). Although this approach helps protect victims' identities, it could undermine the integrity of the data by falsely portraying an area of the city in terms of crime concentration. In other words, when crime data are masked by agencies, it can be good because it helps protect victims' identities, but it can be bad because it may result in information indicating areas of the city have more or less crime than they actually do.

GIS and Crime Mapping Expert—Henri Buccine-Schraeder, MA

Henri Buccine-Schraeder is a research coordinator at Rutgers Center on Public Security at the School of Criminal Justice at Rutgers University, Newark, New Jersey. She studied psychology, sociology, criminal justice, and criminology for her undergraduate degree and criminal justice for her master's degree. Buccine-Schraeder is now studying for her Doctorate in criminal justice. She became interested in working in criminal justice during an undergraduate internship with the New Jersey Department of Corrections, where she was studying sex offenders.

When Buccine-Schraeder started her studies in her master's program, she began working with GIS and RTM as a research assistant for Rutgers Center on Public Security. While in this role, she geocoded and analyzed spatial data, created reports using density mapping, Getis Ord GI*, and RTM. These reports are used to inform interventions with police departments around the country.

As a project manager for Rutgers Center on Public Security, Buccine-Schraeder is in charge of coordinating with grant stakeholders and managing the research assistants who are assigned to the project. For most of these projects, it is important to meet with the police departments and other community partners to bolster the knowledge that is informed from the maps and analysis. In addition to these tasks, she continues the analyses and duties of a research assistant.

Within the role of research coordinator for Rutgers Center on Public Security, it is Buccine-Schraeder's duty to continue to perform the responsibilities of project manager, as well as completing administrative duties, being a liaison between departments, schools, and organizations, project coordination, and overseeing daily operations. Projects while in the role of research coordinator have been within the School of Criminal Justice as well as other projects that have been completed in conjunction with the Psychology Department.

For some of the projects completed by Rutgers Center on Public Security, it has been Buccine-Schraeder's role to conduct literature reviews and meet with stakeholders and project partners. This is an important first step to inform the project that is being undertaken. Next, it is important to collect all data and keep it well organized. Analyses can then begin, including pin mapping, kernel density mapping, and RTM. The results of all analyses are then discussed with all stakeholders and project partners to better understand the story that the maps and analyses are telling. This approach is one that best informs policy and interventions.

Buccine-Schraeder has also worked as a research assistant for Department of Sociology at Rutgers University in New Brunswick, New Jersey. For this project, she worked on acquiring data on cities around the country. She then would take crime data, clean it, and both manually geocode it and use an online geocoder. With all the data and shapefiles that were created, it was important to make sure that everything was well organized.

While tutoring GIS, Buccine-Schraeder shares her spatial expertise with doctoral students needing to use the skill for their dissertation or for work they expect to be doing after graduation. She teaches them how to use ArcGIS from the bottom up. It is important to teach the different options that are available through the use of the software and the different levels of analysis that ArcGIS is able to complete. The most important lesson that is taught through tutoring is how to effectively communicate through maps and how to get their point across to their audience.

Henri has presented at many conferences in cities around the country, including San Diego, Chicago, and Washington, D.C. These conferences include the American Society for Criminology (ASC) conference, the International Association of Chiefs of Police conference, the International Association of Crime Analysts conference (IACA), and the Mensa Annual Gathering. Her presentations have included the examination of environmental risk factors and the use of spatial risk assessments to understand residential locations of registered sex offenders, looking at the spatial influence of ATMs on street crimes, and comparing the environmental risk differences between violent crime incidents that result in arrest and violent crime incidents that do not.

In the future, Buccine-Schraeder hopes to continue to use her mapping skills and knowledge of RTM to help police departments and municipalities to improve their allocation of resources. Furthermore, she hopes to continue to disseminate her knowledge through presentations and publications.

Chapter Wrap-Up

In this chapter, we introduced readers to GIS and crime mapping and analysis as a distinct research methodology by using specific types of data. We explained why researchers and practitioners use GIS and crime mapping techniques to study crime and other crime-related problems. We provided a detailed description of GIS by identifying its four primary components: data, technology, application, and people. Crime analysis conducted by law enforcement agencies was detailed, in the context of administrative, tactical, and strategic rime analysis roles. On the academic side, we presented several techniques and methods commonly used in research. In particular, our discussion focused on spatial crime analysis methods (e.g., crime hot spot mapping, predictive policing, and risk terrain modeling), as well as temporal analysis (e.g., aoristic analysis). We also discussed the repeat and near repeat victimization phenomena as well as geographic profiling. We concluded the chapter with an overview of how results from GIS and crime mapping and analysis should be presented cartographically, identified two of the most common pitfalls, and discussed some of the ethical considerations associated with this approach.

Only one of our featured researchers used crime mapping in her case study: Santos (Santos & Santos, 2016). In her research, she used many of the concepts described here. Her research included an experimental element and hot spots were the units that were assigned to either an experimental or a control group. She was guided in part by the notion that offenders commit crime near, but not too near, their own homes. Santos and colleague's research is a great example of how GIS and crime mapping techniques can both inform our greater understanding of policing and provide findings that inform the way police do their jobs. Table 10.3 offers some information about her work as it relates to GIS and crime mapping.

In the next chapter, we introduce readers to evaluation research. We explain how it differs from other research methodologies, why it is important, and the ways in which it can be conducted. We also explain what the common challenges, pitfalls, and ethical considerations confronted by research conducting evaluation research.

Table 10.3 Featured Research: GIS Techniques, Concepts, and Outcomes

Researcher	Spatial Crime Analysis Method	How Hot Spots Were Defined	Other Geostatistical Concepts	Preparing Hot Spots for Analysis	Outcome
Rachel Santos	Hot Spot Analysis	Administrative boundaries made up of U.S. Census blocks that were combined to create hot spots ($N = 48$). Hot spots were consistent in square mileage and numbers of reported crimes.	Distance decay function and journey to crime algorithms influence the way hot spots were created.	Half of the hot spots in each block were randomly assigned to one of two groups: a treatment group or a control group. In total, there were 6 high crime per offender hot spots, 13 medium crime per offender hot spots, and 5 low crime per offender hot spots, for a total of 24 in each group.	No significant indication that the treatment had an effect on crime or arrest counts, or on repeat arrests of the targeted or nontargeted offenders living in the hot spots.

Applied Assignments

1. Homework Applied Assignment: Crime Mapping and Analysis in Academic Research

Find a map used in a peer-reviewed published academic journal article in criminal justice or criminology. In your thought paper, describe the purpose of this map. What is your overall assessment of it? Identify two aspects or characteristics of the map that you feel could have been done better, given the material presented in this chapter. Describe how you would improve these shortcomings, and explain why your way would be better than the original way in which the data were presented. Conclude your paper by explaining what value you place on data presented cartographically, like the data presented in the map you identified? Turn in the map and your thought paper. Be prepared to discuss your findings in class.

2. Group Work in Class Applied Assignment: Geocoding Campus Crime Data

As a group, go online and obtain a copy of a university's crime log (e.g., UNLV Police Service's Crime Log, located at https://www.unlv.edu/police/crime-log). Whether it's the log from UNLV or from another university, make sure the crime log you obtain contains the reported location of each crime incident. From the same university's website, obtain a copy of a campus map (e.g., the campus map of UNLV, located at http://resnetstc.org/2016/wp-content/uploads/2015/07/CampusMap_new.png).

Taking turns, have each member of the group identify the location of a few incidents recorded by the police and that occurred on or around campus. Plot those locations on the campus map as discrete points. In your group's view, how positionally accurate are the incident locations

(Continued)

you've placed on the campus map? What challenges have you identified with respect to geocoding campus crime data and the lack of detailed reference data that could be used for geocoding campus crime? How might these challenges affect the spatial analysis of campus crime and the subsequent strategies designed to address spatio-temporal patterns of campus crime? Be able to report your group's findings to the class.

3. Internet Applied Assignment: Online Crime Mapping and Analysis

Find a law enforcement agency's website that presents its crime data using an interactive online mapping interface, like the one described earlier in this chapter for the Denver Police Department. Once a website is located, and if the interface allows it, define (a) the area within the agency's jurisdiction you're interested in displaying, (b) the crime type(s) you're interested in investigating, and (c) a date range.

After these parameters are defined and the map is produced, identify the elements on your map that are based on vector data. Can the map be manipulated to also display raster data? If so, how? Also, does the map that you produced from the agency's website incorporate all five map elements that should always been included on a map? If not, which elements are not present, and how do you think the map would be improved if the missing element or elements were included?

Does the interactive map allow the user to conduct any type of analysis based on the information displayed (e.g., hot spot analysis)? If so, can the data be analyzed? if not, how might they be analyzed in ways that would benefit the user? Explain.

Finally, does the interactive map do a good job at balancing the privacy of victims/offenders with public interest? If so, how; if not, why? Explain. Present the answers to these questions in a one-page summary narrative describing the agency's interactive crime mapping system.

Be prepared to discuss your findings in class.

KEY WORDS AND CONCEPTS

Administrative crime analysis 320
Aoristic analysis 329
Boost account 332
Choropleth map 313
Cluster analysis 322
CompStat 321
Crime analysis 320
Crime attractors 328
Crime enablers 328
Crime generators 328
Crime mapping 320
Flag account 332

Geocoding 337
Geographic profiling 335
Hit rate 326
Hot spot mapping 324
Map legend 336
Modifiable Areal Unit Problem (MAUP) 338
North arrow 336
Predictive accuracy index (PAI) 326
Predictive policing 325
Raster 317
Raster data 316

Recapture rate index (RRI) 326
Risk terrain modeling (RTM) 327
Scale bar 336
Self-exciting point process modeling 325
Spatial data 315
Standard deviation 336
Strategic crime analysis 322
Tactical crime analysis 321
Vector data 316

KEY POINTS

- Geographic information systems (GIS) is a field of information technology that deals specifically with the collection, storage, manipulation, analysis, management, and presentation of geographical data; it consists of four distinct parts: data, technology, application, and people.

- GIS allows researchers and practitioners to use complex crime analysis techniques and methods to more easily and quickly identify spatio-temporal patterns of crime, which, in turn, has allowed us to advance our theoretical understanding of when, where, and why crime occurs. GIS has also enabled researchers and practitioners to develop, implement, and test programs and strategies designed to prevent and reduce crime.

- Crime analysts who work in law enforcement agencies generally conduct one of three types of crime analysis: administrative, tactical, or strategic crime analysis.

- Crime hot spot mapping is one of the most popular crime analysis techniques. It involves the use of known locations of recorded crime incidents to identify non-random, relatively high concentrations of crime events within a study area, using advanced spatial-analytic methods.

- Crime forecasting, or predictive policing, involves prospective crime hot spot mapping and can enable law enforcement agencies to identify areas within their jurisdiction that are more likely to experience crime. Risk terrain modeling is similar to predictive policing, but it corporates a broader array of risk factors associated with crime than most predictive policing applications.

- Three of the most commonly used metrics to assess prospective crime hot spot maps include the hit rate,

predictive accuracy index (PAI), and recapture rate index (RRI).

- Aoristic analysis is a crime analysis technique used to identify the temporal patterns in crime data.

- Repeat and near repeat patterns of crime are explained by two completing ideas: the boost and flag accounts.

- Geographic profiling is a method for identifying the most probable area in which a serial offender lives, based on the known locations of crimes that are believed to be committed as part of a series of linked events.

- Whenever results of crime analysis are presented cartographically, the map should always contain a title, north arrow, scale bar, legend, and citation.

- Accurately geocoding crime data, the modifiable areal unit (MAUP) problem, and the ethics involved in striking a balance between protecting the privacy of crime victims and accurately reporting crime-pattern results represent some of the common challenges facing researchers involved in crime analysis.

REVIEW QUESTIONS

1. Why are GIS and crime analysis/mapping a popular research method among academics and practitioners alike?

2. What are the two types of spatial data used in GIS?

3. How can strategic crime analysis be used by a law enforcement agency to study crime patterns? Explain.

4. How can tactical crime analysis be used by a law enforcement agency to study crime patterns? Explain.

5. How does risk terrain modeling differ from other predictive policing methods? Explain.

6. How is aoristic crime analysis used in crime analysis? Explain.

7. Compare and contrast the three commonly used metrics to assess prospective crime hot spot maps.

8. What are the five elements that all maps containing results of crime analysis contain?

9. What are the three ways in which vector data are characterized on a map?

10. How can positional accuracy of geocoded crime incidents affect crime analysis?

CRITICAL THINKING QUESTIONS

1. Imagine you were in charge of a law enforcement agency and wanted to evaluate a crime reduction program that you were about to implement. How could you go about assessing the program using crime mapping and analysis methods? What type of data could you need to collect, including spatial data, and how would you define success. How would you present the results of the evaluation study? Why?

2. Do you think different types of crime might have different types of spatial or temporal patterns? Explain.

3. Suppose you were responsible for creating your city's interactive online crime map. What sort of information would you include on the map? How much detail would you provide in terms of the locations of crime incidents? And how would you balance presenting

accurate information about where crime is occurring with keeping the information about crime victims private?

4. In your opinion, are there ways that data used in crime analysis and mapping projects can be collected that avoids the need for geocoding? Are there any data where geocoding would always be a required part of the analysis? Explain.

5. Which of the two explanations of repeat/near repeat victimization (i.e., flag or boost account) provides a better understanding of this phenomenon, in your opinion? Why?

$SAGE edge™

SAGE edge offers a robust online environment featuring an impressive array of free tools and resources for review, study, and further exploration, keeping you on the cutting edge of teaching and learning. Learn more at **edge.sagepub .com/rennisonrm**.

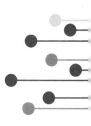

Introduction

This chapter switches gears a bit. We are not looking at specific types of ways to gather data, or at specific approaches to analyzing data, but instead we focus on how *all* of the ways one can gather data can be used to conduct an evaluation. Evaluation is one of the four purposes of research introduced in Chapter 2. Not only does it differ in terms of purpose, but it also differs in several other ways, as we will describe in this chapter. Featured researcher Carlos Cuevas and colleagues' highlighted study (Sabina, Cuevas, & Cotignola-Pickens, 2016) does not include an evaluation component, yet he still finds that evaluation research is particularly attractive because it represents a practical aspect of research. Another one of our featured researchers, Mary Dodge, reiterated the attractiveness of evaluation research by stating in her video interview conducted for this book that it is designed to determine the effectiveness, strengths, and weaknesses of programs. Rod Brunson, yet another featured researcher, agrees with Cuevas and Dodge that conducting evaluation research requires a good understanding of the nuts and bolts of research generally. In conducting evaluations, researchers or evaluators can identify the actual effectiveness of whether something is working. It allows for them to find a way to deal with problems.

To introduce you to evaluation research, this chapter offers a variety of foundational information. First, we discuss why one would use evaluation research. Understanding why evaluation research is important is imperative to grasping the rest of the material in this chapter. Next, we discuss what exactly evaluation research is and how it differs from the research approaches we have described in the text so far. Several specific types of evaluation research as well as the standards of effective evaluation are described. The chapter concludes with a discussion of ethical considerations that must be addressed when conducting an evaluation, as well as of the pitfalls commonly encountered. Finally, we hear from Michael Shively, PhD, an evaluation research expert at Abt Associates. He is focused on conducting evaluations especially related to human trafficking topics. As Shively's work demonstrates, evaluation research is applied, it matters, and it offers

Learning Objectives

After finishing this chapter, you should be able to:

11.1 Identify why someone would use evaluation research, and compare how applied research such as evaluation research differs from basic research.

11.2 Define, describe, and compare the major types of evaluation research and why one would use each.

11.3 Summarize the role of stakeholders, the challenges and benefits they bring, and how they are an important part of any evaluation research.

11.4 Describe what a logic model is, the basic steps associated with logic models, and the ways they can assist in evaluation research.

11.5 Summarize the four major standards of effective evaluations, and offer criteria associated with each.

11.6 Evaluate some of the additional ethical concerns associated with evaluation research. Why are these more significant when conducting this type of research?

a meaningful career path. Perhaps you can see yourself becoming an evaluation research expert where you can make a difference.

Why Use Evaluation Research?

Social programs are all around us. Consider those designed to assist victims of violence. Or a social program to help those coming out of prison integrate back into society. Social programs are designed to help others and ameliorate a social program. It stands to reason that the implementation of a social program should result in beneficial outcomes. Nevertheless, how do we know whether that social program is effective or not? How do we know a program actually helps crime victims or those trying to reintegrate into society? How do we know whether a program is resulting in outcomes and benefits intended? How do we know whether a program is working as it was designed? How can we be sure a program is not resulting in negative unintended consequences or harm to others? You can answer questions like these using evaluation research. With evaluation research (also known as "program evaluation"), you gather systematic, empirical evidence that can be used to find out whether a program leads to the desired beneficial outcomes, is effective, is doing what it is designed to do, or even whether the program leads to negative, unintended consequences (to name a few). At the most extreme, you can use evaluation research to ascertain whether a particular program should be terminated.

The alternative to gathering systematic, empirical data using well-executed research methods is relying on hunches, assumptions, and other nonscientific means. As we saw in the early chapters of this book, using these sources is problematic because they are frequently incorrect and misleading. Because implementing programs cost money, and programs directly affect individuals (both recipients and funders), it stands to reason that quality evaluation research should be an important part of any social program. This can ensure that costs are reasonable and that those who are supposed to be helped by the program are being helped and are not being harmed.

Imagine your university has started a new program requiring all students to attend an orientation. The new orientation program was started with four outcomes or goals in mind:

1. Educate students about the various resources available on campus (e.g., health club, mental health offices, writing centers, computer labs, etc.).

2. Educate students about important policies (e.g., anti-discrimination policies, anti-violence policy, animals on campus policies, etc.).

3. Educate students about the value of a college education (e.g., statistics on earning power, health and victimization risk among those with and without degrees).

4. Build attachment and loyalty to the university for continued support even after graduation.

Each year after the implementation of the required student orientation program, students are surveyed to measure their knowledge of campus resources, important policies, retention in the university, and attachment/loyalty to their university. Included in the survey are questions asking students about their understanding of these resources and policies and whether loyalty has increased, decreased, or remained the same during the last year. In addition, the university gathers data on retention—that is, the number of students who remain in college versus those who have dropped out. By using the survey data and institutional data, administrators can identify whether the orientation is leading to its intended outcomes: increased knowledge of resources and policies, higher retention rates, and increased loyalty to the university. If findings from the analysis of these data show that knowledge, loyalty, and retention are increasing, leadership would conclude that the orientation program is a success because it is providing the benefits intended. If, on the other hand, measurement of these four goals indicates that knowledge of resources and polices, retention, and loyalty are decreasing or even unchanged, leadership may conclude that the new orientation program is not providing the benefits intended. This finding may lead to some modification of the program or to the termination of the program. This fictional (but realistic) example illustrates why someone would use evaluation research.

As a student in the university, you are likely asked to fill out many surveys about your university experience. What do you know about resources at your university?

Evaluation research is useful for many reasons or purposes. As the orientation example indicates, program evaluation can be used to assess a program's performance. Relatedly, program evaluation is useful when a researcher wants to identify whether the program is accomplishing its intended goals. Third, someone can use evaluation research to identify whether the program is effective. In addition, as shown in the "Five Reasons to Use Evaluation Research" box, one reason evaluation research is useful is that can gather data used to provide accountability to those funding the program (e.g., tax-payers, board of directors, university leadership, etc.), those managing the program, or other related administrators. Finally, evaluation research can be used to gather evidence that can be used to educate those in the community about beneficial programs. Those eligible to receive the benefits of a program need to know about it, and those in the community who are indirectly benefiting from a program need to understand its importance as well.

Five Reasons to Use Evaluation Research

1. Assess the performance of a program.

2. Investigate whether a program is achieving its goals.

3. Improve the effectiveness of an existing program.

4. Provide accountability to program funders, program managers, and other administrators.

5. Gather information to educate the public about beneficial programs in the community.

Given the reasons outlined, it should not be a surprise that a great deal of funded social programs now have a required evaluation component. Those providing money for research want to know whether the policies or programs implemented are working as intended. Those providing the money for programs want evidence as to whether the program and its associated costs is worth it. This again points to an opportunity to use these skills in a career. Evaluation research is important, and the demands for those with these skills continue to increase.

What Is Evaluation Research?

We have identified *why* someone would use evaluation research. This section addresses the equally important question: What exactly is evaluation research? Evaluation research is the

Stakeholders: Individuals or organizations who have a direct interest in the program being evaluated.

Develop the research question: Step in the evaluation research process in which the evaluator shares the results of the research with stakeholders.

systematic assessment of the need for, implementation of, or output of a program based on objective criteria. As Cuevas describes it, evaluation research is one of the nicer more practical aspects of research—it is where the rubber meets the road. By using the data gathered in evaluation research, a researcher like you can improve, enhance, expand, or terminate a program. The assessment of a program can be conducted with any and all of the research approaches to research described in this text, including observation, interviews, content analysis, survey research, and secondary data analysis.

Guiding Principles of Evaluation Research

In 2004, the American Evaluation Association published a set of five guiding principles of evaluation research. Before learning more about evaluation research, it is important to understand these foundational elements that guide evaluators. The clear statement of these principles is useful to clients, or stakeholders, who know what to expect. The five principles are taken directly from the American Evaluation Association's statement on the matter (see www .eval.org/p/cm/ld/fid=51):

1. **Systematic Inquiry:** Evaluators conduct systematic, data-based inquiries about whatever is being evaluated.

2. **Competence:** Evaluators provide competent performance to stakeholders.

3. **Integrity/Honesty:** Evaluators ensure the honesty and integrity of the entire evaluation process.

4. **Respect for People:** Evaluators respect the security, dignity, and self-worth of the respondents, program participants, clients, and other stakeholders with whom they interact.

5. **Responsibilities for General and Public Welfare:** Evaluators articulate and take into account the diversity of interests and values that may be related to the general and public welfare.

You should recognize many of these principles already because they are the same principles used in conducting ethical research. With this foundational understanding of what evaluation research is, and what guides it, we can address the major steps taken when conducting this type of research.

Seven Steps of Evaluation Research

Regardless of the specific question guiding evaluation research, several basic steps are used in the evaluation. First, a researcher must **identify and engage stakeholders**. **Stakeholders** are individuals or organizations who have a direct interest in the program being evaluated and can include funders, program administrators, the community in which the program is administered, and clients of the program. Knowing who the stakeholders are, and developing and maintaining a good relationship with stakeholders, is critical during the planning stages, the gathering of data, and the presentation and buy-in of findings. Without the support of stakeholders, evaluation research cannot be successful.

The second basic step in evaluation research is to **develop the research question**. Unlike basic research, in evaluation research, the stakeholder generally provides the research question to the evaluator. For instance, a board of directors may engage a researcher with the express purpose of understanding whether a program is achieving its goals. In this example, the research question is as follows: "Is the program achieving its goals?" Establishing a

Figure 11.1   Seven Basic Steps Used to Conduct Evaluation
               Research

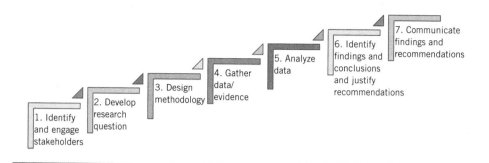

7. Communicate findings and recommendations

6. Identify findings and conclusions and justify recommendations

5. Analyze data

4. Gather data/evidence

3. Design methodology

2. Develop research question

1. Identify and engage stakeholders

research question is just the beginning as earlier chapters in this book demonstrated. It may also be the case that the evaluator works with the client to develop one or more research questions.

The third step in evaluation research is the **design of the methodology**. In using the program goals and research question as a guide, evaluators identify ways to best answer the research question(s). In other words, the evaluator must identify what type or types of data are required to address the research question. The evaluator must also decide how to best collect those data. The data needed may come via observation, content analysis, interviews, surveys, or participation in the program. Dodge argues that good evaluations use multiple methodologies and include both qualitative and quantitative data. Although Dodge's highlighted article in this text does not include evaluation research (Dodge, Starr-Gimeno, & Williams, 2005), Dodge engages in many evaluations. Much of Dodge's evaluation research centers on police agencies. To ascertain how to gather the data needed to conduct those evaluations depends on exactly what the agency needs evaluated. Dodge noted in her video interview that she finds that in some cases, surveys and focus groups are best at gathering the needed data. But, if she is dealing with an agency with sexual harassment issues, face-to-face interviews can be a better approach. Regardless of the issue at hand, Dodge does find that the use of multiple methods is always necessary to gain a better understanding of the issue.

Design of the methodology: Step in the evaluation research process that includes outlining the needed research methodology to answer the research question.

Gather data/evidence: Step in the process of evaluation research in which the evaluator accumulates data and information used to answer the research question.

The fourth step in evaluation research is to **gather data/evidence** that will be used to answer the research question. As noted, having stakeholder buy-in for the evaluation research is critical, especially here. A researcher must work with stakeholders, and they often rely on stakeholders to provide access to data. Having excellent data is an important element in conducting excellent research. Working with stakeholders can be the key to, or hurdle to, gathering the data needed. Once the data are gathered, a researcher can begin the fifth stage of evaluation research: **analyzing the data**. Depending on the research approach used, and the type of data gathered, multiple approaches to analyzing data will be required. The next chapter offers additional insight into analyzing data.

Once the data are analyzed, the researcher **develops findings and conclusions** that answer the guiding research question. Based on these findings, the researcher must then offer recommendations such as modifications to a program, expansion of the program to other places, expansion of the program to additional populations, or termination of the program. In

© dizanna/Canstockphoto

A part of evaluation research is to use the data gathered to ultimately offer recommendations to the client.

Analyzing the data: Step of evaluation research in which the evaluator uses the data and information gathered to answer the research question.

Develop findings and conclusions: Step of evaluation research in which the evaluator uses the data and information gathered to generate findings that address the research question. This includes conclusions about the issue and recommendations for ways to deal with the issue at hand.

Justify these recommendations: Step of the evaluation research process in which the evaluator offers a basis for the recommendations made.

Communicate the findings and recommendations: Final step of evaluation research in which the evaluator shares the results and suggestions arising from the research with stakeholders.

Policy: Principles, rules, and laws that guide a government, an organization, or people.

Program: Developed to respond to policies.

Policy process: Simplified model of the stages of policy making and implementation that includes five major stages: problem identification/agenda setting, policy formation, policy adoption, policy implementation, and policy evaluation. Also called the "policy cycle."

some cases, the researcher works with some client/stakeholders to develop the recommendations. The evaluator must be able to **justify these recommendations** based on the research methodology used and data gathered. Finally, it is not enough to sit in an office, reach a conclusion, and offer recommendations. The researcher must **communicate the findings and recommendations** to the party that requested the evaluation research, as well as to the other stakeholders. Ultimately, someone other than the researcher makes the determination as to whether the recommendations are implemented. With good stakeholder buy-in throughout the process, however, the probability of the recommendations being implemented is increased.

This section described the basic steps taken in evaluation research generally. As discussed in previous chapters, a simple statement such as "gather data" entails many steps and consideration. Having a full understanding of research methods is required for conducting excellent evaluation research. Without that, the evaluation will be poorly done, and the resulting findings will be without value. The next section identifies several specific types of evaluation research. For any one project, the evaluator may use multiple types of evaluation research to address multiple questions.

The Policy Process and Evaluation Research

Understanding program evaluation or evaluation research is easier if you understand basic policy process. Before addressing this, we must first discuss the terms **policy** and **program**. Policies are the principles, rules, and laws that guide a government, organization, or people. Policies are implemented to ameliorate a problem. Programs are developed to respond to policies. A difference between policies and programs is scale. Policies tend to be larger and programs smaller. In some cases, policies involve multiple programs to address an issue. Think of a university that has a policy of "retention maximization." This policy would include many programs, including one that requires attendance at orientation like that discussed earlier. It may also include other programs such as intramural sports, wellness centers, and student clubs. Importantly, both policies and programs can be evaluated. Given their similarity, and that both can be evaluated, we, like many others, will use the terms *policies* and *programs* synonymously in this chapter.

Now that you have an understanding of what a policy and a program is, we move on to the policy process. The **policy process**, also known as the policy cycle, is a simplified representation of the stages of policy making and implementation (see Chapter 13 for an in-depth discussion about the policy process and associated stages). This process includes the implementation and evaluation of programs. In its simplest form, the policy process has five major stages. The first stage in the policy process is problem identification/agenda setting. Problem identification/agenda setting involves the identification of the problem to be solved and the advocating that it be placed on the policy makers' agenda for further consideration. Should a policy issue be taken up by a policy maker and placed on an agenda for further consideration, the next stage in the policy process is policy formation. Policy formation includes the design of multiple approaches, policies, programs, or formal ways to address the problem of interest. After several formal policy options are designed, the policy makers identify and select what they see as the best policy solution, as well as programs of the group. Once the best policy option has been identified, adoption by the appropriate governing body is required. Policy adoption is the third stage in the policy process and refers to the formal adoption, or passage of the policy, which legitimizes the policy. Policy implementation is the fourth stage of the policy process in which agencies operationalize the adopted policy. This includes the drafting of specific programs, procedures, regulations, rules, and guidance to be used by those tasked with carrying out the adopted policy. Finally, the fifth stage in the policy process is policy evaluation. Policy evaluation is used to evaluate the policy and associated programs in ways discussed earlier. Although this illustration suggests that evaluation occurs only at stage five, the truth is that evaluation can occur anywhere during the policy process.

Figure 11.2 Basic Stages of the Policy Process

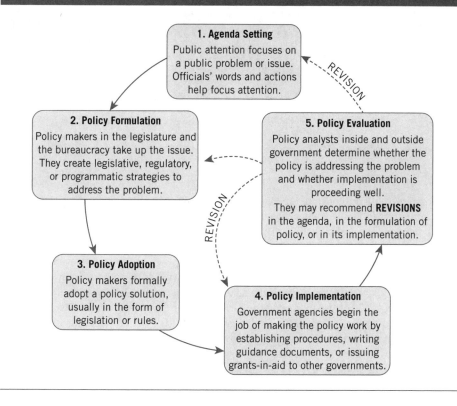

1. Agenda Setting
Public attention focuses on a public problem or issue. Officials' words and actions help focus attention.

2. Policy Formulation
Policy makers in the legislature and the bureaucracy take up the issue. They create legislative, regulatory, or programmatic strategies to address the problem.

5. Policy Evaluation
Policy analysts inside and outside government determine whether the policy is addressing the problem and whether implementation is proceeding well.
They may recommend **REVISIONS** in the agenda, in the formulation of policy, or in its implementation.

3. Policy Adoption
Policy makers formally adopt a policy solution, usually in the form of legislation or rules.

4. Policy Implementation
Government agencies begin the job of making the policy work by establishing procedures, writing guidance documents, or issuing grants-in-aid to other governments.

REVISION

REVISION

Types of Evaluation Research

That program evaluations can occur anywhere along the stages of the policy process indicates the fact that there is no single type of evaluation but many types. Even though it is agreed that there are multiple types of evaluation research, however, no universally agreed-upon *number* of types of evaluation research exists. Some contend there are two types of evaluation research, whereas others identify dozens. Our goal here is to offer an understanding of the types of evaluation research that are frequently used in criminal justice and criminology. Given that purpose, we follow the lead of Scriven (1977) and focus on two principal types of evaluation research, each of which has multiple subtypes (see Table 11.1): formative and summative evaluation research. **Formative evaluation** is evaluation research that occurs in the formative or earlier stages of the development of or modification of a policy or program. It is designed to offer insight about the implementation of a program. The second major type of program evaluation described is **summative evaluation** that occurs after the implementation of the policy or program. Summative evaluations are used to make a comprehensive assessment of a program after program implementation. These primary types of evaluation research, as well as some subtypes, are described next.

Formative Evaluation

Formative evaluations are conducted in the earliest stages of the policy process while a program is being developed. The purpose of a formative evaluation is to ensure the program is

Formative evaluations:
Conducted in the earliest stages of the policy process while a program is being developed with the purpose of ensuring the program is feasible prior to full implementation. Two types of formative evaluations are considered in this text: needs assessments and process evaluations.

Summative evaluation:
One of two major types of program evaluation used to make a comprehensive assessment of a program after the implementation of the policy or program. A summative evaluation is used to ascertain whether a program should be funded and continued or terminated. Two types of summative evaluations are considered in this text: outcome evaluations and impact evaluations.

Table 11.1 Two Primary Types of Evaluation Research

	Formative Evaluation	Summative Evaluation
When?	Before or during the program implementation	After program implementation
Purpose?	Offer information about planning and improving the program	Offer information about whether the program is reaching its objectives

Note: Adapted from Scriven (1977).

feasible prior to full implementation. The idea of a formative evaluation is to gather data that will inform ways to identify whether a program is needed, and to improve the program as it is being implemented before its full-scale implementation. In addition, formative evaluations can occur on an existing program that needs modification, is being used in a new environment, or one being implemented for a different target population. Formative evaluations can be thought of as "trouble-shooting" evaluations in that what is discovered from the evaluation is "fed back" into the program to strengthen or enhance it. Not surprisingly, formative evaluations take place primarily during the early stages of the policy process. Two frequently used subtypes of formative evaluation are considered in this chapter: needs assessments and process evaluations. Each is discussed next.

Needs Assessment

Needs assessments are a type of formative evaluation that are used when the goal of the evaluation is to find out whether there is a problem and how the target population might be better served. A needs assessment provides guidance about whether a program is needed, exactly who may need a program, and the type of program that may be useful for the target population. The findings of a needs assessment allows someone to identify how to effectively target a program to best address a social problem of interest. Engaging in a needs assessment requires deep immersion by the researcher into the environment in which a program may be needed. It requires the researcher to explore and describe the environment, the problem, and the target population comprehensively. A needs assessment follows several steps. First, the evaluator identifies the needs in the target population by working with all involved including the population of interest, funders, administrators, and so on (i.e., stakeholders). Second, the evaluator must identify the size or extent of the problem needing attention.

Needs Assessment Steps

1. Identify the needs in the target population.

2. Estimate the size or extent of the problem leading to the needs: gap analysis to understand difference between what is and what should be.

3. Identify an intervention or program that will best serve the needs of the target population.

This identification of the desired situation versus the actual situation is referred to as a **gap analysis**. The third step in a needs assessment is to identify the sort of intervention or program that will best serve the needs of the target population. This requires consideration of costs and feasibility of addressing the gap between what is and what should be. Many different research approaches including interviews, observations, content analysis, and survey research can be used when doing a needs assessment. This deep dive understanding of the issue allows the researcher to answer whether there is a need, what the needs are, and whose needs are greatest. A needs assessment also allows the researcher to identify the shape and scope of a needed program. Not surprisingly, the needs assessment occurs during the earlier stages of the policy process—during the identification of a needed policy or program.

© halfpoint/Canstockphoto

Process Evaluation

A **process evaluation** is conducted when a program is in operation, and it focuses specifically on whether a program has been implemented and is being delivered as it was designed. A process evaluation can also be used to understand why an existing program has changed over time. Engaging in a process evaluation requires immersion in the program to understand exactly how the program is being delivered. Process evaluation requires full understanding that allows the researcher to identify exactly how the program is being delivered compared with how the process is supposed to be delivered. For these reasons, process evaluations are heavily reliant on methods of gathering qualitative data (e.g., interviews, focus groups, and participant observation). A way to view this is as a trouble-shooting evaluation. The research can identify whether the program is working the best way to meet its full potential. It can identify whether the program is working well and doing what it is supposed to be doing. A process evaluation can also identify where problems are occurring. This comprehensive understanding of the program allows an understanding of what it is compared with what it should be. The findings from a process evaluation can identify inefficiencies in the program delivery that can be addressed.

Logic models play an important role in all evaluation research, but especially so in a process evaluation. Logic models are used to illustrate the ideal about how a program is intended to work. These models depict how the program is supposed to be implemented. Logic models provide an easy-to-understand means to see the causal relationships among program components. Featured researcher Heather Zaykowski has conducted many evaluations and finds that logic models streamline the research. She noted in her video interview that logic models help the client or partner articulate their goals and focus on the important issues. Zaykowski finds working with the clients to develop or clarify their logic model helps them identify their tangible goals and issues. There are multiple benefits of logic models. First, they point to key performance measurement points useful for conducting an evaluation. Second, logic models assist with program design, and make improving existing programs easier, by highlighting problematic program activities. Third, logic models help identify the program expectations. Another featured researcher, Chris Melde, who has conducted numerous evaluations, is a particular fan of logic models and always uses them. If the client doesn't have one (and this is common), Melde spends the time in collaboration with the client to create a logic model. This is often the first part of an evaluation according to Melde.

Logic models in their most basic form include inputs, outputs, short-term outcomes, and long-term outcomes. **Inputs** include things like training or education. The idea is that these inputs should lead to the outputs depicted in the logic model. **Outputs** resulting

Understanding if a need exists, who is affected by that need, and what program can best ameliorate that need are some purposes of a needs assessment. The answers to these and other questions will depend on that needs of the particular target population. How might the needs of these two men differ? How might they be the same?

Gap analysis: Part of a needs assessment in which the evaluator identifies the size or extent of the problem needing attention, as well as the desired situation. Identifying what is and what is desired is the gap analysis.

....

Process evaluation: Type of formative evaluation that is conducted when a program is in operation. Process evaluations focus on whether a program has been implemented and is being delivered as it was designed, or why an existing program has changed over time.

....

Figure 11.3   Proposed Logic Model for Relationship Education Programs for Youth in Foster Care

In this example of a logic model, you can see the inputs, outputs, and short-term and long-term outcomes for a program designed to help youth in foster care.

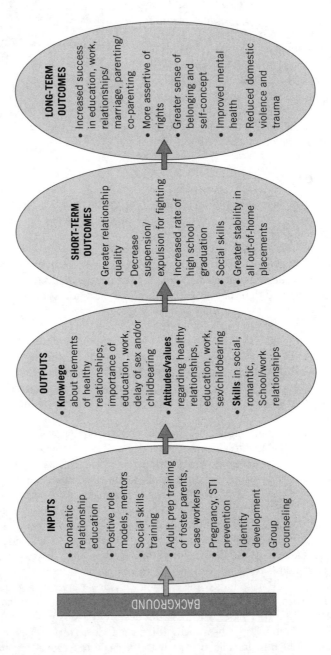

INPUTS
- Romantic relationship education
- Positive role models, mentors
- Social skills training
- Adult prep training of foster parents, case workers
- Pregnancy, STI prevention
- Identity development
- Group counseling

OUTPUTS
- **Knowlege** about elements of healthy relationships, importance of education, work, delay of sex and/or childbearing
- **Attitudes/values** regarding healthy relationships, education, work, sex/childbearing
- **Skills** in social, romantic, School/work relationships

SHORT-TERM OUTCOMES
- Greater relationship quality
- Decrease suspension/ expulsion for fighting
- Increased rate of high school graduation
- Social skills
- Greater stability in all out-of-home placements

LONG-TERM OUTCOMES
- Increased success in education, work, relationships/ marriage, parenting/ co-parenting
- More assertive of rights
- Greater sense of belonging and self-concept
- Improved mental health
- Reduced domestic violence and trauma

BACKGROUND

Source: Exhibit 1, p. 21, from "Putting Youth Relationship Education on the Child Welfare Agenda: Findings from a Research and Evaluation Review." Child Trends December 2012. Reprinted with permission from ChildTrends.

Note: Logic model example found here: http://www.dibbleinstitute.org/wp-content/uploads/2014/01/logic-model.png

from the inputs include things like increased knowledge, changed attitudes or values, and new skills. The notion is that these outcomes will then lead to identified short-term outcomes. **Short-term outcomes** or goals stem from the outputs and include improvements or changes expected to see in a short period. Short-term outcomes or goals include things like improved stability, higher retention rates, reduced recidivism, or fewer arrests. **Long-term outcomes** are the final causal effect of the program. These outcomes are the intended positive benefits resulting from a program that occur further out in time. Long-term outcomes may include safer communities, stable housing, greater educational attainment, lack of arrests, increased justice, and greater satisfaction with life. You should be able to see how a logic model can be useful in trying to understand how a program should be implemented that can guide the evaluator when assessing whether the program is evaluated as intended.

Logic models: Graphic depictions that illustrate the ideal about how a program is intended to work.

Inputs: One of four steps in a basic logic model. Inputs include things like training or education. The idea is that these inputs should lead to the outputs depicted in the logic model.

Summative Evaluation

The second major type of evaluation research considered is the summative evaluation. Summative evaluations provide an overall or summary judgment about program results. This type of evaluation can be used to determine whether a program should be funded and continued or terminated. Unlike formative evaluations that provide information on how to implement or improve a program, the goal of a summative evaluation is to answer questions about the feasibility of continuing, expanding, or discontinuing a program. Summative evaluations occur at the end of the policy process and are concerned with the output and impact of programs. There is no agreement in the literature about the types of summative evaluations. For our purposes, we discuss two types of summative evaluations: outcome evaluations and impact evaluations. Some authors do not distinguish between the two, noting they both focus on results. The differences to focus on here is that outcome evaluations focus on whether the program was effective in terms of the target population in the short and long term, and occur after program completion. In contrast, impact evaluations focus on whether the program met its long-term ultimate goals (which are broader than how they affected the target population) and tend to be conducted years after the program was implemented.

© PixelsAway/Canstockphoto

Summative evaluations are used to make a summary judgement about a program—keep, terminate, or expand?

Outcome Evaluation

Outcome evaluations measure the effectiveness of a program on the *target population*. This type of evaluation is focused on the impacts on the target population specifically versus a summary look at the program. Outcome evaluations focus on the short-term and long-term outcomes among the target population depicted in the logic model. Engaging in an outcome evaluation does not require the deep immersion in the program required in a needs assessment. Rather, an outcome evaluation is more often conducted using quantitative data away from the actual program delivery to measure whether the program is doing what it was intended to do. These data gathering methods include analysis of existing data, surveys, and experiments. Does it show lower rates of recidivism after engaging in the program? Does it increase literacy after going through a program designed to improve literacy?

© KHALED DESOUKI/AFP/Getty Images

Evaluation research skills are used broadly for countless issues.

Does the program lead to higher student retention and greater loyalty after attending a mandatory student orientation? Is the program approaching the desired outcomes? If the answer to these types of questions is "no," then the program may be reassessed or even terminated.

Impact Evaluation

The second type of summative evaluation considered is the impact evaluation. **Impact evaluations** are global evaluations that assess whether a program is achieving its designated goals. Unlike the outcome evaluation, the focus is not on the target population but on the broad goals of the program. An impact evaluation is focused on big-picture questions such as whether the program is achieving its intended results and advancing the social policy it stems from. It identifies the outcomes of the program in terms of intended outcomes and unintended outcomes. Like the outcome evaluation, an impact evaluation is conducted using primarily quantitative data (e.g., focus groups, interviews, and content analysis) without the need for immersion in the program. Rather, an evaluator uses quantitative measurements to answer the question as to whether the program is achieving its goals or not. If not, then the program may be terminated.

As noted earlier, there are additional types of evaluation research that you can conduct including evaluability assessments, implementation evaluations, structured conceptualizations, and cost-effectiveness and cost–benefit analyses. Nevertheless, the formative and summative approaches presented offer a basic understanding of several widely used approaches. When thinking about types of evaluation research, it is important to recognize that no single type is better than another is. In contrast, each type of evaluation research is different and serves a different important purpose. Table 11.2 offers some big picture elements of each of these types of program evaluation approaches.

Distinctive Purposes of Evaluation and Basic Research

Evaluation research is different from the other research purposes described here in many ways. As Stufflebeam (1983) wrote, "[t]he purpose of evaluation is to improve, not prove." Or even more succinctly, Dodge and Zaykowski both highlight the fact that evaluation research differs from basic research because it is applied in nature. Indeed, evaluation research has the purpose or objective of evaluating and improving, but evaluation research is different from other types of research objectives described in this text. Although evaluation research uses the same procedures for gathering, analyzing, and interpreting evidence that other research approaches in this book do, evaluation research is not the same as **basic research** like the descriptive, exploratory, and explanatory research described in this book. In contrast, evaluation research is **applied research**. This section identifies some of the ways this applied versus basic research distinction makes evaluation research stand apart from other research.

Knowledge for Decision Making

Basic research approaches generate knowledge to understand the world better. A researcher engaged in basic research is not conducting research because he or she is answering to a boss. Instead, the basic researcher is answering to no one except his or her own intellectual curiosity that leads to general knowledge. This knowledge created may or may never be used. Alternatively, that knowledge may be used in ways that are wholly disconnected from the researcher who created the knowledge. In contrast, evaluation research is applied research

Table 11.2 Subtypes of Evaluation Research

Evaluation Type	Subtypes of Evaluation	Definition	Purpose	Examples of Questions Addressed
Formative		Evaluates a program during development to make early improvements	Furnish information for funding program improvement when starting a new program	How well is the program being delivered?
		Evaluates an existing program that is being modified, used in a new setting, or used for a new target population	Assist in the shaping or forming of the program during the early phases of program development	What strategies can we use to improve this program?
	Needs Assessment	Determines who needs the program	Alleviate a social problem	To what extent are community needs and standards being met?
		Determines the need for a program	Assess the needs for services of a group	What needs to be done to meet needs and standards?
		Determines the type of program needed		
	Process	Determines whether specific program strategies were implemented as planned	Determine why an established program has changed over time	Did your program meet its goals for recruitment of program participants?
		Focuses on program implementation	Address inefficiencies in program delivery of services	Did participants receive the specified benefits of the program?
		Focuses on program delivery	Accurately portray to outside parties program operations (e.g., for replication elsewhere)	How well is the program operating?
Summative		Provides information on program effectiveness	Used to make a summary judgment on whether to continue or end a program (Scriven, 1977)	Should this program continue to be funded?
		Conducted after the completion of the program design	Help determine whether a program should be expanded to other locations	Should we expand these services to other populations in the community?
	Outcomes	Focuses on the changes in comprehension, attitudes, behaviors, and practices that result from the program	Decide whether program/ activity affects participants outcomes	Did your participants report the desired changes after completing a program cycle?

(Continued)

Table 11.2 (Continued)

Evaluation Type	Subtypes of Evaluation	Definition	Purpose	Examples of Questions Addressed
		Can include both short and long term results	Establish and measure clear benefits of the program	What are the short- or long-term results observed among (or reported by) participants?
			Identify whether the program is having the desired effect on the target population	
	Impact	Broad assessment that focuses on the overall effects of a program.	Influence policy	What changes in your program participants' behaviors are attributable to your program?
		Focuses on long-term, sustained changes as a result of the program activities, both positive/negative and intended/unintended	See impact in longitudinal studies with comparison groups	What effects would program participants miss out on without this program?
		Focuses on both positive/negative and intended/unintended outcomes of the program		Has the program met its long-term goals?

Basic research: Research that generates knowledge motivated by intellectual curiosity to better understand the world.

Applied research: Conducted to develop knowledge for immediate use for a specific decision-making purpose.

that is used to develop knowledge for immediate use for a specific decision-making purpose. In addition, evaluation research is generally conducted because the evaluator is answering to a boss, a client, a funder, or some sort. Evaluation research is not engaged in creating knowledge generally but is engaged in answering a specific question about a program that a stakeholder has posed. It would be incorrect to conclude that basic or applied research is better than the other. They are simply different approaches and serve different purposes. The next sections present many of these differences.

Origination of Research Questions

When conducting basic research, the researcher develops the research question and refines it during the literature review. Research questions can come from myriad places, as described in Chapter 2 and elsewhere. Regardless of the source of the inspiration, the researcher is the one who crafts the research question. In contrast, when conducting evaluation research, the research question is developed by, or in consultation with, the client/stakeholders. The research question is focused on some element of a particular program that the researcher answers on behalf of a stakeholder. In this way, evaluation research and other types of research differ greatly.

Comparative and Judgmental Nature

Basic research is interested in describing the world as it currently exists. It seeks to explore that world or to provide a description or explanation about the world. These findings about "what is" are intended to be used to make improvements in our world in a general sense. Nevertheless, often basic research publishes the research to ultimately make the world a better place. In contrast, evaluation research is more focused. It is focused on "what should be" in comparison with "what is" when examining a specific program or policy. For example, evaluation research may describe how a program is being administered as well as how the program *should* be administered. Such a comparative approach is inherently judgmental, and this aspect of evaluation research sets it apart from basic research.

Working With Stakeholders

A fundamental way that evaluation research differs from basic research is the need to work with a variety of stakeholders. As noted earlier, basic research is undertaken by a researcher desiring to build knowledge and understanding about our world. In general, there is little stakeholder interaction as the researcher conducts his or her investigation. The major exception to this is in the time and effort it can take to get access to data that agencies have. In contrast, evaluation researchers work with stakeholders throughout the process. In fact, conducting evaluation research means the researcher is working collaboratively with, and is dependent on, several stakeholders, some of whom may or may not be cooperative. Knowing who the stakeholders are, and developing and maintaining a good relationship with them, is critical when conducting evaluation research. The researcher needs his or her trust and support to be able to gather the needed data. In addition, the researcher needs the stakeholders' support and trust so that they will be willing to accept and implement the findings from the evaluation conducted. Dodge has found that the failure to establish rapport with stakeholders in the beginning of the evaluation process can kill any evaluation. This rapport must be maintained throughout the process as well, which includes providing a report at the end of the process that is written for the stakeholder audience. An evaluator must always be aware of the relationship with all stakeholders to ensure it remains positive.

Challenging Environment

Basic research takes place in a variety of settings including an office, a laboratory, or the field. In general, those who are being studied or examined in the process of basic research are voluntarily engaging in the research. In general, the relationship between the basic researcher and the research subject is harmonious and cooperative. Evaluation research can differ from this harmonious and cooperative environment. Evaluation research is inevitably about observing or assessing a process or program. The priority of those involved in the program is the program itself, not the evaluation of the program. If gathering data interferes (or is perceived to interfere) with the program, challenges ensue. The evaluator must understand that those involved in the evaluation are aware that what they do in the program is going to be scrutinized, possibly criticized, and conceivably changed because of the evaluation. They understand that the evaluator may identify shortcomings of a program they are dedicated to, and loyal about. In fact, they may fail to see the need for the evaluation. As a result, the environment that some evaluators work in can be hostile, uncooperative, and at times incredibly challenging. Recall the judgmental nature of evaluation research, and the fact that findings may not put the program in the best of lights. At worst, findings may be used to terminate a program some stakeholders believe is useful. This type of environment indicates that an evaluator must not only navigate the challenges of conducting good evaluation research but also must work with others who may not understand or even trust the evaluation or the evaluators. Being mindful of the social implications of the findings from the study is important.

Findings and Dissemination

In general, the way findings are disseminated differs between basic and applied research. Once basic research is completed, researchers tend to draft journal articles to be peer reviewed for consideration of publication in a journal. The manuscripts describe the purpose of the research, relevant literature, methodology, findings, and conclusions. A part of that includes recommendations about future research to continue research on the topic of interest. Once submitted to a journal, the manuscript is sent to three other researchers who assess and comment on the research. Peer review is generally conducted using a **blind review**, meaning those reviewing the research manuscript generally do not know who conducted the research, and those conducting the research generally do not know who is conducting the review. Once the reviews are completed, the reviews are sent to the researcher with a decision by the journal editor as to whether the research will be published (rare without revisions), requires revisions and resubmission to the journal (an R&R), or rejected outright. Should the research manuscript be accepted and published in the journal, the knowledge in the article is available to anyone accessing the journal. Publication in journals can take many months, but more often it takes a one or more years to accomplish.

Evaluation research differs greatly from basic research in that the research report describing the evaluation, findings, and recommendations is submitted to the stakeholders for consideration. As a result, it is important that evaluation reports be written for impact. They must convince the stakeholders that the study just completed made a difference and that positive changes will result from this research. Recommendations in evaluation reports are focused on the program (and not on future research about the findings). Peer review is not used, and broad dissemination is not the goal. This is not to say that evaluation research is never published in journals; it is. In fact, several journals focus specifically on program evaluation. It is just generally not the primary goal of the evaluator to publish for a broader audience.

Characteristics of Effective Evaluations

Four Standards of an Effective Evaluation

1. Utility
2. Feasibility
3. Propriety
4. Accuracy

When conducting any research, the researcher strives for effectiveness. Nevertheless, how do you know whether your research is useful or effective? Peer reviewers can assist with this. Following accepted practices in research methodology when conducting research can assist with this. Unlike basic research, evaluation research is associated with specifically stated and accepted standards to assess the quality, effectiveness, accuracy, ethical, and usefulness of an evaluation. In 1994, the Joint Committee on Standards for Education Evaluation published four standards of effectiveness: utility, feasibility, propriety, and accuracy. Utility focuses on the need that evaluations address significant research questions, provide clearly articulated findings, and make recommendations. Feasibility addresses the need that evaluation research be practical, reasonable, and affordable. Propriety requires evaluations be ethical and legal. Finally, accuracy indicates the need that evaluations be conducted using best research practices, free of biases, and accurate. The Joint Committee on Standards for Education Evaluation also provided multiple criteria for each standard that reflects several of the guiding principles put forth by the American Evaluators Association discussed earlier in this chapter. The specific criteria of effective evaluation, based on the Joint Committee on Standards for Education Evaluation (1994) are discussed next.

Utility

Utility is the first standard of an effective evaluation. **Utility** addresses whether an evaluation responded to the needs of the client and was satisfactory to those using it. Utility can be assessed by focusing on seven specific standards. The first utility criterion is **stakeholder identification**, which requires that an effective evaluation identify and engage all individuals involved in or affected by the evaluation. Identification of all stakeholders is vital to ensure their needs can be, and are, addressed during the course of and after the evaluation. **Evaluator credibility** is a utility standard that indicates that evaluators must be both competent and trustworthy. The presence of competence and trust in the evaluator benefits the evaluation in that findings can be fully credible and accepted. A third utility standard is **information scope and selection,** which requires that the data collected for use in the evaluation must be directly related to the specific purpose of the evaluation. **Values identification** is a utility standard that requires the evaluator to carefully describe the perspectives, procedures, and rationale used to interpret the findings. The foundation for making the value judgments inherent in an evaluation must be clearly articulated. An important utility standard is **report clarity**, which indicates that evaluation reports must clearly articulate multiple elements of the program being evaluated. First, the program itself must be described. In addition, the context and purposes of the program must be articulated. Third, the procedures of the program must be made clear. Finally, the findings of the evaluation must be clearly presented in the report. This detail and clarity ensures all audiences easily understand the evaluation. **Report timeliness and dissemination** is a utility standard that requires that interim and final reports stemming from an evaluation be shared with in a timely fashion to facilitate their use. And the final utility criterion is **evaluation impact**, which is evident when the findings and recommendations are accepted and implemented. The impact goal should guide all elements of the evaluation including evaluation planning, implementation, and reporting. With attention to evaluation impact throughout the process, stakeholders will be more likely to value and use the findings, as well as to implement the recommendations made in the report.

Feasibility

The second major standard of effective evaluation research is feasibility. In other words, is the evaluation research requested possible? The **feasibility** standard focuses on whether an evaluation is both viable and pragmatic. Three specific feasibility standards are considered when assessing an evaluation. These specific standards consider whether the evaluation was practical, realistic, and diplomatic and involved the prudent use of resources. These characteristics are evident based on three criteria. **Practical procedures** is a feasibility standard that indicates that evaluation research should be practical, and it should result in minimal disruption to the program under investigation. For instance, is it practical to get the records of juvenile delinquents given the increased confidentiality under which they are kept? Similarly, **political viability** is a feasibility standard that calls attention to the need to consider the affected stakeholders to gain and maintain their cooperation during all stages of the evaluation. In addition, this standard requires the evaluator to be alert to any stakeholder attempts to thwart, bias, or disrupt the evaluation. The final feasibility standard is **cost-effectiveness**, which requires evaluators to consider the efficient and effective use of resources. In particular,

Utility: One of four standards of an effective evaluation. Refers to whether the evaluation conducted met the needs of and was satisfactory to the people using it.

Stakeholder identification: One of the utility criteria of an effective evaluation. Requires that the evaluator identify all individuals or organizations involved in or affected by the evaluation.

Evaluator credibility: One of the utility criteria of an effective evaluation. Requires that evaluators must be both competent and trustworthy.

Information scope and selection information: One of the utility criteria of an effective evaluation. Requires that the data and information collected for use in the evaluation must speak directly to the specific research questions guiding the program evaluation.

Values identification: One of the utility criteria of an effective evaluation. This criterion requires that an evaluator carefully describe the perspectives, procedures, and rationale used to interpret the findings.

Report clarity: One of the utility criteria of an effective evaluation. This criterion requires that evaluation reports clearly articulate multiple elements of the program being evaluated.

Report timeliness and dissemination: One of the utility criteria of an effective evaluation. Calls for all interim and final reports resulting from the evaluation to be shared with stakeholders in a timely fashion to facilitate their use.

© PlusONE/Shutterstock

this standard guards against engaging in unneeded data gathering and analysis. There is no need to conduct a Ferrari® evaluation (e.g., randomized experimental research) when a less resource-intensive one (e.g., quasi-experimental research) is adequate. Any costs incurred during the evaluation should be directly related to the needs of conducting a useful evaluation.

Propriety

The third major standard of an effective evaluation is propriety. **Propriety** standards offer evidence that the evaluator has conducted an ethical evaluation. Eight specific standards are used to assess propriety, all of which ensure evaluations are legal, ethical, and conducted with regard for the welfare of those involved, as well as anyone else affected by the evaluation. The first of eight propriety standards that provide evidence of an ethical evaluation is **service orientation**, which emphasizes the service nature of evaluation research. Evaluation research should be used to assist organizations, as well as to address and serve the needs of the targeted population affected by the program of interest. A second propriety standard requires the use of **formal agreements.** This standard requires the use of a formal, and written, agreement involving all major parties involved in an evaluation. This written agreement should identify each individual's obligations, how associated tasks will be accomplished, who will conduct required tasks, and when tasks should be completed. Formal agreements are binding unless all parties choose to renegotiate their terms. The next two standards speak to human decency when conducting evaluation research. The **rights of human subjects** focuses on the requirement that evaluation research be planned and conducted using ethical research practices. Evaluation research must be conducted in a way that the rights and welfare of human subjects are respected. The **human interactions** standard dictates the evaluation research be conducted with respect to all individuals associated with the program of interest. No individual should be threatened or harmed, and all engaged must be respected. An important propriety standard calls for **complete and fair assessment.** This standard requires the comprehensive and objective assessment of the strengths and weaknesses of the program. With a comprehensive and fair assessment, the evaluation is useful. Without it, the value of the evaluation is poor. As noted throughout the text, research is only as strong as its weakest part, and in the case of an evaluation, that means that incomplete and biased evaluation would lead to limited, and possibly damaging, outcomes. The **disclosure of findings** is a propriety standard that speaks to the need to ensure all stakeholders—who have put time and effort into the study— deserve to see the findings. In addition, the findings from the evaluation must be made available to those with a legal right to them. During the course of evaluation research, conflict may arise. A propriety standard referred to as **conflict of interest** emphasizes that any conflict of interest that arises must be dealt with transparently and honestly to ensure the evaluation and results are not compromised. And finally, the **fiscal responsibility** propriety standard indicates that funding used during engaging in a program evaluation must be justifiable, ethical, and prudent.

Accuracy

The fourth major evaluation research standard is accuracy. **Accuracy** refers to idea that an effective evaluation should produce correct findings. Twelve standards of accuracy are used,

Most university professors are reviewed annually with regard to teaching. Teaching evaluations can include things such as in-class student evaluations, external reviewer observations, and reviews of syllabi. Students may be more familiar with evaluations found on rate myprofessor.com (RMP). This website rates the easiness, helpfulness, clarity, overall quality, and hotness of professors. A valid question about all of these approaches is whether they measure teaching effectiveness or something else. Johnson and Crews (2013) conducted research on RMP to determine what faculty characteristics determined ratings on the website. This research was guided by several research questions:

1. What faculty characteristics are correlated with RMP scores?

2. What faculty characteristics influence RMP scores after accounting for the easiness and hotness of the faculty?

3. Does the number of raters influence RMP scores given the small sample of self-selected individuals who post evaluations on RMP?

To address these research questions, Johnson and Crews randomly selected 10 states from which to draw the faculty sample. All four-year colleges and universities were included. Next all full-time criminology and criminal justice faculty in these institutions who had been rated on RMP were included in the sample (N = 466). Personal characteristic information about faculty was taken from university websites and the Internet. Information on 59 faculty members could not be found, and they were excluded, leaving 407 criminal justice and criminology faculty members in the sample.

Analyses included univariate descriptives, and ultimately many regressions that could isolate the effect of the independent variables (e.g., race, sex, terminal degree, number of publications, practitioner experience, years of teaching, and employment at an RI university) on the dependent variables. Five regressions were run, one for each dependent variable: easiness, helpfulness, clarity, overall quality, and hotness.

The findings showed that a faculty RMP easiness score was predicted by practitioner experience, employment at a Research I (RI) university, and teaching experience. Specifically, practitioners and those at RI universities were more likely to be rated easy. In contrast, more teaching experience predicted lower ratings in easiness. The regression findings indicated that publication rates and practitioner experience predicted higher helpfulness ratings. In contrast, a doctorate and years of teaching predicted lower scores on helpfulness. A third regression model examined predictors of clarity and found that being White, male, a practitioner, publication count, and number of raters predicted clarity. A doctorate and teaching experience was related to lower clarity scores. Higher ratings for overall quality were associated with Whites, publication count, and practitioner experience. Lower overall quality scores were associated with a doctorate, years teaching, and being at an RI university. Finally, what influences hotness scores? According to this research, none of the independent variables did.

Nevertheless, the researchers continued their examination and found that when they controlled for easiness and hotness ratings, "faculty ascribed characteristics (such as race and sex) explained the greatest proportion of variance in clarity, helpfulness, and overall quality scores. Professional characteristics, such as years of experience, publication rate, and possession of a doctorate were less influential on Ratemyprofessors.com scores."

What sort of policy implications come from this work? First, teaching evaluations are heavily influenced by the easiness of the instructor. Second, faculty ascribed characteristics matter. Third, professional characteristics have only a small influence on RMP ratings. And finally, the number of raters has very little influence on RMP scores. From a policy perspective, these findings point to the need to have teaching evaluated in a variety of ways given that RMP reflects things other than teaching competence and places some groups of faculty at a disadvantage.

Johnson, R. R., & Crews, A. D. (2013). My professor is hot! Correlates of RateMyProfessors.com ratings for criminal justice and criminology faculty members. *American Journal of Criminal Justice, 38,* 639–656.

Political viability: One of the feasibility criteria of an effective evaluation. Requires the evaluators to consider the affected stakeholders to gain and maintain their cooperation during every stage of the evaluation.

Cost-effectiveness: Criterion of feasibility that indicates an effective evaluation. Requires evaluators to consider the efficient and effective use of resources.

Propriety: One of four standards of an effective evaluation. Based on eight criteria that demonstrate that an evaluation was conducted ethically, legally, and with regard for the welfare of those involved, as well as of anyone else affected by the evaluation.

Service orientation: One of the propriety standards of an effective evaluation. Evaluation research should be used to assist organizations and to address and serve the needs of the targeted population affected by the program of interest.

Formal agreements: One of the propriety standards of an effective evaluation that requires the presence of a formal, written agreement involving all principal parties involved in an evaluation.

including presenting the program in context, using systematic procedures, using the appropriate methods, and producing impartial reports with justified conclusions. Each is described next. The accuracy standard focuses largely on the quality of the data used. This should seem logical to you since this book has focused on the need to gather quality data. Without quality data, a piece of research is of limited value. The first accuracy criterion is **program documentation** that requires the program evaluation to include clear, complete, and accurate documentation used in the work. This is documentation about how the evaluation was done as well as about how the documentation was used in the evaluation. In addition, the accuracy standard requires the evaluation to include a **context analysis**. This means that the program must be fully understood in the context in which it exists. The context must be examined in detail by the evaluator so that likely influences affecting the program are known. Third, accuracy standards require the evaluation to **describe purposes and procedures**. An accurate evaluation is one that clearly articulates and outlines the purposes and research methods (aka procedures) of the evaluation. In addition, the stated purposes and research methods of the evaluation should be described in a comprehensive fashion allowing for continual monitoring and assessment. The accuracy standard requires **defensible information sources** that are used in the evaluation be identified and described in detail. Information shared about sources should allow others to assess these data sources. A part of being accurate is that the information used in the evaluation be **valid information**. This accuracy standard requires that the research methods used to gather information and data should ensure a valid interpretation for use in the evaluation. Similarly, **reliable information** is almost a must for effective evaluations. Reliable information requires that the research methods used to gather data and information be designed to provide reliable information for the evaluation. A part of science is the systematic collection of data and information. It is no surprise then that an accuracy standard is the inclusion of **systematic information** and data collection, analysis, and reporting during an evaluation. As with all research, any issues encountered during the information and data gathering should be addressed. The appropriate use of quantitative and qualitative data is required to demonstrate accuracy. As noted in the standards, **analysis of quantitative information** requires the use of appropriate scientific analysis of quantitative data used to address the research question being investigated. Similarly, the **analysis of qualitative information** requires the use of appropriate scientific analysis of qualitative data used to address the research question being considered. An additional accuracy criterion is the presentation of **justified conclusions**. This accuracy standard points to the need that all conclusions and findings be clearly and comprehensively justified based on the data and information analyzed. Justification must allow stakeholders to assess how the justifications were reached. **Impartial reporting** is an accuracy standard that requires care be taken to avoid distortion or bias in findings. The evaluator must strive to report on the evaluation regardless of personal feelings. And finally, **metaevaluation** is an accuracy standard that indicates that evaluation research should be judged on these standards as a means of examining its strengths and weaknesses by stakeholders. Melde summed up these characteristics of an effective evaluation during his video interview conducted for this book by noting that effective evaluations stay true to the principles of good science.

Common Pitfalls in Evaluation Research

Because evaluation research is conducted using any of the research methodologies discussed in this text, the pitfalls associated with each methodology are also relevant here. For example, if interviewing others, you the researcher must establish rapport and ask clear questions. If you are using survey research, care must be taken to avoid double-barreled or leading questions. If you are using a focus group, the moderator must ensure all participants are sharing views and no single attendee is shutting the process down.

Evaluations as an Afterthought

One pitfall associated with evaluation research must be discussed: the afterthought nature of evaluation. That is, evaluation research is too often considered as an afterthought. Although this is not the fault of the researcher, it is something with which many researchers are confronted. Often well-meaning individuals implement a program and only later wonder whether the program is working as they want it to or whether the program is providing the benefits hoped for. At times, no logic model was developed, making the identification of inputs, outputs, and outcomes challenging to discern. In fact, a program may have been launched with no explicit consideration about what success would look like or how the plan was to be delivered.

Dodge finds that waiting until after data are collected to involve a researcher is a common error made by organizations. Dodge shared with us that not including a researcher in the collection of the data (and framing of the evaluation before getting started) often means the quality of the data are problematic. And this means the evaluation is much more challenging than it should be. Alternatively, Dodge finds that many organizations articulate unclear and often unmeasurable goals for the evaluation. Other times, organizations have individuals with clashing ideas about what the goals are. By working with a researcher from the beginning, Dodge noted, feasible, measurable, and useful goals can be agreed to before gathering data.

Dodge also finds that it is too often the case that those implementing a program have collected no data or other information about it. They may not know how many individuals were served. They may not know whether those being served are benefiting. All of these issues point to the value of bringing in a researcher from the beginning.

Zaykowski was brought onto an evaluation at the last minute. The client knew this evaluation was required but failed to act on the evaluation until time was a problem. When she arrived on the project, she found that needed data were not gathered. The grant was supposed to gather data on 80 respondents, but the client had only gathered information on 20. There was no person clearly acting as the leader of the project. The project investigator (PI) of the grant and evaluation was running the program of interest, although she only worked 10 hours a week. This created a perfect storm of evaluation disaster. The problems continued once Zaykowski began working with them as getting access to additional subjects proved difficult. In the end, Zaykowski noted to us that the project was completed but that this episode represents the all-too-common issue that everyone does not know how to conduct an evaluation. Bring in an expert, and bring him or her in early.

Waiting until a program has been launched to consider an evaluation presents several obstacles. For example, it may preclude the use of experimental methods for testing program effects, forcing evaluators to use other less-informative approaches. In addition, early planning for an evaluation tends to make any evaluation that is ultimately conducted take far more time, and this reduces the chances the findings will be used. When a program is being planned is the time to consider evaluation of the program. Failure to do so increases the odds that stakeholders do not buy-in to the work done by the evaluator. This in turn increases the risk that the report, findings, and recommendations of the evaluator are disregarded.

Political Context

A second and related pitfall results from the fact that "evaluation is a rational enterprise that takes place in a political context" (Weiss, 1993, p. 94). Failure to navigate the intersection of the worlds of politics and evaluation will result in major challenges for evaluators. Consider that programs and policies are the result of political decisions. As you are likely aware from your everyday life, few political decisions are arrived at without great and often heated debate, arguments, and challenges. Thus, before a program or policy is launched, it has built-in stakeholders who can be at odds. Recognizing this built-in tension is imperative

Rights of human subjects: One of the propriety standards of an effective evaluation. Requires that evaluation research, be planned and conducted using ethical research practices.

Human interactions: One of the propriety standards of an effective evaluation. Requires that evaluation research be conducted with respect to all individuals associated with the program of interest.

Complete and fair assessment: One of the propriety standards of an effective evaluation. Indicates that an evaluation must offer a complete and fair assessment of the strengths and weaknesses of the program.

Disclosure of findings: One of the propriety standards of an effective evaluation. Indicates that evaluation findings must be made available to those with a legal right to the findings or to those affected by the evaluation.

Conflict of interest: One of the propriety standards of an effective evaluation. Requires that any conflict of interest that occurs must be dealt with transparently and honestly to ensure the evaluation and results are not compromised.

Fiscal responsibility: One of the propriety standards of an effective evaluation. Requires that the use of resources during the course of the evaluation be sound, ethical, and prudent.

for successful evaluation. Recognizing the tangled worlds of evaluation and politics, and that an evaluator must work with all stakeholders, is imperative if you want to be successful in this role.

Trust

Accuracy: One of four evaluation research standards that refers to the notion that an effective evaluation will offer correct findings. Accuracy is evident by presenting the program in context by using systematic procedures, using the appropriate methods, and producing impartial reports with justified conclusions.

Program documentation: Accuracy standard of an effective evaluation that requires that an evaluation be documented clearly, completely, and accurately.

Context analysis: Accuracy standard of an effective evaluation that requires a program to be examined in context as to allow deeper understanding of the program.

A third pitfall is to fail to develop a solid and trusting relationship with stakeholders. Without the buy-in of stakeholders, the evaluation research will be far more difficult to accomplish. Dodge, who has engaged in a great deal of evaluation research, has seen firsthand the challenges that a lack of trust brings, and why it is so important to develop trust early. Dodge finds this especially the case in law enforcement agencies. She noted that "when dealing with law enforcement many of the officers are skeptical that an evaluation can be the impetus for change." Similarly, Dodge finds that trust can be an issue between parties beyond the researcher. She has dealt with situations in which a "city manager or police chief requests an evaluation but then decides not to release the report. Obviously, this happens most when the evaluation shows weakness in the leadership. I always encourage the leadership to make the report available either internally and/or externally. This helps encourage transparency for the department and city." As noted earlier in the chapter, Melde views trust as an essential requirement to have between the researcher and those in the organization. Those in the organization must have trust about the importance of the research design or things can go sideways. Similarly, Zaykowski finds that "the key challenge to evaluation research is that it always involves people outside of academia who don't understand academics. As researchers we want to follow the text book method about how to execute our research and be objective, but from a program's standpoint, they want their program to look good." Zaykowski believes it is good practice to require an MOU (memorandum of understanding) that outlines expectations and states up front that the results may not look like what the client wants them too. Although an MOU doesn't solve all problems, Zaykowski finds it makes these interactions easier.

Overselling Your Skills as an Evaluator

Describe purposes and procedures: Standard of accuracy that requires the evaluator to clearly articulate and outline the purposes and procedures of the evaluation.

A fourth pitfall associated with evaluation research occurs when the evaluator knows nothing about the topic he or she is evaluating. Yes, evaluation research requires the same methodology skills described in this book; nevertheless, as featured researcher Rachel Boba Santos along with Cuevas state, the biggest failures they have witnessed have been when an evaluator is hired to evaluate a program he or she knows nothing about. Santos notes one simply has to know the topic. In these instances, Cuevas has seen these evaluators go into a situation, screw it up due to the lack of substantive understanding, and make a big mess in the end. Santos has seen cases in which a completely incompetent evaluator was hired. The incompetence ended up meaning the evaluation was rushed and poorly done. Both Santos's and Cuevas's advice is not to oversell your skills if you want to conduct an evaluation, to have a realistic plan to avoid rushing, and to be well versed in the topic you are hired to evaluate. To do otherwise is not to provide clients with the service they deserve.

Ethics Associated With Evaluation Research

All research requires continual attention to ethics. Evaluation research is no exception. The many elements of ethics discussed in the book so far apply here. For example, minimizing harm to others, informed consent, confidentiality, fair treatment, and respecting others are all important considerations when conducting evaluation research. Nevertheless, some things should be mentioned to avoid ethical problems when conducting evaluation research. First, even though evaluation research focuses on programs, the evaluator must recognize that people, individuals and groups involved with funding, directing, administering, and receiving benefits from a program—are affected by this activity. Especially vulnerable are those receiving benefits from programs. Consider that according to the Australian Council for International Development (2013, p. 4), failure to consider ethics "can lead to the opposite results intended . . . they can actually worsen the situation for participants in the research and evaluation process, their wider communities and even the evaluators and researchers themselves." Significant consequences that may occur when disregarding ethics are the following:

- A strengthening of discriminatory or unjust social relationships
- The exclusion of key stakeholders
- An increase in participant recriminations
- Unintentional participant identification
- Incorrect findings and recommendations that result in negative programming decisions

Failure to consider ethics can lead to unintended consequences, and all individuals engaged in a program can experience negative outcomes. Consider a summative evaluation that results in the termination of a program. The consequences of this are that people lose jobs and income, and clients of the program lose the benefits they had been receiving. For this reason, we discuss a few ethical issues frequently associated with evaluation research.

Failure to Be Nimble

Melde noted to us that evaluation research takes place in the real world where we often have little control over our environment. Given this, Melde went on to say that "text book evaluation designs rarely work in the real world. You have to be nimble. A researcher has to have a plan b in anticipation of real life." Failure to be nimble and ready to adjust to the real world can lead to an evaluation disaster. A great example of the unexpected was experienced by Santos, who was in the midst of implementing a program, and in the midst of this, the police chief was replaced. The interim chief stopped all research immediately. With an uncooperative interim chief, no plan B could save the research. In the end, the interim chief killed the entire project. Although the implementation and planned evaluation never happened, Santos notes the incident provided great information about working with police chiefs.

Confidentiality

Even though maintaining confidentiality when promised is an ethical consideration for all types of research, it can be a bit trickier in evaluation research. Imagine you are conducting interviews of key stakeholders. They are providing excellent, although negative, information about the program that will be useful in conducting a fair and comprehensive evaluation. There are not many key stakeholders, however, so including this information in the evaluation report without revealing the source of the information may be difficult if not impossible. Alternatively, imagine that as an evaluator you are unable to access certain information due to a challenging gatekeeper. As a result, the evaluator may not be able to assess that information. If there is only one gatekeeper, then maintaining the confidentiality of this individual may be impossible. Dodge echoed this sentiment noting that at times, maintaining confidentiality is nearly impossible. Regardless of the individual involved, if promised confidentiality, the evaluator must strive to honor it.

Defensible information sources: Standard of accuracy requiring the sources of information used to conduct a program evaluation.

Valid information: Accuracy standard that requires that the procedures used to gather information and data used in the evaluation must ensure a valid interpretation.

Reliable information: Accuracy standard that requires that procedures used to gather data and information must be designed and used to provide reliable information for the evaluation.

Systematic information: Accuracy standard that focuses on the need for systematic data and information collection, analysis, and reporting during an evaluation.

Analysis of quantitative information: Accuracy standard requiring the use of appropriate scientific analysis of quantitative data used to address the research question being investigated.

Analysis of qualitative information: Accuracy standard that requires the use of appropriate scientific analysis of qualitative data used to address the research question being considered

Justified conclusions: Accuracy standard that indicates the need for all conclusions and findings be clearly and comprehensively justified allowing stakeholder assessment.

Politics

Impartial reporting: Accuracy standard that calls for care to be taken to avoid distortion or bias in findings.

Metaevaluation: Accuracy standard that refers to the need that the evaluation be judged on these standards to allow an examination of its strengths and weaknesses by stakeholders.

Politics and evaluation research are members of an uneasy marriage. In the middle of this is the evaluator who must act ethically. This can be challenging when the evaluator must work with multiple stakeholders who are at odds. To do so, the evaluator must be guided by the more general ethical requirements associated with research but also by the standards of effective evaluation. In particular, standards of propriety must be maintained. First, the evaluator must be cognizant that his or her role is to serve stakeholders and the targeted population affected by the program. In addition, regardless of any political pressures the evaluator might face, he or she must act with respect to all individuals associated with the program of interest. No individual should be threatened or harmed. Third, regardless of the political pressures faced, the evaluator must provide a comprehensive and fair assessment of the strengths and weaknesses of the program that is disseminated to individuals affected by the evaluation. As Zaykowski stated to us during her video interview, a stakeholder may "want to push back on certain types of findings. It is your role as a researcher to provide fair and objective findings including strengths and weaknesses of the topic of interest." Finally, any conflict of interest that arises must be dealt with transparently and honestly to ensure the evaluation and results are not compromised.

Recognizing this built-in tension between politics and evaluation is imperative to maximize success. The evaluator must remember that evaluation research findings inform political decision makers. In addition, findings about the program are assessed in a larger context of many programs and policies competing for scarce resources and attention. What the evaluation concludes matters. It matters to the program, to recipients of the program, and to those administering the program. Nevertheless, the larger context also matters. Ten years after Weiss's (1993) work was published, Rossi, Lipsey, and Freeman (2003, p. 15) summed up the current and future of the worlds of evaluation and politics: "First, restraints on resources will continue to require funders to choose the social problem areas on which to concentrate resources and the programs that should be given priority. Second, intensive scrutiny of existing programs will continue because of the pressure to curtail or dismantle those that do not demonstrate that they are effective and efficient."

Losing Objectivity and Failure to Pull the Plug

Researchers must be open to the notion that the program they are evaluating is not working or, even worse, is causing unintentional harm. Cuevas offers the example of colleagues who have conducted evaluation research around violence prevention interventions with youth. He has seen situations where some evaluators have not had an open mind, believing that this program—the interventions—was failing and making things worse. People, including researchers, can lose sight of the fact that the program they are evaluating is not effective or beneficial. Still, people have a hard time letting go as they are invested in particular programs. Researchers must be attentive to the ethics around effectiveness of programs, and they must be willing to pull the plug on programs that are doing harm. Recognizing all of these pitfalls in the tangled worlds of evaluation and politics is critical if you want to be successful.

Evaluation Research Expert—Michael Shively, PhD

Michael Shively, PhD, is a senior associate with Abt Associates where he conducts criminal justice, criminology, and victimology program and policy evaluations. In other words, Shively uses the skills you are reading about in this chapter to study policies and programs dealing with human trafficking and prostitution, hate crime, law enforcement, drug trafficking, intimate partner violence, and contextual influences on crime. Shively never thought he would be a researcher, instead, he believed he would work on a boat. Growing up in the Seattle area, he spent a lot of time with his uncle, who was a captain of a tugboat, and on the water in general. When Shively graduated from high school, the economy was in shambles and he could not get a job on any boat. Instead, he went to college. He didn't do well until he found something that really interested him: the social sciences, especially when they focused on crime and justice issues. In those classes, he was drawn to research methods because it allowed an exploration about what was true. He acknowledges that he annoyed some professors when he asked for evidence supporting what they were saying. This is the essence of what research methods offer.

Courtesy of Michael Shively

Shively ultimately earned a BA and an MA from Western Washington University in psychology and sociology, respectively. His sociology PhD was awarded from the University of Massachusetts in Amherst. After graduating, he served as deputy director of research for the Massachusetts Department of Correction and as an assistant professor at Northeastern University's College of Criminal Justice. In addition, he served on the Massachusetts Governor's Commission on Criminal Justice Innovation and on the Massachusetts Criminal History Systems Board; facilitated the Cambridge Neighborhood Safety Task Force; was a founding member of the Regional Human Trafficking Workgroup at the Kennedy School of Government, Harvard University; and was a member of the Massachusetts Attorney General's Human Trafficking Task Force, Subcommittee on Demand.

At Abt, Shively has worked on many interesting projects including research on human trafficking. This is an area that Shively notes where "the ratio of interest, mass media ink, and celebrity advocacy to actual factual information is out of whack." Much remains to be learned about trafficking. One topic in which very little is known is about the actual traffickers. That was the focus on Shively's recent work where he used the presentence reports of people convicted and serving time in federal prison for trafficking. Presentence reports (PSRs) are full of valuable data including (but not limited to) arrest records, aggravated circumstances (e.g., use of weapons), mitigating circumstances (e.g., unknowingly assisted in trafficking), police reports, trial transcripts, interviews with offenders, and interviews with family. In total, 500 PSRs were coded and analyzed. Shively and his team provided understanding about the reasons people traffic, if it is organized or haphazard, what ties an organization together, and whether trafficking represents organizations diversifying or introducing new activities. An example of one enterprise represented the diversification of an existing organized drug smuggling organization. This group recognized that it could add women to cargo on ships headed to the United States to increase profitability. If for some reason the traffickers have to ditch the drugs, they can still recoup costs by forcing these women to work in brothels and strip clubs.

Of the 500 cases reviewed, Shively then randomly selected 50 face-to-face interviews of the incarcerated traffickers. Shively asked the convicts things like, "How did you get started in this? Were you pressured? Did someone suggest it to you? Did you develop this scheme yourself? Who were the people who got you in? How did you perceive risk from law enforcement? What did you worry about? What were the effective and ineffective things police did?" The results of this research are incredibly useful. For law enforcement, they now have an improved understanding about what they do that is effective as well as ineffective. They better understand how criminals evade justice.

Shively offers both general and specific advice to students. First, learn as much as you can because you have no idea what is in your future. Do not turn down any training. Never say that does not apply to you. You never know when you will need that material or skill. Second, learn as much about the career you think you are interested in, and don't believe what you see about it on TV or the media. Some very exciting TV careers comprise crushing boredom in reality. Keep your eyes and options open, and investigate a bit before you commit to a single career path. Third, if you are really passionate about a career, do not let others dissuade you. Investigate it and what it takes to be successful. Shively is a firm believer that "that there is always room for the best in any career."

In terms of specific skills, Shively finds several characteristics and skills that serve students well when they apply for a position like his. The characteristics needed in a successful candidate are those who are personable, organized, deadline oriented, flexible, and smart. In addition, a researcher or evaluator must have foundational understanding of research methods. Shively finds these skills cluster together in their best project managers. The skills he finds critical are research methods skills and quantitative analysis skills. Evaluators and researchers must understand about sampling, validity, reliability, and basic statistics to do well in several roles. Someone looking for work must be able to communicate the basis of research to all types of audiences. What does not work Shively finds are individuals who are content experts—they may know everything about trafficking, but without underlying research methods skills, the content is not useful.

Chapter Wrap-Up

This chapter presents foundational information on evaluation research. Although all of our case study authors do not engage in evaluation research, you should be able to see how their research expertise would be useful in an evaluation. A great example is Brunson, who, to date, has not conducted evaluation research. Yet, Brunson's strong skill set in gathering qualitative data would make him a valuable evaluation research team member. In this chapter, we described why anyone would want to conduct evaluation research. The book began by describing four major purposes for research: exploration, description, explanation, and evaluation. This chapter focuses on the last of those purposes. Evaluation research is useful to understand if a program is needed, if a program is working, if the program has intended or unintended consequences, if the process is efficient or cost effective, and even if the program should be terminated. We also described what evaluation research is, several guiding principles of evaluation research, the seven steps of evaluation research, and how this type of research is connected with the policy process.

A key point in this chapter is that there is no single type of evaluation research but many. Two primary types of evaluation covered in this chapter are formative evaluations and summative evaluations. Formative evaluations, including needs assessments and process evaluations, occur during the formative period of programs and serve as a means to improve programs. In contrast, summative evaluations, including impact evaluations and outcomes evaluations, tend to occur after a program has been implemented. Summative evaluations offer a broader assessment focused on the target population of the program and the success at reaching the goals of the program. Furthermore, no single type of evaluation research is better than another. Each type serves a different, but equally important, purpose.

An overarching theme of this chapter is that evaluation research uses the research approaches focused on in this text such as observations, content analysis, secondary data analysis, and experimental research. Yet, it differs from the material presented in earlier chapters in that it is applied versus basic research. The difference in applied versus basic research is clear when you consider the type of knowledge created, the origination of the research questions, the comparative and judgmental nature of the work, the challenges in working with stakeholders in what can be a noncooperative environment, and how findings are disseminated.

The four standards of effective evaluations were described: utility, feasibility, propriety, and accuracy. In addition, the multiple criteria associated with each of these standards were offered. Evaluation research can be challenging for reasons that other research purposes do not encounter. First, in many cases, an evaluator is called in after the fact. In other words, a program has been launched with little consideration of the purpose of the program and how to assess whether the purpose is being met. In addition, evaluation research must navigate the tricky political context in which it exists. You cannot separate program evaluation from politics, which means you are often dealing with multiple stakeholders who are at odds with each other. Understanding the political nature of this work and that it can present challenges is necessary. Because evaluation research uses all methodologies, it is subject to the ethical concerns that all other research is. There are two ways additional focus on ethics is required. First, confidentiality can be challenging in evaluation research. It may be difficult or impossible to disguise the source of information. In addition, the political pressures that can exert themselves on evaluators must be constantly checked. The evaluator must focus on his or her service-oriented goal and on the standards of propriety.

An evaluation research expert, Michael Shively, PhD, described how he uses research methods skills to conduct real, meaningful evaluation research on topics such as human trafficking. Shively feels that some of the most important questions anyone can ask in any career or role are "Do it make sense to do this?" "Is this designed in a defensible way?" "Is this working as it was intended?" "Does this help?" and "Is it producing results?" These questions fuel evaluation research. People hope that what they do matters. If you are addressing these types of questions, you are making a difference. As the human trafficking case indicates, this type of work is real and not esoteric stuff. It matters.

Several of our case studies included evaluation research. Melde and colleagues' research used data that were collected as a result of a process and outcome evaluation (Melde, Taylor, & Esbensen, 2009). Although his specific research on gang members' fear of crime and perceived risk of being violently victimized did not involve an evaluation, the data came from an evaluative project. Santos and colleague's work was in part a process evaluation designed to ascertain whether intensive policing focused on targeted offenders would influence crime rates in hot spots (Santos & Santos, 2016). Their research involved a mixed-methods practice that is highly desirable according to Zaykowski and the larger literature. Santos and Santos's work is extremely applied, and the outcome of this research directly informs the way the Port St. Lucie, Florida, Police Department approaches policing. Table 11.3 presents some characteristics of each case study with information about their evaluation ties.

The next chapter in this text focuses on analysis. At this point, you have learned about the four purposes of research (explore, describe, explain, and evaluation), and the book has covered many methodology approaches (qualitative research, secondary data analysis, survey research, experimental research, etc.) used to gather data to accomplish those purposes. Next, you need to understand how to analyze the data gathered using those methodological approaches. How do you use the data and information gathered to arrive at findings and conclusions? These are some questions addressed in Chapter 12.

Table 11.3   Featured Research: Types of Evaluation, Logic Models, and the Use of Mixed Methods

Researcher	Type of Evaluation	Logic Models in Final Article?	Mixed Methods Approach Used?
Chris Melde (Melde et al., 2009)	Data were collected as a part of a process and an outcome evaluation. This particular study using these secondary data was not an evaluation itself.	Used, but not provided in final publication	Yes, the data were gathered based on questionnaires, observations, and other means.
Rachel Santos (Santos & Santos, 2016)	Process evaluation.	Used, but not provided in the final publication	Yes, researchers' use of experimental approach, and the use of secondary data included.

The materials presented in this chapter can be used in applied ways. This box presents several assignments to help in demonstrating the value of this material by engaging in assignments related to it.

1. Homework Applied Assignment: Designing an Evaluation of a Program You Are Engaged In

Think of a program you are engaged in. It could be the academic program you are majoring in, a social program (e.g., fraternity, sorority, extramural club, or academic club) or a somewhat formal social club. Whichever group you focus on should have a mission statement associated with it. Now, using that mission statement, design a summative evaluation to see whether the group is meeting its stated goals. Be sure to clearly articulate your research question (given the mission statement and goals). Next identify your research methodology. What data will you gather? How will you gather it? How will you know based on those data the group is achieving its goals and mission? You are welcome to use multiple research approaches in your evaluation. Finally, offer a conclusion that comes from those data about how well your group is doing in meeting its goals. Are there negative consequences from the group? Should the group continue or be terminated? Be prepared to share your paper and findings with the class.

2. Group Work in Class Applied Assignment: Using Secondary Data

The university has hired your group to assess your class. Using the syllabus (where you should have an objective of the class statement), work with your team to devise a plan to assess your class. Keep in mind that you are only offering an evaluation proposal because all data will not be available until the end of the semester. For now, using the objectives outlined on your syllabus, design a summative evaluation to see whether the class is achieving its stated objectives. Be sure to clearly articulate your research question (given the objectives listed). Next identify your proposed research methodology. What data will you gather? How will you gather it? How will you know based on those data the class objectives are being met? You are welcome—and encouraged—to use multiple research approaches in your evaluation. What findings would you expect to see if the class is being successful? What findings would you expect if the class were not meeting its objectives? Be prepared to share your paper and findings with the class.

3. Internet Applied Assignment: Reviewing an Evaluation—No-Drop Policies

Using the Internet, access Smith and Davis's (2004) *An Evaluation of Efforts to Implement No-Drop Policies: Two Central Values in Conflict* found at https://www.ncjrs.gov/pdffiles1/nij/199719.pdf. In a paper, describe the purpose of this evaluation and the background that justifies doing this research. Next, identify the types of evaluation the researchers conducted. Describe the methodology used to conduct this evaluation, including where it happened, types of data gathered, and types of research done. Note the advantages and disadvantages of each approach. Next, describe the findings presented by the researchers. Do you agree or disagree with their conclusions? Should no-drop policies be implemented nationwide, be dropped nationwide, or some combination. Why or why not? What next steps for research do you see are needed? Be prepared to share your findings with the class.

KEY WORDS AND CONCEPTS

Accuracy 362

Analysis of qualitative Information 364

Analysis of quantitative information 364

Analyzing the data 349

Applied research 356

Basic research 356

Blind review 360

Communicate the findings and recommendations 350

Complete and fair assessment 362

Conflict of interest 362

Context analysis 364

Cost-effectiveness 361
Defensible information
    sources 364
Describe purposes and
    procedures 364
Design of the methodology 349
Develop findings and
    conclusions 349
Develop the research question 348
Disclosure of findings 362
Evaluation impact 361
Evaluator credibility 361
Feasibility 361
Fiscal responsibility 362
Formal agreements 362
Formative evaluations 351
Gap analysis 353
Gather data/evidence 349
Human interactions 362

Identify and Engage
    Stakeholders 348
Impact evaluations 356
Impartial reporting 364
Information scope and
    selection 361
Inputs 353
Justified conclusions 364
Justify these recommendations 350
Logic models 353
Long-term outcomes 355
Metaevaluation 364
Needs assessments 352
Outcome evaluations 355
Outputs 353
Policy 350
Policy process 350
Political viability 361
Practical procedures 361

Process evaluation 353
Program 350
Program documentation 364
Propriety 362
Reliable information 364
Report clarity 361
Report timeliness and
    dissemination 361
Rights of human subjects 362
Service orientation 362
Short-term outcomes 355
Stakeholder identification 361
Stakeholders 348
Summative evaluation 351
Systematic information 364
Utility 361
Valid information 364
Values identification 361

KEY POINTS

- Evaluation research is an applied approach to research involving the systematic assessment of the need for, implementation of, or output of a program based on objective criteria. When using the data gathered in an evaluation research, you can recommend improvements, enhancements, expansions, or the termination of a program. The assessment of a program can be conducted by using any of the research approaches described in this text, including observations, interviews, content analysis, survey research, secondary data analysis, and so on.

- Evaluation research involves seven steps: identifying and engaging stakeholders, developing the research question, designing the methodology, gathering data/evidence, analyzing the data, developing findings and conclusions, justifying the recommendations, and communicating findings and recommendations.

- Evaluation research differs from basic research in many ways including the purpose of the research, origination of the research questions, comparative and judgmental nature of the work, working with stakeholders, a challenging environment, and the ways findings are disseminated.

- Stakeholders play an important role in evaluation research and can be the key to success or the key to failure. Stakeholders are any person or organization who has a direct interest in the program being evaluated and can include funders, program administrators, the community in which the program is administered, and clients of the program. Knowing who the stakeholders are, and developing and maintaining a good relationship with stakeholders, is critical during the planning stages, the gathering of data, and presentation and buy-in of findings. Without the support of stakeholders, evaluation research cannot be successful.

- There are two primary types of evaluations: formative and summative. Formative evaluations are conducted in the earliest stages of the policy process while a program is being developed with the purpose of ensuring the program is feasible prior to full implementation. Formative evaluations can be thought of as "trouble-shooting" evaluations in that what is discovered from the evaluation is "fed back" into the program to strengthen or enhance it. Two types of formative evaluations considered in this text are needs assessments and process evaluations. Summative evaluations are used to ascertain whether a program should be funded, continued, or terminated. Two types of summative evaluations are discussed in this text: outcome evaluations and impact evaluations.

- Logic models are graphic depictions that illustrate the ideal about how a program is intended to work. There are three benefits of logic models, including that (1) they point to key performance measurement points useful for conducting an evaluation, (2) that they assist with program design and they make improving existing programs easier by highlighting program activities that are problematic, and (3) that they help identify the program expectations.

- An evaluation is effective when it meets four standards: utility, feasibility, propriety, and accuracy.

- When conducting evaluation research, you must be cognizant of the real-life consequences of their work. Should a program be changed or terminated, individuals lose access to programs, and others may lose jobs.

REVIEW QUESTIONS

1. What distinguishes evaluation research from other types of research?

2. What types of evaluations are there? When are each best used?

3. Who are stakeholders, and why are they important during evaluation research?

4. What value is a logic model? What can it tell someone?

5. What is a gap analysis? How does a gap analysis relate to evaluation research?

6. What does a formative evaluation do? What types of formative evaluations were covered here, and how do they differ from the others?

7. What does a summative evaluation do? What types of summative evaluations were covered here, and how do they differ from the others?

8. What are the four standards of an effective evaluation? What are the standards of each? Why are these important to have?

9. What ethical considerations are important to focus on when conducting evaluation research? Why?

10. What types are common pitfalls are found when conducting evaluation research?

CRITICAL THINKING QUESTIONS

1. You are working with your professor on research projects. She invites you into her office to discuss a new project: a process evaluation of a local program designed to increase literacy. What are some questions you might ask of your professor as you think about what needs to be done?
   What are some of the first steps you should take for this evaluation? What sorts of materials or documents from the client might be useful in planning your evaluation? Why is that?

2. As you discuss this new process evaluation with your professor, you come to learn that the client did not use a logic model. What sorts of difficulties might this mean for the process evaluation? Why would it have been different had a logic model been provided? What additional questions might you ask your client during the planning stages of the evaluation then? Why those questions?

3. You are interning with a local agency that provides résumé assistance for former prisoners. This program is hyped as one that teaches former prisoners how to write

their own résumé, develop excellent interviewing skills, and engage in positive employee behavior. A goal of this program is to increase self-sufficiency and, ultimately, the reduction of recidivism. The funder of this project is a family who strongly believes in these goals. Furthermore, the funder is using its few financial resources to fund this important work. You enjoy working on a meaningful project with this giving family. In the course of your work, you discover that the program is not keeping good records on measures of self-sufficiency or recidivism. In fact, it seems that the information is simply being made up to make the program look successful and to keep the funds flowing. What sorts of measures do you think it should be keeping? What might you do when faced with this dilemma? Who would you tell about this? What guidelines of evaluation research are being violated? What standards of effective evaluations are being compromised? Why?

4. You have spent the last year working on a summative evaluation of a local popular program that assists single teen mothers. You have been working

diligently to follow all guidelines and standards of evaluation research, and you have made your findings. Unfortunately, the findings point to the outcome that the program is not providing any benefit, and it actually seems to be worsening outcomes. You know that if you recommend the termination of the program, several program administrators will lose their jobs. You recognize that this recommendation will also result in some hardship for the clients. How do these things affect your recommendation? Why? What standards or guidelines of evaluation research assist you in making your recommendations?

5. Another person in your class is stating that evaluation research is no different than any other type of research. She notes that the evaluator develops a research question, gathers data, generates findings and conclusions, and then is done. You disagree. What points would you make to demonstrate that she is incorrect? In what ways is evaluation research different than research guided by other purposes? Why do these differences matter?

$SAGE edge™

SAGE edge offers a robust online environment featuring an impressive array of free tools and resources for review, study, and further exploration, keeping you on the cutting edge of teaching and learning. Learn more at **edge.sagepub.com/rennisonrm**.

Analysis, Findings, and Where to Go From There

At this point, you have the data you need to answer your research question or questions. Part 5 of this text addresses the final steps that you as a researcher need to take to complete your research. You must now take your carefully collected data and analyze them to answer your research question(s). Then you need to present your findings in such a way that they are easy to comprehend to all readers of your work. Offering findings and conclusions about your research question requires you to make the findings of your research relevant to more general audiences. Not everyone who consumes your research will be a researcher, so care must be taken to ensure your findings are presented in a way that everyone can understand. To do this, we present three more chapters. Chapter 12 describes an overview of the different ways researchers analyze data. First, the chapter discusses why data must be analyzed. Next the chapter discusses the importance of describing the data you will be analyzing. We then turn to the analysis of quantitative data, followed by a discussion of the analysis of qualitative data (to couple with analysis already discussed in Chapter 6). Chapter 13 focuses on the importance of making your research policy relevant. As we have stressed throughout the text, research matters, and a major way it makes a difference in our lives is by producing research that is policy relevant. Historically, researchers have done a great job of conducting solid research and publishing those results, however, researchers have not focused on making their research relevant to policy. Chapter 13 offers tips to help you make your research and the findings from it shape policy. Finally, the text concludes with Chapter 14, which discusses how you can take your new research skills and use them to begin a meaningful career. Chapter 14 begins with reiterating why research methods skills are beneficial to you. We offer tips on where to look for jobs using these skills, how to create an effective résumé and cover letter, as well as ways you can leverage social media to increase the chances of being invited to an interview. We also discuss the pitfalls associated with job hunting, as well as ethical considerations. Many students don't feel they need this information, but our experience as professors suggests differently. Having all the skills in the world will not matter if you do not have a solid résumé, aren't called in for an interview, and crash-and-burn during an interview. It is true that people hire based on skills. But there are other skills they are looking for when hiring, and this chapter presents them.

Learning Objectives

After finishing this chapter, you should be able to:

12.1 Explain the role of data analysis in the scientific process.

12.2 Identify different types of data analysis commonly used in criminal justice research, and provide examples of when each is used.

12.3 Differentiate between quantitative and qualitative analytic techniques and the software applications that can be used to analyze these data.

12.4 Explain the difference between a case-oriented approach to data analysis, like conjunctive analysis of case configurations (CACC), and traditional, variable-oriented approaches.

12.5 Identify common methods for analyzing geographic data and the software applications commonly used in geographic data analysis.

12.6 Describe some of the ethical challenges researchers face when conducting data analysis.

Deduction: Process of making inferences about a particular instance through the reference to a general principle or law.

Introduction

In Chapter 2, we introduced Wallace's (1971) "wheel of science" to illustrate the recursive process of research. Throughout the book, we have presented information about theory, research questions and purposes, research design, and gathering data using a variety of approaches. At this point in the book, you have data. The next question for you is what to do with these data. Luckily for you, this is the topic of this chapter on data analysis and on the part of the wheel of science called **deduction**.

To this end, we offer an overview of the different ways researchers analyze data. First, we address why you analyze data. Understanding why we analyze our data is the key in understanding the nuts and bolts associated with it. Next, we turn to how data are analyzed focusing on both describing your data and answering more complex research questions. We next turn to the analysis of quantitative data, followed by a brief discussion of the analysis of qualitative data that was provided in Chapter 6. We describe commonly used software applications used in data analysis (i.e., Excel™, SPSS™, STATA™, and SAS). We distinguish between descriptive statistics, correlation analysis, and contingencies. We also discuss configural analysis and geographic analytic approaches and geographic information systems software, not already presented in Chapter 10. As is custom, we then discuss the common pitfalls associated with data analysis and highlight the ethical considerations during the analysis. Finally, we hear from Susan Burton, a senior management analyst supervisor at the Florida Department of Law Enforcement (FDLE). In her role, she uses data analysis to assist law enforcement in her organization.

At the conclusion of this chapter, you will have all of the skills you need to begin conducting your own research. These skills are valuable for many reasons, including making you a critical consumer of information, making you an excellent producer of knowledge, and providing you with real-world skills that will help you begin a rewarding career in research.

The next chapter offers more information about finding that career. For now, we begin our discussion of data analysis in the next section by answering the simple question, "Why analysis?"

Why Analysis?

Why analysis? Why analyze our data? Well, our featured researchers shared their thoughts on this question during their video or phone interviews conducted for this book. Chris Melde, for example, suggests that analyzing data enables us to think systematically and to understand the way we come to the conclusions we reached in our study. It is a key tenant to science, according to Carlos Cuevas. In addition, Rachel Boba Santos notes that it "enables us to avoid relying on anecdotal evidence." Furthermore, Mary Dodge suggests that we analyze our data so that we can make logical conclusions and further our knowledge base, which is a view shared by Rod Brunson, who said that data analysis is needed because it is "a necessary component of evidence gathering, fact finding." Finally, Heather Zaykowski said we analyze data to gain insight into, and answer, our research questions. As the earlier part of the book indicated, coming to a conclusion on something other than systematically gathered data or evidence would lead to erroneous conclusions. As careful researchers, anything less is not good enough.

The simple answer is that all researchers analyze data to answer their research questions. The entire purpose of conducting research is to answer a research question. By analyzing our data, we answer that question. By using data analysis, we can develop findings and make conclusions based on patterns in our data. By using data analysis, we can find support, or fail to find support, for any stated hypothesis. In some types of studies, data analysis and the findings it leads to allow us to generalize our conclusions about patterns in the larger population. By conducting data analysis, we know more about the phenomenon we are investigating. We can then use this scientifically produced knowledge to develop new, or refine existing, theories about why these data patterns were observed. In other words, we conduct data analysis because if we didn't, the scientific process would be incomplete, and the knowledge we hold would be questionable.

How Should Data Be Analyzed?

In the previous section, we said that we conduct data analysis so that we can identify patterns in our data, make claims about research hypotheses, and answer our research questions. Although this explanation addresses the "why" question about data analysis, it does not

© fbatista72/Canstockphoto

address the "how" question. There are many ways to conduct data analysis, and this section of the chapter delves deeper into these approaches. The first thing to keep in mind, and it is worth repeating, is that the purpose of the data analysis is to answer the research question. For example, if your research goal was to describe or explore something, then you need to describe the data you gathered. Describing data allows you to offer findings such as "The average age of my sample is 33 years"; "A theme emerging in the data was abuse of power. This theme was identified by 80% of the sample"; or "The median number of years served

Measures of central tendency are a group of descriptive statistics that numerically describe the "typical" case in data, and include the mean, the median, and the mode.

in prison was eight." The goal with descriptive analysis is to make statements about the something typical in your data.

The next characteristic of your data that drives the type of analysis performed is the nature of the data. Are your data numeric—quantitative? Are they non-numeric—qualitative? Do your data include geospatial information? These are important considerations when selecting the specific approach to data analysis taken. In the next section, we address data analytic techniques specific to quantitative data. After that, we turn to a very brief discussion of approaches used for qualitative data given the treatment of this topic in Chapter 6. Next we offer information on analysis suitable for other types of data. Keep in mind that the purpose of this chapter is to provide your first look at data analytic techniques. To fully answer any research question, you will need to take a statistics course (for quantitative data) or a qualitative research methods course (for qualitative data). Do not be intimidated by the prospect of either of those classes. Once you understand the purpose of these courses—to provide you with tools to answer research questions—you have the framework to be successful.

Analysis of Quantitative Data

All quantitative analysis and findings should begin with a description of the data, regardless of the purpose of the research. This allows you and readers of your research to assess the nature of your sample. For instance, Cuevas and colleagues' research on teen dating violence among Latinos provided this information about the parents of youth taking the survey (Sabina, Cuevas, & Cotignola-Pickens, 2016; see Table 12.1).

Describing your data is an important first step in quantitative data analysis, and there are several ways to do that.

Describing Your Data

Descriptive statistics are one way data can be analyzed. Descriptive statistics, or descriptives, are used to describe your data. Descriptive statistics can be presented using numbers (e.g., an arithmetic average) and visually (e.g., a bar chart). The most basic form of descriptive statistics involves the analysis of a single variable. This type of analysis is **univariate analysis.** The example of parent relationship percentages in Cuevas and colleagues' study is an example of this (Sabina et al., 2016). Univariate analysis can be done in three ways:

Table 12.1 Percentages Table		
Parent Relationship Status	**Wave 1**	**Wave 2**
Single (never married)	12.1%	7.8%
Married	69.2%	70.4%
Cohabitating/committed relationship	8.4%	9.6%
Divorced/separated/widow/other	10.3%	11.8%

(1) show how observations are distributed across a range of categories for a single variable, (2) show the "typical" case in a variable's distribution, and (3) show what all the other cases in a variable's distributions look like, relative to the "typical" case.

Distributions

One of the simplest ways to summarize data for a single variable is using a **frequency distribution**, which is a table that displays the number of times a particular value or category is observed in the data. An example includes asking 15 university students whether they had ever received a speeding ticket while driving. Response categories provided include "Never," "Once," or "More than once." Findings from these data may be presented using a frequency distribution like the one in Table 12.2.

As a reminder, "n" refers to sample size and % refers to percentage. In this example, about half (47%) of students have received more than one speeding ticket, and only one in five (20%) have never received a speeding ticket. This summary makes understanding the data easy. In addition to frequency distributions, researchers often describe other aspects of their data, including what the typical case in a variable's distribution looks like and what all the other cases in a variable's distributions look like, relative to that "typical" case.

Frequency distribution: Used in descriptive statistics, it is a table that displays the number of times a particular value or category is observed in the data for a particular variable.

Measures of central tendency: Group of summary statistics used to numerically describe the "typical" case in a group of observations.

Mean: Measure of central tendency used as a summary statistic. It represents the arithmetic average value of all observations in a data distribution.

Measures of Central Tendency

This is not a statistics textbook, so we do not delve deeply into a conversation about statistics. Nevertheless, data analysis is a key part of the scientific process making it worthwhile to cover some basics. Measures of central tendency are a great place to start. **Measures of central tendency** are a group of descriptive statistics that numerically describe the "typical" case in data and include the mean, the median, and the mode.

Mean

The arithmetic **mean** (or "mean") is the most commonly used measure of central tendency. The mean is a number that describes the typical case in your data. The symbol for a mean is an x with a line or bar over it, and many refer to it as an x-bar. To calculate a mean, you simply add all the observed scores (scores are identified using the symbol x) in a data distribution

Table 12.2   Example of a Frequency Distribution Table

Ticket	n	%
Never	3	20
Once	5	33
More than once	7	47
Total	15	100

Note: It contains summary information that describes the observations across a variable's categories.

(i.e., Σx indicates the need to add the scores) and divide this value by the total number of observations (n). The formula used to calculate a mean is

$$\bar{x} = \frac{\Sigma x}{n}$$

Means should only be calculated on interval- or ratio-level data.[1] For example, if you conducted a study of university students' driving behavior and recorded the number of speeding tickets that 15 different students received since getting their license, the data may look like the following:

Number of tickets = 0, 0, 0, 1, 1, 1, 1, 1, 2, 2, 2, 3, 3, 4, 6

The mean number of speeding tickets in this sample is of university students is $\Sigma x = 27$ and $n = 15$. The average number of speeding tickets ($\bar{x}$) for your sample of 15 university students is 1.8 tickets.

An advantage of the mean is that it uses information from all scores in the distribution. Ironically, it is common for the mean to be a value that is never actually observed in the data. This is ironic because the mean is supposed to be a descriptor of the "typical" case. Another advantage to using a mean is that it tends to be similar when repeated samples are drawn from the same population. This stability is important, especially for when researchers want to use sample statistics like the mean to estimate population parameters. A disadvantage of the mean is that it is sensitive to extreme scores or **outliers**. Outliers are extreme values in a data distribution that are either much lower than or much higher than the other scores in the distribution. This results in pulling the mean down in value lower than normal when there are low extreme scores in a distribution, and inflating the mean when high extreme scores are present. When outliers pull the average in one direction or the other (i.e., higher or lower), we say that distribution of scores is skewed. Another shortcoming of the mean is that it should not be used on all data. For example, when we have nominal-level data (i.e., Race/Hispanic origin [African American, Asian, White, Latino (any race), or Other]) instead of interval-ratio-level data, we should not calculate a mean.

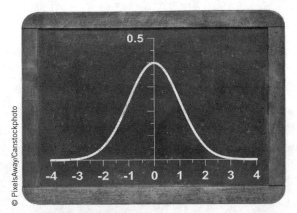

© PixelsAway/Canstockphoto

Median

The **median** represents the numeric center or midpoint of a data distribution. Half of all scores in a data distribution are greater than the median, and half are less than the median. Although many simply use the word *median* to describe a median, some also use the symbol *Mdn*. To calculate a distribution's median, you must first rank the scores from lowest to highest. A common error among students is to fail to rank scores, so don't forget to do this. Next, find the center position (sometimes referred to as the median position [*Mp*]) in the ranked data by adding one to the total number of observations and dividing the total by two:

$$Mp = (n + 1) / 2$$

[1]There are cases when calculating a mean on two-category nominal data is appropriate. This discussion is beyond this textbook and will be discussed in a statistics course.

The final step is to determine which value in the data distribution corresponds to the median position. Returning to our hypothetical university student speeding ticket example:

Number of tickets = 0, 0, 0, 1, 1, 1, 1, 1, 2, 2, 2, 3, 3, 4, 6

This distribution has already been rank-ordered from the fewest to the largest number of speeding tickets. Next, find the median position—$Mp = 8$ (i.e., $[15 + 1] / 2 = 8$). Count from the left 8 scores until we see that the 8th score equals 1. The value that corresponds to the median position for this distribution is one. When the distribution has an even number of observations, the median position (Mp) will not be a whole number. For example, if we had 16 instead of 15 students in our speeding ticket study, the median position would have been 8.5 instead of 8. In these situations, the median is determined by averaging the values above and below the median position. If the median position was 8.5, we would average the values in the 8th and 9th position in the distribution and use this value to represent the distribution's median (Mdn). If we have one more observation in our speeding example (6 tickets), the new distribution would look like this:

Number of tickets = 0, 0, 0, 1, 1, 1, 1, 1, 2, 2, 2, 3, 3, 4, 6, 6

In this case, the median position (Mp) = 8.5 (i.e., $[16 + 1] / 2 = 8.5$), and the values in the 8th and 9th position of the distribution are 1 and 2, respectively. The median is the average the two values = 1.5 (i.e., $[1 + 2] / 2 = 1.5$). An advantage of a median is that it is easily computed and comprehended. Medians are often used instead of means to describe the "typical" case in a data distribution when the data have outliers because medians are not impacted by them like means are. Medians can be used with ratio, interval, or ordinal data, but they are not appropriate for nominal-level data. The biggest shortcoming of medians, however, is that they are more difficult to use in more advanced mathematical calculations.

Mode

The third measure of central tendency is the **mode**, which describes the value that appears most in the data. Some distributions may not have a mode because each value occurs only once, whereas other distributions may have multiple modes. Going back to the original speeding tickets example, the mode of the data is 1 because 1 is observed five times and no other value is observed that often:

Number of tickets = 0, 0, 0, 1, 1, 1, 1, 1, 2, 2, 2, 3, 3, 4, 6

Many simply use the word *mode* when describing the modal category, yet others symbolize it as *Mo*. In our speeding ticket example, *Mo* = 1. An advantage of mode is that it can be used to describe nominal data. Another advantage to using the mode is that it is easiest measure of central tendency to calculate. The primary disadvantage, however, is that the mode of a data distribution does little more than offer a description of data. It cannot be used in statistical analysis because it is not algebraically defined (i.e., it is difficult to use basic arithmetic operations like addition, subtraction, division, etc. on modal values). Not surprisingly, the mode is the least often used measure of central tendency.

Mode: Measure of central tendency used as a summary statistic. It represents the numeric value observed more than any other in a data distribution.

Which measure of central tendency should you use when? Here are some general rules for selecting the most appropriate measure of central tendency to describe a data distribution:

- Use the mode to describe data gathered at any level of measurement.

- Use the median to describe ordinal-, interval-, or ratio-level data that have a skewed data distribution (i.e., distributions with extreme outliers).

- Use the mean to describe interval- and ratio-level data that have a relatively symmetrical distribution.

Measures of Dispersion

Measures of dispersion describe where the other cases in a data distribution are relative to the "typical" case. Measures of dispersion represent how much variation in observed scores is found in the data. Measures of dispersion are important because two distributions of data can have identical means but wildly different degrees of variation. Four common measures of dispersion are the range, interquartile range, variance, and standard deviation. Each of these is described as follows.

Range

The **range** is the most basic measure of dispersion for ordinal-, interval-, and ratio-level variables, and it describes the difference between the largest and the smallest values in a data. The range is calculated by subtracting the largest value from the smallest (Figure 12.1):

$$Range = x_{max} - x_{min},$$

where x_{max} is the largest score in the distribution and x_{min} is the smallest. Going back to our speeding tickets example, if the distribution of speeding tickets for our 15 students was as follows:

Number of tickets = 0, 0, 0, 1, 1, 1, 1, 1, 2, 2, 2, 3, 3, 4, 6

then the range is 6 (i.e., 6 − 0 = 6). Although the primary advantage to using the range to report the variability of a data distribution is that it is easy to calculate, the biggest disadvantage to using it is that it is extremely sensitive to outliers and it does not use all the observations in a distribution to derive its value.

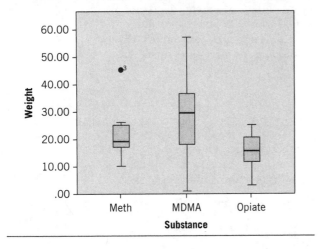

Figure 12.1 Boxplots Show the Spread of Observations for Three Groups

Interquartile Range

A second measure of dispersion is the **interquartile range (*IQR*)**, which indicates the degree of variability based on the difference between the two halves (i.e., the two middle quartiles) of the distribution. The *IQR* can be used with interval- or ratio-level data and is calculated by first determining the median of a data distribution. Next, the medians of both the lower half and the upper half of scores are identified. By identifying these three values in a distribution, the distribution has been split into four groups (i.e., quartiles). The final step in determining the *IQR* is to subtract the upper quartile's (i.e., 3rd quartile) median value from the lower quartile's (i.e., 1st quartile) median value. The results indicate how many scores are found between the 25th percentile and the 75th percentile of scores. The advantage of an inter-quartile range is that it is not sensitive to outliers. The *IQR*'s primary disadvantage is that it's difficult to use in mathematical equations, so it's utility is limited.

Variance

A commonly used measure of dispersion is the **variance,** which indicates how much each score differs, or deviates, from the average score in a data distribution. The variance, which is symbolized as s^2, is used when data are measured at the interval or the ratio level. The variance is calculated by

1. Determining the mean ($\bar{x}$) of the data distribution

2. Subtracting each individual score in the distribution (x_i) from the distribution's mean ($x_i - \bar{x}$), which is called a **deviation score**

3. Squaring each deviation score

4. Adding all the squared deviation scores together ($\sum[x_i - \bar{x}]^2$)

5. Dividing the summed squared deviations scores by $n - 1$, or one less than the total number of observations that make up the sample data distribution

The actual formula for calculating the sample variance is as follows:

$$s^2 = \frac{\sum(x_i - \bar{x})^2}{n - 1}$$

The variance for our distribution of speeding tickets could easily be determined using the formula in Table 12.3.

The variance for our distribution of speeding tickets is 2.74.

The advantages of using a variance to report the variability in a data distribution is that it considers every observation in the distribution and is not too sensitive to extreme scores or outliers. The primary disadvantage of the variance is that it is difficult to interpret because each deviation score is squared.

Standard Deviation

The standard deviation, as introduced in Chapter 10, is the most common measure of dispersion and is the square root of the variance. It's a standardized measure of variability:

$$s = \sqrt{s^2}$$

Revisiting our speeding ticket example where the variance was 2.74, the standard deviation of the distribution (s) is $\sqrt{2.74}$ or 1.66. The main disadvantage of the standard distribution is that it is not a good measure to use with skewed data.

Standard deviations are useful. Zaykowski's (2014) descriptives on victim service use showed that the average age of those using services is 35 years, with a standard deviation of 14.2 years. In contrast, those not using services have an average age of 34.6, with a standard deviation (a measure of dispersion) of 16.2 years. Zaykowski also found much more

Table 12.3 Calculating Sample Variance

	No. of Tickets	Mean	Deviation Score	Squared Deviation Score
	0	1.80	−1.80	3.24
	0	1.80	−1.80	3.24
	0	1.80	−1.80	3.24
	1	1.80	−0.80	0.64
	1	1.80	−0.80	0.64
	1	1.80	−0.80	0.64
	1	1.80	−0.80	0.64
	1	1.80	−0.80	0.64
	2	1.80	0.20	0.04
	2	1.80	0.20	0.04
	2	1.80	0.20	0.04
	3	1.80	1.20	1.44
	3	1.80	1.20	1.44
	4	1.80	2.20	4.84
	6	1.80	4.20	17.64
Mean =	1.80			
n =	15		Sum of deviation scores	= 38.40

s^2 = 38.40 / (15 − 1) or 2.74

variation in physical distress among those seeking services compared with those who did not. This indicates there is more variation in the age of those not using services than in those who do. Similarly, Santos and her colleague used means and standard deviations to ensure their control and experimental hot spots were equivalent (Santos & Santos, 2016). Table 12.4 shows that.

Santos and Santos's (2016) work shows that the crimes per offender in the treatment groups are 1.63 compared with 1.40. It also shows that housing density is 2,304 in treatment areas compared to 2,350 in control groups. Although these numbers appear different, statistical tests (beyond the scope of this book) show them to be equivalent.

Beyond Descriptives

For you to answer your research question(s), you will probably need to do more than describe your data. Typically, answering research questions requires analysis determining whether differences or associations exist between variables. Once differences or associations are identified, you can make broader inferences or empirical generalizations about the larger population. To do this, you need to calculate inferential statistics.

Associations

It is common for researchers to want to know whether variables they have measured are associated with one another. Variables are associated with one another when the values of one variable changes in a systematic (i.e., nonrandom) way with another. Recall this was the topic of association and causation discussed in Chapter 8 focused on experimental research. Associations or relationships can be identified in other ways; for example, if you are working with categorical variables (i.e., nominal- or ordinal-level measures), you can identify an association using cross tabulations and a **chi-square test** of independence (see Figure 12.3). We could, for example, gather data from 100 university students, record their sex and information about whether they ever received a speeding ticket (coded "Never," "Once," and "More than once") and test, using a chi-square test of independence, and identify whether a college student's sex was associated or related to receiving a speeding ticket(s).

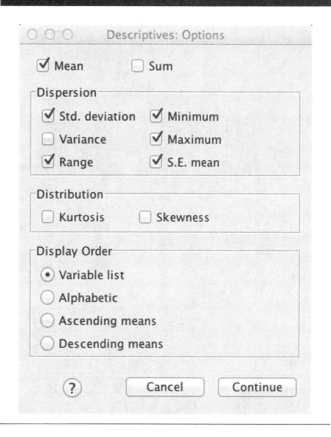

Figure 12.2 Mean and Standard Deviation Can Be Calculated as Part of Univariate Analysis

As noted, Zaykowski (2014) presented a descriptive statistics table that included information about her study's key variables. In addition, she presented descriptives by whether

Table 12.4 Equivalence Analysis of Random Assignment				
	Treatment Areas (*N* = 24)		Control Areas (*N* = 24)	
	M	*SD*	*M*	*SD*
Crime per offender	1.63	1.16	1.40	0.70
Area (sq. miles)	0.58	0.23	0.73	0.44
Population	3,026.58	1,068.05	3,471.38	1,395.98
Housing density	2,304.99	1,071.67	2,350.06	927.48

Chi-square test: Statistical test used to determine whether two categorical variables are independent of one another.

Figure 12.3   Results of a One-Sample Chi-Square Test Produced in SPSS

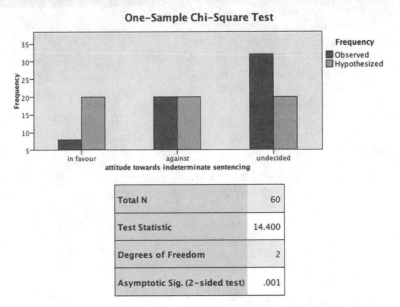

One-Sample Chi-Square Test

Total N	60
Test Statistic	14.400
Degrees of Freedom	2
Asymptotic Sig. (2–sided test)	.001

1. There are 0 cells (0%) with expected values less than 5. The minimum expected value is 20.

Correlation analysis:
Statistical technique used to determine whether two continuous variables are associated with one another.

Regression analysis:
Statistical analysis technique whereby an equation is developed that defines associations between independent and dependent variables. The equation can be used to make predictions about the dependent variable.

individuals who experienced crime reportedly used any type of victim services (Yes/No). She wanted to know whether there is an association between accessing victim services and demographics (i.e., gender, race, income, urban area, etc.). The results of her chi-square test of independent indicated associations between victim services and family problems, sex, type of victimization and whether it was reported to the police. These tests for association were not used to directly answer Zaykowski's research questions but to provide a more in-depth understanding of the data.

Associations that can also be identified between continuous measures using a different analytic approach are necessary. **Correlation analysis** is used to determine whether associations exist between interval- and ratio-level data (see Figure 12.4). As described in Chapter 8, correlations can be either positive (as the value of one variable increases, the value of the other variable also increases) or negative (as the value of one variable changes, the value of the other variable changes in the opposite direction). In addition to the direction of a correlation (i.e., positive or negative), the strength of correlations can be established through statistical analysis. Associations measured by correlation analysis range between 1 and –1, and variables that are more strongly correlated to one another are those that are closer to these two extremes. It's important to note, however, that even if a researcher establishes a very strong correlation between two variables, the association between them does not prove a causal relationship (see Chapter 8).

Perhaps the most common way researchers aim to establish associations between variables is by conducting regression analysis. **Regression analysis** allows researchers to make *predictions* about a particular outcome or dependent variable using information from all independent variables. Zaykowski (2014), Santos (Santos & Santos, 2016), Cuevas (Sabina et al., 2016), and Melde (Melde, Taylor, & Esbensen, 2009) each used regression analysis

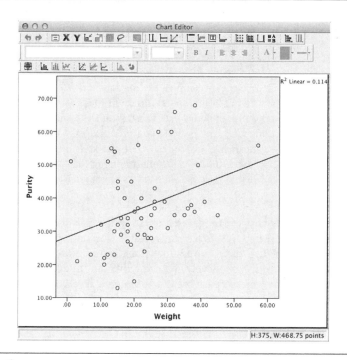

to answer at least one of their research questions. The findings from Zaykowski's (2014, p. 367) regression indicated, among other things, that "predictors of service usage included female victim, sexual assault victim, reported to the police, and several categories of victim offender relationship: intimate, family, acquaintance, unknown relationship, and more than one offender. Victims who had job problems and physical distress were more likely to contact victim services." In addition, Zaykowski's findings point to the need for additional research to understand the mechanism of police involvement in connecting victims with services. Zaykowski's findings indicate a need to better understand whether the police understand what services are available, and why they seem to point only some types of victims toward services.

The findings from Cuevas and colleagues' indicated psychological dating violence was the predominate type of violence found among Latino youth, as 15% reported it (Sabina et al., 2016). These findings also showed that 72% of Latinos reported no dating violence at either wave of data collection: 11% reported no violence at Wave 1 but did at Wave 2, 9% of Latino teens reported victimization at Wave 1 but not at Wave 2, and, finally, 8% reported victimization at both waves. Regression analyses indicated that older youth were more likely to be in the group that had no violence at Wave 1 but did at Wave 2, as well as those who experienced violence at both waves. In addition, one finding was that "cultural variables largely did not distinguish between the four groups except for immigrant status being associated with diminished risk of being in the group" that began experiencing violence at wave 2 (Sabina et al., 2016, p. 12).

Melde et al.'s (2009) research involved two types of regression to answer their research questions. Analysis of their data shows that "after controlling for the prevalence of prior victimization, males report a significantly higher increase in victimization than females" after joining a gang (pp. 581–583). Regression output also show that "[c]ompared with those students who reporting being non-Hispanic/white, only Hispanic respondents reported less overall victimization at time 2" (p. 583). And finally, the results suggest that gang membership at Time 2 is associated with a significant increase in victimization. In sum, "gang members repot higher levels of actual victimization and perceptions of victimization risk than non-gang-involved youth. Gang membership is associated with reduced level of fear however" (p. 565).

Santos and her colleague (2016) used several types of regression to address her multiple research questions. Contrary to her expectations, the findings did not offer strong evidence of the effects of high-intensity policing in hot spots. Although these findings were not as anticipated, they do point to the promise of additional research on the topic. Even though there are various types of regression analysis, which are beyond the scope of this book, each of these researchers established answers to his or her respective research questions using regression analysis as an analytic method to identify associations and potential causality in their data.

Differences

In addition to discovering answers to research question through the identification of associations, researchers often find answers to their research questions by determining whether group differences exist in their data. Group differences can be tested when one variable is measured at the nominal or interval level (i.e., using different categories to group observations) and another variable is measured at the ratio or interval level (i.e., using discrete values [e.g., number of tickets] or continuous values [e.g., temperature]). When two groups are being compared, researchers often use t tests, whereas analysis of variance (ANOVA) is used to compare groups when there are more than two groups.

As with regression analysis, there are several different types of t tests used to detect group differences, and a discussion of each is well beyond the scope of this text. Suffice it to say that despite the type of t tests used, they are all fundamentally doing the same thing: testing whether one group is different from a second group. Typically, group comparisons are based on a comparison between the two groups' means. For example, in going back to our speeding ticket example, we could test whether the average number of speeding tickets (measured as whole numbers) for female students was significantly less than the average number of tickets for male students using a t test. For the continuous variables used in her study, Zaykowski (2014) presented group (mean) differences for those who reportedly used victim services (Yes/No) as part of her descriptive statistics table. This was similar to what she did for the chi-squared analysis, but she used a t test for the independent variables that were not categorical (i.e., Age, Household size, Mental distress, and Physical distress).

When more than two groups are being tested for differences, t tests cannot be used. Instead, researchers use a type of statistical test called **analysis of variance (ANOVA)**. ANOVA can be thought of as a test similar to the t test, but it is used when making comparisons between three or more groups. For example, if we want to know whether class status (i.e., Freshmen, Sophomores, Juniors, or Seniors) is related to driving ability, we could conduct an ANOVA test to see whether the mean number of speeding tickets for each group of students differed significantly.

Qualitative Data Analysis

The methods used to organize and analyze qualitative data were described in Chapter 6. Because qualitative data analysis does not use statistics and related analyses, it does not require the space in that chapter to discuss them. There are some things to note about qualitative analysis, however. First, providing a separate chapter for collecting qualitative data, and analyzing qualitative data, creates a false dichotomy. Why? Because qualitative data analysis cannot be separated from quantitative data collection. As we noted in Chapter 6, analyzing qualitative data begins as soon as the first data are collected because even then the researcher is watching for patterns or relationships. Once data collection has ended, the researcher continues with the analysis. The first step is to organize the data. Next is a focused analysis that requires the researcher to engage in the iterative process of reducing, condensing, and coding the data into broader categories or themes.

This was the approach used by Dodge and colleagues (Dodge, Starr-Gimeno, & Williams, 2005). They gathered data from their policewomen about working as decoys. As they began gathering the data, they adjusted later interviews to incorporate their findings. At some point, Dodge and her colleagues reached saturation and were not gathering new data. For Dodge et al.'s research, saturation occurred after 25 women were interviewed. From the data gathered, they identified several themes that framed their findings:

- "The decoys," which considered how officers viewed this work

- "Cops: too pretty to prostitute," which described how decoys should look at behave

- "Negotiating the deal," which described the need for decoys to "dirty talk" and be familiar with jargon

- "Johns of all types," which described the huge variety of men arrested for soliciting a prostitute and how the officers viewed them

- "Safety concerns," which dealt with the real danger this work entails

- "Who's the victim?" which described the widespread impact of prostitution on people, neighborhoods, homeowners, and businesses

- "Effectiveness from a decoy's perspective," which described the decoys' views of deterrent effect of this type of police activity

Brunson and colleague's work was conducted similarly (Brunson & Weitzer, 2009). After gathering data from the 45 young men in the three neighborhoods, Brunson and his colleague organized, sorted, and identified themes. In addition, they came up with two primary findings: first, that "white youth had a less troubled relationship with and more positive views of the police than Black youth" (p. 864) and, second, that "[p]olice treatment of residents appeared to be less problematic in the White neighborhood (Mayfield) and more problematic in the Black neighborhood (Barksdale), with the mixed neighborhood (Hazelcrest) falling in between" (p. 864). Major themes were identified and included unwarranted stops, verbal abuse, physical abuse, police corruption, racially biased policing, and police accountability. These themes are especially interesting when you consider this research was done a few years before the August 2014 shooting of Michael Brown in Ferguson, Missouri (which is situated less than 5 miles from these neighborhoods).

Although neither Dodge nor Brunson and their respective colleagues analyzed their data with the assistance of software programs (Brunson & Weitzer, 2009; Dodge et al., 2005), others do. As noted in Chapter 6, qualitative software programs cannot take the place of the researcher, yet they may provide some time-saving approaches to data analysis. Some of those programs are described in the sections that follow.

Data Analysis Software

Collectively, the different statistical methods described thus far in this chapter are part of a broader group of analytic methods used in research. Many of these statistical methods can be applied to data through the use of statistical analysis software applications. Some software applications are designed to be more useful for data analysis associated with quantitative research, whereas other software applications are specifically designed for analysis of data produced from qualitative studies. A description of these applications, starting with quantitative analytic software applications, including a description of some of their unique features and benefits, is provided first.

Software Applications Used in Quantitative Research

Software applications give researchers the ability to analyze large numerical data sets used in quantitative research. Although there are many quantitative statistical software applications on the market, the particular program that researchers choose to use to analyze their data often depends on the aim of the research project, the research questions that must be answered, and the researcher's familiarity with the software. The following subsections provide an overview of some of the more commonly used applications used in quantitative criminological research.

Excel

Most people have heard of Microsoft® Excel™ and know it as a useful electronic **spreadsheet** for keeping track of the family budget, stock investments, and small business income and expenses or for creating charts and graphs used in class presentations. Technically, a spreadsheet is a type of document used to arrange data in rows and columns within a grid. Electronic spreadsheets, like those contained in Excel, can be manipulated and used to make myriad calculations (e.g., averages, standard deviations, chi-square tests, etc.) based on formulas created by the user. Data contained in Excel can also be used to create visual displays such as bar charts, line graphs, and pivot tables. More detailed information about visually displaying data is provided later in this chapter (see the section titled "Reporting Findings From Your Research"). The Excel interface resembles the image provided in Figure 12.5.

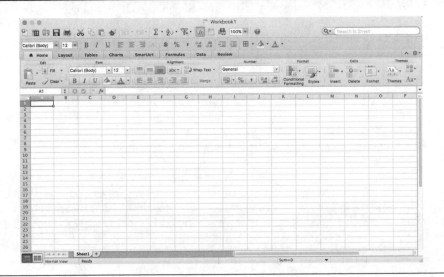

Figure 12.5   Blank Spreadsheet in Microsoft Excel

An Excel spreadsheet comprises columns (i.e., the vertical boxes in Figure 12.5 that are labeled A, B, C, etc.), and rows (i.e., the horizontal boxes in Figure 12.5 that are labeled 1, 2, 3, etc.). At the intersections of each row and column are cells, and together the cells comprise a single spreadsheet. Users can enter numbers, texts, dates, or formulas into the spreadsheet's cells to keep track of data, analyze data, or display data visually.

For example, in Figure 12.6, the hypothetical speeding ticket data has been entered into an Excel spreadsheet in cells D3 through D17 (the highlighted cells). At the top of the list, the title "Tickets" has been entered into cell D2. Cell E6 is titled, Mean, and underneath it, in cell E7 is a formula that has been entered: (=AVERAGE(D3: D17)). This particular formula will automatically calculate the average number of tickets entered into cells D3 through D17. One advantage of using Excel to calculate the average number of tickets automatically in cell E7 is that if the researcher changes the data entered into cells D3 through D17, or adds more data to the list of existing observations, the average can be recalculated quickly and easily (i.e., on the fly).

Just like any new software application, the more time spent using Excel, the more familiar it will become, and the easier it is to use. Fortunately, Excel is so popular that thousands of recourses are available online to help those interested in learning more about how to use it to analyze quantitative data. A great place to start is YouTube®. There are all sorts of "how-to" videos for all levels of Excel users, from the novice to the more advanced.

SPSS

SPSS is a widely used data analysis software application that was first released in 1968 as the Statistical Package for the Social Sciences (SPSS). Acquired by IBM in 2009, SPSS is now officially named IBM® SPSS Statistics™, and it remains a popular and powerful data analysis tool. Unlike simple electronic spreadsheets, SPSS is designed specifically for conducting analysis of data produced

Figure 12.6 Excel Spreadsheet Calculated the Mean Number of Students' Speeding Tickets

	Tickets	var	var	var
1	0			
2	0			
3	0			
4	1			
5	1			
6	1			
7	1			
8	1			
9	2			
10	2			
11	2			
12	3			
13	3			
14	4			
15	6			
16				

from quantitative research. Melde, Santos, and Cuevas use SPSS as their primary software application for data analysis associated with their research.

SPSS is designed around three primary interfaces: a Data Editor, a Syntax Editor, and an Output Viewer. The Data Editor is the most commonly used interface of the three, and it consists of two components: a data viewer and a variable viewer. The data viewer looks very much like an Excel spreadsheet and is where you can see your data. In the SPSS data viewer, columns represent variables and rows represent each observation from the unit of analysis. For example, Figure 12.7 is a SPSS data view window that shows the data collected for one variable (Tickets) from 15 students (one observation for each of the 15 students surveyed). The variable viewer allows the researchers to view the structure of each variable contained in his or her data set. For example, information about the type of variable (i.e., numeric or text), the variable's name, and its level of measurement can all be accessed in the variable viewer.

Researchers use the SPSS Syntax Editor to create SPSS syntax (i.e., code) that can be run within the SPSS environment. SPSS syntax is a programming language that allows researchers to manipulate and analyze data in SPSS, as well as to document how their data are analyzed, without having to rely on using the built-in drop-down menus. Researchers can save their SPSS syntax files for future use or even share them with colleagues with whom they might collaborate on research projects. For example, Figure 12.8 show the SPSS syntax that could be run on the Hypothetical Study data file to produce the average number of speeding tickets (along with the standard deviation, minimum value, and maximum value) for our 15 university students surveyed in our study.

The third SPSS interface is the Output Viewer. As the name suggests, this is where the results of procedures run, either through the use of SPSS menu items or in the Syntax Editor, and are presented as output. When the syntax shown in Figure 12.8 is run on the Hypothetical Study data on university students' driving, the output shown in Figure 12.9 is produced.

From a series of intuitively designed drop-down menus, researchers can conduct hundreds of analytic procedures in SPSS, including univariate analysis (i.e., frequency distributions,

Figure 12.8   SPSS Syntax That Could Be Run on the Hypothetical Study Data File to Produce the Average Number of Speeding Tickets

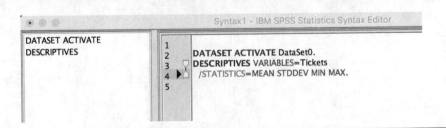

Figure 12.9 SPSS Output Shows Descriptive Statistics for Hypothetical Study Data File

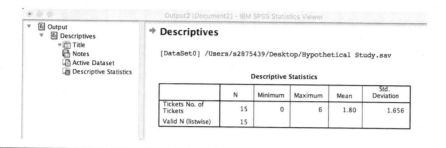

Output2 [Document2] - IBM SPSS Statistics Viewer

Output
Descriptives
Title
Notes
Active Dataset
Descriptive Statistics

→ **Descriptives**

[DataSet0] /Users/s2875439/Desktop/Hypothetical Study.sav

Descriptive Statistics

	N	Minimum	Maximum	Mean	Std. Deviation
Tickets No. of Tickets	15	0	6	1.80	1.656
Valid N (listwise)	15				

descriptive statistics, or cross tabulations), bivariate analysis (i.e., correlations, *t* tests, and ANOVA), and multivariate analysis (i.e., linear regression). The SPSS learning curve is steeper compared with Excel, but the quantitative analytic tools available in SPSS are more powerful.

Other Commercial Packages

In addition to SPSS, many other commercial software applications are commonly used in quantitative data analysis. Two of the most prominent are STATA™ and SAS®. Like SPSS and Excel, STATA (statistics + data = STATA) is a commercial software application from StataCorp® that has been around for several decades and can be run on both the Microsoft® Windows™ and Apple® Mac™ operating systems. Although STATA uses a different graphical interface, like SPSS, researchers can analyze data in STATA using either the built-in menu items or by typing in commands on the STATA command line (similar to the Syntax Editor in SPSS). Another similarity between STATA and SPSS is that both can import myriad data file formats, including Excel-formatted spreadsheets (i.e., .xlxs or .csv files) and other commonly used data file types (i.e., .asc, .dbf., and .txt).

SAS, which stands for Statistical Analysis Systems, is another commercial statistical analysis software package distributed by the company "SAS" commonly used in the field of criminology and criminal justice to analyze quantitative data. SAS was first developed in 1966 at North Carolina State University and since then has become one of the biggest advanced analytics products on the market. In 2005, Alan Acock compared SAS with SPSS and STATA to answer the following question: "Which software analysis package is the best?" Based on his findings, Acock (2005, p. 1093) explained, "SAS programs provide extraordinary range of data analysis and data management tasks," but they were difficult to use and learn. In contrast, SPSS and STATA were both easier to learn in part because of their better documentation, but they had fewer analytic abilities. Acock further noted that these limitations could be expanded with paid (in the case of SPSS) or free (in the case of STATA) add-ons. So which product was considered the best? Acock concluded that of the three, SAS was best for "power users," while occasional users would benefit most from SPSS and STATA.

Software Applications Used in Qualitative Research

The assumptions that the world we live in operates according to general laws and that these laws have properties and relationships that can be observed and measured are at the heart of *quantitative* research. Through rigorous observation and measurement, and the

Qualitative data analysis (QDA): Approach to data analysis that emphasized open-ended research questions and moves from these toward greater precision, based on information that emerges during data analysis.

Coding sorts: In qualitative data analysis, they represent compilations of similarly coded blocks of text from different sources that are converted into a single file or report.

Theme: In qualitative data analysis, it refers to an idea category that emerges from grouping lower level data points together as part of the analytic process.

Characteristics: In qualitative data analysis, they represent a single item or event in a text, similar to an individual response to variables used in quantitative data analysis.

Second-order analysis: In qualitative data analysis, it is the process that involves identifying *recurrent* themes and respondent clusters. It also can be used to build event sequences and to develop new hypotheses.

application of reason and logic, quantitative research aims to produce an empirical understanding of the world in which we live. In contrast to this positivist, quantitative-oriented approach to knowledge discovery, *qualitative* researchers believe that our focus should be on understanding the totality of a phenomenon, based on an interpretive philosophy. This understanding is derived from careful, detailed analysis of structured and unstructured text founded in writings, news articles, books, conversations, interview transcripts, audio or video recordings, social media posts, and electronic news feeds.

Qualitative data analysis (QDA) often starts with a broad, open-ended question(s) compared with the explicit questions associated with quantitative research. From this starting point, researchers move toward greater precision or greater refinement of the original question, based on information that emerges during QDA, in what typically is a four-step process. The first step in QDA usually involves organizing the data that the researcher have collected from texts, conversations, recordings, posts, and so on. This process may involve transcription, translation, or cleaning data.

Next, the researcher will identify a QDA framework that he or she will use to analyze the data. The framework may be an explanatory framework (i.e., guided by the research question), or it may be an exploratory framework (i.e., guided by the data). Part of this framework will involve the researcher identifying a coding plan for his or her data. In other words, the researcher will determine how he or she will structure, label, and define the data.

Step 3 of QDA involves coding the data and sorting it into the researcher's framework, which is typically done through the use of a QDA software application. In this context, coding refers to the process of attaching labels to lines of text so that the researcher can group and compare similar or related pieces of information; **coding sorts** are compilations of similarly coded blocks of text from different sources that are converted into a single file or report.

Step 4 involves a researcher using the framework developed in Step 2 for descriptive analysis of his or her data, based on themes that are identified in the analytic process. In qualitative data analysis, a **theme** refers to an idea category that emerges from grouping lower level data points together as part of the analysis, which is often developed around specific characteristics that are identified in qualitative data. **Characteristics** represent a single item or event in a text, which is similar to an individual response to variables used in quantitative data analysis.

If the QDA is not exploratory in nature, step 4 can also involve the researcher conducting **second-order analysis** as part of the final step. Second-order analysis involves identifying *recurrent* themes, patterns in the data, and respondent clusters. It also can be used to build event sequences and to develop new hypotheses.

Just like there are many different software applications commonly used in quantitative data analysis, several qualitative data analysis software packages are available to researchers. Because we discuss quantitative and qualitative *research* in greater detail in Part 4, we provide details of some of the most popular *applications* used in criminology and criminal justice research that are qualitative in nature in the following subsections, including QDA Miner™, NVivo™, ATLAS.ti™, and HyperRESEARCH™. In doing so, we highlight some of their more noteworthy features and the benefits of each.

QDA Miner

QDA Miner is a qualitative data analysis software application developed by Provalis Research®. This commercial software was first made available in 2004 and is available for the Windows operating system. In 2012, a "Lite" version of QDA Miner was released for free but with reduced functionality. QDA Miner is used in the field of criminology and criminal justice by those who conduct qualitative studies and who typically study data produced from journal articles, radio or television scripts, social media or RSS feeds, images, or interview transcripts derived from focus groups or in-depth interviews.

Research in Action
Reducing Bullying in Schools

Bullying continues to be a problem for many in the educational system. The purpose of this research by Hart, Hart, and Miethe (2013) was to better understand the situational contexts of bullying so that focused policies could be implemented to reduce this violence. This study was guided by the following three research questions:

1. Is school bullying characterized by situational clustering, or is it uniformly distributed across contexts?

2. How much contextual variability is associated with the dominant situational profiles of school bullying?

3. What are the particular individual and contextual factors most commonly found within these dominant situational contexts?

To address these research questions, situational contexts of school bullying were constructed using National Crime Victimization Survey (NCVS) School Crime Supplement (SCS) data. The NCVS's SCS collects data about school-related victimizations so that policy makers, academic researchers, and practitioners can make informed decisions concerning policies and programs. The data come from SCS interviews completed by 6th through 12th graders during the 2005, 2007, and 2009 school years ($N = 16,244$). Predictors of bullying included individual predictors (i.e., gender, grade level, and race), behavioral characteristics (i.e., externalizing and internalizing behavior and academic performance), school climate, and peer influence. Analysis of these data was accomplished using conjunctive analysis of case configurations (CACC).

Combining each of the response categories for these predictors leads to a possible 512 situational contexts of bullying (e.g., one context is a female victim, freshman,

White, etc.). The analysis offered support for situational clustering of bullying (research question 1). The findings showed that school bullying occurs in, or clusters among, 156 situational contexts out of the possible 512. In other words, all bullying incidents in the data were found in 30% of all possible situational profiles. The findings also indicated that there is extreme contextual variability ranging from a low of 7% to a high of 100% associated with the dominant situational profiles of school bullying (research question 2). Finally, risk factors such as gender, grade, externalizing/internalizing behaviors, and academic achievement, as well as other contextual factors such as fairness in the application of school rules and a student's involvement in extracurricular activities—*when considered in conjunction with all factors simultaneously*—are not consistent determinants of higher than average bullying victimization. The researchers concluded that the context within which the risk factors appear are more important to understanding bullying victimization risk than the individual risk factors themselves.

These findings led to important school policy recommendations regarding bullying. Specifically, the researchers suggest that "results of our conjunctive analysis illustrate the wide variability in the prevalence of student bullying victimization across contexts. In particular, these findings suggest that the likelihood of these incidents depend on complex social situations that are not easily summarized in terms of a single variable(s) that holds across all contexts. Instead, to understand when bullying occurs policy analysts must explore the nature of the different situational contexts that underlie them" (Hart et al., 2013, p. 66).

Hart, T. C., Hart, J. L., & Miethe, T. D. (2013). Situational context of student bullying victimization and reporting behavior: A conjunctive analysis of case configurations. *Justice Research and Policy, 15*(2), 43–73.

The features in QDA Miner allow researchers to graphically view the codings of a document, providing them with an easy-to-understand glimpse of the spatial distribution of their coding. **Link analysis** is also available in QDA Miner. In qualitative data analysis, link analysis refers to a technique used to evaluate relationships (i.e., connections) between various types of nodes (i.e., objects), including organizations, people, and transactions; it is used primarily to (a) find matches in data for known patterns of interest, (b) find anomalies where known patterns are violated, and (c) find new patterns of interest.

QDA Miner allows researchers to import files with different formats such as PDF, Microsoft Word™, Excel, HTML, RTF, SPSS, and JPEG. It offers text retrieval tools such as keyword retrieval and cluster extraction. It even permits basic analytic functions such as coding frequencies and sequences, cluster analysis, coding by variables, and visualization tools such as multidimensional scaling, choropleth and hot spot maps, correspondence analysis graphics, and proximity plots. QDA Miner also allows researchers to extract **meta data** from image files for analysis. Meta data refers to data that describe data. For example, when a picture is taken with a smartphone, the image often has the geographic coordinates of where the phone was located when the picture was taken and is included as part of the image file's meta data.

NVivo

NVivo is a qualitative data analysis software package produced by QSR International®. Originally developed in 1999 as NUD*UST™, NVivo is available for both the Windows and Mac operating systems. NVivo is designed for qualitative researchers who work with very rich text-based data or data derived from multimedia information. Dodge says NVivo is the software she uses most often in her research, when she uses software. Dodge finds that it assists in classifying, sorting, and arranging qualitative information quickly and easily. As useful as it is though, Dodge reveals that she prefers to analyze her qualitative data without the use of software programs. Instead, Dodge prefers doing it the old-fashioned way by organizing, sorting, and thinking about the themes that her data reveal themselves. Qualitative researchers can also use the software to examine relationships in data and combine analysis with linking, shaping, searching, and modeling techniques commonly used in qualitative data analysis. A researcher or an analyst can also test theories, identify trends, and cross-examine information in myriad ways using NVivo's search engine and query functions. Like QDA Miner, NVivo supports several data formats such as audio files, videos, digital photos, Word, PDF, spreadsheets, rich text, plain text, and Web and social media data. NVivo users can also interchange data with applications like Excel, Word, SPSS, and SurveyMonkey™.

ATLAS.ti

ATLAS.ti is a qualitative data analysis software application developed by Scientific Software Development GmbH®. It is available on both the Windows and Mac operating systems. The software has even been designed for Apple® iOS™ and Google® Android™ mobile devices. ATLAS.ti allows researchers to analyze large amounts of textual, graphical, audio, and video data across a wide range of media types, including Word documents (i.e., .doc and .docx files), plain text files (i.e., .txt file), and PDF files (i.e., .pdf files). The software allows researchers to conduct automated searches across one or multiple documents to auto-code and extract meaning from the existing content. The software also allows researchers to work with dozens of graphic and audio formats (e.g., .wav, ,mp3, .wma, etc.) as well as with most common video types (e.g., .avi, .mp4, .wmv, etc.). Researchers can even import data from Evernote™ or Twitter® for analysis in ATLAS.ti. The software also provides researchers with several different ways to visualize findings, for example, through the use of **mind maps**. A mind map is a graphical way to represent ideas and concepts by structuring information visually so that analysis, comprehension, synthesis, and recall are improved. Files created in ATLAS.ti can be exported in SPSS, HTML, CSV, and Excel formats.

NVIVO/© QSR International Pty Ltd

ATLAS.ti Scientific Software Development GmbH

HyperRESEARCH

HyperRESEARCH is a QDA software application designed by ResearchWare® in 1991. It can be run on both the Windows and Mac operating systems and is designed to help conduct qualitative data analysis. HyperRESEARCH enables researchers to examine and organize textual, audio, video, and image data through multiple user interfaces. For example, the Study Window is the main HyperRESEARCH window; it is where you can view your cases and code references. It also shows you how many cases are currently in your study, how cases are filtered, and how many cases are filtered when a filter is applied, as well as how many code references have been coded to the current case. Figure 12.10 shows HyperRESEARCH's Report builder interface, which allows you to create and test theoretical models, identify patterns, and summarize results of their qualitative data analysis quickly and easily. Similarly, the Code Map window in HyperRESEARCH provides you with a tool to explore the graphical representations of relationships between codes in your data. Alternatively, information about the data can be displayed through other windows, like information relating to the frequency with which specific words appear in content. Figure 12.11 shows an example of HyperRESEARCH's Word Counter Cloud Viewer and depicts the most common words that appear more than 150 times in the six text files being analyzed.

The software is flexible, supporting both case-base and source-based qualitative methodologies or combinations, which according to the company makes its product well suited for mix-method approaches to qualitative research. As with the qualitative data analysis software applications previously discussed, HyperRESEARCH supports myriad file types and formats, including text files, image files (e.g., .jpg, .gif, and .png), audio files, and video files. And like many of the other applications previously discussed, HyerRESEARCH offers those interested in the software a free trial version that can be downloaded from the Internet.

Figure 12.10 HyperRESEARCH's Report Builder Interface, Used to Create and Test, for Example, Theoretical Models

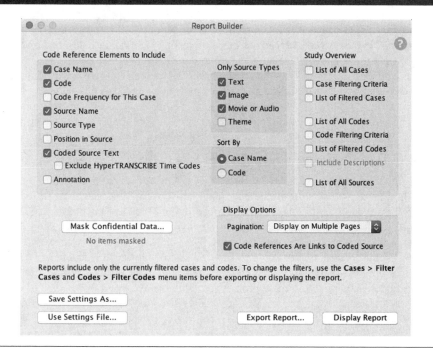

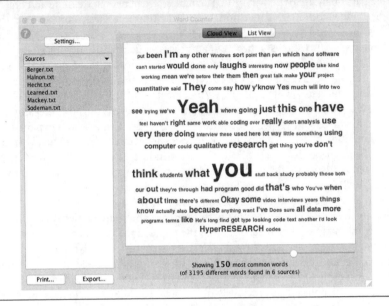

Figure 12.11 HyperRESEARCH's Word Counter Cloud Viewer Shows the Most Common Words in a File of Text That Is Being Analyzed

Alternative Analytic Approaches

Conjunctive analysis of case configurations (CACC): Used to analyze both small and large data sets, focuses on reducing data into meaningful statistical information (e.g., frequency distributions and percentages), and assesses empirical observations with formal statistical tests (e.g., chi-square test of independence).

Situational contexts: Used in conjunctive analysis of case configurations as the unit of analysis that is defined by the combinations of variable attributes believed to influence that outcome. Also referred to as "case configurations."

A newer approach to data analysis is **conjunctive analysis of case configurations (CACC)**. CACC can be used to analyze both small and large data sets, focus on reducing data into meaningful statistical information (e.g., frequency distributions and percentages), and assess empirical observations with formal statistical tests (e.g., chi-square test of independence). In terms of qualitative analysis, CACC focuses on the complex causal recipes or causal pathways that define particular outcomes. In other words, instead of focusing on people (i.e., victims, offenders, and police), places (i.e., crime hot spots, crime attractors, and crime generators), or events (i.e., homicides, robberies, and executions) and variables that explain the variance in these observations, CACC builds **situational contexts** of particular outcomes, from an existing data file, defined by the combinations of variable attributes believed to influence that outcome. An overview of this process follows, along with information that can be used in popular software applications to conduct CACC.

Conjunctive Analysis of Case Configurations (CACC)

Miethe, Hart, and Regoeczi (2008) introduced CACC as a new way to explore criminal justice data to find patterns that more traditional, quantitative techniques can struggle to identify. Since its introduction, CACC has been developed into a versatile data analytic tool that has been used to study myriad topics within criminology and criminal justice. Recently, Hart, Rennison, and Miethe (2017) described CACC as an "easy-to-follow" three-step process involving (1) the construction of a CACC "truth table" from an existing data file, (2) the identification of unique situational profiles among these data, and (3) the labeling of the sources of contextual variability within these profiles (i.e., situational contexts).

When researchers want to use CACC to analyze data, they begin by constructing a data matrix—also referred to as a "truth table." This matrix contains all the possible combinations of the data, measured at the nominal or ordinal level contained in an existing data file. For example, Table 12.5 provides an illustration of a hypothetical data matrix containing

Table 12.5	Hypothetical CACC Data Matrix With Eight Case Profiles, Adapted From Miethe et al. (2008)				
Profile #	X_1	X_2	X_3	N	Y
1	0	0	0	nc_1	y_1/nc_1
2	0	0	1	nc_2	y_2/nc_2
3	0	1	0	nc_3	y_3/nc_3
4	0	1	1	nc_4	y_4/nc_4
5	1	0	0	nc_5	y_5/nc_5
6	1	0	1	nc_6	y_6/nc_6
7	1	1	0	nc_7	y_7/nc_7
8	1	1	1	nc_8	y_8/nc_8

information about a particular outcome variable (Y) and predictor variables (X_1, X_2, and X_3), all of which are dichotomized as "0" or "1" in this example. Each row of the matrix—identified by its Profile #—reflects all the possible combinations (i.e., case configurations) of predictor-variable attributes that the researcher could observe in the existing data file. For example, if three independent variables are included in a CACC and each has two attributes (i.e., "0" or "1"), then a total of eight profiles *could* be observed in the data matrix (i.e., 2^3) that is constructed.

Although eight possible profiles could be observed in the existing data file, once the data matrix is generated, it will only contain case configurations that are actually *observed* in the existing data file. This is important because it gives the researcher some indication of the extent to which the phenomenon he or she is studying (i.e., the outcome) demonstrates patterns of situational clustering. By examining the patterns of observed case configurations and their relative prevalence, CACC builds complex causal pathways from existing data, which reflect empirically observed patterns of causality.

Step 2 of CACC involves examining the distribution of case configurations contained in the data matrix. For example, the frequency of unique case configurations (i.e., nc_1, nc_2, nc_3, etc. in Table 12.5) can be evaluated to determine the percentage of all observations in the existing data file cluster within dominant case configurations (i.e., configurations observed at least 10 times), and whether the distribution of observed profiles among the dominant profiles differs significantly from what is expected. This can be assessed using a chi-square test.

Step 3 of CACC involves researchers assessing the relative influence of individual factors contained within dominant case configurations. To do this, boxplots are commonly used to visually display the differences in the likelihoods of outcomes between *matched pairs* of case profiles. For example, in Table 12.5, Profile #s 1 and 2, 3 and 4, 5 and 6, and 7 and 8 are all identical profiles, except for the values associated with one predictor variable (i.e., X_3). The impact that a change in X_3's value has across matched profiles can be calculated by calculating the difference in the likelihood of outcome Y associated with the matched profiles (i.e., $[y_1/nc_1] - [y_2/nc_2]$; $[y_3/nc_3] - [y_4/nc_4]$; $[y_5/nc_5] - [y_6/nc_6]$; and $[y_7/nc_7] - [y_8/nc_8]$) can be illustrated visually, for example, as a boxplot.

SPSS

CACC is a data analytic technique that can be performed using many of the software applications discussed previously in this chapter. For example, in SPSS, a CACC truth table can be created on an existing data file by using the *Sort Cases* and *Aggregate* functions. The following syntax illustrates this process that involves three hypothetical independent variables (X_1, X_2, and X_3) and a dependent variable (Y):

SORT CASES BY X_1(A) X_2(A) X_3(A).

AGGREGATE

/OUTFILE = 'cacc_file'

/BREAK = X_1 X_2 X_3

/Y_mean = MEAN(Y)

/N_Cases = N.

STATA

In STATA, the same procedure could be executed using the following code, once the existing data file is sorted by the three independent variables:

egen N_Cases = count(Y), by (A B C D)

collapse (count) N_Cases (mean) Y_MEAN = Y, by (A B C D)

list A B C D Y_MEAN N_Cases

SAS

In SAS, the code would look like this:

```
proc means data = yourdata nway;
class a b c d;
var y;
output out = cdmatrix(drop=_type_ _freq_) mean = n= / autoname;
run;
proc print data = cdmatrix;
run;
```

R

And in R, the code would look like this:

```
n <- 100
file_name <- data.frame(X1 = sample(LETTERS[1:3],n, replace = TRUE),
```

X2 = sample(LETTERS[1:3],n, replace = TRUE),

X3 = sample(LETTERS[1:2],n, replace = TRUE),

Y = sample(c("yes,""no"),n, replace = TRUE))

Once a CACC truth table has been created from an existing data file, statistical tests of the distributions of case configurations (i.e., chi-square tests) can be conducted in the software application. Once completed, tables and figures can be created that provide visual descriptions of important aspects of the configural patterns (i.e., situational clustering or isolated effects of a single independent variable).

Geostatistical Approaches

Chapter 10 focuses specifically on GIS and crime mapping. Although we've already introduced some of the common crime analysis techniques (e.g., hot spot mapping, predictive policing, risk terrain modeling, and repeat/near repeat victimization), our discussion of geostatistical analysis was limited. We consider **geostatistical analysis** to be any mathematical technique that uses the geographical properties of data as part of a statistical or analytic method. Unlike many of the well-established statistical methods used with non-geographic data, and discussed previously in this chapter, some of the spatial statistical methods presented in the following subsections, and used by researchers in the field of criminal justice and criminology, are still being developed and improved. Some of the more common geostatistical techniques, and the software available to apply these methods, are discussed.

> We consider geostatistical analysis to be any mathematical technique that uses the geographical properties of data as part of a statistical or analytic method.

Geostatistical analysis: Any mathematical technique that uses the geographical properties of data as part of a statistical or an analytic method.

Spatial descriptions: Group of spatial statistics that describes the overall *spatial* distribution of geographic data.

Introduction to Spatial Statistics

Many of the spatial statistics used in geostatistical analysis are extensions of traditional statistical methods discussed earlier in this chapter. For example, we have already outlined how descriptive statistics can help you summarize your data in a succinct and meaningful way. We also explained that you could describe your data using univariate analyses to produce measures of central tendency (i.e., mean, median, and mode) and measures of dispersion (i.e., variance and standard deviation). These statistics are intended to describe the "typical" case, and all the other cases relative to the "typical" case in a data set, respectively. Similar descriptive statistics are used in spatial statistics.

Spatial Description

In geostatistical analysis, **spatial descriptions** refer to a group of spatial statistics that describe the overall *spatial* distribution of geographic data (i.e., how data in a data set are distributed throughout a study area). Mean center and standard distance, the standard deviational ellipse, and the convex hull are three examples of spatial descriptive statistics.

Mean Center

Imagine that the locations of four crime incidents in a given area were depicted by the four dots shown in the box to the left in Figure 12.12.

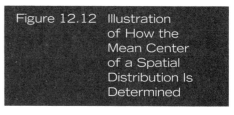

Figure 12.12 Illustration of How the Mean Center of a Spatial Distribution Is Determined

Mean center: Average x- and y-coordinates of all the features in the study area.

Standard distance: Summary measure of the distribution of features around any given point.

Convex hull: Smallest polygon that can be drawn around the outer points of all the data in a data distribution of geographic locations.

First Law of Geography: Also known as "Tobler's Law," it states that everything is related to everything else, but near things are more related than distant things.

Spatial dependency: Measure used in geostatistical analysis to define the spatial relationship between *values* of geographical data.

Spatial autocorrelation: Degree to which geographic features are similarly arranged in space.

You could find the "average location" of these four crimes by calculating their **mean center**. In the box on the right of Figure 12.12, the mean center location of the four purple dots is represented by the black dot and is determined by computing the average of the four X-coordinates and the average of the four Y-coordinates for all four incidents' X–Y-coordinate pairs. Finding the average location for a set of geogrphic data can be very useful for tracking changes of locations of things over time or between different things in the same area. For example, crime analysts can determine whether the mean center for burglaries in their jurisdiction is different for those that occur during the daytime compared with where nighttime burglaries occur.

Standard Distance

Standard distance is a spatial description method that is reported along with the mean center. The **standard distance** is used to describe the *compactness* of geographic data, and it is used in a similar way to how the standard deviation is used with nongeographic data. Standard distance is often represented as a single radius (measured in units of feet, miles, meters, kilometers, etc.) that surrounds the mean center location of a distribution of geographic data. Concentric radii can also be used to display 1, 2, and 3 standard distances from the mean center location. The standard distance is calculated using the X- and Y-coordinates for all the geographic data in a distribution, using the following equation:

$$SD = \sqrt{\frac{\sum_{i=1}^{n}\left(x_i - \overline{x}\right)}{n} + \frac{\sum_{i=1}^{n}\left(y_i - \overline{y}\right)}{n}},$$

where x_i and y_i are the X- and Y-coordinates for each individual data point (i) and $\overline{x}$ and $\overline{y}$ represents the mean center location for each data point. The symbol n denotes the total number of data points in a file.

Convex Hull

A convex hull is third common way to describe the distribution of geographic data. A **convex hull** or convex envelope can be thought of as the smallest polygon that can be drawn around the outer points of all the data in a data distribution of geographic locations. The convex hull is commonly known as the minimum convex polygon and can be used by researchers to define a particular study area, one that encompasses all the phenomena that were studied and represented in a geographic data set. Convex hull is the least common of the three types of spatial description methods used in geostatistics.

Spatial Dependency and Autocorrelation

In 1970, Waldo Tobler famously said, "Everything is related to everything else, but near things are more related than distant things" (p. 236). Tobler's statement about how things are related to each other in space has since become known as Tobler's Law or the **First Law of Geography**; it is the foundation for understanding patterns of spatial dependency and spatial autocorrelation that may be present in spatial data.

In spatial statistics, **spatial dependency** is a measure used to define the spatial relationship between *values* of geographical data. Most statistical tests used in spatial data analysis assume that the data being analyzed do not have spatial dependence. In other words, they assume spatial *independence*. The assumption of spatial independence is assessed through the various tests of **spatial autocorrelation**, including the Moran's "I" statistic, Geary's "C" statistic, and the Get-Ord "G" statistic. All of these spatial statistics are used on count data (e.g., number of burglaries) that have been aggregated to a larger unit of analysis (e.g., census blocks) to determine whether the assumption that observations are spatially independent of one another has been violated. Assessing the underlying assumptions of statistical tests is an important part of data analysis, and the concept of spatial autocorrelation is one of the most important in spatial statistics.

Spatial Interpolation and Regression

Two other types of spatial statistical analysis include methods involving spatial interpolation and regression. **Spatial interpolation** techniques refer to a group of geostatistical techniques that rely on the known recorded values of phenomena at specific locations to estimate the unobserved values of the same phenomenon at other locations.

Kernel density estimation (KDE), used in crime hot spot analysis, is an example of a spatial interpolation method. In crime hot spot mapping, for example, KDE is used to estimate the density of crime across an entire study area, based on the known locations of discrete events. KDE begins by overlaying a grid over the entire study area and calculating a density estimate based on the center points of each grid cell. Each distance between an incident and the center of a grid cell is then weighted based on a specific method of interpolation and bandwidth (i.e., search radius). Figure 12.13 illustrates the KDE process and shows several parameters that must be considered before a density estimate can be produced. These parameters include the grid cell size, the method of interpolation (i.e., the kernel function), and the bandwidth.

When the kernel function is placed over a grid cell centerpoint, the number of crime incidents within the function's bandwidth is used to determine the density estimate assigned to each cell. Although KDE is the most common spatial interpolation method used in criminology and criminal justice research, other methods of spatial interpolation used in geostatistical analysis include inverse distance weighting and kriging.

Earlier in this chapter, we described regression analysis as a popular method for predicting a particular outcome based on variables believed to be associated with the outcome, using a linear equation. This approach to quantitative data analysis can be extended and applied to spatial data in geostatistical analysis. One of the most common approaches

Spatial interpolation: Group of geostatistical techniques that relies on the known recorded values of phenomena at specific locations to estimate the unobserved values of the same phenomenon at other locations.

Figure 12.13 Visual Illustration of the Parameters That Define the Process of Kernel Density Estimation (KDE)

Visual Process of Kernel Density Estimation (KDE)

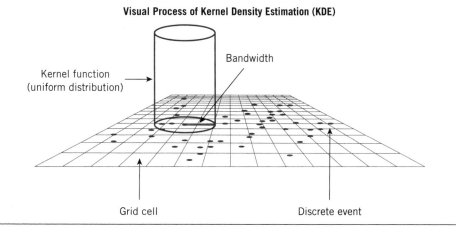

to applying regression analysis to spatial data is through a technique called **geographically weighted regression (GWR)**.

GWR is similar to linear regression analysis in that the technique involves using a set of predictor variables to estimate their relationship to an outcome variable or dependent variable. GWR is unique in that the regression analysis in GWR also considers the spatial relationships among predictor variables and estimates the relationships of predictor variables to an outcome variable for every feature on a map. For example, in Figure 12.14, GWR was used to estimate the likelihood of crime in each census tract within Clark County, Nevada, based on indicators of neighborhood characteristics, including the rate of foreclosure. The map in Figure 12.14 shows areas of the county where the GWR model does a very good job in explaining crime rates (i.e., dark gray areas located on the western side of the map), compared with areas of the county where the GWR model doesn't perform as well (i.e., dark gray areas located on the eastern side of the map). GWR is a powerful and popular geostatistical analysis tool, useful for developing prediction models that rely on spatial data.

Reporting Findings From Your Research

You have data. You have the analysis. What do they tell you? How do you answer the research questions with this? How will you share those findings with others? It is not enough to conduct analysis and be done. You must share those findings in ways that non-research-oriented people can understand. When it comes time to disseminating findings from your research,

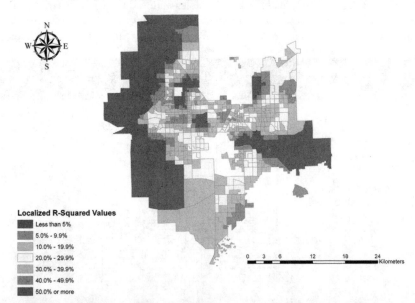

Figure 12.14 Results of a Geographic Weighted Regression (GWR) Analysis

Geographically Weighted Regression Results

Localized R-Squared Values
- Less than 5%
- 5.0% - 9.9%
- 10.0% - 19.9%
- 20.0% - 29.9%
- 30.0% - 39.9%
- 40.0% - 49.9%
- 50.0% or more

Results of a Geographic Weighted Regression (GWR) analysis show areas within Clark County, Nevada, associated with neighborhoods where the GWR model does a god job of predicting crime (dark gray areas on the western side of the map), compared with areas where it does a poorer job (dark gray areas on the eastern side of the map).

several options should be considered. Which option you choose will depend, in large part, on what the original aim of your study was. If, for example, you conducted an evaluation of a program or a project, you may be required to report your findings to the funding agency or organization that sponsored the evaluation. Often when findings of an evaluation project are provided to the stakeholders that sponsored the project, the report is written in a way that is appropriate for that audience. It may include an executive summary, highlighting the key findings of the project. It may also avoid including a lot of technical content such as mathematical equations or discussions of esoteric theoretical concepts. It may also rely on several charts, graphs, or maps to quickly and easily convey important findings to the reader. The key to disseminating research findings effectively, according to Santos and Cuevas, is to "know your audience."

The aim of many research projects is simply to advance our empirical understanding of something. When the aim of research is to contribute to the existing body of scientific knowledge, the approach to disseminating findings is somewhat different than when sponsored evaluations are conducted. The findings from empirical studies are often disseminated as peer-reviewed academic journal articles, which have a much more formal and rigid structure (see, for example, the structure of a Literature Review section of journal articles presented in Chapter 3). Although sometimes tables, graphs, charts, and maps are incorporated in peer-reviewed articles, they consist mostly of text organized by a specific structure that often includes a justification for why the study was conducted, the data and methods used to conduct the research, a formal presentation of findings, and conclusions the authors reached based on their results.

Another popular method used to disseminating research findings is a conference presentation. Professional conferences are organized meetings of professionals within a specific industry or with a shared interest. The American Society of Criminology (ASC), American Criminal Justice Society (ACJS), the Environmental Criminology and Crime Analysis (ECCA), and the International Association of Crime Analysts (IACA) conferences are annual professional meetings attended by criminology and criminal justices professionals. Conferences tend to be convened over several days. Each day usually consists of several sessions that focus on a particular topic or area of interest.

Depending on how large a conference is, several sessions can run simultaneously each day. Most conference sessions consist of 3 to 4 short, concise presentations that last about 20 to 30 minutes. The presentations are overviews of research or projects that have been undertaken and that are specific to the topic of the session. Presenters typically use a Microsoft PowerPoint™ presentation to deliver their material to the audience. When all the presenters have delivered their work, the session usually concludes with a question-and-answer period or a general discussion of how all the research relates to the session topic.

Poster sessions—where a researcher displays a summary of his or her project or research findings as a single poster, along with several other researchers and their posters, simultaneously—are workshops that are also common features of most professional conferences. Regardless of whether researchers disseminate their work through technical reports, peer-reviewed articles, or conference presentations, important messages may get lost if their work is not presented in a clear, organized, and concise manner. Tables can be used to help to convey effectively research findings to a large audience. The next section provides some general guidelines and tips to displaying research results.

Tables

A table is an effective way to display data. Tables can be used to display summary statistics, results of formal statistical tests, or myriad other information. Tables should be used to support the text they accompany and not to offer redundant information or to provide additional

Poster session: Method of disseminating research findings at a professional conference, where the information being disseminated is summarized on a single poster.

information not found in text. If a table doesn't make a unique contribution to the paper and doesn't effectively communicate the information it contains, it shouldn't be included. Tables are usually used to present numerical information that is arranged in columns and rows. Figure 12.15 is an example of a well-designed table, and it is used as an example to discuss some of the important table elements.

Table Number: Every table should be numbered, and if more than one table appears in your work, each table should be numbered in the order in which it is presented.

Title: A brief title that conveys to the reader what information is presented in the table should always be included as part of your tabular information.

Headings, Stubs, and Spanners: Headings, stubs, and spanners are used together to organize how tabular data are presented. Column heads, stub heads, and column spanners define, often with a single word or symbol, the information that is presented underneath them. For example, in Figure 12.15, "Statistics" is used as a column spanner, and the specific statistics presented in the table are denoted using statistical symbols as column headings (i.e., *n, %,* Min, Max, *Mdn,* and *SD*).

Dividers and Notes. Table dividers are solid lines used to separate the body of a table from the reset of the tabular information contained in it. Notations are also common information included in a table and should come below a table's bottom most divider. Notes should be clear, concise, and necessary information that helps the reader better understand information presented in Figure 12.15.

Figures

Figures are another useful methods for visually displaying data to the reader. Many different types of figures can be used this way, including graphs (e.g., line graphs), charts (e.g., bar charts), maps (e.g., crime hot spot map), or photographs. Because so many different figures can be used to present data or information, there aren't "one size fits all" rules for creating and presenting figures. Instead, authors should follow these general guidelines:

- Like tables, figures should be used to support text. Avoid creating figures that are essentially redundant information.

- Avoid subjective visuals; instead, use figures to present objective, factual information.

- Only include information that is necessary in a figure. A good example of this is not to include a legend on a line graph and *also* label each line in the graph. Both the legend and the labels aren't needed. Pick one.

- Be sure that all elements of a figure are easy to read and symbolized clearly and logically. For example, it's a good idea not to give a choropleth hot spot map more than seven color-coded categories (see, for example, Figure 12.14) as too many categories can make it difficult for the reader to differentiate between groups.

- Whenever possible, make sure that a figure contains words that are written in the same type font as the rest of the document.

- Make sure that units of measurement are clearly defined and that graph axes are clearly labeled.

When these guidelines are followed, charts, graphs, maps, and photographs can be used as efficient and effective ways to display data.

Figure 12.15 Example of Tabular Data

Summary statistics for Gold Coast Community Survey (GCCS) participants

COLUMN HEAD

Statistics

Characteristic — STUB HEAD — STUB — COLUMN SPANNER — DIVIDER

Characteristic	n	%	Min	Max	Mdn	SD
Demographics						
Gender						
Male	254	36.1				
Female	449	63.9				
Australian born						
No	234	32.8				
Yes	476	67.2				
Currently married[a]						
No	209	29.8				
Yes	492	70.2				
Age (years)	692		18	93	57.0	15.9
Time at residence (months)	691		1	1062	81.2	23.4

Note: Key elements that should be included in tables are noted in ALL CAPS. Values under the percentage columns reflect the percentage of valid responses.

[a]Currently married includes *de facto* marriage.

Common Pitfalls in Data Analysis and Developing Findings

Garbage In, Garbage Out (GIGO): Notion in research that findings produced from data analysis are only as good as the data being analyzed.

Let's face it; mistakes happen. But we can do our best to avoid making mistakes, including common mistakes made during data analysis, if we understand the common pitfalls made during this important phase of scientific discovery. Many mistakes made during data analysis are made because of problems related to either data quality or other limitations to the data that a researcher fails to recognize. Remember, at the heart of much research is our ability to accurately and reliability measure concepts that are directly unobservable (i.e., guardianship, social disorganization, fear of crime, etc.). Proper measurement and data collection are essential, and if the measures we use in research are bad, or if we collect data using poor methods, then any statistic we produce will be meaningless. Data that are nonsensical, incomplete, or imprecise will lead to faulty statistics and conclusions based on bad analysis: **Garbage In, Garbage Out (GIGO)**. Major sources of inaccurate data in criminological research include poor measures of concepts and bad sampling designs.

Most researchers understand the GIGO problem and do their best to avoid it by constructing good measures and implementing good sampling protocols. Even when valid and reliable data are collected, using appropriate sampling methods, mistakes can be made. Here is a list of what we think are the four most common, and easily avoidable, mistakes made in data analysis:

1. *Correlation does not imply causation:* As noted previously in this chapter, researchers often analyze data to determine (or refute) whether two variables are associated, or correlated, to each other. Nevertheless, just because two variables are correlated does not mean a *causal* relationship exists. For example, each of the following relationships is strongly correlated, but it would be silly to think that these relationships are causally related:

   - U.S. spending on science, space, and technology is strongly correlated with suicides by hanging, strangulation, and suffocation ($r = .998$).

   - The number of people who drowned by falling into a pool is strongly correlated with films in which Nicolas Cage has appeared ($r = .667$).

   - The number of people who die by becoming entangled in their bed sheets is strongly correlated with the per capita consumption of cheese ($r = .947$).

   - Marriage rates in Kentucky are strongly correlated with the number of people who drown after falling out of fishing boats ($r = .952$).

Source: Tylervigen.com (n.d).

Granted, it's obvious that these correlations do not represent causal relationships. Nevertheless, it's not uncommon for researchers to think that when a correlational relationship is found in data that it somehow represents a causal relationship, but this is incorrect and is a mistake in logic that can be easily avoided.

2. *Knowing a technique, but not knowing the data:* Too often researchers know how to analyze data, but they lack a firm grasp or understanding of the data they're analyzing. This can especially be true when secondary data analysis is being conducted. The "Datasaurus" presented in Figure 12.16 provides an excellent example of this common pitfall. Datasaurus was created by Alberto Cairo (2016) as a lesson he uses to illustrate the importance of data visualization techniques (e.g., box plots, scatterplots, histograms, etc.), which are tools that you can use to "get to know" your data. Albert gives his students a data file containing two variables. The first variable has a mean of 54.26 ($SD = 16.77$); variable two has a mean of 47.83 ($SD = 26.94$). If the students want to use these variables and test whether the two means are significantly different, they should visualize the data before running analysis to identify any problems or anomalies. When this is done, using a scatterplot, the two variables produce an image like the one shown in Figure 12.16.

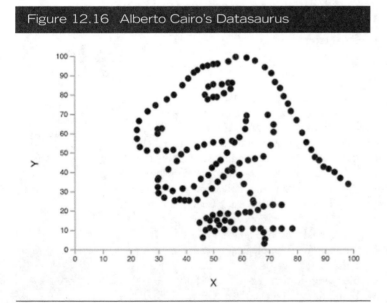

Figure 12.16   Alberto Cairo's Datasaurus

Note: Reprinted from Cairo (2016).

Obviously, there's a problem with these two variables, and a researcher who wants to use them to conduct a *t* test of mean differences, for example, should think twice. This is a lighthearted example of problems associated with knowing a technique but not knowing your data. Even so, the bottom line is this: Without "getting to know" your data, you're likely to make a mistake either during the data analysis process or in presenting findings. This can occur even if you know how to properly conduct the analysis you want to run.

Statistical significance: When the outcome of a research hypothesis test indicates a true difference (or association) between the observed and hypothesized values that are not likely to occur based on chance alone.

Substantive significance: Whether statistically significant findings are substantively meaningful.

3. *Not applying the appropriate analytic method:* Researchers much pay careful attention to (a) how a study is designed and (b) whether the analytic methods being used fit with the design that was implemented. If not, mistakes will likely be made. For example, suppose you collected data from our group of students mentioned previously in this chapter about their driving patterns. You collected information on two variables: how many tickets they've ever received and their sex. Suppose you entered their responses into a data set and coded all the students who identified as male with a value of "0" and all the students who identified as female with a value of "1." Technically, you could compute a mean for the variable sex (i.e., add up all the 1s and 0s and divide by 15 or the number of students in the study). But what would that mean . . . mean? The answer is "Nothing!" Computing an average on a nominal- (e.g., gender) or interval-level measure is a mistake. The results are meaningless and an example of not applying the appropriate analytic method to the data.

4. *Thinking statistical significance means substantive significance:* When studies are conducted to test specific research hypotheses, investigators make a determination about patterns observed in their data and the likelihood similar patterns would be observed in the broader population from which the research sample was drawn. **Statistical significance** is a term often used in these types of studies and refers to when the outcome of a research hypothesis test indicates a true difference between the observed and hypothesized values; in other words, that the differences or relationships in the data are not likely to occur based on chance alone.

In contrast, **substantive significance** refers to the importance of observed differences or associations. It indicates whether differences (or associations) between observed sample values and hypothesized values are large enough to be meaningful to criminologists or the public. Researchers may lose sight of whether significant findings are also substantive findings when reporting results of their investigations. Nevertheless, the difference between statistical and substantive significance must be considered. Large differences in small samples may be substantively important but statistically insignificant. Conversely, small differences in large samples may be statistically significant but substantively trivial. The best practice is to balance these two concerns. Do not use statistical significance as the only indicator of substantive differences, especially when you have very small or very large samples.

Ethics Associated With Analyzing Your Data and Developing Your Findings

You may have heard of the old saying "There are three kinds of lies: lies, damned lies, and statistics." Many believe former British prime minister Benjamin Disraeli (1874–1880) was the first to utter this phrase; others attribute it Mark Twain. Regardless of who said it first, the statement rings true with many, especially in today's world of "big data." The problem with the statement, however, is that it fails to acknowledge the fact that statistics are just numbers and that they can neither lie nor tell the truth. It is the researcher's responsibility to not only engage in research that is of the highest ethical standards but also to produce results from data analysis that is not unscrupulous.

Many ethical guidelines exist for conducting data analysis, but few are as clear and concise as those developed by Rachel Wasserman (2013). Those most relevant to the field of criminology and criminal justice include the following:

1. Researchers must be competent and sufficiently trained in the techniques they use and/or only delegate analysis responsibilities to other members of the research team that are competent. If an analyst doesn't know how to properly conduct data analysis, then he or she risks producing and reporting inaccurate or misleading information.

2. Analysis should only be conducted with software designed to conduct the specific analysis required to answer the researcher's research question(s).

3. Researchers should choose a minimally sufficient analysis based on the research question and assumptions of the statistical technique.

4. Researchers must "know their data" (i.e., how the data were collected, and how the data were prepared for analysis, including proper exploratory analyses).

5. Changes made to raw data should always be documented, along with the reasons that the changes were made.

6. Don't cherry-pick findings. In other words, researchers should avoid "mining the data" for answers that support their personal views.

7. Researchers should make it clear to the research team that high ethical standards are valued and that it is everyone's responsibility to apply this standard to all aspects of the research project—including data analysis.

Cuevas provides an excellent summary of the importance of maintaining high ethical standards when conducting data analysis. He put it this way during his video interview conducted for this book: "We can do analysis quickly and easily now because of computers, but that can give you a false sense of security. Everything has to be done well and to a high ethical standard before, during, and after the data analysis . . . if the results of the analysis are good."

Analysis and Findings Expert—Sue Burton

Sue Burton has been the director of Florida's Statistical Analysis Center (FSAC) at the Department of Law Enforcement since 1995. She holds a degree in business management from Florida State University, yet her 20+ years of experience working with administrative criminal justice data across the criminal justice system has fueled her career in criminal justice statistical analysis. She currently serves on the U.S. Department of Justice's Science Advisory Board, appointed by former U.S. Attorney General, Eric Holder. She's serving a five-year term. Burton's many years of collaboration with the Bureau of Justice Statistics, specifically to illustrate the value of using existing operational or administrative criminal justice data sources to answer research questions, put her in the "spotlight" for this appointment.

As the director of FSAC, her goal is to document, analyze, and explain criminal justice data (i.e., criminal histories, uniform crime reports [UCR], corrections, officer employment, etc.) for policy and operational purposes. The most common type of research performed by the Center involves descriptive statistics. As mentioned in this chapter, the exploration of data sources requires data analysis, which can serve to prepare data for in-depth research projects or to answer a policy question, by simply creating a frequency or distribution of the certain data elements.

Courtesy of Susan Burton

The Statistical Analysis Center supports policy decision making by providing information about the state's crime picture to federal agencies, the state legislature, operational agencies like law enforcement, corrections, juvenile justice and the judicial offices, as well as local law enforcement agencies. To be a valuable partner, the center has to maintain an intimate knowledge of the available data and cultivate a skill set to make use of analytical tools such as SAS, STATA, and even Excel.

SAS is the primary tool for the Center staff. Data that the Center "mines" are often large and complex (e.g., the entire state criminal history files that go back to the 1920s). Before any research question is broached, a statistical description of the relevant data elements is created to scope the project and to identify any data limitations. Statistical procedures to identify the amount of missing data are performed, along with the more basic frequencies and cross-tabulations of relevant variables.

An equally important element of any analysis conducted at FSAC is consulting with data experts and those familiar with the processes that generate data. The center often meets with internal operational staff or research staff of the departments of corrections, juvenile justice, and the courts to make sure staff members understand the data source and their limitations.

Over the years, the center has established data-sharing agreements with the departments that maintain data, which includes additional information about the individuals in the state's criminal justice system that are not found in criminal history files. Information sharing between departments is crucial. Burton says, "Data sharing helps us complete the picture of what happens in the criminal justice system. Our Center uses the state's criminal history files to gain an overall understanding of crime in Florida, with a focus on arrest events. Sometimes it helps to fill some gaps from other criminal justice data sources." Her group has integrated data from various criminal justice data systems to create a research-friendly information source about crime and punishment in the state of Florida.

The center's integrated database contains criminal history records for the last 100 years, including monthly updates of about 100,000 new arrest and judicial records. The information has been used for various research projects, including a project that combined data from the Department of Correction's Sentencing Guidelines database to create severity scores to quantify offender seriousness. The center's ability to place criminal history data into research formats makes it a valuable resource that is used by the state's research units to measure the success of programs that seek to decrease recidivism rates among other measures important to the state's policy maker.

Chapter Wrap-Up

In this chapter, our focus was on ways to analyze data produced from qualitative and quantitative studies. We explained why data analysis is important and the role data analysis plays in the creation of new, empirically based knowledge. Data description methods, including measures of central tendency (e.g., mean, median, and mode) and measures of dispersion (e.g., range, variance, and standard deviation), were introduced. We also presented information about quantitative approaches to data analysis and some of the common software applications you can use to conduct statistical analysis. We also provided an overview of qualitative methods and applications used in criminology and criminal justice research. Conjunctive analysis of case configurations (CACC) was also discussed as an alternative approach to traditional analytic methods, providing specific details of how to run CACC in SPSS, STATA and SAS. Approaches to analyzing geospatial data were also presented in this chapter, along with a discussion of some of the most common spatial statistical methods used in our field. Guidance to students on how to effectively and efficiently display findings from their research with tables and in figures was also offered. This chapter concluded with an overview of some of the most common errors made in data analysis, along with strategies that can be used to overcome these pitfalls. We also discussed some of the important ethical considerations associated with data analysis.

Regardless of the purpose of their research, our case studies analyzed their data and developed findings to answer their research questions. Table 12.6 offers that information in one place to show that even though research purposes, questions, and approaches vary, the overall purpose is to answer a research question. In the next chapter, we focus on making your research relevant by explaining how to translate research into language that is nontechnical so that non-research-oriented people can understand it. We place particular emphasis on the importance of relationships and networking. We also introduce readers to evaluation research, explaining how it differs from other research methodologies. We discuss why this particular research method is important and the ways in which it can be conducted. Finally, we explain the common challenges, pitfalls, and ethical considerations confronted by research conducting evaluation research.

Table 12.6 Featured Research: Type of Data Used, Analytic Techniques, and Findings			
Researcher	**Type of Data Used**	**Analytic Techniques Used**	**Findings Include . . .**
Rod Brunson (Brunson & Weitzer, 2009)	Qualitative Data	Transcriptions were used to extract themes where they were grouped into conceptual domains based on generalized statement contents.	Our study builds on the ecological literature with qualitative evidence regarding the experiences and attitudes of youths who reside in three disadvantaged neighborhoods that differ by racial composition. The findings suggest that, holding neighborhood socioeconomic context constant, race makes a difference in how youth are treated by police and in their perceptions of officers.
Carlos Cuevas (Sabina et al., 2016)	Quantitative Data	Descriptive statistics. Estimated risk ratios of dating violence. Multinomial logistic regression was used to assess the influence of independent variables while holding other variables constant.	Generally, those who experienced Wave 1 dating violence victimization were 2.59–7.98 times more likely to experience dating violence victimization in Wave 2 than those who did not experience Wave 1 dating violence victimization. Sexual dating violence victimization in Wave 1 significantly increased the risk of any physical and sexual dating violence victimization in Wave 2. Psychological dating violence victimization in Wave 1 significantly increased the risk of any and stalking dating violence victimization. Risk ratios show that Wave 1 dating violence victimization did not significantly increase the risk of conventional crime, child maltreatment, peer/sibling victimization, sexual victimization, polyvictimization, or stalking victimization.

Researcher	Type of Data Used	Analytic Techniques Used	Findings Include . . .
Mary Dodge (Dodge et al., 2005)	Qualitative Data	Each interview was recorded, and the tapes were transcribed and analyzed by the researchers. Themes were extracted, and typical quotes were highlighted to represent those themes.	Women officers interviewed for this research enjoyed the excitement and variety of the assignment. With limited opportunities, the role of a prostitute decoy in a reverse prostitution sting may represent the best avenue for gaining valuable undercover experience in order to move to other coveted positions in the department.
Chris Melde (Melde et al., 2009)	Quantitative Data	Descriptive statistics.	Gender differences in victimization rates were found in Wave 1, with boys reporting higher levels of any dating violence victimization, physical dating violence victimization, sexual dating violence victimization, and psychological dating violence victimization. At Wave 2, gender differences were not apparent, except for girls reporting significantly higher levels of sexual dating violence victimization than boys. Those who experienced Wave 1 dating violence victimization were 2.59–7.98 times more likely to experience dating violence victimization in Wave 2, than those who did not experience Wave 1 dating violence victimization. Results show that Wave 1 dating violence victimization did not significantly increase the risk of conventional crime, child maltreatment, peer/sibling victimization, sexual victimization, polyvictimization, or stalking victimization.
Rachel Santos (Santos & Santos, 2016)	Quantitative Data	Descriptive statistics. Negative binomial models. Ordinary least-squares regression.	At the descriptive level, the four measures show that there was a decrease of reported burglaries and thefts from vehicles in both treatment and control areas. The arrest counts and ratios collected for each hot spot showed contrasting results. Both control and treatment areas had a large increase in arrest counts during the intervention period—149% and 78%, respectively. The control areas also had a significantly higher ratio of arrests per individuals arrested (a 30% increase), whereas the treatment areas saw a slight but insignificant reduction (6%). None of the six models revealed significant results to indicate whether the presence of the intervention or the intervention dosage had an effect on crime or arrests. Two very conservative conclusions suggest that the intervention may have had some influence on the targeted offenders and in the hot spots.
Heather Zaykowski (2014)	Quantitative Data	Descriptive statistics. Logistic regressions.	Although service providers address and treat traumatic stress resulting from criminal victimization, very few victims actually have contact with these services. Victim services were more likely to be used when the incident was known to the police, the victim was female, and the relationship involved greater intimacy.

Applied Assignments

1. Homework Applied Assignment: Descriptive Statistics

Find three different papers published in three different peer-reviewed academic journals in criminal justice or criminology. Each paper must include a table of descriptive statistics. Begin your thought paper by comparing and contrasting the measures of central tendency and measures of dispersions used to describe the researchers' data. Next, identify the primary research question associated with each study and the particular analytic technique used to answer them. If identified, also report the software application used to analyze the researchers' data. Finally, express in your own opinion whether the final results of the researchers' analysis were presented efficiently and effectively (i.e., did the authors use tables, charts, figures, maps, etc. to present their findings), and explain why or why not. Be prepared to discuss your thought paper in class.

2. Group Work in Class Applied Assignment: Conjunctive Analysis of Case Configurations

Form a group with four other students in your class. With your professor's permission, walk around campus and have each member of your group, including yourself, ask five different students (a) their class (i.e., freshman, sophomore, junior, senior, or other), (b) whether they're currently in a fraternity/sorority, and (c) whether they've ever received a speeding ticket. Once data have been collected from 25 students, construct a CACC truth table of all *possible* student profiles that could be observed. There are 20 possible combinations (i.e., 5 class ranks, 2 affiliations [Yes or No], and 2 speeding responses [Yes or No]; or 5 × 2 × 2 = 20). Next, identify the specific profile each of the 25 students interviewed is associated with. Continue this process until your entire sample of interviewed students has been allocated to a single profile. Once this process is complete, tally the count and compute the percentage for each observed profile that is actually *observed* in your data.

Of the 20 possible profiles that could have been observed, what percentage was actually observed in your data? Which profile was the profile observed most often? What percentage of all profiles did the dominant profile comprise? What other patterns did your group observe in your data? Be able to report your group's findings to the class.

3. Internet Applied Assignment: Bad Stats

Go online and find a website that presents, what you believe to be, "bad statistics" related to some crime or justice-related issue or problem. Explain why you feel the statistical information presented on the website is "bad." Is it a matter of GIGO, a suggestion of causality based on correlations, an apparent misunderstanding of the data upon which the report is based, using the wrong analytic method, or some other reason? Explain. Are the findings or information discussed on the website based on data analysis results that are both statistically and substantively significant? Finally, are there any ethical issues you think that the presenters of this information failed to consider or overlook? Discuss. Be prepared to discuss your findings in class.

KEY WORDS AND CONCEPTS

Analysis of variance (ANOVA) 390
Characteristics 396
Chi-square test 387
Coding sorts 396
Conjunctive analysis of case configurations (CACC) 400
Convex hull 404

Correlation analysis 388
Deduction 378
Descriptive statistics 380
Deviation score 385
First Law of Geography 404
Frequency Distribution 381
Garbage In, Garbage Out (GIGO) 409

Geographically weighted regression (GWR) 406
Geostatistical analysis 403
Interquartile range (IQR) 384
Link analysis 398
Mean 381
Mean center 404

Measures of central tendency 381
Measures of dispersion 384
Median 382
Meta data 398
Mind maps 398
Mode 383
Outliers 382
Poster session 407

Qualitative data analysis (QDA) 396
Range 384
Regression analysis 388
Second-order analysis 396
Situational contexts 400
Spatial autocorrelation 404
Spatial dependency 404
Spatial descriptions 403

Spatial interpolation 405
Spreadsheet 392
Standard distance 404
Statistical significance 411
Substantive significance 411
Theme 396
Univariate Analysis 380
Variance 385

KEY POINTS

- Data analysis is generally classified into two groups: descriptive statistics and inferential statistics. Descriptive statistics involve analyzing data so that numerical descriptors of the typical case, or all the other cases relative to the typical case, are produced. Inferential statistics involve data analysis designed to test research hypotheses.

- Many quantitative statistical methods can be applied to data using myriad statistical analysis software applications. Popular applications include Microsoft Excel, SPSS, STATA and SAS.

- Qualitative data analysis (QDA) often begins with a broad, open-ended question(s). Next, data are collected from texts, conversations, recordings, and posts around a well-defined framework. QDA frameworks typically include, among other things, a data-coding plan, which is used to sort data and report findings from descriptive analysis based on themes identified by the researcher. If the QDA is not exploratory in nature, researchers conduct second-order analysis.

- Conjunctive analysis of case configures (CACC) is an approach to data analysis that focuses on reducing data into meaningful statistical information (e.g., frequency distributions and percentages) and that assesses empirical observations with formal statistical tests (e.g., chi-square test of independence). CACC builds situational contexts of particular outcomes, from an existing data file, defined by the combinations of variable attributes believed to influence that outcome.

- Geostatistical analyses are mathematical techniques that use the geographical properties of data as part of a statistical or analytic method and include spatial descriptions, spatial dependency and autocorrelation, and spatial interpolation and regression methods.

- Research findings are disseminated in myriad ways, including in reports to sponsors of research, academic journals, and conference presentations and workshops. Tables and figures are used to visually display data in ways that effectively and efficiently support text.

- Proper measurement and data collection are essential to good data analysis. If the measures we use in research are bad, or if we collect data using poor methods, then any statistic we produce will be meaningless. Data that are nonsensical, incomplete, or imprecise will lead to faulty statistics and conclusions based on bad analysis: Garbage In, Garbage Out (GIGO).

- Statistical significance does not always mean findings have substantive significance.

- It is the researcher's responsibility to not only engage in research that is of the highest ethical standards but also to produce results from data analysis that adhere to high ethical standards. One way to achieve this goal is to make it clear to the research team that high ethical standards are valued and that it is everyone's responsibility to apply this standard to all aspects of the research project—including data analysis.

REVIEW QUESTIONS

1. Why do researchers conducted data analysis, and how does it fit within the process of generating empirical knowledge?

2. Describe some of the common measures of central tendency and measures of dispersion used in data analysis.

3. Provide examples of research questions that would require correlational analysis, and contrast them with research questions that would require analytic approaches that assess group differences. Do you think one approach to statistical analysis is better than the other? Explain.

4. Describe some of the common statistical software applications used to analyze quantitative data. Provide an example of when one application may be more or less appropriate to use than another.

5. Describe the four general steps in conducting qualitative data analysis.

6. Describe some of the common statistical software applications used to analyze qualitative data. Provide an example of when one application may be more or less appropriate to use than another.

7. Describe some of the spatial descriptions, spatial dependency and autocorrelation, and spatial

interpolation and regression techniques commonly used in geostatistical analysis.

8. Identify a key part of a table, and explain how it is used in a table to help organize and visually display data.

9. Explain what the phrase "Garbage In, Garbage Out" means, and apply it to the analysis of criminal justice data.

10. Describe some of the steps researchers can take to ensure results produced from data analysis are of a high ethical standard.

CRITICAL THINKING QUESTIONS

1. The following information was obtained online from the FBI's UCR website. It represents the frequency distribution of violent crimes recorded by law enforcement agencies that occurred on Florida's college and university campuses in 2015 (see Table 12.9).

Table 12.7 Violent Crimes Recorded on Florida's College/University Campuses in 2015	
University/College	Violent Crimes
Florida A&M University	10,241
Florida Atlantic University	30,297
Florida Gulf Coast University	14,473
Florida International University	49,610
Florida South Western State College	15,389
Florida State University	41,226
New College of Florida	834
Pensacola State College	10,317
Santa Fe College	15,055
Tallahassee Community College	13,049
University of Central Florida	60,767
University of Florida	49,459
University of North Florida	15,984
University of South Florida	46,429
University of West Florida	12,602

Choose three measures of central tendency and three measures of dispersion, and report the values of each and explain why you chose them. You may use Excel or another software application (i.e., SPSS, SAS, STATA, etc.) to help analyze the data if needed.

2. Explain how conjunctive analysis of case configurations (CACC) is similar to quantitative data analysis. Also provide examples of how CACC is similar to qualitative data analysis. Finally, create a research question that you think would be an interesting topic to examine using the CACC method, and explain why.

3. Many of the standard statistical methods used to analyze nonspatial data can be used to analyze geospatial data. Identify three methods discussed in this chapter, and explain how they are similar and how they are different.

4. Convert the tabular data presented in Question 1 into a bar chart by hand or using Excel (or any other software application) for any of the five colleges or universities. Exchange your figure with someone else's in your class. Critique each other's work.

5. Rachel Wasserman (2013) argued that researchers must avoid cherry-picking findings as part of their data analysis. Explain how the distribution of violent crime presented in Question 1 could be "cherry-picked" to produce evidence in support of or again a specific research question.

Learning Objectives

After finishing this chapter, you should be able to:

13.1 Define policy-relevant research, and contrast it with research that is not policy relevant.

13.2 Summarize the policy process, and describe each stage. Identify which stages enable researchers to influence policy makers.

13.3 Identify who policy makers are and why they are important in conducting policy-relevant research.

13.4 Evaluate the parts of a policy brief, and compare and contrast a journal article and a policy brief.

13.5 Identify and summarize the competing sources of influence on policy makers, and describe why researchers need to understand this.

13.6 Describe and explain the activities a researcher wishing to conduct policy-relevant research should engage in.

Introduction

Featured researchers Rod Brunson, Rachel Boba Santos, Chris Melde, Heather Zaykowski, Mary Dodge, and Carlos Cuevas conduct research because their findings will matter and will be used to build knowledge, as well as to make the world a better place. Research can matter in many ways that have been described in this book. First, research can make a difference by adding to our general knowledge and our understanding of the world. Santos and colleague's research increased our understanding about the effect of intensive policing (Santos & Santos, 2016). Brunson and colleague's work offers insight into how police interactions differ for White and Black youth living in similar communities (Brunson & Weitzer, 2009). Dodge and colleagues' work provides a greater understanding about how female officers deal with being an undercover prostitute, their views of the works, the participants, danger, and even the effectiveness of these stings (Dodge, Starr-Gimeno, & Williams, 2005). As this book has shown, the findings from exploratory and descriptive research provide understanding about crime, incarceration, reentry, victimization, police discretion, use of force by police, and an infinite number of criminal justice topics.

Explanatory research makes a difference as well in that it allows for us to better understand connections between those topics as well as the role that gender, years in prison, age, times victimized, race, and education play on some criminal justice outcome. Zaykowski's (2014) research provides insight into the important role that reporting victimization to the police plays in whether the victim seeks assistance. This work shows that reporting to the police increases the odds of accessing victim services by three times. In addition, given Zaykowski's research, we know that police reporting increases the odds of accessing victim services by more than four times for those attacked by an intimate partner compared with a stranger.

A second important way research matters is that it provides valuable information about programs. As Chapter 11 showed, evaluation research allows for researchers to ascertain whether policies and their associated programs are operating as intended, policies or programs should be expanded or discontinued, and policies and programs are cost effective (to name a few goals of evaluation research). A third way research can matter or make a difference is by producing research that is policy relevant. That is, our research can be used to shape policy. Historically, researchers have done a great job of conducting solid research and publishing those results; nevertheless, researchers have not conducted as much research that is policy relevant. Santos, in a video interview conducted for this book, stated that she believes this is in large part because making your research relevant is challenging. It is not enough to say, "My research is relevant"; we must offer clear reasons how it is relevant. Therefore, this chapter discusses ways to make your research relevant. It defines policy, policy makers, and describes the policy process. In addition, it presents the challenges with getting your research findings to policy makers, and it offers tips as to how you as a researcher can maximize the chances that your research will be policy relevant.

Congress is one body in the United States that establishes policy. We elect policy makers to go to Washington, D.C., to produce policy to improve our lives. If you want to produce policy relevant research, would it benefit you to know who in congress is dealing with certain policies? How do you propose they learn about your research if you don't even know who they are?

Why Conduct Policy-Relevant Research?

Policies directly influence all of our lives in many ways on a daily basis. For example, policies reflected in speed limits affect how fast we each drive (at least when we do not think a police officer is around). Policies determine at what age we can drink alcohol, serve in the military, and marry. Policies dictate not only when we can marry but who we can and cannot marry. Policies affect student loan availability and repayment schedules.

The late 1960s saw an alarming increase in crime. In response, the Law Enforcement Assistance Administration (LEAA; the precursor to the Office of Justice Programs; see Chapter 9) was established in part to advance the criminal justice discipline. A part of this included funding research to influence criminal justice policy. Today, as a result of this work, you are likely familiar with many criminal justice policies. Some controversial policies include the three-strikes policies in effect in 28 states that require a person who is found guilty of committing a violent felony after having been convicted of two previous crimes to be imprisoned for life. Also widely known are sex offender registry policies. Although the specific policy differs by jurisdiction, sex offender policies require convicted sex offenders to register with their local law enforcement agencies. The amount of information they must provide differs, but the purpose of the registries is to allow law enforcement to better monitor these individuals, as well as to allow the public to be aware of potential risks who may live near them.

Another widely known criminal justice policy concerns mandatory arrest resulting from a domestic violence incident. Mandatory arrest policies require the arrest of a person when the law enforcement officer has probable cause that an individual committed a violent act against a domestic partner. In these instances, the officer does not need a warrant, and the officer did not need to witness the violence.

It seems reasonable to expect that policies we all live with such as three-strikes, sex offender registries, and mandatory arrest were designed and implemented based on findings from a body of well-conducted research. Although that is reasonable, it does not always happen. Not many of us would be comfortable to learn that our lives are affected by policies crafted based on a single piece of research (no research is perfect, so using a body of research findings is important), a policy maker's whims, political or other ideology, or random chance. Most of us hope or assume that decisions about what policies to implement, and the shape

of those policies, were based on our understanding about what is best for the public and those involved given a body of research findings.

It almost seems silly to state clearly that we want our policy to be based on a body of good research. Nevertheless, it has to be stated because in reality, policy design and implementation is guided by more than good research. In the past, it has been guided by a single imperfect piece of research, political or religious ideology, and other seemingly random factors. This means that policies that affect your life are not always influenced by the best research available. This can lead to unnecessary suffering, expensive approaches to social issues that do not work, and a failure to ameliorate a problem of interest. In sum, we want research to be policy relevant because we want to solve problems and make the world a better place. We want to live under policies that improve the world and not worsen it for anyone.

Mandatory arrest policies adopted widely mandate officers to make an arrest with probable cause, but no warrant in domestic violence cases, even if the violence was not witnessed. Are these policies based on well-conducted research? What might explain the adoption of the consequential policies?

What Is Policy-Relevant Research?

Policy-relevant research is research that directly influences policy makers or agency personnel who are developing and implementing policy. Policy-relevant research can be used to provide an understanding about what societal problems exist and why those problems are important to solve, what policies are needed, how policies should be shaped, how policies should be implemented, how existing policies should be adjusted, and what policies are not beneficial to the group they are designed to assist (to name a few purposes). Policy-relevant research can be used by policy makers to inform and address policy needs in two ways. First, policy-relevant research can be used by policy makers to identify and develop needed policies focused on important issues. Second, policy-relevant research can be used by policy makers to improve and enhance existing policies. Policy-relevant research is not research on a policy but research that directly affects or influences policy.

Policy-relevant research: Research that directly influences the development of and implementation of the principles, rules, and laws that guide a government, an organization, or people by informing and influencing policy makers.

To be clear, no single piece of research can (or should) change the direction of policy. Rather, a body of research should inform policy design and implementation. Producing policy-relevant research means generating research that adds to a body of literature that influences policy makers and that influences small policy changes on the margin.

What Is Policy?

Before further discussing policy-relevant research, it is useful to clearly identify what we mean by policy. As is the case with complex topics, there is no one widely agreed upon definition of policy. Policy is multifaceted, making it difficult to define. Here are several common definitions:

- "A definite course or method of action selected from among alternatives and in light of given conditions to guide and determine present and future decisions." (Merriam Webster Dictionary Online, n.d.)

- "A definite course of action adopted for the sake of expediency, facility, etc." (Dictionary.com, n.d.)

- An "action or procedure conforming to or considered with reference to prudence or expediency." (Dictionary.com, n.d.)

- "Prudence or wisdom in the management of affairs." (Merriam Webster Dictionary Online, n.d.)

- "Management or procedure based primarily on material interest." (Merriam Webster Dictionary Online, n.d.)

- "A high-level overall plan embracing the general goals and acceptable procedures especially of a governmental body." (Merriam Webster Dictionary Online, n.d.)

- "The basic principles by which a government is guided." (Business Dictionary Online, n.d.)

- "The declared objectives that a government or party seeks to achieve and preserve in the interest of national community." (Business Dictionary Online, n.d.)

- "A course or principle of action adopted or proposed by an organization or individual." (Oxford Dictionary Online, n.d.)

© Svetlana_Smirnova/iStockphoto.com

By blending elements of these commonly available definitions, we offer a simple definition of **policy** as the principles, rules, and laws that guide a government, an organization, or people. Examples of criminal justice policies, as described earlier, include three-strikes policies, sex-offender policies, and mandatory arrest policies. Policy is broad and includes actions or the adoption of principles, rules and laws in governments, nonprofits, quasi-governmental agencies, and the private sector. A more specific type of policy is public policy. **Public policy** refers to policy designed and implemented by governmental agencies specifically. Policy expert Paul Cairney (n.d.) defines public policy as the "the sum total of government actions, from signals of intent, to the final outcomes." It too is broad, but it is limited to policy actions in a government. Given this information about policy, we can expand our earlier definition of policy-relevant research to be research that influences the design and implementation of principles, rules, and laws that guide a government, an organization, or people.

When thinking about policy, you may hear a variety of terms such as policies, procedures, and guidelines. This section offers some insight into what each of these terms means, although they bleed together. In some ways, they all refer to policies but with different levels of specificity. As noted, policies are the principles, rules, and laws that guide a government, an organization, or people. In general, we think of policies as being broad statements containing little detail that are formally adopted by the appropriate board or authorizing group. At times, however, a policy is produced that is very detailed that gives almost no discretion to the regulatory agency in promulgating regulations. On the other hand, policy makers have also at other times written legislation and policies that are very brief (e.g., a page long) that leave nearly all of the nuance and discretion to the agency responsible for the policy. In general, **procedures** are more detailed protocols, standard operating procedures, or the step-by-step processes that should be followed to accomplish the spirit of the policy. Although policies are formally adopted by a body given the power to do so, procedures are generally crafted by a different group of individuals. Finally, a **regulation, rule,** or **guideline** offers recommendations about how to accomplish the step-by-step procedures. Regulations, rules, and guidelines outline the expected behavior and actions one should take in following the procedures. Regulations, rules, and guidelines frequently provide examples of how to deal with specific instances an individual may encounter. Unlike policies and procedures, rules, regulations, and guidelines are not compulsory, but they are suggestions or best practices.

What do you want influencing policy? Would you be okay to learn that horoscopes influenced the design and implementation of policy? Would you prefer policy be based on well-conducted research? What can you do to ensure the later happens more than the former?

Policy: Principles, rules, and laws that guide a government, an organization, or people.

Public policy: Policy designed and implemented by governmental agencies specifically.

Procedures: Step-by-step or standard operating procedures, that should be followed to accomplish the policy.

Regulations: Recommendations about the expected behavior during the course of following procedures, with examples of how to deal with specific instances one may encounter.

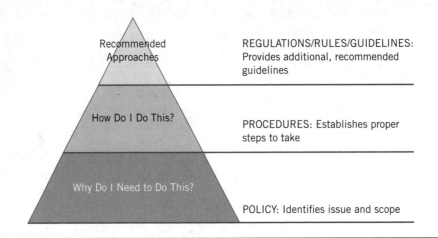

Figure 13.1 Relationship Between Policy, Procedures, and Guidelines

Recommended Approaches

REGULATIONS/RULES/GUIDELINES: Provides additional, recommended guidelines

How Do I Do This?

PROCEDURES: Establishes proper steps to take

Why Do I Need to Do This?

POLICY: Identifies issue and scope

Who Are Policy Makers?

Rules: Recommendations about the expected behavior during the course of following procedures, with examples of how to deal with specific instances one may encounter.

Guidelines: Recommendations about the expected behavior during the course of following procedures, with examples of how to deal with specific instances one may encounter.

Policy makers: Individuals in a position who create the principles, rules, and laws that guide a government, an organization, or people that are carried out by a government or business groups.

For your research to influence policy makers, you know who the policy makers are. Most broadly, **policy makers** are individuals in a position with the authority to decide the principles, rules, and laws that guide a government, organization, or people. For much of Santos's (Santos & Santos, 2016), Brunson's (Brunson & Weitzer, 2009), and Dodge's (Dodge et al. 2005) research, police chiefs are the policy makers. For much of Melde's research (Melde, Taylor, & Esbensen, 2009), policy makers are school superintendents. And is Cuevas's (Sabina, Cuevas, & Cotignola-Pickens, 2016) and Zaykowski's (2014), policy makers are generally those at the state and the federal level who can change policies related to victimization. For example, Cuevas and colleagues' published research (Sabina et al., 2016) focused on sexual violence assault against Latina women was used in congressional briefing documents. Zaykowski's continued relationship with those in the Department of Justice who focus on victimization means her work (Zaykowski, 2014) will be influential in policy going forward. Many of our featured authors engage in evaluation research, which by definition is relevant. By using the findings from this work, programs or policies are influenced. Policy is so complex that it cannot be managed by only a handful of people. This means that policy makers can be found in a multitude of places. Policy makers exist at the local, state, and federal levels. Policy makers can be elected officials, bureaucrats, civil servants, or individuals appointed to important roles in the community. Policy makers are found at the International Association of Chiefs of Police (IACP), the U.S. Senate, county commissioner offices, and university presidential suites. Policy makers may also be individuals who work closely with those just named. Policy makers can lead agencies in the executive, legislative, and court branches of government, and they can be found in think tanks, lobbying groups, professional organizations, or other organizations. Brunson argues that we all have the potential to be policy makers. Are you a community leader? Do you work in a place that has influence over others? Are you a member of a social club or religious organization? A policy maker, Brunson notes, is just a person who is positioned politically, or socially, to have his or her directives and recommendations put into practice. That may be you.

Who a policy maker is depends on the particular issue or research of interest. Consider the research conducted by Santos and Santos (2016) that focuses on intensive policing. Who would the appropriate policy maker be in this case? It would not be someone in the courts. And it would not be someone working at a think tank who focuses on energy issues. Rather, for Santos and colleague's work on intensive policing, local police chiefs are the policy makers they would want to work with, educate, and influence. Think of the work by Melde and his colleagues (2009) on the protective function of gang membership among adolescents. Consider a body of research that finds that one program minimizes risk of violence to students. Which policy maker would need to learn about this? Obvious policy makers would be school district superintendents and members of school boards. For others, policy makers may be city council members, mayors, Homeland Security directors, U.S. senators, influential think tanks, or governors. At the federal level, policy makers include members of the House, Senate, and many individuals leading departments and bureaus in the executive, legislative, and judicial branches. In regard to criminal justice policy, the attorney general is one policy maker. In addition, there are other policy makers leading bureaus in the Office of Justice Programs. Those crafting prison and jail policy would also be of interest for some research. Policy makers and those who support them are critical in making policy-relevant research in that they can support your research throughout the policy process.

Policy makers can be found everywhere. In this image, environmental policy maker Ivonne A-Baki, secretary of state for Yasuni-ITT Initiative, Republic of Ecuador, gives a lecture at the The Issam Fares Institute's Climate Change and Environment in the Arab World Program in 2016.

The Policy Process

Earlier in the chapter we noted that researchers have not been as successful at using their research to influence policy as they have been at generating general knowledge and at evaluating existing programs. There are many reasons for this lack of success. Understanding the reasons, and avoiding them, is important to maximize the chances that your research will be policy relevant. A reason for some lack of success is the failure of many researchers to understand the stages of the policy process and where in that process researchers can exert some influence. For example, during the agenda setting stage, a researcher can conduct a needs assessment. During the policy formulation stage, a literature review or meta-analysis is valuable. During the policy implementation stage, a formative evaluation is influential. And finally during the policy evaluation stage, a summative evaluation provides essential evaluative information. The policy process was introduced in Chapter 11 given its connection with evaluation research. In this chapter, we revisit it and provide greater detail.

The policy process, also known as the policy cycle, is a simplified representation of the stages of policy making and implementation. An illustrated version of the policy cycle is useful as a learning tool, but it is important to recognize that policy is not created in the real world in this way (see Figure 13.2). Nonetheless, a consideration of this tidy representation of the policy process is instructive. As Cairney (n.d.) notes, the policy process is unrealistic and useful at once. This presentation of the policy process is based on five major stages: problem identification/agenda setting, policy formation, policy adoption, policy implementation, and policy evaluation. Although Figure 13.2 illustrates the five discrete stages, in fact, these stages overlap and influence one another. In addition, the policy process is a continuous loop in which each stage informs the others, but it also goes backward and forward among all the stages. As we learn more about a particular policy at one stage, we can make adjustments at other stages of the policy process to improve attention to the issue of interest.

Figure 13.2 Policy Making and Implementation

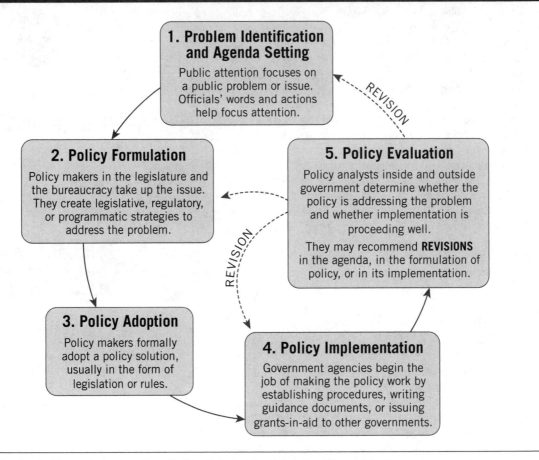

1. **Problem Identification and Agenda Setting**
Public attention focuses on a public problem or issue. Officials' words and actions help focus attention.

2. **Policy Formulation**
Policy makers in the legislature and the bureaucracy take up the issue. They create legislative, regulatory, or programmatic strategies to address the problem.

5. **Policy Evaluation**
Policy analysts inside and outside government determine whether the policy is addressing the problem and whether implementation is proceeding well.
They may recommend **REVISIONS** in the agenda, in the formulation of policy, or in its implementation.

3. **Policy Adoption**
Policy makers formally adopt a policy solution, usually in the form of legislation or rules.

4. **Policy Implementation**
Government agencies begin the job of making the policy work by establishing procedures, writing guidance documents, or issuing grants-in-aid to other governments.

REVISION

Source: Reprinted with permission from Texas Politics Project at the University of Texas at Austin.

Problem Identification/Agenda Setting

Problem identification/ agenda setting: First stage of the policy process that occurs when the public brings an issue to the attention of policy makers and demands something be done to address this issue.

Focusing event: Event that captures the attention of policy makers, the public, and the media simultaneously like a major disaster or other crises.

The first stage in the policy process is problem identification/agenda setting. **Problem identification/agenda setting** occurs when an issue is brought to the attention of policy makers with demands, or evidence (e.g., 9/11 terrorist attack) that something be done to address the issue. In plain language, this stage involves the identification of the problem to be solved and the advocating that it be placed on the policy makers' agenda for further consideration. Many individuals or groups can bring something to the attention of a policy maker including members of the researchers, public, elites, the media, advocacy groups, interest groups, think tanks, university groups, or a focusing event among others. A **focusing event** is an event that captures policy makers, public attention, and media attention simultaneously like a major disaster or other crises. The Patriot Act and 9/11 is an example of a focusing event.

Think of the many criminal justice issues that you believe demand policy attention but are not getting adequate attention. Perhaps you are thinking about intensive policing. Or maybe you are focused on policing strategies especially as they relate to the role that race may play in that. Rather, your issue of great interest may center on youth joining gangs and how that affects their risk of being violently victimized. You may want to see policies that implement programs in schools to help adolescents. Maybe you are most concerned about victims failing to get the assistance they needed, or maybe you are most concerned about college student victimization and campus safety. If these are important issues, then bringing them to the attention of a policy maker, and emphasizing the importance of adding the issue to the agenda for more consideration, is the first stage.

This initial stage of policy identification and agenda setting is one in which researchers and their research can be influential if heard among other voices bringing issues to the attention of policy makers. It is at this stage that policy makers can be informed and educated about what research findings and recommendations indicate about an issue. Nevertheless, bringing an issue to the attention of a policy maker is only one part of the problem identification and agenda setting stage. The policy maker must sift through all the competing issues to decide which ones to move forward in the policy process. Think back to the issues just described. If you were a policy maker, which of these issues would you focus on given your limited time, expertise, and space on an agenda. Which would you pay less (or no) attention to? What would lead you to focus on one issue over another? Researchers and their research are only one of a competing sea of voices trying to get the attention of policy makers about a myriad of issues.

Policy formation: Second step in the policy process that includes the design of one or multiple approaches to solve the problem of interest.

Policy adoption: Third stage in the policy process that refers to the formal adoption of the policy often in the form of a law.

Policy Formulation

Should a policy issue be taken up by a policy maker and placed on an agenda for further consideration, the next stage in the policy process is policy formation. **Policy formation** is the second stage in the policy process, and it includes the design of multiple approaches, policies, programs, or formal ways to address the problem of interest. After several formal policy options are designed, the policy makers then identify and select what they see as the best policy solution of the group. This stage in the policy process requires compromise among policy makers and other parties to select the final policy that will be either adopted or rejected by the appropriate governing body. Policy formulation has a tangible goal of a bill or policy that goes before the policy making authority for formal adoption.

Let's imagine that policy makers in the state in which you live have decided to develop a policy to deal with the increasing opioid crisis. The opioid crisis affects the criminal justice system as law enforcement officers respond to calls about overdoses, robberies, violence, and burglaries caused by the drug. Judges deal with the opioid crisis in that they face those who have been arrested for using or dealing this drug. The correctional system then faces an onslaught of those convicted of these crimes, as well as those who are in jail because they cannot post bail (or were not offered bail). Finally, victims of crimes committed as a result of those seeking resources for more drugs are clearly affected by this crisis. What types of policies would you recommend be considered to address this issue? Given this issue goes beyond the criminal justice system (e.g., child maltreatment, foster care, public health, etc.), what sorts of policies would you design if you were a policy maker? How would you choose which one to ultimately consider for adoption?

Researchers and their research can be influential during the policy formation stage. Researchers can offer substantive expertise about what research indicates will and will not be effective as a policy. Researchers can educate policy makers about the various policies before them for consideration.

Policy Adoption

Once the best policy option has been identified, adoption by the appropriate governing body is required. **Policy adoption** is the third stage in the policy process, and it refers to the formal adoption or passage of the policy, which legitimizes the policy. Policies are often

© Joe Raedle/Getty Images

adopted in the form of a law. Even if one bill manages to be adopted by one policy-making body, it may need to be passed or adopted by another. It may be that any policy will have to be successfully adopted by multiple groups before it is formally adopted. Researchers who have a dialogue with policy makers could influence and educate policy maker's votes on policy adoption. These researchers can also find themselves at the table of stakeholders who work toward policy adoption. Their dialogue, based on research, can include what benefits and limitations the policy offers.

Policy Implementation

Policy implementation is the fourth stage of the policy process in which agencies (generally not the bodies that formulated or adopted the policies) operationalize the adopted policy. Adopted policies are not detailed about *how* the policy is to be implemented. Thus, policy implementation includes the drafting of specific procedures, regulations, rules, and guidance to be used by those tasked with carrying out the adopted policy. The policy implementation stage is yet another place that researchers and their research can be influential. Policy-relevant research can provide guidance about specific procedures, regulations, and guidelines considered to lead toward the best way to implement the policy. Policy implementation often involves research that analyzes the cause-and-effect relationships between the problem (i.e., prison riots) and the solution (i.e., solitary confinement) to understand what works and what does not work to solve problems.

Policy Evaluation

The fifth stage in the policy process is policy evaluation. **Policy evaluation** includes activities designed to determine whether a policy and its associated programs are addressing the problems they were intended to address, if the policy as implemented is cost effective, the presence of any negative unintended consequences, and whether the implementation occurred as it was designed. The findings from policy evaluation are useful for adjusting all stages of the policy process. The evaluation may identify problems such as parts of the problem that are not being addressed. The evaluation may provide feedback by identifying a new problem and altering the policy agenda. Policy evaluation may highlight issues with policy formation as noted by negative unintended consequences. And policy evaluation can identify whether the policy implementation needs adjustment as well. The findings from a policy evaluation provide the feedback needed that results in policy improvement over time. As demonstrated in Chapter 11, policy evaluation is a place in which researchers can be influential.

Challenges of Getting Research to Policy Makers

The policy process reveals many places that a researcher can introduce policy-relevant research findings to influence policy design and implementation. Simply understanding the stages of the policy process, and the stages where influence by research is an option, however, is not enough. A researcher must also understand the additional challenges that make getting policy-relevant research—research that actually influences policy—to the policy makers. This section identifies many of those challenges.

Relationship and Communication Barriers

A common error that researchers make with regard to getting policy-relevant research to policy makers is that researchers frequently have no communication or relationship with policy makers. For many reasons, **communication** between researchers and policy makers is frequently lacking. First, researchers and policy makers exist in different, too frequently disconnected, worlds, and both researchers and policy makers have failed to bridge that gap. If you as a researcher want your work to be policy relevant, you must develop and maintain relationships with policy makers. Of course, this requires that the researcher know who the policy makers are, and many researchers do not know them. A researcher must know the individuals and groups who are policy makers on the topic of interest in order to share their research and expertise.

A good way to start a relationship with a policy maker is to pick up the phone and schedule a meeting to meet with him or her. Share your research and how that information can benefit the policy maker. In any meeting with a policy maker, you must be concise and clear, and you must verbally convey your information in plain English in a condensed document. A policy brief is a great example of this and will be discussed later in the chapter.

Another related way to develop and nurture relationships with policy makers is through networking. **Networking** is linking with, interacting with, and developing relationships with others to exchange information to achieve a goal. Networking may lead you to individuals you did not realize were influential, but they are. A great way to network is to attend policy-related events. Attend legislative functions that governmental agencies host. Attend events by think tanks and other interest groups. Attend or host university events that bring individuals interested in the topic as well as policy makers. Plus, networking is great for future career opportunities. Offer to present your research at these events.

The failure to communicate between researchers and policy makers goes both ways. If policy makers want to develop and implement policies informed by a body of well-conducted research, they must reach out to those who can share what the research says as well. That is usually people who have conducted that research. Nevertheless, policy makers may not even know that there is relevant research or researchers studying the topic of interest. Most researchers are more than happy to share their expertise about a topic if asked. Make knowing who is researching the policy-relevant topics easy for them to find. Most university websites have faculty and student pages that highlight research being conducted and research expertise. Calls to the deans of relevant schools and departments can identify students and faculty working on particular topics. Policy makers can also gain insight about subject matter experts by reading university communications (websites, newsletters, etc.) that highlight relevant ongoing research and areas of interest. One limitation to the idea that policy makers will reach out is simply that it rarely happens. As a result, it is your responsibility as a researcher to let the policy makers know you exist. Make sure you have a page highlighting your research. Make sure the university is sharing your research in its communications. Send an e-mail with a brief description of your research to policy makers. You can include your résumé with that e-mail, but don't only send your vita or résumé. Provide a brief description about why the policy maker needs you, and then follow up with a request for a meeting. This relationship, if nurtured, will be valuable in your quest for making your research policy relevant.

Communication: Reporting of findings to policy makers.

Networking: Linking with, or interacting with, others to exchange information to achieve a goal.

Nonaccessible Presentation of Research

Policy brief: Short two-to-four page document of about 1,500 words that in plain English presents research findings and policy recommendations to a nonacademic audience. Policy briefs include five sections: executive summary, introduction, approach and results, conclusion, and implications and recommendations.

Another common communication-related error that prevents research from being policy relevant is the failure to present your research findings in an accessible way for policy makers and others. Handing over a research paper or a journal article for policy makers to read all but guarantees it will be tossed out as soon as you leave. Research must be translated and formatted in easy-to-access and understandable ways for nonacademic audiences.

Three characteristics of effective communication are useful to keep in mind. First, make the message of your policy brief clear. State it early, state it often, and state it clearly. If the reader remembers one thing about your research, make sure it is this message. Second, think about the audience. Write the research for that audience. Avoid jargon and overly technical details. Many refer to the "mom test." That is, if your mom can read and understand it, then you have accomplished your goal.* Clearly, many moms can read technical, complex documents, but the point is that the writing must be easily accessible. Write it with the intended audience in mind. Finally, ensure that the document is attractive and inviting. Make a reader want to pick it up and begin reading. Make the reader want to continue reading once they begin.

As a researcher, you cannot sit back and passively hope that policy makers will find your amazing research and findings and understand how it can benefit them. That is not going to happen. Why? Because as a new researcher, your research is likely seen by no one aside from your professor. Of if you are working with a professor, your research might be published in a peer-reviewed journal. Policy makers most likely won't find your research in a journal. Journal access requires costly subscriptions. While you are in college you may have access, but once you have graduated and moved on, that access to journals is usually severed because of the high cost. This is the case for the general population as well who generally does not have access to journals or who is unwilling to pay for them.

This is problematic, but as noted, even if journals were widely available to policy makers and the public, it is unlikely they will wade through the 1,000s of journals available to find your nuggets of wisdom. How often do you as a student do this for your classes? Do you really expect a busy policy maker to do it? If you want to produce policy-relevant research, you must package that information for easy consumption by others. This does not include providing copies of your papers or articles to the policy maker. More must be done to translate the work for their consumption.

An excellent way to follow the three characteristics of effective communication and make your research easily accessible and easily understandable to policy makers and others is by writing a **policy brief**. A policy brief is an attractive, two- to four-page document of about 1,500 words. In this space, a researcher presents, in plain English, his or her research to a nonacademic audience. Policy briefs must be free of jargon, and they must simplify, clarify, and make understanding the research, findings, and policy implications easy. The policy brief must clearly state what the problem you addressed is, what current knowledge exists, and what gap you addressed. Findings and policy recommendations must be stated prominently and clearly so the policy maker can easily find them. Providing useful photos and graphs to make your point is a plus and encourages further reading. Figures are especially useful as the adage notes, "A picture is worth a thousand words." If technical information must be included, it should be included in an appendix. Policy briefs are critical. They must be written. The other voices competing for the attention of policy makers are writing them, so you must do the same to hope to be heard.

Remember, policy makers are busy people, and as the policy process highlights, you and your research are competing with other issues and voices. No one, including policy

---

*While many refer to the "mom test" this is not to suggest that moms are dumb. It refers to the possibility that your mom will not be an expert in the substantive area of your research only. She is however an expert in many other ways and must explain that information to you using the "kid test."

makers, wants to read walls of text filled with jargon to figure out what your research offers them. The key is to communicate with policy makers in a way that accessing and understanding your research is easy, uncomplicated, and has clear policy implications spelled out. Sharing policy briefs at meetings and networking events will maximize the chances that your work as a researcher will be read. The "Making a Policy Brief" box provided later in this chapter offers additional information about constructing a policy brief.

Competing Sources of Influence

Another challenge making it difficult to get policy-relevant research to policy makers mentioned in this chapter is that researchers are only one voice in a sea of competing voices faced by a policy maker. Therefore, research is often kept from influencing policy because it is not heard by a policy maker who is bombarded with other powerful, overlapping sources of influence, including the media, fear, ill-informed perceptions, advocacy groups, ideology, and budgets that influence personal opinions. This section addresses each of these topics in greater detail.

"I want you to draft the bill with all your usual precision and flair. Explain its purposes, justify its expenditures, emphasize how it fits the broad aims of democratic progress. And one other thing: Can you make it sound like a tax cut?"

Media

The media is a major voice being heard by policy makers. The influence of the media can keep policy-relevant research from affecting policy. In the United States, we made a policy decision to not have publicly supported media (with a few exceptions such as NPR or PBS), so our media must make profits to remain in business. This means advertising is important to them. As a result, the purpose of the **media** is to deliver viewers to its advertisers (contrary to what any media outlet tells you). This is most effectively done by showing viewers things that keep them coming back to watch more. Crime, violence, and mayhem are extremely effective at getting viewers to return to a media source repeatedly. For this reason, media outlets, including news outlets and non-news shows, are dominated by stories of crime and violence.

Unfortunately, this immersion in crime, gore, and violence in the media leads to a gross misunderstanding of the actual nature of crime, victimization, and the criminal justice system. As a result, the public develops misperceptions about and a warped sense of important criminal justice issues. The public then takes these issues to policy makers (who themselves are influenced by the media) and demands policies to address them. Unfortunately, these demands are often based on poor information, raw emotion, and little fact.

Fear

Related to the media's portrayal of crime and violence is fear. Fear is something that can keep policy-relevant research from affecting policy. Research shows that the criminal justice information portrayed in the media is associated with heightened fear among the public. Melde reminds us that a certain amount of fear of violence and crime is healthy. He noted in his video interview for this book, "Would we find it problematic if people were not afraid of secondhand smoke? No. Being fearful of that is important." What is unhealthy is that many parts of the public have a disproportionate amount of fear of crime in relation to their risk of victimization. When the public consults the media and sees violence committed all over the world, and sees the same violent incidents played over and over again (**looping**), members of the public come to believe that crime is worse than it really is. In this way, fear often drives what the public thinks policy makers should be focused on.

In the case of producing policy relevant research, avoid jargon. The goal when sharing research findings is for the public to be able to understand you.

Media: Competing voice heard by policy makers that has the goal of delivering viewers to their advertisers.

Looping: Tactic used by the media where a particular crime or violent event is repeated over and over again.

Advocacy group: Collection of individuals who operate to influence public opinion, policy makers, regarding particular criminal justice issues that require immediate attention and policy. Also known as an "interest group."

Furthermore, this saturation in viewing violence also tends to make the public feel that violence and crime are worse than they have ever been. This is the source of demands for policies that will return us to the "good old days." Ironically, the good old days had substantially higher rates of violence and property crime than we experience today. By using FBI Uniform Crime Reporting System data, as well as the National Crime Victimization Survey data, we can see that there is no question that rates of property and violent crime have declined drastically since the early 1990s. Regardless, the public seems to believe that crime is out of control and our society less safe than it has ever been. The public fails to recognize that given technology, they are now immersed in violent media portrayals of the world that was not accessible so easily in the good old days. Policy makers are themselves often unclear about the current and former rates of violence and property, and many of them fall prey to this same fear. In addition, some willingly take advantage of this fear and promise "tough-on-crime" policies should they be elected to an official position. The result is that both the public and policy makers clamor for tough-on-crime policies even when the available body of research shows the many of the demanded policies are unneeded, ineffective, or, worse, destructive and costly.

Advocacy and Interest Groups

A third important influence that can keep policy-relevant research from affecting policy are **advocacy groups,** also known as interest groups, that operate with the goal of affecting policy makers and ultimately policy. An advocacy or interest group is an organization of individuals who seek to influence public opinion, policy makers, and policy. Advocacy and interest groups lobby policy makers and the public to persuade them that particular criminal justice issues require immediate attention and policy solutions. An example of an innovative nonprofit advocacy group is Breaking Silence. With offices in Colorado and California (see www.breakingsilenceco.org), Breaking Silence has a mission that "engages and inspires communities to take action and recognize their responsibility for the impact interpersonal violence (IPV) has on our culture. The organization is committed to promoting empathy,

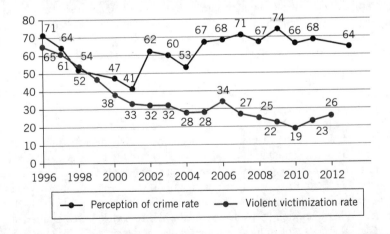

Figure 13.3 U.S. Violent Crime Rate vs. Americans' Perception of Crime Rate vs. a Year Ago

Source: Adapted from "Most Americans Still See Crime Up Over Last Year," Justin McCarthy, *Gallup News,* November 21, 2014.

healing and open dialogue through a traveling interactive exhibit in which the stories of survivors are brought to life with chilling realism."

A well-known advocacy group affecting criminal justice policy is the National Rifle Association (NRA). The NRA was founded in 1871 to "promote and encourage rifle shooting on a scientific basis" (NRA, n.d., para. 1). Even though the NRA continues to be a force dedicated to firearm education, it has expanded its influence to include other activities including lobbying. The NRA began direct lobbying in 1975 with the formation of the Institute for Legislative Action (ILA). The ILA lobbies policy makers to implement assorted policies in response to what it perceives as ongoing attacks on the Second Amendment. Today, the NRA views itself as the oldest operational civil rights organization, and it is a major political force when it comes to firearm policy in the United States. For example, the NRA successfully lobbied policy makers in Congress who then required that "none of the funds made available for injury prevention and control at the Centers for Disease Control and Prevention may be used to advocate or promote gun control" (Luo, 2011, para. 11; NRA-ILA, 2001). This example shows how some advocacy and interest groups can influence policy by drowning out the voices of some researchers, and can even prevent research from being conducted although it might inform important criminal justice policies.

Researchers compete with advocacy and interest groups to influence policy makers and, ultimately, policy. Although there is competition with these groups for the attention of policy makers, it is not necessarily the case that researchers and advocacy and interest groups are at odds with one another. In fact, many researchers and advocacy groups have interests that align, which could suggest a collaborative opportunity.

Ideology

Ideology, whether religious, economic or political, is another powerful influence on policy makers that can keep policy-relevant research from affecting policy. **Ideology** is a set of ideas that creates one's economic, political, or social view of the world. Ideology is powerful and can blind someone to contrary evidence found in research. It can prompt members of the public and other groups to lobby policy makers for wanted policy. Ideology can cause a policy maker to even doubt whether research is valuable at all. It is challenging to make your research policy relevant when policy makers themselves do not believe in research and research findings or that it can offer valuable policy implications. Consider the role of political ideology on incarceration policy. Most liberals believe that the criminal justice system should focus on rehabilitation, which means policies promoting less incarceration. Conservatives generally opt for a punitive approach requiring longer, and tougher, prison terms be given to those convicted of crimes. What is your viewpoint? Should we focus on rehabilitation, or should we focus on a harsher imprisonment? Why do you think that? Is it your ideology, or are you aware of what research has to say about this topic? When ideology guides your decision making, it may do so in a way that is contrary to the findings of a large, rich body of research on the same topic. As a result, ideology can influence policy in ways that may worsen versus ameliorate an important social issue.

The NRA successfully lobbied policy makers in Congress who enacted policies requiring "none of the funds made available for injury prevention and control at the Centers for Disease Control and Prevention may be used to advocate or promote gun control." How might this affect policy on gun violence in the United States?

Ideology: Set of ideas and ideals that form one's economic, political, or social views of the world.

Budget Constraints

Budget constraints are something that can keep policy-relevant research from affecting policy. We live in a world with finite financial resources. This means that even when the best

Although defendants are entitled to effective assistance of counsel, research by Williams (2017) suggests appointed counsel in particular often fail to provide effective assistance, and negative case outcomes (e.g., conviction, longer sentences) result. The purpose of this research is to investigate whether the types of counsel—public defender versus retained—influences bail decisions. The following three hypotheses were addressed in this research:

1. There is no relationship between type of counsel and whether or not defendants are denied bail.

2. Defendants with public defenders are less likely to be released prior to case outcome than are defendants with retained counsel.

3. Defendants with public defenders will be assigned higher bail amounts than will defendants with retained counsel.

To conduct this research, Williams (2017) used the 1990 to 2004 State Court Processing Statistics data set collected by the U.S. Department of Justice's Bureau of Justice Statistics. These secondary data were downloaded from ICPSR and include felony defendant data from the nation's 75 most populated counties. For the purposes of this study, the researchers focused on counties in Florida because it allows for indigent defendants who may be facing incarceration the right to appointed counsel at bail hearings.

Analytic techniques include first describing the data (using descriptives) followed by a series of regressions to address the hypotheses. An examination of whether the type of attorney influences whether bailed was denied showed that the odds of bail being denied was 1.8 times higher for defendants with public defenders compared with those with retained counsel. This finding does not offer support for Hypothesis 1. The second regression investigated whether attorney type influences whether a defendant was released. The findings show that defendants with public defenders were less likely to be released prior to case outcome than were defendants with retained counsel. This finding supports the second hypothesis. And finally, regression output indicated that defendants with public defenders had lower bail amounts than had defendants with retained counsel, which does not support Hypothesis 3.

This research has important policy implications. First, the difference between appointed and retained counsel is vital in the earlier stages of a case when decisions are made regarding a defendant's fate. Although most attention considers case outcome, this research highlights the need to be alert to disadvantages throughout the process. Yet, the news reported here is not all bad. Even though defendants with public defenders were more likely to be denied bail and less likely to be released, they also benefited from lower bail amounts and from nonfinancial release options. All defendants deserve equal representation regardless of the stage of the process and the type of attorney representing them.

Williams, M. R. (2017). The effect of attorney type on bail decisions, *Criminal Justice Policy Review, 28*(1), 3–17.

Budgets: Provide information about how much money and other resources can be spent on an items. Policies are subject to budget constraints.

body of research points to a particular policy that would produce excellent outcomes, it may be too expensive to implement. **Budgets** provide information about how much money and other resources can be spent in any given period. Budgets are important considerations when it comes to policy design and implementation. Consider a policy that offers free housing, education, and job training to those convicted of a crime after the are released from prison in order to greatly reduce recidivism. Although research may show that this type of intensive intervention leads to far better outcomes, funding such an approach may be prohibitive. This is just one example of budgets and limited funds getting in the way of research findings influencing policy.

Maximizing Chances of Producing Policy-Relevant Research

So far, we have identified all those things that make getting policy-relevant research to policy makers challenging. This section take a more positive view and offers actions that you as a researcher can do to maximize the chance that your research will gain the attention of the policy maker and ultimately influence policy.

Plan to Be Policy Relevant From the Start

One way you can maximize the probability that your research will be policy relevant is by thinking of policy relevance early when the research project is being designed. A common error that researchers make in regard to producing policy-relevant research is not considering policy relevance until the research is complete. A researcher must think about the policy relevance of their research at the earliest stages of planning the research. Waiting until research is complete may be too late, or at best, it will minimize the chances that the research will be policy relevant. You as a researcher must understand existing policy and policy gaps that require research attention to produce policy-relevant research. You as a researcher must formulate research questions that are useful to policy makers. You as a researcher must have a relationship with policy makers before research has begun. In some cases, including a policy maker on the research team is beneficial for all parties. The researchers gain a great deal of understanding of what is important to policy makers. And policy makers as research partners feel some ownership of the research. This relationship means the researcher and the research has the assistance in getting the attention needed to influence the policy process. By thinking about policy relevance in the planning stages of research, you can maximize the chances that your work will be useful in the design and implementation of policy.

Relationship

Another "must do" to maximize the chance of producing policy-relevant research is to develop and maintain a relationship with policy makers relevant to your research interests. First, you must learn who the policy makers relevant to your area of research are. You must learn where they are. Then you must reach out and make contact with those policy makers. This may happen on a one-on-one basis or at a networking event. Should you get some one-on-one time with the policy maker, be prepared to share, in plain English, what your research is about, how it relates to the policy of interest, and how your research can guide the policy maker. Offer the policy maker policy briefs of your work. And make clear that you are available to the policy maker for her future needs. Access to a policy maker can also be made through his or her associates. Find out who they are as well. Reach out to them and develop a relationship with them. Include them on research projects. Be respectful of the policy maker and his or her staff's time as they are busy and have many competing issues and voices making demands of them. Your goal is to let them know how you can help them and make their lives easier.

Translating Your Research

And third, translate your research and findings to policy makers to maximize the chances it will be policy relevant. Do not expect policy makers to find you and your research. It is up to you as a researcher to find them and let them know you and your work is available and important to them. One option is for researchers to submit their research that bridges the academic and policy/general audience population at the following website: https://theconversation.com. This website is also used by the media when it is looking for an expert to speak with on a specific topics. A good example of an accessible piece of research is found at https://theconversation.com/what-do-special-educators-need-to-succeed-55559, regarding an education topic.

As a researcher, you must present your results in a way that allows policy makers to use them to make their own arguments convincing to others. Writing in an accessible way and providing an accurate, but compelling, statistic are some ways to accomplish this.

Ideally, you will have an ongoing relationship with policy makers and their associates. You need to provide them information in an easy-to-use format that is jargon free to help policy makers and other audiences see how your research can inform policy. As noted, using policy briefs is ideal. Additional means to communicate policy-relevant research to policy makers exist. One is to attend or host a policy forum or, ideally, a series of forums where policy makers are invited to both attend and to participate on a panel dedicated to a particular topic. Additional, you can produce a regularly published newsletter, or blog, focused on policy issues and related policy findings that is disseminated to policy makers. For example, the Alaska Justice Forum offers a large assortment of policy publications that make connecting with policy makers (and the public) easy (see https://www.uaa.alaska.edu/academics/college-of-health/departments/justice-center/alaska-justice-forum/). Providing clear and concise information about the issue and clear policy recommendations that they can take back and implement maximizes the chances that your research is valuable to policy makers who are busy and thrive on easy to access to, and easily digestible, policy information.

Common Pitfalls in Producing Policy-Relevant Research

Several common pitfalls associated with attempts at producing policy-relevant research have been emphasized in this chapter but bear repeating here. These include believing all research is policy relevant (it is not), failing to address policy-relevant questions, and waiting too long to consider the policy relevance of your research.

Producing Research That Is Not Policy Relevant

Researchers often mistakenly believe that all research they conduct is policy relevant. It is not. Every piece of research conducted and published is not useful to policy makers. Cuevas has witnessed some researchers who try to shoehorn everything they do into policy work when it simply does not fit the bill. If you as a researcher have that relationship with relevant policy makers, then they can help in developing research questions that will allow researchers to address policy questions.

To know whether your research is policy relevant, consider these questions. Does your research address a policy need? Which policy? How does it address the need? Have you as a researcher educated yourself about existing policies related to your research topic? What policy gaps exist? How does your research fill those gaps? What new information does your research offer? If you as a researcher cannot answer these questions, and you cannot identify the policies your work is related to, then you have work to do before you can produce policy-relevant research. Although it may be true that your research may be picked up and used to influence policy, your chances are better if you design your work with an eye toward existing policies and whether your research addresses policy gaps.

Failing to Recognize How Your Research Is Relevant

Policy-relevant research focuses on specific research questions that produce findings of interest to policy makers. Recall earlier chapters where we discussed several types of research guided by different questions. We described exploratory research as useful when little or nothing is known about a topic. The purpose or goal of exploratory research is to answer questions such as "What is it?" "How is it done?" or "Where is it?" Descriptive research is similar to explanatory research, although it is much more narrowly focused on a topic given knowledge gained from earlier exploratory research. Descriptive research addresses questions such as "What is it?" "What are the characteristics of it?" or "What does it look like?" In contrast, explanatory research provides explanations about a topic to answer questions such as "Why is it?" "How is it?" "What is the effect of it?" "What causes it?" or "What predicts it?" Exploratory and descriptive research offers some insight into what social problems exist. In this way, they can inform the agenda setting part of the policy cycle. Nevertheless, all the rich descriptive and exploratory research in the world cannot inform policy implementation or implications. If your goal is to bring attention to a social problem, descriptive and explanatory research questions are useful, yet this work cannot offer insight into implementation and implications.

In earlier chapters, we described explanatory research as useful for identifying what characteristics are related to a topic, as well as what impacts, causes, or influences a particular outcome or topic of interest. In addition, through explanatory research, you can gain understanding about how to predict outcomes or topics of interest. Explanatory research is ideal for policy-relevant research because it focuses on more or improved understanding of complex causation associated with an issue. For example, explanatory research can provide new ideas about what works and what doesn't work regarding a policy. Explanatory research can offer new information about what works for different people in different circumstances regarding a policy. Research that influences the design implementation and implications is based on more complex research questions, making explanatory approaches ideal. Explanatory research can provide an understanding as to why something is the way it is (which requires an understanding of what causes it) or what predicts something. This type of information is useful in the creation of and implementation of a policy.

Failure to Know Relevant Policy Makers

Another common pitfall is to not have a relationship with policy makers. If you don't know who policy makers are, you can't take your findings to them. To think that policy makers will find your research is fantasy. You must take the findings to them. This pitfall is related to the fourth pitfall, which is to fail to produce information about the research for more general audiences. Handing someone your journal article to read means it won't be read (try this at a party and see how it goes). Handing a policy maker a journal article ends the same way. One must create policy briefs or develop other means of communication of the research that is easy to access and easy to understand.

Going Beyond Your Data and Findings

And finally, a pitfall of producing policy-relevant research is to go beyond your data and findings. This is true of all research as well. A researcher must base his or her findings and policy recommendations on the data gathered. And a researcher must base his or her policy recommendation on the findings from those data. A good researcher does not go beyond the evidence and information he or she has systematically gathered and analyzed to develop the conclusions and policy recommendations presented. Other influences such as ideology, intuition, or personal beliefs have no place in a policy discussion. As a researcher, the policy maker relies on you to provide information based on evidence and data. Your expertise is valuable—your unrelated opinions are not.

Another pitfall is that researchers too often assume that science and evidence should and can trump politics. Policy decisions are inherently political decisions, and therefore, the policy makers must consider trade-offs between values, evidence, economics, and so on. Although this may seem frustrating and disappointing, it is a part of the process. It should not mean that you as a researcher should not interface with policy makers, even if it doesn't always translate to the outcomes our research points to.

Ethics and Conducting Policy-Relevant Research

Being guided by ethics is a constant in all research we conduct. When one is producing and sharing policy-relevant research that does not change. This section offers some ethical considerations to keep in mind when conducting policy-relevant research. First, whether in writing or verbally, you as a researchers must always be clear about the limitations of your research. No research is perfect, including yours. Policy makers may hope that your research offers some important information regarding a policy, and it is up to you to ensure that the policy maker understands exactly what your research can and cannot be used to support. Never go beyond your data and findings regardless of the temptation to do so.

Research, including policy-relevant research, requires replication. A policy should never be established or altered based on a single study. Again, no research is perfect. Only through replication can we gain more confidence in our outcomes. A classic error in establishing policy based on a single study (against the advice of the researcher) is the Minneapolis Domestic Violence Experiment conducted in 1981–1982. This single study was used to support the adoption of mandatory arrest policies throughout the United States. Later replication of this study in five additional locations with the policy in practice demonstrated that mandatory arrest policies are extremely problematic. The findings from the five replications showed some evidence of the benefits of mandatory arrest, yet others found that mandatory arrest is associated with more repeat offending. Yet, most policies that are adopted are difficult to end. The mandatory arrest policy is no different. The point is that replication is the key, and no one research study should be used to implement a policy. Maybe policy makers do not know this. It is up to you as the researcher to make it clear.

Santos points out another ethical issue that one must consider when producing policy-relevant research. That is, researchers must guard against whether the policy advice they are providing is biased by their personal opinions. Or it may be that a researcher feels pressure to produce research that supports a particular group's point of view. Both of these issues indicate a lack of objectivity and straying from the principles of scientific research. This risk means that researchers must continually question whether what they are finding is based on the evidence or on an opinion. As Brunson stated in his phone interview conducted for this book, if you as a researcher "are helping guide policy, you have to be more diligent and committed to adhering to the rules and expectations of conducting good science." All our case study researchers made this point during their interviews. For example, Dodge stated that "a researcher must make conclusions based on their data and analysis only."

At times, working with nonresearchers such as policy makers can present challenges. Nonresearchers may not understand the process or the importance of research methodology and want you to find the finding they want versus the finding that comes from the data. As a researcher, you must remain ethical and maintain your objectivity. You do not want to become known as a "hired gun" type of researchers who gives policy makers what they want. Nothing is worth your integrity.

Policy Expert—Katie TePas

Katie TePas never knew what she would do when she grew up, but she was certain it would be working with people in a social justice capacity. She has always been certain that every person has a right to have a life full of joy, happiness, and health like she has had, and she has always wanted to be a part of making that happen. She was raised with the expectation that she would work with people and make the world a better place for others. Little did she know that her path would take her to working with state troopers in Alaska, helping survivors of violence against women across Alaska, and even advising the governor of Alaska on policy-relevant research.

Currently, TePas is consulting and taking time off to travel the world. Before this, however, her path was varied. She graduated from college and worked in Fairbanks at a sexual assault and domestic violence center. After spending time there, she knew she wanted to pursue a master's degree. After completing that, she returned to Alaska and got a job with the state troopers where she managed a Violence Against Women grant and operated as the Alaska state trainer for 11 years. This eventually put her in Governor Sean Parnell's circle where she advised on policy. When Governor Parnell was not reelected, TePas returned to the State Trooper's Association for several years. She now works as a consultant when she isn't traveling to Mongolia or other amazing destinations to develop programs designed to reduce violence against women and offer services to those who have experienced it.

The nexus between policy and research is a critical influence in her work. For example, while working with the State Trooper's Association, TePas recognized she needed concrete data to get the troopers to where she wanted them to be in terms of sexual assault response and investigations. To get the needed data, she turned to Andre Rosay, PhD, a professor and the director of the Justice Center at the University of Alaska Anchorage. Designing the methodology to collect the needed data was easy, but it took years to develop the necessary relationship and trust among all stakeholders to support the collection of these data. Finally, a leader in the State Trooper's Association was confident enough to know the data could show how well they were doing, as well as to point to areas for improvement. With this relationship, the project launched.

Courtesy of Katie Tepas

The first project included an evaluation of domestic violence and sexual assault cases. This research then spun off onto a study on prosecution rates. In the end, this work provided the evidence to hire village public safety officers, which was especially beneficial in rural areas. People began reporting victimization early and using services more frequently, which led to even more public safety officers being funded. Another part of this partnership was the launching of the first Alaska Victimization Survey. This statewide victimization survey provided the baseline data of violence that resulted in additional funding and in more useful policies, procedures, and practices. The national study led to regional victimization surveys that allowed policy changes at the community level. All of this work, and other research not mentioned, resulted from meaningful dialogue and research that pulled back the curtain of violence in Alaska. With this problem in the open, TePas and her colleagues were able to reduce the amount of violence. Although the domestic violence rates in Alaska continue to be the highest in the nation, she knows that by using policy-relevant research, people's lives have been improved. Some have even been saved.

Today, the Justice Center and TePas continue to have a great relationship with the Alaska legislative body. They testify frequently to help policy makers understand the best policies to serve the population. The researchers are well respected because of their relationship with policy makers and because they can be counted on as an objective third party. Their research continues to be translated into attainable policy implications.

TePas has advice for students today. First, she encourages all students to ask the hard questions when you see a research finding. Where did the data come from? How were concepts measured? What methods were used? She notes the importance of finding and reading the original study because you cannot trust anyone else's depiction of that research. See it for yourself, and make an assessment of the original.

Second, TePas strongly encourages all students to intern and work in the field. It is only through this experience that you can see whether you belong there or whether your skills and passions are better suited elsewhere. For instance, she is now in social work but once thought she'd do clinical work. While working at the domestic violence shelter, however, she found she was frustrated with existing policy. She knew that had to change to make these survivors' lives better. Without that internship and employment at the shelter, she would have never taken the path she is on. Her passion remains the same, but how she used it changed.

Third, TePas implores students to learn early the importance of relationship building. A constant in her success is relationships. She notes that the relationships she built along the way have always proved valuable. Not only have they allowed her to be effective in all of her roles, but they have also led to other great opportunities. She has come to recognize the power of relationships and social networking. It is the key.

Finally, TePas encourages people to embrace the open doors that their relationships offer. Go through that door and see what is on the other side. It may be a chance to work with the governor (or become governor!) and to use research to make policy that matters.

Chapter Wrap-Up

This text has described many skills associated with research methodology. Something they all have in common are that they are important skills that are demand in the job market. This chapter focuses on yet another very important but frequently overlooked skill—making research relevant. To do so, you must understand research methods and you must be able to translate that information into language that nontechnical and non-research-oriented people can understand. This key skill can get you a job. Not only that, it is a skill that helps to make the world a better place. If research is informing policy, then we all win. Another

Making a Policy Brief

In this chapter, we discussed the importance of preparing policy briefs to give to and educate policy makers. In this box, we offer more detailed instructions on how to construct a policy brief based largely on the toolbox provided by the International Development Research Centre (IDRC).

An overarching goal of the policy brief is to educate the busy policy maker in a way that is easy. This is accomplished by using plain English, making it pleasing to the eye, using subtitles so finding information is fast and easy, and including interesting elements that compels the reader to keep reading. The policy brief must do more than convey information. It must make the reader want to keep reading. This is accomplished by using titles with verbs and attractive graphs and photos, as well as by enhancing particularly important points in sidebars or boxes. The Internet has a plethora of policy brief templates that offer ideas on how to make an attractive brief.

In terms of the substance, a policy brief should include five primary sections:

- Executive Summary

- Introduction

- Approach and Results

- Conclusion

- Implications and Recommendations

The **executive summary** should tell busy policy makers the overall purpose and findings of the policy brief. An executive summary should hook the reader and compel them to keep reading. The executive summary should have a front-and-center place in the policy brief such as on the cover or on the top of the first page. The fact of the matter is, many people will read no more than the executive summary, so it needs to be compelling and easy to find and offer the reader a clear, but basic, understanding about the research, findings, and conclusions. Like most summary sections in a paper, the executive summary is written last.

The **introduction section of a policy brief** accomplishes several important tasks including why the reader should care about this topic. This is accomplished by first addressing clearly why this research is important. It is not enough to assume the reader will see why this topic is important. It must be stated clearly in the policy brief. The introduction section of the policy brief must explain the significance or urgency of the issue. This part of the brief should tell the policy maker what will happen if this issue is ignored. It should also identify in plain English the objectives of the research that was conducted. This information must be clear, yet it is ideal if the researcher create a sense of curiosity in the reader to compel him or her to keep reading.

The **approach subsection** and the **results subsection** often fall under one section called "Approach and Results." The subsections are set off using subtitles for ease of reading. In the "approach" subsection, the policy brief needs to describe how the study was conducted. It should describe relevant background information, including the context of the study. By using

(Continued)

Executive summary: First section in a policy brief that is generally written last. This section should tell busy policy makers the overall purpose and findings of the policy brief.

Introduction section of a policy brief: Second section of a policy brief that tells the reader why he or she should care about the topic of the brief.

Approach subsection: Subsection in a policy brief that describes relevant background information including the context of the study. Through the use of nontechnical terms, the approach subsection should identify the research methods used to collect the data.

Results subsection: Part of a policy brief usually presented with the approach subsection. The results subsection conveys what was learned from the research and is best accomplished beginning with the broadest statements about the findings, before moving on to more specifics.

(Continued)

nontechnical terms, the approach subsection should identify the research methods used to collect the data. In contrast, the results subsection should convey what was learned from the research. When presenting findings, it is best practice to begin with the broadest statements about the findings and then to move to more specifics. Ideally, the first statement in a paragraph will offer the broadest summary of the details in the paragraph. The use of figures and photos is helpful in conveying results (plus they are attractive to the reader). Both the results and conclusions subsections must be derived from the data gathered. Policy briefs should never offer results or conclusions that go beyond the data from which they came.

The **conclusions section of a journal article** in a policy brief should answer the general question, "What does it all mean?" In the conclusions section, the researcher must interpret the data and offer concrete conclusions. Ideas must be balanced and defensible, as well as expressed strongly.

The final section in a policy brief comprises the **implications subsection** and the **recommendations subsection** that fall under one subsection called "Implications and Recommendations." Information in each subsection must flow from the conclusions, and the statements in each of these subsections must be supported by the data or evidence gathered. The implications subsection should identify what *could* happen. As a result, the implications subsection frequently uses "if–then" statements. The implications subsection is also where the researcher describes what the consequences of this issue are. The recommendations subsection should be more concrete in that it should describe what *should* happen given the findings of the research. The recommendations subsection is best described using precise steps that are relevant, credible, and feasible. Remember that the steps described here are those that should be useful to the policy maker.

key theme in this chapter is the importance of relationships and networking. These too are skills that will benefit you greatly. Don't wait until you are done with your research, start now. Engage policy makers and develop relationships with them so you can partner in your research.

This chapter also spent time covering the policy process or the policy cycle. This is important for you to understand because it demonstrates the many times during the process when research can be informative. Keep in mind, however, that the tidy illustration of the policy process is an oversimplification of the policy process. In reality, there are feedback loops as all stages inform others. It is similar to research. We can offer all the pretty illustrations of research with neat stages, but engaging in research requires nimbleness, creativity, and the ability to solve the real issues that pop up—and they always pop up—when actually engaging in research.

Some of the bumps in the road you should expect when making your research policy relevant are the competing voices. There are interest groups, the media, and even personal opinion that are fighting for the attention of policy makers. Knowing this can better prepare you for this challenge. One way we discussed to be "heard" is using policy briefs. These short, succinct, and clear documents describe research and how it can be useful to policy makers. If done well, policy makers will read them, and your research is more likely to be influential.

We also heard from Katie TePas who works with researchers to produce findings that are useful to policy makers in Alaska. Her work, and her relationships with researchers and policy makers, has allowed her to make real changes in policies affecting people's lives in Alaska for the better. You can do the same in your community.

All of our case study researchers are involved in policy-relevant research. Brunson and Weitzer's (2009) research findings have direct implications for training police officers about how the public perceives and experiences them. Furthermore, by sharing that the perceptions and experiences differ by the race of the civilian, officers can be trained to focus on any unconscious (or conscious) biases they hold and act upon. Santos and Santos's (2016) research has direct implications on how to police high-risk offenders. Guided by theory and experience, Santos and her colleague were able to test whether this approach influenced four different outcomes focused on offenders and hot spots. Although the findings were not what was expected, the research points to the need to continue investigating high-intensity policing capitalizing on what was learned in this research.

Dodge et al.'s (2005) exploratory work provided an almost immediate policy outcome. By better understanding what women officers posing as prostitutes deal with, both as a decoy but also as a female officer, upper management acted. One finding noted that for women officers, working as a prostitution decoy is one of the few ways to gain undercover work to be promoted. Recognizing the imbalance in opportunities, management promoted a detective with this undercover experience to be the first female SWAT commander in the nation.

Melde et al.'s (2009) work on gang members and fear identified the crux of the seemingly contradiction of gang members joining gangs for safety when it is clear that gang members are far more likely to be violently victimized. The research confirms findings that gang membership is associated with higher risk of violent victimization, but it also shows that membership in a gang is associated with a reduced fear of victimization, which appears to serve as an emotional protection of sorts. These findings are useful in designing training and prevention programs, and they indicate an intervention point by focusing on the fear of victimization. Zaykowski's (2014) work is contributing to a body of literature to better understand those things associated with accessing victim services. Her research points to the role of reporting to the police and raises questions about police discretion in sharing these services. Zaykowski's work also indicates the need to ensure that police understand what services are available, and that all victims are deserving of available services. More research is needed to ultimately design training and education around accessing services, as well as to treat victims evenly. Cuevas and colleagues' work (Sabina et al., 2016) contributes to our understanding about Latino teen dating violence. The findings mirror other work focused on other populations, but they still indicate many ways in which training and prevention programs can be adjusted to reflect this work. Among those findings are that the different types of violence can be covered in the same trainings, as well as the need for male and female youth to be involved in trainings as they are both victims of dating violence. Table 13.1 presents some characteristics of each case study related to their policy implications. As you look at these, do you see additional implications that are not mentioned here?

The next chapter—the final chapter—in this text focuses on taking all of these skills and using them to begin your career. You can be as skilled as the best person out there, but if you don't understand what jobs to look for, where to look for jobs, and how to look for jobs, you will not be employable. So although Chapter 14 is not research methods specific, it is invaluable in helping you take your new research skills to the real world.

Table 13.1 Featured Research: Connecting Research to Policy, Policy Makers, and the Public

Researcher	What Policies Might This Research Affect?	How Research Reached Policy Makers	Policy Brief Available?	Next Steps in Making This Available to Policy Makers
Rod Brunson (Brunson & Weitzer, 2009)	This research can be useful in training police officers. It can demonstrate that the interactions between them and communities are perceived to be, and experienced, differentially.	Public presentations of this work in the communities in which the research was conducted. Presentation of findings at conferences. Publication in journals. Interviews by the media, especially with the recent events in Ferguson, MO.	No	Sitting with policing agencies to talk about these findings directly.
Carlos Cuevas (Sabina et al., 2016)	Policies focused on training and prevention efforts can benefit from this research. In particular, the research shows that prevention efforts that target child maltreatment, conventional crime, and/or peer/sibling victimization may work to prevent dating violence as well. Findings suggest that prevention and intervention can be combined across forms of violence, and that early intervention is best. Males and females should both be included in prevention/ intervention efforts, as both are affected by this violence. Findings show that the family unit is an appropriate point of intervention.	Because these data were collected using federal grant money, the findings are presented to the funding authority (USDOJ) and the public in a non-journal article format. Journal articles and conference presentations were also used. Cuevas and colleagues also engage with media to discuss this research. Because the data are archived at ICPSR, the data are available for others to use to study similar topics. The work was picked up in congressional hearings.	No	Continuing engaging with stakeholders and policy makers on dating violence among Latino youth.
Mary Dodge (Dodge et al., 2005)	Policies that affect how women officers are promoted. In general, promotion requires undercover work, but undercover work opportunities are rarer for women compared to men officers.	Research was conducted with individuals at the police departments (i.e., collaborators). Findings were taken to officers and officials in the departments. Conference presentations. Journal article published.	No	No additional steps planned on this specific topic. As a result of this research, a police chief appointed a female officer as the first SWAT commander in the United States.

Chris Melde (Melde et al., 2009)	Reiterates findings that gang membership is associated with higher risk of violent victimization—this can continue to inform educational programs designed to steer people away from gangs. This work also demonstrates how being in a gang is associated with a reduced fear of victimization—an emotional protection of sorts. This too can be used to inform training and prevention programs. The research also offers insight into a possible intervention point which is by focusing on the fear of victimization. This focus may ultimately lead to members disassociating from gangs.	Journal articles. Conference presentations. Continued relationship with and interaction with gang associations (e.g., Eurogang) who can benefit from this work globally.	No	Continuing engaging with stakeholders and policy makers as research on adolescent gangs continues. Continued strong networking with global gang researchers.
Rachel Santos (Santos & Santos, 2016)	The way that policing is conducted.	The researchers worked directly with the police department and this relationship ensured the policy makers were aware of the research and findings. In addition, conference presentations and journal articles.	No	Continued attention to this issue through additional research and networking with the police department, and national level policing policy
Heather Zaykowski (2014)	This research offers greater information about what influences a victim to seek victim services. Findings show that victims of intimate and family violence are most likely to get assistance, but it cannot address the reasons why. Possible reasons include police perceptions about how to handle views, and police perceptions of "worthy" victims. Policies that can be influenced include police training about sharing victims services information with all victims regardless of personal views.	Journal articles and conference presentations.	No	Additional work to unpack the "why" questions regarding police informing victims of services. A focus on understanding police discretion as a mechanism connecting victims to services can provide additional insight, and has clear policy implications.

Applied Assignments

The materials presented in this chapter can be used in applied ways. This box presents several assignments to help in demonstrating the value of this material by engaging in assignments related to it.

1. Homework Applied Assignment: Making a Policy Brief

Select an article from one of our case studies. By using the guide in this chapter, design and write a policy brief that would share these findings with policy makers. Be sure to include all of the sections described, and be sure to use language that is jargon free and easy for the general public to use. In addition, remember that a policy brief should be attractive. Many online policy brief templates can assist with this assignment. On a cover sheet, identify who you believe the local policy makers in your community are that would benefit from this research. Be prepared to discuss your findings in class.

2. Group Work in Class Applied Assignment: Field Observation as a Group

You are a member of a policy group at your university. Each of you was appointed to sit on this committee by the provost given your research methods skills. The committee's mission is to identify policies that are not working well and to identify the data and research needed to inform how the policy can be improved. Your task today is to as a group identify a policy that is not working well at the university. Next, identify issues with that policy you believe need to be changed. As a group, you need to identify the methodology used to gather data needed to inform ways to improve the policy. How do you think those data will help? What if the data do not suggest change is needed? Are there other data you should gather then? How will you share your findings and conclusions with your provost who doesn't know anything about research methods or policy? Be prepared to share you findings with the class.

3. Internet Applied Assignment: Gathering and Analyzing Online Qualitative Data

Search the Internet for a policy being considered at the state level. Once you find that policy, write a paper summarizing it and noting whether any data were used (that you can find) to influence the policy. Next, identify the type of methodology you think is needed to gather data you think would be useful for this policy and why. Describe the steps you would take to alert the state-level policy makers about the data you'd like to gather. Be prepared to share your findings with the class.

KEY WORDS AND CONCEPTS

Advocacy groups 432
Approach subsection 441
Budgets 434
Communication 429
Conclusions section of a journal article 442
Executive summary 441
Focusing event 426
Guidelines 423
Ideology 433
Implications subsection 442

Introduction section of a policy brief 441
Looping 431
Media 431
Networking 429
Policy 423
Policy adoption 427
Policy brief 430
Policy evaluation 428
Policy formation 427
Policy implementation 428
Policy makers 424

Policy-relevant research 422
Problem identification/ agenda setting 426
Procedures 423
Public policy 423
Recommendations subsection 442
Regulations 423
Results subsection 441
Rules 423

KEY POINTS

- Research used to influence policy makers when they design and implement policy is policy-relevant research. Historically, researchers have done a great job of conducting solid traditional research and of publishing those results; nevertheless, researchers have not been as successful at producing policy-relevant research.

- Policy comprises the principles, rules, and laws that guide a government, an organization, or people. Public policy refers to policy in the government arena. Policies differ from procedures, regulations, and rules.

- Policy affects all aspects of our lives on a daily basis. As someone living under many policies, it reasonable to want policy to be based on well-conducted research. That is, it is reasonable to hope for criminal justice research to be policy-relevant research.

- The policy process, also known as the policy cycle, is a simplified representation of the stages of policy making and implementation. Although many descriptions of the policy process are available, we focus on a policy process based on five major stages, including problem identification/agenda setting, policy formation, policy adoption, policy implementation, and policy evaluation.

- Researchers must develop and maintain relationships with policy makers to get their research seen by them.

- Researchers must translate their research to make it accessible to policy makers and others. An excellent way to do that is by writing policy briefs.

- A policy brief is a short two- to four-page document of about 1,500 words. In this space, a researcher presents, in plain English, the purpose, findings, and policy implications (among other things) to a nonacademic audience. Policy briefs must be free of jargon, and they must simplify, clarify, and make understanding the research easy.

- A researcher can maximize the probability that his or her research will be policy relevant by thinking about it at the beginning of a research project. This means the researcher can use a suitable research question, be versed in the policy of interest, be aware of policy gaps, and perhaps even include a policy maker on the research team.

- Not all research produced is policy relevant, and policy makers will not find your work. As a researcher, you must reach out and bring your research to policy makers.

REVIEW QUESTIONS

1. What is policy, and how does it differ from public policy? What are examples of policies you like? What are examples of policies you do not like?

2. Who are policy makers you would want to influence with your criminal justice and criminology research?

3. How does policy-relevant research differ from other types of research? Why isn't all research policy relevant?

4. Which research questions are best for policy-relevant research? Why is that?

5. Why is a depiction of the policy process useful but at the same time unrealistic?

6. What are the stages of the policy process, and how can researchers influence policy makers at each stage?

7. What common mistakes do researchers make when it comes to making policy-relevant research? How might they maximize the chances that their research is influential?

8. What is a policy brief, and how does it differ from an academic journal article or even a research paper? What are the characteristics of a well-constructed policy brief?

9. What are ways that researchers can connect with policy makers? Why is this so important?

10. What are common pitfalls that occur when one is trying to conduct policy-relevant research? How might these be avoided?

CRITICAL THINKING QUESTIONS

1. A professor shares her most recent journal publication with the class as an assigned reading. She also mentions that she sent it to a local lawmaker since it is related to a policy under consideration. You hear students commenting that the article is full of jargon and that they are not sure how the research describing a proposed policy is policy relevant. If the professor asks, what suggestions would you give her to make it more policy relevant and accessible?

2. You are working as a research assistant with a professor who studies the three-strikes policy in your state. He writes many journal articles on this topic but is frustrated that his excellent research is not being used in policy making. What five specific suggestions would you offer him to help him make his work more policy relevant?

3. You are working on your Honor's thesis that focuses on mandatory arrest policy in your city. You are passionate about producing research that will be policy relevant so you have developed a relationship with a local council member who is also passionate about this topic. You have invited him to be a collaborator on this research. Your research shows that in your city, mandatory arrest has actually reduced repeat arrest by offenders. In other words, it appears to be a beneficial policy in place. The council member does not believe it and pressures you to make changes in your findings. What do you do in a situation like this? How might you change your research?

4. Santos and Santos's (2016) research indicated that intensive policing did not statistically affect their outcome measures. In other words, it did not appear to have much an effect, although the authors noted that the direction of the findings was positive. You have developed a relationship with the local police chief who is aware of your familiarity with this research. She is asking what sort of policy implications come from this work. What suggestions would you provide the chief? Why?

5. Meanwhile, in your hometown, the police chief finds Brunson and Weitzer's (2009) work. The chief is very interested in the topic but is disappointed that he cannot understand some of the research jargon. He pays you to consult with him about this so he can make any needed policy changes. As a consultant, what would you produce and share with this police chief? Why?

$SAGE edge™

SAGE edge offers a robust online environment featuring an impressive array of free tools and resources for review, study, and further exploration, keeping you on the cutting edge of teaching and learning. Learn more at **edge.sagepub .com/rennisonrm**.

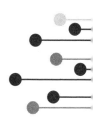

CHAPTER 14

Research Methods as a Career

Introduction

This book has introduced you to the various research methods used in criminal justice and criminology. A question many students have when they show up for this class is, "Why do I have to take this class?" We have tried to make clear the many reasons you should take the course and, even more importantly, the many reasons you should *want* to take this course. The material in this course makes you a better consumer of information, and it makes you a better producer of information. Finally, the material in the class provides access to the technical and critical thinking skills that will make you employable. We have covered the elements focused on technical and critical thinking skills so far. This last chapter does not present material on research methods. Rather, in this last chapter, we offer information and strategies on how you can use the knowledge learned in this book and your class to find and secure a job using these skills. To that end, this chapter begins with why these skills are beneficial to you. Next, we turn to where to look for jobs. Tips on how to create an effective résumé and job cover letter are also presented, as well as ways you can leverage social media to increase the chances of being invited to an interview and, ultimately, of being offered a job. We also discuss the pitfalls to watch out for when job hunting and some of the ethical considerations to be aware of when searching for the career that is right for you. To begin, we examine many of the tools you will need to find your dream job.

Why Research Methods as a Career?

Throughout this book, we have emphasized the fact that research methods skills are important, highly desired, and can lead to a career in the "real world." **Skill** is defined as having the ability to do something well. A **professional skill set** represents a particular group of skills that employers desire in their employees, which a person usually develops through

Learning Objectives

After finishing this chapter, you should be able to:

14.1 Explain why research methods skills are valuable and beneficial to your career.

14.2 Describe some of the key differences between public- and private-sector jobs.

14.3 Identify where to look for jobs online and how to use social media to increase the likelihood of getting an interview or a job offer.

14.4 Create a professional looking résumé and cover letter that can be used when applying for jobs.

14.5 Understand what defines a good job interview and how to prepare yourself for one every time.

14.6 Describe the common pitfalls associated with career searches and the ethical dilemmas that you may confront when job hunting.

Skill: Defined as having the ability to do something well.

Professional skill set: Particular group of skills that employers desire in their employees, which a person usually develops through training and education.

449

© Stacy Revere/Getty Images

Possessing professional skills that employers want—and are willing to pay for—is the key to landing your dream job. This book offers those professional skills to you. Will you take them?

training and education. Possessing professional skills that employers want—and are willing to pay for—is the key to landing your dream job. This book offers those professional skills to you. Will you take them?

Consider Major League Baseball, for example. In 2016, the league's players had an overall batting average of .284. This means that for every 100 times at bat, on average, league players managed to get a hit less than 29 times. Nevertheless, the ability to get a hit fewer than 29 out of 100 times at the plate represents a remarkable skill, a professional skill that earned Major League Baseball players an average salary of over $4 million that year.

The ability to conduct research in the field of criminology and criminal justice will not earn you anything close to what professional baseball players make, but the professional skill set associated with being able to conduct criminological research is extremely marketable. In fact, as featured researcher Carlos Cuevas told us in his video interview conducted for this book, research method skills are "the most transferrable skill you can develop." He knows they can be applied and are desirable in any industry, not just in academics, and not just in the criminal justice or criminology fields.

Think back to the experts we have heard from at the end of each chapter throughout this book. They include Sharon Devine, Chris Keating, Carol Peeples, Sean McCandless, Brenidy Rice, Sam Gallaher, Jenna Truman, Michael Shively, Bridget Kelly, Henri Buccine-Schraeder, Sue Burton, Katie TePas, and Nora Scanlon. They all started out just where you are: in a class focused on research methods. Maybe they all started that class wondering why they had to take that class too. Since then, they have each continued gaining a variety of educational training and experiences. Some have PhDs, while others do not. Not one of our experts works as a professor, although some work in a university setting. In fact, several of these individuals thought they wanted to become a professor only to learn it was not as appealing as they once thought. Today, all of these experts work outside of academia where they use research methods skills daily in a rewarding career that makes a difference in our world. Some are self-employed, and others work for agencies. Seeing these experts, what they do, and the skills they use should help, in part, demonstrate why you should focus on excelling at the research methods skills presented in this text.

Even if you do not go on to work in a capacity to create new knowledge, you will likely find yourself in a position where you have to understand research findings. In this role, you will need to understand the research methodology that goes into the research findings to properly assess that work. Having research methods skills makes you a more adept manager or leader in the role you find yourself in. We know that, and using learning research methods skills can change the trajectory of your life, leading you to a meaningful career using them.

Where Do I Get Started?

The best time to get started thinking about a career is long before you earn your degree. If you wait until the degree is awarded to think about your career, you may have made things a little more difficult for yourself. Why? Because part of getting a job is developing networks, relationships, and as many skills as possible. Both networking and relationships take time to develop and nurture, meaning you should start on this early. The relationships you develop in college will be useful to you because professors and those you interact with as a student will know that you, a qualified and professional soon-to-be minted graduate, will soon be looking for a career. These people will call you when they know a job is coming available. They will share with their colleagues that there is a great potential employee in you. If these leaders in the field know you, and if they know you are skilled, professional, and someone they would want in their organization, you have just made finding a job that much easier. There is nothing easier than having a job come looking for you.

An often overlooked advantage of thinking about your career early is that you will view your professors differently. You need to view your professors as mentors who cannot just help you *while* you are in college but also help you even *after* you graduate. Professors can help you decide on good locations to intern. They can help guide you through challenging situations you may be unfamiliar with while attending college. Also, you may not believe it, but your professors are strongly connected to the real world. They may very well have come from the real world just like both authors of this text. They know who is in the field across the nation, and those working in the real world know them too. You need your professors for other reasons too. Will you need a committee for a thesis or dissertation? Which professors will sit on that committee? Professors are not required to sit on your committee, but they do so because they want to see you succeed. Sitting on a committee does not bring a professor more money or prestige—just more work. Professors do this to help you succeed.

Conversely, if you are a student who has proven to be difficult, failed to work in their classes, and created general discord, you may very well struggle putting together a committee. You may also struggle when it is time to go on the job market. Remember, you will need letters of recommendation from your professors, and you want them to be able to write strongly positive letters on your behalf. It would be wrong to think that any letter a professor writes is a positive one. We write honest letters. It is important also that you recognize that even if you do not ask your professor for a letter of recommendation, people in the field will call them to ask their thoughts about applicants anyway. This happens all the time. Be the student that everyone is eager to assist in your goals. Remember that throughout your career, you want to develop good relationships with them all.

Another advantage of thinking about your career very early in your college years is that it allows you to take advantage of opportunities that can benefit you when it is time to look for a job. For example, internships are invaluable and put you in the presence of potential employers and their clients (who are also potential employers). Many students hate interning, and they grumble at the fact that interning is a requirement for many degrees. It is common for students to complain that they already have experience or that they have hardships (we all have hardships) that make getting to an internship challenging. Nonetheless, the most common expression of gratitude coming from students is often a result of their internship. The internship is designed to allow you to network and meet and work with people in the field—people who hire students like you. Interning allows you to show people outside of academia what skills you have to offer. Internships allow you to develop new methodological skills and professional skills that were not covered in your courses.

Internships also provide students with professional skills. If you have not been in a professional work setting, you may not be familiar with the culture, and you may not know exactly how to conduct yourself around other working professionals. Many students scoff at this advice only to learn that they really did not understand the culture. One student showed up at her internships at a police agency trying to sell personal pleasure devices (her side business). She was escorted from the building, and her internship was halted immediately. In discussions with her, she continued to be baffled and resisted the notion that her behavior was not professional. Knowing how to dress properly can also be a mystery for some. Ask your professor or other professional contacts what you should wear to your internship. Making repeated errors in this way can also lead to the loss of an internship and all it has to offer. Another student continued showing up to her internships in revealing blouses and flip-flops. Her internship was in a state court building. She lost this opportunity as a result as well. As an intern, you can learn about these sorts of things, with minimal consequences

While you are still in college, attend functions on topics you care about. Go to discussion panels on topics that you are interested in.

Cover letter: Formal correspondence, written to a hiring official, explaining a candidate's interest in an employment opportunity with his or her organization.

should things go wrong, as long as you heed the advice of those trying to help you.

A final overlooked, but massive, benefit of internships is that students can add experience on their résumé that they may not be able to get otherwise. This is critical. Many students get frustrated when looking for jobs because most job advertisements require experience. Students lament that they cannot get experience because they can't get a job, but they can't get a job because they don't have relevant experience. Internships provide that needed experience. Although some degree programs require internships to graduate, you do not have to depend on that to intern. Do it yourself. Find an agency or organization that interests you, call it, and ask if the agency accepts interns. Do not wait for others to make you do this; do it for yourself. This shows excellent initiative.

Also, while you are still in college, attend functions on topics you care about. Go to discussion panels on topics that you are interested in. Do not just attend these events, but introduce yourself to the speakers and thank them for their time and expertise. Introduce yourself as a student who hopes to get a job in the field you care about when you graduate. You can even buy your own business cards to hand out so these experts and leaders in the field can contact you again. People attending these talks, or sitting on the panels of these talks, are connected. It is true, and no exaggeration, that it is a small world, so becoming known as an eager, energetic, and absolutely qualified person can pay off hugely when it comes to starting your career.

Finally, recall the advice that Michael Shivley, offered earlier in the book: "Get all the training you can, and learn everything you can." Attend workshops on Microsoft® Excel™. Attend workshops on interviewing. Attend workshops on résumé writing. Become more of an expert on programs like IBM® SPSS™ by watching YouTube® videos. You cannot attend too many workshops, and you cannot be overtrained or overprepared. You never know when this information and these skills will come in handy. Anything you learn is guaranteed to come in handy. If you take advantage of the opportunities the university offers you, and you view your professors as allies, you will be well situated and have given yourself many advantages when it is time to look for the first job in your rewarding career.

Career Search Documents

Almost every position you apply for will require you to produce a variety of documents as part of your job application. It is advisable that you have these documents complete and polished prior to starting your job search in earnest. Although they may be ready to go, each application will require tweaks to those documents. Keep in mind it is easier to tweak a document than it is to develop a new document when you might be up against a deadline for submission of an application. Three of the most important job-related documents you'll need to provide at some point during the application process are (1) a cover letter, (2) a professional résumé, and (3) letters of recommendation.

Cover Letters

When it is time to start looking for a job, and a potential employment opportunity is identified, one of the first things that an applicant should do is prepare a job cover letter. A **cover letter** is formal correspondence, written to the hiring official, explaining your interest in an employment opportunity with his or her organization. There are several reasons why job applications are accompanied by cover letters. Cover letters do the following:

1. Introduce you to the organization and the hiring official

2. Present a clear, concise, and compelling case for why you are the best person for the advertised job

3. Fill in gaps and elaborate on aspects of your résumé that would strengthen your application

Although each cover letter is a unique chance to "sell" yourself to the employer, they all share similar characteristics. A strong cover letters begin by clearly conveying the job applicant's contact information followed by the current date. The hiring official's contact information, including his or her title, name of organization/company, and the organization's address should also be available. The letter itself begins with a salutation, which should be personalized and respectful—avoid the all-too-common "To Whom It May Concern" as most job advertisements show the name and title of the person the application should be submitted to. You must take the time to ensure the salutation is correct in terms of both the title and the preferred gender pronoun: Dr. Hart, Dr. Rennison, Ms. Smith, Mr. Johnson, Ms. Schwartz, and so on.

Because a cover letter "supports" or "clarifies" other information in your application, it should be clear and concise. Keep in mind the person hiring (or committee hiring) has many applications to go through. In some cases, there are hundreds of applications to go through. To be one of the applications considered, the body of your cover letter should consist of only two or three paragraphs. The opening paragraph should be designed to grab the hiring official's attention. It should state why you are applying, the position to which you are applying, and the advertised job announcement number (if applicable). The second paragraph should promote you as the applicant, emphasizing your knowledge, skills, and abilities. The final paragraph should reinforce your "fit" for the job, restating your interest in the position and referencing your résumé. Each paragraph must be able to stand on its own, each supporting an application in a unique way.

A cover letter always ends with a complimentary close. In this context, a **complimentary close** is a polite ending to the cover letter. In job cover letters, common closes include Warmest Regards, Regards, Sincerely, and Best Wishes (for some examples). A quick search of the Internet will produce numerous examples of high-quality examples of cover letters that you can use when applying for your next job.

Figure 14.1 shows an example of an excellent cover letter.

It is no exaggeration to state that cover letters can make or break a job candidate's application. The authors of this text have sat on countless job search committees and have more stories about botched cover letters than you can imagine. A surprisingly frequent error we see is addressing the letter to the wrong place—to the wrong city even! It is never useful to say in your cover letter how you have always dreamed of working in Boulder, Colorado, when the job is located in Denver, Colorado. They are very different places! Another common fatal error is addressing the hiring authority using the wrong pronoun. Is the hiring authority a doctor? Is so, address him or her accordingly. Do not assume all hiring authorities are male either. Do not assume all women use the title of Mrs. This error is common and a reason to throw away an application when attention to detail is part of the job requirements. If these basic things are botched, the hiring committee wonders else about the applicant's ability to do the job he or she will foul up when

What Makes a Great Résumé?

A great résumé

- Answers the question, "What do I have to offer the employer?"

- Provides personal contact information

- Contains a clear and concise goal statement

- Lists current and past employment, demonstrating employability

- Contains details of formal educational achievements, including the names and addresses of the institutions awarding the degree(s) and time spent at that institution

- Presents key skills that an employer desires

Figure 14.1   Cover Letter Example

Dear Hiring Manager:

It is with great enthusiasm that I submit my application for the position of Junior Crime Analyst for the Ethical Law Enforcement Agency. As a student who interned at the Quality Law Enforcement Agency for one year, I know my diverse skills and qualifications will make me an asset to the Ethical Law Enforcement Agency team.

As you will see from the attached résumé, I've spent my time at the university building my skill set so I can contribute to an organization like yours. I not only interned for a year with Quality, but I also attended five panel discussions on the use of crime data to predict and combat crime. In addition, as president of the Alpha Phi Sigma chapter at my university, I planned the final panel focused on strategic crime analysis in our community. I'm not only used to wearing many hats, I sincerely enjoy doing it; I thrive in an environment where no two work days are the same, but all are used to improve our community.

In addition to being flexible and responsive, I'm also a fanatic for details, particularly when it comes to presentations. One of my recent projects involved writing a 20-page crime analysis report. I proofed and edited several of the narratives that contributed to that report, as well as proofed the data spreadsheets in Excel to ensure the findings were accurate. Finally, I created the PowerPoint presentation that has been used to share our findings with the community and law enforcement leadership. I believe in applying this same level of attention to detail to tasks as visible as prepping the materials for a top-level meeting and as mundane as making sure the copier never runs out of paper.

Last, but certainly not least, I want you to know that I'm a passionate law enforcement fan and a longtime supporter of our community's officers. I've been following the Quality and Ethical agencies since the earliest days of their "We all Matter" campaign, and I am so excited to see this vision becoming a reality. I'm a follower of your website and of the awarding of new grants by the National Institute of Justice to continue our campaign to combat crime in our downtown area.

In closing, I am thrilled at the possibility of being a Junior Crime Analyst in the Ethical Law Enforcement Agency. I have long dreamed of being a part of your organization and have focused my studies around being the best analyst I can be. I welcome the opportunity to meet with you and discuss the value that I can bring to your organization. I appreciate your consideration and look forward to hearing from you.

Warmest regards,
Catelyn Toya Johnson

Résumé: Written summary of your educational record, work history, certifications, memberships, and accomplishments that often accompanies a job application.

he or she can't get these simple things correct. Seemingly small errors like this will get your application a one-way trip to the trash. That is no exaggeration.

Résumés

In preparing to go on the job market, one must also craft a résumé. The following sections explain what a résumé is, why you need one, and what it should (and shouldn't) contain. This section concludes with a sample résumé that can be used as a guide when crafting your own.

What is a résumé? A **résumé** is a written summary of your educational record, work history, certifications, memberships, and accomplishments that often accompanies a job application. Potential employers can use applicants' résumés to filter out those not meeting the criteria of the job so they can develop a "short list" of those people who will be interviewed for the opening. Therefore, it is vital to develop a very good résumé, one that presents a strong and convincing argument that you are the right person for that job you are applying for.

Given the gravitas of a résumé, and how it can stand between getting an interview or not, you should make sure your résumé is designed with a few important objectives in mind. First, your résumé should provide clear, straightforward, and easy-to-find answers to a very important question: "What are the main things that I have to offer which will benefit this employer and that are relevant for this job?" In short, the résumé should tell prospective employers everything that might interest them but nothing that will waste their time. Know your audience!

Second, your résumé should provide your personal details, including your name and, most important, your contact information (e.g., your home address, mobile phone number, and e-mail address). It is shocking the number of résumés that are submitted with no contact information![1] Make sure that if you include an e-mail address, that the e-mail address is appropriate. You wouldn't want to risk missing an interview opportunity because your e-mail address suggested you might not be the right person for the job (e.g., allnightparty monster@gmail.com; qqqq@yahoo.com; lazybarfly@hotmail.com; reefermania@ganga.com; xxxxlips@aol.com). In terms of personal information, be aware that there are some things that you are legally not required to include on your résumé (or in an interview) such as your gender, date of birth, nationality, ethnicity, or marital status.

Third, a résumé should contain a clear and concise objective statement. This is usually a single sentence that describes the role and field in which you wish to work. For instance, you may want to indicate that you wish to be a crime analyst in the Lincoln, Nebraska, Police Department (assuming you are applying to the Lincoln, Nebraska, Police Department). Be careful that this objective statement isn't too broad or too vague. The more focused it is on a specific job, the stronger it will be. If you just tell prospective employers that you are hardworking and want to work in their field, it doesn't really add much value to your résumé. Instead, use this space to give them a specific understanding of what you are looking to achieve and why you are the best person to do so.

Fourth, your résumé should include a section presenting your current and past employment. Documenting all of your paid work, including part-time, temporary, and internship work, demonstrates your experience and employability. If you have completed volunteer work or an internship, include that information as long as it is relevant to your employer's interests. In addition, note that it was voluntary or an internship. To pass this off as a paid position would be unethical. When presenting your employment history, it is a good idea to present it in reverse chronological order. This means your employment history should start at the top of the résumé with your present or most recent employment, going back in time down the page.

In addition to stating where you worked or for whom, the employment history section of your résumé should include the following:

1. Year and the month you started and stopped working there (if applicable)

2. Job position or title

3. Employer's name and location

4. Duties and responsibilities of your position

When describing your job duties, it is a good idea to present the information in succinct sentences that begin with past-tense action verbs (e.g., "developed, "administered," and "organized"). A good example is something like this:

- Developed an automated daily reporting system using Microsoft Word, Excel, and Outlook, saving the company time and money. (To make this statement even stronger, add specific quantitative information, if you can, such as just how much time and money you saved; e.g., "saving the company $5K/year and 2 days/week spent on reporting.")

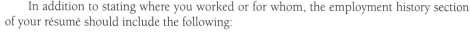

[1]There is one caveat regarding contact information, however: Because most résumés are being uploaded onto public spaces now, contact information, such as mailing address and phone number, are often being left off in those cases, and only an e-mail address and/or LinkedIn profile URL is provided. Therefore, consider having a version that can be sent directly to employers with your full contact information and another that can be placed online with just the e-mail and LinkedIn URL.

Referee: Person who can write a letter of recommendation on a candidate's behalf to a potential employer.

- Entered survey data from a survey distributed to a sample of 5,000 students at the University of Minnesota. (If the survey led to some significant findings or policy changes, don't leave that out!)

- Created a PowerPoint presentation of evaluation research findings focused on a program designed to increase quality of life. (You could enhance this by also stating how the presentation was used and to whom it was presented.)

Keep in mind when crafting these statements that the main focus should be on things that are relevant to the job you are applying for and would be of upmost interest to the prospective employer. This means that you should not be writing a "one size fits all" résumé. You want to be tailoring it to each position and each organization as much as you can or when you can. Again, the more you know your audience, the more you can speak directly to them!

Fifth, a good résumé should also include information about your formal education. In this section, the degree earned (i.e., High School Diploma, Bachelor of Arts, Master of Science, etc.), the name and address of the institution awarding the degree, and the time spent at that institution should be included as part of the educational history reported on your résumé. (Please note that as you get further along in your career, however, you will want to remove your high school information unless it is useful for the job you are applying for, for example, you are applying to a job at your high school or you want to show you were locally born and raised in the area.)

Sixth, it is vital that your résumé include information about what computer skills you possess. In this section, include those computer programs you are proficient in that will be essential to know for that job. Also, be sure to include specific examples of how you have used particular applications in the past and your level of expertise. Do not "oversell" or lie about your skills here. It is okay if your skills are basic. Many jobs require no more than basic skills in SPSS, Excel, or other software. The following two examples illustrate a "good" and "bad" way to present information about computer skills on your résumé:

Good

Highly proficient in Microsoft Excel, with the ability to create complex formulas, pivot tables, charts, and graphs.

Bad

Know Excel.

Finally, your résumé should include information for a list of **referees** or references that include the name, professional position, and contact information of people who can vouch for your employability.[2] A referee might be a current or former professor, co-worker or supervisor, or the head of an organization, club, or society to which you belong. Potential employers will contact your referees to verify employability usually after they have decided they want to hire you but prior to making you the job offer. It is imperative that you ask the referees you put on your résumé if they are willing to serve in this capacity. Do not let them get a surprise call about a reference ever. You do not want that reference to spend time on that call trying to figure out who you are. This doesn't look good to the person gathering references.

---

[2]As noted earlier in Footnote 1, however, if you are placing your résumé online, you will want to leave off your referee information so that their names and phone numbers are not shown publicly. As suggested, you can have one version of your résumé that you send directly (and privately) to an employer with your referee information and another you post online without it.

Most students studying criminal justice are interested in traditional career pathways associated with their degree, choosing to work in law enforcement, corrections, courts, or victim services organizations. The study by Tripp and Cobkit (2013) demonstrates alternative career pathways that criminal justice graduates may not have considered. And although there might not be direct policy implications, the findings and the authors' conclusions upon which they are based offer helpful guidance to those who will be hitting the job market after graduation.

The researchers conducting the current study were guided by two primary research questions:

1. What jobs are available for criminal justice students outside of the criminal justice system?

2. What are the requirements for obtaining a position outside of the criminal justice system?

Keep in mind that you and your friends could probably come up with your own answers to these questions, and you may be correct in your response to them, but the current study sought to answer these questions by applying a systematic, scientific approach using the methods and techniques already discussed in this text.

Data used to answer Tripp and Cobkit's (2013) questions were obtained from analyzing the content of job postings listed on popular job recruiting websites (i.e., CareerBuilder, Monster, Juju, Indeed, SimplyHired, and the job portions of the International Association of Law Enforcement Intelligence Analysts and the Department of Labor websites) from May through August 2012. Specifically, keyword searchers on "private investigator," "private security," "intelligence analyst," "criminal justice," and ""criminology" were entered into the websites' search engines. "Corporate investigator," "law office investigator," and "victim advocate" were also used. Next, as the researchers explained, "a Google search for private law firms, private investigation companies, and private securities corporations was conducted. This search for the specified private corporations was used as a supplement to the career search engines due to their lack of presence." Information about the specific job opportunity, including degree requirements, was culled from announcements for analysis.

Once the private firms were identified, information on current job opportunities was obtained from the individual sites. To complement this information, additional specialized searches for a variety of corporations were conducted, including job searchers with the top 60 companies of the Fortune 500, the top 25 U.S. defense contractors, nongovernmental organizations, nonprofits related to criminal justice, and criminal justice research institutes and professional organizations. Possible jobs with the United Nations and intelligence analyst jobs with the federal government were included. In total, the researchers analyzed data collected from 63 different companies, offering 89 separate jobs that criminal justice students could be qualified for.

The findings from the current study by Tripp and Cobkit (2013) revealed several types of job opportunities for criminal justice graduates, including jobs in investigations with Amazon.com, Target, Citigroup, Boeing, and Northrop Grumman; legal assistance jobs with Google, IBM, and the YWCS; intelligence analysts jobs with the CIA, NSA, and BAE Systems; and research positions with RAND Corp, LexisNexis, and CAN Analysis and Solutions. Job prospects for large, top-tier Fortune 500 companies even looked bright: 21% of the first 60 companies of the Fortune 500 had job opportunities for criminal justice students.

The take-away message from this study is simple: When it comes to careers for criminal justice students graduates, many will choose traditional pathways (i.e., law enforcement, corrections, courts, or victim services organizations). Students should be aware, however, that myriad opportunities await them with companies that they may not have even thought would be looking for graduates like them. Their knowledge, skills, and abilities are in high demand!

Tripp, T., & Cobkit, S. (2013). Unexpected pathways: Criminal justice career options in the private sector. *Journal of Criminal Justice Education, 24*(4), 478–494.

Other information can be included in a résumé if it is relevant to the job you are pursuing. For example, if you are proficient in a foreign language or you have a particular hobby or interest that sets you apart from other applicants, it is worthwhile including this information on your résumé.

Sample Résumé

One of the best ways to develop a strong résumé is to use others as a guide. Figure 14.2 shows an example of a professional résumé you can use as a model for creating your own.

It is imperative that you proofread your résumé. This means to check, double-check, and triple-check your résumé for accuracy. Are the phone numbers current? Are the addresses correct? Have you spelled everything correctly? Are there sneaky typos such as "asses" instead of "assess" or "pubic" versus "public"? These happen and are job application killers.

One good proofreading tip is to read your résumé backward. You've likely read through the document so many times your eyes now just glance over the words. So it's a good idea to change the way you look at it. Start at the bottom and move up the page, right to left. It will help you see things like missing periods or odd spacing. You just might be surprised by the glaring typos you find even though you have looked at the document a 100 times and have run spell-check!

Like the cover letter, an error on your résumé will likely be a death sentence for your chance at getting an interview. Hiring officials typically have so many applications for a single position that they can afford to remove your application from the pool even for what you might think are minor issues. Think back to Chapter 4 when we discussed how variables are used to measure abstract concepts. In a job search scenario, the résumé and cover letter are tangible measures of the underlying concept of "accurate, careful, detailed, and thoughtful." Have you had multiple people proofread your résumé after you think it is perfect? They should. The consequences of having easy-to-correct errors on your job search documents are too consequential.

Letters of Recommendation

In addition to a cover letter and professional résumé, letters of recommendation are important job-related documents that you will need to provide (or at least request from the letter writer) during the application process. We next turn to a description of recommendation letters, why applicants need them, what they should include, and how to ask for them.

A **letter of recommendation**, which is also a letter of reference, is a document in which a person known to the applicant assesses the qualities, characteristics, and capabilities of the applicant. Letters of recommendation should speak directly to the applicant's abilities to perform the tasks and to his or her level of professionalism associated with the job for which he or she is applying. Just like some of the other documents already discussed in this chapter, a letter of recommendation can make or break your job application. Good letters of recommendation can mean the difference between getting your foot in the door and being granted an interview and receiving the dreaded rejection letter (if you are lucky enough to apply to a place that still sends rejection letters). Therefore, it is important to know who to contact to be a referee, or the person writing the recommendation letter, and what he or she will include in the letter.

Identifying a good referee is one of the first things you should do when you have identified a job you wish to apply for. The best types of people to approach to author letters on your behalf are those that have both the time and the skills to write an effective correspondence to a hiring official. It is also necessary to contact those whom you would like to write letters on your behalf to make sure they are willing to do so. Finally, it is a good idea to provide your references or referees with a sample of what it is you would have them focus on when they

Figure 14.2 Résumé Example

Pat Smith
1234 Main St.
Anytown, XX 99999
KimDoe@notsnail.com
(123) 456-7890

CAREER GOAL

To be a part of an energetic and effective team of professionals dedicated to identifying and resolving social justice problems in my community.

EDUCATION

2016 – Current   University of Some Great State, Wonderfulville, XX

                        Bachelors of Arts

                        Major: Criminology and Criminal Justice

Relevant courses: Research Methods, Statistics, Advanced Principles of Criminal Justice; Law and Legal Process; Law and Society; Criminological Theory; Social Justice in Contemporary Society.

2012–2016   Impressive High School, Impressive City, XX

                        High School Diploma

EMPLOYMENT HISTORY

2016–Present   Waiter (Part-time)

                        Upmarket Restaurant and Bar, Wonderfulville, XX

                        Responsibilities – Effectively communicating with patrons in order to ensure they were served the meals they ordered, precisely they way they ordered them. Serving up to 60 customers per evening, developing the ability to work efficiently and effectively under pressure, in challenging circumstances. Developed strong time management skills.

2016–2018   Research Assistant

                        Department of Criminology, Some Great State University

                        Responsibilities – Assisted Dr. Smartypants and his research team with data collection and cleaning routines on information gathered as part of their NIJ-funded project, *Some Awesome Grant Funded Research Project*. Quickly and accurately transferred information from survey instruments into SPSS. Conducted univariate analysis, bivariate analysis on data to be used in the report to NIJ.

2014–2016   Internship

                        Executive Director's Assistant

                        Impressive City Homeless Shelter, Impressive City, XX

                        Responsibilities – Supporting the Executive Director in the day-to-day operation of the shelter though filing paperwork, developing spreadsheets in Excel used to tract information related to the number of homeless served at the shelter; and assisting with serving meals to the homeless, washing dishes, and cleaning up the Center.

COMPUTER SKILLS

Microsoft Excel   Able to create spreadsheets using complex formulas, pivot tables, charts, and graphs.
(Highly Proficient)

Microsoft Word   Able to create advanced documents that incorporate complex formatting structures, multiple layouts, and the
(Highly Proficient)   inclusion of graphics and images.

(Continued)

Figure 14.2 (Continued)

PowerPoint
(Highly Proficient)

Able to create complex presentations that incorporate audio files, video links, and animation.

HTML
(Proficient)

Able to create websites and their common features such as forms, cascading style sheets, and dynamic image files.

MEMBERSHIPS

2016 – Present	Greenpeace
2015 – Present	Social Justice International
2014 – 2016	National Honor Society

REFERENCES

Professor I.M. Smartypants
Department of Criminal Justice
University of Some Great State
Wonderfulville, XX
i.m.smart@nomail.com
(123) 456-7890

Professor U.R. Overworked
Department of Criminal Justice
University of Some Great State
Wonderfulville, XX
u.r.overworked@nomail.com
(123) 456-7891

Mrs. Jane Smith
Executive Director
Impressive City Homeless Shelter
Impressive City, XX
j.smith@blahhoo.com
(123) 456-7890

write their letters. It allows them to focus on the things that you feel will benefit your application the most. You should consider the following:

1. Former relevant employers

2. Former or current university professors

3. Leaders in the community (e.g., your pastor, head of the organization for which you volunteers, etc.)

It is a good practice to ask the letter writer if he or she would offer a letter of recommendation. It is also good practice to share with the letter writer your résumé and a clear statement as to why you think you are qualified for the position. You must give the letter writer adequate time to write the letter. This means weeks if possible. A day or two is not enough time for a solid letter (or any letter) to be written. In many cases, the letters of recommendation go directly to the hiring authority and the applicant never sees them. If this is the case, you must provide the letter writer the name, address, title, and deadline for the letter. In short, make writing the letter as easy as possible for the reference. If you put together a strong employment application for the position you want, and it includes a well-crafted résumé, a clear and concise cover letter, and letters of recommendation that provide testimony to your knowledge, skills, and abilities, there is a good chance you will be invited to be interviewed for a job you are qualified for. Now that you have your documentation in order, it is time to discuss where to look for good jobs.

Public- Versus Private-Sector Jobs

If you are ready to start a career in criminology and criminal justice, and you are looking for a job opportunity that allows you to apply your knowledge of research methodology and the related skills you have developed through education and training, one of the first things you'll need to consider is where you want to work, not only in terms of a particular city or particular company but also in terms of the company or agency you would like to be a part of. Both public- and private-sector jobs that require research skills are available, and both present unique opportunities and challenges. One of the first things you should consider in terms of "where" you want to work is whether you want to work in the public or the private sector.

Working in the Public Sector

Public-sector employees in the federal, state, and local governments are responsible for keeping the public safe among other things. Maintaining public safety is a challenging task, one that requires a diverse, well-trained, and professional workforce. As a result, many public-sector employers are looking for individuals with the knowledge, skills, and abilities to conduct criminological research. This, of course, includes expertise and experience in research methods. Public-sector jobs can be found at the local, state, and federal level. Happily, though, most advertise for open positions in the same places. We discuss the places public-sector jobs are commonly advertised, and we provide examples of jobs that require research methods skills posted on these sites.

USAJOBS

According to the Bureau of Labor Statistics (BLS), the U.S. federal government employs more than 20 million people. If you are interested in working for the federal government, then you will want to visit USAJOBS.gov, where all federal employment opportunities are posted. There are two types of federal government jobs: permanent positions and temporary positions. When an applicant is first hired in a permanent position, he or she is generally classified as career-conditional. Under this classification, employees typically must complete a one-year probationary period and a total of three years continuous service to attain "permanent" employee status. The federal government also hires people to fill temporary roles. In this type of position, employees are appointed for a specified period, not to exceed one year, or a specified period that is at least more than one year but no more than four years. In either case, the temporary position does not give the employee permanent status.

Applying for a job with the federal government is relatively easy. First, applicants must create a profile on the USAJOBS.gov website. Once you create an account, you can search for job openings and review job announcements. Next, you can prepare a job application in the USAJOBS.gov website. Applications are submitted directly to an agency's human resources department, through the USAJOBS.gov website. It is important to note, however, that at some point, you could be asked to submit a "federal" résumé. For details on what to include on a federal résumé, check out https://www.usajobs.gov/Help/faq/application/documents/resume/what-to-include/. Federal positions might also require you to respond to knowledge, skills, and abilities (KSA), otherwise known as "general employee competencies" questions at some

point during the application/interview process. For more information on KSAs, check out www
.fedcareerinfo.com/ksa.htm.

Figure 14.3 is an example of a position advertised on the USAJOBS.com website.

There are a few details of the example position worth mentioning. For example, every
position with the U.S. federal government has the following:

1. A position title (e.g., Statistician)

2. A job series (e.g., GS-1530) and grade (e.g., 09/11)

3. Where the position is located (e.g., Office of the Inspector General)

4. Eligibility requirements

Figure 14.3 Job Advertisement Found on USAJOBS.gov

Statistician
US Department of Justice
Office of the Inspector General
Series & Grade
GS-1530-09/11

Who May Apply

Recent Graduates - Applicants within 2 years of receiving their degree or certificate. Veterans precluded from applying due to military service, must be within 6 years of receiving their degree or certificate. Students may apply if meeting the education requirements no later than August 31, 2017.

Duties

Specific duties at the GS-9 level include:

Applying statistical theories, concepts and principles to the work.

Using standard methodology in obtaining and analyzing data and information on a broad range of issues.

Exercising independent responsibility for applying established technology in routine ways to well defined, moderate-sized mathematical statistics projects, or in support of a larger project.

Preparing preliminary reports according to established procedures.

Education

For the GS-9 position, two years of progressively higher level graduate education leading to a Ph.D. degree or Ph.D. or equivalent doctoral degree: that included 15 semester hours in statistics (or in mathematics and statistics, provided at least 6 semester hours were in statistics), and 9 additional semester hours in one or more of the following: physical or biological sciences, medicine, education, or engineering; or in the social sciences including demography, history, economics, social welfare, geography, international relations, social or cultural anthropology, health sociology, political science, public administration, psychology, etc.

Required Documents

The following documents are required:

Resume showing relevant training and experience

Cover letter (optional)

Veteran preference documentation, if applicable

ICTAP documentation, if applicable

An unofficial college transcript (Note: If you are selected for this position, official transcript(s) will be required prior to your first day.).

Applicants should use all of this information to determine whether they are interested in and qualified for the job.

Furthermore, all jobs within the U.S. federal government are classified by the **General Schedule (GS)**, which determines the pay scale for most federal employees, especially those in professional, technical, administrative, or clerical positions. The GS pay scale consists of 15 grades, from GS-1, the lowest level, to GS-15, the highest level (see Table 14.1). Within each scale, there are 10 steps. The table shows the 2017 GS pay scale for federal employees (in $1,000 increments). For the Statistician's position presented earlier in Figure 14.3, the salary range would be between $43,300 (GS-9, Step 1) and $68,000 (GS-11, Step 10).

Pay close attention to the job qualifications listed in the job advertisement. Use those same words in your application. If they note that you need proficiency with SPSS, then you need to put in your application that you are proficient in SPSS (if this is true). Key words are important and a quick and easy way to find applicants who are qualified.

General Schedule (GS): Determines the pay scale for most federal employees especially those in professional, technical, administrative, or clerical positions.

Applying to State and Local Positions

Many state and local governments hire employees who are competent in conducting research or who possess strong research methods and data analysis skills. State and local agency positions are also posted online. Applicants can go directly to the state or municipal website to peruse announcements, or they can use a website like Governmentjobs.com, which searches government job websites and compiles government job listings in one place.

Table 14.1 General Schedule (GS) Pay Scale (in $1,000) for Federal Employees (2017)

Grade	Steps									
	1	2	3	4	5	6	7	8	9	10
1	18.5	19.1	19.8	20.4	21.0	21.4	22.0	22.6	22.6	23.2
2	20.8	21.3	22.0	22.6	22.9	23.5	24.2	24.9	25.5	26.2
3	22.7	23.5	24.2	25.0	25.8	26.5	27.3	28.0	28.8	29.5
4	25.5	26.4	27.2	28.1	28.9	29.8	30.6	31.5	32.3	33.2
5	28.5	29.5	30.4	31.4	32.4	33.3	34.3	35.2	36.2	37.1
6	31.8	32.9	33.9	35.0	36.1	37.1	38.2	39.2	40.3	41.4
7	35.4	36.5	37.7	38.9	40.1	41.3	42.4	43.6	44.8	46.0
8	39.2	40.5	41.8	43.1	44.4	45.7	47.0	48.3	49.6	50.9
9	43.3	44.7	46.1	47.6	49.0	50.5	51.9	53.3	54.8	56.2
10	47.6	49.2	50.8	52.4	54.0	55.6	57.2	58.7	60.3	61.9
11	52.3	54.1	55.8	57.6	59.3	61.0	62.8	64.5	66.3	68.0
12	62.7	64.8	66.9	69.0	71.1	73.2	75.3	77.4	79.5	81.5
13	74.0	77.1	79.6	82.0	84.5	87.0	89.5	92.0	94.5	97.0
14	88.1	91.1	94.0	97.0	99.9	102.8	105.8	108.7	111.6	114.6
15	103.7	107.1	110.6	114.0	117.5	121.0	124.4	127.9	131.3	134.8

Figure 14.4 is an example of a municipal job you can find on the Governmentjobs.com website. This particular announcement is for a Crime Analyst position with the City of Round Rock, Texas. Notice that the some of the skills, experience, and training the city is looking for relate specifically to several of the topics covered in this text as they pertain to criminological research. The ideal candidate will have the ability to do the following:

- Evaluate data

- Analyze findings

- Write comprehensive reports

- Think critically with respect to sources, research methods, and document creation

- Develop a variety of analytical products

- Facilitate the transfer of information between local, state, and federal agencies

- Use a variety of software applications and resources—most at an intermediate level

Working in the Private Sector

As described in the previous section, public-sector employees are individuals who work for some sort of government agency, at either the federal, the state, or the municipal level. **Private-sector employees**, in contrast, are individuals who work primarily for private-sector businesses or companies. Although jobs in both the private and public sectors may sometimes require similar professional skills, there are important distinctions.

Public-sector employers are government agencies; therefore, certain constitutional rights are afforded to public-sector employees. Often private-sector employees do not enjoy similar legal protections. On the other hand, because public employees often hold positions of trust in the society (e.g., law enforcement), some constitutional rights (e.g., union activity and speech) may be limited so that the government agencies may perform their day-to-day functions. One of the biggest distinctions between private-sector and public-sector employment, however, relates to job security. Most private-sector workers are considered to be "at-will" employees. This means that they can be fired from a business or organization for almost any reason. It is currently unconstitutional to be fired because of your race or gender or for exercising rights provided by statutes (e.g., workers' compensation or truthfully testifying in court). This is not the case in the public sector, however. Government agencies are not allowed to discipline, demote, or fire an employee unless there is "cause" (e.g., violating rules governing the workplace, dishonesty, misconduct, or poor performance).

Despite the differences between public- and private-sector jobs, both provide excellent career opportunities for job seekers. Jobs in both arenas offer job seekers like you the chance to apply your knowledge, skills, and abilities related to conducting research in a professional position. Figure 14.5 shows excerpts from a job advertisement for a Fraud Detection Specialist at Square, Inc., a mobile payment company based in San Francisco. This particular position seeks an employee to help identify and protect clients against financial loss.

Understanding the difference between public and private employment is important. It is also good to understand what kind of jobs might be available in each sector that gives employees the opportunity to apply their research skills. Knowing the best way to find and apply for these positions is equally important. The next section focuses specifically on where to begin looking for that dream job, one that will start you down your chosen career path.

Figure 14.4   Crime Analyst Position Advertised on Governmentjobs.com

5/34/2017   Job bulletin

CITY OF ROUND ROCK

invites applications for the position of:
Crime Analyst
An Equal Opportunity Employer

SALARY:

Hourly
$20.32 - $25.40

OPENING DATE: 05/12/17

CLOSING DATE: 05/28/17 11:59 PM

DESCRIPTION:

Under general supervision, the Crime Analyst performs crime and intelligence analysis for reporting and presenting crime information, statistical trends, and criminal intelligence in support of the Police Department.

EXAMPLES OF DUTIES:

Evaluate information, select essential elements, and correlate new information with existing information. Analyze findings, make interpretations, and white comprehensive reports based on these data.

Performs tactical crime and intelligence analysis to support investigations and patrol efforts. Works as part of a team with other analysts, sworn personnel, and personnel from other agencies to provide analytical assistance, collect and disseminate intelligence, and share resources.

Thinks critically, questions assumptions, and avoids bias with respect to sources, research methods, and document creation.

Develops a variety of analytical products and facilitates the transfer of information between local, state, and federal agencies.

Uses a variety of software applications and resources – most at an intermediate level.

Demonstrates continuous effort to improve operations, decrease turnaround times, streamline work processes, and wo

EXPERIENCE AND TRAINING:

Graduation from an accredited four (4) year college or university with major course work in Criminal Justice, Social Science, or in a related field. Experience may substitute for education on a year to year basis up to a maximum of four years.

Minimum two (2) year required in research, crime or intelligence analysis, and/or the interpretation of law enforcement data. A Master's Degree in a relevant field of study may be substituted for two (2) years of experience.

CERTIFIED AND LICENCES REQUIRED:

Valid class C driver's license. Ability to pass a background investigation. May be required to obtain federal secret security clearance.

Preferred:

Certification by the International Association of Crime Analysts or the International Association of Law Enforcement Intelligence Analysts.

The City of Round Rock operates under the legal doctrine of "employment-at-will" and is an equal opportunity employer.

The City values diversity and a strives to attract a responsible, qualified and diverse workforce that represents the community that we serve.

http://agency.govermentjobs.com/roundrock/job_bulletin.cfm?jobID=127051&sharedWindow=0

Figure 14.5 Fraud Detection Specialist Job Announcement

Fraud Detection Specialist
San Francisco, CA
Full-time

Job Description

Square's Fraud Operations team is seeking a highly motivated Fraud Detection Specialist to mitigate transactional fraud within the merchant commerce space. In this role, you will perform detailed analysis of high-risk purchases/transactions via real-time queues to identify unauthorized transactions across different types of payments (card, ACH, and mobile payments). This position analyzes unrecognizable risk patterns and communicates with our clients in cases where additional information is required. All candidates must be flexible with their schedule; having the ability to work nontraditional shifts as well as some holidays.

Job Responsibilities

- Monitor numerous real-time queues and review high-risk transactions from specified points-of-sale requiring demonstrated decision making and critical thinking skills

- Use departmental policies to determine if transactions are fraudulent or risky and should be canceled and refunded, or are legitimate and should be processed and fulfilled on the largest dollar amounts

- Maintain or exceed established service level agreements (SLAs) and guidelines for timely resolution of queued transactions to minimize potential revenue losses

- Contact and effectively communicate with customers and internal partners to ensure all SLAs are achieved with little or no supervision

- Effectively manage incoming communication via multiple channels (phone, email, and Customer Relationship Management systems) from both internal and external customers; resolve all issues within established service level agreements

- Conduct analysis of transactional and customer records to link unidentified transactions and accounts to known fraudulent activity

- Interact with other Risk teams on developing fraud prevention strategy and processes

Qualifications

- Strong communication skills, self-motivation and results-oriented approach

- Demonstrated customer service, organizational, and analytical skills

- Flexibility to adapt and able to manage multiple assignments while working independently

- Strong Internet research, Google Docs, and overall PC skills; SQL experience a plus;

- Bachelor's degree required (B.A. or B.S) preferably in Criminology, Psychology, or a quantitative field

- Experience: 3+ years in a risk-related role that includes direct customer support

Where to Look for a Career

Before you start looking for a career, there are a few things worth considering. For example, Featured researcher Chris Melde suggests students think through *why* they want a job and be prepared to understand what their limits are. Understanding what you are (and are not) qualified to do is important to know before looking for a job. Rachel Boba Santos shares similar thoughts. She suggests that students make sure that the job they're after is one they are qualified to have; students should read job announcements carefully. But the bottom line is this: To find the perfect job to start your career, you need to know who is hiring and what jobs they are looking to fill. As some of the information presented in this chapter has already implied, a great place to look for answers to these questions is the Internet. There are myriad ways to search the Web to find jobs, and some approaches are more effective than others. In this section, we provide some suggestions for finding the right job for you, quickly and easily.

Online Job Searches

Long gone are the times when we looked for jobs in the classified section of the newspaper. Most jobs these days are found online. Online job advertising allows employers to reach a much broader applicant pool than classified newspaper ads. Employers can use Web-based analytics to determine the effectiveness of their online ads, and they can develop strategies based on this information to target specific pools of applicants in more effective ways.

For those looking to be hired, online ads offer real-time information about who's hiring and for what kinds of jobs. In addition, online ads often are linked to application sites that allow people to submit their résumés to the hiring company's human resources department immediately (e.g., USAJOBS.gov). In short, online job advertising has changed the way potential employees look for work, and how employers recruit the best applicants.

Three of the most common job search sites are (1) Indeed.com, (2) Careebuilder.com, and (3) Monster.com. The trick to finding your dream job on these, or on any of the other online job listing sites, according to Alison Doyle (2016), founder and CEO of CareerToolBelt.com, is to understand and effectively use **keyword** searches.

A keyword, in the context of an online job hunt, is a word or phrase that is particular to the job you're looking for and that will narrow your search to include only those that you're interested in applying for. For example, in the federal government position provided in Figure 14.3, "1530" is a keyword. Using keywords can enable you to search online job sites more efficiently and effectively; here are six tips for using keywords while scouring job search sites:

- **Field or industry:** Begin by putting in the field or industry you would like to work in, such as "criminology" or "research" or "GIS" or "analysis."

- **Location:** It is up to you how precise you would like to be. You can put in a state, city, town, or even a zip code.

- **Desired job title:** You can try putting in your desired title (e.g., crime analyst), but keep in mind that not all companies use the same title, so it is good practice to search on related or alternative titles a company might use.

- **Industry-specific skills, tools, and jargon:** As well as searching by job titles, you can search by the functionality required by a job (e.g., SPSS).

- **Company names:** If you happen to have a dream company that you would like to work for—or a giant multinational company that you know has a lot of job openings at any one time—you can search directly by the company name.

- **Job type:** Narrow search results by putting in full time, part time, contract, and so on.

© Boogich/iStockphoto.com

Online job advertising allows employers to reach a much broader applicant pool than classified newspaper ads.

When using social media to find and apply for jobs, there are several general guidelines that you should follow.

In addition to websites specifically designed to disseminate information about available jobs, social media represents a fantastic way to learn about who's hiring. Facebook®, LinkedIn®, and Twitter® are the biggest names in social media platforms, and they can be used to help identify and land that perfect job.

Social Media

When using social media to find and apply for jobs, there are several general guidelines that you should follow. One of the first things you will want to do is to "clean" your Internet image. For example, if you "Google" your name right now, what sort of information would be returned? If you've used various social media sites to rate former professors or employers, posted less-than-flattering images of you and your friends, or hosted a website that not everyone would appreciate, you may want to consider removing anything that a potential employer might find and use to disqualify you from employment consideration.

A wide variety of applications are available for searching, finding, and cleaning/removing unwanted content from the Internet. It is worthwhile checking for content that may create problems for you as a job applicant and removing unwanted content before applying for a job. Nevertheless, be aware that things on the Web really are forever. For example, if you check out the Wayback Machine (https://archive.org/web/), you can see that pages are archived forever. Still, cleaning up what you can is better than leaving everything you are not proud of today posted for your prospective employer to see. And don't doubt it, your prospective employer will "Google" you. That is guaranteed.

It is also a good idea to limit your social media exposure to the platforms that are important. Facebook, LinkedIn, and Twitter are the platforms most likely to be checked by a potential employer. Having a social media presence on other platforms is going to cost you precious time to maintain and will not likely return a substantial contribution of your time on that investment. Relatedly, all your social media accounts and e-mails associated with them should reflect your real name, not a nickname that only your friends know you by, especially if it is less than flattering or may be offensive to a potential employer.

Finally, it is a good idea to use your social media accounts to steer potential employers back to one place—a place where your full story can be told. A great way to do this is to develop your own professional webpage that includes content that will help potential employers learn more about what you can offer their company or organization as an employee. Linking all your social media accounts to a single website—your professional webpage—could potentially help get your job application moved to the top of the stack.

In addition to these general ideas about leveraging social media to improve your chances of getting an interview and landing the job you're after, there are there other things that you can do that are specific to particular social media platforms, such as Facebook, LinkedIn, and Twitter that can benefit you in your employment search.

Facebook

According to a recent survey by Jobvite, an IT software and services company, 83% of people looking for a job and 65% of employment recruiters said that they use Facebook in their job searches and announcements. Susan Adams (2012, 2014), a writer for *Forbes* magazine, suggests four ways to use Facebook to maximize your chances of finding a great job. The following are excerpts of her recommendations:

1. **Fill out your profile with your professional history**. Facebook has an easy way to add your work credentials to your profile. First, go to your own page (not the newsfeed page). Then, click on the "about" page and select "edit profile." Here you can include information about your work history and education history. If you want to make yourself known to the 65% of recruiters who troll for job candidates on Facebook, fill out this information accurately and without typographic errors.

2. **Classify your friends**. If you go to your list of friends, you will see a "friends" box next to each friend. Click on that box, and you should see a roster of lists—the default of which has "close friends," "acquaintances," and "start a new list." Click on "start a new list," and title it "Professional" or "Work." After that list is created, you should find all of your friends who you would consider professional contacts and add them to that list. This way, you can target your work-related status updates.

3. **Post content and respond to other people's professional postings**. There is value in online contact, so pay attention to your professional friends' postings. "Like" their posts and make insightful comments about the things they share. Users can now access five additional animated emoji with which to express themselves. Each emotive icon is named for the reaction it's meant to convey. "Like" you already know—say hello to "love," "haha," "wow," "sad," and "angry."

4. **Find networking connections**. Type the company name you are interested in into the Facebook search bar. Then choose the "People" tab located under the search bar. Next, from the menu on the left of the screen, click "+ Choose a Company. . ." from the Filter Results by Work option. Enter the name of the company in the search window that appears and click Enter/Return. Results that are produced are a list of people who work at the company whose name you entered. This is a networking goldmine.

There is a good chance that you are already using Facebook in some manner as a job search tool. If you incorporate these tips into your job-hunting routines, you will better leverage Facebook's potential.

LinkedIn

LinkedIn was launched in 2003 as a business- and employment-oriented social networking service. Its parent company is Microsoft, and it currently has over 100 million active users. Because of its popularity, specifically among those looking for jobs and among those looking to hire, LinkedIn should definitely be used when it comes time to look for perfect place to work. The popular Women's magazine, *Marie Claire* (2017), recently provided readers with advice on how to best use LinkedIn to land their dream jobs. Here is a list of our five favorite recommendations:

1. **Treat LinkedIn like more than a paper CV**. Be sure to include previous work, videos, or presentations that demonstrate the versatility of your knowledge, skills, and abilities on your LinkedIn profile.

2. **Make it easy for them to find you**. Put yourself in an employer's shoes and think about how someone is likely to come across your profile. Consider what recruiters are likely to search, and incorporate this information into your profile headline.

3. **Hand-pick the right skills.** Make sure that your LinkedIn profile reflects the specific skills you possess. If you have "connections" on LinkedIn, they can endorse these skills. Previous employers can also reference them in recommendations that they give on your profile.

4. **Follow your dream companies.** There are over 3 million Company Pages on LinkedIn, so follow the ones you may want to work for some day. You will get updates when people leave or join the company, and you will get notified when that company posts jobs. LinkedIn Company Pages also show you if any of your contacts know people who work at those companies.

5. **Build your network**. It is an unwritten rule that 50 is the minimum number of contacts needed for a successful LinkedIn profile, but the more connections you are able to build, the more you will start to show up in sidebars and searches. Family, friends, colleagues and peers are all valuable connections. When requesting to connect, keep it personal instead of the standard message LinkedIn can send—the personal touch helps forge a relationship.

If you are just starting to look for jobs that will get you started on your career, you may not have set up a LinkedIn profile, but like Facebook, LinkedIn's reach makes it a powerful tool for finding that perfect job! Get your LinkedIn page up today.

Twitter

Twitter is another popular social media platform that you're probably familiar with and likely use. But have you ever thought about using Twitter to find that dream job, networking with industry insiders, or building your personal brand so that potential employers will want to hire you? If not, here are some tips, offered by Pamela Skillings (2017), co-founder of Big Interview, on how you might use Twitter to accomplish these goals. Skillings suggests four easy-to-follow steps for finding "hidden jobs" on Twitter: (1) Start following people in your field and organizations you would like to work for and their employees, (2) join the conversation when it is relevant to your industry, (3) take advantage of hashtags (#), and (4) get help. When it comes to looking for job leads on Twitter, you do not have to go it alone. There are plenty of apps available that will help you identify potential employment opportunities. And there are plenty of websites that will help assist you in finding jobs on Twitter.

Skillings (2017) also suggests that one of the keys to using Twitter effectively to find a job is to become someone worth following. This may seem easier said than done, but she suggests that your number of followers will likely start to grow if you routinely share tips and industry-related questions quickly but thoughtfully. You should also be actively sharing valuable links and ideas. Whenever possible, engage Twitter peers at industry events, conventions, or during other networking opportunities in person. Finally, Skillings says that "spammers" who fill up your feed with unnecessary links for their services or goods should be avoided as this can have adverse effects on your followers.

Twitter should also be used to build your personal brand if you're using it as a social media platform to find that dream job. Skillings (2017) suggests using Twitter to get more proactive in your networking efforts. For some, it could mean creating a blog on a niche area of interest and tweeting about it directly to users of that blog. This might help to build your credibility within the industry and solidify your brand with potential employers. Alternatively, you may want to consider using hashtags to announce that you are available for work. Some consider it a little self-righteous but not if you have presented yourself as a professional, made the appropriate contacts, and established your credibility. If that is the case, it could be the perfect time to use a little self-promoting hash-tagging to let potential employers know you're available (e.g., #HireMe #MBA #Candidate #JobSearching #Hire [insert college nickname or mascot]). Regardless of whether or not you feel comfortable promoting yourself on Twitter to build your name brand, it is a powerful social media platform that should not be ignored. It can enhance your efforts to find that dream job and should be used to position yourself as a promising candidate to potential employers.

Internships

We introduced internships earlier in the chapter, but they are worth revisiting. Internships offer one of the best ways to land a full-time job; they benefit companies and organizations too. One of our featured researchers, Mary Dodge, recommends students pursue as many internships opportunities as possible, whenever the chance arises. Whether paid or unpaid, an internship provides a company with an opportunity to "test drive" potential employees at a low cost. If the organization also creates an enjoyable environment and experience for interns, it may also benefit from a positive word-of-mouth effect. When this occurs, it may result in a greater number of highly qualified and motivate pool of applicants for jobs the organization advertises in the future.

Interviewing Well

Why do employers conduct interviews? The answer is simple: They need to make sure that the applicant has the skills they're looking for and because they are assessing whether the applicant is "fit" to be successful in their company or organization. Interviewing is a two-way street. Applicants should see interviews as an opportunity to determine whether the company or organization is a good "fit" for them. During the interviewing process, the applicant must confirm to the employer that they have the knowledge, skill set, and ability to do the job. This only can be accomplished if the applicant quickly establishes a good rapport with the interviewer(s). Therefore, going into a job interview with a clear profile of what the employer is looking for in a successful candidate is essential for landing the job.

Before the Interview

The job market is changing quickly, and the way in which interviews are conducted has also changed considerably in recent years. When applying for a job, applicants should consider what types of interview will be conducted. The traditional one-on-one, face-to-face interview is popular, but other types of interviews are also common. Group interviews, interviews conducted over the telephone or via Skype®, or even interviews that involve large assessment centers are not uncommon.

Top Twitter Job Search Hashtags

- #Hiring or #NowHiring
- #Jobs
- #Careers
- #TweetMyJobs
- #JobOpening
- #JobListing
- #JobPosting
- #HR
- #Graduate Jobs

Tips on Turning an Internship Into a Full-time Job

- Choose an internship that allows you to make a meaningful contribution to the organization.
- Act professionally at all times during your internship.
- Establish networks while at the organization.
- Ask questions that demonstrate your interest in your job and the organization.
- Set goals that let you to demonstrate your skills during your internship.
- Volunteer without overextending yourself.
- Follow up after your internship is completed.

Source: Smith (2012).

Succeeding in a job interview requires considerably preplanning and preparation.

One of the keys to a successful job interview is being prepared for any type of interview the employer uses.

Succeeding in a job interview requires considerable preplanning and preparation. If you got on an elevator with someone, could you quickly and accurately describe yourself to him or her before reaching your floor? If not, then you need to develop your "elevator pitch" before going on an interview. Knowing what skills you possess, what makes that skill set unique, and how a potential employee views that skill set is a necessary part of preparing for an interview. But how are you supposed to know whether an employer will think your skills are attractive to an interviewee? The answer is simple: by researching the company.

Researching the company that you've applied to is an integral part of any preinterview preparation process. Going online and visit the company's website. Find its Mission Statement, Strategic Statement, Forward-thinking Objectives, and similar "About Us" information. Figuring out a way to link your skill sets with a company's strategic vision during an interview can pay big dividends! It demonstrates that you are not just looking for a job but that you are looking to make a contribution to the company or organization.

Preparing Questions by (and for) the Interviewer

Preparing for a job interview should also involve (a) identifying questions you will likely be asked and (b) developing a memorable question to ask the interviewer. There are questions that an interviewer will almost always ask an interviewee. They might be open questions (e.g., tell me a bit about yourself), behavioral questions (e.g., tell me about a time when you . . .), or hypothetical-based questions (e.g., what would you do in the following situation . . .). Some of the other most common ones are

- Where do you see yourself in five years?
- What is your greatest strength?
- What is your greatest weakness?
- Why should we hire you?
- What are your salary expectations?
- Why are you leaving or have left your job?
- Why do you want this job?
- How do you handle stress and pressure?

If you cannot answer these questions quickly and confidently, then you need more practice.

During the Interview

Most job interviews begin as soon as the applicant and the employer meet, before either side says a single word to one another. Therefore, it's vital to be on time for a job interview and to be dressed appropriately. A confident introduction and handshake is also important for a successful interview. Finally, assuring you are engaged with the interviewer by maintaining constant eye contact and confident body language is also a must.

These are some of the little things that an interviewee can do to set themselves apart (in a good way) from other applicants during the interview process. If you really want to set yourself apart, however, think of a good question to ask the interviewer when he or she turns the tables on you and says, "Is there anything you would like to ask us about this job opportunity?"

Asking the Right Questions

A memorable question could be something like "If I asked the person I'd be working closest with at my job, what are three things he or she likes most about working for your company and three things he or she likes least? What do you think he or she would say?"

This is a good way to turn the typical "What's your greatest strength/weakness" question back on the interviewer, and his or her answer to this sort of question could be eye opening. The bottom line is this: When given a chance to ask an interviewer questions about the company or the job for which you're applying, don't pass up the opportunity. In fact, ask a memorable question—one that shows a genuine interest in the job!

On the flip side, certain questions are best not asked during a job interview. For example, during the job interview, it's not a good idea to ask what your salary would be, how many days off you will get, and if you sign a contract and get a better job offer, if you can renegotiate your offer. It's also not a good idea to ask a question that can be answered by spending a little time doing some basic research on the Internet. Doing this will make you appear lazy and a high maintenance employee.

Your Professional Portfolio

Putting together a professional portfolio to present during a job interview is something all job candidates should consider doing. A **professional portfolio** is a carefully crafted set of documents and material that showcases the work of a professional and is used, for example, during job interviews to provide evidence of employability and fit with an organization or company. Obviously, certain documents should always be part of a professional portfolio, including a résumé and copies of your reference letters. The following items are also worth considering incorporating into a professional portfolio:

- **Introductory Statement**: A one-page summary statement providing an overview of the contents in your portfolio

- **Statement of Professional Preparation:** A brief description of your preparedness to work in the field

- **Professional Commitment Essay**: A two- to three-page essay focused on the relevance of your education to the job that you're applying for

- **Reflections on Documents**: A summary of your major accomplishments and outcomes that is relevant to the job that you're applying for

- **Appendix**: Contains full documents referenced or discussed in other sections of the portfolio

Whatever you decide to include in your professional portfolio, make sure it is well organized and presented cleanly and concisely. Both physical portfolios (i.e., documents contained in a three-ring binder) and electronic portfolios are acceptable formats.

Remember, it's also important to get feedback on your portfolio once it's created. This means you may want to have an academic advisor or mentor review your portfolio before

Professional portfolio: Carefully crafted set of documents and material that showcases the work of a professional and is used, for example, during job interviews to provide evidence of employability and fit with an organization or company.

heading out to an interview. Also, be prepared to give your portfolio to a potential employer during an interview, so it's a good idea to make multiple copies.

After the Interview

A successful job application may hinge as much on what an applicant does *after* a job interview as on what he or she does before or during it. Each postinterview situation is different, but there are certain things an interviewee should always consider doing after their interview is over—even if he or she doesn't follow through on each one. For example, as the interview ends, the applicant should get the card of the interviewer before leaving. This will make sure the applicant has the necessary information to follow up directly with the hiring agent.

Once the interviewer is back at home, it is a good idea to reflect on his or her performance. Reflecting on an interview can involve asking questions like "What did I say or do, specifically, that impressed the hiring official?" "Is there anything that I could have said or done better in response to any of the questions I was asked?" and "How will I respond to similar questions during my next interview?" Writing down the answers to these questions can help improve future job interviews.

In most situations, it is appropriate to follow up the job interview by writing a thank-you e-mail and sending it to the hiring official that conducted the interview. It is important to make sure the e-mail conveys more than the generic "thank you for your time" message. Including information that reminds the hiring official of who you are is the kind of information that should go into a follow-up thank-you e-mail. In other words, make it personal. (If you really want to go a step further, consider sending a handwritten note in a thank-you card. So few candidates do this, and it can add to the personal touch.)

Finally, if it's appropriate, try leveraging social media to reinforce your interview. For example, you can use LinkedIn to send a connection request to the hiring manager. (Note, however, that not all hiring managers will accept your request to connect as a matter of policy, but there is no harm in trying!) Keep in mind, however, that you should not be too quick to follow up after your interview. If you do, you could come across as too impatient. Also keep in mind that following up with a hiring official after a job interview may not always be appropriate. If you have any doubt, check in with a mentor to get his or her advice.

Professional Interviewing Tips

Each of our featured researchers has his or her own thoughts about what makes a good interview, and they were willing to share their top three interviewing tips with us. Here is what they had to say:

Chris Melde: (1) Be prepared and understand the organization you want to work for (e.g., their history). (2) Have questions ready to ask them (do your homework). (3) Clean up your social media accounts.

Rachel Boba Santos: (1) Dress appropriately. (2) Look people in the eye. (3) Bring a portfolio. One other thing: Read and study the job description. Understand what the job is that you are applying for. Read news articles. Read an organization's website. Do research on that organization and that job!

Carlos Cuevas: (1) Be genuine, and do not try to pass yourself off as someone or something you're not. This means being honest about what you can and cannot do. (2) Be aware of how well you "fit" the organization; it goes both ways. (3) Learn how to shake hands.

Mary Dodge: (1) Dress appropriately. (2) Remove any unusual jewelry. (3) Avoid using the word *like*.

Rod Brunson: If you are looking for a job in academics: (1) Be informed about the institution and department. (2) Know about what people do (i.e., the topics they specialize in). (3) Understand where faculty place their work (i.e., where they are published).

Heather Zaykowski: (1) Do not lie on a résumé. (2) Dress nicely. (3) Behave appropriately (e.g., have good posture and pretend you want a job).

National Association of Colleges and Employers (NACE): National professional organization that aims to facilitate the hiring of college graduates.

Pitfalls and Career Searches

Like any task, there are specific pitfalls to avoid. When it comes to job searching, avoiding pitfalls means the difference between getting a job and being rejected for a dream position. A common pitfall when it comes to job searches is believing you will leave the university with a bachelor's degree—or even a master's degree—and land a position as a six-digit salaried manager in an organization. This does not happen. *All* people, regardless of their educational attainment, must work their way up through the ranks. An education can speed that process, but it is unrealistic to believe that a BA in criminal justice will make you a manager of all crime analysts at an agency. In any role, you have to pay your dues.

A second and related pitfall is to enter any job and believe you have nothing left to learn. The university provides a solid foundation of information that provides an advantage to you. Nevertheless, you will find in any role you take, there is much to be learned. Be open to learning it. By being open and eager to learn even more, you will position yourself for future opportunities.

A pitfall that happens too often has to do with honesty. When filling out application materials, writing your résumé, or in an interview, you must be truthful. Do not claim your internship was full-time employment. Do not claim to have experience that you do not. Do not claim you have a master's degree if you do not. Especially in the field of criminal justice and criminology, dishonesty is absolutely unacceptable. If you are viewed as dishonest, you will not be considered a viable candidate.

It was discussed in the text of this chapter but deserves repeating: Clean up your social media. Those considering hiring you will look at your social media. What will they see? A foul-mouthed party animal? Someone with bigoted views? A misogynist? Make sure that when people look at all of your social media, they see a professional, respectful, and mature person. Finally, a pitfall we wish we did not have to highlight relates to being a jerk. Do not be a jerk. No one wants to hire a jerk. No one wants to work with a jerk. Be a kind and respectful person—the sort of person you want to work with.

Ethics and Career Searches

The **National Association of Colleges and Employers (NACE)** is a national professional organization that aims to facilitate the hiring of college graduates. One area upon which NACE focuses its efforts is the principles and practices of the hiring process. To this end, NACE has developed three career planning and recruitment principals that it hopes its members will follow during the hiring process:

1. Maintain an open and free selection of employment and experiential learning opportunities in an atmosphere conducive to objective thought, where job candidates can choose to optimize their talents and meet their personal objectives.

2. Maintain a recruitment process that is fair and equitable.

3. Support informed and responsible decision making by candidates.

NACE also recognized the importance of supporting professional development programs and of conducting salary and demographic trend surveys as part of assuring that these principals are upheld, as they are intended to provide employers and members with a framework to promote professionalism. An important component of promoting professionalism is the adherence to certain ethical standards related to recruiting, hiring, and employment. Students entering the job market should also follow a set of ethical standards. The Center for Career Exploration and Success at Miami University outlines clear ethical guidelines that they encourage their students to follow during the job search process:

- Interview only if you are sincerely interested in the position.

- Do not use interviews as "practice."

- Be certain to provide accurate information on your background, including work experience, GPA, major, etc.

- Respond promptly to invitations for on-site or second interviews.

- Never interview just to get a free trip to the job location.

- Follow established procedures if you must cancel an interview.

- Exercise prudence in your interview expenditures and be sure to keep receipts for travel and lodging expenses.

- Carefully discuss offers with employers to verify terms and reach mutually acceptable response deadlines.

- Acceptance of an employment offer should be made in good faith and honored as a contractual agreement with the employer.

- Do not continue to interview after accepting an offer, and be certain to notify other employers with offers pending.

- Notify our office when you accept an offer so we may better assist students still seeking positions. (Miami University's Career Services, 2017, para. 4)

Failing to follow these standards when job hunting may adversely impact your employment opportunities. The result could range from slight embarrassment to being disqualified from consideration, or even to having your employment terminated if a breach of ethics is discovered after you've been hired and it is severe (e.g., purposefully providing inaccurate background information).

Research Methods as a Career Expert—Nora Scanlon, MA

Nora Scanlon is an academic advisor and program coordinator and instructor at the University of Colorado Denver (CU Denver), School of Public Affairs. Scanlon studied criminology for her undergraduate degree from the University of Denver and Criminal Justice and Public Administration for her dual master's degrees from the CU Denver. Currently she advises approximately 300 undergraduate criminal justice students from the point they begin their academic careers through graduation at CU Denver. In addition, she teaches the Criminal Justice Internship course, which is focused on professional development and preparation for entering the job search process and workplace.

Courtesy of Nora Scanlon

Scanlon is an expert when it comes to helping students convert their academic skills into a career. She begins with basics such getting involved on campus. She shares events, internship opportunities, and chances to meeting with faculty during lunch with students. As advising continues, she works with students on résumé writing. Scanlon notes that there are numerous ways to apply research methods skills to a successful job search. For example, when writing your résumé, consider including a section in the middle of your résumé titled "Special Projects/ Research" where you highlight and briefly explain a research project in which you took part. Include the title of your research project, the purpose, and the required skills needed to make the project successful. Your explanation of the project should be no longer than two sentences.

An example of the professional development Scanlon offers is holding mock interviews. She recommends answering interview questions by drawing from your research experience. Scanlon points to the 2014 Job Outlook from the National Association of Colleges and Employers (NACE) that rated the following 10 characteristics as somewhere between very important and extremely important during an interview:

1. Ability to work in a team structure

2. Ability to make decisions and solve problems

3. Ability to plan, organize and prioritize work

4. Ability to verbally communicate with persons inside and outside the organization

5. Ability to retain and process information

6. Ability to analyze quantitative data

7. Technical knowledge related to the job

8. Proficiency with computer software programs

9. Ability to create and edit written reports

10. Ability to sell or influence others

Scanlon encourages students to challenge themselves to think of a way they have engaged in each of these skills throughout the course of a research project, course, or internship. For example, she asks whether you worked in a team structure (#1)? Yes! Another example, do you have experience analyzing quantitative data (#6) and creating and editing written reports (#9)? Yes! Next, how do you explain your experience in a clear and concise way during an interview? Being prepared to make these statements about yourself before the interview is the key. Practice interviewing is a great way to be prepared.

An excellent piece of advice Scanlon shares with all students is a framework to structure interview answers using the STAR approach (Table 14.2). STAR works especially well for behavioral-based interview questions, which focus on experiences, skills, and knowledge that are related to the job in which one is applying. Employers ask these questions because they may believe that past behaviors predict future behaviors. STAR stands for, Situation, Task, Action, and Result. The University of Colorado Denver's Career Center has created Table 14.2 explaining STAR.

Table 14.2   University of Colorado Denver, Career Center, Interview With a Purpose Brochure

When answering behavioral-based questions, use the STAR INTERVIEWING TECHNIQUE:

Situation or Task	Describe the situation/problem that you were in or the task that you needed to accomplish. You mush describe a specific event or situation, not a generalized description of what you have done in the past. Be sure to give enough detail for the interviewer to understand. The situation can be from a previous job, from a volunteer experience, or any relevant event. Focus areas of interviews are: Leadership, Teamwork, Personal Development, and Management Interaction.
Action you took	Describe the action you took and be sure to keep the focus on you. Even if you are discussing a group project or effort, describe what you did, not the efforts of the team. Don't tell what you might do, tell what you did.
Results you achieved	What did you accomplish? What were the results? How did the event end? What did you learn?

Scanlon asks, "Do you remember the NACE characteristics that employers ranked as very important and extremely important? In Table 14.3, pick three of the characteristics on the left and using STAR explain, through your research project, how you've obtained, or improved these skills." For example, with team structure, an interviewer may ask, "Tell me about a time you've solved a problem with a team." Applying STAR, you would describe the research project and a problem you faced, the skills it took to overcome that problem and what the end result was, as well as what you learned. Even when discussing a group or team structure, you should continue to focus on your efforts versus the group as a whole. Not only does this framework provide concise and relevant answers; it also keeps you as an applicant from rambling on and appearing scattered.

Using the STAR framework in conjunction with the top skills listed earlier will help the employer more clearly understand your skills and, hopefully, will help him or her to visualize you as part of the team. By focusing on your research project or internship, you are providing information about a specific experience versus speaking in generalities. This approach, states Scanlon, leads to a stronger answer, and the employer will have a more solid connection with you. When it comes time for the employer to review the various applicants interviewed, it is easy to forget someone who fails to bring themselves, as an individual, to the table. Employers will rarely spend excessive amounts of time trying to piece together an applicant's background, skills, and experience. Instead, they will move on to the applicant who best pieces it all together for them. Scanlon states, "What's the good news? You, as the applicant, have a lot of control over this process!" Use it to your advantage.

Scanlon recommends that students be familiar with the Bureau of Labor Statistics (BLS) and its information about jobs. For example, the average 2016 median pay for Statisticians was $80,500/year or $38.70 per hour. BLS projects the employment of statisticians to grow 34% from 2014 to 2024, which is "much faster than the average for all occupations" (https://www.bls.gov/ooh/math/statisticians.htm). The average starting salary for a crime analyst is $40,620, and the growth in this field is also double-digit. Maybe you are not interested in becoming a crime analyst or a statistician. Remember that the NACE survey does not just survey employers regarding statistical or analytical positions; it surveys all kinds of employers,

Table 14.3 STAR Method Matrix for Demonstrating Your Professional Skills			
	Situation or Task	Action	Result
Team structure			
Make decisions and solve problems			
Plan, organize, and prioritize work			
Verbal communication skills			
Retain and process information			
Analyze quantitative data			
Technical knowledge			
Computer software programs			
Create and edit written reports			
Sell or influence others			

Source: Used with permission from The Career Center, The University of Colorado, Denver.

organizations, and positions. This means the skills you are learning and developing during the course of your research methods course can be applied to other positions, organizations, and employers (even outside of the criminal justice field). Research methods skills are transferrable skills. The ability to work in a team structure is not a skill just limited to those interested in pursuing a criminal justice career. This skill set is desired across fields and sectors. Interviewing as a probation officer or as a victim advocate? Be prepared to address your abilities to work in a team structure, and remember you can draw on your research methods experiences to answer many kinds of interview questions.

Chapter Wrap-Up

In this chapter, our focus was on pursuing careers in the field of criminology and criminal justice research. We explained why professional skills related to conducting research are important and why they are desirable to potential employers. We differentiated public- versus private-sector jobs. We also identified specific places job seekers can look for a career, focusing specifically on online job search sites, social media platforms, and internships. We've provided readers with detailed information about preparing key documents applicants need to prepare when going onto the job market: a cover letter, a résumé, and letters of recommendation. Guidance on how to interview well, including what to do before the interview, during the interview, and after the interview, is offered. We concluded this chapter with an overview of some of the most common errors made during job searches, including common ethical issues and pitfalls applicants may face.

Applied Assignments

1. Homework Applied Assignment: Creating a Job Résumé

Create a job résumé, or update your existing résumé, based on the guidance we've provided you within this text. Pay particular attention to the information we presented about "What Makes a Great Résumé?" in the Résumés section. Be sure your new résumé answers the question, "What do I have to offer the employer?"; provides personal contact information; contains a clear and concise goal statement; lists current and past employment, demonstrating employability; contains details of formal educational achievements, including the names and addresses of the institutions awarding the degree(s) and time spent at that institution; and presents key skills that an employer desires. Be prepared to discuss your résumé in class.

2. Group Work in Class Applied Assignment: Interviewing for a Job

Form a group with other students in the class so that your group has an even number of students. Then divide the group in half. Half of the group will act as a job-hiring official, and the other half of the group will act as job applicants. Both the applicants and the officials should prepare three questions for a mock job. The questions can be open questions (e.g., tell me a bit about yourself), behavioral questions (e.g., tell me about a time when you . . .), or hypothetical-based questions (e.g., what would you do in the following situation . . .).

Have the hiring official ask the job hunters their questions and then vice versa. Then, switch roles. Each of you develop three NEW questions, and repeat the Q&A process. After all students have had an opportunity to ask (and answer) questions as both a hiring official and a job candidate, discuss with your partner what you liked/didn't like about your responses and how this exercise could help you prepare for your next job interview. Prepare to share your experiences with the class.

3. Internet Applied Assignment: Locating a Job Using an Online Search Tool

Visit any online job search website and search for a type of job that you may be interested in perusing after you graduate. Go to two other job search websites and find two other (different) jobs. In a reflective narrative, compare and contrast the knowledge, skills, and abilities that all three jobs have in common and that are unique, respectively. Next, identify the professional skills that these jobs desire and that you currently possess or are developing as part of your degree program. Also identify those professional skills that these jobs desire but that you lack. Finally, explain ways that you could overcome these deficiencies so that they are skills you have developed when it comes time to enter the job market. Be prepared to discuss your paper in class.

KEY WORDS AND CONCEPTS

Complimentary close 453
Cover letter 452
General Schedule (GS) 463
Keyword 467
Letter of recommendation 458

National Association of Colleges and
  Employers (NACE) 475
Private-sector employees 464
Professional portfolio 473
Professional skill set 449

Public-sector employees 461
Referee 456
Résumé 454
Skill 449

KEY POINTS

- The professional set of skills associated with the ability to conduct research in criminology and criminal justice is attractive to employers.

- Jobs in both the public and private sectors need employees who are able to think logically about social problems, apply scientifically rigorous approaches to knowledge discovery, and can communicate empirically based evidence to a broad array of stakeholders.

- Online job search tools are a quick and easy way to find out who's hiring, and what jobs they're looking to fill. Three of the most common job search sites are (1) Indeed.com, (2) Careebuilder.com, and (3) Monster.com.

- Social media platforms, such as Facebook, LinkedIn, and Twitter, can be leveraged to help you find your dream job.

- Internships often lead to full-time employment; they offer both the intern and the organization the opportunity to "test drive" each other before making a more permanent commitment.

- Three of the most important job-related documents you'll need to provide at some point during the application process are (1) a cover letter, (2) a professional résumé, and (3) letters of recommendation.

- A job interview is a crucial part of landing a good job. Interviews give employers an opportunity make sure that applicants have the skills their looking for and whether applicants are "fit" to be successful in their organizations. Applicants should see interviews as an opportunity to determine whether the company or organization is a good "fit" for them as well.

REVIEW QUESTIONS

1. Why are research methods skills beneficial to you?

2. What are the similarities and differences between public- and private-sector jobs?

3. What are some types of *public*-sector jobs that would require an employee to use some of the professional skills associated with conducting research?

4. What are some types of *private*-sector jobs that would require an employee to use some of the professional skills associated with conducting research?

5. What are the names of some of the most common job search sites?

6. How can some of the most common social media platforms (e.g., Facebook, LinkedIn, and Twitter) be used to identify and apply for jobs?

7. Why do internships offer a great opportunity to gain full-time employment with the company an intern works for?

8. What is a job résumé, and what are some of the things it should (and shouldn't) include?

9. What is a letter of recommendation, and who are some of the people you should ask to be your referee?

10. What are some of the "things to remember" before, during, and after a job interview?

11. What are some of the common pitfalls that should be avoided when searching for your dream job?

CRITICAL THINKING QUESTIONS

1. What are some of the professional skills that could be associated with each of the different stages depicted in Wallace's Wheel of Science (see Figure 2.1 in Chapter 2) and that employers would want in any job candidate?

2. Log onto USAJobs.com and type "Justice + Research" into the search box. Click on a few results that are returned, and investigate the kinds of skills that are listed under the section titled "Preferred Qualifications." What are some of the common skills

desired for these positions, and how do they relate to skills related to research?

3. Compare and contrast Facebook, LinkedIn, and Twitter in terms of their abilities to identify and apply for jobs. In your opinion, is one social media platform better than the others? Is there a platform you would avoid using? If so, why or why not?

4. Go online and find a job posting using an online job search site (e.g., Monster.com). Create a cover letter for the advertised position. What were the important points stressed in the letter you wrote? What did you decide to leave out? For this position, whom would you ask to write a letter of recommendation on your behalf? Why?

5. With a partner from class, go online and find a job posting using an online job search site (e.g., Monster .com). One of you choose to be the hiring agent for this position and the other choose to be the job applicant. Spend a few minutes preparing questions for each other that you would ask during an interview. Then have the interviewer conduct an interview. After the interview is over, both the hiring agent and the job seeker should evaluate the interview. What went well, and what went horribly wrong? What lessons have you learned that will better prepare you for your next job interview?

$SAGE edge™

SAGE edge offers a robust online environment featuring an impressive array of free tools and resources for review, study, and further exploration, keeping you on the cutting edge of teaching and learning. Learn more at **edge.sagepub .com/rennisonrm**.

Appendix

Random Numbers Table

```
76066 60044 08110 37354 23064 92492 57648 62180 01701 56580 65384 92088
11978 52308 78202 53635 27336 79675 22659 20264 74334 38681 72198 45090
52971 02769 53376 74998 63248 98496 92751 36545 78606 25863 10650 03174
25604 58312 86747 28000 04242 22400 67925 57907 14518 18127 80743 19455
29877 45494 25200 86083 03433 04501 01296 10910 55512 68589 82474 40817
65789 64316 95292 02364 07705 91683 39749 68993 54703 24132 89288 93819
33340 88220 97024 23727 17059 83947 09841 58716 58976 11314 27741 51903
05973 43763 03837 50171 84611 34408 85015 06637 94888 30136 97833 41626
10246 30945 42290 34813
```

Specs: This table of 100 random numbers was produced according to the following specifications: Numbers were randomly selected from within the range of 0 to 99999. Duplicate numbers were allowed. This table was generated on 9/21/2017.

Glossary

1-in-*k* method: Most commonly used systematic sampling approach that is based on the formula $k = N / n$.

Abstract: First section of a journal article that provides, in a concise paragraph of approximately 150 to 250 words, the purpose, method, findings, and conclusions of the research.

Accidental sampling: Nonprobability sampling approach where a sample is gathered simply based on convenience and ease of finding it. Also known as "convenience sampling" and as "haphazard sampling."

Accuracy: One of four evaluation research standards that refers to the notion that an effective evaluation will offer correct findings. Accuracy is evident by presenting the program in context by using systematic procedures, using the appropriate methods, and producing impartial reports with justified conclusions.

Administrative crime analysis: One of three types of crime analysis performed by law enforcement personnel, typically involving long-range projects that are internal to the agency.

Advocacy group: Collection of individuals who operate to influence public opinion, policy makers, regarding particular criminal justice issues that require immediate attention and policy. Also known as an "interest group."

American Community Survey (ACS): Second largest survey administered by the Census Bureau that involves more than 3 million people living in America every year. Data on income and education levels as well as on employment status and housing characteristics are gathered during the ACS.

Analysis of qualitative information: Accuracy standard that requires the use of appropriate scientific analysis of qualitative data used to address the research question being considered.

Analysis of quantitative information: Accuracy standard requiring the use of appropriate scientific analysis of quantitative data used to address the research question being investigated.

Analysis of variance (ANOVA): Statistical analysis technique used to compare the group averages among three or more groups or across three or more points in time.

Analyzing the data: Step of evaluation research in which the evaluator uses the data and information gathered to answer the research question. The specific type of analysis is contingent on the research methodology used to gather the data/information.

Anonymity: Refers to situations where the researcher cannot link the data gathered to the respondent or does not gather identifying information about the respondent.

Aoristic analysis: Crime analysis method used for determining the 24-hour rhythm of crimes when the exact time of crime event is unknown.

APA: American Psychological Association's publication style. This style was created almost a century ago to standardize scientific writing. APA guidelines dictate every element of a scientific paper, including how citations are handled both in text and in the references, the required sections in a paper, heading formats, and punctuation.

Applied research: Conducted to develop knowledge for immediate use for a specific decision-making purpose. Evaluation research is a type of applied research. In contrast, basic research generates knowledge for the sake of knowledge.

Approach subsection: Subsection in a policy brief that describes relevant background information including the context of the study. Through the use of nontechnical terms, the approach subsection should identify the research methods used to collect the data. It is usually presented with the results subsection.

Assent: Agreement by a child to participate in research that will likely benefit him or her. To gain assent, the child must be able to comprehend and understand what it means to be a participant in research.

Assessment of risk and benefits: Second requirement of ethical research stated in the Belmont Report. It is required that all parties engaged in research examine whether the benefits of the study outweigh the risks. It is the researcher's responsibility to properly design a study and to ensure that the selection of subjects is fair and just. It is a review committee's responsibility to identify whether any risks to the participants are justified. Participants must assess whether they will or will not participate.

Association: One of three criteria needed to establish causation, which is found when the values in the independent variable and the values in the dependent variable move together in a pattern.

Attributes: Categories or grouping of the data collected for a particular measure.

Authoritative sources: Knowledge based on information accepted from people or sources that are trusted such as parents, clergy, news sources, bloggers, social media, or professors.

Availability sampling: Nonprobability sampling approach where a sample is gathered simply based on convenience and ease of finding sampling elements. It is also known as "convenience sampling," "accidental sampling," and "haphazard sampling."

Axial coding: In this step, the researcher focuses on these preliminary analytic categories or labels to identify relationships between the categories. The attention during this stage is not on the raw data but on the summarized labels of the data.

Basic research: Research that generates knowledge motivated by intellectual curiosity to better understand the world. In contrast, applied research, such as evaluation research, is used to develop knowledge for immediate use for a specific decision-making purpose.

Before-and-after design: Quasi-experimental design that has no random assignment and no comparison group. It does, however, include a pretest and a posttest. This design has marginal internal validity given the inability to control for confounding factors making claims of causality challenging. In addition, external validity is also poor.

Behaviorally specific question: In research, a question that tends to be more graphic in nature, which leaves little doubt in the mind of the respondent about the type of information the research is after.

Belmont Report: Ethical Principles and Guidelines for the Protection of Human Subjects and Research: Report that outlined the principles of human subjects research including respect for persons, beneficence, and justice.

Beneficence: Second principle of ethical research outlined in the Belmont Report. It states that researchers are obligated to do no harm, to maximize possible benefits, and to minimize possible harms to all participants in a study. Study participants include respondents, researchers, and bystanders.

Bias: Describes a sample that fails to include a particular type of individual or particular groups found in the population.

Biased sample: Indicates that the sample fails to include a particular type of individual or some groups found in the population.

Blind review: Method of reviewing journal manuscripts in which neither the reviewers nor the manuscript writer knows the identity of the other.

Block groups: Geographic area used by the Census Bureau for aggregating population data that is typically defined by a population of 600 to 3,000 people.

Block matching: Type of matching used in some true experiments that includes the creation of subgroups of the subjects or units of interest based on a block variable. The experiment is then conducted separately on each block. By conducting the experiment on two groups or blocks, the researcher has controlled for the effect of the characteristic making up the block.

Block variables: Those variables the researcher believes will affect response to the treatment. Block variables are used to create blocks used in block matching.

Boolean operators: Connect or exclude particular search terms or phrases used in an electronic search. Use of Boolean operators enables the searcher to narrow or broaden a search for material.

Boost account: One of two explanations of the repeat victimization phenomenon. It suggests that repeat/near repeat victimization is a result of the same offender returning to where he or she succeeded at committing the initial offense because the initial offense increased the offender's perception of reward and decreased the risk (i.e., "boosted" his or her confidence).

Budgets: Provide information about how much money and other resources can be spent on an items. Policies are subject to budget constraints.

Bureau of Justice Statistics (BJS): Part of the Office of Justice Programs (OJP), it is responsible for collecting, analyzing, and publishing data related to crime in the United States, which is gathered from the 50,000 agencies that comprise the U.S. justice system.

Cargo theft: According to the FBI (2015, "What is cargo theft?," para. 1), "[t]he criminal taking of any cargo including, but not limited to, goods, chattels, money, or baggage that constitutes, in whole or in part, a commercial shipment of freight moving in commerce, from any pipeline system, railroad car, motor truck, or other vehicle, or from any tank or storage facility, station house, platform, or depot, or from any vessel or wharf, or from any aircraft, air terminal, airport, aircraft terminal or air navigation facility, or from any intermodal container, intermodal chassis, trailer, container freight station, warehouse, freight distribution facility, or freight consolidation facility."

Categorical variable: Variables characterized by a nominal level of measurement.

Causal relationship: Purpose of experimental research because it can provide evidence of if and how one variable affects, causes, influences, or predicts another variable.

Causation: Exists when the variation in one variable causes variation in another variable. Three criteria must be present to establish a causal relationship: temporal ordering, association, and no spurious relationships.

Census Bureau: Federal agency in the United States responsible for administering the decennial census, which is used to allocate seats in the U.S. House of Representatives based on states' populations.

Census: Gathering of data from a collective that includes every element of the population.

Centers for Disease Control and Prevention (CDC): Part of the Department of Health and Human Services, located just outside of Atlanta, Georgia. The CDC gathers data valuable to criminal justice researchers.

Chain referral sampling: Specific type of purposive sampling approach in which sample subjects are selected based on referrals from prior subjects. Also called "networks," "snowball sampling," or "reputational sampling."

Characteristics: In qualitative data analysis, they represent a single item or event in a text, similar to an individual response to variables used in quantitative data analysis·

Chi-square test: Statistical test used to determine whether two categorical variables are independent of one another.

Choropleth map: Type of thematic map that uses shaded or patterned areas in proportion to the measurement of the statistical variable being displayed on the map, such as population density or per-capita income.

Chronologically based literature reviews: Organized to describe changes and growth in our understanding of a topic over time. The changes described may be based on relevant substantive themes, focused on change in methodology, change in theory, or any other relevant theme.

Cloning: Type of plagiarism involving the direct copying and pasting of others' words without citing the original author.

Closed-ended question: Type of survey question that requires respondents to select an answer from a list of response categories.

Cluster: Part of cluster sampling that refers to a sampling element where a researcher or more of the desired units of observation are found or associated. Clusters take on many forms such as states, cities, universities, schools, housing units, census blocks, counties, etc.

Cluster analysis: Crime analysis technique that involves the identification of similar types of crime that "cluster" in space or time.

Cluster sampling: Probability sampling approach where groups or clusters (where a researcher will find the units of observation needed for the research) are first sampled, and then each unit within each cluster is used to gather data.

Codebook: Documentation for a data set that explains how the data files are structured, how the variables are contained in the data set, and the type of coding of specific variables is also available for each data set.

Coding: Coding can refer to converting a respondent's answers into a numerical value that can be entered into a database. In qualitative data analysis, it is the process of attaching labels to lines of text so that the researcher can group and compare similar or related pieces of information.

Coding sorts: In qualitative data analysis, they represent compilations of similarly coded blocks of text from different sources that are converted into a single file or report.

Common Rule: Common name of Subpart A of the HHS regulations of 1991.

Communicate the findings and recommendations: One of seven evaluation research steps in which the evaluator shares the results and suggestions arising from the research with stakeholders. The sharing includes a comprehensive accounting of the research process.

Communication: Reporting of findings to policy makers. Communication must be done on their terms. Sharing information in the form of journal articles is not appropriate. Rather, the use of a policy brief or other type of communication is necessary.

Complete and fair assessment: One of the propriety standards of an effective evaluation. Indicates that an evaluation must offer a complete and fair assessment of the strengths and weaknesses of the program. Without a complete and fair assessment, the usefulness of the evaluation is limited.

Complete observer: Role conception in which the researcher only observes, and does not participate, or conduct interviews at all. The role of the observer is to observe and to take meaning from what is seen. Those being watched are unaware of the presence of the researcher.

Complete participant: Role conception in which the researcher keeps hidden his or her true identity and purpose from those being observed. The researchers' goal is to interact in this natural setting as naturally as possible to gather data and meaning.

Complimentary close: Polite ending to a letter. In job cover letters, common closes include "Regards," "Sincerely," and "Best Wishes."

Comprehensible: Requirement from the Belmont Report of the information given possible study participants. That the information be comprehensible is required before the participant can offer informed consent.

CompStat: Organizational management approach used by police departments to proactively address crime problems, which relies heavily on crime analysis and mapping.

Computer-assisted qualitative data analysis (CAQDAS): Tool available to qualitative researchers for assistance in analyzing qualitative data. It cannot replace the role of the researcher.

Computer-assisted telephone interviewing (CATI): Computerized system that guides the interviewer through the survey on a computer. The system prompts the interviewer about exactly what to ask.

Concept: Abstract, mental pictures of things that exist only in our minds. Examples include gender, victim, injury, recidivism, and rehabilitation.

Conceptual definition: Precise, accurate, comprehensive, and clear definitions resulting from conceptualization.

Conceptualization: Process of precisely, accurately, comprehensively, and clearly defining what is meant by a particular concept. The resulting definition from this process is a conceptual definition.

Conclusions: Found at the end of journal articles and are generally short sections that briefly summarize the overall conclusions of the research, and why the findings are important. In many cases, the discussion and conclusion sections are combined.

Conclusions section in a policy brief: Acts to answer the general question, "What does it all mean?" In the conclusions section, the researcher must interpret the data and offer concrete conclusions.

Confidentiality: When the researcher knows and can identify individual respondents but promises to keep that information private.

Conflict of interest: One of the propriety standards of an effective evaluation. Requires that any conflict of interest that occurs must be dealt with transparently and honestly to ensure the evaluation and results are not compromised.

Confounders: Variables that the researcher seeks to control or eliminate in experimental research. Control of confounders can be accomplished via random assignment of subjects or units to control and experimental groups.

Confounding factor: Third variable at work in a spurious relationship that is causing what appears to be a relationship between two other variables.

Conjunctive analysis of case configurations (CACC): Used to analyze both small and large data sets, focuses on reducing data into meaningful statistical information (e.g., frequency distributions and percentages), and assesses empirical observations with formal statistical tests (e.g., chi-square test of independence). In terms of qualitative analysis, CACC focuses on the complex causal recipes or causal pathways that define particular outcomes. In other words, instead of focusing on people (i.e., victims, offenders, police), places (i.e., crime hot spots, crime attractors, crime generators), or events (i.e., homicides, robberies, executions) and variables that explain the variance in these observations, CACC builds situational contexts of particular outcomes, from an existing data file, defined by the combinations of variable attributes believed to influence that outcome.

Content analysis: Type of document analysis that does not have a widely agreed upon definition. Most do agree that it is both quantitative and qualitative in nature. The most widely acknowledged definition is posited by Neuendorf as "a summarizing, quantitative analysis of messages that relies on the scientific method, including attention to objectivity/intersubjectivity, a priori design, reliability, validity, generalizability, replicability, and hypothesis testing" (2002, p. 10).

Content validity: Type of validity established when a measure captures the meaning of the abstract concept based on the conceptual definition.

Context analysis: Accuracy standard of an effective evaluation that requires a program to be examined in context as to allow deeper understanding of the program. With this knowledge, a researcher is more likely to provide findings that influences the program.

Continuous variable: Additional way to describe a ratio or interval level of measurement. Continuous variables use numerical measurement and are not restricted to whole numbers. That is, they can be expressed using decimals (e.g., 1.3, 27.85, 1,079.453).

Control group: Group of subjects or other units of interest that does not receive any treatment during experimental research.

Control variable: Type of independent variable included in research to better isolate the role of an independent variable of interest (frequently referred to as CVs).

Convenience sampling: Nonprobability sampling approach where a sample is gathered simply based on convenience and ease of finding. Also known as "accidental sampling" and as "haphazard sampling."

Convex hull: Smallest polygon that can be drawn around the outer points of all the data in a data distribution of geographic locations.

Correlation analysis: Statistical technique used to determine whether two continuous variables are associated with one another.

Cost-effectiveness: Criterion of feasibility that indicates an effective evaluation. Requires evaluators to consider the efficient and effective use of resources. Any costs incurred should be directly toward producing information needed to conduct a useful evaluation.

County Business Patterns (CBP): Data that contain annual economic information by industry and that can be used to support studies that consider economic activity of small areas as part of their research question.

Cover letter: Formal correspondence, written to a hiring official, explaining a candidate's interest in an employment opportunity with his or her organization.

Crime analysis: When used in geographic information systems (GIS), it refers to spatial analysis methods used on crime data to understand where and when events occur so that patterns can be systematically identified and reduction and prevention strategies implemented.

Crime attractors: Places that are attractive to offenders simply due to the nature of the activity that occurs at that particular location.

Crime enablers: Locations that have little or no regulation of behavior. The lack of control increases the likelihood for crime to occur.

Crime generators: Places that attract large numbers of both offenders and victims, such as shopping malls, sporting events, parades, and other festivities.

Crime mapping: Research methodology used to identify spatio-temporal patterns in crime data.

Criterion validity: Type of validity established when one's measures correspond to existing measures (aka criteria).

Cross-sectional data: Data collected at the same point of time or without regard to differences in time.

Current Population Survey (CPS): Monthly survey of about 60,000 U.S. households sponsored by the Bureau of Labor Statistics. Its primary aim is to gauge the monthly unemployment rate in the United States, providing one of many indicators of economic health of the nation.

Data: Information that takes a variety of forms, such as words, observations, measurements, descriptions, and numbers. The individual pieces of information or evidence gathered, analyzed, and used to answer the research question. Data can be numeric and non-numeric in nature.

Data codebooks: Collection of all data gathered by a particular data set. Many criminal justice and criminology data codebooks are available online at no charge.

Deduction: Process of making inferences about a particular instance through the reference to a general principle or law.

Deductive reasoning: Approach in which the researcher begins with broad or general statements that are used to derive more specific statements. Used in research that begins more generally and works to more specificity. Commonly used in research using quantitative data.

Defensible information sources: Standard of accuracy requiring the sources of information used to conduct a program evaluation. Information shared about sources used in the evaluation should be detailed enough to allow others to assess these sources.

Definition: Clarifying the precise meaning of a particular concept when used in research. For example, in one piece of research, injury may be defined as physical harms perpetrated to another person against his or her will. In some other piece of research, injury may be defined as physical, emotional, psychological, and financial harms perpetrated against another person against his or her will.

De-identified data: Data that have been stripped of all identifiable data so that there is no way they could be linked back to the subjects from whom it was originally collected.

Demographic questions: Questions that ask about basic characteristics of the person such as gender, age, race, ethnicity, income, and so on.

Dependent variable: Type of variable that is the outcome of interest and focus of the research.

Describe purposes and procedures: Standard of accuracy that requires the evaluator to clearly articulate and outline the purposes and procedures of the evaluation. In addition, the stated purposes and procedures of the evaluation should be described comprehensively to allow continual monitoring and assessment of the evaluation.

Descriptive literature review: Organization format for a literature review that identifies the major elements of contemporary understanding about a particular topic.

Descriptive research: Focused description of a topic that answers questions such as "What is it?" "What are the characteristics of it?" and "What does it look like?" It is similar to exploratory research, but it is narrower given knowledge gained by exploratory research.

Descriptive statistics: Branch of statistics that involves the use of numbers to summarize the characteristics of data.

Design of the methodology: Step in the evaluation research process that includes outlining the needed research methodology to answer the research question. This includes items such as identifying the program goals, identifying ways to best measure if those goals are being met, and identifying what type or types of data are required to address the research question. Those data may come via observation, content analysis, interviews, surveys, or participation in the program.

Develop findings and conclusions: Step of evaluation research in which the evaluator uses the data and information gathered to generate findings that address the research question. In addition, this includes conclusions about the issue and recommendations for ways to deal with the issue at hand.

Develop the research question: Final step of seven steps in the evaluation research process in which the evaluator shares the results of the research with stakeholders. The other steps include identifying and engaging stakeholders, developing the research question, designing the methodology, gathering data/evidence, analyzing the data, developing findings and conclusions, justifying the recommendations, and finally, communicating findings and recommendations.

Deviation score: Difference between an individual score in a data distribution and the average of all scores in the same distribution.

Disclosure of findings: One of the propriety standards of an effective evaluation. Indicates that evaluation findings must be made available to those with a legal right to the findings or to those affected by the evaluation.

Discrete variable: Additional way to describe interval- and ratio-level variables. These variables use numeric measurement and are restricted to only whole numbers.

Discussion: Section found near the end of a journal article that follows the findings section. Discussion sections are used to discuss the findings and to place them into the context of the existing literature.

Document analysis: Systematic collection, review, evaluation, synthesizing, and interpretation of documents to gain meaning and understanding, regardless of whether the document is printed or available in electronic form. Documents include numerous sources of text and images including cartoons, advertisements, books, letters, maps, public records, scripts, meeting minutes, and so on.

Don A. Dillman: Expert in survey methodology at Washington State University who has written extensively on survey design and ways to minimize survey nonresponse.

Double-barreled questions: Questions that ask about more than one issue in a single question. This makes it unclear which part of the question the response refers to.

Ecological fallacy: Error in logic where a researcher applies conclusions based on a group or an organization to an individual. This fallacy assumes all individuals in a collective are characterized by the larger collective's average characteristic.

Ecological momentary assessments (EMA): Research that comprises a unique type of methodology, designed for real time/real place data collection. That is, when taking a survey, the data gathered extends beyond the answers to the questions.

Ecological validity: Extent to which data reflect the "real world."

Elements: Individual parts that when aggregated form a population.

Empirical: Type of research based on systematic observations, experimentations, or experiences.

Empirical peer-reviewed journal articles: Type of original or primary source that is useful in constructing a literature review. This research is based on systematic observation and has undergone rigorous peer review prior to publication.

Encryption: Process in which data and information are encoded making unauthorized access impossible.

Ethics: Norms for behavior that distinguish between what is and is not acceptable. Ethics are not necessarily what our feelings or laws direct us to do but what the common norms of moral behavior in society dictate.

Ethnographic interviews: Also called "unstructured interviews." They are conducted conversationally and are based on very few broad, guiding questions that provide a basic framework to the interview. An unstructured interviewing approach allows a researcher to gather data about the topic based on the respondent's experiences and perceptions. Respondents can share with the researcher what is important versus the researcher asking the respondent about what the researcher believes is important.

Ethnography: A type of systematic qualitative research in which the researcher's goal is to gather a comprehensive and holistic understanding of the culture, environment, and social phenomenon associated with a group or with individuals in a group. Ethnography involves a researcher immersing him- or herself into a culture for a prolonged period.

Evaluation impact: One of the utility criteria of an effective evaluation. Is present when the findings and recommendations of an evaluation are accepted and implemented by key stakeholders.

Evaluation research: Applied systematic assessment of the need for, implementation of, or output of a program based on objective criteria. By using the data gathered in evaluation research, the researcher can improve, enhance, expand, or terminate a program. Evaluation research involves seven basic steps: identifying and engaging stakeholders, developing the research question, designing the methodology, gathering data/evidence, analyzing the data, developing findings and conclusions, justifying the recommendations, and communicating findings and recommendations.

Evaluator credibility: One of the utility criteria of an effective evaluation. Requires that evaluators must be both competent and trustworthy. The presence of competence and trust in the evaluator benefits the evaluation in that findings can be fully credible and accepted.

Executive summary: First section in a policy brief that is generally written last. This section should tell busy policy makers the overall purpose and findings of the policy brief. An executive summary should hook the reader and compel them to keep reading.

Exempt research: That which does not have information about respondents, is publicly available, and has no more than minimal risk.

Exhaustive: Desirable characteristic in response categories meaning every possible response option is offered.

Exhaustiveness: Measurement requirement that there be an attribute available for every possible response.

Expedited review: Review by the institutional review board (IRB) committee chair (and perhaps one or two other members). This is not necessarily a fast review but one that does not require the full board.

Experimental group: Group of subjects or other units of interest that receives the treatment in experimental research.

Experimental mortality: Threat to internal validity of experimental research that occurs when subjects from either the control or the experimental group drop out of the research at differential rates for reasons related to features of the study.

Explanatory research: Research that provides explanations about a topic by addressing question such as "Why is it?" "How is it?" "What is the effect of it?" "What causes it?" and "What predicts it?"

Exploratory research: Research that addresses questions such as "What is it?" How is it?" and "Where is it?" This approach is used when little or nothing is known about a topic.

External validity: Related to the generalizability of experimental findings to other people in other situations. External validity is often at odds with internal validity.

Face validity: Type of validity that indicates a measure *appears* to measure the concept it is designed to measure.

Face-to-face interviews: Also referred to as "in-person interviews." They represent another popular survey modality in which the interviewer asks the respondent questions and records the respondent's answer.

Farfel and Chisolm: Researchers at John Hopkins University in the 1990s who conducted experiments on lead paint abatement techniques. This experiment exposed young children, who are most vulnerable to the pernicious effects of lead contamination. Although some children in the experiment experienced a decline in lead toxicity, others experienced an increase.

Feasibility: One of four major standards of effective evaluations that focuses on whether an evaluation is viable, pragmatic, realistic, diplomatic, and involves the prudent use of resources.

Federal Bureau of Investigation (FBI): Domestic intelligence and security service of the United States, which serves as the nation's prime federal law enforcement agency.

Federal Policy for the Protections of Human Subjects: Set of regulations developed by the Department of Health and Human Services (HHS) in 1991 that guides most contemporary research today. These regulations build on foundational documents such as the Nuremberg Code and the Belmont Report. When developed, this policy contained four Subparts: A (aka Common Rule), B, C, and D. In 2009, a fifth subpart (Subpart E) was added.

FedStats: Data repository that offers open access to a wide range of statistical data generated by the federal government.

Field notes: Most basic and most important data recording technique used in qualitative research. They should be used regardless of the approach used, and they can be supplemented by other data recording approaches such as audio or video recordings. Field notes should include everything a researcher observes. The researcher uses words to describe the environment, time, weather, sounds, smells, and sights in as much detail as possible. No detail is too small, or occurrence too unimportant, to be included.

Fielded: Term used to mean that a survey has been distributed or administered and data are being collected.

Filters: Used in electronic searches to place restrictions on or refine a search. Common filters used are on the type of source needed (e.g., journal articles) and date range of publication (e.g., last five years).

Findings: Section that reports the findings of a piece of research. In this section, the research questions are answered.

First Law of Geography: Also known as "Tobler's Law," it states that everything is related to everything else, but near things are more related than distant things.

Fiscal responsibility: One of the propriety standards of an effective evaluation. Requires that the use of resources during the course of the evaluation be sound, ethical, and prudent.

Flag account: One of two explanations of the repeat victimization phenomenon. The flag account suggests it is the characteristics of the person/target that entice potential offenders but that these characteristics remain constant over time.

Focus group: Collections of people involved in the discussion of a predetermined set of short, clear, and nonbiased questions. Led by a moderator, a focus group generally lasts from 45 minutes to 2 hours.

Focusing event: Event that captures the attention of policy makers, the public, and the media simultaneously like a major disaster or other crises.

Formal agreements: One of the propriety standards of an effective evaluation that requires the presence of a formal, written agreement involving all principal parties involved in an evaluation. This written agreement should identify clearly each individual's obligations, how associated tasks are to be done, who is to conduct required tasks, and when tasks will be completed. Formal agreement is binding unless all parties choose to renegotiate the terms of it.

Formative evaluation: Conducted in the earliest stages of the policy process while a program is being developed with the purpose of ensuring the program is feasible prior to full implementation. Formative evaluations can be thought of as "trouble-shooting" evaluations in that what is discovered from the evaluation is "fed back" into the program to strengthen or enhance it. Two types of formative evaluations are considered in this text: needs assessments and process evaluations.

Frequency distribution: Used in descriptive statistics, it is a table that displays the number of times a particular value or category is observed in the data for a particular variable.

Full board review: All research that is not exempt or expedited and requires the review of the full institutional review board (IRB).

Full enumeration: Another term used for a census because all members of the population were used to gather data.

Gap analysis: Part of a needs assessment in which the evaluator identifies the size or extent of the problem needing attention, as well as the desired situation. Identifying what is and what is desired is the gap analysis.

Garbage In, Garbage Out (GIGO): Notion in research that findings produced from data analysis are only as good as the data being analyzed.

Gather data/evidence: Step in the process of evaluation research in which the evaluator accumulates data and information used to answer the research question. Data can come from multiples sources, including observations, interviews, surveys, and content analysis.

Generalizability: Desirable characteristic of findings from research indicating that the results from a sample can be applied to the larger population from which the sample was taken.

General Schedule (GS): Determines the pay scale for most federal employees especially those in professional, technical, administrative, or clerical positions. The GS pay scale consists of 15 grades, from GS-1, the lowest level, to GS-15, the highest level.

Geocoding: In GIS and crime analysis, it is the process of assigning an XY coordinate pair to the description of a place (i.e., an address) by comparing the descriptive location-specific elements of nonspatial data to those in reference data that have existing spatial information associated with it.

Geographic information systems (GIS): Branch of information technology that involves collecting, storing, manipulating, analyzing, managing, and presenting geospatially referenced data.

Geographic profiling: Crime analysis method used for identifying the most probable area in which a serial offender lives, based on the known locations of crimes that are believed to be committed as part of a series of linked events.

Geographic regions: Units of analyses and the who or what being studied. These may include city blocks, census tracks, cities, counties, states, or countries.

Geographically weighted regression (GWR): Spatial analysis technique similar to linear regression analysis involving the use of predictor variables to estimate their relationship to an outcome variable or dependent variable.

Geospatial data: Data containing spatially referenced information (e.g., the latitude and longitude coordinates) included as part of all the data contained in a data set.

Geostatistical analysis: Any mathematical technique that uses the geographical properties of data as part of a statistical or an analytic method.

Going native: Phrase devised by Gold (1958), occurs when the field researcher actually becomes the role he or she is playing and is no longer able to observe the situation with any objectivity.

Gold standard: Phrase used to describe true experimental research designs given their ability to establish causality.

Grounded theory: Systematic methodology that leads to the construction of theory through the coding and analysis of qualitative data.

Group: Unit of analysis used to indicate that the who or what being studied is a group. For example, a Boy Scout troop is a group that may be the who or what being studied. Treated the same as organizations.

Guidelines: Recommendations about the expected behavior during the course of following procedures, with examples of how to deal with specific instances one may encounter.

Haphazard sampling: Nonprobability sampling approach where a sample is gathered simply based on convenience and ease of finding. Also known as "accidental sampling."

Hate Crime Statistics Act of 1990: Out of this act, the FBI publishes an annual hate crime statistics report that is congressionally mandated.

Hawthorne Effect: Identified in 1953, refers to possible impact on behavior of those who are aware they are being observed and studied. It is a type of reactivity meaning that individual will hide or exaggerate behaviors when he or she is aware of being observed.

History: Threat to the internal validity of an experiment that refers to the occurrence of an external event during the course of an experiment that affects subjects' response to the treatment and as a result the findings of the research.

Hit rate: Measure of predictive accuracy used in predictive policing, which is defined by the number of crime incidents that actually fall within a predicted crime hot spot, based on past crime events. The hit rate is expressed as a simple percentage that ranges from 0% to 100%.

Holmesberg Prison: Pennsylvania prison where Dr. Albert Kligman performed unethical skin experiments on prisoners from 1951 to 1974.

Hot spot mapping: Various, advanced, spatial-statistical methods and techniques that use the known locations of recorded crime incidents to identify nonrandom, high concentrations of crime events within a study area.

Human interactions: One of the propriety standards of an effective evaluation. Requires that evaluation research be conducted with respect to all individuals associated with the program of interest. No individual should be threatened or harmed, and all engaged must be respected.

Human subject: According to the Common Rule refers to a living individual.

Hypothesis: Testable statement about the relationship between variables.

Identify and Engage Stakeholders: First step of the evaluation research process in which the evaluator scans the environments to identify those who are affiliated with and affected by the program of interest. Once identified, those stakeholders must be engaged in the process to maximize buy-in and, ultimately, the success of the project.

Ideology: Set of ideas and ideals that form one's economic, political, or social views of the world.

Impact evaluations: One of two summative evaluations considered in this text. Impact evaluations are global examinations that assess whether a program is achieving its designated goals. These evaluations identify the output of the program in terms of intended outputs, as well as in terms of unintended outputs.

Impact factors: Scores assigned to journals theoretically indicating the journal's quality. The higher the score, the higher the quality.

Impartial reporting: Accuracy standard that calls for care to be taken to avoid distortion or bias in findings. The evaluator must strive to report on the evaluation regardless of personal feelings.

Implications subsection: Subsection of a policy brief that identifies what *could* happen and frequently includes "if, then" statements.

Incentives: Used in survey research when eligible participants are given something of value in return for their participation.

Independent variable: Type of variable that is believed or hypothesized to influence, be associated with, or cause the variation in an outcome or dependent variable.

Individual: Most common unit of analysis used in criminology and criminal justice research that indicates that the who or what being studied is an individual. This could be any person in the population or specific individuals such as students, offender, or law enforcement officers.

Individualist fallacy: Also known as "reductionism" or as "reductionist fallacy." It is a reasoning error that occurs when a researcher applies conclusions based on research using an individual unit of analysis to a group or an organization.

Inductive reasoning: Used in research that begins more specific and works to greater generality. Commonly used in research using qualitative data.

Inferences: Conclusions about the population based on evidence and reasoning about sample data.

Information scope and selection information: One of the utility criteria of an effective evaluation. Requires that the data and information collected for use in the evaluation must speak directly to the specific research questions guiding the program evaluation. This criterion mandates that the data and information must be responsive to the interests of the stakeholders.

Information: Required by the Belmont Report for ethical research. Those considering participating in research must be provided information about the study they are considering.

Informed consent: First requirement of ethical research stated in the Belmont Report. Informed consent indicates participants can choose what shall or shall not be done to them. To obtain informed consent, the research participant must be given comprehensible information about the study, from which he or she can volunteer to participate.

Inputs: One of four steps in a basic logic model. Inputs include things like training or education. The idea is that these inputs should lead to the outputs depicted in the logic model.

Institutional review boards (IRBs): Committee convened and tasked with reviewing, approving, and monitoring health and social science research involving humans in the United States. With few exceptions, all research that is supported in any fashion by the U.S. federal government requires IRB oversight; other funding sources may also require IRB approval for human subjects research.

Instrumentation: Threat to the internal validity of an experiment that refers to how instruments used in an experiment may be unreliable and affect the findings of an experiment.

Interaction effect of testing and experimental variables: Also known as the "reactive effect of testing." It is a threat to the external validity of experiments that results from subjects responding differentially to the treatment, or being sensitized to the treatment, in unnatural ways affecting the findings.

Interaction of experimental arrangements and experimental variables: Threats to the external validity of experimental research that refers to how the artificially controlled situations in which experiments are conducted may jeopardize one's ability to generalize findings to a nonexperimental setting.

Interaction of selection biases and experimental variables: Threats to the external validity of experimental research resulting from the sample used in experimental research. If the sample differs from the population in ways such as willingness to volunteer for research, aptitude, intelligence, or other characteristics, the ability to generalize findings from the research is jeopardized.

Interaction of testing and experimental variables: Also known as the reactive effects of testing, it is a threat to the external validity of an experiment that results from subjects responding differentially to the treatment or being sensitized to the treatment in ways that affect the findings.

Interest group: Collection of individuals who operate to influence public opinion and policy makers on particular criminal justice issues that require immediate attention and policy. Also known as an "advocacy group."

Internal validity: Related to the degree to which a researcher can conclude a causal relationship among variables in an experiment. Internal validity is often at odds with external validity.

Interquartile range (*IQR*): Measure of dispersion used as a summary statistic. It indicates how much variability there is in a data distribution based on the difference between the two halves (i.e., two middle quartiles) of the distribution.

Inter-rater reliability: Way to establish the presence or absence of reliability by measuring the degree to which different raters or observers offer consistent assessments of the same phenomenon.

Inter-university Consortium for Political and Social Research (ICPSR): Association of universities and institutions that maintains and provides access to social science data for research and instruction. There are over 8,000 discrete studies/surveys and more than 65,000 data sets in the ICPSR archives.

Interval: Level of measurement that indicates that attributes of a measure can be rank-ordered and have known and equal differences between categories. Interval-level measures do not have a meaningful zero.

Intervening variable: Variable that is situated between the two other variables in time, creating a type of a spurious relationship.

Interviewer bias: When the survey participant is influenced by the presence or actions of an interviewer.

Interviews: Conversations between the researcher and an individual or a group of individuals. Interviews also represent a type of survey mode that involves the researcher (i.e., the interviewer) directly engaging with the survey participant during the data collection process.

Introduction section of a journal article: First section of the text (after the abstract) that identifies the purpose of the research and why it is important.

Introduction section of a policy brief: Second section of a policy brief that tells the reader why he or she should care about the topic of the brief.

Intuition: Knowledge developed based on a feeling or gut instinct.

Items: Questions contained on a survey instrument.

Justice: Third principle of ethical research outlined in the Belmont Report. This principle indicates that research subjects must be treated reasonably, justly, and fairly. Selection of participants should not be conducted in which some, due to their easy availability, their compromised position, or their manipulability are taken advantage of or shoulder the bulk of the costs of the research. Selection of subjects in research should be related directly to the problem being studied, and the costs and benefits of the research should be shouldered fairly.

Justified conclusions: Accuracy standard that indicates the need for all conclusions and findings be clearly and comprehensively justified allowing stakeholder assessment.

Justify these recommendations: Step of the evaluation research process in which the evaluator offers a basis for the recommendations made. The evaluator must indicate that the recommendations were based on appropriate well-gathered data and that biases did not influence the recommendations.

Key words: Major concepts of greatest importance found in a journal article. They are generally found on the first page of the article.

Keyword: In the context of an online job hunt, it is a word or phrase that is particular to the job sought after and that will narrow a search to include only those that a candidate is interested in applying for.

Dr. Albert Kligman: Researcher who performed unethical skin experiments on prisoners confined at the Holmesburg Prison in Pennsylvania from 1951 to 1974. Without the prisoners' understanding, they were exposed to chemicals including toothpaste, shampoos, eye drops, hair dye, detergents, mind-altering drugs, radioactive isotopes, dioxin (an exceedingly toxic compound), herpes, staphylococcus, and athlete's foot, among other things. The subjects were paid in such a way as to raise doubt that they were not coerced.

Knowledge: In this context, it is defined as information believed to be true and reliable. Knowledge can come from a variety of sources both scientific and nonscientific. This text is focused on assessing and creating scientific knowledge.

Law Enforcement Management and Administrative Statistics (LEMAS): National survey sponsored by the Bureau of Justice Statistics (BJS) that gathers data from state and local law enforcement agencies that employ 100 or more sworn officers (i.e., "large" law enforcement agencies).

Law Enforcement Officers Killed and Assaulted (LEOKA): Uniform Crime Reports (UCR) Program that includes information on incidents resulting in the assault and killing of on-duty officers.

Leading questions: Questions that contain a controversial or unjustified assumption that leads a respondent to answer in a particular way that may not reflect his or her true feelings. Also known as a "loaded question."

Letter of recommendation: Also referred to as a "letter of reference." It is a document in which the writer assesses the qualities, characteristics, and capabilities of the person being recommended.

Level of measurement: Nature of the data gathered for a particular variable.

Likert-type scale: Commonly used measurement approach in which the response format includes ordered attributes such as "very unsatisfied," "unsatisfied," "satisfied," and "very satisfied."

LimeSurvey: Online survey software program that is a free and open-source online survey application. It is written in a scripting language called "PHP."

Link analysis: In qualitative research, it refers to a technique used to evaluate relationships (i.e., connections) between various types of nodes (i.e., objects). It is used primarily to (a) find matches in data for known patterns of interest, (b) find anomalies where known patterns are violated, and (c) find new patterns of interest.

Literature review journal articles: Type of original or primary source valuable for constructing a literature review. A published literature reviews, presents, organizes, and synthesizes existing understanding on a topic.

Literature review: Review, summary, and synthesis of extant knowledge on a topic. Literature review sections in journal articles review, present, organize, and synthesize existing understanding on a topic at the time the research was conducted. They are used to place the published research into context and to demonstrate how it adds to our understanding of a topic.

Loaded questions: Questions that contain a controversial or unjustified assumption that leads a respondent to answer in a particular way that may not reflect his or her true feelings. Also known as a "leading question."

Logic models: Graphic depictions that illustrate the ideal about how a program is intended to work. Logic models provide an easy-to-understand means to see the causal relationships among program components. There are four benefits of logic models: They point to key performance measurement points useful for conducting an evaluation, they assist with program design, they make improvement of existing programs easier by highlighting program activities that are problematic, and they help identify program expectations.

Long-term outcomes: One of four causal steps in a logic model, referring to the intended positive benefits resulting from a program that are expected to occur further in the future. Long-term outcomes may include reduced victimization, stable housing, greater educational attainment, a lack of arrests, and greater satisfaction with life.

Longitudinal data: Data collected from the same sample at different points in time.

Looping: Tactic used by the media where a particular crime or violent event is repeated over and over again. This leads the public to believe that crime and violence is worse than it is, which affects what the public views as important criminal justice issues.

Mail and written surveys: Mode of surveying that involves providing a written survey to an individual. This survey can be sent via the mail or handed out in person.

Manipulation of an independent variable: One of three characteristics of true experimental research. The control or manipulation of the independent variable must be done by the researcher.

Map legend: Required element of a map used to explain what symbols on a map represent.

Margin of error: Maximum expected deviation expected between a sample statistic and a population parameter.

Matched pairs design: Also called "paired-matching." It is a matching approach used in true experiments in which the researcher create pairs of subjects or units of interest based on relevant characteristics that are identified prior to the experiment. Once pairs are established, one unit in the pair is randomly assigned to the experimental group, and the other is assigned to the control group.

Matching: Randomization technique that eliminates the possibility that differences between subjects based on the matching variables can affect results. Matching can be accomplished via block matching or pair matching.

Matrix question: Question that includes multiple closed-ended questions sharing the same response categories.

Maturation: Threat to the internal validity of an experiment that refers to the natural changes that happen to subjects participating in experimental research, including hunger, boredom, or aging.

Maximum variation sampling: Purposeful sampling approach in that subjects are selected to maximize or increase the variation or heterogeneity of relevant characteristics in the sample. Rather than seeking some sort of representativeness of the sample, the goal is to seek maximum variation in the sample to provide insight into how a topic is viewed and processed by subjects in a variety of settings under a variety of conditions.

MEAL: Writing strategy in which one begins with a *m*ain point, offers *e*vidence, *a*nalyzes the evidence, and then *l*inks that material to the main point.

Mean: Measure of central tendency used as a summary statistic. It represents the arithmetic average value of all observations in a data distribution.

Mean center: Average x- and y-coordinates of all the features in the study area.

Measure: Tools used to gather data that represent an abstract underlying concept. Data are gathered in the same way some tools in a garage are used.

Measurement: Process of quantifying a concept. Measurement can be conducted in a variety of ways such as through survey questions (e.g., on a scale from 1 to 10, how happy are you today? How many cigarettes have you smoked this week? and What is your current GPA?), counting behaviors during observation, taking blood pressure measurements, or recording one's age.

Measures of central tendency: Group of summary statistics used to numerically describe the "typical" case in a group of observations.

Measures of dispersion: Group of summary statistics used to numerically describe the variability in observed scores among a group of observations.

Media: Competing voice heard by policy makers that has the goal of delivering viewers to their advertisers. Media is most effective at achieving its goal by showing viewers things that keep them coming back to watch more, including misrepresentations of crime and violence. This drives what the public believes are important criminal justice issues.

Median: Measure of central tendency used as a summary statistics. It represents the numeric "center" of a data distribution or the value that represents the score that half of all other scores in a data distribution are greater than and half are less than.

Meta data: Data used to describe other data.

Metaevaluation: Accuracy standard that refers to the need that the evaluation be judged on these standards to allow an examination of its strengths and weaknesses by stakeholders.

Method: Sections in journal articles that outline in detail the approach taken to answer the research question. Information shared includes the source of the data used (e.g., sample), the approach taken to gather the data (e.g., survey, observations, interviews), and the analytic techniques used to analyze these data (e.g., descriptives, regression).

Mind maps: Graphical representation of ideas and concepts by structuring information visually so that analysis, comprehension, synthesis, and recall are improved.

Missing data: When no data are recorded for a particular variable. Missing data come in two broad forms. First, it can refer to when a person was supposed to include information and did not do so.

Mobile survey: Mode of survey research whereby a questionnaire is delivered to an eligible participant via the Internet and completed on a smartphone or tablet, usually through a Web browser or a mobile application (i.e., app).

Mode: Measure of central tendency used as a summary statistic. It represents the numeric value observed more than any other in a data distribution.

Modifiable Areal Unit Problem (MAUP): In geographic information systems (GIS), it is a problem arising from the imposition of artificial units of spatial reporting on continuous geographical phenomenon, which results in the generation of artificial spatial patterns.

Mosaic plagiarism: Form of plagiarism in which one takes another person's text and replaces some words with synonyms without citing the originator of the idea. In addition, mosaic plagiarism also occurs when one strings together verbatim fragments from multiple authors or sources without citing the original authors.

Multistage sampling: Not really a probability sampling approach, but instead it is the use of multiple probability sampling techniques to draw a sample. For example, a researcher may first randomly sample housing units (first stage; sampling a cluster of housing) and then randomly select people to interview in each of the selected clusters.

Mutually exclusive: Measurement requirement that the attributes offered must not overlap in meaning.

National Archive of Criminal Justice Data (NACJD): Specialized data archive sponsored by the Bureau of Justice Statistics (BJS), National Institute of Justice (NIJ), and the Office of Juvenile Justice and Delinquency Prevention (OJJDP). The purpose of the archive is to preserve and distribute crime and justice data for secondary data analysis.

National Association of Colleges and Employers (NACE): National professional organization that aims to facilitate the hiring of college graduates.

National Commission for the Protection of Human Subjects of Biomedical and Behavioral Research: Also known as "The Commission." The purpose of The Commission was to develop policies related to human subject research guidelines.

National Crime Victimization Survey (NCVS): Nationally representative survey sponsored by the Bureau of Justice Statistics (BJS) that gathers data about property and violence victimization occurring in the United States to persons age 12 or older living in housing units. NCVS data are one of the nation's sources of crime data, which includes both crime that is and is not reported to the police. NCVS data demonstrate a drop in violent and property crime since the early 1990s.

National Criminal Justice Information and Statistics Service (NCJISS): Became the Bureau of Justice Statistics (BJS) in 1979, with the passage of the Justice System Improvement Act. The mission of NCJISS, and later of BJS, is to gather and analyze crime data, publish crime reports, and make available this information to the public, policy makers, media, government officials, and researchers.

National Incident Based Reporting System (NIBRS): Incident-based crime that includes the nature and types of crime committed during each incident, victim(s) and offender(s) characteristics, type and value of stolen and recovered property, and characteristics of arrested individuals.

National Institutes of Health (NIH): Federal collection of 27 institutes and centers engaged in biomedical research. NIH offers free online training in human subjects research.

National Research Act of 1974: Created by the National Commission for the Protection of Human Subjects of Biomedical and Behavioral Research. The purpose of this act was to develop human subjects research guidelines.

National Vital Statistics System (NVSS): Program that provides data on vital events including deaths (but also births, marriage, divorces and fetal deaths). Mortality data, including that on homicide, from the NVSS are a widely used source of cause-of-death information. It offers advantages of being available for small geographic places over decades, allowing comparisons with other countries.

Natural experiments: Occur outside of laboratories or other artificial locations and in the natural world. Natural experiments have a control and an experimental group, but they do not include randomization or researcher control of the treatment.

Near Repeat Calculator (NRC): Developed by Jerry Ratcliffe at Temple University, and funded by the U.S. Department of Justice, the NRC is a free software tool that can be used to identify repeat/near repeat patterns in crime data.

Needs assessments: Type of formative assessments with the goal of understanding the needs of a target population. Needs assessments provide guidance about whether a program is needed, exactly who may need a program, and the type of program that may be useful for the target population. The findings of a needs assessment allow someone to identify how to effectively target a program to best address a social problem of interest. Engaging in a needs assessment requires deep immersion by the researcher into the environment in which a program may be needed.

Neonate: Newborn.

Network sampling: Specific type of purposive sampling approach in which sample subjects are selected based on referrals from prior subjects. Also called "snowball sampling," "chain referral," or "reputational sampling."

Networking: Linking with, or interacting with, others to exchange information to achieve a goal. Networking with policy makers is necessary to maximize the chances your research will be policy relevant.

Nominal: Level of measurement that indicates attributes or categories differ in name only. Nominal levels of measurement have inherent ordering between named categories or attributes, and the categories cannot be placed on a continuum with a meaningful zero. Variables with nominal levels of measurement are frequently called "categorical variables."

Nonequivalent control groups design: Most commonly used quasi-experimental design that uses nonrandomly generated control and experimental groups.

Nonprobability sampling: Process of selecting a subset of elements in the population without the presence of a comprehensive list of population members. By using nonprobability sampling, some members of the population have a zero chance of being selected into the sample, and the probability of being selected into a nonprobability sample is frequently unknown. This is most widely used in qualitative research.

Nonrandomized designs: Also known as "quasi-experimental research designs." They are used when random assignment to a control or an experimental group is not possible, impractical, or unethical. Referred to by Campbell as "queasy experiments."

North arrow: Required element of a map that is used to orient the map for the reader.

Notification letters: Letters mailed to those in the sample to alert them that they will be receiving a survey. Notification letters are effective tools for increasing response rates.

Nuremberg Code: After the research atrocities perpetrated in Nazi Germany, the Nuremberg Code was enacted in 1947 to outline 10 ethical principles to guide research.

Observation and fieldwork: One of three primary forms of qualitative research that involved the researcher going into the field to observe, and possibly participate in, the topic of interest.

Observer as participant: One of four role conceptions available for field research. The researcher's presence and purpose is known by those being observed. While all know the purpose of the researcher, the duration of the observation is brief, and any interaction between the observer and the topic is minimal.

Office of Justice Programs (OJP): Agency in the U.S. Department of Justice that focuses on crime prevention through research and development, assistance to state, local, and tribal criminal justice agencies.

One-group pretest–posttest design: Pre-experimental design that includes only one group (no comparison group), no randomization, and no researcher control of the treatment.

One-shot case design: Pre-experimental design in which one investigates only one group that experienced some type of treatment (not administered by the researcher) believed to have been related to some outcome. The researcher compares the findings of the posttest to personal expectations of the measurement had the treatment not been administered.

Online survey: Mode of survey research whereby a questionnaire is delivered to an eligible participant via the Internet and completed on a personal computer, usually through a Web browser.

Open coding: Refers to a researcher reading the complete set of raw data multiple times to organize and summarize the data (whether it be words, sentences, paragraphs, or illustrations) into preliminary groupings of analytic categories.

Open-source geographic information systems (GIS): Free GIS software that can be used in crime analysis and mapping. Open-source projects include QGIS, MapWindow GIS, and GRASS GIS.

Open-ended questions: Designed to give the respondent the opportunity to answer in his or her own words. These are similar to essay questions on exams. Open-ended questions are ideal for gathering qualitative data.

Operationalization: Process in which a researcher identifies *how* each concept will be measured based on the conceptual definition.

Ordinal: Level of measurement that indicates that attributes of a measure have an inherent order to them. A level of measurement in which attributes can be rank-ordered.

Organization: Unit of analysis used to indicate that the who or what being studied is an organization. For example, fraternities and sororities are organizations that may be the who or what being studied. Treated the same as groups.

Original sources: Also known as "primary sources." They are primarily peer-reviewed journal articles. There are three basic forms of original source journal articles: peer-reviewed empirical journal articles, theoretical journal articles, and literature review journal articles.

Outcome evaluations: Type of summative evaluation that measures the effectiveness of a program on the target population. This type of evaluation is focused on the impacts on the target population specifically versus the program. Outcome evaluations focus on the short-term and long-term outcomes among the target population depicted in the logic model.

Outliers: Extreme values within a data distribution.

Outputs: One of four steps in a basic logic model. Outputs are those intended consequences resulting from inputs and include things like increased knowledge, changed attitudes or values, and new skills.

Paired-matching: Also called "matched pairs design." It is a matching approach used in true experiments in which the researcher creates pairs of subjects or units of interest based on relevant characteristics that are identified prior to the experiment. Once pairs are established, one unit in the pair is randomly assigned to the experimental group, and the unit other is assigned to the control group.

Partial enumeration: Another term used for "sample": not all members of the population are included.

Participant as observer: One of four role conceptions in which the researcher and his or her primary contact(s) in the field are the only ones aware of the researcher's actual role and purpose for the observation. While the researcher's role is known to a select few, the researcher engages with the group as a member or a colleague.

Participant observation: Combination of observation with some degree of participation by the researcher. It is characterized by four types of participant observation described on a continuum of role conceptions.

Peer-reviewed journal articles: Published articles that were rigorously peer-reviewed before being published in an academic journal. These are an excellent source of information used in a literature review.

Periodicity: Potential issue when using systematic sampling approaches that refers to a pattern hidden in the sampling frame. Periodicity occurs when a characteristic relevant to the study being conducted is found in the sampling frame and when that characteristic appears on a cyclical basis that matches the interval used in systematic sampling. Failure to account for periodicity will lead to bias in the sample drawn.

Permission: Frequently, but not always, required by at least one parent when a child participates in research.

Personal experience: Knowledge accepted based on one's own observations and experiences.

Peter Buxtun: Person responsible for leaking information regarding the Tuskegee Syphilis Experiment to journalists after the sponsoring agency refused to act on it.

Phrase: Particular series of terms or words. Phrases used in electronic searches are identified using quotation marks.

Pilot study: Used to identify problems with a survey questionnaire before it is fielded to the sample of respondents. To conduct a pretest, the researcher asks a small group of people to complete the survey instrument so errors and issues can be rectified. Also called a "pretest."

Plagiarism: Fraud and theft of another person's words, thoughts, ideas, or other creations (e.g., songs, artwork), and the presentation of that material as one's own.

Policy: Principles, rules, and laws that guide a government, an organization, or people.

Policy adoption: Third stage in the policy process that refers to the formal adoption of the policy often in the form of a law.

Policy brief: Short two- to four-page document of about 1,500 words that in plain English presents research findings and policy recommendations to a nonacademic audience. Policy briefs include five sections: executive summary, introduction, approach and results, conclusion, and implications and recommendations.

Policy cycle: Simplified model of the stages of policy making and implementation that includes five major stages: problem identification/agenda setting, policy formation, policy adoption, policy implementation, and policy evaluation. Also called the "policy process."

Policy evaluation: Fifth stage in the policy process that addresses whether the policy and its associated programs are addressing the problems it was intended to address, if the policy as implemented is cost effective, the presence of any negative unintended consequences, and whether the implementation occurred as it was designed.

Policy formation: Second step in the policy process that includes the design of one or multiple approaches to solve the problem of interest.

Policy implementation: Fourth stage in the policy process that includes the drafting of specific procedures, regulations, rules, and guidance to be used by those tasked with carrying out the adopted policy.

Policy makers: Individuals in a position who create the principles, rules, and laws that guide a government, an organization, or people that are carried out by a government or business groups.

Policy process: Simplified model of the stages of policy making and implementation that includes five major stages: problem identification/agenda setting, policy formation, policy adoption, policy implementation, and policy evaluation. Also called the "policy cycle."

Policy-relevant research: Research that directly influences the development of and implementation of the principles, rules, and laws that guide a government, an organization, or people by informing and influencing policy makers.

Political viability: One of the feasibility criteria of an effective evaluation. Requires the evaluators to consider the affected stakeholders to gain and maintain their cooperation during every stage of the evaluation. In addition, the evaluator must be alert to stakeholder attempts to thwart, bias, or disrupt the evaluation.

Population: Collection of all elements that, when aggregated, make up that collective.

Population parameter: Summary of something in the greater population.

Poster session: Method of disseminating research findings at a professional conference, where the information being disseminated is summarized on a single poster.

Potentially vulnerable populations: Any population that may be more vulnerable to coercion or undue influence. For example, the Veteran's Administration views veterans as a potentially vulnerable population. Depending on the research, a potentially vulnerable population may include students, employees, educationally disadvantaged people, minorities, or older persons.

Practical procedures: One of the feasibility criteria of an effective evaluation. Requires that evaluation research be practical, and it should result in minimal disruption to the program under investigation.

Predatory journals: Illegitimate journals that are in business to take fees from unsuspecting authors. In general, elements of the journal are fabricated (e.g., impact factor scores, editorial boards, peer review, location of offices and office holders). Information taken from predatory journals should not be used in academic literature reviews.

Predatory publishers: Illegitimate publishers of predatory journals. In general, elements of the publisher are fabricated (e.g., impact factor scores, editorial boards, journal holdings, peer-review, location of offices and office holders). Predatory publishers are not a source of quality academic information.

Predictive accuracy index (PAI): Used to assess the quality of prospective hot spot maps that is calculated as the ratio of the hit rate to the proportion of the study area that has been in a hot spot in the past. A higher PAI value reflects greater predictive accuracy.

Predictive policing: Application of analytic techniques to identify likely targets for police intervention and prevent crime or solve past crimes by making statistical predictions.

Predictor variables: Also known as "independent variables" in experimental research.

Pre-experiments: Experiments that fail to include most elements of a true experiment. In general, pre-experiments lack both control and experimental groups, lack random assignment, and frequently lack researcher control of the treatment. While useful as preliminary steps to see whether additional research is warranted, pre-experiments represent poor designs.

Pretest: Used to identify problems with a survey questionnaire before it is fielded to the sample of respondents. To conduct a pretest, the researcher asks a small group of people to complete the survey instrument so errors and issues can be rectified. Also called a "pilot."

Primary data collection: Also known as "original data collection." When research methodologies are used in the collection of original data.

Primary sources: Also known as "original sources." They are primarily peer-reviewed journal articles. There are three basic forms of primary source journal articles: peer-reviewed empirical journal articles, theoretical journal articles, and literature review journal articles.

Private-sector employees: Individuals who work primarily for businesses or nonprofit agencies.

Probability sampling: Process of selecting a subset of elements from a comprehensive list of the population. This approach requires that every population element have a known, nonzero chance of being selected.

Probing: Subtle phrase or follow-up question that interviewers use to encourage survey participants to elaborate on previous responses.

Problem identification/agenda setting: First stage of the policy process that occurs when the public brings an issue to the attention of policy makers and demands something be done to address this issue.

Procedures: Step-by-step or standard operating procedures, that should be followed to accomplish the policy.

Process evaluation: Type of formative evaluation that is conducted when a program is in operation. Process evaluations focus on whether a program has been implemented and is being delivered as it was designed, or why an existing program has changed over time. A way to view this is as a trouble-shooting evaluation that can identify whether the program is working the best way to meet its full potential, or where problems or inefficiencies in the process are occurring.

Professional portfolio: Carefully crafted set of documents and material that showcases the work of a professional and is used, for example, during job interviews to provide evidence of employability and fit with an organization or company.

Professional skill set: Particular group of skills that employers desire in their employees, which a person usually develops through training and education.

Program: Developed to respond to policies.

Program documentation: Accuracy standard of an effective evaluation that requires that an evaluation be documented clearly, completely, and accurately.

Propriety: One of four standards of an effective evaluation. Based on eight criteria that demonstrate that an evaluation was conducted ethically, legally, and with regard for the welfare of those involved, as well as of anyone else affected by the evaluation.

Public policy: Policy designed and implemented by governmental agencies specifically. It is defined by policy expert Paul Cairney (n.d.) as the "the sum total of government actions, from signals of intent, to the final outcomes."

Public-sector employees: Individuals who work for some sort of government agency either at the federal, state, or municipal level.

Public use data: Data that are prepared with the intent of making them available to anyone (i.e., the public).

Purpose of the research: Overarching goal of the research. Broadly, there are four categories of purposes of research: exploratory, descriptive, explanatory, and evaluation.

Purposive sampling: Nonprobability sampling approach in which the sample is selected based solely on a particular characteristic of the case. Samples gathered using this approach are selected because the respondents have particular information needed to conduct the research.

Qualitative data: Non-numerical data. Researchers using qualitative data generally use inductive reasoning. Qualitative data are available in numerous formats, including texts, narratives, published documents, videos, music, photos, recordings, observations, participating, body language, and so on.

Qualitative data analysis (QDA): Approach to data analysis that emphasized open-ended research questions and moves from these toward greater precision, based on information that emerges during data analysis.

Qualitative research: Uses non-numeric data to answer what are frequently exploratory research questions designed to provide detailed and nuanced understanding of a topic. Qualitative research is not focused on counting, quantifying, or measuring anything about a topic.

Qualtrics: Paid software program (i.e., it is not free although your university may have a contract with it making it free for you to use) that is easy to use, offering a "drag-and-drop" interface that lets researchers quickly add advanced online survey options and analysis features to questionnaires.

Quantitative data: Numerical data. Research using quantitative data generally uses deductive reasoning.

Quasi-experimental research: Also known as "non-randomized designs." They are used when random assignment to a control or an experimental group is not possible, impractical, or unethical. Referred to by Campbell as "queasy experiments."

Questionnaires: Written, printed, or electronic survey instruments that a respondent fills out on his or her own.

Question-order effect: When the ordering of questions on a survey influences responses given to later questions.

Quota sampling: Nonprobability sampling approach in which a researcher gathers cases for the sample that have specific characteristics such as urban, suburban, and rural households. This is roughly the nonprobability sampling equivalent to stratified sampling.

Random assignment: Characteristic of a true experiment in which subjects or units of interest are randomly placed in an experimental or a control group. The random nature of the assignment maximizes the chances that the experimental and control groups are equivalent.

Random digit dialing (RDD): Method for selecting people for involvement in telephone surveys by generating telephone numbers at random, which has the potential for including unlisted numbers.

Range: Measure of dispersion used as a summary statistic. It reflects the difference between the largest and smallest values in a data distribution.

Raster: Matrix of cells (i.e., pixels) that are organized into rows and columns, like a grid. This grid is overlaid on a study area.

Unlike vector data, each raster cell contains a value that represents some aspect or characteristic of the data being depicted on a map.

Raster data: Type of geospatial data represented as a matrix of cells (i.e., pixels) that is organized into rows and columns, like a grid.

Ratio: Level of measurement that indicates that attributes of a measure can be rank-ordered, have known and equal differences between categories, and be nonarbitrary and meaningful zero. Any measure gathering count data is ratio in nature.

Reactive effect of testing: Also known as the "interaction effect of testing." It is a threat to the external validity of experiments that result from subjects responding differentially to the treatment, or being sensitized to the treatment, in unnatural ways affecting the findings.

Reactivity threats: Threats to external validity that refer to how the novelty of participating in research, and being aware that one is being observed during the experiment, influences one's behaviors and views.

Recall bias: When the survey participant's responses to questions lack accuracy or completeness because they are unwilling or unable to "recall" events or information from the past.

Recapture rate index (RRI): Metric used to determine the quality of crime hot spot predictions. The RRI is based on the ratio of hot spot density for the present time and the previous time, standardized for changes in the total number of crimes in each year.

Recency effects: Stems from question ordering on a survey. This question-order effect occurs when the ordering of questions on a survey influences responses given to later questions.

Recommendations subsection: Part of a policy brief that describes in concrete fashion what *should* happen given the findings of the research. The recommendations subsection is best described using precise steps that are relevant, credible, and feasible.

Referee: Person who can write a letter of recommendation on a candidate's behalf to a potential employer. He or she can vouch for employability and might be a former professor, co-worker or supervisor, or the head of an organization, club, or society to which the candidate belongs.

Reference: Section in journal article offers the full citation information for every source cited in the body of a journal article.

Regression analysis: Statistical analysis technique whereby an equation is developed that defines associations between independent and dependent variables. The equation can be used to make predictions about the dependent variable.

Regulations: Recommendations about the expected behavior during the course of following procedures, with examples of how to deal with specific instances one may encounter.

Reliability: Refers to consistency of measurement. This includes the quality of measurement taken across a group of subjects over repeated administrations (assuming no real change has occurred), as well as consistency of findings from an experiment conducted repeatedly under the same conditions. In this case, reliability helps establish validity.

Reliable information: Accuracy standard that requires that procedures used to gather data and information must be designed and used to provide reliable information for the evaluation.

Replication: Repeating of a piece of research.

Report clarity: One of the utility criteria of an effective evaluation. This criterion requires that evaluation reports clearly articulate multiple elements of the program being evaluated. First, the program itself must be described. In addition, the context and purposes of the program must be articulated. Third, the procedures of the program must be made clear. And finally, the findings of the evaluation must be clearly presented in the report. This detail and clarity ensure the evaluation is easily understood by all audiences.

Report timeliness and dissemination: One of the utility criteria of an effective evaluation. This criterion calls for all interim and final reports resulting from the evaluation to be shared with stakeholders in a timely fashion to facilitate their use.

Representative: Desirable characteristic of a sample that indicates it accurately represents or reflects the population from which it came.

Reputational sampling: Specific type of purposive sampling approach in which sample subjects are selected based on referrals from prior subjects. Also called "networks," "snowball sampling," or "chain referral sampling."

Request for proposals (RFP): Formal statement asking for research proposals on a particular topic.

Research: According to the Common Rule refers to a systematic investigation or examination that will contribute to generalizable knowledge.

Research methods: Methods, processes, or steps used to conduct social science research.

Research question: Question that guides research designed to generate knowledge. This question guides the research endeavor.

Research topic: Subject about which one is intellectually curious and wishes to investigate to develop additional knowledge.

Respect for persons: First principle of ethical research outlined in the Belmont Report. It states that individuals should be treated as autonomous agents and that autonomy must be acknowledged. Persons with diminished autonomy are entitled to protection, and protection is required of those with diminished autonomy.

Respondent burden: Effort needed in terms of time and energy required by a respondent to complete a survey. As a researcher, you must minimize respondent burden in all ways possible.

Respondents: Individuals participating in a survey.

Response categories: List of options available from which a respondent selects an answer.

Response rate: Way to measure the success of a survey and, subsequently, how well the participants represent the larger population they are intended to reflect. Rates are typically reported as the percentage of all eligible subjects asked to complete a survey and are computed by dividing the number of participants by the total number of eligible participants and by multiplying that proportion by 100.

Results subsection: Part of a policy brief usually presented with the approach subsection. The results subsection conveys what was learned from the research and is best accomplished beginning with the broadest statements about the findings, before moving on to more specifics.

Résumé: Written summary of your educational record, work history, certifications, memberships, and accomplishments that often accompanies a job application.

Right to service: Instances in which a subject is denied potentially beneficial treatment in an experiment. This may be violating the ethical principle of minimizing harm to subjects. For example, consider the subjects in the Tuskegee Syphilis Experiment and their shielding from penicillin.

Rights of human subjects: One of the propriety standards of an effective evaluation. Requires that evaluation research, like all research, be planned and conducted using ethical research practices. Evaluation research must be conducted such that the rights and welfare of human subjects are respected.

Risk terrain modeling (RTM): Crime analysis technique used to identify risks that come from features of a landscape. RTM models how these risk factors are co-located to result in unique behavior settings for crime.

Role conceptions: Four roles a researcher can take while engaging in field research and observation. They include (1) complete observer, (2) observer as participant, (3) participant as observer, and (4) complete participant.

Rules: Recommendations about the expected behavior during the course of following procedures, with examples of how to deal with specific instances one may encounter.

Sample: Subset of a population of interest from which information or data is gathered. Samples are often composed of people, but they can also be other things including geographic areas (e.g., cities or organizations) or documents (e.g., newspaper reports).

Sample statistics: Summaries of data gathered from a sample.

Sampling: Selecting a subset of elements from the larger population.

Sampling elements: Individual items found on sampling frames. Specific sampling elements are selected for samples.

Sampling error: Error between sample statistics and population parameters.

Sampling frame: Comprehensive list that includes all elements of the population. It is from the sampling frame that probability sampling selects the sampling elements.

Sampling interval: Number, or the distance between, each sampling elements selected to be in a systematically drawn sample. Stated differently, a researcher picks every nth element from a sampling frame for inclusion in the sample.

Sampling without replacement: Any sampling element can appear in a sample only once. Should, during the selection of a sample, an element be selected a second (or more) time, a researcher should simply move on with the sample selection.

Saturation: Has several related meanings, one of which involves searching for sources for a literature review. In particular, it indicates the search for sources is complete because one finds no new information on a topic and the same studies and authors repeatedly are discussed.

Saturation: Point in which gathering data from additional respondents or cases does not lead to additional data.

Scale bar: Required element of a map that is used to orient the map-reader with respect to distance.

Science: Challenging and much debated definition that is defined here as a branch of knowledge derived from observable and falsifiable information, data, or evidence gathered in a systematic fashion.

Secondary data analysis: Research methodology that involves the reanalysis of data collected by someone else, for some other purpose, to answer a new research question or to test a new research hypothesis.

Second-order analysis: In qualitative data analysis, it is the process that involves identifying *recurrent* themes and respondent clusters. It also can be used to build event sequences and to develop new hypotheses.

Selection bias: Potential threat to the internal validity of experimental research that refers to differences that may exist between the control and experimental group unbeknownst to the researcher.

Selection of subjects: Third requirement in the Belmont Report that requires that subjects in research should be fairly selected and that the benefits and risks of the research should be fairly distributed.

Selective coding: In this coding step, the research reviews all raw data and the previous codes or labels for several purposes. First, the researcher makes contrasts and comparisons among themes or labels. Second, during this secondary stage, the researcher identifies overarching and broad variables that describe connections and relationships among some of the labels or themes.

Self-administered questionnaire: Type of survey, administered either in paper or in electronic form, which a survey participant completes on his or her own.

Self-exciting point process modeling: Analogous to the aftershocks of an earthquake. In the context of crime, think of an increase in likelihood of a second crime after an initial crime within a particular area.

Semistructured interviews: Interviews in which all respondents are asked the same set of questions. By asking the same questions across respondents, the research can compare responses. Although a set of questions is posed to every respondent, a semistructured interview still allows and requires follow-up questions and probing on interesting responses given.

Service orientation: One of the propriety standards of an effective evaluation. Evaluation research should be used to assist organizations and to address and serve the needs of the targeted population affected by the program of interest.

Sheridan and King (1972): Study designed to ascertain whether Milgram's (1963) finding regarding obedience to authority would extend to administering actual painful shocks to a "cute, fluffy, puppy." Milgram's initial findings were supported as the puppy was repeatedly shocked by 26 "teachers."

Short-term outcomes: One of four causal steps in a logic model, referring to the intended positive benefits resulting from a program that are expected to occur quickly. Short-term outcomes stem from the outputs and include improvements or changes expected to see in a short period such as improved stability, higher retention rates, reduced recidivism, or fewer arrests.

Simple random sampling: Type of probability sampling in which each element in the population has a known, and equal, probability of being drawn or selected into the sample.

Situational contexts: Used in conjunctive analysis of case configurations as the unit of analysis that is defined by the combinations of variable attributes believed to influence that outcome. Also referred to as "case configurations."

Skill: Defined as having the ability to do something well.

Skip-and-fill patterns: Also known as "conditional logic statements." A type of survey in which the questions asked are contingent on answers to previous questions.

Snowball sampling: Nonprobability sampling approach in which current respondents are asked for contact information of others having the needed characteristics to participate in the study. Also called "networks," "chain referral sampling," or "reputational sampling."

Social artifacts: Units of analyses and the who or what being studied. These include social products such as opinion pieces in newspapers, books, movies, commercials, social media posts, songs, vehicles, mug shots, and other such items.

Social interactions: Type of unit of analysis—or the who or what being studied—that includes interactions such as victimization, marriages, and aggression.

Social science research: Area of science focused on society and human relationships in society. Criminal justice, criminology, and sociology are a few disciplines within the social sciences.

Solomon Four Group: True experimental design that includes four randomly generated groups of subjects. It has all the benefits of a two-group pretest–treatment–posttest design; plus it offers information about whether the results were affected by the presence of a pretest.

Spatial autocorrelation: Degree to which geographic features are similarly arranged in space.

Spatial data: Data that have geographic coordinates associated with a corresponding physical location. The coordinates associated with spatial data are the key.

Spatial dependency: Measure used in geostatistical analysis to define the spatial relationship between *values* of geographical data.

Spatial descriptions: Group of spatial statistics that describes the overall *spatial* distribution of geographic data.

Spatial interpolation: Group of geostatistical techniques that relies on the known recorded values of phenomena at specific locations to estimate the unobserved values of the same phenomenon at other locations.

Spreadsheet: A type of document used to arrange data in rows and columns within a grid.

Spurious relationship: Relationship among variables in which it appears that two variables are related to one another, but instead a third variable is the causal factor.

Stakeholder identification: One of the utility criteria of an effective evaluation. Requires that the evaluator identify all individuals or organizations involved in or affected by the evaluation. Identification of all stakeholders is vital to ensure their needs can be, and are, addressed during the evaluation.

Stakeholders: Individuals or organizations who have a direct interest in the program being evaluated and can include funders, program administrators, the community in which the program is administered, and clients of the program. Knowing who the stakeholders are, and developing and maintaining a good relationship with stakeholders, is critical during the planning stages, the gathering of data, and presentation and buy-in of findings. Without the support of stakeholders, evaluation research cannot be successful.

Standard deviation: Measure of dispersion used as a summary statistic. It is the square root of the variance.

Standard distance: Summary measure of the distribution of features around any given point (similar to the way a standard deviation measures the distribution of data values around the statistical mean).

Stanford Prison Experiment: Haney, Banks, and Zimbardo's (1973) classic example of unethical research in which participants took on the roles of guards or prisoners in a makeshift jail. Guards quickly became abusive, and prisoners quickly exhibited clear signs of trauma. Although they were told they could leave the experiment at any time, participants were prevented from doing so.

Stanley Milgram (1963): Responsible for a series of studies, the first of which was conducted in 1961. This research focused on obedience to authority and illustrated the willingness of people to obey authority figures even when that behavior conflicted with a person's conscience.

State Administering Agency (SAA): State agency responsible for distributing formula grant funds from the U.S. Department of Justice's Office of Justice Programs (OJP) to agencies within the SAA's state.

Static-group comparison design: Pre-experimental design that includes a nonrandomly assigned control and experimental group, no researcher control of the treatment, and a posttest.

Statistical Analysis Centers (SACs): State agencies created by legislation or executive order that collect, analyze, and disseminate criminal justice data at the state level.

Statistical regression: Threat to internal validity of some experimental research where groups have been selected for participation in an experiment based on extreme scores that refers to tendency for extreme scores to move toward the mean over repeated measures.

Statistical significance: When the outcome of a research hypothesis test indicates a true difference (or association) between the observed and hypothesized values that are not likely to occur based on chance alone.

Strata: Subdivisions or subgroups of the sampling frame created in stratified sampling.

Strategic crime analysis: Crime analysis technique used in law enforcement that is focused on operational strategies of the organization in an attempt to develop solutions to chronic crime-related problems.

Stratified sampling: Probability sampling approach that requires the sampling frame to be first divided into mutually exclusive and exhaustive subgroups meaningful to the research. The second step is to independently and randomly sample from each stratum.

Subpart A: One subpart of the Department of Health and Human Services (HHS) regulations that outlines the fundamental procedures for conducting human subject research including the framework for institutional review boards (IRBs) and informed consent. It is colloquially referred to as the Common Rule.

Subpart B: One subpart of the Department of Health and Human Services (HHS) regulations that outlines additional protections for pregnant women, neonates, and fetuses proposed to participate in research.

Subpart C: One subpart of the Department of Health and Human Services (HHS) regulations that outlines additional protections for prisoners proposed to participate in research.

Subpart D: One subpart of the Department of Health and Human Services (HHS) regulations that outlines additional protections for children proposed to participate in research.

Subpart E: Most recently added subpart of Department of Health and Human Services (HHS) regulations that outlines registration requirements of institutional review board (IRB) committees. This subpart was added in 2009.

Substantive significance: Whether statistically significant findings are substantively meaningful.

Summary Reporting System (SRS): Formerly called Uniform Crime Report (UCR) data, it offers *counts* of murder and non-negligent manslaughter, rape, robbery, aggravated assault, burglary, larceny/theft, motor vehicle theft, and arson.

Summative evaluation: One of two major types of program evaluation used to make a comprehensive assessment of a program after the implementation of the policy or program. A summative evaluation is used to ascertain whether a program should be funded and continued or terminated. Two types of summative evaluations are considered in this text: outcome evaluations and impact evaluations.

Supplementary Homicide Reports (SHR): Federal Bureau of Investigation (FBI) data that provide detailed information on murder (both justifiable and not), including the victim's age, sex, and race; the offender's age, sex, and race; weapon type (if any); victim–offender relationship; and the circumstances that led to the murder.

Survey: Instrument, or tool, used to gather data. The survey includes questions that are either open-ended or closed-ended and can be administered in multiple ways such as self-administration, telephone, face-to-face interviews, and online.

Survey fraud: When participants, during online and mobile surveys, sign up to be part of a survey panel just for the incentives offered.

Survey modes: Ways in which surveys can be administered. There are four primary types of survey modes or means of distribution: mail/written, phone, face-to-face, and the Internet.

Survey nonresponse: When sample respondents who choose to complete and return surveys differ in meaningful ways from those who are chosen but do not participate in the survey.

Survey panels: Existing samples that a researcher can pay to get access to.

Survey processing: Process of converting survey responses into useful data via coding so they can be analyzed.

Survey research: Research methodology that involves gathering qualitative and quantitative data from a sample of survey participants, known as "respondents," using a survey instrument.

Systematic information: Accuracy standard that focuses on the need for systematic data and information collection, analysis, and reporting during an evaluation. As with all research, any issues encountered during the information and data gathering should be addressed.

Systematic sampling: Probability sampling approach in which the sample is constructed by selecting sampling elements from a sampling frame using a sampling interval.

Tactical crime analysis: Type of crime analysis used in law enforcement that emphasizes collecting data, identifying patterns, and developing possible leads so that criminal cases can be cleared quickly.

Telephone surveys: Common interview modality used to collect original survey data over the telephone. Telephone surveys are inexpensive to administer, and they collect data quickly.

Temporal ordering: One of three requirements of causation that refers to the requirement that the variation in the independent variable occur *prior* to the variation in the dependent variable.

Term: Single word used in an electronic search.

Testing: Threat to the internal validity of an experiment that refers to the effect that taking one test can have on another; the results of a later test. In terms of experimental research, this means the researcher must be aware that the act of taking the pretest may affect one's performance on the posttest.

Testing threat: Threats to the external validity of experimental research due to the use of pre- or posttests that may lead

subjects to respond differently or to be sensitized in unnatural ways to the treatment during the course of the experiment.

Test–retest reliability: Way to establish the presence or absence of reliability by using the same measure repeatedly over time.

Thematically constructed literature review: Review focused on the ideas found in the literature, not on the particular articles or authors.

Theme: In qualitative data analysis, it refers to an idea category that emerges from grouping lower level data points together as part of the analytic process. They are often developed around specific characteristics that are identified in qualitative data.

Theoretical journal article: Type of primary or original source that is of great value in constructing an academic literature review. A theoretical journal article evaluates an existing theory, proposes revisions to an existing theory, or proposes a new theory.

Theoretical sampling: Theoretical sampling is accomplished using an iterative approach where the researcher simultaneously collects, codes, and analyzes data and then by using that information decides what data to collect next.

Theory: Explanation about how things work. A set of interrelated propositions, assumptions, and definitions about how the world is expected to work or about how the people living in it are supposed to behave.

Tradition, customs, and norms: Knowledge or beliefs passed on from person to person over time. This knowledge is thought to be true and valuable because people have always believed it to be true and valuable.

Treatment: Researcher's manipulation of the independent variable.

Triangulation: Use of multiple methods, researchers, theory, or data—different "lines of action" to conduct a study. This goal is not just to use multiple lines of action but also to use the multiple lines of action together to remove threats to validity associated with any single line of action. By using triangulation, a researcher can offer evidence to strengthen support for conclusions.

True experiment: Research design that has three defining characteristics: (1) at least one experimental and one control group, (2) assignment to the experimental and control groups via randomization, and (3) treatment administered to the experimental group via manipulation of an independent variable (aka the predictor variable) by the researcher.

Tuskegee Syphilis Experiment: Unethical research sponsored by the U.S. government in which impoverished Black males infected with syphilis were prevented from obtaining penicillin as a cure. Many participants died but not before infecting spouses and children with syphilis.

Two-group posttest-only design: True experimental design including randomly assigned experimental and control groups and manipulation of the independent variable by the researcher. Posttests are used to compare groups after the treatment.

Two-group pretest–treatment–posttest design: True experimental design including randomly assigned experimental and control groups, and manipulation of the independent variable by the researcher. Pretests and posttests are used to compare groups after the treatment enabling a more precise assessment of the treatment.

USA Patriot Improvement and Reauthorization Act of 2005: This act mandated the Federal Bureau of Investigation (FBI) to collect data on cargo theft.

U.S. Department of Commerce (USDOC): Federal executive department of the U.S. government responsible for creating jobs, promoting economic growth, encouraging sustainable development, and improving standards of living for all Americans.

U.S. Department of Justice (USDOJ): Federal executive department of the U.S. government responsible for the enforcement of the law and administration of justice.

Uniform Crime Reporting (UCR) Program: Local, state, tribal, and federal law enforcement program that provides one of the two national measures of crime in the United States.

Unit of analysis: What or who that is being studied and analyzed in a particular piece of research. It is the unit being studied and the level of social life that the research question is focused on. These sometimes differ from the unit of observation.

Unit of observation: Unit from which data are collected to answer a research question focused on the unit of analysis. Units of observation can be, but are not always, the same as the units of analysis.

Univariate analysis: Most basic form of descriptive statistics involves the analysis of a single variable.

Unstructured interviews: Also called "ethnographic interviews." They are conducted conversationally and are based on very few broad, guiding questions that provide a basic framework to the interview. An unstructured interviewing approach allows a researcher to gather data about the topic based on the respondent's experiences and perceptions. Respondents can share with the researcher what is important versus the researcher asking the respondent about what the researcher believes is important.

Utility: One of four standards of an effective evaluation. Refers to whether the evaluation conducted met the needs of and was satisfactory to the people using it. Utility in evaluation research is based on the presence of seven utility criteria including a focus on those affected by the evaluation, the quality and quantity of data collected to perform the evaluation, the values used to assess the findings, and the clarity and timeliness of the completed evaluation report.

Valid information: Accuracy standard that requires that the procedures used to gather information and data used in the evaluation must ensure a valid interpretation.

Validity: Sought-after characteristics in research that indicate that one's measures and variables correspond as accurately as possible to the underlying concepts they represent.

Values identification: One of the utility criteria of an effective evaluation. This criterion requires that an evaluator carefully describe the perspectives, procedures, and rationale used to interpret the findings. By articulating the foundation for making the value judgments inherent in an evaluation, someone can identify the values used to reach conclusions.

Variable: Labels applied to measures used to represent the concepts of interest. Variables act as proxies for the abstract concepts they represent.

Variance: Measure of dispersion used as a summary statistic. It represents the degree to which each observation differs from the average value in a data distribution.

Vector data: Type of geospatial data used to represent the characteristics of the real world in one of three ways: as points, lines, or polygons.

Voluntary participation: Required in ethical research. A participant's engagement in a study must be grounded in having received comprehensible information about the study. Only after receiving this can a participant voluntarily agree to engage in the study.

Vulnerable populations: Those that receive an additional layer of review when proposed to participate in research. According to Department of Health and Human Services (HHS) regulations, pregnant women, human fetuses and neonates, prisoners, and children are vulnerable populations. These populations are considered vulnerable in that they may be more vulnerable to coercion or undue influence.

Wheel of science: Diagram developed by Walter Wallace (1971) that illustrates the recursive nature of the scientific process of developing empirical knowledge.

Wikipedia: Online encyclopedia that can be edited by anyone. Wikipedia is not an acceptable source of information for academic literature reviews.

References

Chapter 1

Best, J. (2012). *Damned lies and statistics: Untangling number from the media, politicians, and activist* (Reprinted ed.). Berkeley: University of California Press.

Brunson, R., & Weitzer, R. (2009). Police relations with Black and White youths in different urban neighborhoods. *Urban Affairs Review, 44*(6), 858–885.

Butler, H. D., Steiner, B., Makarious, M. D., & Travis, L. F. (2017). Assessing the effects of exposure to supermax confinement on offender postrelease behaviors. *The Prison Journal, 97*(3), 275–295.

Cantor, D., Fisher, B., Chibnall, S., Townsend, R., Lee, H., Bruce, C., & Thomas, C. (2015). *Report on the AAU campus climate survey on sexual assault and sexual misconduct.* Rockville, MD: Westat. Retrieved from https://www.aau.edu/uploadedFiles/AAU_Publications/AAU_Reports/Sexual_Assault_Campus_Survey/AAU_Campus_Climate_Survey_12_14_15.pdf

Dodge, M., Starr-Gimeno, D., & Williams, T. (2005). Puttin' on the sting: Women police officers' perspectives on reverse prostitution assignments. *The International Journal of Police Science & Management, 7*(2), 71–85.

Federal Bureau of Investigation. (2014). *Crime in the United States.* Washington, DC: U.S. Department of Justice, Federal Bureau of Investigation. Retrieved from https://www.fbi.gov/about-us/cjis/ucr/crime-in-the-u.s/2014/crime-in-the-u.s.-2014/tables/table-1

Haney, C., Banks, C., & Zimbardo, P. (1973). A study of prisoners and guards in a simulated prison. *Naval Research Reviews, 30,* 4–17.

Health and Human Services. (2009). 45 CFR 46: Code of federal regulations, title 45 public welfare, part 46 protection of human subjects. Retrieved from https://www.hhs.gov/ohrp/regulations-and-policy/regulations/45-cfr-46

Ivy, A. C. (1948). The history and ethics of use of human subjects in medical experiments. *Science, 108*(2792), 1–5.

Krebs, C., & Lindquist, C. (2014, December 14). Setting the record straight on '1 in 5.' *Time Magazine.* Retrieved from http://time.com/3633903/campus-rape-1-in-5-sexual-assault-setting-record-straight/

Krebs, C., Lindquist, C. H., Warner, T. D., Fisher, B. S., & Martin, S. L. (2007). *The Campus Sexual Assault (CSA) Study.* Washington, DC: U.S. Department of Justice, National Institute of Justice. Retrieved from https://www.ncjrs.gov/pdffiles1/nij/grants/221153.pdf

Melde, C., Taylor, T., & Esbensen, F. (2009). "I got your back": An examination of the protective function of gang membership in adolescence. *Criminology, 47*(2) 565–594.

Milgram, S. (1963). Behavioral study of obedience. *Journal of Abnormal and Social Psychology, 67*(4), 371–378.

Milgram, S. (1975). *Obedience to authority.* New York, NY: Harper Torchbooks.

National Commission for the Protection of Human Subjects of Biomedical and Behavioral Research. (1979, April 18). *The Belmont report: Ethical principles and guidelines for the protection of human subjects and research.* Washington, DC: U.S. Department of Health, Education and Welfare. Retrieved from http://www.fda.gov/ohrms/dockets/ac/05/briefing/2005-4178b_09_02_Belmont%20Report.pdf

National Research Act of 1974. (2009). Retrieved from http://www.hhs.gov/ohrp/regulations-and-policy/regulations/45-cfr-46/index.html

Office of History, National Institutes of Health. (n.d.). *Nuremberg Code.* Retrieved from https://history.nih.gov/research/downloads/nuremberg.pdf

Perez-Pena, R. (2015, September 21). 1 in 4 women experience sex assault on campus. *The New York Times.* Retrieved from http://www.nytimes.com/2015/09/22/us/a-third-of-college-women-experience-unwanted-sexual-contact-study-finds.html

Sabina, C., Cuevas, C. A., & Cotignola-Pickens, H. M. (2016). Longitudinal dating violence victimization among Latino teens: Rates, risk factors, and cultural influences. *Journal of Adolescence, 47,* 5–15.

Santos, R. B. (2016). *Crime analysis with crime mapping* (4th ed.). Thousand Oaks, CA: Sage.

Santos, R. B., & Santos, R. G. (2016). Offender-focused police intervention in residential burglary and theft from vehicle hot spots: A partially blocked randomized control trial. *Journal of Experimental Criminology, 12,* 373–402.

Sheridan, C. L., & King, R. G. (1972). Obedience to authority with an authentic victim. *Proceedings of the Annual Convention of the American Psychological Association, 80,* 165–166.

Truman, J. L., & Langton, L. (2015, August). *Criminal victimization, 2014.* Washington, DC: U.S. Department of Justice, Bureau of Justice Statistics. Retrieved from http://www.bjs.gov/content/pub/pdf/cv14.pdf

U.S. Public Health Service (USPHS). (1966). *Surgeon General's directives on human experimentation.* Washington, DC: Author. Retrieved from https://history.nih.gov/research/downloads/surgeongeneral directive1966.pdf

Zaykowski, H. (2014). Mobilizing victim services: The role of reporting to the police. *Journal of Traumatic Stress, 27*(3), 365–369.

Chapter 2

Brunson, R., & Weitzer, R. (2009). Police relations with Black and White youths in different urban neighborhoods. *Urban Affairs Review, 44*(6), 858–885.

Cao, L. (2004). *Major criminological theories: Concepts and measures.* Belmont, CA: Wadsworth Thomson.

Cohen, L. E., & Felson, M. (1979). Social change and crime rate trends: A routine activity approach. *American Sociological Review, 44,* 588–608.

Dodge, M., Starr-Gimeno, D., & Williams, T. (2005). Puttin' on the sting: Women police officers' perspectives on reverse prostitution assignments. *The International Journal of Police Science & Management, 7*(2), 71–85.

Farfel, M. R., & Chisolm, J. J. Jr. (1991). Health and environmental outcomes of traditional and modified practices for abatement of residential lead-based paint. *American Journal of Public Health, 80,* 1240–1245.

Health and Human Services. (2009). 45 CFR 46: Code of federal regulations, title 45 public welfare, part 46 protection of human subjects. Retrieved from https://www.hhs.gov/ohrp/regulations-and-policy/regulations/45-cfr-46

Melde, C., Taylor, T., & Esbensen, F. (2009). "I got your back": An examination of the protective function of gang membership in adolescence. *Criminology, 47*(2) 565–594.

Milgram, S. (1963). Behavioral study of obedience. *The Journal of Abnormal and Social Psychology, 67*(4), 375, 377.

Miraglia, G. (2007). *Coming out from behind the badge: Stories of success and advice from police officers "Out" on the job.* Bloomington, IN: AuthorHouse.

National Commission for the Protection of Human Subjects of Biomedical and Behavioral Research. (1979, April 18). *The Belmont report: Ethical principles and guidelines for the protection of human subjects and research.* Washington, DC: U.S. Department of Health, Education and Welfare. Retrieved from http://www.fda.gov/ohrms/dockets/ac/05/briefing/2005-4178b_09_02_Belmont%20Report.pdf

Office of History, National Institutes of Health. (n.d.). *Nuremberg Code.* Retrieved from https://history.nih.gov/research/downloads/nuremberg.pdf

Policastro, C., Teasdale, B., & Daigle L. E. (2015). The recurring victimization of individuals with mental illness: A comparison of trajectories for two racial groups. *Journal of Quantitative Criminology, 32,* 675–693.

Rennison, C. M., & Dodge, M. (2012). Police impersonation: Pretenses and pretenders. *American Journal of Criminal Justice, 37*(4), 505–522.

Sabina, C., Cuevas, C. A., & Cotignola-Pickens, H. M. (2016). Longitudinal dating violence victimization among Latino teens: Rates, risk factors, and cultural influences. *Journal of Adolescence, 47,* 5–15.

Santos, R. B., & Santos, R. G. (2016). Offender-focused police intervention in residential burglary and theft from vehicle hot spots: A partially blocked randomized control trial. *Journal of Experimental Criminology, 12,* 373–402.

Sieber, J. E. (2001). *Summary of human subjects protection issues related to large sample surveys* (NCJ 187692). Washington, DC: USGPO.

Wallace, W. (1971). *The logic of science in sociology.* New York, NY: Aldine.

Winstanley, A. (2009). *Burglars in blue.* Bloomington, IN: AuthorHouse.

Zaykowski, H. (2014). Mobilizing victim services: The role of reporting to the police. *Journal of Traumatic Stress, 27*(3), 365–369.

Chapter 3

American Psychological Association (APA). (2010). *Publication manual* (6th ed.). Washington, DC: Author.

Brunson, R., & Weitzer, R. (2009). Police relations with Black and White youths in different urban neighborhoods. *Urban Affairs Review, 44*(6), 858–885.

Dodge, M., Starr-Gimeno, D., & Williams, T. (2005). Puttin' on the sting: Women police officers' perspectives on reverse prostitution assignments. *The International Journal of Police Science & Management, 7*(2), 71–85.

Mazières, D., & Kohler, E. (2005). Get me off your fucking mailing list. Unpublished paper. Retrieved from http://www.scs.stanford.edu/~dm/home/papers/remove.pdf

Melde, C., Taylor, T., & Esbensen, F. (2009). "I got your back": An examination of the protective function of gang membership in adolescence. *Criminology, 47*(2) 565–594.

Ramcharan, R. (2006). Regressions: Why are economists obsessed with them? *Finance and Development, 43*(1). Retrieved from http://www.imf.org/external/pubs/ft/fandd/2006/03/basics.htm

Rennison, C. M., & Dodge, M. J. (2012). Police impersonation: Pretenses and predators. *American Journal of Criminal Justice, 37,* 505–522.

Sabina, C., Cuevas, C. A., & Cotignola-Pickens, H. M. (2016). Longitudinal dating violence victimization among Latino teens: Rates, risk factors, and cultural influences. *Journal of Adolescence, 47,* 5–15.

Santos, R. B., & Santos, R. G. (2016). Offender-focused police intervention in residential burglary and theft from vehicle hot spots: A partially blocked randomized control trial. *Journal of Experimental Criminology, 12,* 373–402.

SPSS Inc. (2009). Corporate history. Retrieved from http://www.spss.com.hk/corpinfo/history.htm

U.S. District Court, District of Nevada. (2016). Federal trade commission. Retrieved from https://www.ftc.gov/system/files/documents/cases/1608260micscmpt.pdf.

Zaykowski, H. (2014). Mobilizing victim services: The role of reporting to the police. *Journal of Traumatic Stress, 27*(3), 365–369.

Chapter 4

Bollen, K. A. (1989). *Structural equations with latent variables.* Hoboken, NJ: Wiley.

Brunson, R., & Weitzer, R. (2009). Police relations with Black and White youths in different urban neighborhoods. *Urban Affairs Review, 44*(6), 858–885.

Dodge, M., Starr-Gimeno, D., & Williams, T. (2005). Puttin' on the sting: Women police officers' perspectives on reverse prostitution assignments. *The International Journal of Police Science & Management, 7*(2), 71–85.

Melde, C., Taylor, T., & Esbensen, F. (2009). "I got your back": An examination of the protective function of gang membership in adolescence. *Criminology, 47*(2) 565–594.

Sabina, C., Cuevas, C. A., & Cotignola-Pickens, H. M. (2016). Longitudinal dating violence victimization among Latino teens: Rates, risk factors, and cultural influences. *Journal of Adolescence, 47,* 5–15.

Santos, R. B., & Santos, R. G. (2016). Offender-focused police intervention in residential burglary and theft from vehicle hot spots: A partially blocked randomized control trial. *Journal of Experimental Criminology, 12,* 373–402.

Schweitzer, K., & Nunez, N. (2017). Victim impact statements: How victim social class affects juror decision making. *Violence and Victims, 327*(3), 521–532.

Stevens, S. S. (*1946, June 7*). On the theory of scales of measurement. *Science, 103*(2684), 677–680.

Techopedia. (2017). Cybercrime. Retrieved from https://www.techopedia.com/definition/2387/cybercrime.

Zaykowski, H. (2014). Mobilizing victim services: The role of reporting to the police. *Journal of Traumatic Stress, 27*(3), 365–369.

Chapter 5

Alker, H. A., Jr. (1969). A typology of ecological fallacies. In M. Dogan & S. Rokkan (Eds.), *Quantitative ecological analysis* (pp. 69–86). Cambridge: Massachusetts Institute of Technology.

Brunson, R., & Weitzer, R. (2009). Police relations with Black and White youths in different urban neighborhoods. *Urban Affairs Review, 44*(6), 858–885.

Cantor, D., Fisher, B., Chibnall, S., Townsend, R., Lee, H., Bruce, C., & Thomas, C. (2015). *Report on the AAU campus climate survey on sexual assault and sexual misconduct.* Rockville, MD: Westat. Retrieved from https://www.aau.edu/uploadedFiles/AAU_Publications/AAU_Reports/Sexual_Assault_Campus_Survey/AAU_Campus_Climate_Survey_12_14_15.pdf

Craig, J. M., & Piquero, N. L. (2016). The effects of low self-control and desire-for-control on white-collar offending: A replication. *Deviant Behavior, 37,* 1308–1324.

Dodge, M., Starr-Gimeno, D., & Williams, T. (2005). Puttin' on the sting: Women police officers' perspectives on reverse prostitution assignments. *The International Journal of Police Science & Management, 7*(2), 71–85.

Groves, R. M., Fowler, F. J., Jr., Couper, M. P., Lepkowski, J. M., Singer, E., & Tourangeau, R. (2004). *Survey methodology.* Hoboken, NJ: Wiley.

Koss, M. P., & Oros, C. J. (1982). Sexual Experiences Survey: A research instrument investigating sexual aggression and victimization. *Journal of Consulting and Clinical Psychology, 50*(3), 455–457.

Krebs, C., Lindquist, C. H., Warner, T. D., Fisher, B. S., & Martin, S. L. (2007). *The Campus Sexual Assault (CSA) Study.* Washington, DC: U.S. Department of Justice, National Institute of Justice. Retrieved from https://www.ncjrs.gov/pdffiles1/nij/grants/221153.pdf

Melde, C., Taylor, T., & Esbensen, F. (2009). "I got your back": An examination of the protective function of gang membership in adolescence. *Criminology, 47*(2) 565–594.

Niles, R. (n.d.). Survey sample sizes and margin of error. Retrieved from http://www.robertniles.com/stats/margin.shtml

Robinson, W. S. (1950). Ecological correlations and the behavior of individuals. *American Sociological Review, 15,* 351–357.

Sabina, C., Cuevas, C. A., & Cotignola-Pickens, H. M. (2016). Longitudinal dating violence victimization among Latino teens: Rates, risk factors, and cultural influences. *Journal of Adolescence, 47,* 5–15.

Santos, R. B., & Santos, R. G. (2016). Offender-focused police intervention in residential burglary and theft from vehicle hot spots: A partially blocked randomized control trial. *Journal of Experimental Criminology, 12,* 373–402.

Zaykowski, H. (2014). Mobilizing victim services: The role of reporting to the police. *Journal of Traumatic Stress, 27*(3), 365–369.

Chapter 6

Bowen, G. A. (2009). Document analysis as a qualitative research method. *Qualitative Research Journal, 9*(2), 27–40.

Brunson, R., & Weitzer, R. (2009). Police relations with Black and White youths in different urban neighborhoods. *Urban Affairs Review, 44*(6), 858–885.

Cobbina, J. (2008). Race and class differences in print media portrayals of crack cocaine and methamphetamine. *Journal of Criminal Justice and Popular Culture, 15*(2), 145–167.

Creswell, J. W. (2013). *Qualitative inquiry and research design: Choosing among five approaches* (3rd ed.). Thousand Oaks, CA: Sage.

Denzin, N. K. (1978). *The research act.* New York, NY: McGraw-Hill.

Denzin, N. K., & Lincoln, Y. S. (1994). *The handbook of qualitative research.* Thousand Oaks, CA: Sage.

Denzin, N. K., & Lincoln, Y. S. (2005). *The Sage handbook of qualitative research* (3rd ed.). Thousand Oaks, CA: Sage.

Denzin, N. K., & Lincoln, Y. S. (Eds.). (2011). *The Sage handbook of qualitative research* (4th ed.). Thousand Oaks, CA: Sage.

Dodge, M., Starr-Gimeno, D., & Williams, T. (2005). Puttin' on the sting: Women police officers' perspectives on reverse prostitution assignments. *The International Journal of Police Science & Management, 7*(2), 71–85.

Glaser, B. G., & Strauss, A. L. (1967). *The discovery of grounded theory: Strategies for qualitative research.* London: Aldine Transaction.

Gold, R. L. (1958). Roles in sociological field observations. *Social Forces, 36*(3), 217–223.

Jacob, E. (1987). Qualitative research traditions: A review. *Review of Educational Research, 57,* 1–50.

Junker, B. H. (1952). Some suggestions for the design of field work learning experiences. In E. C. Hughes et al. (Eds.), *Cases on field work,* Part III-A. Chicago, IL: University of Chicago Press.

Lancy, D. F. (1993). *Qualitative research in education: An introduction to the major traditions.* New York: Longrnan.

Marshall, C., & Rossman, G. (2010). *Designing qualitative research* (5th ed.). Thousand Oaks, CA: Sage.

McCambridge, J., Witton, J., & Elbourne, D. R. (2014). Systematic review of the Hawthorne effect: New concepts are needed to study research participation effects. *Journal of Clinical Epidemiology, 67,* 267–277.

Miles, M. B., & Huberman, M. (1994). *Qualitative data analysis: An expanded sourcebook* (2nd ed.). Thousand Oaks, CA: Sage.

Morse, M. (1994). Designing funded qualitative research. In N. K. Denzin & Y. S. Lincoln (Eds.), *Handbook of qualitative research* (pp. 220–235). Thousand Oaks, CA: Sage.

Moustakas, C. (1994). *Phenomenological research methods.* Thousand Oaks, CA: Sage.

Munhall, P. L., & Oiler, C. (Eds.). (1986). *Nursing research: A qualitative perspective.* Norwalk, CT: Appleton-Century-Crofts.

Neuendorf, K. A. (2002). *The content analysis guidebook.* Thousand Oaks, CA: Sage.

Patton, M. Q. (2015). *Qualitative research and evaluations methods.* Thousand Oaks, CA: Sage.

Sabina, C., Cuevas, C. A., & Cotignola-Pickens, H. M. (2016). Longitudinal dating violence victimization among Latino teens: Rates, risk factors, and cultural influences. *Journal of Adolescence, 47,* 5–15.

Saldaña, J. (2011). *Fundamentals of qualitative research.* Oxford, England: Oxford University Press.

Sanjari, M., Bahramnezhad, F., Fomani, F. K., Shoghi, M., & Cheraghi, M. A. (2014). Ethical challenges of research in qualitative studies: The necessity to develop a specific guideline. *Journal of Medical Ethics and History of Medicine, 7*(14). Retrieved from https://www.ncbi.nlm.nih.gov/pmc/articles/PMC4263394/

Santos, R. B., & Santos, R. G. (2016). Offender-focused police intervention in residential burglary and theft from vehicle hot spots: A partially blocked randomized control trial. *Journal of Experimental Criminology, 12,* 373–402.

Slife, B. D., & Williams, R. N. (1995). *What's behind the research? Discovering hidden assumptions in the behavioral sciences.* Thousand Oaks, CA: Sage.

Straus, A. L. (1987). *Qualitative analysis for social scientists.* Cambridge, England: Cambridge University Press.

Strauss, A., & Corbin, J. (1990). *Basics of qualitative research: Grounded theory procedures and techniques.* Newbury Park, CA: Sage.

Chapter 7

Blumberg, S. J., & Luke, J. V. (2015). *Wireless substitution: Early release of estimates from the National Health Interview Survey, January–June 2015.* Washington, DC: National Center for Health Statistics, USGPO.

Bradford, B., Stanko, E. A., & Jackson, J. (2009). Using research to inform policy: The role of public attitude surveys in understanding public confidence and police contact. *Policing, 39*(2), 139–148.

Brunson, R., & Weitzer, R. (2009). Police relations with Black and White youths in different urban neighborhoods. *Urban Affairs Review, 44*(6), 858–885.

Crawford, S., Mick, D., Couper, P., & Lamias, M. J. (2001). Web surveys: Perceptions of burden. *Social Science Computer Review, 19*(2), 146–162.

Daly, J. M., Jones, J. K., Gereau, P. L., & Levy, B. T. (2011). Nonresponse error in mail surveys: Top ten problems. *Nursing Research and Practice, 2011,* 1–5.

Dillman, D. A. (2000). *Mail and internet surveys: The tailored design method.* Hoboken, NJ: Wiley.

Dillman, D. A., Smyth, J. D., & Christian, L. M. (2008). *The tailored design method* (3rd ed.). Hoboken, NJ: Wiley.

Dillman, D. A., Smyth, J. D., & Christian, L. M. (2009). *Internet, mail and mixed-mode surveys: The tailored design method* (3rd ed.). Hoboken, NJ: Wiley.

Dodge, M., Starr-Gimeno, D., & Williams, T. (2005). Puttin' on the sting: Women police officers' perspectives on reverse prostitution assignments. *The International Journal of Police Science & Management, 7*(2), 71–85.

Kochanek, K. D., Murphy, S. L., Xu, J., & Tejada-Vera, B. (2016). Deaths: Final data for 2014. *National Vital Statistics Reports, 65*(4).

Melde, C., Taylor, T., & Esbensen, F. (2009). "I got your back": An examination of the protective function of gang membership in adolescence. *Criminology, 47*(2) 565–594.

Miethe, T. D., Lieberman, J. D., Sakiyama, M., & Troshynski, E. I. (2014). Public attitudes about areial drone activities: Results of a national survey. Center for Crime and Justice Police, University of Nevada, Las Vegas, CCJP 2014–02.

Ransley, J., Hart, T., & Barlett, D. (2017). Evaluation of the Queensland Police Service's trial of hub policing. *Queensland Police Service.* Retrieved from https://www.griffith.edu.au/criminology-law/griffith-criminology-institute/our-projects/evaluation-of-the-qps-hub-policing-trial

Sabina, C., Cuevas, C. A., & Cotignola-Pickens, H. M. (2016). Longitudinal dating violence victimization among Latino teens: Rates, risk factors, and cultural influences. *Journal of Adolescence, 47,* 5–15.

Santos, R. B., & Santos, R. G. (2016). Offender-focused police intervention in residential burglary and theft from vehicle hot spots: A partially blocked randomized control trial. *Journal of Experimental Criminology, 12,* 373–402.

Zaykowski, H. (2014). Mobilizing victim services: The role of reporting to the police. *Journal of Traumatic Stress, 27*(3), 365–369.

Chapter 8

Campbell, D. T., & Stanley, J. C. (1963). *Experimental and quasi-experimental designs for research.* Boston, MA: Houghton Mifflin.

Dodge, M., Starr-Gimeno, D., & Williams, T. (2005). Puttin' on the sting: Women police officers' perspectives on reverse prostitution assignments. *The International Journal of Police Science & Management, 7*(2), 71–85.

Melde, C., Taylor, T., & Esbensen, F. (2009). "I got your back": An examination of the protective function of gang membership in adolescence. *Criminology, 47*(2) 565–594.

Sampson, R. J. (2010). Gold standard myths: Observations on the experimental turn in quantitative criminology. *Journal of Quantitative Criminology, 26,* 489–500.

Santos, R. B., & Santos, R. G. (2016). Offender-focused police intervention in residential burglary and theft from vehicle hot spots: A partially blocked randomized control trial. *Journal of Experimental Criminology, 12,* 373–402.

White, M., Goldkamp, J., & Robinson, J. (2006). Acupuncture in drug treatment: Exploring its role and impact on participant behavior in the drug court setting. *Journal of Experimental Criminology, 2*(10), 45–65.

Chapter 9

Bureau of Justice Statistics. (2017). *All data collections.* Washington, DC: U.S. Department of Justice, Office of Justice Programs.

Federal Bureau of Investigation. (2015). *Cargo theft.* Washington, DC: U.S. Department of Justice, Federal Bureau of Investigation. Retrieved from https://ucr.fbi.gov/crime-in-the-u.s/2015/crime-in-the-u.s.-2015/additional-reports/cargo-theft/cargotheft-report_-2015-_final

Health and Human Services. (2009). Code of federal regulations, subpart A, basic HHS policy for protection of human research subjects 45 CFR 46: Author. Retrieved from https://www.hhs.gov/ohrp/regulations-and-policy/regulations/45-cfr-46

Johnson, S. D., Summers, L., & Pease, K. (2009). Offender as forager? A direct test of the boost account of victimization. *Journal of Quantitative Criminology, 25*(2), 181–200.

Melde, C., Taylor, T., & Esbensen, F. (2009). "I got your back": An examination of the protective function of gang membership in adolescence. *Criminology, 47*(2) 565–594.

Sabina, C., Cuevas, C. A., & Cotignola-Pickens, H. M. (2016). Longitudinal dating violence victimization among Latino teens: Rates, risk factors, and cultural influences. *Journal of Adolescence, 47,* 5–15.

Santos, R. B., & Santos, R. G. (2016). Offender-focused police intervention in residential burglary and theft from vehicle hot spots: A partially blocked randomized control trial. *Journal of Experimental Criminology, 12,* 373–402.

US Bureau of the Census. (2016). *Small Area Income and Poverty Estimates (SAIPE) Program, Dec. 2016* (Figure 1). Washington, DC: Author. Retrieved from https://www.census.gov/did/www/saipe/data/highlights/files/2015/Figure1.pdf

U.S. Department of Commerce. (n.d.). Mission statement. Retrieved from https://www.commerce.gov/tags/mission-statement

U.S. Department of Justice. (n.d.). Home page. Retrieved from https://www.justice.gov/about

Zaykowski, H. (2014). Mobilizing victim services: The role of reporting to the police. *Journal of Traumatic Stress, 27*(3), 365–369.

Chapter 10

Brantingham, P., & Brantingham, P. (1999). Theoretical model of crime hot spot generation. *Studies on Crime and Crime Prevention, 8,* 7–26.

Clarke, R., & Eck, J. (2005). *Crime analysis for problem solvers in 60 small steps.* Washington, DC: U.S. Government Printing Office.

Daley, D., Bachmann, M., Bachmann, B. A., Pedigo, C., Bui, M., & Coffman, J. (2016). Risk terrain modeling predicts child maltreatment. *Child Abuse & Neglect, 62,* 29–38.

Eck, J., Chainey, S., Cameron, J., & Wilson, R. (2005). *Mapping crime: Understanding hotspots.* Washington, DC: U.S. Government Printing Office.

Heywood, D. I., Cornelius, S., & Carver, S. (2002). *An introduction to geographical information systems* (4th ed). New York: Addison Wesley Longman.

Lo, C. P., & Yeung, A. K. W. (2002). *Concepts and techniques of geographic information systems.* Upper Saddle River, NJ: Prentice Hall.

Perry, W. L., McInnis, B., Price, C. C., Smith, S. C., & Hollywood, J. S. (2013). *Predictive policing: The role of crime forecasting in law enforcement operations.* Washington, DC: Rand Corporation.

Ratcliffe, J. H. (2000). Aoristic analysis: The spatial interpretation of unspecific temporal events. *International Journal of Geographical Information Science, 14*(7), 669–679.

Rhind, D. (1989). *Why GIS? ARC News* (Vol. 11, No. 3). Redlands, CA: Environmental Systems Research Institute, Inc.

Rossmo, D. K. (1997). Geographic profiling. In J. L. Jackson & D. A. Bekerian (Eds.), *Offender profiling: Theory, research and practice* (pp. 159–175). Hoboken, NJ: Wiley.

Santos, R. B. (2017). *Crime analysis with crime mapping* (4th ed.). Thousand Oaks, CA: Sage.

Santos, R. B., & Santos, R. G. (2016). Offender-focused police intervention in residential burglary and theft from vehicle hot spots: A partially blocked randomized control trial. *Journal of Experimental Criminology, 12,* 373–402.

U.S. Geological Survey. (2007). *Geographic information systems.* Reston, VA: Author. Retrieved from https://webgis.wr.usgs.gov/globalgis/tutorials/what_is_gis.htm

Chapter 11

Australian Council for International Development. (2013). *Principles for ethical research and evaluation in development.* Deakin: Author. Retrieved from http://ethics.iit.edu/codes/ACFID%202016.pdf

Dodge, M., Starr-Gimeno, D., & Williams, T. (2005). Puttin' on the sting: Women police officers' perspectives on reverse prostitution assignments. *The International Journal of Police Science & Management, 7*(2), 71–85.

Johnson, R. R., & Crews, A. D. (2013). My professor is hot! Correlates of RateMyProfessors.com ratings for criminal justice and criminology faculty members. *American Journal of Criminal Justice, 38,* 639–656.

Joint Committee on Standards for Educational Evaluation. (1994). *Program evaluation standards: How to assess evaluations of educational programs* (2nd ed.). Thousand Oaks, CA: Sage.

Melde, C., Taylor, T., & Esbensen, F. (2009). "I got your back": An examination of the protective function of gang membership in adolescence. *Criminology, 47*(2) 565–594.

Rossi, P. H., Lipsey, M. W., & Freeman, H. E. (2003). *Evaluation: A systematic approach* (7th ed.). Thousand Oaks, CA: Sage.

Sabina, C., Cuevas, C. A., & Cotignola-Pickens, H. M. (2016). Longitudinal dating violence victimization among Latino teens: Rates, risk factors, and cultural influences. *Journal of Adolescence, 47,* 5–15.

Santos, R. B., & Santos, R. G. (2016). Offender-focused police intervention in residential burglary and theft from vehicle hot spots: A partially blocked randomized control trial. *Journal of Experimental Criminology, 12,* 373–402.

Scriven, M. (1977). The evaluation of teachers and teaching. In G. Borich (Ed.), *The appraisal of teaching: Concepts and process* (pp. 186–193). Reading, MA: Addison-Wesley.

Smith, B. E., & Davis, R. C. (2004). *An evaluation of efforts to implement no-drop policies: Two central values in conflict* (NCJ 199719). Washington, DC: National Criminal Justice Reference Service.

Stufflebeam, D. L. (1983). The CIPP Model for program evaluation. In G. F. Madaus, M. Scriven, & D. L. Stufflebeam (Eds.), *Evaluation models: Viewpoints on educational and human services evaluation*, 117–141. Boston: Kluwer Nijhof.

Weiss, C. H. (1993). Where politics and evaluation research meet. *Evaluation Practice, 14*(1), 93–106.

Chapter 12

Acock, A. C. (2005). SAS, Stata, SPSS: A comparison. *Journal of Marriage and Family, 67*(4), 1093–1095.

Brunson, R., & Weitzer, R. (2009). Police relations with Black and White youths in different urban neighborhoods. *Urban Affairs Review, 44*(6), 858–885.

Cairo, A. (2016, August 29). Download the Datasaurus: Never trust summary statistics alone; always visualize your data [Blog post]. *The Functional Art*. Retrieved from http://www.thefunctionalart.com/2016/08/download-datasaurus-never-trust-summary.html

Dodge, M., Starr-Gimeno, D., & Williams, T. (2005). Puttin' on the sting: Women police officers' perspectives on reverse prostitution assignments. *The International Journal of Police Science & Management, 7*(2), 71–85.

Hart, T. C., Hart, J. L., & Miethe, T. D. (2013). Situational context of student bullying victimization and reporting behavior: A conjunctive analysis of case configurations. *Justice Research and Policy, 15*(2), 43–73.

Hart, T. C., Rennison, C. M., & Miethe, T. D. (2017). Identifying patterns of situational clustering and contextual variability in criminological data: An overview of conjunctive analysis of case configurations (CACC). *Journal of Contemporary Criminal Justice, 33*(2), 112–120.

Melde, C., Taylor, T., & Esbensen, F. (2009). "I got your back": An examination of the protective function of gang membership in adolescence. *Criminology, 47*(2) 565–594.

Miethe, T. D., Hart, T. C., & Regoeczi, W. C. (2008). The conjunctive analysis of case configurations: An exploratory method for discrete multivariate analyses of crime data. *Journal of Quantitative Criminology, 24*(2), 227–241.

Sabina, C., Cuevas, C. A., & Cotignola-Pickens, H. M. (2016). Longitudinal dating violence victimization among Latino teens: Rates, risk factors, and cultural influences. *Journal of Adolescence, 47*, 5–15.

Santos, R. B., & Santos, R. G. (2016). Offender-focused police intervention in residential burglary and theft from vehicle hot spots: A partially blocked randomized control trial. *Journal of Experimental Criminology, 12*, 373–402.

Tobler, W. (1970). A computer movie simulating urban growth in the Detroit region. *Economic Geography, 46*(2), 234–240.

Tylverfigen.com. (n.d.). Spurious correlations [Website]. Retrieved from http://www.tylervigen.com/spurious-correlations

Wallace, W. (1971). *The logic of science in sociology*. New York: Aldine.

Wasserman, R. (2013). Ethical issues and guidelines for conducting data analysis in psychological research. *Ethics & Behavior, 23*(1), 3–15.

Zaykowski, H. (2014). Mobilizing victim services: The role of reporting to the police. *Journal of Traumatic Stress, 27*(3), 365–369.

Chapter 13

Brunson, R., & Weitzer, R. (2009). Police relations with Black and White youths in different urban neighborhoods. *Urban Affairs Review, 44*(6), 858–885.

Business Dictionary Online. (n.d.). Definition of "policy." Retrieved from http://www.businessdictionary.com/definition/policy.html

Cairney, P. (n.d.). Politics & public policy: 1000 words. *Wordpress.com*. Retrieved from https://paulcairney.wordpress.com/1000-words/

Dictionary.com. (n.d.). Definition of "policy." Retrieved from http://www.dictionary.com/browse/policy

Dodge, M., Starr-Gimeno, D., & Williams, T. (2005). Puttin' on the sting: Women police officers' perspectives on reverse prostitution assignments. *The International Journal of Police Science & Management, 7*(2), 71–85.

Luo, M. (2011, January 25). NRA Stymies firearms research, scientists say. *The New York Times*. Retrieved from http://www.nytimes.com/2011/01/26/us/26guns.html?pagewanted=1&_r=0

Melde, C., Taylor, T., & Esbensen, F. (2009). "I got your back": An examination of the protective function of gang membership in adolescence. *Criminology, 47*(2) 565–594.

Merriam Webster Dictionary Online. (n.d.). Definition of "policy." Retrieved from https://www.merriam-webster.com/dictionary/policy

National Rifle Association. (n.d.). A brief history of the NRA. Retrieved from https://home.nra.org/about-the-nra/

NRA-ILA. (2001, December 11). 22 times less safe? Anti-gun lobby's favorite spin re-attacks guns in the home. Retrieved from https://www.nraila.org/articles/20011211/22-times-less-safe brantigun-lobbys-f

Oxford Dictionary Online. (n.d.). Definition of "policy." Retrieved from: https://en.oxforddictionaries.com/definition/policy

Sabina, C., Cuevas, C. A., & Cotignola-Pickens, H. M. (2016). Longitudinal dating violence victimization among Latino teens: Rates, risk factors, and cultural influences. *Journal of Adolescence, 47,* 5–15.

Santos, R. B., & Santos, R. G. (2016). Offender-focused police intervention in residential burglary and theft from vehicle hot spots: A partially blocked randomized control trial. *Journal of Experimental Criminology, 12,* 373–402.

Williams, M. R. (2017). The effect of attorney type on bail decisions, *Criminal Justice Policy Review, 28*(1), 3–17.

Zaykowski, H. (2014). Mobilizing victim services: The role of reporting to the police. *Journal of Traumatic Stress, 27*(3), 365–369.

Chapter 14

Adams, S. (2012). Odds are your internship will get you a job. *Forbes.com*. Retrieved from https://www.forbes.com/sites/susanadams/2012/07/25/odds-are-your-internship-will-get-you-a-job/#2d66d11962e5

Adams, S. (2014). 4 ways to use Facebook to find a job. *Forbes.com*. Retrieved from https://www.forbes.com/sites/susanadams/2014/02/06/4-ways-to-use-facebook-to-find-a-job/#426a83301fab

Doyle, A. (2016). Best keywords to use in your job search. *The Balance*. Retrieved from https://www.thebalance.com/best-keywords-to-use-in-your-job-search-2062028

Marie Claire. (2017). 13 ways you can use your LinkedIn profile to get your dream job. *MarieClaire.com*. Retrieved from http://www.marieclaire.co.uk/life/work/10-ways-you-can-use-your-linkedin-profile-to-get-your-dream-job-98464

Miami University's Career Services. (2017). Ethical considerations to guide your job search. *Miami University's Enrollment Management & Student Success Center for Career Exploration & Success*. Retrieved from https://miamioh.edu/emss/offices/career-services/internship-job-search/ethical-considerations/index.html

Skillings, P. (2017). How to use twitter to find a job. *BigInterview.com*. Retrieved from https://biginterview.com/ blog/2015/03/twitter-jobs.html

Tripp, T., & Cobkit, S. (2013). Unexpected pathways: Criminal justice career options in the private sector. *Journal of Criminal Justice Education, 24*(4), 478–494.

Index

A-Baki, Ivonne, 425
Abstracts:
  defined, 74
  examples, 75, 93
  research articles and, 74–75
Accessibility, of research findings, 430–431
Accidental sampling, 148, 154–155, 160
Accuracy standard, evaluation research, 362, 364, 368
Acock, Alan, 395
ACSII, 283
Adams, Susan, 468
Administrative crime analysis, 320
Advocacy groups, policy makers and, 432–433
Agenda setting, problem identification, 426–427
Aggression and Violent Behavior (journal website), 66
American Community Survey (ACS), 291
American Criminal Justice Society (ACJS), 407
American Evaluation Association, 348, 361
American Fact Finder (website), 291
American Journal of Criminal Justice, 65
American Psychological Association (APA) style, 77, 79
American Society of Criminology (ASC),
      65 (website), 407
Americans with Disabilities Act (ADA) Regulations, 284
Analysis of qualitative information, 364, 370
Analysis of variance (ANOVA), 390
Annual Parole Survey, 284, 289
Annual Probation Survey, 289
Anonymity, 230
ANOVA (analysis of variance), 390
Aoristic analysis, 329–332
APA. *See* American Psychological Association
Apple®, 217
Apple® iOS™, 398
Apple® Mac™, 395
Applied research, 356, 360
Approach subsection, policy brief, 441–442
ArcGIS™ software, 318, 334
Assent, child participation and, 52, 53
Assessment of risk and benefits, 21
Association:
  causation is not, 245–247
  defined, 245
  variables, correlated examples, 246
Association of American Universities (AAU), 5
Associations:
  correlation analysis and, 388
  quantitative data analysis and, 387–390
  regression analysis and, 388–390
ATLAS.ti, Scientific Software Development GmbH®,
      software, 398–399

Attributes:
  defined, 118
  ethics and, 127–128
  levels of measurement, 121–123
  mutually exclusive/exhaustiveness, 120–121
  response categories, 118–120
Attrition, subject loss and, 268
Audio recorders, field notes and, 195
Australian Council for International Development, 367
Authoritative sources, knowledge and, 9
Availability sampling, 148, 154–155, 160
Axial coding, 197
Azavea®, 325, 326

Bachmann, B. A., 334
Bachmann, M., 334
Bail decisions, attorney type and, 434
Banks, C., 17–18
Basic research, 356, 360
Beall, Jeffrey, 67
Before-and-after design, 266, 271
Behaviorally specific questions, 5
Belmont Report, 48
  principles of, 19
  requirements for human subjects, 19
*Belmont Report: Ethical Principles and Guidelines for the
      Protection of Human Subjects and Research*
      (the Commission), 19, 48
Beneficence, 19, 48
Bias:
  interviewer, survey research and, 214
  nonresponse, 215
  recall, 216
  sampling and, 142–143
Biased sample, 142–143
Big Interview, 470
Blind review, 360
Block groups, 291
Block matching, 250–251
Block variables, 250–251
Blogs, as source, 68
Body language, interviews and, 189
Boolean operators, 71–73
Boost account, 332
Booth, Charles, 313, 315
Boxplot, 384
Bradford, B., 228
Brantingham, Patricia, 327
Brantingham, Paul, 327
Breaking Silence (advocacy group), 432
British Crime Survey (BCS), 228

British Journal of Criminology, 314
Brunson, Rod, 22
    abstract example, 93
    conceptualization, 106
    controlled experiments, 257
    data analysis/coding, 196
    data analysis/techniques/findings, 414
    data collection, 101–102
    ethics, policy-relevant research, 439
    example abstract, 75
    exploratory research, 40
    featured research, 25, 57, 203
    geographic information systems (GIS), 314
    gold standard, 253
    grounded theory, theme identification and, 198–199
    hypotheses/concepts/variables, 131
    inductive reasoning, 182
    interviews, 188
    job interview tips, 475
    policy makers and, 424
    policy-relevant research, 444
    population/sample, 139, 168
    qualitative data, 177–179, 183
    qualitative data analysis, 391
    research questions, 46
    sample size, research type and, 163
    secondary data analysis, 276, 300
    source saturation, 73–74
    survey, descriptive research, 211–212
    survey research types/modes, 239
    topic development method, 33
    variables, research questions and, 110, 111
Buccine-Schraeder, Henri, 339–340
Budget constraints, policy maker influence, 433–435
Budgets
Bui, M., 334
Bullying, reducing school, 397
Bureau of Justice Statistics. *See* U.S. Bureau of Justice
    Statistics (BJS)
Bureau of Labor Statistics. *See* U.S. Bureau of Labor
    Statistics (BLS)
Burglars in Blue (Winstanley), 37
Burton, Sue, 412–413
Butler, H. D., 11
Buxton, Peter, 15

CACC. *See* Conjunctive analysis of case
    configurations (CACC)
Cairney, P, 425
Cairney, Paul, 423
Cairo, Alberto, 410
Cameron, J, 324
Campbell, D. T., 257, 260, 263, 265

Campus law enforcement agencies, survey, 290
Campus Sexual Assault (CSA) Study (Krebs et al), 4–6, 164
Cantor, D., 5–6, 164
Cao, L., 35
Capital punishment, data on, 289
Caplan, Joel, 327
CAQDAS. *See* Computer-assisted qualitative data analysis
Career, research methods as, 467–468
    criminal justice graduates, 457
    ethics and, 475–476
    expert (Nora Scanlon), 476–479
    internships and, 451–452, 471
    interviews and, 471–475
    job search, documents needed for, 452–461. *See also*
        Documents, job searches and
    networking/relationships, getting started, 450–452
    online job searches, 467–468
    private sector, 464–466
    public sector, 461–464
    skills/professional skills and, 449–450
    social media job searches, 468–471
Careerbuilder.com, 467
CareerToolBelt.com, 467
Cargo theft, 288
Cartographic boundary shapefiles, 292
Case studies:
    qualitative data and, 177
    researchers and, 21
Categorical variable, 121
CATI. *See* Computer-assisted telephone interviewing
Causality, criteria for claiming, 267
Causal relationships, 243
Causation:
    association is not, 245–247
    correlation and, 410
    defined
    defining criteria for, 244–245
    importance of establishing, 247
Census:
    advantages/disadvantages, 140
    defined, 140
    sample, 139–140
Census Bureau. *See* U.S. Bureau of the Census
Center for Career Exploration and Success at
    Miami University, 476
Centers for Disease Control and Prevention (CDC),
    293–294, 433
    National Health Interview Survey, 219
Chainey, S., 324
Chain referral sampling, 148, 156, 157, 161
Characteristics, QDA and, 396
Chicago Manual of Style, 77
Chicago Tribune, 191

Children, use in research, 52–53
Chisolm, J. J., 52–53
Chi-squared test:
    of independence, 387
    one-sample, 388
Choropleth map, 313, 314, 334
Christian, L. M., 224
Chronologically based literature reviews, 84
Citations:
    cloning and, 90
    in-text, 79
    plagiary and, 90
    summarizing original source, 78
Clarke, R., 328
Cloning (copy & pasting words of others), 90
Closed-ended questions:
    qualitative data and, 178–179
    survey research, 222–223
Cluster analysis, 322
Clustering, 328
Cluster sampling (probability), 148, 151–153, 159
Cobbina, J., 191
Cobkit, S., 457
Codebook, 283
Coding data:
    axial, 197
    grounded theory and, 196–197
    mail or written surveys and, 215
    open coding, 197
    qualitative, grounded theory and, 196–197
    qualitative data and, 180
    selective coding, 197
Coding sorts, 396
Coffman, J., 334
Cohen, L. E., 36
Coming Out from Behind the Badge (Miraglia), 37
Common Rule, HHS research ethics regulations, 48–50
Communicate findings/recommendations, evaluation
        research, 350
Communication, policy makers and:
    barriers, policy makers and, 429
    effective, characteristics of, 430
    nonaccessible presentation, 430–431
    policy brief, 430–431
    translating findings, 436
Competence, evaluation research and, 348
Complete and fair assessment, propriety standard, 362, 367
Completeness, geocoding, 337
Complete observer, 193
Complete participant role, 192
Complimentary close, cover letter, 453
Comprehensible, Belmont Report, 19, 21
CompStat tactical crime analysis, 321–322

Computer-assisted qualitative data analysis (CAQDAS), 199
Computer-assisted telephone interviewing (CATI), 219–220
Concepts:
    case study examples, 104
    defined, 103–105
    ethics and, 127–128
    examples, 103–105
    expert (Brenidy Rice), 128–129
    featured research examples, 131–133
    measurable elements of, 104
    non-varying, as pitfall, 127
    stages from concept to variables, 102, 126
Conceptual definition, 106
Conceptualization:
    concept to variables stage, 102
    defined, 106
    ethics and, 127–128
    example, 106–107
Conclusions:
    empirical research journal articles, 77
    policy brief and, 442
    report, 14
Conditional logic statements, 217
Conference Series, LLC, 68
Confidentiality:
    field notes and, 195
    survey research and, 230
Conflict of interest, propriety standard, 362, 367
Confounders, 250
Confounding factor, causality, 245
Conjunctive analysis of case configurations (CACC),
        400–401
Consent, observation and, 192
Content analysis, 194–195
    accuracy standard, 364
    evaluation research, 368
Content validity, 124
Context, qualitative data and, 177, 180
Context analysis, accuracy standard, 364, 368
Continuous variables, 123
Control group:
    defined, 249
    example, 269
    nonequivalent, 265–266
    pre-experiments and, 263–264
    See also True experiment
Control variables, 113–115
Convenience sampling, 148, 154–155, 160
Convex envelope, 404
Convex hull, 404
Corbin, J., 185
Correlation, causation and, 410
Correlation analysis, 388

Cost:
  data entry/processing, 232
  qualitative data collection, 180
Cost-effectiveness, evaluation research, 362, 365
Count data, 313
County Business Patterns (CBP), 292
Cover letters, job searches, 452–454 (example)
Craig, J. M., 144
Crews, A. D., 363
Crime analysis:
  administrative, 320
  aoristic, 329–332
  defining, 320
  geographic profiling, 335
  hot spot mapping, 324
  predictive policing, 325–327
  repeat victimization/near repeat victimization, 332–334
  research and, 323–324
  risk terrain modeling (RTM), 327–329
  strategic, 322–323
  tactical, 321–322
  See also Crime mapping; Geographic information
      systems (GIS)
Crime attractors, 328
Crime & Delinquency, 65
Crime enablers, 328
Crime generators, 328
Crime mapping:
  administrative crime analysis, 320
  defining, 13, 320
  ethics and, 338–339
  expert (Buccine-Schraeder), 339–340
  geocoding process, 337
  history of GIS and, 313–314
  Modifiable Areal Unit Problem (MAUP), 337–338
  report findings, 335–336
  strategic analysis, 322–323
  tactical crime analysis and, 321–322
  See also Geographic information systems (GIS)
Crime pattern analysis, 322
Crime pattern theory, 327
CrimeStatIV, 335
Criminal Justice and Behavior, 65
Criminal justice graduates, 457
Criminal justice policies, 423
Criminal Justice Review, 65
Criminology, 65
Criminology, Justice Quarterly, 314
Criminology & Public Policy, 65
Criterion validity, 124
Cross-sectional data, 305
Cuevas, Carlos, 22–23
  abstract example, 93
  associations, regression analysis, 389

causation, 244
concept examples, 103
data analysis/techniques/findings, 414
data characteristics/sources, 306
ethics, reporting findings and, 412
evaluation research, 366
example abstract, 75
explanatory research, 41, 268
featured research, 25, 57
geographic information systems (GIS), 314
gold standard, 253
hot spot mapping, 324
hypotheses/concepts/variables, 132
IBM® SPSS Statistics™, 394
job interview tips, 474
literature review, 63
operationalization example, 107, 109
policy makers and, 424
policy-relevant research, 444
population/sample, 139
population/sampling considerations, 168
qualitative data, 175–176, 178
questions, data and, 224
randomization, 252
requests for proposals, 36
research method skills, 450
research questions, 47, 100–101
sampling approach, 148
sampling importance, 137
secondary data, 277, 300, 301
source saturation, 74
survey, explanatory research, 213
survey research types/modes, 239
unit of analysis, 143
variable, research question, 110
Current Population Survey (CPS), 291
Customs, as knowledge source, 9
CV. *See* Control variable

Daigle, L. E., 38
Daley, D., 334
Daly, J. M., 215
Data:
  accurate portrayal of, 91
  attributes and, 118–121
  census bureau collection, 290–292
  collect at highest measurement, 123
  collecting/types of, 13
  concepts and, 103–105
  conceptualization and, 105–107
  crime statistics, 6–9
  deductive reasoning and, 100
  defined, 2, 3
  differences in construction of violent crime rates, 8

discrete/continuous variables, 123
encryption, 237
everyday life, 4
expert (Brenidy Rice), 128–129
FBI sources of, 288–290
inductive reasoning and, 101
levels of measurement and, 121–123
measures, 115–118
operationalization and, 107, 109
qualitative, 101
quantitative, 100–101
research question and, 101–102
secondary, research using. See Secondary data research
sources of, 34–35
spatial/geographical, GIS and, 315–317
understanding research using quantitative/qualitative, 105
U.S. Department of Commerce collection, 290–292
validity and, 123–124
variables and, 109–115
See also Data analysis; Statistics; and entries for specific types of data
Data analysis:
conjunctive analysis of case configurations (CACC), 400–401
ethics, reporting findings and, 411–412
evaluation research, 349, 350
expert (Sue Burton), 412–413
findings, reporting. See Findings, reporting
geostatistical, 403
qualitative data, 390–391
quantitative data, 380–390
spatial statistics, 403–406
Data analysis software:
qualitative research, 395–400
quantitative research, 392–395
See also Software
Data codebooks, 34–35
Data collection, summarize method, 78
Data entry, survey processing, 231–232
Data Sharing for Demographic Research (DSDR), 282
Datasuarus, Alberto Cairo, 410
Dating Violence among Latino Adolescents (DAVILA) survey, 213
DAVILA, 277
Deaths in Custody Reporting Program (DCRP), 289
Decision-making, evaluation research and, 356, 358
Deduction, 378
Deductive reasoning:
data collection and, 100
illustrated, 182
inductive v., 101, 181
Defensible information source, accuracy standard, 364, 368
Definition(s):
concepts and, 106
defined, 5

De-identified data, 302
Demographic questions, 227
Denzin, N. K., 186, 187
Department of Health and Human Services (HHS), 48
lead paint study, 52–53
research regulations, 49–50
Department of Justice (DOJ), See U.S. Department of Justice (DOJ)
Dependent variable, 111–112, 115
Describe purposes/procedures, accuracy standard, 364, 368
Descriptive literature review, 81
Descriptive research, 41, 42, 211–212
Descriptive statistics, 380
Design of the methodology, evaluation research, 349
Design research. See Research design
Develop findings/conclusions, evaluation research, 349–350
Develop research question, evaluation research, 348
Deviation score, 385
Devine, Sharon, 55–56
Dillman, Don A., 215, 224–226, 231, 232
Dillman et al.'s 19 principles for writing survey questions, 225–226
Disclosure of findings, propriety standard, 362, 367
Discrete variables, 123
Discussion section, empirical journal article, 77
Disraeli, Benjamin, 411
Distribution, mail and written survey, 214–215
Dividers, in tables, 408
Document analysis, 193–194
Documents, job searches and:
cover letter, 452–454 (example)
letter of recommendation, 458, 460–461
professional portfolio, 473–474
résumé, 453–460
STAR Method Matrix, demonstrating professional skills, 479
Dodge, Mary, 23, 39
abstract example, 93
concept examples, 103–105
convenience sampling, 155
data analysis approach, 196
data analysis/techniques/findings, 415
data collection, 101–102
ethics, policy-relevant research, 439
evaluation research, 349, 356, 365, 366, 368
example abstract, 75
experimental research, 268
exploratory research, 40
featured research, 25, 57
geographic information systems (GIS), 314
gold standard, 253
hypotheses/concepts/variables, 132
internships, 471
interviews, 188

job interview tips, 475
NVio, QSR International® software, 398
objectivity/going native, 200
policy makers and, 424
policy-relevant research, 444
population/sampling considerations, 169
purpose/research questions/sampling/analysis, 203
qualitative data, 176–179, 183
qualitative data analysis, 391
qualitative inquiry, 181
research example, 69–70, 73
sampling approach, 148
secondary data, 300, 301
snowball sampling, 157
source saturation, 73
survey, exploratory research, 211
survey research types/modes, 239
topic research method of, 37
type of research, 162
unit of analysis, 143, 146
Double-barreled questions, 223
Doyle, Alison, 467
DV. *See* Dependent variable

Early relevance, policy-relevant research, 435
Eck, J., 324, 328
Ecological fallacy:
    sample size and, 164
    units of analysis and, 146–147
Ecological Momentary Assessment (EMA), 218
Ecological validity, 218
Edit, literature review writing, 87
Effectiveness, research, 261
Elements, 139
EMA. *See* Ecological Momentary Assessment
Emergency room statistics, 289
Empirical, 65
Empirical generalizations, wheel of science, 31
Empirical peer-reviewed journal articles, 65
Empirical research journal articles:
    abstracts and, 74–75
    conclusions section, 77
    discussion section, 77
    findings section, 77
    introduction section, 76
    keywords, 76
    literature review of, 76–77
    method section, 77
    references section, 77
    style guides, 77
Employment interviews, 471–475
Encryption, data, 237
Environmental Criminology and Crime Analysis
    (ECCA), 407

Equivalence analysis, random assignment, 387
Errors:
    findings, reporting, 409–410
    online/mobile data entry, 217
    surveys, mail and written self-administered, 216
Errors, writing literature review:
    examples, 88–89
    failure to focus on themes, 88
    not allowing enough time, 87–88
    organization/structure, lack of, 88
    proposed research, failure to justify need for, 89
    purpose, not knowing, 92
    quoting problems, 88
Esbensen, Finn-Aage, 34, 80
Esri® software, 318
Ethics:
    Belmont Report principles of, 19
    career searches and, 475–476
    children, use in research, 52–53
    Common Rule, IRB role and, 49–50
    concepts/operationalizations/measurements/
        variables/data, 127–128
    confidentiality and, 367
    defined, 3, 14
    evaluation research and, 366–367
    experimental research and, 268–269
    expert (Sharon Devine), 55–56
    fieldwork and, 192
    findings, reporting and, 411–412
    GIS/crime mapping and, 338–339
    HHS regulations, 49
    human participation, Belmont Report, 19
    human subjects, protecting, 54–55
    informed consent, 19
    Internal Review Board, role, 20–21
    IRB role and, 49–50
    legislation, 19
    Milgram teacher/learner study and, 48–49
    plagiary and, 89–90
    policy-relevant research and, 438–439
    predatory journals/publishers and, 68
    pregnant women/human fetuses, neonates, 51
    prisoners use in research, 51–52
    qualitative data research and, 200–201
    research principles/requirements, 18–20
    respect for persons, benefice, and justice, 48
    sampling and, 164
    secondary data analysis and, 301–302
    survey research and, 236–237
    unethical research examples, 14–18
    veterans in research, 53–54
    vulnerable populations and, 50
Ethnographic interviews, 188, 189
Ethnography, data collection, 190

Evaluation impact, 361, 364
Evaluation research, 41, 42
  accuracy standard, 362, 364
  afterthought nature of, 365
  comparative/judgmental nature, 359
  confidentiality, 367
  decision-making, knowledge for, 356, 358
  defining, 347–348
  effective, four standards of, 360–361
  environmental challenges, 359–360
  ethics and, 366–367
  expert (Michael Shively), 368–370, 452
  feasibility standard of, 361–362
  featured researchers, 371
  findings/dissemination, 360
  flexibility, importance, 367
  formative, 351–355
  guiding principles of, 348
  objectivity, losing/failure to end study, 368
  policy process and, 350–351
  political context, 365–366
  politics and, 368
  professional knowledge of subject matter, 366
  propriety standard of, 362
  reasons to use, 346–347
  research questions, origination of, 358
  seven basic steps used to conduct, 349
  stakeholders, working with, 359
  steps of, 348–350
  summative, 355–356
  survey, 213
  trust/ethics, 366
  types of, 351
  utility standard of, 361
Evaluator credibility, 361
Evernote™, 398
Evidence, MEAL strategy and, 83–87
Excel™, 283, 392–393
Executive summary, policy brief, 441
Exempt research, 54
Exhaustive, 120
Exhaustiveness, attributes and, 120–121
Expedited review, 54
Experimental group, 249, 269. See also True experiment
Experimental mortality, 257
Experimental research:
  association, not causation, 245–247
  causality pitfall, 267
  causation, defining criteria for, 244–245
  defining, 248
  design characteristics, 271
  design effectiveness, 261
  ethics and, 268–269
  experimental/control group use in, 269

  expert (Chris Keating), 269–270
  external validity threats, 260–262
  featured researchers, 272
  internal validity, threats to, 257–260
  natural experiments, 266–267
  pre-experiments, 263–265
  reliability, 262
  threats to external validity, 260, 262
  threats to internal validity, 257–260
  true experiments, 248–256
  validity types, 256–257
  why conduct?, 244
  See also entries for individual categories
Experimental variables, interaction of testing and, 262
Experts:
  Buccine-Schraeder, Henri (crime mapping), 339–340
  Burton, Sue (data analysis/findings), 412–413
  Devine, Sharon (IRB), 55–56
  Gallaher, Sam (sampling), 165–166
  Keating, Chris (experimental research), 269–270
  Kelly, Bridget (survey research), 237–238
  McCandless, Sean (literature review), 91–92
  Peeples, Carol (qualitative data research), 201–202
  Rice, Brenidy (data concepts), 128–130
  Scanlon, Nora (research methods career), 476–479
  Shively, Michael (evaluation research), 368–370, 452
  TePas, Katie (policy-relevant research), 439–440
  Truman, Jenna (secondary data), 302–305
Explanatory research, 41, 42, 212–213
Exploratory research, 40–41, 42, 211
External validity:
  defining, 256–257
  threats to, 252 (cartoon), 260, 262

Facebook®, 282, 468–469
Face-to-face (in-person) interviews:
  advantages, 221
  defined, 221
  disadvantages, 221–222
Face validity, 123–124
Farfel, M. R., 52–53
Farfel and Chisolm, 52–53
FBI's Interstate Identification Index (III), 289
Fear, looping and, 431–432
Feasibility standard, evaluation research, 361–362, 364
Featured research:
  abstracts, 93–94
  data analysis techniques/findings, 414–415
  evaluation research, 371
  experimental designs, characteristics, 272
  GIS techniques/concepts/outcomes, 341
  hypothesis/concepts/variables, 131–133
  policy-relevant research, 444–445
  population and sampling considerations, 168–169

purpose/research questions, sampling and analysis, 203
qualitative research, 185–187
sources of, generalizability of data used, 306–307
survey types and modes used, 239
topic/purpose/research questions/IRB approval, 57
Federal Bureau of Investigation (FBI):
    cargo theft statistics, 288
    data compilation/secondary source, 288–290
    hate crime statistics, 286, 288
    Law Enforcement Officers Killed and Assaulted
        (LEOKA), 286
    National Incident-Based Reporting System
        (NIBRS), 285–286
    Summary Reporting System (SRS/UCR), 285
    Supplementary Homicide Reports (SHR), 285
    Uniform Crime Reports (UCR), 8
    USA Patriot Improvement and Reauthorization Act
        of 2005, 288
    violent crime statistics, 6–9
    website, crime statistics, 66
Federal Coordination and Compliance Section of the
    Department of Justice's Civil Rights Division, 284
Federal Policy for the Protections of Human Subjects (HHS):
    children and, 52–53
    departments/agencies and, 50
    IRB role, 49–50
    pregnant women/human fetuses/neonates, 51
    prisoners, 51–52
    subparts/common rule of, 49
    veterans, 53–54
    vulnerable populations, 50
Federal Statistical System (FedStats), 283–284
Federal Trade Commission (FTC), 68
Felson, M., 36
Feminist Criminology, 65
Feminist Theory (journal website), 66
Fetuses (human) research ethics and, 51
Fielded, 212
Fielding the survey, 231
Field notes, recording qualitative data, 195–196
Field research, Junker's role conceptions of, 190
Field work:
    data collection and, 184, 187
    ethics and, 192
    observation, data collection, 190, 192
Figures, research findings using, 408–409
Filters, search, 71, 72
Findings:
    defined
    develop, 13
    report, 14
    secondary data, reporting, 298–299
    section, empirical research journal articles, 77
    summarizing sources, 79

Findings, reporting:
    accessibility of, policy makers and, 430–431
    data, knowledge of, 410–411
    errors/pitfalls, 409–410
    ethics and, 411–412
    expert (Sue Burton), 412–413
    figures, 408–409
    garbage in/garbage out, 409–410
    methods of, 406–407
    policy makers and. See Policy makers, getting research to
    poster sessions, 407
    presentations, 407
    statistical significance, 411
    substantive significance, 411
    tables, 407–408
    translating, 436
First draft, 87
First Law of Geography, 404–405
First rough draft, organizing, 81–84
Fiscal responsibility, propriety standard, 362, 367
Fisher, B., 4–6, 164
Flag account, 332
Fletcher, Joseph, 313
Flow, of survey, 227
Fly, The (film), 248, 263
Focus groups, 189
Focusing event, policy-making process, 426–427
Foreign languages spoken, résumé and, 458
Formal agreements, propriety standard, 362, 365
Formative evaluation, 357, 364, 368
    defined, 351–352
    needs assessment, 352–353
    process evaluation, 353–355
Frankenstein (film), 248
Freeman, H. E., 368
Frequency data, 313
Frequency distributions, 380–381
Frequency distribution table, 381
Full board review, 54
Full enumeration, 140

Gallaher, Sam, 165–166
Gap analysis, 353
Garbage In, Garbage Out (GIGO), 409–410
Gather data/evidence, evaluation research, 349
Geary's C statistic, 324, 404
Gedela, Srinubabu, 68
Generalizability:
    defined
    qualitative data, 180
    sample size and, 164
    units of analysis and, 141
General Schedule (GS), public sector employment, 463
Geocoding process, 337

Geographically weighted regression (GWR), 405
Geographic information systems (GIS):
    application component, 319
    defining, 292, 314–315
    ethics and, 338–339
    expert (Henri Buccine-Schraeder), 339–340
    featured researchers, 341
    geocoding process and, 337
    hardware/software technology of, 317–318
    history of crime mapping and, 313–314
    Modifiable Areal Unit Problem (MAUP), 337–338
    people component, 319–320
    report findings, 335–336
    spatial/geographical data, 315–317
    See also Crime mapping
Geographic profiling, 335
Geographic regions (unit of analysis), 145
Geospatial data, 291–292
Geostatistical data analysis, 403
    mean center, 403–404
    spatial descriptions, 403
    spatial interpolation/regression and, 405–406
    standard distance, 404
Gereau, P. L., 215
Get-Ord statistic, 404
GIS. See Geographic information systems (GIS)
Github (website), 235
Global statistical test, 324
Going native, researchers and, 190, 200
Gold, R. L., 190, 192
Gold standard, experimental research, 252–253
Google®, 282
Google® Android™, 398
Government departments/agencies, common rule adoption
        and, 50
G-Power Software, 267
Graphics, data visualization and, 198
GRASS GIS software, 318
Grounded theory analysis:
    coding qualitative data using, 196–197
    defined, 196
Group (unit of analysis), 145
    experimental/control, 249
    randomly assigned experimental/control, 253–254
    two-group pretest-treatment-posttest design, 254–255
Guerry, André-Michel, 313
Guidelines, 423–424
GWR (geographically weighted regression), 406

Haney, C., 17–18
Haphazard sampling, 148, 154–155, 160
Hardware technology, GIS and, 317–318
Hart, J. L., 397
Hart, T. C., 397, 400

Hash-tagging, Twitter® job searches and, 470–471
Hate Crime Statistics Act of 1990, 286
Hawthorne Effect, 192–193, 262
Headings, in tables, 408
Heat Map questions, 234
HHS. See Department of Health and Human Services
History, 257–258
Hit rate, 326
Holder, Eric, 412
Holmesberg Prison skin experiments, 51, 52
Homicide Studies, 65
Honesty, evaluation research and, 348
Hot spot analysis, 322, 323
Hot spot mapping, 324
Hot spot mapping techniques, 324
Huberman, M., 186
Human interactions, propriety standard, 362, 366
Human subjects:
    defined, 49, 50
    ethics and, 46–54
    secondary data analysis, ethics and, 301–303
    training in protection of, 46–55
    See also Ethics; Respect for persons;
            Vulnerable populations
Human trafficking reporting system, 289
HunchLab™, 325, 326
HyperRESEARCH, ResearchWare®, software, 399–400
Hypotheses:
    defined, 31
    testing, with qualitative data, 178
    wheel of science, 31

IBM® SPSS Statistics™, 393–395, 452
ICPSR. See Interuniversity Consortium for Political and
        Social Research
ICPSR Summer Program in Quantitative Methods of Social
        Research, 282
Identifiable information, 302
Identify/engage stakeholders, evaluation research, 348
Ideology, policy makers and, 433
iMedPub, LLC, predatory journal, 68
Impact evaluation, summative, 356, 358, 359
Impact factors, 67, 68
Impartial reporting, accuracy standard, 364, 370
Implications subsection, policy brief, 442
Inappropriate sources, 68
Incentives, survey research, 230
Indeed.com, 467
Independence, Chi-squared test of, 387
Independent variables, 112–113, 115, 252
Individualist fallacy:
    defined
    sample size and, 164
    units of analysis and, 147

Individual (unit of analysis), 143, 144
Inductive reasoning:
　deductive v., 101, 181
　defined, 101
　illustrate, 182
　qualitative, 182
Inferences, 136–137
Information, Belmont Report, 19, 20
Information scope and selection information, evaluation
　　research, 361
Informed consent:
　Belmont Report, ethics, 19
　defined, 20
Initial primary source, 73–74
In-person interviews, 188–189
　advantages, 221
　defined, 221
　disadvantages, 221–222
Inputs, 353
Inquiry, qualitative data and, 181
Institute for Legislative Action (ILA), 433
Institutional review board (IRB):
　defining, 20, 22
　exempt/expedited/full panel review, 54
　expert (Sharon Devine), 55–56
　HHS research ethics regulations and, 49–50
　human subjects, protecting, 54–55
　role of, 20–21
Instrumentation, threat to internal validity, 258
Integrated Public Use Microdata Series (PUSM)
　　(website), 291
Integrity, evaluation research and, 348
Intentional violence statistics, 289
Interaction effect of testing, 262
Interaction of experimental arrangements and experimental
　　variables, 260, 262
Interaction of selection biases and experimental variables,
　　validity testing, 260
Interaction of testing and experimental variables,
　　262, 280–283
Interest groups, policy makers and, 432–433
Internal validity:
　defining, 256–257
　maturation, threat to, 258–259
　selection bias, 259
　threats to, 252. See also Threats to internal validity
International Association of Chiefs of Police (IACP), 424
International Association of Crime Analysts (IACA), 407
International Development Research Center (IDRC), 441
International Journal of Advanced Computer Technology
　　(IJACT), 67
Internet:
　identify research topics on, 40
　online surveys, 216–218

Qualtrics, 233–235
SurveyMonkey®, 233
survey research and, 210
See also Websites entries
Internships, research careers and, 451–452, 471
Interpersonal violence (IPV) impact, 432
Interquartile range (IQR), measure of
　　dispersion, 384–385
Inter-rater reliability, 124–125
Interuniversity Consortium for Political and Social Research
　　(ICPSR), website, 278, 279, 282, 302
Interval level of measurement, 122, 383
Intervening variable, causation and, 245, 247
Interviewer bias, survey research and, 214
Interviews:
　defined, 187
　employment, 471–475
　ethnographic, 188, 189
　face-to-face (in-person), 221–222
　focus groups, 189
　individual, 188–189
　qualitative data and, 180
　qualitative data collection, 187–188
　semistructured, 188, 189
　survey research and, 210
　unconstructed, 188
In-text citation, 79
Introduction section:
　empirical research journal articles, 76
　policy brief, 441
Intuition, as knowledge source, 10
iPad™, 217
IRB. See Institutional review board (IRB)
Items, defined, 209
Iterative process, use in search, 71
IV. See Independent variable

Jackson, J., 228
Jacob, E., 185
Jail inmate census, 289
Job interviews:
　asking right questions, 473
　confidence, eye contact/body language, 472–473
　post interview reflection, 474
　preparing/research for, 471–472
　professional portfolio, 473–474
　questions, preparing for interviewer, 472
　STAR interviewing technique, 478
　tips from professionals, 474–475
Job search:
　documents for. See Documents, job searches and
　ethics and, 475–476
　hash-tagging, 470–471
　internships, turning into full-time jobs, 471

interviews and, 471–475
mistakes to avoid, 474
online, 467–468
social media, 468–471
Jobvite, 468
Johnson, R. R., 363
Johnson, S. D., 287
Joint Committee on Standards for Education Evaluation, 360, 361
Jones, J. K., 215
Journal of Contemporary Criminal Justice, 65
Journal of Crime and Justice, 65
Journal of Experimental Criminology (website), 273
Journal of Interpersonal Violence, 65
Journal of Quantitative Criminology, 65, 314
Journal of Research in Crime and Delinquency, 65, 314
Journals:
assessing, 67–68
predatory, avoid, 67–68
restricting searches in, 73
topic source, 33
See also Empirical research journal articles
Journey-to-crime assumptions, 335
Judgmental sampling, 148, 156, 162
Junker, B. H., 190
Junker's Role Conceptions of a Field Research Continuum, 190
Justice, Belmont Report, 19, 20, 48
Justice Quarterly, 65
Justified conclusions, accuracy standard, 364, 370
Justify recommendations, evaluation research, 350

Keating, Chris, 269–270
Kelly, Bridget, 237–238
Kennedy, Les, 327
Kernel density estimation (KDE), 328, 334, 405
Key words, empirical research journal articles, 76
Keywords, online job searches, 467–468
King, R. G., 17
Kligman, Albert, 52
Knowledge:
authoritative sources, 9
create/assess, 3–4
creators/consumers of, 3
defined, 2
evaluation research generates, 41
intuition as source of, 10
personal experience as, 9
tradition/customs/norms as, 9
See also Research methods
Knowledge, skills, and abilities (KSAs), 461–462
Kohler, E., 67
Koss, M. P., 154
Krebs, C., 4–6, 164

Labels:
pitfalls of, 127
selective coding and, 197
Lancy, D. F., 185
Law enforcement agencies, state/federal census, 289
Law Enforcement Assistance Administration (LEAA), 288, 421
Law Enforcement Management and Administrative Statistics (LEMAS) survey, 212
Law Enforcement Officers Killed and Assaulted (LEOKA), 286
Layers, 328
Layout, survey research, 227, 229
LEAA. *See* Law Enforcement Assistance Administration
Leading question, survey research, 223
Lead paint experiment, 52–53
Legislation, ethical research and, 19
LEMAS. *See* Law Enforcement Management and Administrative Statistics
LEMAS survey, U.S. Bureau of Justice Statistics, 212
Letters of recommendation, 458, 460–461
Levels of measurement:
defined, 121
interval, 122
nominal, 121
ordinal, 121–122
ratio, 122–123
Levy, B. T., 215
Likert-type scale, 122, 128
LimeSurvey, 235
Lincoln, Y. S., 186, 187
Lindquist, C. H., 4–6, 164
Linear association, 389
Link analysis, QDA Miner, Provalis Research® software, 398
Linking, MEAL strategy and, 83–87
Linking known offenders to past crimes, 322
Lipsey, M. W., 368
Listening, topic identification and, 39
Literature review:
abstracts, reading, 74–75
chronologically organized, 84
conduct, 12–13
descriptive, 81
descriptive literature review, 81
edit/proof/polish, 87
empirical research journal articles, 76–77
errors, common, 87–89
existing research, accurate portrayal of, 90–91
expert (Sean McCandless), 91–92
first draft, 87
first rough draft, organize/prepare for, 83–84
identify initial primary sources, 73–77
inappropriate sources, 68
main point, constructing, 81
MEAL strategy, 83–87

plagiary and, 89–90
predatory publishers/journals, avoid, 67–68
primary sources and
reasons for, 63
roadmap for, 64
search terms, develop, 71–73
sources, types of, 64–65
steps in, 64–65
style guides, 77
summarize original sources, 78–90
thematically constructed literature review, 81–82
topic, previous focus on, 81
See also Primary Sources; Sources
Literature review journal article, 66
Loaded questions, survey research, 223
Lobbying activities, policy makers and, 433
Local indicators of spatial association statistics, 324
Local statistical agencies, websites, 295–296
Logic models, 353, 354, 356
Longitudinal data, 305
Longitudinal Perspective on Physical and Sexual Intimate
    Partner Violence Against Women, 284
Longitudinal study, 213
Long-term outcomes, 355, 359
Looping, media tactic, 431
Low self-control/desire for control, crime and, 144

Magazines, as source, 68
Mail and written surveys (postal surveys):
    advantages, 214
    defined, 214
    disadvantages, 215–216
    reasons not received/completed, 216
    self-administered, 216
Main point:
    constructing, 81
    MEAL strategy and, 83–87
Major periods of understanding, 82
Major themes, open coding and, 197
Makarious, M. D., 11
Manipulation of an independent variable (treatment), 252
MapInfo™, 318
Map legend, 336
MapWindow GIS software, 318
Margin of error, 157, 162
Marie Claire magazine, 469
Marshall, C., 186
Martin, S. L., 4–6, 164
Matched pairs design, 250–251
Matching, 250–252
Matrix question, 224
Maturation, threat to internal validity, 258–259
MAUP. *See* Modifiable Areal Unit Problem (MAUP)
Maximum variation sampling, 183

Mazières, D., 67
McCall, 250
McCandless, Sean, 63, 91–92
McCarthy, Justin, 432
MEAL strategy, writing literature review, 83–87
Mean:
    calculating with standard deviation, 387
    quantitative data analysis and, 381–382
Mean center, of spatial distribution, 403–404
Measure:
    defined, 115
    examples, 115, 117
    how many to use, 117–118
Measurement:
    data collection at highest, 123
    defined, 5
    discrete/continuous variables, 123
    ethics and, 127–128
    levels of, 121–123
    Likert-type scale, 122, 128
    operationalize using low level of, 127
    relationship of reliability/validity, 125
    reliability and, 124–125
    validity and, 123–124
    See also Levels of measurement
Measures of central tendency, 379, 381
Measures of dispersion:
    interquartile range, 384–385
    quantitative data analysis and, 384
    range, 384
    standard deviation, 385–386
    variance, 385
Media:
    competing source of policy influence, 431
    viewing, topic identification and, 39
Median, 382–383
Melde, Chris, 24
    abstract example, 93
    administration of treatment, randomization, 263
    associations, regression analysis, 389–390
    causation, 247
    concept examples, 103
    control group, 268
    data analysis/techniques/findings, 415
    data characteristics/sources, 306
    evaluation research, 367, 371
    experimental design, 272
    featured research, 25, 57
    geographic information systems (GIS), 314
    history, validity and, 258
    hypotheses/concepts/variables, 132
    IBM® SPSS Statistics™, 394
    inductive reasoning, 181
    job interview tips, 474

logic models, 353
policy makers and, 424, 425
policy-relevant research, 445
population/sampling considerations, 169
research questions, 46, 100
sampling, 138–139
sampling approach, 147–148
summarization example, 80
survey, explanatory research, 213
survey research types/modes, 239
topic identification method, 33–34
two-group posttest-only, 253
variables, research questions and, 110, 111
video interviews, randomization, 267–268
Memorandum of understanding (MOU), 366
Mental illness, revictimization and, 38
Mentors, 193
Meta data, QDA Miner, Provalis Research® software, 398
Metaevaluation, accuracy standard, 364, 370
Method section, empirical research journal articles, 77
Metropolitan Police's Public Attitude Survey (PAS), 228
Microsoft® Excel™, 330, 392–393
Microsoft® PowerPoint™, 407
Microsoft® Windows™, 395
Microsoft® Word™, 318
Miethe, T. D., 397, 400
Miles, M. B., 186
Milgram, Stanley, 15–17, 48–49
Milgram's Obedience to Authority, 15–17, 48–49
Mind maps, ATLAS.ti, Scientific Software Development
    GmbH® and, 398–399
Minneapolis Domestic Violence Experiment, 438
Miraglia, Greg, 37
Missing data, 301
Mobile phones, telephone surveys and, 219
Mobile surveys:
    advantages, 217–218
    defined, 216–217
    disadvantages, 218
Mode, 383–384
Modifiable Areal Unit Problem (MAUP), 328, 337–338
Monster.com, 467
Moral panic, 191
Moran's I statistic, 324, 404
Morse, M., 185
Mosaic plagiarism, 90
Moustakas, C., 185
Multistage sampling, 148, 153–154, 159
Munhall, P. L., 185
Mutually exclusive attributes, 120–121

Narrow research questions, 45–46
National Addiction & HIV/AIDS Digital Archive Program
    (NAHDAP), 282

National Archive of Criminal Justice Data (NACJD), 280
National Archive of Data on Arts & Culture (NADAC), 282
National Association of Colleges and Employers
    (NACE), 475–476
National Center for Injury Prevention and Control, 293
National Commission for the Protection of Human Subjects
    of Biomedical and Behavioral Research, 19
National corrections reporting program, 289
National Crime Victimization Survey (NCVS):
    data of, 7, 8, 34, 91, 109, 212, 277–280, 288, 289,
        397, 432
    potentially vulnerable populations and, 53–54
National Criminal Justice Information and Statistics Service
    (NCJISS), 288
National Criminal Justice Reference Service (NCJRS)
    (research website), 66
National Incident-Based Reporting System
    (NIBRS), 285–286
National Institute of Justice (NIJ), 280
National Institutes of Health (NIH):
    protecting human subjects, training, 55
    website, 53, 59
National judicial reporting program, 290
National prisoner statistics program, 290
National Research Act of 1974, 19, 20
National Rifle Association (NRA), 433
National survey of DNA crime laboratories, 290
National Vital Statistics System (NVSS), 293
National White-Collar Crime Center, 144
Natural experiments, 266–267, 271
Nazi research, concentration camp prisoners, 14
NCAA Student-Athlete Experiences Data Archive, 282
NCVS. See National Crime Victimization Survey
Nearest Neighbor Index, 324
Near Repeat Calculator (NRC), 332, 333
Near repeat victimization (NRV), 332–334
Needs assessment, formative evaluation, 352–353, 357
Neonates, research ethics and, 51
Networking:
    careers in research and, 450–452
    policy makers, getting research to, 429
Network sampling, 148, 156, 157, 161
Neuendorf, K. A., 194
Newspapers, as source, 68
New York Times, 5, 191
NIH. See National Institutes of Health
NOIR (levels of measurement), 121, 122
Nominal level of measurement, 121
Nonequivalent control groups design, 265–266, 271
Non-numerical data (qualitative), 101
Nonprobability sampling, 148, 151, 156, 161
    convenience/accidental/availability/haphazard, 148,
        154–155, 160
    defining, 148, 151

probability *v.*, 148
  purposive/judgmental, 148, 156, 161
  quota sampling, 148, 155–156, 160
  snowball, 148, 156, 157, 161
Nonrandomized designs, 265
Nonrelevent research, 436–437
Nonresponders, follow-up, 231
Nonresponse bias, 215
Nonverbal responses, interviews and, 189
Norms, as knowledge source, 9
North arrows, 336
Notes, in tables, 408
Notification letters, survey research, 230–231
NUD*UST™ (NVio, QSR International®), 398
Nunez, N., 108
Nuremberg Code, 18–19, 48
NVio, QSR International®, software, 398

Objectivity, researcher loss of, 200, 368
Observation:
  complete observer, 193
  consent, ethics and, 192
  data collection and, 184, 187
  ethnography and, 190
  fieldwork, data collection and, 190, 192
  observer as participant, 193
  participant, 190
  participant as observer, 192–193
  theory and, 35
  wheel of science, 31
Observation and fieldwork, 190
Observer as participant, 193
Office of Justice Programs (OJP), 288
Office of Juvenile Justice and Delinquency Prevention
    (OJJDP), 280
Oiler, C., 185
OMICS Groups, Inc., predatory journal, 68
One-group pretest-posttest design, 264
One-group pretest-treatment-posttest, 271
1-in-*k* method (systematic sampling), 150
One-sample Chi-square test, 388
One-shot case design, 264, 271
Online job searches, 467–468
Online surveys:
  advantages, 217–218
  defined, 216–217
  disadvantages, 218
Open coding, 197
Open-ended nature, qualitative data, 178
Open-ended questions:
  qualitative data, 178–179
  survey research and, 215, 222
Open-source geographic information systems (GIS)
    software, 318

Operating systems, software applications and, 395
Operationalization:
  concept to variables stage, 102
  defined, 107
  example, 107, 109
  low levels of measurement and, 127
  measures and, 116–117
  multiple measures, 118
Ordinal level of measurement, 121–122
Organization, first rough draft, 81–84
  chronologically organized, 84
  descriptive literature review, 81
  lack of, 88
Organization (unit of analysis), 145
Organizing data, coding and, 196–198
Original sources, 64
Outcome evaluations, summative, 355–359
Outliers, 382
Outputs, 353–354, 358

Page numbers, in-text citations, 79
Pair-matching, 250–251
Paragraph numbers, in-text citations, 79
Parameters (population), 138
Parental permission, child participation and, 52, 53
Partial enumeration, 138–139
Participant as observer, 192–193
Participant observation, 190
Participant safety, qualitative data research and, 200–201
Patton, M. Q., 176, 178, 194
Pay scale, federal employees, 463
Pease, K., 287
Pedigo, C., 334
Peeples, Carol, 201–202
Peer-reviewed research:
  empirical research journal articles, 65
  journal articles, 64–65
  literature review journal article, 66
  predatory publishers/journals, avoid, 67–68
  theoretical journal articles, 66
  See also Literature review
Percentages table, 380
Periodicity (sampling), 150
Permission, parental, child participation and, 52, 53
Personal experience:
  knowledge source, 9
  topic identification and, 36–37
Pew Research Center, 219
Phone interviews, 188–189
PHPSurveyor, 234
Phrase (search), 71, 72
Pilot study, 154
Piquero, N. L., 144
Pitney Bowes®, 318

Piza, Eric, 327
Plagiarism, 89–90
Policastro, C., 38
PoliceAnalyst software, 330–331
Police impersonation, in United States, 69–70
Police-public contact survey, 290
Policy, defining, 350, 422–424
Policy adoption, 426, 427–428
Policy brief, 430–431, 441–442
Policy cycle, evaluation research, 350–351, 425–426
Policy evaluation/revisions, 426, 428
Policy formation, 426, 427
Policy implementation, 426, 428
Policy implications, 14
Policy makers, getting research to:
    failure to know relevant, 437
    nonaccessible presentation of research, 430–431
    policy brief, 430–431, 441–442
    relationship/communication barriers and, 429
    relationships with, 435
    stages/challenges of, 428–429
    translate findings for, 436
Policy makers, influences on:
    advocacy/interest groups and, 432–433
    budget constraints, 433–435
    fear of crime, 431–432
    ideology, 433
    lobbying activities, 433
    media as, 431
Policy makers, policy-relevant research and, 424–425
Policy-making process:
    adoption, 427–428
    defining, 425–426
    evaluation, 428
    focusing event, 426–427
    formation, 427
    implementation, 428
    problem identification/agenda setting, 426–427
Policy process, evaluation research, 350–351
Policy-relevant research:
    criminal justice policy, 423
    defining, 422
    early relevance, 435
    ethics and, 438–439
    expert (Katie TePas), 439–440
    failure to know relevant policy makers, 437
    failure to recognize relevance, 437
    going beyond data/findings, error of, 438
    nonrelevance, 436–437
    policy definitions, 422–424
    policy makers and, 424–425
    policy process, 425–428
    public policy, 423
    regulation, rule, guidelines and procedures, 423–424

relationships with policy makers and, 435
translating research, 436
why conduct, 421–422
    See also Policy makers, getting research to;
        Policy-making process
Political context, evaluation research, 365–366
Political viability, evaluation research, 361–362, 364
Politics, evaluation research and, 368
Population:
    census/sample or, 139–140
    defined, 139
    full enumeration/census, 140
    generalizability, 141
    margin of error and, 162
    nature of, sample size and, 163
    samples and, 139
Population parameter, 137, 138
Positional accuracy, 337
Poster sessions, reporting research findings, 407
Postrelease behavior, supermax confinement and, 11
Potentially vulnerable populations, 53–54
Practical procedures, evaluation research, 361, 364
Predatory journals, 67–68
Predatory publishers, 67–68
Predictive accuracy index (PAI), 326
Predictive policing, 325–327
Predictor variable, 248
PredPol® predictive policing, 325
Pre-experimental design, 271
    defining, 263–264
    one-group pretest-posttest, 264
    one-shot case, 264
    static-group comparisons, 265
Pre-experiments, 263–265
Pregnant women, research ethics and, 51
Presentations, research findings and, 407
Presentence reports (PRs), 369
Pretest, 154, 229–230
Primary data collection, 276
Primary sources:
    abstracts, read, 74
    Boolean operators, 71–73
    defined, 64
    empirical research journal articles, 74–77
    identify initial/saturation and, 73–74
    sample abstracts, 75
    sample introduction, 76
    search terms, develop, 70–71
    summarizing, 78–90
    thematically constructed literature review, 81–82
    topic, previous focus on chosen, 81
    See also Sources
Prisoners, use in research ethics, 51–52
Privacy, GIS/crime mapping and, 338–339

Private-sector employees
Private sector employment, 464–466
Probability sampling:
    cluster, 148, 151–153, 159
    defined, 148
    multistage, 148, 153–154, 159
    nonprobability v., 148
    simple random, 148–150, 158
    stratified, 148, 151, 152, 158
    systematic, 148, 150–151, 158
Probing, 181
Problem analysis, 322
Problem identification, agenda setting, 426–427, 426
Procedures, 423–424
Process evaluation, formative evaluation, 353–355, 357
Process Tracing in Qualitative and Mixed Methods
        Research, 282
Professional portfolio, 473–474
Professional skills, 449–450, 479
Professors, working/researching with, 39–40
Program, defined, 350
Program documentation, accuracy standard, 364, 368
Project investigator (PI), 365
Project on Human Development in Chicago Neighborhoods
        (PHDCN), 282
Proof, literature review writing, 87
Propriety standard, evaluation research, 362, 365
Provalis Research® QDA Miner, 396, 398
PROVE predictive policing software, 325–327
Psychology of Violence, 65
Public policy, 423
Public sector employees
Public sector employment, 461–464
    advertisement example, 462
    federal employee pay scale, 463
    General Schedule (GS), 463
    governmentjobs.com sample, 465
    knowledge, skills and abilities (KSAs), 461–462
    private v., 464
    state/local positions, 463–464
    USAJOBS.gov, 461–463
Public use data, ethics and, 301
Public welfare, evaluation research and, 348
Published research, topic identification and, 32–34
Publishers, predatory, avoid, 67–68
Punishment & Society, 65
Purdue University Online Writing Lab (OWL) (website), 77
Pure theory testing approach, 35
Purpose of research:
    descriptive, 41
    evaluation, 41
    example, 69
    explanatory, 41
    exploratory research, 40–41

featured researchers, examples, 203
    identify, 32
    not knowing, as common error, 92
    sample size/margin of error and, 157, 162
    summarize source, 78
    surveys and, 211–213
    type of and, 162–163
Purposive sampling, 148, 156, 161

QDA. *See* Qualitative data analysis
QDA Miner, Provalis Research®, software, 396, 398
QGIS software, 318
QSR International®, NVio software, 398
Qualitative data:
    abstract topic using, 176
    benefits/limitations of, 180–181
    coding process, grounded theory and, 197–198. *See also*
            Coding data
    collection tools, 175
    complete observer, 193
    complete participant, 192
    computer-assisted qualitative data analysis (CAQDAS), 199
    content analysis, 194–195
    defining, 101
    defining research using, 178–179
    document analysis, 193–194
    ethics and, 200–201
    expert (Carol Peeples), 201–202
    focus groups, 189
    how things work, 176–177
    individual interviewing, 188–189
    inductive reasoning and, 182
    inquiry, 181
    interviews and, 187–188
    methods of gathering, 184–187
    objectivity, loss of/going native pitfalls, 200
    observation and fieldwork, 190, 192
    observer as participant, 193
    organizing/analyzing, 196–198
    participant as observer, 192–193
    recording, field notes, 195–196
    sample size and, 183–184
    sampling considerations, 182–183
    stages of research using, 179
    terminology of, 175
    understanding research using, 105
    why research using, 175–178
    See also Data; Qualitative data analysis (QDA)
Qualitative data analysis (QDA):
    characteristics and, 396
    defining, 390–391
    second-order analysis, 396
    steps in, 395–396
    theme and, 396

Qualitative data analysis (QDA), software applications:
  ATLAS.ti, Scientific Software Development GmbH®, 398–399
  defining QDA, steps in, 395–396
  HyperRESEARCH, ResearchWare®, 399–400
  NVio, QSR International®, 398
  QDA Miner, 396, 398
Qualitative inquiry. *See* Qualitative data
Qualitative research, 100–101, 105, 174. *See also* Qualitative
    data analysis (QDA)
Qualtrics®, online survey, 209, 213, 224, 233–235
Quantitative data, 100
Quantitative data analysis:
  associations and, 387–390
  describing your data, 380
  differences, 390
  distributions, 380–381
  interquartile range and, 384–385
  mean, 381–382
  measures of central tendency, 381
  median, 382–383
  mode, 383–384
  range, 384
  regression analysis, 388–390
  software applications for, 392–395
  standard deviation, 385–386
  variance, 385
Quantitative data analysis software applications:
  Excel™, 392–393
  IBM® SPSS Statistics™, 393–395
  SAS®, 395, 402
  STATA™ StataCorp®, 283, 395, 402
Quasi-experimental research design:
  before-and-after, 266
  defining, 265
  example, 271
  nonequivalent groups, 265–266
Questionnaires:
  defined, 209–210
  design/layout, 227, 229
Question-order effect, surveys, 216
Question(s):
  behaviorally specific, 5
  closed-ended, 179
  construct research, 43–44
  demographic, 227
  descriptive research and, 41
  double-barreled, 223
  evaluate research, 44–46
  explanatory research, 41
  exploratory research, 40
  featured researchers, examples, 203
  Heat Map, 234
  identify research, 32
  items, survey research and, 209

job interview, 472, 473
  leading, 223
  loaded/leading surveys and, 223
  matrix, survey, 224
  open/closed ended, qualitative data and, 178–179
  open/closed ended, surveys and, 222–223
  opened-ended, 178
  principles for writing (Dillman), 225–226
  Qualtrics survey, 233–235
  research, develop, 10, 12
  skip-and-fill, 217
  types/purposes/answered in research, 42
  why create research, 44
Quetelet, Adolphe, 313, 314
Quota sampling, 148, 155–156, 160
Quotation marks, in-text citations, 79

R, in CACC code, 402–403
Race:
  Holmesberg Prison experiments and, 51, 52
  mental illness, revictimization and, 38
  moral panic, drug use and, 191
  Tuskegee Syphilis Experiment, 15
Rand Corporation, 325
Random assignment, 250
  equivalence analysis of, 387
  quasi-experimental research and, 265–266
  Solomon Four Group research design, 256
Random digit dialing (RDD), 148, 219–220
Randomization:
  defined, 250
  matching and, 250–252
  true experiments and. *See* True experiment
Randomized designs, 265. *See also* Quasi-experimental
    research design
Randomly assigned control group (RC), 253–254
Randomly assigned experimental group (RE), 253–254
Random number generator (website), 149
Random number table, 483
Range, measure of dispersion, 384
Raster, 316
Raster data (spatial), 316–317
Ratcliffe, Jerry, 325, 329, 332
Ratemyprofessor.com, 363
Ratio level of measurement, 122–123, 383
Reactive effects of testing, 262
Reactivity threats, 262
Reading, topic research and, 37
Recall bias, 216
Recapture rate index (RRI), 326
Recency effects, surveys, 216
Recommendations subsection, policy brief, 442
Recording qualitative data, field notes, 195–196
Reductionism, 147

Reductionist fallacy, 147
Referees, résumé and, 456, 458, 460–461
References, résumé and, 456, 458, 460–461
References section, journal articles, 77
Refine topic, 43
Regoeczi, W. C., 400
Regression, spatial interpolation and, 405–406
Regression analysis, 388–390
Regression output, associations and, 389–390
Regulations, 423–424
Relationships, policy makers and, 429, 435
Relevance, policy and, 436–437
Reliability:
    experimental research and, 262
    inter-rater, 124–125
    measurement and, 124–125
    test-retest, 125
    validity relationship, 125
Reliable information, accuracy standard, 364, 369
Repeatability, geocoding, 337
Repeat incident analysis, 322
Repeat victimization (RV), 332–334
Replication of research, 162–163
Report clarity, propriety standard, 361, 362
Reporting findings. See Findings, reporting
Report timeliness and dissemination, evaluation research, 361, 364
Representative sample, 141
Reputational sampling, 148, 156, 157, 161
Requests for proposals (RFPs), 36
Research:
    common rule definition, 49, 50
    crime analysis in, 323–324. See also Crime analysis
    defined, 2
    ethical requirements, 18–20
    existing, accurate portrayal of, 90–91
    experimental. See Experimental research
    IRB submission problems, 56
    legislation for ethical, 19
    policy makers and. See Policy makers entries
    policy-relevant. See Policy-relevant research
    purpose of. See Purpose of research
    qualitative, 174–175
    summarize importance of, 78
    types/purposes/questions answered in, 42
    unethical. See Unethical research examples
    victim impact statements, 108
Research design:
    effectiveness, 261
    experimental, 271
    pre-experiments, 263–266. See also
        Pre-experimental design
    survey, 227, 229
    true experimental research, 252–256

wheel of science, 31
    See also Pre-experimental design
Researcher control of administration of treatment.
        See True experiment
Researchers:
    applicant skills/hiring good, 128–130
    Carlos Cuevas, 22–23
    case studies and, 21
    Chris Melde, 24
    complete participant role, 192
    going native, 190, 192
    Heather Zaykowski, 24
    loss of objectivity/going native, 200
    Mary Dodge, 23
    observer as participant, 193
    participant as observer, 192–193
    Rachel Boba Santos, 21–22
    research of, 25
    Rod Brunson, 22
    See also entries for individual researchers
Research methods:
    Campus Sexual Assault (CSA) Study, 4–6
    careers. See Career, research methods as
    defining, 2–3
    everyday life data, 4
    knowledge/ways of knowing, 3–4
    sources of knowledge, 9–10
    violent crime, in United States, 6–9
Research question:
    answering, example, 69
    construct, 43–44
    control variables, 113–115
    data collection and, 100–101
    data type decisions and, 101–102
    dependent variable, 111–112
    develop, 10, 12, 32
    evaluate feasibility, 44–46
    examples, case studies, 46–47
    illustrated, 112
    independent variables, 112–113
    measures and, 115–118
    origination of, 358
    research statement and, example, 43
    variables and, 109–110
    what is really being asked?, 110–111
    why create?, 44
    See also Question(s)
Research stages:
    data collection, 13
    design, 13
    literature review, conduct, 12–13
    report findings/conclusions/policy implications, 14
    research question, develop, 10, 12
    select analytical approach /develop findings, 13

Research topic:
abstract, 176
avoid pitfalls, 47
comprehensive understanding of, 180
data codebook and, 34–35
ethics and, 48–49
Internet, 40
listening, 39
personal experiences, 36–37
previous work on, 81
professors, working/researching with, 39–40
published research, 32–34
reading, 37
refine, 43
requests for proposals (RFPs), 36
theory, 35
viewing, 39
ResearchWare®, HyperRESEARCH software, 399–400
Resources, sample size and, 163
Respect for persons:
Belmont Report, 19, 48
evaluation research and, 348
See also Ethics; Human subjects
Respondent burden, survey research, 222
Respondents, survey, 209
Response categories:
attributes, 118–120
survey research, 223
Response rates:
notification letters and, 230–231
survey, 215
Results subsection, policy brief, 441–442
Résumé:
computer skills, 456
defining, 454
education, 456
foreign languages spoken, 458
personal information to include, 455–456
professional portfolio and, 473–474
references/referees, 456
sample, 458, 459–460
what makes a great, 453
Review, IRB, 54
Revisions, policy evaluation and, 426
Rhind, D., 314
Rice, Brenidy, 128–130
Rights of human subjects, propriety standard, 362, 366
Right to service, 268
Risk/benefits assessment, Belmont Report, 19, 21
Risk terrain modeling (RTM), 327–329, 334
Risk Terrain Modeling Diagnostics Utility (RTMDx),
328–329, 334
Robinson, J., 261
Role conceptions, Junker's, 190

Rolin, Bernard, 19n3
Rossi, P. H., 368
Rossman, G, 186
Rossmo, Kim, 335
Rough draft, 81–84
Routine Activity Theory, 36
Rules, 423–424

Sabrina, Chiara, 277
Saldaña, J., 186–187
Sample:
advantages/disadvantages, 140–141
bias and, 142–143
census or, 139–140
defined, 5
population and, 139
relationships with populations/parameters/statistics, 138
representative, 141
summarize size/how attained, 78
See also other Sample *and* Sampling *entries*
Sample size:
ethics and, 164
generalizing ungeneralizable findings, 164
margin of error and, 157, 162
nature of population and, 163
purpose of research and, 157, 162
qualitative data and, 181
qualitative data/inquiry and, 183–184
resources available and, 163
sampling error and, 142
type of research, 162–163
Sample statistic, 137
Sample variance, calculating, 386
Sampling:
approach, choosing, 147–149
defining, 138–139
expert (Sam Gallaher), 165–166
fallacies, ecological/individualistic, 164
featured researchers, examples, 203
importance of, 136–138
maximum consideration, 183
probability, 148–149
qualitative data and, 182–183
random-digit dialing, 148
relationships among populations, 138
sample size and. *See* Sample size
theoretical, 183
units of analysis, 184
Sampling elements, 148–149
Sampling error:
defined, 141
examples, 141–142
sample size and, 142
Sampling frame, 148–149

Sampling interval, 150
Sampling without replacement, 149
Sampson, R. J., 253
Santos, Rachel Boba, 21–22
    abstract example, 94
    concept examples
    conceptualization example, 109
    confidentiality, survey notification letter, 231
    data analysis/techniques/findings, 415
    data characteristics/sources, 307
    data collection, 102
    ethics, policy-relevant research, 438
    evaluation research, 41, 366, 371
    experimental research, 244, 268, 272
    featured research, 25
    geographic information systems (GIS), 314, 341
    hypotheses/concepts/variables, 132
    IBM® SPSS Statistics™, 394
    job interview tips, 474
    level of measurement, 123
    manipulation of treatment, 252
    means/standard deviations, 386
    participant safety, ethics and, 201
    policy makers and, 424–425
    policy-relevant research, 445
    population/sample, 139
    population/sampling considerations, 170
    qualitative data, 178
    randomization, 250–252
    regression analysis, 390
    research questions, 47
    sample introduction, 76
    sampling importance, 137
    secondary data, 277–279
    topic research method of, 34, 37
    true experiments, 248–249
    two-group pretest-treatment-posttest
        design, 255
    unit of analysis, 146
SAS® software, 283, 395, 402
Saturation:
    research type/replication, 162–163
    source, 73–74
Scale bar, 336
Scanlon, Nora, 476–479
Scatterplot, 389, 410
School Crime Supplement (SCS) data, 397
Schweitzer, K., 108
Science, defined, 2
Scientific process, as recursive process, 31
Scientific Software Development GmbH®,
        ATLAS.ti, 398–399
Search engines, Boolean operators and, 71–73
Search terms, finding primary sources, 70–71

Secondary data analysis:
    Centers for Disease Control and Prevention
        (CDC), 293–294
    defining, 276, 277
    disadvantages/limitations of using, 296–297
    ethics and, 301–302
    expert (Jenna Truman), 302–305
    featured researchers, 306–307
    Federal Statistical System (FedStats), 283–284
    geographic data, 291–293
    local statistical agencies (Websites), 295–296
    missing data, 301
    pitfalls/problems, 300–301
    public use data, 301
    reporting findings, 298–299
    Statistical Analysis Centers (SACs), 294–295
    U.S. Department of Commerce collection, 290–292
Secondary data research:
    analysis, 276
    defining, 277–280
    Federal Bureau of Investigation (FBI), 284–286, 288
    ISPSR, 280–283
    U.S. Department of Justice (USDOJ), 284
    why conduct, 277–278
Second-order analysis, 396
Selection bias, threat to internal validity, 259, 260
Selection of subjects, Belmont Report, 19, 22
Selective coding, 197
Selective stage, coding, 197
Self-administered mail surveys, 216, 232
Self-administered questionnaire, 214
Self-exciting point process modeling, 325
Semistructured interviews, 188, 189, 210
Service orientation, propriety standard, 362, 365
Setting, observation and, 190
Sexual Abuse, 65
Sheridan, C. L., 17
Sheridan and King (1972), 17
ShinyApp, 331–332
Shiveley, Michael, 368–370, 452
Short-term outcomes, 355, 358
Similarities/differences, qualitative data and, 178
Simple random sampling, (probability), 148–150, 158
Situational contexts, CACC and, 400–401
Skillings, Pamela, 470
Skills, 449–450
Skip-and-fill patterns, 217
Skype®, 188, 471
Slife, B. D., 186
Smartphones, mobile and online surveys, 217
Smyth, 224
Snowballing sample, 148, 156, 157, 161
Social artifacts (unit of analysis), 145–146
Social interactions (unit of analysis), 145–146

Social media, job searches and, 468–471
    Facebook®, 468–469
    LinkedIn, 469–470
    Twitter®, 470–471
Social science research, 2
Software:
    ArcGIS™, 318
    ATLAS.ti, Scientific Software Development
        GmbH®, 398–399
    Excel™, 392–393
    geocoding, 337
    geographic profiling, 335
    G-Power Software, 267
    GIS technology and, 317–318
    GRASS GIS, 318
    HyperRESEARCH, ResearchWare®, 399–400
    IBM® SPSS Statistics™, 393–395
    LimeSurvey, 235
    NVio, QSR International®, 398
    MapWindow GIS, 318
    operating systems, 395
    PoliceAnalyst, 330–331
    predictive policing, 325–327
    professional skills with, résumé and, 456
    PROVE predictive policing, 327
    QDA Miner, Provalis Research®, 396, 398
    QGIS, 318
    qualitative research analysis, 395–400
    quantitative data analysis, 392–395
    Qualtrics, 233–235
    Risk Terrain Modeling Diagnostics Utility, 328–329, 334
    SAS®, 395, 402
    ShinyApp, 331–332
    STATA™ StataCorp®, 283, 395, 402
    SurveyMonkey®, 233
Software, survey:
    G-Power, 267
    LimeSurvey, 235
    Qualtrics, 233–235
    SurveyMonkey®, 233
Solomon Four Group research design, 255–256, 271
Sources:
    abstracts and, 74
    empirical peer-reviewed journal articles, 65
    government research/reports/policy briefs, 66
    inappropriate, 68
    literature review journal article, 66
    predatory standalone journals, danger of, 67–68
    primary. See Primary sources
    saturation, 73–74
    summarizing original, 78–90
    theoretical journal articles, 66
    types of, 64–65
Spanners, in tables, 408

Spatial autocorrelation, 404–405
Spatial data, 315–317
Spatial dependency, 404–405
Spatial descriptions
    convex hull, 404–405
    defined, 403
    mean center, 403–404
    standard distance, 404
Spatial independence, 404–405
Spatial interpolation, 405
Spatial statistics, spatial description, 403
Spreadsheet, 392
SPSS™ software (Statistical Package for the Social Sciences),
    283, 393–395, 401–402
Spurious relationship, 245, 247
Spurlock, Morgan, 248
Stakeholder identification, evaluation research, 361
Stakeholders, 348
Standalone predatory journals, 67–68
Standard deviation, 336, 385–387
Standard distance, geographical data, 404
Stanford Prison Experiment, 17–18, 248
Stanford University, 15–17
Stanko, E. A., 228
Stanley, J. C., 257, 260, 263
STAR interviewing technique, 477–479
STAR Method Matrix, 479
StataCorp®, STATA™ software, 283, 395, 402
STATA™ StataCorp® software, 283, 395
State Administering Agency (SAA), 294, 295
Static-group comparison pre-experimental design, 265, 271
Statistical Analysis Centers (SACs), 294–295
Statistical Package for the Social Sciences (SPSS):
    CACC and, 401–402
    data analysis software, 283, 393–395
Statistical regression, 259
Statistical significance, 411
Statistics:
    crime websites, 66
    relationships among parameters/populations/samples and, 138
    violent crime in United States, 6–9
    See also Data
Steiner, B., 11
Stevens, S. S., 121
Strata, 151
Strategic crime analysis, 322–323
Stratified sampling (probability), 148, 151, 152, 158
Strauss, A., 185, 196
Street geocoding, 337
Stubs, in tables, 408
Stufflebeam, D. L., 356
Style guides:
    criminal justice, 77
    in-text citations, 79

Subject loss, 268
Subject selection, Belmont Report, 19, 22
Subpart A, HHS research ethics regulations, 48–50
Subpart B, HHS research ethics regulations, 49
Subpart C, HHS research ethics regulations, 49
Subpart D, HHS research ethics regulations, 49
Subpart E, HHS research ethics regulations, 49
Substance Abuse and Mental Health Data Archive
    (SAMHDA), 282
Substantive significance, 411
Subthemes, data analysis and, 196–197
Summarize original sources, 78–90
Summary Reporting System (SRS/UCR), 285
Summary table, thematically constructed literature
    review, 81–82
Summative evaluation, evaluation research:
  defined, 355
  impact, 356, 359
  outcome, 355–356
  subtypes of, 357–358
Summers, L., 287
Supermax confinement, postrelease behavior and, 11
Supersize Me (film), 248
Supplementary Homicide Reports (SHR), 285
Survey, defining, 209
Survey administration:
  fielding, 231
  follow-up to nonresponders, 231
  notification letters, 230–231
  processing/data entry, 231–232
  timing of survey correspondence, 232
Survey fraud, online/mobile surveys and, 218
Survey modes, distribution, 214
SurveyMonkey®, 209, 233
Survey nonresponse, 215
Survey panels, 217
Survey processing, data entry, 231–232
Survey research:
  defined, 209
  descriptive, 211–212
  design/layout, 227, 229
  distribution, survey modes, 214
  Ecological Momentary Assessment (EMA), 218
  ethics and, 236–237
  evaluation, 213
  expert (Bridget Kelly), 237–238
  explanatory, 212–213
  exploratory research and, 211
  face-to-face (in-person), 221–222
  featured researchers, types/modes used, 239
  interviewer bias and, 214
  interviews, 210
  LEMAS, 212
  LimeSurvey, 235

longitundinal study, 213
  mail and written (postal surveys), 214–216
  online/mobile, 216–218
  pitfalls in, 236
  pretesting instruments, 229–230
  Qualtrics software, 233–235
  questions, types for, 222–224
  response rates, 215
  skip-and-fill example, 217
  software for, 232–235
  steps in, 210–211
  SurveyMonkey®, 233
  telephone, 218–220
  tools for, 209
  why conduct?, 209
  writing questions for (Dillman), 225–226
Systematic information, accuracy standard, 364, 369
Systematic inquiry, evaluation research and, 348
Systematic sampling (probability), 148, 150–151, 158
Systems function, qualitative data and, 177

Table number, 408
Tables, reporting research findings, 407–408
Tabular data, example, 409
Tactical crime analysis, 321–322
Tailored Design Method, The (Dillman), 215
Target populations, 355
Taylor, Terrance, 34, 80
Teasdale, B., 38
Technology, geographic information systems (GIS) and,
    317–318
Telephone surveys:
  advantages, 220
  computer-assisted telephone interviewing (CATI),
    219–220
  defined, 218–219
  disadvantages, 220
  landline/cell phone use, 219
  random digit dialing, 219–220
Temporal ordering, causation and, 244–245
TePas, Katie, 439–440
Term, search, 71, 72
Testing, internal validity threat, 259–260
  interaction of, experimental variables and, 262
  reactive (interaction) effect of, 262
Testing threat, external validity, 260
Test-retest reliability, 125
Textbooks, as source, 68
Thematically constructed literature review, 81
Themes:
  data analysis and, 196–197
  QDA and, 396
  qualitatively derived, examples of, 198–199
Theoretical journal articles, 66

Theoretical sampling, 183
Theory:
    criminological, 31
    research topic identification and, 35
    routine activity, 36
    wheel of science, 31
Threats to external validity:
    interaction of experimental arrangements/variables, 260, 262
    interaction of selection biases, experimental variables and, 260
    interaction of testing and experimental variables, 262
    reactivity, 262
Threats to internal validity:
    experimental mortality, 257
    history, 257–258
    instrumentation, 258
    maturation, 258–259
    selection bias, 259
    statistical regression, 259
    testing, 259–260
TIGER Geodatabases, 292
TIGER/Line Shapefiles, 292
TIGER/Line with Selected Demographic and Economic Data, 292
TIGERweb, 292
Title examination, in topic identification, 33
Titles, in tables, 408
Tobler, Waldo, 404–405
Tobler's Law, 404–405
Topic. *See* Research topic
Topologically Integrated Geographic Encoding and Referencing (TIGER) program, 292
Townsley, Michael, 331
Tradition, as knowledge source, 9
Training, protecting human subjects, 55
Trauma, Violence & Abuse (journal website), 66
Travis, I. F., 11
Treatment (manipulation of an independent variable), 252, 268
Treatment group, 268–269
Trend analysis, 322
Triangulation, 184, 187
Tripp, T., 457
True experiment, 271
    block matching, example, 251
    defining, 248–249
    designs, 252–253
    experimental/control group, 249
    manipulation of independent variable (treatment), 252
    matched pair example, 250
    matching in, 250–252
    random assignment, 250
    reliability, 262

Solomon Four Group design, 255–256
    two-group posttest-only design, 253–254
    two-group pretest-treatment-posttest design, 254–255
    See also Threats to external validity; Threats to internal validity
Truman, Jenna, 302–305
Trust, evaluation research and, 366
Tuskegee Syphilis Experiment, 15, 293
Twain, Mark, 411
Twitter®, 398, 470–471
Two-group posttest-only research design, 253–254, 271
Two-group pretest-treatment-post-test, 254–255, 271

Understanding, in field, 82
Unethical research, examples:
    Holmsberg prison, 51, 52
    lead paint research, 52–53
    Milgram's Obedience to Authority, 15–17, 48–49
    Nazi research, concentration camp prisoners, 14
    Stanford Prison Experiment, 17–18
    Tuskegee Syphilis Experiment, 15
Uniform Crime Reports (UCR) (FBI), 8, 281, 295, 432
United States:
    incarceration rates in, 11
    police impersonation in, 69–70
    violent crime in, 6–9
Unit of analysis:
    defined, 143
    ecological fallacy and, 146–147
    geographic regions, 145
    groups/organizations, 145
    identifying individuals when sampling, 184
    individual, 143, 145
    individualist fallacy, 147
    social artifacts/interactions, 145–146
    unit of observation v., 146
Unit of observation, unit of analysis v., 146
Univariate analysis, 380, 387
University of Colorado Denver, Career Center, 478
Unstructured interviews, 188, 210
U.S. Bureau of the Census:
    data collection, 290–291
    2010 Census, 227, 230
U.S. Bureau of Justice Statistics (BJS):
    data collection, 280, 288–290, 314, 434
    LEMAS survey, 212
    website, 66
U.S. Bureau of Labor Statistics (BLS), 478
U.S. Congress, 421
U.S. Department of Commerce (USDOC):
    Census Bureau data, 290–292
    data collection, 290–292
    geographic data, 291–293
U.S. Department of Health and Human Services, 293, 302

U.S. Department of Justice (DOJ), 6–9, 36, 412–413, 424, 434
  literature review source, 66
  Office of Justice Programs (OJP), 294
  website, 284
U.S. Federal Register, 19
U.S. Geological Survey (USGS), 315
U.S. Office of Naval Research, 17–18
U.S. Public Health Service (USPHS), 20
U.S. Senate, 424
U.S. Statistical Program, 283
USAJOBS.gov, public sector employment, 461–463
USA Patriot Improvement and Reauthorization
    Act of 2005, 288
Utility standard, evaluation research, 361

Valid information, accuracy standard, 364, 369
Validity:
  content, 124
  criterion, 124
  defined, 123
  face, 123–124
  internal/external threats to, 252
  relationship reliability, 125
  threats to external, 260, 262
  threats to internal, 257–260
  types of, 256–257
Values identification:
  evaluation research, 361
  propriety standard, 362
Variables:
  associated/correlated examples, 246
  association and, 245
  block, 250–251
  categorical, 121
  causal relationships and, 243
  concept, stages from to, 102, 126
  confounders, 250
  continuous, 123
  control, 113–115
  defined, 109
  dependent, 111–112
  discrete, 123
  ethics and, 127–128
  featured research examples, 131–133
  independent, 112–113
  intervening, 245
  manipulation of independent, 252
  memorizing types of, ineffective, 115
  research questions and, 109–110
  research questions using same, 116
  spurious relationship and, 245
Variance:
  analysis of (ANOVA), 390
  defined, 382

measure of dispersion, 385
  standard deviation and, 385–386
Vector data (spatial), 316
Verbatim text, cloning, 90
Veterans, potentially vulnerable population, 53–54
Veterans Administration, 54
Victim impact statements, research, 108
Victimization risk, 328
Video conference interviews, 188–189
Video recorders, field notes and, 195
Viewing media, topic identification and, 39
Violence Against Women, 65
Violence and Victims, 65
Violent crime:
  differences in construction of rates of, 8
  in United States, 6–9
Violent victimizations, 7
Voluntary participation, Belmont Report, 19, 20
Vulnerable populations, 50
  children, 52–53
  potentially vulnerable, 53–54
  pregnant women/human fetuses/neonates, 51
  prisoners, 51–52

Wallace, Walter, 30–32, 378
Wallace's wheel of science, 30–32
Warner, T. D., 4–6, 164
Washington Post, 191
Wasserman, Rachel, 412
Websites, 66. *See also* Internet *entries*
Weiss, C. H., 368
Weitzer, R, 75. *See also* Brunson
What is really being asked? (variable), 110–111
Wheel of science, 30–32
Wheel of science (Wallace), 378
White, M. Goldkamp, 261
Wikipedia, 68
Williams, M. R., 434
Williams, R. N., 186
Wilson, R., 324
Winstanley, Art, 37

YouTube®, 393, 452

Zaykowski, Heather, 24, 25
  abstract example, 94
  associations, regression analysis and, 388–389
  causation, 247
  concept examples, 103
  conceptualization example, 109
  data analysis/techniques/findings, 415
  data characteristics/sources, 307
  dependent variable, 111–112
  descriptive analysis, 387–388

differences, analysis of variance, 390
empirical research article, 74
evaluation research, 356, 365, 366, 368
explanatory research, 41
geographic information systems
    (GIS), 314
hypotheses/concepts/variables, 133
independent variables, 113
job interview tips, 475
logic models, 353
plagiary, 90
policy makers and, 424
policy-relevant research, 445
population/sample, 139
population/sampling considerations, 170
qualitative data, 178

quotations, 88
reliability, 262
reporting findings, secondary data, 298–299
research questions, 46
sampling importance, 137
secondary data, 277, 278, 279–280
source saturation, 74
standard deviation, 385–386
summarization example, 80
survey, explanatory research, 212–213
survey research types/modes, 239
topic research method of, 34, 40
unit of analysis, 143, 146
variables, research questions and, 110
Zimbardo, P., 17–18
Zoom®, 188